RACE AND ETHNIC RELATIONS 98/99

Eighth Edition

Editor

John A. Kromkowski

Catholic University of America

John A. Kromkowski is president of The National Center for Urban Ethnic Affairs in Washington, D.C., a nonprofit research and educational institute that has sponsored and published many books and articles on ethnic relations, urban affairs, and economic revitalization. He is Assistant Dean of the College of Arts and Sciences at the Catholic University of America, and he coordinates international seminars and internship programs in the United States, England, Ireland, and Belgium. He has served on national advisory boards for the Campaign for Human Development, the U.S. Department of Education Ethnic Heritage Studies Program, the White House Fellows Program, the National Neighborhood Coalition, and the American Revolution Bicentennial Administration. Dr. Kromkowski has edited a series sponsored by the Council for Research in Values and Philosophy titled *Cultural Heritage and Contemporary Change*. These volumes include scholarly findings and reflections on urbanization, cultural affairs, personhood, community, and political economy.

Annual Editions

A Library of Information from the Public Press

Dushkin/McGraw·Hill

Sluice Dock, Guilford, Connecticut 06437

Visit us on the Internet—http://www.dushkin.com/

The Annual Editions Series

ANNUAL EDITIONS, including GLOBAL STUDIES, consist of over 70 volumes designed to provide the reader with convenient, low-cost access to a wide range of current, carefully selected articles from some of the most important magazines, newspapers, and journals published today. ANNUAL EDITIONS are updated on an annual basis through a continuous monitoring of over 300 periodical sources. All ANNUAL EDITIONS have a number of features that are designed to make them particularly useful, including topic guides, annotated tables of contents, unit overviews, and indexes. For the teacher using ANNUAL EDITIONS in the classroom, an Instructor's Resource Guide with test questions is available for each volume. GLOBAL STUDIES titles provide comprehensive background information and selected world press articles on the regions and countries of the world.

VOLUMES AVAILABLE

ANNUAL EDITIONS

Abnormal Psychology
Accounting
Adolescent Psychology
Aging
American Foreign Policy
American Government
American History, Pre-Civil War
American History, Post-Civil War
American Public Policy
Anthropology
Archaeology
Astronomy
Biopsychology
Business Ethics
Canadian Politics
Child Growth and Development
Comparative Politics
Computers in Education
Computers in Society
Criminal Justice
Criminology
Developing World
Deviant Behavior
Drugs, Society, and Behavior
Dying, Death, and Bereavement

Early Childhood Education
Economics
Educating Exceptional Children
Education
Educational Psychology
Environment
Geography
Geology
Global Issues
Health
Human Development
Human Resources
Human Sexuality
International Business
Macroeconomics
Management
Marketing
Marriage and Family
Mass Media
Microeconomics
Multicultural Education
Nutrition
Personal Growth and Behavior
Physical Anthropology
Psychology
Public Administration
Race and Ethnic Relations

Social Problems
Social Psychology
Sociology
State and Local Government
Teaching English as a Second
  Language
Urban Society
Violence and Terrorism
Western Civilization, Pre-Reformation
Western Civilization, Post-Reformation
Women's Health
World History, Pre-Modern
World History, Modern
World Politics

GLOBAL STUDIES

Africa
China
India and South Asia
Japan and the Pacific Rim
Latin America
Middle East
Russia, the Eurasian Republics, and
  Central/Eastern Europe
Western Europe

Cataloging in Publication Data
Main entry under title: Annual editions: Race and ethnic relations. 1998/99.
      1. Race relations—Periodicals. 2. United States—Race relations—Periodicals. 3. Culture conflict—United States—Periodicals. I. Kromkowski, John A., comp. II. Title: Race and ethnic relations.
ISBN 0–697–39194-9   305.8'073'05   ISSN 1075–5195

Eighth Edition

Cover: Martin Luther King Jr. leads the civil rights march from Selma to Montgomery, Alabama, in March 1965.
© Ivan Massar/Black Star.

Printed on Recycled Paper

Printed in the United States of America   1234567890BAHBAH901234098

Editors/Advisory Board

Members of the Advisory Board are instrumental in the final selection of articles for each edition of ANNUAL EDITIONS. Their review of articles for content, level, currentness, and appropriateness provides critical direction to the editor and staff. We think that you will find their careful consideration well reflected in this volume.

EDITOR

John A. Kromkowski
Catholic University of America

ADVISORY BOARD

Staff

To the Reader

In publishing ANNUAL EDITIONS we recognize the enormous role played by the magazines, newspapers, and journals of the *public press* in providing current, first-rate educational information in a broad spectrum of interest areas. Many of these articles are appropriate for students, researchers, and professionals seeking accurate, current material to help bridge the gap between principles and theories and the real world. These articles, however, become more useful for study when those of lasting value are carefully *collected, organized, indexed,* and *reproduced* in a *low-cost format,* which provides easy and permanent access when the material is needed. That is the role played by ANNUAL EDITIONS. Under the direction of each volume's *academic editor,* who is an expert in the subject area, and with the guidance of an *Advisory Board,* each year we seek to provide in each ANNUAL EDITION a current, well-balanced, carefully selected collection of the best of the public press for your study and enjoyment. We think that you will find this volume useful, and we hope that you will take a moment to let us know what you think.

The information explosion, which has led to an expansion of knowledge about the range of diversity among and within societies, has increased awareness of ethnicity and race. During previous periods of history, society was discussed in terms of a universal sense of common humanity. Differences between societies and the arrangements of economic production were noted, but they were usually explained in terms of theories of progressive development or of class conflict. Consciousness of the enduring pluralism expressed in ethnic, racial, and cultural diversity has emerged throughout the world. The dimensions of diversity are significantly, if not essentially, shaped by social, economic, cultural, and, most important, political and communitarian processes. Creativity, imagination, and religion influence ethnic and racial relations.

This collection was designed to assist you in understanding ethnic and racial pluralism in the United States and in several other countries. Unit 1, for example, illustrates how the most basic legal principles of a society—and especially the U.S. Supreme Court's historical interpretation of them—are especially significant for the delineation of ethnic groups, for the acceptance of cultural pluralism, and for the political and moral foundations from which contemporary challenges to the promise of American liberties may be addressed. The immigration of people, the focus of unit 2, into a relatively young society such as America is of particular concern, because the fragility of social continuity is exposed by the recognition of changes in the ethnic composition of American society.

The contemporary experiences of indigenous groups, including Native Americans, are described in unit 3. Discussion of the experiences of the descendants of the earliest groups and the most recently arrived ethnic populations and the legal framework for participating in America is extended in unit 4 on Hispanic/Latino Americans and unit 5 on African Americans. Unit 6 explores various dimensions of the Asian American experience. The experiences of these ethnicities form a cluster of concerns addressed in the traditional literature that focused on marginality, minority, and alienation. Unit 7, titled "The Ethnic Legacy," articulates neglected dimensions of ethnicity derived from the industrial and urban development of America and a pluralistic vision of diversity and cosmopolitan and catholic moral imagination.

Unit 8, "The Ethnic Factor: International Challenges for the 1990s," extends prior concerns and addresses national and international implications of ethnic exclusivity and the imperatives of new approaches to group relations. Unit 9 focuses on understanding the origins of racialism and the religious and ethical origins that shape consciousness of group affinities and, especially, the emergence of scientific claims of racialism and religious exclusion in public affairs.

The American experience, especially those legal protections that are most sacred, has been explained by many as the development of personal freedom. This focus is not entirely valid. For nearly eight decades, Americans have become increasingly aware of the ways that group and personal identity are interwoven, forming a dense network of culture, economy, polity, and sociality. This perspective on the American reality was fashioned from the necessity and the moral imagination of the children and grandchildren of immigrants to the United States. Their contribution was developed in the urban experience and its valuation of a new form of pluralism—one beyond the dichotomous divide of white-Negro/freeman-former slave. Thus, their language of ethnic relations aspired to refashion the dichotomous logic of social divisiveness that is historically derived from race-slavery and color consciousness and their institutional legacies. This reinterpretative project opts for a more complex matrix of ethnicities and an appreciation of the cultures that constitute our common humanity.

New to this edition of *Annual Editions: Race and Ethnic Relations* are *World Wide Web* sites that can be used to further explore article topics. These sites are cross-referenced by number in the topic guide.

Readers may have input into the next edition of *Annual Editions: Race and Ethnic Relations* by completing and returning the prepaid article rating form in the back of the book.

John A. Kromkowski
Editor

Contents

UNIT 1

Race and Ethnicity in the American Legal Tradition

Six articles in this section include Supreme Court decisions that established the legal definitions of race, citizenship, and the historic landmarks of equal protection and due process, as well as discussions of civil rights doctrine and implementation and the rise of new critical legal theories that challenge traditional remedies.

The concepts in bold italics are developed in the article. For further expansion please refer to the Topic Guide and the Index.

UNIT 2

Immigration and the American Experience

Four articles in this section review the historical record of immigration and current concerns regarding patterns of immigration and the legal, social, cultural, and economic issues that are related to immigrants in the American experience.

UNIT 3

Indigenous Ethnic Groups

Six articles in this section review the issues and problems of indigenous peoples. They portray the new relationship that indigenous people are forging with concurrent governments and the processes that protect indigenous traditions within pluralistic societies.

The concepts in bold italics are developed in the article. For further expansion please refer to the Topic Guide and the Index.

vi

UNIT 4

Hispanic/Latino Americans

Five articles in this section reveal the demographics of Hispanic/Latino Americans as well as the economic and political cultural dynamics of these diverse ethnicities.

The concepts in bold italics are developed in the article. For further expansion please refer to the Topic Guide and the Index.

UNIT 5

African Americans

Five articles in this section review historical experiences derived from slavery and segregation and then explore current contexts and persistent concerns of African Americans.

UNIT 6

Asian Americans

Four articles in this section explore dimensions of pluralism among Asian Americans and their issues related to the cultural, economic, and political dynamics of pluralism.

The concepts in bold italics are developed in the article. For further expansion please refer to the Topic Guide and the Index.

UNIT 7

The Ethnic Legacy

Five articles in this section examine neglected dimensions of ethnic communities, their intersection with each other, and the influence of interethnic protocols within American society.

The concepts in bold italics are developed in the article. For further expansion please refer to the Topic Guide and the Index.

UNIT 8

The Ethnic Factor: International Challenges for the 1990s

Five articles in this section look at the intersections of ethnicities and the impact of ethnic conflict and cooperation on international affairs and the prospect of peace.

UNIT 9

Understanding Cultural Pluralism

Five articles in this section examine the origins of misunderstandings regarding human variety, indicate the influence of race and ethnic opinions in selected contexts, and discuss the range of challenges that must be addressed to forge new approaches to understanding cultural pluralism.

The concepts in bold italics are developed in the article. For further expansion please refer to the Topic Guide and the Index.

x

The concepts in bold italics are developed in the article. For further expansion please refer to the Topic Guide and the Index.

Topic Guide

This topic guide suggests how the selections in this book relate to topics of traditional concern to students and professionals involved with the study of race and ethnic relations. It is useful for locating articles that relate to each other for reading and research. The guide is arranged alphabetically according to topic. Articles may, of course, treat topics that do not appear in the topic guide. In turn, entries in the topic guide do not necessarily constitute a comprehensive listing of all the contents of each selection. **In addition, relevant Web sites, which are annotated on the next two pages, are noted in bold italics under the topic articles.**

TOPIC AREA	TREATED IN	TOPIC AREA	TREATED IN
Affirmative Action	5. Strange Politics of Affirmative Action 6. One America in the 21st Century 25. Understanding Integration 26. America's Caste System 35. End of the Rainbow 43. Color Blind 44. How to Mend Affirmative Action *(3, 6, 8, 16, 17, 18, 19, 34)*	**Demography**	2. Racial Restrictions in the Law of Citizenship 8. We Asked . . . You Told Us 10. Newcomers and Established Residents 12. American Indians in the 1990s 17. Specific Hispanics 18. There's More to Racism than Black and White 26. America's Caste System 27. Misperceived Minorities 30. Challenge for U.S. Asians 31. Migrations to the 13 British North American Colonies 32. Settlement of the Old Northwest 36. Racial Classifications in U.S. Census *(4, 5, 12, 13, 14, 15, 22, 29, 30, 33, 35)*
Asian/Indian Americans	2. Racial Restrictions in the Law of Citizenship *(20, 25)*		
Canada Rights	11. 12th Session of UN Working Group 13. Canada Pressed on Indian Rights 39. Outcasts Once Again *(16, 21)*	**Desegregation**	3. *Brown v. Board of Education* 4. Retreat into Legalism 5. Strange Politics of Affirmative Action 6. One America in the 21st Century 10. Newcomers and Established Residents 11. 12th Session of UN Working Group 12. American Indians in the 1990s 22. 10 Most Dramatic Events 23. Black Politics, the 1996 Elections 24. Understanding Afrocentrism 25. Understanding Integration 26. America's Caste System 27. Misperceived Minorities 33. Italian Americans 43. Color Blind *(1, 3, 6, 8, 9, 16, 17, 19, 21, 22, 24, 29, 32, 34, 35)*
Chinese Americans	30. Challenge for U.S. Asians *(20, 25)*		
Civil Rights	1. *Dred Scott v. Sandford* 2. Racial Restrictions in the Law of Citizenship 3. *Brown v. Board of Education* 4. Retreat into Legalism 5. Strange Politics of Affirmative Action 6. One America in the 21st Century 10. Newcomers and Established Residents 11. 12th Session of UN Working Group 12. American Indians in the 1990s 16. Different Kind of Justice 18. There's More to Racism 22. 10 Most Dramatic Events 25. Understanding Integration 26. America's Caste System 33. Italian Americans 34. If Names Could Kill 39. Outcasts Once Again 40. Eugenics, Anyone? 43. Color Blind 44. How to Mend Affirmative Action *(1, 2, 3, 4, 6, 8, 9, 22, 32, 34)*	**Discrimination**	1. *Dred Scott v. Sandford* 2. Racial Restrictions in the Law of Citizenship 3. *Brown v. Board of Education* 4. Retreat into Legalism 5. Strange Politics of Affirmative Action 6. One America in the 21st Century 22. 10 Most Dramatic Events 25. Understanding Integration 26. America's Caste System 27. Misperceived Minorities 33. Italian Americans 34. If Names Could Kill 36. Polish Americans and the Holocaust 39. Outcasts Once Again 43. Color Blind *(1, 3, 4, 6, 8, 12, 14, 15, 16, 17, 18, 19, 20, 21, 22, 24, 27, 28, 29, 34, 36, 37)*
Courts	1. *Dred Scott v. Sandford* 2. Racial Restrictions in the Law of Citizenship 4. Retreat into Legalism 5. Strange Politics of Affirmative Action 16. Different Kind of Justice *(6, 7, 8, 9)*	**Economy**	10. Newcomers and Established Residents 12. American Indians in the 1990s 14. Profile: Rebecca Adamson 20. Balancing Act 27. Misperceived Minorities *(16, 17, 18, 19, 20, 21, 30, 31)*
Culture	9. Ethnicity v. Assimilation 12. Newcomers and Established Residents 14. Profile: Rebecca Adamson 15. Cape Town's District Six Rises Again 21. Tickled Brown 24. Understanding Afrocentrism 25. Understanding Integration 33. Italian Americans 37. Belonging in the West 45. Hip-Hop Nation *(16, 17, 18, 19, 20, 21, 24, 27, 31, 35, 36, 37)*	**Education**	3. *Brown v. Board of Education* 4. Retreat into Legalism 10. Newcomers and Established Relationships 20. Balancing Act 22. 10 Most Dramatic Events

Selected World Wide Web Sites for
AE: Race and Ethnic Relations

All of these Web sites are hot-linked through the *Annual Editions* home page: *http://www.dushkin.com/annualeditions* (just click on this book's title). In addition, these sites are referenced by number and appear where relevant in the Topic Guide on the previous two pages.

Some Web sites are continually changing their structure and content, so the information listed may not always be available.

General Sources

1. Library of Congress—*http://www.loc.gov/*—Examine this extensive Web site to learn about resource tools, library services/resources, exhibitions, and databases in many different fields related to race and ethnicity. See, for example, the site's information on the exhibition entitled "African American Odyssey" at *http://lcweb2.loc.gov/ammem/aaohtml/aohome.html*.

2. Social Science Information Gateway—*http://sosig.esrc.bris.ac.uk*—Access an online catalogue of thousands of Internet resources relevant to social science education and research at this site. Every resource is selected and described by a librarian or subject specialist.

3. SocioSite—*http://www.pscw.uva.nl/sociosite/TOPICS/Women.html*—Open this enormous site of the University of Amsterdam's Sociology Department to gain insights into a number of social issues. It provides links in affirmative action, race and ethnic relations, and much more.

4. University of Pennsylvania/Library— *http://www.library.upenn.edu/resources/social/sociology/sociology.html*—This site provides a number of valuable indexes of culture and ethnic studies, population and demographics, and statistical sources.

5. WWW Virtual Library: Demography & Population Studies—*http://coombs.anu.edu.au/ResFacilities/DemographyPage.html*—At this Web site you can find a definitive guide to demography and population studies. A multitude of important links to information about global poverty and hunger are available.

Race and Ethnicity in the American Legal Tradition

6. American Civil Liberties Union (ACLU)—*http://www.aclu.org/*—This site contains links to the ACLU's archives of information about civil rights in the United States and around the world, now and historically. Consult the index to find discussions of such topics as racial equality and immigrants' rights.

7. Human Rights Web—*http://www.hrweb.org/*—The history of the human-rights movement, text on seminal figures, landmark legal and political documents, and ideas on how individuals can get involved in helping to protect the rights of all peoples around the world can be found at this valuable site.

8. Supreme Court/Legal Information Institute—*http://supct.law.cornell.edu/supct/index.html*—Open this site for current and historical information about the Supreme Court. The archive contains many opinions issued since May 1990 as well as a collection of nearly 600 of the most historical decisions of the Court.

9. The White House—*http://www.whitehouse.gov/WH/Welcome.html*—Visit the home page of the White House for direct access to information about commonly requested federal services, the White House Briefing Room, and the presidents and vice presidents. The Virtual Library allows you to search White House documents, listen to speeches, and view photos.

Immigration and the American Experience

10. American Psychological Association (APA)—*http://www.apa.org/psychnet/*—By exploring the APA's PsychNET, you will be able to find links to an abundance of articles and other resources that are useful in understanding the factors that are involved in the development of prejudice.

11. Child Welfare League of America (CWLA)—*http://www.cwla.org/*—The CWLA is the United States' oldest and largest organization devoted entirely to the well-being of vulnerable children and their families. This site provides links to information about issues related to the process of becoming multicultural.

12. The Gallup Organization—*http://www.gallup.com/*—Open this Gallup Organization home page for links to an extensive archive of public opinion poll results and special reports on a huge variety of topics related to race and ethnicity in American society.

13. National Immigrant Forum—*http://www.immigrationforum.org/national.htm*—This pro-immigrant organization offers this page to examine the effects of immigration on the U.S. economy and society. Click on the links for discussion of underground economies, immigrant economies, and other topics.

14. The National Network for Immigrant and Refugee Rights (NNIRR)—*http://www.nnirr.org/*—The NNIRR serves as a forum to share information and analysis, to educate communities and the general public, and to develop and coordinate plans of action on important immigrant and refugee issues. Visit this site and its many links to explore these issues.

15. U.S. Immigration and Naturalization Service (INS)—*http://www.ins.usdoj.gov/*—This is the home page of the INS. Visit this site to learn U.S. official policy vis-à-vis immigrants, laws and regulations, and statistics.

Indigenous Ethnic Groups

16. American Indian Science and Engineering Society (AISES)—*http://spot.colorado.edu/~aises/aises.html*—This AISES "Multicultural Educational Reform Programs" site provides a framework for learning about science, mathematics, and technology by which underrepresented minority students and their teachers can make meaningful cultural connections to teaching and learning. There are useful links to programs for Native American education.

Hispanic/Latino Americans

17. Latino On-Line—*http://www.latinoonline.org/*—The purpose of this site is to empower Latinos. The site and its links address such topics of concern to Latinos as immigration, housing, employment, ethnicity, and income.

18. National Council of La Raza (NCLR)—*http://www.nclr.org/*—Explore NCLR's home page for links to discussions of important health and education issues in the Hispanic community. Many other economic, political, and social concerns are also covered at this site.

African Americans

19. National Association for the Advancement of Colored People (NAACP)—*http://www.naacp.org/*—Open this home page to explore the NAACP's stances regarding many topics in race and ethnic relations. Many links to other organizations and resources are provided.

Asian Americans

20. Asian Community Online Network—*http://www.igc.apc.org/acon/links/index.html*—Search through the links presented here for information on the political, historical, legal, and other concerns and interests of a wide variety of Asian American groups.

The Ethnic Legacy

21. African American Heritage Preservation Foundation—*http://www.preservenet.cornell.edu/aahpf/home page.htm*—Explore this site for information about ongoing and planned projects in preserving historical African American sites. This home page of the African American Heritage Preservation Foundation provides information about and links to related archaeological digs.

22. American Indian Ritual Object Repatriation Foundation—*http://www.repatriationfoundation.org/*—Visit this home page of the American Indian Ritual Object Repatriation Foundation, which aims to assist in the return of sacred ceremonial material to the appropriate American Indian nation, clan, or family; and to educate the public about the importance of culture and repatriation.

23. American Studies Web—*http://www.georgetown.edu/crossroads/asw/*—This eclectic site provides links to a wealth of resources on the Internet related to race and ethnic relations. It is of great help when doing research in demography and population studies.

24. Carfax—*http://www.carfax.co.uk/subjeduc.htm*—Look through this superb index for numerous articles as well as links to education publications such as *Journal of Beliefs and Values, Educational Philosophy and Theory, European Journal of Intercultural Studies*, and *Race, Ethnicity, and Education*.

25. The International Center for Migration, Ethnicity, and Citizenship—*http://www.newschool.edu/icmec/*—The Center is engaged in scholarly research and public policy analysis bearing on international migration, refugees, and the incorporation of newcomers in host countries. Explore this site for current news and to learn of resources for research.

The Ethnic Factor:
International Challenges for the 1990s

26. Africa News Online—*http://www.africanews.org/*—Open this site for *Africa News* on the Web. This source provides extensive, up-to-date information on all of Africa, with reports from Africa's leading newspapers, magazines, and news agencies. Background documents and Internet links are among the resource pages.

27. Cultural Survival—*http://www.cs.org/*—This nonprofit organization, founded in 1972, works to defend and protect the human rights and cultural autonomy of indigenous peoples and oppressed ethnic minorities around the world. Explore this site to learn about policies intended to avoid genocide and ethnic conflict and to promote tolerance and respect.

28. Human Rights and Humanitarian Assistance—*http://info.pitt.edu/~ian/resource/human.htm*—Through this site, part of the World Wide Web Virtual Library, you can conduct research into a number of human rights concerns around the world. The site provides links to many topics of interest in the study of race and ethnicity.

29. The North-South Institute—*http://www.nsi-ins.ca/info.html*—Searching this site of the North-South Institute—which works to strengthen international development cooperation and enhance social equity—will help you find information on a variety of issues related to international race and ethnicity issues.

30. U.S. Agency for International Development—*http://www.info.usaid.gov/*—This Web site covers such broad and overlapping issues as democracy, population and health, race and ethnicity, and economic growth. It provides specific information about different regions and countries.

31. World Wide Web Virtual Library: International Affairs Resources—*http://info.pitt.edu/~ian/ianres.html*—Surf this site and its extensive links to learn about specific countries and regions; to research various think tanks and international organizations; and to study such vital topics as international law, economic development, human rights, and peacekeeping.

Understanding Cultural Pluralism

32. American Scientist—*http://www.amsci.org/amsci/amsci.html*—Investigating this site will lead you to a variety of articles and other resources of value in exploring issues and concepts related to race and ethnicity.

33. Anthropology Resources Page, University of South Dakota—*http://www.usd.edu/anth/*—Many cultural topics can be accessed from this site from the University of South Dakota. Click on the links to find information about differences and similarities in values and lifestyles among the world's peoples.

34. National Center for Policy Analysis—*http://www.public-policy.org/~ncpa/pd/pdindex.html*—Through this site, you can read discussions on an array of topics that are of major interest in the study of American politics and government from a sociological perspective, from affirmative action to income disparity.

35. National Geographic Society—*http://www.nationalgeographic.com/*—This site provides links to National Geographic's huge archive of maps, articles, and other documents. There is a great deal of material related to social and cultural topics, of great value to those interested in the study of cultural pluralism.

36. Patterns of Variability: The Concept of Race—*http://www.as.ua.edu/ant/bindon/ant101/syllabus/race/race1.htm*—This site provides a handy, at-a-glance reference to the prevailing concepts of race and the causes of human variability since ancient times. It can serve as a valuable starting point for research and understanding into the concept of race.

37. STANDARDS: An International Journal of Multicultural Studies—*http://stripe.colorado.edu/~standard/*—This fascinating site provides access to the STANDARDS archives and a seemingly infinite number of links to topics of interest in the study of cultural pluralism.

We highly recommend that you review our Web site for expanded information and our other product lines. We are continually updating and adding links to our Web site in order to offer you the most usable and useful information that will support and expand the value of your Annual Editions. You can reach us at: *http://www.dushkin.com/annualeditions/*.

Race and Ethnicity in the American Legal Tradition

• The Foundations (Articles 1–3)
• The Civil Rights Era (Articles 4–6)

The legal framework established by the original U.S. Constitution illustrates the way that the American Founders handled ethnic pluralism. In most respects, they ignored the cultural and linguistic variety within and between the 13 original states, adopting instead a legal system that guaranteed religious exercise free from government interference, due process of law, and freedom of speech and the press. The founders, however, conspicuously compromised their claims of unalienable rights and democratic republicanism with regard to the constitutional status of Africans in bondage and indigenous Native Americans. Even after the Civil War and the inclusion of constitutional amendments that ended slavery provided for political inclusion of all persons and specifically mandated the loss of representation in the House of Representatives for those states that denied equal protection of the laws to all, exclusionary practices continued. Decisions by the U.S. Supreme Court helped to establish a legal system in which inequality and ethnic discrimination—both political and private—were legally permissible. The Supreme Court's attempt to redress the complex relationship between our constitutional system and the diverse society it governs is mediated by a political leadership that has not persistently sought "equal justice under the law" for all persons.

Moreover, the history of American immigration legislation, from the Alien and Sedition Laws at the founding to the most recent statutes, reveals an ambiguous legacy. This legal framework continues to mirror the political forces that influence the definition of citizenship and the constitution of ethnic identity and ethnic groups in America.

The legacies of African slavery, racial segregation, and ethnic discrimination established by the Constitution and by subsequent Court doctrines are traced in the following abbreviated U.S. Supreme Court opinions.

In *Dred Scott v. Sandford* (1856), the Supreme Court addressed the constitutional status of an African held in bondage who had been moved to a state that prohibited slavery. U.S. Supreme Court Chief Justice Roger B. Taney attempted to resolve the increasingly divisive issue of slavery by declaring that the "Negro African race"—whether free or slave—was "not intended to be included under the word 'citizens' in the Constitution, and can therefore claim none of the rights and privileges that instrument provides for and secures to citizens of the United States." Contrary to Taney's intentions, however, *Dred Scott* further fractured the nation, ensuring that only the Civil War would resolve the slavery issue.

In *Plessy v. Ferguson* (1896), the Supreme Court upheld the constitutionality of "Jim Crow" laws that segregated public facilities on the basis of an individual's racial ancestry. The Court reasoned that this "separate but equal" segregation did not violate any rights guaranteed by the U.S. Constitution, nor did it stamp "the colored race with a badge of inferiority." Instead, the Court argued that if "this be so, it is not by reason of anything found in the act but solely because the colored race chooses to put that construction upon it." In contrast, Justice John M. Harlan's vigorous dissent from the Court's *Plessy* opinion contends that "our Constitution is color-blind, and neither knows nor tolerates classes among citizens." The history of the Courts's attention to citizenship provides a view of a culturally embedded character of color consciousness and the strict textual dependence of the Justices that interpreted the Constitution. Another perspective, however, emerges from the congressional debate that occurred when a civil rights law ensuring equal protection and voting rights was passed shortly after the Civil War. That legislative history is cited extensively in *Shaare Tefila/ Al-khasraji (1987)*. This expansive view of protection for all ethnic groups cited in these decisions and the origin of these views in congressional intention voiced by elected legislators are indications of the Court's new directions. The Court's dependence on statutes rather than on the exercise of constitutional authority as the judiciary, and thus as a policymaker and initiator, appears to be waning. Moreover, the Court, under the influence of a color-blind doctrine, seems ready to challenge policies that significantly rely on race and ethnicity, thus changing the landscape as well as the discussion of race and ethnicity, inviting all of us to reexamine both the intentions and outcomes of all legislation in this field.

In *Brown v. Board of Education of Topeka* (1954), the Supreme Court began the ambitious project of dismantling state-supported racial segregation. In *Brown*, a unanimous Court overturned *Plessy v. Ferguson,* arguing that

"in the field of public education the doctrine of 'separate but equal' has no place," because "separate educational facilities are inherently unequal."

However, this era of civil rights consensus embodied in the landmark actions of the Supreme Court has been challenged by contemporary plaintiffs who have turned to the Court for clarification regarding specific cases related to the significance of race and ethnic criteria in public affairs. The lack of popular support for the administration and implementation of policies and the judicial leadership of those policies in California emerged in Proposition 209. This issue of popular concern was played out in the referendum which was supported by the electorate, but their decision will be played out in the Court as the country braces itself for another cycle of tension and acrimony between the will of the people in a particular state and the rule and supremacy of national law. The mediation between law and popular expression, the political nexus of state and federal legitimacy, will no doubt be challenged by these contentions.

The impact of these reconsiderations and of the remedies that should be applied will undoubtedly contribute to the Presidential Initiative on Race and the national conversation designed to fashion a fresh understanding of race relations and the various ways an America united can be developed. The implementation of the desegregation remedies, affirmative action, and voting rights remedies have been challenged in the judicial rulings as well as the decision to avoid court action that might compromise hard won gains for minority populations. The politics of affirmative action advocates and opponents has become more strident and has exacerbated racial and ethnic competition for public participation.

In the late 1960s, proposals that sought to depolarize race issues argued for a policy of benign neglect, meaning that although equal protection and opportunity were essential, economic and education policy should focus on the needs of persons and groups and regions, not on their race, and that these should be the driving criteria and the redistributive thrust of a national policy of remediation. What does this philosophy of public policy contribute to the current context?

Looking Ahead: Challenge Questions

Comment on the idea that the American political process has relied too extensively on the Supreme Court, and forecast the outcomes of the Presidential Initiative on Race.

The U.S. Congress is the lawmaking institution that authorized national policies of equal protection that are constitutionally guaranteed to all. What explains the disparity between the patently clear proclamation of equality and the painfully obvious practices of racial/ethnic discrimination?

Why has the constitutional penalty of reducing the number of representatives in Congress found in Article 14, Section 2, not been applied?

DRED SCOTT V. SANDFORD

December Term 1856.

MR. CHIEF JUSTICE TANEY delivered the opinion of the court.

This case has been twice argued. After the argument at the last term, differences of opinion were found to exist among the members of the court; and as the questions in controversy are of the highest importance, and the court was at that time much pressed by the ordinary business of the term, it was deemed advisable to continue the case, and direct a re-argument on some of the points, in order that we might have an opportunity of giving to the whole subject a more deliberate consideration. It has accordingly been again argued by counsel, and considered by the court; and I now proceed to deliver its opinion.

There are two leading questions presented by the record:

1. Had the Circuit Court of the United States jurisdiction to hear and determine the case between these parties? And

2. If it had jurisdiction, is the judgment it has given erroneous or not?

The plaintiff in error, who was also the plaintiff in the court below, was, with his wife and children, held as slaves by the defendant, in the State of Missouri; and he brought this action in the Circuit Court of the United States for that district, to assert the title of himself and his family to freedom.

The declaration is in the form usually adopted in that State to try questions of this description, and contains the averment necessary to give the court jurisdiction; that he and the defendant are citizens of different States; that is, that he is a citizen of Missouri, and the defendant a citizen of New York.

The defendant pleaded in abatement to the jurisdiction of the court, that the plaintiff was not a citizen of the State of Missouri, as alleged in his declaration, being a negro of African descent, whose ancestors were of pure African blood, and who were brought into this country and sold as slaves.

To this plea the plaintiff demurred, and the defendant joined in demurrer. The court overruled the plea,

and gave judgment that the defendant should answer over. And he thereupon put in sundry pleas in bar, upon which issues were joined; and at the trial the verdict and judgment were in his favor. Whereupon the plaintiff brought this writ of error.

Before we speak of the pleas in bar, it will be proper to dispose of the questions which have arisen on the plea in abatement.

That plea denies the right of the plaintiff to sue in a court of the United States, for the reasons therein stated.

If the question raised by it is legally before us, and the court should be of opinion that the facts stated in it disqualify the plaintiff from becoming a citizen, in the sense in which that word is used in the Constitution of the United States, then the judgment of the Circuit Court is erroneous, and must be reversed.

It is suggested, however, that this plea is not before us; and that as the judgment in the court below on this plea was in favor of the plaintiff, he does not seek to reverse it, or bring it before the court for revision by his writ of error; and also that the defendant waived this defence by pleading over, and thereby admitted the jurisdiction of the court.

But, in making this objection, we think the peculiar and limited jurisdiction of courts of the United States has not been adverted to. This peculiar and limited jurisdiction has made it necessary, in these courts, to adopt different rules and principles of pleading, so far as jurisdiction is concerned, from those which regulate courts of common law in England, and in the different States of the Union which have adopted the common-law rules.

In these last-mentioned courts, where their character and rank are analogous to that of a Circuit Court of the United States; in other words, where they are what the law terms courts of general jurisdiction; they are presumed to have jurisdiction, unless the contrary appears. No averment in the pleadings of the plaintiff is necessary, in order to give jurisdiction. If the defendant objects to it, he must plead it specially, and unless the fact on which he relies is found to be true by a jury, or admitted to be true by the plaintiff, the jurisdiction cannot be disputed in an appellate court.

Now, it is not necessary to inquire whether in courts of that description a party who pleads over in bar, when a plea to the jurisdiction has been ruled against him, does or does not waive his plea; nor whether upon a judgment in his favor on the pleas in bar, and a writ of error brought by the plaintiff, the question upon the plea in abatement would be open for revision in the appellate court. Cases that may have been decided in such courts, or rules that may have been laid down by common-law pleaders, can have no influence in the decision in this court. Because, under the Constitution and laws of the United States, the rules which govern the pleadings in its courts, in questions of jurisdiction, stand on different principles and are regulated by different laws.

This difference arises, as we have said, from the peculiar character of the Government of the United States. For although it is sovereign and supreme in its appropriate sphere of action, yet it does not possess all the powers which usually belong to the sovereignty of a nation. Certain specified powers, enumerated in the Constitution, have been conferred upon it; and neither the legislative, executive, nor judicial departments of the Government can lawfully exercise any authority beyond the limits marked out by the Constitution. And in regulating the judicial department, the cases in which the courts of the United States shall have jurisdiction are particularly and specifically enumerated and defined; and they are not authorized to take cognizance of any case which does not come within the description therein specified. Hence, when a plaintiff sues in a court of the United States, it is necessary that he should show, in his pleading, that the suit he brings is within the jurisdiction of the court, and that he is entitled to sue there. And if he omits to do this, and should, by any oversight of the Circuit Court, obtain a judgment in his favor, the judgment would be reversed in the appellate court for want of jurisdiction in the court below. The jurisdiction would not be presumed, as in the case of a common-law English or State court, unless the contrary appeared. But the record, when it comes before the appellate court, must show, affirmatively, that the inferior court had authority, under the Constitution, to hear and determine the case. And if the plaintiff claims a right to sue in a Circuit Court of the United States, under that provision of the Constitution which gives jurisdiction in controversies between citizens of different States, he must distinctly aver in his pleading that they are citizens of different States; and he cannot maintain his suit without showing that fact in the pleadings.

This point was decided in the case of *Bingham v. Cabot,* (in 3 Dall., 382,) and ever since adhered to by the court. And in *Jackson v. Ashton,* (8 Pet., 148,) it was held that the objection to which it was open could not be waived by the opposite party, because consent of parties could not give jurisdiction.

It is needless to accumulate cases on this subject. Those already referred to, and the cases of *Capron v. Van Noorden,* (in 2 Cr., 126) and *Montalet v. Murray,* (4 Cr., 46,) are sufficient to show the rule of which we have spoken. The case of *Capron v. Van Noorden* strikingly illustrates the difference between a common-law court and a court of the United States.

If, however, the fact of citizenship is averred in the declaration, and the defendant does not deny it, and put it in issue by plea in abatement, he cannot offer evidence at the trial to disprove it, and consequently cannot avail himself of the objection in the appellate court, unless the defect should be apparent in some other part of the record. For if there is no plea in abatement, and the want of jurisdiction does not appear in any other part of the transcript brought up by the writ of error, the undisputed averment of citizenship in the declaration must be taken in this court to be true. In this case, the citizenship is averred, but it is denied by the defendant in the manner required by the rules of pleading, and the fact upon which the denial is based is admitted by the demurrer. And, if the plea and demurrer, and judgment of the court below upon it, are before us upon this record, the question to be decided is, whether the facts stated in the plea are sufficient to show that the plaintiff is not entitled to sue as a citizen in a court of the United States. . . .

We think they are before us. The plea in abatement and the judgment of the court upon it, are a part of the judicial proceedings in the Circuit Court, and are there recorded as such; and a writ of error always brings up to the superior court the whole record of the proceedings in the court below. And in the case of the *United States v. Smith,* (11 Wheat., 172) this court said, that the case being brought up by writ of error, the whole record was under the consideration of this court. And this being the case in the present instance, the plea in abatement is necessarily under consideration; and it becomes, therefore, our duty to decide whether the facts stated in the plea are or are not sufficient to show that the plaintiff is not entitled to sue as a citizen in a court of the United States.

This is certainly a very serious question, and one that now for the first time has been brought for decision before this court. But it is brought here by those who have a right to bring it, and it is our duty to meet it and decide it.

The question is simply this: Can a negro, whose ancestors were imported into this country, and sold as slaves, become a member of the political community formed and brought into existence by the Constitution of the United States, and as such become entitled to all the rights, and privileges, and immunities, guaranteed by that instrument to the citizen? One of which rights is the privilege of suing in a court of the United States in the cases specified in the Constitution.

It will be observed, that the plea applies to that class of persons only whose ancestors were negroes of the African race, and imported into this country, and sold and held as slaves. The only matter in issue before the court, therefore, is, whether the descendants of such slaves, when they shall be emancipated, or who are born of parents who had become free before their birth, are citizens of a State, in the sense in which the word citizen is used in the Constitution of the United States. And this being the only matter in dispute on the pleadings, the court must be understood as speaking in this opinion of that class only, that is, of those persons who are the descendants of Africans who were imported into this country, and sold as slaves.

The situation of this population was altogether unlike that of the Indian race. The latter, it is true, formed no part of the colonial communities, and never amalgamated with them in social connections or in government. But although they were uncivilized, they were yet a free and independent people, associated together in nations or tribes, and governed by their own laws. Many of these political communities were situated in territories to which the white race claimed the ultimate right of dominion. But that claim was acknowledged to be subject to the right of the Indians to occupy it as long as they thought proper, and neither the English nor colonial Governments claimed or exercised any dominion over the tribe or nation by whom it was occupied, nor claimed the right to the possession of the territory, until the tribe or nation consented to cede it. These Indian Governments were regarded and treated as foreign Governments, as must so as if an ocean had separated the red man from the white; and their freedom has constantly been acknowledged, from the time of the first emigration to the English colonies to the present day, by the different Governments which succeeded each other. Treaties have been negotiated with them, and their alliance sought for in war; and the people who compose these Indian political communities have always been treated as foreigners not living under our Government. It is true that the course of events has brought the Indian tribes within the limits of the United States under subjection to the white race; and it has been found necessary, for their sake as well as our own, to regard them as in a state of pupilage, and to legislate to a certain extent over them and the territory they occupy. But they may, without doubt, like the subjects of any other foreign Government, be naturalized by the authority of Congress, and become citizens of a State, and of the United States; and if an individual should leave his nation or tribe, and take up his abode among the white population, he would be entitled to all the rights and privileges which would belong to an emigrant from any other foreign people.

We proceed to examine the case as presented by the pleadings.

The words "people of the United States" and "citizens" are synonymous terms, and mean the same thing. They both describe the political body who, according to our republican institutions, form the sovereignty, and who hold the power and conduct the Government through their representatives. They are what we familiarly call the "sovereign people," and every citizen is one of this people, and a constituent member of this sovereignty. The question before us is, whether the class of persons described in the plea in abatement compose a portion of this people, and are constituent members of this sovereignty? We think they are not, and that they are not included, and were not intended to be included, under the word "citizens" in the Constitution, and can therefore claim none of the rights and privileges which that instrument provides for and secures to citizens of the United States. On the contrary, they were at that time considered as a subordinate and inferior class of beings, who had been subjugated by the dominant race, and, whether emancipated or not, yet remained subject to their authority, and had no rights or privileges but such as those who held the power and the Government might choose to grant them.

It is not the province of the court to decide upon the justice or injustice, the policy or impolicy, of these laws. The decision of that question belonged to the political or law-making power; to those who formed the sovereignty and framed the Constitution. The duty of the court is, to interpret the instrument they have framed, with the best lights we can obtain on the subject, and to administer it as we find it, according to its true intent and meaning when it was adopted.

In discussing this question, we must not confound the rights of citizenship which a State may confer within its own limits, and the rights of citizenship as a member of the Union. It does not by any means follow, because he has all the rights and privileges of a citizen of a State, that he must be a citizen of the United States. He may have all of the rights and privileges of the citizen of a State, and yet not be entitled to the rights and privileges of a citizen in any other State. For, previous to the adoption of the Constitution of the United States, every State had the undoubted right to confer on whomsoever it pleased the character of citizen, and to endow him with all its rights. But this character of course was confined to the boundaries of the State, and gave him no rights or privileges in other States beyond those secured to him by the laws of nations and the comity of States. Nor have the several States surrendered the power of conferring these rights and privileges by adopting the Constitution of the United States. Each State may still confer them upon an alien, or any one it thinks proper, or upon any class or description of persons; yet he would not be a citizen in the sense in which that word is used in the Constitution of the United States, nor entitled to sue as such in one of its courts, nor to the privileges and immunities of a citizen in the other States. The rights which he would acquire would be restricted to the State which gave them. The Constitution has conferred on Congress the right to establish a uniform rule of naturalization, and this right is evidently exclusive, and has always been held by this court to be so. Consequently, no State, since the adoption of the Constitution, can by naturalizing an alien invest him with the rights and privileges secured to a citizen of a State under the Federal Government, although, so far as the State alone was concerned, he would undoubtedly be entitled to the rights of a citizen, and clothed with all the rights and immunities which the Constitution and laws of the State attached to that character.

It is very clear, therefore, that no State can, by any act or law of its own, passed since the adoption of the Constitution, introduce a new member into the political community created by the Constitution of the United States. It cannot make him a member of this community by making him a member of its own. And for the same reason it cannot introduce any person, or description of persons, who were not intended to be embraced in this new political family, which the Constitution brought into existence, but were intended to be excluded from it.

The question then arises, whether the provisions of the Constitution, in relation to the personal rights and privileges to which the citizen of a State should be entitled, embraced the negro African race, at that time in this country, or who might afterwards be imported, who had then or should afterwards be made free in any State; and to put it in the power of a single State to make him a citizen of the United States, and endue him with the full rights of citizenship in every other State without their consent? Does the Constitution of the United States act upon him whenever he shall be made free under the laws of a State, and raised there to the rank of a citizen, and immediately clothe him with all the privileges of a citizen in every other State, and in its own courts?

The court think the affirmative of these propositions cannot be maintained. And if it cannot, the plaintiff in error could not be a citizen of the State of Missouri, within the meaning of the Constitution of the United States, and, consequently, was not entitled to sue in its courts.

It is true, every person, and every class and description of persons, who were at the time of the adoption of the Constitution recognised as citizens in the several States, became also citizens of this new political body; but none other; it was formed by them, and for them and their posterity, but for no one else. And the personal rights and privileges guarantied to citizens of this new sovereignty were intended to embrace those only who were then members of the several State communities, or who should afterwards by birthright or otherwise become members, according to the provisions of the Constitution and the principles on which it was founded. It was the union of those who were at that time members of distinct and separate political communities into one political family, whose power, for certain specified purposes, was to extend over the whole territory of the United States. And it gave to each citizen rights and privileges outside of his State which he did not before possess, and placed him in every other State upon a perfect equality with its own citizens as to rights of person and rights of property; it made him a citizen of the United States.

It becomes necessary, therefore, to determine who were citizens of the several States when the Constitution was adopted. And in order to do this, we must recur to the Governments and institutions of the thirteen colonies, when they separated from Great Britain and formed new sovereignties, and took their places in the family of independent nations. We must inquire who, at that time, were recognised as the people or citizens of a State, whose rights and liberties had been outraged by the English Government; and who declared their independence, and assumed the powers of Government to defend their rights by force of arms.

In the opinion of the court, the legislation and histories of the times, and the language used in the Declaration of Independence, show, that neither the class of persons who had been imported as slaves, nor their descendants, whether they had become free or not, were then acknowledged as a part of the people, nor intended to be included in the general words used in that memorable instrument. . . .

Racial Restrictions in the Law of Citizenship

Ian F. Haney Lopez

The racial composition of the U.S. citizenry reflects in part the accident of world migration patterns. More than this, however, it reflects the conscious design of U.S. immigration and naturalization laws.

Federal law restricted immigration to this country on the basis of race for nearly one hundred years, roughly from the Chinese exclusion laws of the 1880s until the end of the national origin quotas in 1965.[1] The history of this discrimination can briefly be traced. Nativist sentiment against Irish and German Catholics on the East Coast and against Chinese and Mexicans on the West Coast, which had been doused by the Civil War, reignited during the economic slump of the 1870s. Though most of the nativist efforts failed to gain congressional sanction, Congress in 1882 passed the Chinese Exclusion Act, which suspended the immigration of Chinese laborers for ten years.[2] The Act was expanded to exclude all Chinese in 1884, and was eventually implemented indefinitely.[3] In 1917, Congress created "an Asiatic barred zone," excluding all persons from Asia.[4] During this same period, the Senate passed a bill to exclude "all members of the African or black race." This effort was defeated in the House only after intensive lobbying by the NAACP.[5] Efforts to exclude the supposedly racially undesirable southern and eastern Europeans were more successful. In 1921, Congress established a temporary quota system designed "to confine immigration as much as possible to western and northern European stock," making this bar permanent three years later in the National Origin Act of 1924.[6] With the onset of the Depression, attention shifted to Mexican immigrants. Although no law explicitly targeted this group, federal immigration officials began a series of round-ups and mass deportations of people of Mexican descent under the general rubric of a "repatriation campaign." Approximately 500,000 people were forcibly returned to Mexico during the Depression, more than half of them U.S. citizens.[7] This pattern was repeated in the 1950s, when Attorney General Herbert Brownwell launched a program to expel Mexicans. This effort, dubbed "Operation Wetback," indiscriminately deported more than one million citizens and noncitizens in 1954 alone.[8]

Racial restrictions on immigration were not significantly dismantled until 1965, when Congress in a major overhaul of immigration law abolished both the national origin system and the Asiatic Barred Zone.[9] Even so, purposeful racial discrimination in immigration law by Congress remains constitutionally permissible, since the case that upheld the Chinese Exclusion Act to this day remains good law.[10] Moreover, arguably racial discrimination in immigration law continues. For example, Congress has enacted special provisions to encourage Irish immigration, while refusing to ameliorate the backlog of would-be immigrants from the Philippines, India, South Korea, China, and Hong Kong, backlogs created in part through a century of racial exclusion.[11] The history of racial discrimination in U.S. immigration law is a long and continuing one.

As discriminatory as the laws of immigration have been, the laws of citizenship betray an even more dismal record of racial exclusion. From this country's inception, the laws regulating who was or could become a citizen were tainted by racial prejudice. Birthright citizenship, the automatic acquisition of citizenship by virtue of birth, was tied to race until 1940. Naturalized citizenship, the acquisition of citizenship by any means other than through birth, was conditioned on race until 1952. Like immigration laws, the laws of birthright citizenship and naturalization shaped the racial character of the United States.

 From *White by Law: The Legal Construction of Race*, 1996, Chapter 2, pp. 37-47, 235-240. © 1996 by New York University Press. Reprinted by permission.

Birthright Citizenship

Most persons acquire citizenship by birth rather than through naturalization. During the 1990s, for example, naturalization will account for only 7.5 percent of the increase in the U.S. citizen population.[12] At the time of the prerequisite cases, the proportion of persons gaining citizenship through naturalization was probably somewhat higher, given the higher ratio of immigrants to total population, but still far smaller than the number of people gaining citizenship by birth. In order to situate the prerequisite laws, therefore, it is useful first to review the history of racial discrimination in the laws of birthright citizenship.

The U.S. Constitution as ratified did not define the citizenry, probably because it was assumed that the English common law rule of *jus soli* would continue.[13] Under *jus soli,* citizenship accrues to "all" born within a nation's jurisdiction. Despite the seeming breadth of this doctrine, the word "all" is qualified because for the first one hundred years and more of this country's history it did not fully encompass racial minorities. This is the import of the *Dred Scott* decision.[14] Scott, an enslaved man, sought to use the federal courts to sue for his freedom. However, access to the courts was predicated on citizenship. Dismissing his claim, the United States Supreme Court in the person of Chief Justice Roger Taney declared in 1857 that Scott and all other Blacks, free and enslaved, were not and could never be citizens because they were "a subordinate and inferior class of beings." The decision protected the slave-holding South and infuriated much of the North, further dividing a country already fractured around the issues of slavery and the power of the national government. *Dred Scott* was invalidated after the Civil War by the Civil Rights Act of 1866, which declared that "All persons born . . . in the United States and not subject to any foreign power, excluding Indians not taxed, are declared to be citizens of the United States."[15] *Jus soli* subsequently became part of the organic law of the land in the form of the Fourteenth Amendment: "All persons born or naturalized in the United States, and subject to the jurisdiction thereof, are citizens of the United States and of the state wherein they reside."[16]

Despite the broad language of the Fourteenth Amendment—though in keeping with the words of the 1866 act—some racial minorities remained outside the bounds of *jus soli* even after its constitutional enactment. In particular, questions persisted about the citizenship status of children born in the United States to noncitizen parents, and about the status of Native Americans. The Supreme Court did not decide the status of the former until 1898,

when it ruled in *U.S. v. Wong Kim Ark* that native-born children of aliens, even those permanently barred by race from acquiring citizenship, were birthright citizens of the United States.[17] On the citizenship of the latter, the Supreme Court answered negatively in 1884, holding in *Elk v. Wilkins* that Native Americans owed allegiance to their tribe and so did not acquire citizenship upon birth.[18] Congress responded by granting Native Americans citizenship in piecemeal fashion, often tribe by tribe. Not until 1924 did Congress pass an act conferring citizenship on all Native Americans in the United States.[19] Even then, however, questions arose regarding the citizenship of those born in the United States after the effective date of the 1924 act. These questions were finally resolved, and *jus soli* fully applied, under the Nationality Act of 1940, which specifically bestowed citizenship on all those born in the United States "to a member of an Indian, Eskimo, Aleutian, or other aboriginal tribe."[20] Thus, the basic law of citizenship, that a person born here is a citizen here, did not include all racial minorities until 1940.

Unfortunately, the impulse to restrict birthright citizenship by race is far from dead in this country. Apparently, California Governor Pete Wilson and many others seek a return to the times when citizenship depended on racial proxies such as immigrant status. Wilson has called for a federal constitutional amendment that would prevent the American-born children of undocumented persons from receiving birthright citizenship.[21] His call has not been ignored: thirteen members of Congress recently sponsored a constitutional amendment that would repeal the existing Citizenship Clause of the Fourteenth Amendment and replace it with a provision that "All persons born in the United States . . . of mothers who are citizens or legal residents of the United States . . . are citizens of the United States."[22] Apparently, such a change is supported by 49 percent of Americans.[23] In addition to explicitly discriminating against fathers by eliminating their right to confer citizenship through parentage, this proposal implicitly discriminates along racial lines. The effort to deny citizenship to children born here to undocumented immigrants seems to be motivated not by an abstract concern over the political status of the parents, but by racial animosity against Asians and Latinos, those commonly seen as comprising the vast bulk of undocumented migrants. Bill Ong Hing writes, "The discussion of who is and who is not American, who can and cannot become American, goes beyond the technicalities of citizenship and residency requirements; it strikes at the very heart of our nation's long and troubled legacy of race relations.[24] As this troubled legacy reveals, the triumph over racial discrimination in the laws of citizenship and alienage came slowly and only recently. In the campaign for the "control of our borders," we are once again debating the citizenship of the native-born and the merits of *Dred Scott*.[25]

Naturalization

Although the Constitution did not originally define the citizenry, it explicitly gave Congress the authority to establish the criteria for granting citizenship after birth. Article I grants Congress the power "To establish a uniform Rule of Naturalization."[26] From the start, Congress exercised this power in a manner that burdened naturalization laws with racial restrictions that tracked those in the law of birthright citizenship. In 1790, only a few months after ratification of the Constitution, Congress limited naturalization to "any alien, being a free white person who shall have resided within the limits and under the jurisdiction of the United States for a term of two years."[27] This clause mirrored not only the de facto laws of birthright citizenship, but also the racially restrictive naturalization laws of several states. At least three states had previously limited citizenship to "white persons": Virginia in 1779, South Carolina in 1784, and Georgia in 1785.[28] Though there would be many subsequent changes in the requirements for federal naturalization, racial identity endured as a bedrock requirement for the next 162 years. In every naturalization act from 1790 until 1952, Congress included the "white person" prerequisite.[29]

The history of racial prerequisites to naturalization can be divided into two periods of approximately eighty years each. The first period extended from 1790 to 1870, when only Whites were able to naturalize. In the wake of the Civil War, the "white person" restriction on naturalization came under serious attack as part of the effort to expunge *Dred Scott*. Some congressmen, Charles Sumner chief among them, argued that racial barriers to naturalization should be struck altogether. However, racial prejudice against Native Americans and Asians forestalled the complete elimination of the racial prerequisites. During congressional debates, one senator argued against conferring "the rank, privileges, and immunities of citizenship upon the cruel savages who destroyed [Minnesota's] peaceful settlements and massacred the people with circumstances of atrocity too horrible to relate."[30] Another senator wondered "whether this door [of citizenship] shall now be thrown open to the Asiatic population," warning that to do so would spell for the Pacific coast "an end to republican government there, because it is very well ascertained that those

people have no appreciation of that form of government; it seems to be obnoxious to their very nature; they seem to be incapable either of understanding or carrying it out."[31] Sentiments such as these ensured that even after the Civil War, bars against Native American and Asian naturalization would continue.[32] Congress opted to maintain the "white person" prerequisite, but to extend the right to naturalize to "persons of African nativity, or African descent."[33] After 1870, Blacks as well as Whites could naturalize, but not others.

During the second period, from 1870 until the last of the prerequisite laws were abolished in 1952, the White-Black dichotomy in American race relations dominated naturalization law. During this period, Whites and Blacks were eligible for citizenship, but others, particularly those from Asia, were not. Indeed, increasing antipathy toward Asians on the West Coast resulted in an explicit disqualification of Chinese persons from naturalization in 1882.[34] The prohibition of Chinese naturalization, the only U.S. law ever to exclude by name a particular nationality from citizenship, was coupled with the ban on Chinese immigration discussed previously. The Supreme Court readily upheld the bar, writing that "Chinese persons not born in this country have never been recognized as citizens of the United States, nor authorized to become such under the naturalization laws."[35] While Blacks were permitted to naturalize beginning in 1870, the Chinese and most "other non-Whites" would have to wait until the 1940s for the right to naturalize.[36]

World War II forced a domestic reconsideration of the racism integral to U.S. naturalization law. In 1935, Hitler's Germany limited citizenship to members of the Aryan race, making Germany the only country other than the United States with a racial restriction on naturalization.[37] The fact of this bad company was not lost on those administering our naturalization laws. "When Earl G. Harrison in 1944 resigned as United States Commissioner of Immigration and Naturalization, he said that the only country in the world, outside the United States, that observes racial discrimination in matters relating to naturalization was Nazi Germany, 'and we all agree that this is not very desirable company.'"[38] Furthermore, the United States was open to charges of hypocrisy for banning from naturalization the nationals of many of its Asian allies. During the war, the United States seemed through some of its laws and social practices to embrace the same racism it was fighting. Both fronts of the war exposed profound inconsistencies between U.S. naturalization law and broader social ideals. These considerations, among others, led Congress to begin a process of piecemeal reform in the laws governing citizenship.

In 1940, Congress opened naturalization to "descendants of races indigenous to the Western Hemisphere."[39] Apparently, this "additional limitation was designed 'to more fully cement' the ties of Pan-Americanism" at a time of impending crisis.[40] In 1943, Congress replaced the prohibition on the naturalization of Chinese persons with a provision explicitly granting them this boon.[41] In 1946, it opened up naturalization to persons from the Philippines and India as well.[42] Thus, at the end of the war, our naturalization law looked like this:

The right to become a naturalized citizen under the provisions of this Act shall extend only to—

(1) white persons, persons of African nativity or descent, and persons of races indigenous to the continents of North or South America or adjacent islands and Filipino persons or persons of Filipino descent;
(2) persons who possess, either singly or in combination, a preponderance of blood of one or more of the classes specified in clause (1);
(3) Chinese persons or persons of Chinese descent; and persons of races indigenous to India; and
(4) persons who possess, either singly or in combination, a preponderance of blood of one or more of the classes specified in clause (3) or, either singly or in combination, as much as one-half blood of those classes and some additional blood of one of the classes specified in clause (1).[43]

This incremental retreat from a "Whites only" conception of citizenship made the arbitrariness of U.S. naturalization law increasingly obvious. For example, under the above statute, the right to acquire citizenship depended for some on blood-quantum distinctions based on descent from peoples indigenous to islands adjacent to the Americas. In 1952, Congress moved towards whole-sale reform, overhauling the naturalization statute to read simply that "[t]he right of a person to become a naturalized citizen of the United States shall not be denied or abridged because of race or sex or because such person is married."[44] Thus, in 1952, racial bars on naturalization came to an official end.[45]

Notice the mention of gender in the statutory language ending racial restrictions in naturalization. The issue of women and citizenship can only be touched on here, but deserves significant study in its own right.[46] As the language of the 1952 Act implies, eligibility for naturalization once depended on a woman's marital status. Congress in 1855 declared that a foreign woman automatically acquired citizenship upon marriage to a U.S. citizen, or upon the naturalization of her alien husband.[47] This provision built upon the supposition that a woman's social and political status flowed from her husband. As an 1895 treatise on naturalization put it,

"A woman partakes of her husband's nationality; her nationality is merged in that of her husband; her political status follows that of her husband."[48] A wife's acquisition of citizenship, however, remained subject to her individual qualification for naturalization—that is, on whether she was a "white person."[49] Thus, the Supreme Court held in 1868 that only "white women" could gain citizenship by marrying a citizen.[50] Racial restrictions further complicated matters for noncitizen women in that naturalization was denied to those married to a man racially ineligible for citizenship, irrespective of the woman's own qualifications, racial or otherwise.[51] The automatic naturalization of a woman upon her marriage to a citizen or upon the naturalization of her husband ended in 1922.[52]

The citizenship of American-born women was also affected by the interplay of gender and racial restrictions. Even though under English common law a woman's nationality was unaffected by marriage, many courts in this country stripped women who married noncitizens of their U.S. citizenship.[53] Congress recognized and mandated this practice in 1907, legislating that an American woman's marriage to an alien terminated her citizenship.[54] Under considerable pressure, Congress partially repealed this act in 1922.[55] However, the 1922 act continued to require the expatriation of any woman who married a foreigner racially barred from citizenship, flatly declaring that "any woman citizen who marries an alien ineligible to citizenship shall cease to be a citizen."[56] Until Congress repealed this provision in 1931,[57] marriage to a non-White alien by an American woman was akin to treason against this country: either of these acts justified the stripping of citizenship from someone American by birth. Indeed, a woman's marriage to a non-White foreigner was perhaps a worse crime, for while a traitor lost his citizenship only after trial, the woman lost hers automatically.[58] The laws governing the racial composition of this country's citizenry came inseverably bound up with and exacerbated by sexism. It is in this context of combined racial and gender prejudice that we should understand the absence of any women among the petitioners named in the prerequisite cases: it is not that women were unaffected by the racial bars, but that they were doubly bound by them, restricted both as individuals, and as less than individuals (that is, as wives).

Notes

1. U.S. COMMISSION ON CIVIL RIGHTS, THE TARNISHED GOLDEN DOOR: CIVIL RIGHTS ISSUES IN IMMIGRATION 1–12 (1990).

2. Chinese Exclusion Act, ch. 126, 22 Stat. 58 (1882). *See generally* Harold Hongju Koh, *Bitter Fruit of the Asian Immigration Cases*, 6 CONSTITUTION 69 (1994). For a sobering account of the many lynchings of Chinese in the western United States during this period, *see* John R. Wunder, *Anti-Chinese Violence in the American West, 1850–1910*, LAW FOR THE ELEPHANT, LAW FOR THE BEAVER: ESSAYS IN THE LEGAL HISTORY OF THE NORTH AMERICAN WEST 212 (John McLaren, Hamar Foster, and Chet Orloff eds., 1992). Charles McClain, Jr., discusses the historical origins of anti-Chinese prejudice and the legal responses undertaken by that community on the West Coast. Charles McClain, Jr., *The Chinese Struggle for Civil Rights in Nineteenth Century America: The First Phase, 1850–1870*, 72 CAL. L. REV. 529 (1984). For a discussion of contemporary racial violence against Asian Americans, *see* Note, *Racial Violence against Asian Americans*, 106 HARV. L. REV. 1926 (1993); Robert Chang, *Toward an Asian American Legal Scholarship: Critical Race Theory, Post-Structuralism, and Narrative Space*, 81 CAL. L. REV. 1241, 1251–58(1993).

3. Act of July 9, 1884, ch. 220, 23 Stat. 115; Act of May 5, 1892, ch. 60, 27 Stat. 25; Act of April 29, 1902, ch. 641, 32 Stat. 176; Act of April 27, 1904, ch. 1630, 33 Stat. 428.

4. Act of Feb. 5, 1917, ch. 29, 39 Stat. 874.

5. U.S. COMMISSION ON CIVIL RIGHTS, *supra*, at 9.

6. *Id. See* Act of May 19, 1921, ch. 8, 42 Stat. 5; Act of May 26, 1924, ch. 190, 43 Stat. 153.

7. U.S. COMMISSION ON CIVIL RIGHTS, *supra*, at 10.

8. *Id.* at 11. *See generally* JUAN RAMON GARCIA, OPERATION WETBACK: THE MASS DEPORTATION OF MEXICAN UNDOCUMENTED WORKERS IN 1954 (1980).

9. Act of Oct. 2, 1965, 79 Stat. 911.

10. Chae Chan Ping v. United States, 130 U.S. 581 (1889). The Court reasoned in part that if "the government of the United States, through its legislative department, considers the presence of foreigners of a different race in this country, who will not assimilate with us, to be dangerous to its peace and security, their exclusion is not to be stayed." For a critique of this deplorable result, *see* Louis Henkin, *The Constitution and United States Sovereignty: A Century of Chinese Exclusion and Its Progeny*, 100 HARV. L. REV. 853 (1987).

11. For efforts to encourage Irish immigration, *see, e.g., Immigration Act of 1990, § 131, 104 Stat. 4978 (codified as amended at 8 U.S.C. § 1153 (c) [1994]). Bill Ong Hing argues that Congress continues to discriminate against Asians. "Through an examination of past exclusion laws, previous legislation, and the specific provisions of the Immigration Act of 1990, the conclusion can be drawn that Congress never intended to make up for nearly 80 years of Asian exclusion, and that a conscious hostility towards persons of Asian descent continues to pervade Congressional circles." Bill Ong Hing*, Asian Americans and Present U.S. Immigration Policies: A Legacy of Asian Exclusion, *ASIAN AMERICANS AND THE SUPREME COURT: A DOCUMENTARY HISTORY 1106, 1107 (Hyung-Chan Kim ed., 1992).*

12. Louis DeSipio and Harry Pachon, Making Americans: Administrative Discretion and Americanization, *12 CHICANO-LATINO L. REV. 52, 53 (1992).*

13. CHARLES GORDON AND STANLEY MAILMAN, IMMIGRATION LAW AND PROCEDURE § 92.03[1][b] (rev. ed. 1992).

14. Dred Scott v. Sandford, 60 U.S. (19 How.) 393 (1857). For an insightful discussion of the role of Dred Scott *in the development of American citizenship, see JAMES KETTNER, THE DEVELOPMENT OF AMERICAN CITIZENSHIP, 1608–1870, at 300–333 (1978); see also KENNETH L. KARST, BELONGING TO AMERICA: EQUAL CITIZENSHIP AND THE CONSTITUTION 43–61 (1989).*

15. Civil Rights Act of 1866, ch. 31, 14 Stat. 27.

16. U.S. Const. amend. XIV.

17. 169 U.S. 649 (1898).

18. 112 U.S. 94 (1884).

19. Act of June 2, 1924, ch. 233, 43 Stat. 253.

20. Nationality Act of 1940, § 201(b), 54 Stat. 1138. See generally GORDON AND MAILMAN, supra, at § 92.03[3][e].

21. Pete Wilson, Crack Down on Illegals, USA TODAY, Aug. 20, 1993, at 12A.

22. H. R. J. Res. 129, 103d Cong., 1st Sess. (1993). An earlier, scholarly call to revamp the Fourteenth Amendment can be found in PETER SCHUCK and ROGER SMITH, CITIZENSHIP WITHOUT CONSENT: ILLEGAL ALIENS IN THE AMERICAN POLITY (1985).

23. Koh, supra, *at 69–70.*

24. Bill Ong Hing, Beyond the Rhetoric of Assimilation and Cultural Pluralism: Addressing the Tension of Separatism and Conflict in an Immigration-Driven Multiracial Society, *81 CAL. L. REV. 863, 866 (1993).*

25. Gerald Neuman warns against amending the Citizenship Clause. Gerald Neuman, Back to Dred Scott? *24 SAN DIEGO L. REV. 485, 500 (1987).* See also Note, The Birthright Citizenship Amendment: A Threat to Equality, *107 HARV. L. REV. 1026 (1994).*

26. U.S. Const. art. I, sec. 8, cl. 4.

27. Act of March 26, 1790, ch. 3, 1 Stat. 103.

28. KETTNER, supra, *at 215–16.*

29. One exception exists. In revisions undertaken in 1870, the "white person" limitation was omitted. However, this omission is regarded as accidental, and the prerequisite was reinserted in 1875 by "an act to correct errors and to supply omissions in the Revised Statutes of the United States." Act of Feb. 18, 1875, ch. 80, 18 Stat. 318. See *In re Ah Yup, 1 F.Cas. 223 (C.C.D.Cal. 1878) ("Upon revision of the statutes, the revisors, probably inadvertently, as Congress did not contemplate a change of the laws in force, omitted the words 'white persons.' ").*

30. Statement of Senator Hendricks, 59 CONG. GLOBE, 42nd Cong., 1st Sess. 2939 (1866). See also *John Guendelsberger, Access to Citizenship for Children Born Within the State to Foreign Parents, 40 AM. J. COMP. L. 379, 407–9 (1992).*

31. Statement of Senator Cowan, 57 CONG. GLOBE, 42nd Cong., 1st Sess. 499 (1866). For a discussion of the role of anti-Asian prejudice in the laws governing naturalization, see generally *Elizabeth Hull,* Naturalization and Denaturalization, *ASIAN AMERICANS AND THE SUPREME COURT: A DOCUMENTARY HISTORY 403 (Hyung-Chan Kim ed., 1992)*

32. The Senate rejected an amendment that would have allowed Chinese persons to naturalize. The proposed amendment read: "That the naturalization laws are hereby extended to aliens of African nativity, and to persons of African descent, and to persons born in the Chinese empire." BILL ONG HING, MAKING AND REMAKING ASIAN AMERICA THROUGH IMMIGRATION POLICY, 1850–1990, at 239 n.34 (1993).

33. Act of July 14, 1870, ch. 255, § 7, 16 Stat. 254.

34. Chinese Exclusion Act, ch. 126, § 14, 22 Stat. 58 (1882).

35. Fong Yue Ting v. United States, 149 U.S. 698, 716 (1893).

36. Neil Gotanda contends that separate racial ideologies function with respect to "other non-Whites," meaning non-Black racial minorities such as Asians, Native Americans, and Latinos. Neil Gotanda, "Other Non-Whites" in American Legal History: A Review of Justice at War, 85 COLUM. L. REV. 1186 (1985). Gotanda *explicitly identifies the operation of this separate ideology in the Supreme Court's jurisprudence regarding Asians and citizenship. Neil Gotanda,* Asian American Rights and the "Miss Saigon Syndrome," *ASIAN AMERICANS AND THE SUPREME COURT: A DOCUMENTARY HISTORY 1087, 1096–97 (Hyung-Chan Kim ed., 1992).*

37. Charles Gordon, The Racial Barrier to American Citizenship, *93 U. PA. L. REV. 237, 252 (1945).*

38. . MILTON KONVITZ, THE ALIEN AND THE ASIATIC IN AMERICAN LAW 80–81 (1946) (citation omitted).

39. Act of Oct. 14, 1940, ch. 876, § 303, 54 Stat. 1140.

40. Note, The Nationality Act of 1940, *54 HARV. L. REV. 860, 865 n.40 (1941).*

41. Act of Dec. 17, 1943, ch. 344, § 3, 57 Stat. 600.

42. Act of July 2, 1946, ch. 534, 60 Stat. 416.

43. Id.
44. Immigration and Nationality Act of 1952, ch. 2, § 311, 66 Stat. 239 (codified as amended at 8 U.S.C. 1422 [1988]).
45. Arguably, the continued substantial exclusion of Asians from immigration not remedied until 1965, rendered their eligibility for naturalization relatively meaningless. "[T]he national quota system for admitting immigrants which was built into the 1952 Act gave the grant of eligibility a hollow ring." Chin Kim and Bok Lim Kim, Asian Immigrants in American Law: A Look at the Past and the Challenge Which Remains, *26 AM. U. L. REV. 373, 390 (1977)*.
46. See generally *Ursula Vogel*, Is Citizenship Gender-Specific? *THE FRONTIERS OF CITIZENSHIP 58 (Ursula Vogel and Michael Moran eds., 1991)*.
47. Act of Feb. 10, 1855, ch. 71, § 2, 10 Stat. 604. Because gender-based laws in the area of citizenship were motivated by the idea that a woman's citizenship should follow that of her husband, no naturalization law has explicitly targeted unmarried women. GORDON AND MAILMAN, supra, *at § 95.03[6] ("An unmarried woman has never been (statutorily barred from naturalization.")*.
48. PRENTISS WEBSTER, LAW OF NATURALIZATION IN THE UNITED STATES OF AMERICA AND OTHER COUNTRIES 80 (1895).
49. Act of Feb. 10, 1855, ch. 71, § 2, 10 Stat. 604.
50. Kelly v. Owen, 74 U.S. 496, 498 (1868).
51. GORDON AND MAILMAN, supra at § 95.03[6].
52. Act of Sept. 22, 1922, ch. 411, §2, 42 Stat. 1021.
53. GORDON AND MAILMAN, supra at § 100.03[4][m].
54. Act of March 2, 1907, ch. 2534, § 3, 34 Stat. 1228. This act was upheld in MacKenzie v. Hare, 239 U.S. 299 (1915) (expatriating a U.S.-born woman upon her marriage to a British citizen).
55. Act of Sept. 22, 1922, ch. 411, §3, 42 Stat. 1021.
56. Id. The Act also stated that "[n]o woman whose husband is not eligible to citizenship shall be naturalized during the continuance of the marriage."
57. Act of March 3, 1931, ch. 442, §4(a), 46 Stat. 1511.
58. The loss of birthright citizenship was particularly harsh for those women whose race made them unable to regain citizenship through naturalization, especially after 1924, when the immigration laws of this country barred entry to any alien ineligible to citizenship. Immigration Act of 1924, ch. 190, § 13(c), 43 Stat. 162. See, e.g., Ex parte (Ng) Fung Sing, 6 F.2d 670 (W. D. Wash. 1925). In that case, a U.S. birthright citizen of Chinese descent was expatriated because of her marriage to a Chinese citizen, and was subsequently refused admittance to the United States as an alien ineligible to citizenship.

BROWN et al.

v.

BOARD OF EDUCATION

OF TOPEKA et al.

347 U.S. 483 (1954)

MR. CHIEF JUSTICE WARREN delivered the opinion of the Court.

These cases come to us from the States of Kansas, South Carolina, Virginia, and Delaware. They are premised on different facts and different local conditions, but a common legal question justifies their consideration together in this consolidated opinion.[1]

In each of the cases, minors of the Negro race, through their legal representatives, seek the aid of the courts in obtaining admission to the public schools of their community on a nonsegregated basis. In each instance, they had been denied admission to schools attended by white children under laws requiring or permitting segregation according to race. This segregation was alleged to deprive the plaintiffs of the equal protection of the laws under the Fourteenth Amendment. In each of the cases other than the Delaware case, a three-judge federal district court denied relief to the plaintiffs on the so-called "separate but equal" doctrine announced by this Court in *Plessy v. Ferguson*, 163 U.S. 537. Under that doctrine, equality of treatment is accorded when the races are provided substantially equal facilities, even though these facilities be separate. In the Delaware case, the Supreme Court of Delaware adhered to that doctrine, but ordered that the plaintiffs be admitted to the white schools because of their superiority to the Negro schools.

The plaintiffs contend that segregated public schools are not "equal" and cannot be made "equal," and that hence they are deprived of the equal protection of the laws. Because of the obvious importance of the question presented, the Court took jurisdiction.[2] Argument was heard in the 1952 Term, and reargument was heard this Term on certain questions propounded by the Court.[3]

Reargument was largely devoted to the circumstances surrounding the adoption of the Fourteenth Amendment in 1868. It covered exhaustively consideration of the Amendment in Congress, ratification by the states, then existing practices in racial segregation, and the views of proponents and opponents of the Amendment. This discussion and our own investigation convince us that, although these sources cast some light, it is not enough to resolve the problem with which we are faced. At best, they are inconclusive. The most avid proponents of the post–War Amendments undoubtedly intended them to remove all legal distinctions among "all persons born or naturalized in the United States." Their opponents, just as certainly, were antagonistic to both the letter and the spirit of the Amendments and wished them to have the most limited effect. What others in Congress and the state legislatures had in mind cannot be determined with an degree of certainty.

An additional reason for the inconclusive nature of the Amendment's history, with respect to segregated schools, is the status of public education at that time.[4] In the South, the movement toward free common schools, supported by general taxation, had not yet taken hold. Education of white children was largely in the hands of private groups. Education of Negroes was almost nonexistent, and practically all of the race were illiterate. In fact, any education of Negroes was forbidden by law in some states. Today, in contrast, many Negroes have achieved outstanding success in the arts and sciences as well as in the business and professional world. It is true that public school education at the time of the Amendment had advanced further in the North, but the effect of the Amendment on northern States was generally ignored in the congressional debates. Even in the North, the conditions of public education did not approximate those existing today. The curriculum was usually rudimentary; ungraded schools were common in rural areas; the school term

From *U.S. Reports*, 1954. Opinion of the Supreme Court, 1954.

was but three months a year in many states; and compulsory school attendance was virtually unknown. As a consequence, it is not surprising that there should be so little in the history of the Fourteenth Amendment relating to its intended effect on public education.

In the first cases in this Court construing the Fourteenth Amendment, decided shortly after its adoption, the Court interpreted it as proscribing all state-imposed discriminations against the Negro race.[5] The doctrine of "separate but equal" did not make its appearance in this Court until 1896 in the case of *Plessy v. Ferguson, supra,* involving not education but transportation.[6] American courts have since labored with the doctrine for over half a century. In this Court, there have been six cases involving the "separate but equal" doctrine in the field of public education.[7] In *Cumming v. County Board of Education,* 175 U.S. 528, and *Gong Lum v. Rice,* 275 U.S. 78, the validity of the doctrine itself was not challenged.[8] In more recent cases, all on the graduate school level, inequality was found in that specific benefits enjoyed by white students were denied to Negro students of the same educational qualifications. *Missouri ex rel. Gaines v. Canada,* 305 U.S. 337; *Sipuel v. Oklahoma,* 332 U.S. 631; *Sweatt v. Painter,* 339 U.S. 629; *McLaurin v. Oklahoma State Regents,* 339 U.S. 637. In none of these cases was it necessary to re-examine the doctrine to grant relief to the Negro plaintiff. And in *Sweatt v. Painter, supra,* the Court expressly reserved decision on the question whether *Plessy v. Ferguson* should be held inapplicable to public education.

In the instant cases, that question is directly presented. Here, unlike *Sweatt v. Painter,* there are findings below that the Negro and white schools involved have been equalized, or are being equalized, with respect to buildings, curricula, qualifications and salaries of teachers, and other "tangible" factors.[9] Our decision, therefore, cannot turn on merely a comparison of these tangible factors in the Negro and white schools involved in each of the cases. We must look instead to the effect of segregation itself on public education.

In approaching this problem, we cannot turn the clock back to 1868 when the Amendment was adopted, or even to 1896 when *Plessy v. Ferguson* was written. We must consider public education in the light of its full development and its present place in American life throughout the Nation. Only in this way can it be determined if segregation in public schools deprives these plaintiffs of the equal protection of the laws.

Today, education is perhaps the most important function of state and local governments. Compulsory school attendance laws and the great expenditures for education both demonstrate our recognition of the importance of education to our democratic society. It is required in the performance of our most basic public responsibilities, even service in the armed forces. It is

the very foundation of good citizenship. Today it is a principal instrument in awakening the child to cultural values, in preparing him for later professional training, and in helping him to adjust normally to his environment. In these days, it is doubtful that any child may reasonably be expected to succeed in life if he is denied the opportunity of an education. Such an opportunity, where the state has undertaken to provide it, is a right which must be made available to all on equal terms.

We come then to the question presented: Does segregation of children in public schools solely on the basis of race, even though the physical facilities and other "tangible" factors may be equal, deprive the children of the minority group of equal educational opportunities? We believe that it does.

In *Sweatt v. Painter, supra,* in finding that a segregated law school for Negroes could not provide them equal educational opportunities, this Court relied in large part on "those qualities which are incapable of objective measurement but which make for greatness in a law school." In *McLaurin v. Oklahoma State Regents, supra,* the Court, in requiring that a Negro admitted to a white graduate school be treated like all other students, again resorted to intangible considerations: " . . . his ability to study, to engage in discussions and exchange views with other students, and, in general, to learn his profession." Such considerations apply with added force to children in grade and high schools. To separate them from others of similar age and qualifications solely because of their race generates a feeling of inferiority as to their status in the community that may affect their hearts and minds in a way unlikely ever to be undone. The effect of this separation on their educational opportunities was well stated by a finding in the Kansas case by a court which nevertheless felt compelled to rule against the Negro plaintiffs:

> "Segregation of white and colored children in public schools has a detrimental effect upon the colored children. The impact is greater when it has the sanction of the law; for the policy of separating the races is usually interpreted as denoting the inferiority of the negro group. A sense of inferiority affects the motivation of a child to learn. Segregation with the sanction of law, therefore, has a tendency to [retard] the educational and mental development of negro children and to deprive them of some of the benefits they would receive in a racial[ly] integrated school system."[10]

Whatever may have been the extent of psychological knowledge at the time of *Plessy v. Ferguson,* this finding is amply supported by modern authority.[11] Any language in *Plessy v. Ferguson* contrary to this finding is rejected.

We conclude that in the field of public education the doctrine of "separate but equal" has no place. Separate educational facilities are inherently unequal. Therefore, we hold that the plaintiffs and others similarly situated for whom the actions have been brought are, by reason of the segregation complained of, deprived of the equal protection of the laws guaranteed by the Fourteenth Amendment. This disposition makes unnecessary any discussion whether such segregation also violates the Due Process Clause of the Fourteenth Amendment.[12]

Because these are class actions, because of the wide applicability of this decision, and because of the great variety of local conditions, the formulation of decrees in these cases presents problems of considerable complexity. On reargument, the consideration of appropriate relief was necessarily subordinated to the primary question—the constitutionality of segregation in public education. We have now announced that such segregation is a denial of the equal protection of the laws. In order that we may have the full assistance of the parties in formulating decrees, the cases will be restored to the docket, and the parties are requested to present further argument on Questions 4 and 5 previously propounded by the Court for the reargument this Term.[13] The Attorney General of the United States is again invited to participate. The Attorneys General of the states requiring or permitting segregation in public education will also be permitted to appear as *amici curiae* upon request to do so by September 15, 1954, and submission of briefs by October 1, 1954.[14]

It is so ordered.

NOTES

1. In the Kansas case, *Brown v. Board of Education,* the plaintiffs are Negro children of elementary school age residing in Topeka. They brought this action in the United States District Court for the District of Kansas to enjoin enforcement of a Kansas statute which permits, but does not require, cities of more than 15,000 population to maintain separate school facilities for Negro and white students. Kan. Gen. Stat. § 72–1724 (1949). Pursuant to that authority, the Topeka Board of Education elected to establish segregated elementary schools. Other public schools in the community, however, are operated on a nonsegregated basis. . . .

In the South Carolina case, *Briggs v. Elliott,* the plaintiffs are Negro children of both elementary and high school age residing in Clarendon County. They brought this action in the United States District Court for the Eastern District of South Carolina to enjoin enforcement of provisions in the state constitution and statutory code which require the segregation of Negroes and whites in public schools. . . .

In the Virginia case, *Davis v. County School Board,* the plaintiffs are Negro children of high school age residing in Prince Edward County. They brought this action in the United States District Court for the Eastern District of Virginia to enjoin enforcement of provisions in the state constitution and statutory code which require the segregation of Negroes and whites in public schools. . . .

In the Delaware case, *Gebhart v. Belton,* the plaintiffs are Negro children of both elementary and high school age residing in New Castle county. They brought this action in the Delaware Court of Chancery to enjoin enforcement of provisions in the state constitution and statutory code which require the segregation of Negroes and whites in public schools. . . .

2. technical footnote deleted.
3. technical footnote deleted.
4. technical footnote deleted.
5. technical footnote deleted.
6. technical footnote deleted.
7. technical footnote deleted.
8. technical footnote deleted.
9. technical footnote deleted.
10. technical footnote deleted.
11. K. B. Clark, Effect of Prejudice and Discrimination on Personality Development (Midcentury White House Conference on Children and Youth, 1950); Witmer and Kotinsky, Personality in the Making (1952), c. VI; Deutscher and Chein, The Psychological Effects of Enforced Segregation: A Survey of Social Science Opinion, 26 J. Psychol. 259 (1948); Chein, What are the Psychological Effects of Segregation Under Conditions of Equal Facilities?, 3 Int. J. Opinion and Attitude Res. 229 (1949); Brameld, Educational Costs, in Discrimination and National Welfare (MacIver, ed., 1949), 44–48; Frazier, The Negro in the United States (1949), 674–681. And see generally Myrdal, An American Dilemma (1944).
12. technical footnote deleted.
13. technical footnote deleted.
14. technical footnote deleted.

Retreat Into Legalism:
The Little Rock School Desegregation Case in Historic Perspective

David L. Kirp, *University of California, Berkeley*

Law and order are not here to be preserved by depriving the Negro children of their constitutional rights. . . . The right of a student not to be segregated on racial grounds is indeed so fundamental and pervasive that it is embraced in the concept of due process of law.

Cooper *v.* Aaron *(1958)*

During the 1970s and 1980s, a word disappeared from the American vocabulary. That word is segregation.

Douglas Massey and Nancy Denton, American Apartheid *(1993)*

In the waning days of the summer of 1957, the nation's attention was riveted on an unfolding drama in Little Rock, Arkansas. There, Governor Orval Faubus, who earlier had cultivated a reputation as a racial moderate, had declared in flat contradiction of a federal court order that nine black students—the first black students to be admitted to a white school in Little Rock—would not be permitted to enroll in Central High School. "Blood will run in the streets," Faubus warned, if the youngsters tried to enter the school, and the first intrepid black student was driven off, the vengeful crowd shouting "Get her! Lynch her! . . . Get a rope and drag her over to this tree."

Although the impasse was broken when, after three weeks of violence, President Eisenhower finally ordered army paratroopers to escort the black youngsters into Central High, the military presence didn't mean peace. When harassment of the nine students continued unabated, the federal trial judge, fearful of yet

more "chaos, bedlam and turmoil," shifted course, agreeing to postpone integration for two years, until 1960; meanwhile, the nine black students who had survived a year at Central High would be reassigned to the all-black high school (Irons 1988, 111).

It was this order, appealed by the NAACP, that the Supreme Court took up in special session in September 1958. This was four weeks before the Court Term was scheduled to begin, and the timing of the oral argument was meant to dramatize the significance of the case: only three times before in the Court's history had the justices convened during a recess (Irons and Guitton 1993, 249–263). While this was not the first occasion on which a Dixie official had vowed to perpetuate the regime of school segregation struck down in *Brown v. Board of Education* (1954), it represented the most direct and frontal defiance of the federal judiciary, and so the Court felt compelled to respond swiftly. Barely 24 hours after oral arguments, the justices ordered that integration in Little Rock proceed without delay; two weeks later, it issued a more detailed decree in *Cooper v. Aaron* (1958).

The opinion in the Little Rock case is remarkable neither for its rhetorical flourishes nor for its constitutional boldness. Unlike the Segregation Cases, there is no heartstrings-tugging plea to end segregation in order not to inflict damage upon the "hearts and minds" of the young, no tacit overruling of a sixty-year-old precedent. Instead, what makes *Cooper* memorable is the declaration of judicial

will that is so palpably on display, the jurists' insistence on their right to the last word in matters of constitutional law. This is less *Brown* revisited than *Marbury v. Madison* (1803) *redux.*

Often in its history, the Supreme Court has been called upon to act as "teacher in a vital national seminar" (Rostow 1952); so too here. Each of the justices individually signed the opinion in *Cooper v. Aaron*, and that remarkable gesture—Earl Warren as John Hancock in this declaration of judicial independence—was a tangible manifestation of the justices' determination to prevail. The Segregation Cases, the Court insisted, embodied the law of the land to which government officials and ordinary citizens alike owed allegiance.

Fast Forward

Shift time and geography some 30 years to DeKalb County, Georgia; then, a few years later, shift once more to Kansas City, Missouri (*Freeman* v. *Pitts* 1992; *Missouri* v. *Jenkins* 1995). These are the most recent school desegregation cases to be heard by the Supreme Court, and their contrast with *Cooper v. Aaron* could not be plainer. The justices, so pointedly unanimous about the right course of action in Little Rock, have become badly split and publicly querulous, disinclined even to conceal their disdain for their colleagues' opposing views. The issues to be decided have much less to do with great principles—simple justice (Kluger 1976)—than with the details of political and judicial management. Whatever the Supreme Court may

From *PS: Political Science and Politics,* September 1997, pp. 443–447. © 1997 by David L. Kirp and the American Political Science Association. Reprinted by permission.

Escorting students to Central High School, Little Rock.   Courtesy of the Library of Congress

subsequently say about desegrega-tion, these opinions confirm what has been apparent for years: that an era during which the Court em-braced an integrationist vision of racial fairness has ended. The persis-tence of segregation, it seems, no longer troubles the sleep of the jus-tices.

In DeKalb County, a leafy Atlanta suburb, school officials sought an end to pupil busing mandated by the trial court which, decades after the original litigants had graduated from high school, was still issuing supple-mentary orders. These officials in-sisted that they had done their job. The public schools were "unitary" according to the standards laid down by the Court. The fact that some schools in the county remained mostly black while others were mainly white was not government's fault, but rather a matter of housing prices and individual preferences—factors entirely outside public offi-cals' control. It was time, they be-lieved—long past time, really—to be freed from court oversight.

In Kansas City, a quarrel over money had broken out between the city and the state over who should pay for enticements to integration. Missouri objected to having to un-derwrite the costs of magnet schools, specially designed institutions which offered everything from Olympic size swimming pools to the latest in electronic gadgetry in order to lure white suburbanites to the almost entirely black urban school system.

In the DeKalb County litigation, the school board prevailed; and the state got its way in Missouri. The array of opinions in these two cases reveals desegregation to be in full retreat. The integrationist-minded justices who once ruled the Court became fixated on the minutiae of school board behavior in DeKalb County and the precise terms of the legal complaint in Kansas City. It was the opponents who displayed passion and summoned principle to defend individual liberty and assail judicial paternalism. As a matter of rhetoric, these moments belong to Clarence Thomas, who has gentrified Orval Faubus' angry sentiments, rendering them the stuff of constitutional law.

How could the death of the integrationist ideal have happened so swiftly?

Just Schools

"No single issue has more moral force than *Brown*," wrote J. Harvie Wilkinson, III a generation ago in *From Brown to Bakke*. "Few struggles have been morally more significant than the one for racial integation of American life. Yet school integration may be the most political item on the Court's agenda" (Wilkinson 1979, 151).[1] From a matter of high principle in *Brown*, desegregation rapidly descended into the swamp of defiance (as in Little Rock), evasion, avoidance, and delay. The Court, frustrated by the success of these tactics, sought a clear standard against which to measure compliance with its orders. It settled upon a numerical standard which took racial balance as its starting point.

In *Green v. County School Board* (1968), freedom of choice, the justification the rural Virginia district proferred for having accomplished only token integration, was simply a euphemism for evading *Brown*. It made obvious sense to order that the district's two elementary schools reflect the racial composition of the

school district—that there be "a system without a 'white' school and a 'Negro' school, but just schools." However, when in the *Swann* (1971) case this same "just schools" standard was applied in formulaic fashion to urban, residentially segregated Charlotte, North Carolina, thousands of students had to be bused to school over substantial distances.

Until *Swann*, desegregation occupied the unchallenged moral high ground in national discourse. *Brown* enjoyed near-iconic status; while justices might disagree among themselves about the constitutional status of civil rights demonstrations, to dissent in a school case was a sacrilege. But *Swann* changed all that. The ruling evoked a national chorus of complaint, whipped up by chief chorister Richard Nixon. It didn't matter that pupils had been bused to school since Henry Ford's time— that, as the NAACP pithily and accurately pointed out, "It's Not the Distance, It's the Niggers" (Mills 1973, 322) which best explained the anti-busing sentiment. The Supreme Court's decision to discuss the issue entirely in terms of numbers—racial balance substituting for historically-rooted understandings of racial justice, on the one hand and educationally rooted understandings of equal opportunity on the other—proved to be a fatal misrepresentation of the problem.

Just one year after *Swann*, and nearly twenty years after *Brown*, the first dissents were registered in a Supreme Court desegregation case (*Wright v. City Council of Emporia* 1972), when Nixon's appointees voted as a bloc to loosen judicial control. A year later, in the Denver case, the justices, again divided made numbers rather than principle the heart of their first ruling on segregation in the North (*Keyes v. Denver School District* 1973).

An incautious Supreme Court, willing to confront the full measure of school segregation, might have advanced "a sweeping and interconnected view of American racial history. It might have seen school segregation as a product of prejudice in jobs, housing, politics, public facilities, the military, with discrimination and segregation in each part of

American life reverberating through the whole" (Wilkinson 1979, 140; see generally, Myrdal 1972). With much less strain on their constitutional role as interpreters of the law, the justices could have decided that fixing a single national standard for school segregation was both legally and morally right (Hochschild 1984).

In 1954, when the opinion in the Segregation Cases was announced, North and South seemed to occupy different moral universes, and merging those universes required a second Reconstruction (Orfield 1969; Rodgers and Bullock 1976). The Supreme Court refused even to hear a desegregation case from the North throughout the 1960s, as if waiting for the apparently intractable legal and political issues posed by those lawsuits to be tamed in lower court opinions.

By the 1970s, however, it could plausibly be said that the racial situation in Denver was not so different from Charlotte, either in fact or law. On both sides of Mason's and Dixon's line, the constitutional injustice stemmed from government-sanctioned—indeed, government-promoted—segregation in housing, which combined with school boards' use of racially distinct neighborhoods to define attendance zones, resulting in segregated public schools. While Northern officials piously contended that such segregation was *de facto*— that it just happened—since government officials drew these attendance zones, the government was always a player, never an innocent party. As Justice Douglas bluntly pointed out in *Keyes*, the Denver case, "the State is barred from creating by one device or another ghettoes that determine the school one is compelled to attend" (*Keyes v. Denver School District* 1973, 205).

A few years earlier, in the Charlotte case, the justices had come close to adopting such a nationwide standard, but when it became clear that such an opinion would not command unanimous assent the majority, still bewitched by unanimity, backed off. Never again would there be a majority on the high court for such a ruling.

To cobble together a solid majority in the Denver case, Justice Brennan, the avatar of racial liberalism, wrote an opinion that combined the by-now familiar fixation on numbers with a hyper-legalist analysis. Before a federal court could order desegregation in the North, Brennan announced, there had to be proof of intentional past wrongdoing on the part of local school officials which substantially affected the racial composition of the schools. Even as the segregation-promoting character of housing policy was ignored in this equation, burdens of pleading and burdens of proof became the order of the day. The result was Dickensian litigation, daunting to all but the most experienced and best-financed litigants.[2] The outcomes of such litigation varied from place to place in the North—what to one judge was illicit official behavior seemed entirely innocent to another—and this inconsistency made for more popular unhappiness with the courts. Why us, the citizens of San Francisco asked, and not them, referring to San Jose, and the question was really unanswerable (Kirp 1982; Kirp and Jensen 1984).

Brown had deliberately been written in language fit for the Sunday newspaper supplements. In *Keyes*, by contrast, the lack of a persuasive rationale anchored in a morally-driven conceptualization of official wrong-doing made the decision seem a crude imposition of judicial will, not necessarily the right thing to do.

The triumph of artlessly executed hyper-legalism over simple justice became complete in *Milliken v. Bradley* (1975). In that case, the justices overturned, by a 5-4 vote, an order requiring desegregation, not just for the city of Detroit but for the surrounding suburbs as well. This opinion ignored mountains of evidence concerning the complicity of state and suburban officials in walling off Detroit from the surrounding suburbs, evidence on which the trial judge based his decree. *Milliken* sent an unmistakable message—urban apartheid would not be overcome through judicial decree.

The Detroit decision effectively spelled the end of judicial activism in public school desegregation. The constitutional war was over. DeKalb County, Georgia and Kansas City, Missouri were merely mopping-up operations.

Back to the Future

Racial justice acquired meaning outside as well as inside the courtroom during these years. What had seemed so simple in Little Rock in 1957—that nine intrepid black adolescents should not be turned away from a public high school because of their race—had become more complicated by the 1970s. In both the South and the North, residential segregation had increased, making school desegregation logistically harder to accomplish. Nor was it so clear that, in terms of educational outcomes, busing was worth the political and social price (St. John 1975). New black voices were being heard, many of them unsympathetic to the desegregation project. Some black leaders had come to reject integration in favor of black-run schools (Levin 1970; Fantini, Gittell and Magat 1970), even as others grew impatient while waiting, seemingly forever, for the promise of *Brown* to be realized in their communities (Bell 1978). Anyplace where desegregation landed on the agenda, it became *the* issue, demanding massive amounts of time, energy and money. During the past generation, issues having more to do with pedagogy and educational philosophy, less to do with racial justice—the back-to-basics movement; the push for educational excellence; the demand, through vouchers or charter schools, for greater choice of school—have seized the spotlight.

The Supreme Court cannot be faulted for failing to make good on its promise, implicit in Little Rock and spelled out a decade later in *Green*, that state-inflicted segregation would be eliminated "root and branch." To accomplish this would have required the active support of other branches of government and ultimately the citizenry (Hochschild 1995; Kirp 1984; Kirp, Dwyer, and Rosenthal 1996). But the Court can fairly be criticized for announcing a universal obligation to desegregate America's schools, then through its busing decrees imposing the burden selectively; as well as for failing to risk greatly to preserve its integrationist ideal of racial justice, instead bowing (in *Keyes*, *Milliken* and the later cases) to the pragmatics of pol-

itics in a way the justices had rejected in *Cooper v. Aaron*. If the achievement of a unitary society was really beyond the capacity of justices, the past generation's desegregation decisions have nonetheless undercut the moral authority of constitutional law.

The 40 year-old story of Little Rock has come full circle—like parent, like child. Even as the children of Linda Brown, the named plaintiff in the Segregation Cases, went to segregated schools in Topeka, it's unlikely that the offspring of those nine remarkable teenagers in Little Rock attended integrated public schools. There is a difference between then and now, though: Now hardly any voices are raised in protest.

Notes

1. Even in the Little Rock case, conventionally regarded as the most uncompromising of the Court's rulings, Justice Frankfurter was moved to plead for the cooperation of elected officials in achieving desegregation. Success meant "working together . . . in a cooperative effort," he declared in a concurring opinion, not the imposition of judicial rule (*Cooper v. Aaron* at 20).

2. Having been Director of the Center for Law and Education and a legal strategist in several of these cases, I have a first-hand sense of the enormity of these litigation burdens.

References

Bell, Derrick. 1978. "Waiting on the Promise of *Brown*." *Law and Contemporary Problems* 39:341.

Brown v. *Board of Education*. 1954. 347 U.S. 483.

Cooper v. *Aaron*. 1958. 358 U.S. 1.

Fantini, Mario, Marilyn Gittell, and Richard Magat. 1970. *Community Control and the Urban School*. New York: Praeger.

Freeman v. *Pitts*. 1992. 503 U.S. 467.

Green v. *County School Board*. 1968. 391 U.S. 430.

Hochschild, Jennifer. 1984. *The New American Dilemma: Liberal Democracy and School Desegregation*. New Haven: Yale University Press.

———. 1995. *Facing Up to the American Dream: Race, Class, and the Soul of the Nation*. Princeton: Princeton University Press.

Irons, Peter. 1988. *The Courage of Their Convictions*. New York: Free Press.

———, and Stephanie Guitton, eds. 1993.

May It Please the Court. New York: New Press.

Missouri v. *Jenkins.* 1995. 515 U.S. 70.

Keyes v. *Denver School District.* 1973. 413 U.S. 189.

Kirp, David. 1977. "School Desegregation and the Limits of Legalism." *Public Interest* 47:101

———. 1982. *Just Schools: The Idea of Racial Equality in American Education.* Berkeley and Los Angeles: University of California Press.

———, John Dwyer, and Larry Rosenthal. 1996. *Our Town: Race, Housing, and the Soul of Suburbia.* New Brunswick, NJ: Rutgers University Press.

———, and Donald Jensen, eds. 1984. *School Days, Rule Days.* London and Philadelphia: Falmer Press.

Kluger, Richard. 1976. *Simple Justice.* New York: Knopf.

Levin, Henry, ed. 1970. *Community Control of Schools.* Washington DC: Brookings Institution.

Marbury v. *Madison.* 1803. 5 U.S. 137.

Massey, Robert, and Nancy Denton. 1993. *American Apartheid.* Cambridge, MA: Harvard University Press.

Milliken v. *Bradley.* 1975. 418 U.S. 717.

Mills, Nicholas, ed. 1973. *The Great School Bus Controversy.* New York: Teachers College Press.

Myrdal, Gunnar, ed. 1972. *An American Dilemma: The Negro Problem and Modern Democracy.* New York: Pantheon.

Orfield, Gary. 1969. *The Reconstruction of Southern Education.* New York: John Wiley.

———. 1996. *Dismantling Desegregation: The Quiet Reversal of Brown v. Board of Education.* New York: New Press.

Peltason, Jack. 1961. *Fifty-Eight Lonely Men.* Urbana IL: University of Illinois Press.

Rodgers, Harvey Jr., and Charles S. Bullock, III. 1976. *Coercion to Compliance.* Lexington MA: D.C. Heath.

Rosenberg, Gerald. 1991. *The Hollow Hope: Can Courts Bring about Social Change?*

Chicago: University of Chicago Press.

Rostow, Eugene. 1952. "The Democratic Character of Judicial Review." *Harvard Law Review* 66:208.

St. John, Nancy. 1975. *School Desegregation: Outcomes for Children.* New York: Wiley.

Swann v. *Charlotte-Mecklenberg Board of Education.* 1971. 302 U.S. 1.

Symposium. 1976. "Is School Desegregation Still a Good Idea?" *School Review* 84:309.

Wilkinson, J. Harvie, III. 1979. *From Brown to Bakke: The Supreme Court and School Integration: 1954–1978.* New York: Oxford University Press.

Wright v. *City Council of Emporia.* 1972. 407 U.S. 451.

About the Author

David L. Kirp is professor of public policy, University of California-Berkeley.

The Strange Politics of Affirmative Action

Few issues in American politics are more hotly debated than affirmative action. Yet the programs themselves are only one source of controversy, our author writes. Another is the new style of politics that has accompanied the rise of affirmative action and other issues, a politics of "weak membership," maximum publicity, and sharp confrontation.

by Peter Skerry

Not long ago, a California labor organizer complained to me about how hard it was to create a Latino caucus in the state employees' union. She recounted how time and again, after helping a member with a grievance, she would go back and ask the person to lend a hand to her effort, or at least to contribute a few dollars. The response was almost always the same: "Thanks, but I got what I deserved here. I don't see any need to contribute to your caucus."

Researchers with the Diversity Project at the University of California at Berkeley heard something similar from a Chicana undergraduate: "Yeah, I do belong at Cal. Affirmative action may have helped me get my foot in the door, but I walked through the door by myself."

A new kind of political leader has come to the fore, media-savvy and eager for conflict, often fitting the mold of New York's flamboyant Rev. Al Sharpton.

Or listen to the words of the young black executive quoted by Yale University law professor Stephen Carter in *Confessions of an Affirmative Action Baby* (1991): "I've made it because I'm good."

When we hear such claims, we tend to focus on the word "good"—the speaker's self-conscious claim of accomplishment and achievement, of meritocratic virtue. But we should also pay attention to the "I"—the individualistic claim that *I* made it because of my own hard work and effort.

Vignettes such as these remind us that, as sociologist Seymour Martin Lipset observes, "affirmative action policies have forced a sharp confrontation between two core American values: egalitarianism and individualism." And, as these illustrations show, it is not only white Americans who feel the conflict. Affirmative action poses a challenge to the individualistic values of its minority beneficiaries as well. This is not to say that these beneficiaries reject affirmative action. But it does force them to confront unsettling questions: How do members of minority groups reconcile the benefits they receive from affirmative action with their own individualistic values? Does their individualism pose problems for minority leaders trying to attain group objectives?

These questions point to a paradox that lies at the heart of affirmative action. Even though they are frequently criticized for granting "group rights" to designated minorities, affirmative action programs do nothing of the sort. They in fact grant benefits to individuals—directly—without their having to belong to a formally constituted group or organization. Yes, one must be a member of a designated minority, but these minority groups have no official membership rolls or criteria. So in contemporary America it is possible to benefit from "group rights" without formally belonging to a group—and without having to give anything back to it.

Critics such as George Will may in some sense be justified in characterizing affirmative action as "racial spoils." Yet in American political history, the "spoils system" refers to a quid pro quo between victorious politicians and their loyal supporters. This is the Tammany Hall tradition, the system that fueled machine politics from Boston to San Antonio, where fealty to the local ward heeler might lead to a reduced property tax assessment or maybe even a

personal loan to get through a rough patch. But with affirmative action there is no organizational tie—no reciprocal connection of reward (and restraint) between individual beneficiaries and leaders.

Only if one looks at how group boundaries are defined and policed in other nations does the curious nature of affirmative action in the United States become clear. In Malaysia, for example, the federal constitution establishes membership criteria for Malays and other protected groups. Those who wish to take advantage of employment and educational preferences must produce documentary proof that they are members of the appropriate groups. Similarly, in the former Soviet Union (as well as present-day Russia), each citizen is assigned a nationality at the age of 16, typically on the basis of the mother's nationality. An individual can belong to one and only one nationality, which is recorded on his or her passport and cannot be changed. Such tightly regulated groups and official membership criteria simply do not fit with fundamental American notions of individual liberty and choice. The American alternative to officially recognized groups has always been voluntary associations.

To be sure, in the past the status and composition of minority groups, especially of the black population, were not matters of individual choice but were rigidly defined and policed by the state. But this is hardly the situation today. Indeed, it is striking that under affirmative action we leave it to potential beneficiaries themselves to declare if they are members of a favored group. Similarly, the U.S. census tallies racial and ethnic data based on how individuals identify themselves to the government, not on how the government identifies them.

In short, affirmative action is not a system of officially designated groups with enforced boundaries and memberships. Affirmative action is an example of American exceptionalism, another unique but typically American hybrid: rights are afforded to groups that are weakly constituted. To put it differently, these are group rights in which the benefits are received by individuals without the mediation of any meaningful organizational effort or tie. The group rights of affirmative action get

refracted through our individualistic political culture. The result is neither as compatible with American values as its supporters suggest, nor as balkanizing as its critics assert.

Yet this very ambiguity may help explain why affirmative action is so contentious. To be sure, much of the controversy surrounding affirmative action can be traced to the challenge it presents to long-held American values. But a good deal of that controversy can also be attributed to the specific institutional context within which we conduct our political business today. In other words, the continuing controversy over affirmative action has as much to do with the nature of contemporary American politics as with the state of race relations. And while some comfort can be had in this finding, it also suggests that the controversy will be all the more difficult to resolve.

The fierce national debate over affirmative action has obscured the fact that members of minority groups share the traditional American attachment to individualism. Analyzing all the available survey data on affirmative action, political scientists Lee Sigelman and Susan Welch conclude that "blacks, like whites, believe in merit as the major criterion in hiring." Yet they also report that "blacks are more supportive of affirmative action than whites." How can this be? Sigelman and Welch argue that blacks are caught between their very American commitment to individual merit and their belief that racism and discrimination hinder its realization. The authors conclude that blacks and whites define affirmative action differently: "Most blacks concede that preferential treatment is unfair, but still support the other components of affirmative action [specified by the authors as compensation for past racism and assurance of future fairness]." Whites, however, tend to see preferential treatment as a damning "central component" of affirmative action. There is no question, however, that there is a significant commitment to individual merit among black Americans.

Of course, individualism among blacks competes with intense pressures for conformity or, to use a more positive term, solidarity. Sociologist Elijah Anderson captures some of these crosscurrents in *Street Wise: Race, Class, and Change in an Urban Community* (1990), a study of a racially and ethnically diverse big-city neighborhood. Anderson identifies two social types among blacks. One type, generally working- and

PETER SKERRY, *a former Wilson Center Fellow, is a Visiting Fellow at the Brookings Institution. He is the author of* Mexican Americans: The Ambivalent Minority *(1993). Copyright © 1997 by Peter Skerry.*

lower-middle-class in character, tends to "view the social world mainly in terms of ethnicity and color." Its members see "retaining their racial identity, or 'blackness,'" as a central problem in their lives. The other type, more typically middle-class, includes those who "are inclined to see themselves as 'individuals' and thus to choose their friends not so much by color as by apparent social attitudes, interests, and affinities." But as political scientist Terri Susan Fine concludes from her analysis of the survey data, such educated, individualistic, and self-reliant blacks are the most likely to back affirmative action. Far from being antithetical to black individualism, support for affirmative action actually correlates with it.

The two distinct types identified by Anderson can and do coexist within individuals. For testimony to this fact one need look no further than the recent spate of well-received memoirs by prominent black writers. To varying degrees, Carter's *Confessions*, Brent Staples's *Parallel Time* (1994), Gerald Early's *Daughters* (1994), and Henry Louis Gates's *Colored People* (1994) are portraits of successful people struggling with the contest between the individualism of mainstream America (however imperfectly realized) and the group ties of black America.

Yet the point here is not psychological or even sociological, but political—rather, it concerns the character of political organization in contemporary minority politics. Whatever their personal values, the beneficiaries of affirmative action encounter few, if any, organizational ties that would oblige them to acknowledge that they owe at least part of their success to someone or something outside themselves. Such individuals are what economists call *free-riders*—beneficiaries of efforts to which they have not contributed.

Many of today's minority leaders seem acutely aware of this phenomenon. New York activist Rev. Al Sharpton recently scolded minority journalists attending a convention in Atlanta for criticizing the civil rights movement: "The movement created options for many of you to get the jobs you have. You come in and condemn something that really sponsored your careers." John Jacob, former president of the National Urban League, observes that "we have now raised a generation of young people who've never known poverty, who've never lived in our 'segregated' communities, who went—by America's

definition—to the finest schools and who have come to believe that their achievement is predicated on the fact that they are smart." Or, as a middle-aged Mexican-American politician once said to me about the younger generation, "There's no way to make them feel guilty."

Curiously, this free-rider problem was anticipated by black nationalists in the 1960s. As Stephen Carter recounts in his memoir, leaders of the black power movement considered affirmative action nothing more than an attempt by the terrified white power structure to co-opt "the talented tenth": "By opening to them the rewards that corporate capitalism bestows upon those at the top, the system would skim off the cream while leaving essentially unchanged the situation of those at the bottom."

The excesses of the 1960s black nationalists should not keep us from appreciating their prescience about the negative impact of integration and affirmative action on disadvantaged blacks. Black nationalists also worried about the destructive impact of American individualism—a concern demonstrated by Harold Cruse's use of the phrase "Individualism and 'The Open Society'" as the title of the first chapter of his 1970 polemic, *The Crisis of the Negro Intellectual*. Cruse did not object to integration out of any hatred of whites or even race pride—though there is an undeniable strain of the latter in his writing. Rather, his objection was based on his preoccupation with the contradiction between America's formal regime of individual rights and the political power actually exercised by groups:

America, which idealizes the rights of the individual above everything else, is in reality, a nation dominated by the social power of groups, classes, in-groups and cliques—both ethnic and religious. The individual in America has few rights that are not backed up by the political, economic, and social power of one group or another. . . . Thus it can be seen that those Negroes . . . who have accepted the full essence of the Great American Ideal of individualism are in serious trouble trying to function in America.

For Cruse, "the crisis of the Negro intellectual" was precisely that black intellectuals, and the middle class from which they emerge, are more susceptible than other blacks to the attractions of individualism and its rewards. If they succumbed, he feared, ordinary blacks would be deprived

of the leadership critical to forging the political solidarity necessary for genuine advancement in America.

Echoing Cruse, Charles Hamilton and Stokely Carmichael based their case for black power (in their 1967 book by that title) explicitly on the experience of European immigrants. What was the model for black power? Irish power. "Italians vote for Rubino over O'Brien; Irish for Murphy over Goldberg, etc.," they wrote. "This phenomenon may seem distasteful to some, but it has been and remains today a central fact of the American political system."

It was only a short step from this insight to an embrace of the white ethnics' instrument of political advancement: the political machine. Writing in the late 1960s, Hamilton and Carmichael were predictably critical of what was left of the machines, but they also held a grudging respect for their adversaries' modus operandi.

This should come as no surprise. The political machine provided what black nationalists understood to be missing in programs like affirmative action: an institutional mechanism to bridge the gap between the upwardly mobile and those left behind. In other words, a mechanism to tax the free-riders and bind the fates of the two groups together. One can exaggerate the extent to which machines served this function. But for countless immigrants through decades of American history they did provide a means of preserving ethnic ties despite the atomizing effects of assimilation.

Today, of course, the machines are gone—in great measure because their ethnic-group loyalties offended the ethos of American individualism. At the same time, however, Americans have developed extraordinarily high expectations about including minorities, the poor, and other previously excluded groups in the political process. Minority leaders thus feel acutely the lack of disciplined, community-based institutions capable of mobilizing the disadvantaged and maintaining their loyalty.

Faced with an enormous gap between means and ends, these leaders and their allies have done what might have been predicted: they have created new organizations with drastically reduced membership costs—costs measured not merely in dollars but in commitments of time, energy, and loyalty. In some instances, those costs have been reduced to zero.

The quintessential example is the Mexican American Legal Defense and Educational Fund (MALDEF), which seeks to represent not only all Mexican Americans but all of the nation's 27 million Latinos. This claim is widely accepted, and the organization has played a prominent role in recent debates over immigration and affirmative action. Yet MALDEF has no members. It gets most of its funding from corporations and foundations, especially the Ford Foundation, which played the critical role in establishing it in the late 1960s. Lacking members, MALDEF has no real bonds of accountability to the communities it strives to represent.

With *no* membership base, MALDEF is an extreme case. But it differs more in degree than in kind from other organizations representing minorities, such as the National Council of La Raza and the National Urban League.

And the phenomenon is hardly confined to minority politics. For MALDEF and similar organizations are part of a broad public-interest movement that since the 1960s has sought to represent a variety of otherwise unrepresented interests or constituencies. These groups span the spectrum, ranging from Common Cause to Mothers Against Drunk Driving, from the Center for Individual Rights to the Children's Defense Fund.

All of these groups represent interests that are difficult to organize and that do not ordinarily get articulated. The individuals concerned may lack the resources—money, time, skills—to create a vehicle to advance their interests. Or they may be stymied by being geographically dispersed and not in easy or frequent contact with one another. Indeed, they may not even be aware of one another's existence and common interests. Finally, the broad interests concerned may be relatively marginal to the day-to-day, narrowly defined, and explicitly self-interested concerns that conventional interest or professional groups typically pursue.

In overcoming such obstacles, public interest organizations invariably assume certain characteristics. As I have already suggested, they may not actually enroll members. If they do, the members do not typically provide a substantial share of the money necessary to run the organization. Such organizations have what political scientist Jeffrey Berry refers to as "cheap membership," consisting of little more than writing a check for annual dues. Indeed, as Harvard University political scientist Robert

Putnam observes, public interest organizations are low in "social connectedness." As Putnam noted in his controversial 1995 article, "Bowling Alone," members of such groups typically do not attend meetings, and in fact "most are unlikely to ever (knowingly) encounter any other member." Their ties "are to common symbols, common leaders, and perhaps common ideals, but not to one another."

The weak membership ties of public interest organizations also reinforce the tendency, present in any organization, for the leadership or headquarters staff to dominate. Not surprisingly, the leaders of these organizations are more accountable to the wealthy patrons, foundations, and government agencies that provide the bulk of their resources than to the constituents whose interests are being represented. And to the extent constituents or members are dispersed across the nation or even the world, the need to maintain contact with them causes leaders to rely on high-tech communications (such as computerized direct mail, fax machines, and Web sites), which further devalue whatever social and communal resources the grassroots might be able to muster.

Public interest organizations also tend to supplement the quiet, inside lobbying of traditional interest groups with "outside" strategies that involve attracting public—especially media—attention. One reason why is suggested in a study of public interest law firms by Burton Weisbrod and his colleagues at the University of Wisconsin at Madison. They point out that because the services of such firms are not for sale in the market, their sponsors assess performance in terms of positive media attention rather than revenues. Unlike conventional law firms, public interest firms end up maximizing publicity, not profit.

Political scientist Jack Walker, of the University of Michigan at Ann Arbor, points to another factor feeding the public interest groups' appetite for publicity. Because these organizations are not rooted in the face-to-face interactions of individuals who live or work together, they must rely on the media to keep their widely dispersed members (and patrons) informed. To keep all these parties engaged, public interest leaders resort to a kind of high-pitched revivalism, continually and publicly recommitting the organization to its lofty goals—and in the process pointing out threats from enemies. Some of the media that leaders use are

internal, such as newsletters, but the incentives to reach out by grabbing the attention of TV, radio, and newspapers are strong. After all, as Walker argues, those drawn to public interest activities expect to see results in the *public* arena.

Such regrettable tendencies may emerge in any political endeavor. Yet they consistently characterize public interest politics. And while public interest organizations hardly dominate contemporary American politics, they have helped acclimate us to a style of politics in which the participants are "organizations" virtually in name only and in which posturing and confrontation play a central role.

More to the point, the curious and often perverse dynamics of public interest politics shape controversies involving race and affirmative action. The 1994 ouster of Benjamin Chavis as executive director of the National Association for the Advancement of Colored People (NAACP) is a good example. The internal rift over Chavis's management of the organization's $3.8 million debt was widely reported in the press. But it was seldom noted that his removal was instigated not by the membership but by the Ford Foundation, which withheld a major grant until the NAACP's finances were put in order. One of the few observers who did note it was *Washington Post* columnist William Raspberry, who wrote: "The obvious question is how such a venerable organization, still 600,000 members strong, has come to the point not just of being in debt but also of being beholden to a private foundation for its survival?" Answering his own question, Raspberry cited the NAACP's "inability to ask its natural constituency for what it needs." Such is the effect of foundation patronage even on a well-established organization that—unlike MALDEF—has a substantial membership base.

The use of outside strategies to make up for weak organizational ties to minority constituents shows up in other controversies, such as the disputes in 1980 and 1990 over the undercounting of minorities by the U.S. census. As noted earlier, the census gathers racial and ethnic data based on the self-identification of individual respondents. In 1990, minority leaders spent considerable resources—theirs as well as the government's—urging their constituents to "make yourself count." That meant not only filling out and returning census forms but checking the boxes identifying themselves as members of the appropriate racial and eth-

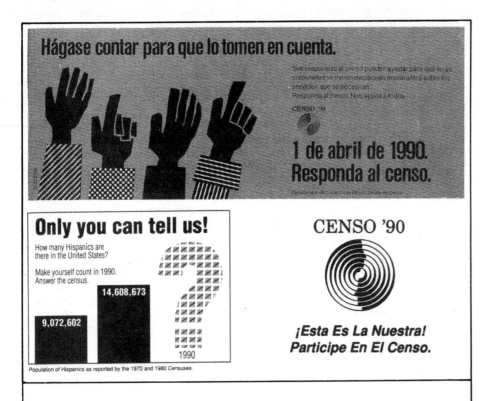

Organizations with weak membership must use publicity to reach their constituents, as Hispanic groups did in a "make yourself count" campaign during the 1990 census.

On an optimistic note, the contrast between the politics of affirmative action and the politics bred by rigid group boundaries in other parts of the world should remind us that, however daunting our racial and ethnic problems, the United States is not Bosnia, or even Quebec. The elixir of American individualism is still too powerful to permit such intense and overriding group loyalties to flourish.

Yet neither should this analysis offer any false hope. It may be tempting to conclude that the principle of individual merit is so fundamental to our way of life that it will eventually undermine affirmative action. But this assumes that black Americans and members of other minority groups are not really committed to affirmative action. I believe that they are, albeit by means of a specific, and perhaps strained, interpretation of how such programs work.

Still, the forces of individualism in America are so strong that they create other problems—and this is my real point. For the irony is that just when America sees itself as a society rent by hostile groups and verging on balkanization, the reality is that the barriers between groups have probably never been lower. Despite some trouble signs, Americans still enjoy substantial social, economic, and residential mobility. One of the most telling indicators—intermarriage rates—is strikingly high. Demographer Barry Edmonston of the National Academy of Sciences and his colleagues report that 12 percent of married Asians in 1990 had non-Asian spouses, while 19 percent of married Hispanics had non-Hispanic spouses. For the children and grandchildren of Asian and Hispanic immigrants, intermarriage rates are much higher. To be sure, the intermarriage rate for black Americans was only six percent in 1990, but even this figure is higher than it was a generation ago.

The catch is that the high degree of mobility among Americans helps weaken the ties between individuals and larger groups, fueling the intense group competition and conflict that we are enduring today. Precisely because many political leaders have such anemic ties to those they seek to represent, they must resort to the publicity-seeking, media-oriented tactics that are so inflammatory. The lack of strong, organized bases of support also helps explain why black leaders have been willing to dilute their historically unique claims on the American

nic groups. As part of the same high-profile effort, minority advocates also launched lawsuits challenging the Census Bureau's methods of counting. In a world of more traditional membership-based organizations, it would have been a relatively simple matter to pass the word to cooperate with the census. But now passing the word means mounting an expensive and often divisive public relations blitz.

A similar dynamic was evident, if not obvious, in the 1991 controversy over Clarence Thomas's nomination to the Supreme Court. In that battle, minority leaders and their allies tried to block Thomas's nomination because he held to a conservative judicial philosophy. They were outraged by Thomas's position on affirmative action, not simply because he opposed it but because, though an admitted beneficiary, he refused to pay his dues by supporting the very policy that had aided him. In essence, Clarence Thomas was saying, "I made it because I'm good." And he was effectively urging other minority-group members to say the same thing.

In a public drama like this, appearances are not always what they seem. We tend to assume that minority leaders make waves in order to sway the majority. Yet in our strange new political world, minority leaders must go to extraordinary lengths to convince their own constituents that they owe them—the leaders—a debt. Since they have no power to sanction those who benefit from the programs they have fought for, minority leaders aim their rhetoric not just at guilty (and not-so-guilty) whites but at all those beneficiaries out there who are even tempted to follow Clarence Thomas's example.

What may we conclude from this analysis? Does the peculiar admixture of individualism and group rights that we have concocted bode well or ill for the ability of America to sort out its racial affairs at the end of the 20th century?

conscience by accepting women, Hispanics, and the handicapped as equal claimants for the benefits of affirmative action. Deprived of the organizational resources formerly available to leaders that allowed them to discipline as well as reward constituents, minority leaders today resort to rhetoric and ideology to enforce conformity. Shorn of patronage, they resort to passion.

The lesson, then, is a sobering one. Our problems with affirmative action may be more intractable than we realize. If we assume, as I believe we must, that the political aspirations of minorities are not about to abate (or be sublimated, as some have urged, into economic activity), then it is clear that those aspirations will continue to be channeled through the kinds of socially disconnected, funder-dominated organizations that I have examined here. There are not many alternatives on the horizon.

A glimmer of hope is represented by the work of the Industrial Areas Foundation (IAF), founded more than 50 years ago by Saul Alinsky. Infused since the 1960s with a new generation of leaders, the IAF attempts to build genuine grassroots organizations in minority and nonminority neighborhoods around the nation. Outfits such as Communities Organized for Public Service in San Antonio and East Brooklyn Churches in New York manage to avoid many of the problems that beset weak-membership groups. Still, the IAF approach is hardly without difficulties, not the least of which is a dearth of skilled organizers. But the bigger problem is that the IAF is fighting a lonely uphill battle against powerful social, cultural, and political trends.

These trends explain why Californians, having just approved the anti–affirmative action Civil Rights Initiative, may now find that it is easier to eliminate affirmative action *programs* than to temper the excesses of affirmative action *politics*. For the same reasons, there is cause to be suspicious of claims that class-based affirmative action would be significantly less rancorous and divisive than race-based efforts. The unhappy imperatives of politics in contemporary America would certainly remain unchanged. Indeed, class-based affirmative action might pull even more of us into the maelstrom.

ONE AMERICA IN THE 21ST CENTURY: THE PRESIDENT'S INITIATIVE ON RACE

"In the end, more than anything else, our world leadership grows out of the power of our example here at home, out of our ability to remain strong as one America. . . . We are the world's most diverse democracy, and the world looks to us to show that it is possible to live and advance together across those kinds of differences. . . . Building one America is our most important mission . . . money cannot buy it. Power cannot compel it. Technology cannot create it. It can only come from the human spirit."

—President Clinton, February 4, 1997

WHAT IS THE PRESIDENT'S RACE INITIATIVE?

This initiative is a year-long effort, led by the President, to present to the nation his vision of a stronger, more just and more united American community, offering opportunity and fairness for all Americans. The President's initiative will combine constructive dialogue, study, and action. It will examine the current state of race relations and our common future, look at the laws and policies that can help to ensure that we remain One America, and enlist individuals, communities, businesses and government at all levels in an effort to understand our differences as we appreciate the values that unite us.

WHY A MAJOR INITIATIVE ON RACE, AND WHY NOW?

President Clinton's personal, life-long commitment. Growing up in the South, the President saw for himself the great harm caused by racial discrimination, and the difference that can be achieved by changing both policies and attitudes. That longstanding, deeply personal commitment has led him to make this initiative one of his major second-term priorities. He knows that America can reach its full potential only by enlisting the full energies of all our people, and giving all our citizens, of every background, the chance to make the most of their own God-given talents.

Not a crisis, but an opportunity. This effort builds on the President's record throughout his first term (defending affirmative action, major speeches on race and reconciliation, etc.). But unlike previous Presidential efforts in this area, President Clinton's initiative is the result not of a crisis, but of a unique opportunity:

America is strong enough to look to the future. Having moved aggressively in the first term to get the country back on the right track—reversing the rising tide of crime, welfare, budget deficits, unemployment and income inequality—the President believes that it is time for America to address these issues as we prepare for the 21st Century. Many "wedge" issues have been defused. On many of the issues that had been used to divide the country—such as crime and welfare—the President has begun to change the terms of the debate, pointing to solutions instead of pointing fingers, and defusing tensions so that an honest dialogue about race can begin.

Responsibility, community and citizenship. This initiative will encourage Americans to take responsibility—for ourselves and our families, for our community and at home with one another. It is a call to citizenship, because the President believes that being a good citizen includes recognizing the promise of America—an America free of destructive bigotry, a nation that welcomes those who play by the rules, serve their community and reach out to make all Americans feel at home. This is a great nation, and the true measure of our greatness is in the human heart.

WHAT ARE THE INITIATIVE'S GOALS AND METHODS?

The initiative will have five central goals:

1. To articulate the President's vision of racial reconciliation and a just, unified America;
2. To help educate the nation about the facts surrounding the issue of race;
3. To promote a constructive dialogue, to confront and work through the difficult and controversial issues surrounding race;
4. To recruit and encourage leadership at all levels to help bridge racial divides;
5. To find, develop and implement solutions in critical areas such as education, economic opportunity, housing, health care, crime and the administration of justice—for individuals, communities, corporations and government at all levels.

The President hopes to achieve these goals through the following methods:

Presidential leadership. The President will begin a national examination of race and reconciliation—explaining why the goal of One America is so important to preparing for the 21st Century, addressing the facts about race, encouraging others to discuss difficult racial issues that we too often avoid and reaching out to Americans of every race to get them engaged in the process. Unlike previous national efforts, this initiative will be led directly and personally by the President throughout.

Dialogue, study and action. Through dialogue, study and action, we will increase our understanding of race, and propose and promote policies and solutions that can make a difference.

Dialogue. Dialogue can help to inform, and to build support for constructive solutions to the issues of race. For an entire generation growing up after the civil rights movement, there has been little or no public articulation of the values and ideals of racial reconciliation. (And too often the rhetoric has been negative, helping to confirm derogatory stereotypes.) This initiative will employ the power of the Presidency to encourage open, candid debate about difficult issues and to highlight actions by individuals, communities, businesses and government that are working in this area now.

Study. The issues to be addressed will include: different perceptions and experiences of Americans of different races, confronting harmful stereotypes and examining serious problems. While the initiative will be largely forward-looking, it is also important to help educate Americans about the past—so that the nation has a clear sense of what has come before, recognizing the unique experience of African Americans throughout our history.

Action. Throughout this effort, attention will go to policies that can make a difference and solutions that can be implemented by individuals, community groups, state and local governments and the federal government. Examples of issues to be addressed include the lack of economic progress among Hispanic Americans and the greatly reduced number of black and Hispanic students in California. This nation has made real progress, but we know that there is more that must be done.

- An example of dialogue, study and action is the President's 5/16/97 apology to the survivors of the Tuskeegee Study, which was combined with concrete actions and further study (establishing a bioethics center at Tuskeegee; studying ways to involve minority communities in research and health care; new training materials for medical researchers on ethics and how to apply them to diverse populations; and new postgraduate fellowships in bioethics for minorities).

ELEMENTS OF THE PRESIDENT'S INITIATIVE

Advisory Board. This small, diverse group will advise the President and assist him in outreach efforts and consultations with experts. They were chosen based on their outstanding leadership on this issue and their contributions to America's ongoing dialogue about race and reconciliation.

Significant Presidential events/actions throughout the year. Events held throughout the year will include town hall meetings in different regions of the country, meetings with the advisory board and other events which will enable the President to carry out his goals for the initiative.

Outreach, consultation and leadership recruitment. The effort will include outreach to community leaders, religious leaders, state and local elected officials, members of Congress, business leaders and individuals, encouraging them to become involved in reconciliation and community-building projects.

The President's Report to the American People. The President will issue a report next summer, in which he will:

- Present his vision of One America, including an illustration and assessment of the growing diversity of our nation and of his consultations with his advisory board;
- Reflect [on] the work that has occurred during the year, including the conversations and suggestions made at town hall meetings and other venues;
- Report on how the nation has evolved on the issue of race over the past 30 years, including the studies commissioned for the initiative;
- Provide recommendations and solutions that enable individuals, communities, businesses, organizations and government to address difficult issues and build on our best possibilities.

Immigration and the American Experience

The history of immigration and ethnic group diversity is embedded in the history of America from earliest times. These social historical facts have often been ignored and nearly forgotten.

To the European and Asian immigrant, America represented freedom from the constraints of state-bound societies whose limits could not be overcome except through emigration. Yet this historical pathway to liberty, justice, and opportunity came to be perceived as a "tarnished door" when the deep impulses of exclusion and exclusivity came to the fore. The victims were aliens who, ironically, achieved the American promise but were denied the reward of acceptance and incorporation into the very culture they helped to fashion. The following articles describe the immigrant experience and raise once again the issues that every large-scale multiethnic regime must address: How can unity and diversity be channeled into political, economic, and cultural well-being? What are the legitimate limits and strengths of ethnic groups in the expression of policy regarding countries toward which some affinity may be attributed?

The history of immigration law does not champion American ethnic groups. Immigration laws include the Chinese Exclusion Acts of the 1880s, the National Origins Quota System of the 1920s, the Mexican Repatriation Campaign of the 1950s, and the McCarran-Walter Act in 1952. A new era began with the inclusiveness of the mid–1960s. The findings of the 1990 U.S. Census indicate a range of demographic, economic, and social indicators in this most recent era of immigration in the United States. Both the immediate impact of present-day newcomers and the changes in America that can be attributed to the conflicts and contributions of previous immigrants appear to be facets of nearly every contemporary social issue.

The U.S. Census documents the consequences of decades and generations of immigration. The Census enables us to discern the spectrum of American ethnicities and the regional patterns of ethnic settlement. The stories of new immigrants are aspects of a worldwide drama. The European and American contexts discussed in this unit provide perspectives on immigrant adjustment and their reception in various regimes and cultures. The ongoing issue of cultural formation through language and the political artifices used to heighten or diminish ethnicity as a political factor are explored. The movement of people induces change and growth that poses great po-

tential for well-being and economic development. Nevertheless, the influx of persons and cultures requires awareness of our cultural diversity and common humanity as well as energy, mutual openness to talent, and participation of all in the experience of being and becoming Americans.

Full employment and social-economic mobility in countries from which persons are coming to the United States would decrease incentives for migration. Political and religious freedom in other countries would negate another cause for the movement of people from oppressive regimes to democratic and liberal societies.

Changes in the U.S. immigration laws in 1965 contributed to the growing number of Central American, South American, and Asian immigrants who have entered the country. The flow of population also includes persons who have entered without governmental authorization. Extreme violence and political turmoil have contributed to the number of refugees seeking asylum in the United States.

As the unit articles make clear, immigration not only has an impact on the receiving country but also affects nations that lose the talents, skills, and loyalty of disaffected migrants. Immigration, moreover, contributes to an already complex process of intergenerational relationships and the socialization of persons whose experiences of profound cultural change are intensified by competition, patterns of settlement, options for mobility, and the consciousness of ethnic traditions that conflict with dominant cultural and educational institutions.

Michael Piore's assessment of children born to immigrant workers suggests an interesting lens through which the following articles may be read. Dr. Piore writes:

There is nothing in the immigration process that ensures that this second generation will be able to move up to the higher level jobs toward which they aspire. Indeed, historically industrial societies appear consistently to disappoint the expectations of the second generation in this regard. That disappointment has in turn been the source of enormous social tension. The sit-down strikes in the late thirties which sparked the industrial unions movement in the United States may in large measure be attributed to the reaction of the children of pre-World War I European immigrants to their labor market conditions. Similarly, the racial disturbances in Northern urban ghettos in the middle and late 1960s may be looked upon as

a revolt of the black migrants against a society bent upon confining them to their parents' jobs.

As a guide for your own study, the U.S. Commission on Civil Rights has noted that increased immigration raises the following issues for both recent arrivals and Americans by birth:

Employment: The areas of occupation selected by or imposed upon various ethnic populations trace ethnic group mobility strategies and ethnic succession in the workplace, especially in manufacturing, hospitals, restaurants, and maintenance and custodial positions. Some ethnic populations appear to have greater numbers of highly educated persons in professional or semiprofessional positions.

Institutional and societal barriers: The job preferences and discrimination against the ethnic enclaves and persons in small communities that are isolated from mainstream English-speaking society suggest the value of second-language competencies. Mutual accommodation is required to minimize the effect of inadequate language skills and training, and difficulties in obtaining licenses, memberships, and certification.

Exploitation of workers: The most common form is the payment of wages below minimum standards. Alien workers have been stereotyped as a drain on public services. Such scapegoating is insupportable.

Taking jobs from Americans: Fact or fiction?: The stunning fact is that immigrants are a source of increased productivity and a significant, if not utterly necessary, addition to the workforce as well as to the consumer power that drives the American economy.

Looking Ahead: Challenge Questions

In what respects are the historical experiences of America relevant to contemporary immigration issues and policies?

A decade ago, American national policy advisers discussed the claims of irredentist populations as an ethnic/political issue of comparison between Poland and Germany and the United States and Mexico. How has the globalization of the economy—NAFTA and the European Community—changed the relationships among countries and their perceptions of one another?

On December 10, 1996, the Mexican government passed a law to allow dual citizenship to persons living in the United States. What does this policy portend for the relationship between Mexico and the United States? Should statehood for Northern Mexico become an option? At present, is this law of citizenship a threat to or an opportunity for ethnic group relations?

Why do periods of economic crisis appear to exacerbate tensions and strain relations among ethnic groups?

The clustering of ethnic populations in various regions of America has produced patterns that are worth pondering. Discuss the importance of locality to understanding American ethnicities. In what respect is the immigration question really a local issue, not a national concern?

What remedies for language diversity are acceptable in a democratic society? Is the argument about stereotypic language compelling? Prescriptive? Misleading? Why?

Immigration: Bridging Gap Between Ideas and Action

Tightened borders are gaining support; experts debate costs, benefits of newest arrivals

If the 104th Congress does not enact major new laws on immigration, it will not be for lack of suggestions: Various members want to boost border patrols and deportations; impose border fees, worker identification cards and new immigration ceilings; stem public benefits for non-citizens; and end citizenship for the children of illegal aliens.

Lawmakers are exploring these new restrictions amid concerns that the costs of new arrivals outweigh the advantages they provide.

Illegal immigrants are the primary target. "People are fed up," said Sen. Alan K. Simpson, R-Wyo., chairman of the Judiciary Committee's immigration panel and an advocate of new restrictions. "They see people violating our law come here and be treated hospitably."

There is also a new skepticism toward legal immigration, which has surged in recent years. Already, House lawmakers have voted to restrict public benefits for lawful immigrants who have not become citizens — triggering an emotional debate about the rights of recent arrivals vs. the native-born.

"It's simply targeting people because of their political vulnerability,"

By Holly Idelson

said Lincoln Diaz-Balart of Florida, a Cuban-born Republican who split with his party leadership on the issue.

At a minimum, lawmakers and the Clinton administration are prepared to invest more in policing the nation's borders and deporting illegal entrants. They may do more, such as creating a national computer registry to identify work status or narrowing the channels for legal immigration.

But the policy landscape is not as straightforward as the desire for action.

Increased border patrols, for example, cost money — at a time when Republicans are trying to curb government spending. National registries raise civil liberties issues among liberals — and also alarm conservatives hostile to the idea of increased government oversight in the workplace.

It is not clear that immigrants pose an economic threat: Some economists say that immigrants overtax public services while making it harder for the native-born to find jobs. But other studies indicate that immigrants are an economic windfall, or even a necessity, for the United States.

And economics cannot answer some of the social questions at the heart of immigration policy in a nation founded by immigrants: Who deserves to be in the United States? What are immigrants supposed to bring to the country, and how much are they allowed to take?

Some of the strongest voices for restrictions have come from within the Republican Party, where some complain that immigrants are overburdening public services or creating a balkanized community by failing to learn English and otherwise assimilate.

Other Republicans, however, argue that newcomers inject critical vitality into the nation's economy. They are wary of proposals that send a restrictionist or anti-foreign message, which could be perceived as racist and could jeopardize the party's appeal among ethnic communities—such as Cuban-American—that share many Republican values.

"This is one of those issues that really threatens to tear the Republican Party in half," said Stephen Moore, an economist specializing in immigration at the libertarian CATO Institute.

For their part, Democrats must balance their traditional allegiances to minority and civil rights organizations against the public appetite for immigration restrictions that those groups may find offensive.

As California Goes

The impetus for national action on immigration begins with California.

From *Congressional Quarterly*, April 15, 1995, pp. 1065-1071. © 1995 by Congressional Quarterly, Inc. Reprinted by permission.

Anti-immigration sentiment often tracks hard economic times, as it did during the 1990 recession. Much of the nation has pulled out of that slump, but California is still reeling. It also hosts more legal and illegal immigrants than any other state.

The combination has been explosive. It prompted the now widely known Proposition 187, a successful 1994 state ballot initiative to deny most public services to illegal aliens. The Proposition 187 argument spilled into the national political debate, nurturing seeds of discontent already planted by publicized abuses in the asylum system and other aspects of the immigration system.

Rep. Howard L. Berman, D-Calif., said such problems have generated public agitation even in areas with few immigrants. "It's almost a national test of will of the effectiveness of government to enforce its laws," he said. Proposition 187 is on hold pending a court challenge, but the issue remains on the nation's front burner.

California and five other states also have tried to sue the federal government for billions of dollars in reimbursement for providing services to illegal aliens. Their claims focus attention on the costs of immigration in increased public services or displaced workers.

Academics generally agree that illegal immigrants take more in public services than they pay in taxes (although they typically pay some taxes and contribute indirect economic benefits that may make them an overall plus).

The fiscal picture for legal immigrants is more confusing. Donald Huddle, an economics professor at Rice University, estimates that legal immigrants directly cost taxpayers about $17 billion more in 1993 than they paid in taxes. But researchers at the Urban Institute, a nonpartisan public policy research and education organization, have calculated these immigrants as a net plus for taxpayers. And many economists say the contribution from immigrants is even more positive when broader economic factors are included — such as their strong record of starting and sustaining small businesses, or the health of industries that benefit from their labor.

Disputed cost estimates notwithstanding, analysts generally agree that the direct economic benefits from immigrants flow disproportionately to the federal government in the form of payroll taxes, while the major direct costs, such as education, are borne primarily by states and localities.

And states have little power to legislate their way out of these costs. The federal courts, and sometimes state constitutions, dictate that states cannot discriminate against non-citizens when providing welfare benefits. In some cases — public education, for example — they must provide services to illegal aliens as well.

That financial scenario helps account for some of the political pressure — particularly from governors and state legislatures — for Congress to do more to stem new arrivals.

But money is not the only concern among politicians and voters.

The current wave of immigration is not only large, but also culturally distinct from earlier influxes. In 1965, Congress adjusted immigration laws to place less emphasis on nationality — which had favored Europeans — and more on admitting relatives of U.S. citizens or legal residents. Over time, that policy has worked to bring in ever greater proportions of immigrants from Asia and Latin America.

Their arrival has been met with disquiet in some communities, where some native-born citizens complain that newcomers are not assimilating.

Daniel Stein, executive director of the Federation for American Immigration Reform (FAIR), said that culture shock may be particularly pronounced when it coincides with low birth rates or shifting demographics among the native-born. "Suddenly, what used to be their own neighborhood shopping strip, there's not a sign in English," said Stein, whose 70,000-member group supports restrictions on immigration.

The resulting disorientation helps feed public apprehension about more immigrants, who can become easy scapegoats for economic or cultural problems in the community.

Moore, of the Cato Institute, also connects anti-immigration sentiment with an inward-looking mood he perceives in certain foreign policy arguments, such as calls to defeat the North American Free Trade Agreement. "I think there is a real danger in this country in terms of a re-emerging economic nationalism," he said.

Political Heat

The desire for political action brewed throughout the 103rd Congress, popping up on spending bills and on spontaneous floor amendments. When Congress approved emergency earthquake aid to California, for example, lawmakers sought to stop most of the assistance from going to illegal aliens. *(1994 Weekly Report, p. 319)*

The Clinton administration proposed sizable budget increases for the Immigration and Naturalization Service (INS) and an overhaul of the rules for processing asylum claims. These efforts won credit even from some Republicans, who conceded that the INS had languished under GOP administrations.

But other GOP lawmakers said President Clinton did not go far enough.

Congress moved no major legislation on immigration, in part because Clinton and some Democratic congressional leaders were reluctant to take on the issue in such a politically charged climate.

Republicans are showing far less hesitancy.

Immigration politics do not fall along party lines, but the recent calls to restrict immigration — legal and illegal — have been more potent within the Republican Party. Republicans are typically less dependent on support from Hispanics and other minority groups that are sensitive to potential discrimination, and sometimes perceive racist undercurrents in restrictionist proposals.

Moreover, the Republican takeover in Congress has delivered the House and Senate Judiciary committees on immigration policy into the hands of two lawmakers with a longstanding interest in tightening the nation's borders: Sen. Simpson and Rep. Lamar Smith, R-Texas.

Simpson already has introduced a major proposal on illegal immigration (S 269) and plans to offer a bill addressing legal immigration later this year.

Smith is holding hearings on the issue and is expected to craft his own comprehensive bill.

The administration plans to weigh in with a legislative package on illegal immigration, relying in part on recent recommendations from the bipartisan U.S. Commission on Immigration Reform, created by the 1990 Immigration Act (PL 101-649) and chaired by former Texas Democratic Rep. Barbara Jordan.

Bright Line

The starting point for the debate is cracking down on illegal immigrants. Government officials estimate that about 4 million people are living in the United States illegally, many of them concentrated in a few states.

Tightening the border has become an automatic cause for most politi-

Proposals Would Crack Down on Illegals...

Congress is likely to take up an array of immigration-related proposals as part of a comprehensive legislative package. Many measures are aimed at keeping — or throwing — illegal immigrants out of the country. Others would change the terms for legal immigrants to enter and live in the United States. Below are key proposals:

Illegal Immigration

● **Border security.** Many lawmakers support increased resources to secure the nation's borders. Most of the attention is on expanding staff and equipment for the Border Patrol along the U.S.-Mexico border. The Immigration and Naturalization Service (INS) currently employs about 4,500 Border Patrol agents; lawmakers want to boost that to as high as 10,000, although some are concerned about the cost and potential human rights abuses by the patrols.

The Clinton administration originally suggested a border crossing fee to help finance border security and processing for legal entrants but retreated amid howls of protest from some affected communities and their congressional representatives, who feared it would squelch commerce in the border region. Clinton is now suggesting a voluntary crossing fee plan, with enhanced border services going to those communities that "opt in." Some key congressional voices on immigration, such as Sens. Alan K. Simpson, R-Wyo., and Dianne Feinstein, D-Calif., support the idea.

Lawmakers also want to explore ways to improve compliance with visa regulations or tighten qualifications for receiving entry visas. Officials estimate that about half the illegal immigrant population entered the country legally but overstayed their visas. Ideas include giving the State Department more resources to screen visa applications or requiring applicants to post a financial bond to help ensure that they will return to their home country.

Some lawmakers may want to reconsider the current Visa Waiver Program (PL 103-416), which allows short-term tourists and business travelers to enter the United States without a visa if they are from countries that have a low rate of denials and violations on U.S. visas. How-

ever, this program is popular as a means to promote tourism and commerce.

● **Employer sanctions.** The 1986 Immigration Reform and Control Act (PL 99-603) for the first time made it illegal to hire undocumented aliens, with punishments including civil fines and, in egregious cases, jail time. But so far the federal government has devoted few resources to enforcing the provisions, and there is widespread agreement that the law has had little effect in deterring illegal immigration. Policy-makers differ on what to do now. The Clinton administration and some lawmakers propose putting new resources into enforcing employer sanctions as well as general labor laws upholding minimum workplace standards. But others are hostile to increased government interference in the workplace or skeptical that the program can work. In the past, lawmakers such as Senate Judiciary Chairman Orrin G. Hatch, R-Utah, and Sen. Edward M. Kennedy, D-Mass., have called for scrapping employer sanctions, citing claims that the law has led to incidents of job discrimination against citizens who look "foreign."

● **Verification.** Closely related to the employer sanctions debate is the question of verification. Momentum is increasing behind proposals to create a national registry enabling employers to check the legal status of potential employees. The proposal — which would probably rely on Social Security numbers and could be accompanied by some sort of enhanced Social Security or work authorization card — has long been anathema to certain minority groups and civil libertarians, who fear it would be costly and inaccurate and lead to discrimination against those who appear foreign-born. However, members of both parties are interested in the idea as perhaps the only way to curtail employment of illegal aliens. The Clinton administration is proposing several pilot programs for a national registry, in keeping with recent recommendations by the bipartisan Commission on Immigration Reform.

Lawmakers have also proposed tougher penalties for those who use or manufacture fraudulent visas or other documents for immigrants.

● **Reimbursement.** Six states are suing the federal government to recover money spent on services to illegal

cians — either as a prelude to cutbacks in legal immigration or as an attempt to forestall them.

The result has been a virtual bidding war among policy-makers pledging to expand personnel and equipment along the southwest border. The Border Patrol now consists of about 4,700 agents. Lawmakers are talking seriously about doubling that.

Many policy-makers and analysts also say the government must look beyond the borders to what primarily draws immigrants across — jobs.

The administration wants to improve enforcement of the law that prohibits hiring undocumented workers, targeting industries known for relying on them.

Clinton officials and many Democrats also call for tougher enforcement of general labor laws, saying that illegal aliens are often attractive hires because they are afraid to challenge exploitative working conditions that legal citizens would not tolerate.

"You can drive up and down the state of California on Highway 89 . . .

and the people working the crops are still not U.S. citizens," said Xavier Becerra, D-Calif., a member of the House Judiciary Committee's immigration panel.

"If we were to just follow some of our own labor standards, you'd see a change," Becerra said.

But some conservatives are skeptical about increased government intervention in the workplace. That extends to proposals to create a national registry to verify that a job applicant can work legally.

...And Tighten Rules for Legal Immigrants

aliens. While the legal actions are not expected to prevail, the federal government is moving to quell some of the irritation. Pending anti-crime legislation (HR 667 — H Rept 104-21) would guarantee a total of $650 million annually from fiscal 1996 through 2000 for the costs of incarcerating illegal aliens, building on money already approved in the 1994 crime law (PL 103-322). The Clinton administration's fiscal 1996 budget proposed $250 million to help affected states pay for certain medical and education expenses for immigrants.

Legal Immigration

● **Immigration ceilings.** While much political attention has been focused on illegal immigration, some lawmakers insist that the United States also must scale back the number of newcomers it allows to enter each year through lawful channels. Regular legal immigration has climbed to more than 800,000 people annually, including refugees, relatives of U.S. citizens and those admitted because they have work skills in high demand. Simpson, chairman of the Senate immigration subcommittee, last session proposed dropping those levels to about 600,000; other lawmakers advocate steeper cuts or a temporary moratorium on immigration.

Besides questioning the overall numbers, lawmakers are likely to consider changing the priorities for who gains legal admission. Family reunification now accounts for more than half of all legal immigration. Several members have suggested that the United States should emphasize admitting people with needed work skills or language proficiency and cut back on the ability of citizens or legal permanent residents to bring in relatives. Family reunification currently can apply to siblings and adult children. Some lawmakers have suggested limiting the provision to members of the nuclear or immediate family.

Simpson also wants to repeal the 1966 Cuban Adjustment Act, which lets any Cuban who arrives on U.S. soil qualify for work papers and legal status after one year.

● **Benefits.** House Republicans have passed a bill (HR 4) to prohibit or restrict welfare and other federal benefits for many legal immigrants who have not become U.S. citizens. In some cases these aliens would be banned outright from receiving benefits; in others, their access would be restricted by stepping up requirements that their sponsors' financial resources be taken into account (a process known as "deeming") when determining the applicant's eligibility. The legislation also would clarify that illegal aliens cannot receive most federal benefits. (That is generally the case now.) Republicans are touting the proposal as a way to save money and draw a closer connection between benefits and full citizenship. But it has generated fierce opposition in several camps, including among governors who say states will be forced to pick up the cost when needy immigrants who have been receiving federal aid turn to state programs for increased help. Key Senate Republicans appear cool to the proposal. (Weekly Report, p. 872)

There is broader support for the more general principle of requiring sponsors to help support new immigrants who need assistance. Sponsors currently sign an affidavit promising to provide their charges with financial support, but these pledges are not legally enforceable.

Related Concerns

● **Deportation.** Several lawmakers have proposed ways to send more immigrants home, faster. The primary focus is on steps to speed deportation of aliens — both legal and illegal — who commit serious crimes. But there are also proposals to expedite deportation for asylum seekers without valid claims, for would-be entrants who are apprehended at sea, and for newcomers who enter legally but quickly become dependent on public assistance. Current law allows for deportation of immigrants who become dependent on government benefits, but this "public charge" provision is rarely enforced.

● **Citizenship.** One of the most dramatic proposals is to deny automatic U.S. citizenship to the children of illegal aliens born in this country. California Gov. Pete Wilson has proposed a constitutional amendment to this effect. On Capitol Hill, members have proposed making that change by constitutional amendment or by statute.

—Holly Idelson

This puts conservative organizations in an odd political alliance with various minority and civil liberties groups, who have long decried such proposals as tantamount to a national identification card that would be wielded primarily against those who appear "foreign."

Cecilia Muñoz, an immigration policy specialist at the National Council of La Raza, a national Hispanic group, said those types of abuses are already occurring in the wake of Proposition 187. "There are people getting carded in grocery stores in California."

Still, the political tide seems to be going the other way.

Both the Clinton administration and the Jordan Commission have called for pilot programs to test verification methods. Many lawmakers in both parties say they do not understand what the fuss is about, because citizens are routinely asked to provide their Social Security numbers and other identification for tasks official and mundane.

"If we can protect a $2 charge at Kmart," said Rep. Elton Gallegly, R-Calif., "we should be able to protect American jobs." Gallegly chairs an immigration task force appointed by House Speaker Newt Gingrich, R-Ga.

Another key proposal is to cut illegal immigrants' access to government benefits. These aliens are not legally entitled to most federal aid, but some lawmakers say they tap into the system anyway.

Rooting out such abuses, however, will require costly or otherwise controversial improvements to government records that verify immigration status.

History of Immigration Policy

Immigration policy has not followed a steady course toward either liberalization or exclusion. Lawmakers instead have sought to alter the flow of newcomers to favor certain groups at certain times, including immigrants from specific countries, skilled workers and family members of U.S. residents. Refugees — those who leave their country on a non-voluntary basis — generally have been addressed as a separate issue.

Congress cleared the first comprehensive immigration law in 1891, excluding immigrants considered "likely to become public charges." But as the number peaked around the turn of the century, Congress passed further measures allowing for deportation of aliens who had become a public burden after five years' residence.

In 1921, a quota system based on national origins was enacted. It limited immigration from each country to 3 percent a year of the total number of immigrants from that country who lived in the United States in 1910. Afterward, immigration levels — which had been running as high as a million a year — plummeted to 164,000.

The McCarran-Walter Act of 1952 (PL 82-414), passed at the height of the Cold War over President Harry S Truman's veto, extended the grounds for excluding or deporting aliens to include issues of national security. It allotted Great Britain, Germany and Ireland more than two-thirds of the quota of 155,000 annual immigrant slots, while allowing fewer than 200 apiece for Japan and China.

Quota System

Immigration and Nationality Act of 1965. Every president after Truman sought elimination of the national origins quota system. Lyndon B. Johnson in particular found the quotas discriminatory. In 1965, ethnic groups' 40-year effort to end country-by-country quotas succeeded with the enactment of the Immigration and Nationality Act (PL 89-236).

The act established an overall annual limit of about 320,000, with immigrants selected at random on the basis of personal qualities, favoring foreigners with immediate relatives in the United States. Since 1967, European and Canadian immigration, which had accounted for about 85 percent of the total from 1820 to 1960, has fallen to 17 percent, while immigration from Asia and Latin America has risen to 81 percent.

The bill allotted 6 percent of the total legal immigration pool to refugees from communist or Middle Eastern countries — who previously were excluded if a country had reached its quota.

Refugee Act of 1980. This bill (PL 96-212) defined "refugee" to include people from any part of the world, not just communist countries and the Middle East, and tripled the number of refugees allowed to enter the United States each year, from 17,400 to 50,000. Currently, the State Department grants political or other asylum to nearly 250,000 people annually. (*1980 Almanac, p. 378*)

Immigration Reform and Control Act of 1986. With support from the Reagan administration, Congress in 1986 passed an immigration bill (PL 99-603) to impose sanctions on people who hire illegal immigrants.

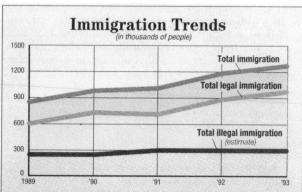

Immigration Trends
(in thousands of people)

Total immigration

Total legal immigration

Total illegal immigration *(estimate)*

In 1993, immigration totaled about 1.3 million people, including about 1 million legal immigrants and an estimated 300,000 illegals. Most legal immigrants are admitted to join family members in the U.S. Others are admitted because of their work skills or for humanitarian reasons. Not shown in this chart are 2.7 million illegal immigrants who became legal under the 1986 Immigration Reform and Control Act (PL 99-603) between 1989 and 1993. The figures for asylees reflect the number of claims filed rather than granted.

Annual Immigration *(in thousands)*

	1989	1990	1991	1992	1993
Family-related	341.6	446.2	453.2	500.9	539.5
Employment-based	52.8	56.7	58.0	119.8	149.2
Humanitarian	179.5	186.4	168.1	220.8	246.9
Refugees	107.2	122.3	112.8	132.1	119.5
Asylees	61.3	58.9	49.6	83.2	120.3
Cuban Program	11.0	5.2	5.7	5.5	7.1
Special Categories	29.1	42.0	32.5	41.6	36.3
Total Legal Immigration	603.0	731.3	711.8	883.1	971.9
Illegal Immigration	250.0	250.0	300.0	300.0	300.0
Total Immigration	853.0	981.3	1,011.8	1,183.1	1,271.9

SOURCE: Center for Immigration Studies, May 1994

MARILYN GATES-DAVIS

For the first time, employers faced fines — and in flagrant cases, jail terms — for knowingly hiring such immigrants. But the bill also created a mechanism for granting legal status to millions of longtime illegal immigrants already in the country. (*1986 Almanac, p. 61*)

Immigration Act of 1990. In 1990, Congress raised the legal immigration ceiling from about 500,000 to about 700,000 annually. The bill (PL 101-649) created a category of "diversity" visas to benefit nationals of countries adversely affected by the 1965 law — primarily those European countries that immigration laws had previously favored. In 1990, all but about 10 percent of the people who obtained visas came from Asia and Latin America. The bill also aimed to encourage workers with special skills and education to immigrate to the United States. (*1990 Almanac, p. 474*)

—Alan Greenblatt

The acid test will be whether lawmakers, in tight budget times, put up the money required for any or all of these initiatives. As Susan Martin, executive director of the Jordan Commission, told the Senate Judiciary Committee: "No solution to the problem of illegal immigration is going to come cheap."

Closing the Front Door

Some lawmakers say that legal immigration has also gotten out of hand. It is at historic highs, with between 700,000 and 1 million people lawfully admitted each year from 1990 to 1993. During that time, the government also legalized more than 2 million people already living in the United States, under the terms of the 1986 Immigration Reform and Control Act (PL99-603). (Chart, History of Immigration Policy)

That is more new legal residents per year than the boom immigration years of the early 1900s, although they represent a smaller proportion of the native population.

"We don't need all these people," said Stein of FAIR, which advocates a temporary moratorium on immigration, then greatly reduced levels of admission with more emphasis on immigrants who provide needed job skills.

Sen. Simpson has called for more modest changes, but also wants to lower legal immigration ceilings and rethink who gets preference for admission.

On the House side, Smith also is inclined to curtail legal immigration, although he speaks of "trimming around the edges" rather than dramatic cutbacks.

Smith's caution may reflect the ambivalence within his party leadership about tackling legal immigration. Gingrich says he sees no need to cut immigration ceilings. Nor is Gallegly interested: "We've got enough work to do to address the illegal problem."

Others are quick to affirm their enthusiastic support for lawful immigration, saying it has brought the country economic and cultural vitality. "Legal immigration is a great plus for this country and it continues to be," said Sen. Paul Simon, D-Ill., a member of the Judiciary Committee's immigration panel.

INS Commissioner Doris Meissner said the administration is withholding judgment on proposed changes in legal immigration until the Jordan Commission releases its recommendations on that issue in June.

Considering Citizenship

Despite such skittishness about overhauling the rules for legal immigration, a new examination of citizenship seems inevitable.

Already, the welfare reform debate has revealed a willingness to adjust the contract between legal immigrants, their sponsors and the government. The House welfare bill (HR 4) would greatly restrict legal aliens' access to certain federal programs, either by banning them outright or by requiring sponsors to assume greater financial accountability. Some Republican advocates of the change suggested these non-citizens were making excessive use of the benefits. *(Weekly Report, p. 872)*

Studies do indicate that elderly immigrants and refugees rely on some federal benefits at a higher rate than the native-born. Other immigrants traditionally have been somewhat less likely to make use of federal assistance programs, although that may be changing.

Gallegly is among those who think Congress should draw a connection between citizenship and public benefits. "If they don't want to pledge their allegiance to the United States," he said, "they shouldn't be eligible for food stamps."

But numerous Democratic lawmakers said the welfare plan is being promoted primarily as a way to free up funds — about $20 billion over four years — for other GOP priorities. They are indignant about denying benefits to legal immigrants who generally bear the burdens of full citizenship, such as paying taxes.

"If you are a legal immigrant in this country, you are working here, you are paying taxes, and bad times come to you, you ought to be entitled to everything else that every American has," Jim McDermott, D-Wash., said during floor debate on the welfare proposal. The Jordan Commission likewise came down against denying benefits to legal immigrants.

Still, even some critics are uneasy about the many legal immigrants who do not seek to become citizens.

Rep. John Bryant, D-Texas, put the question this way at a February hearing: "Are you coming here because

you love us or are you just coming here to make money?"

Smith says it is this question of allegiance that drives controversial movements such as efforts to make English the country's official language. While critics see the language movement as an intolerant swipe at the foreign-born, Smith says it is motivated by a desire to promote a unified culture.

Across the Capitol, Simpson agrees: "The magic of America, corny as hell as it sounds, is common flag, common language, public culture."

Yet Frank Sharry, executive director of the National Immigration Forum, an umbrella group for pro-immigration organizations, believes fears about non-assimilation are often ill-founded: "People don't give up everything they've known to come to the United States so they can reject it."

There are several reasons why many legal immigrants do not pursue citizenship, including emotional ties to their homeland, skittishness about interacting with government officials and difficulty passing the English or history tests for naturalization.

INS Commissioner Meissner said her agency is making a push to promote naturalization, an issue that often has been ignored. And as politicians step up talk of cutting benefits to non-citizens, record numbers of legal immigrants are applying for citizenship.

Meanwhile, some immigration advocates say lawmakers should not lose sight of what immigrants stand for — whether or not they are on the track to formal citizenship. When it comes to hard work, determination and other values extolled by politicians, said Becerra, "they do the things that we talk about at a higher clip than the citizen population."

> Simpson and Smith have a longstanding interest in tightening the borders. "People are fed up," Simpson says of illegal immigration. Smith talks of "trimming around the edges" rather than dramatic cutbacks in legal immigration.

We asked...
You told us
Ancestry

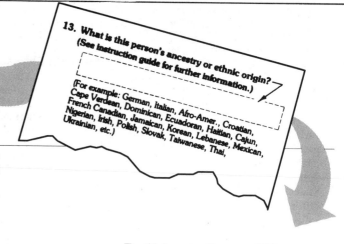

13. What is this person's ancestry or ethnic origin?
(See instruction guide for further information.)

(For example: German, Italian, Afro-Amer., Croatian, Cape Verdean, Dominican, Ecuadoran, Haitian, French Canadian, Jamaican, Korean, Lebanese, Mexican, Nigerian, Irish, Polish, Slovak, Taiwanese, Thai, Ukrainian, etc.)

The Census Bureau conducts a census of population and housing every 10 years. This bulletin is one of a series that shows the questions asked in the 1990 census and the answers that you, the American people, gave. Each bulletin focuses on a question or group of questions appearing on the 1990 census questionnaires.

In question **13** on the 1990 census forms, **we asked** people to write in their ancestry. Ancestry refers to a person's ethnic origin, heritage, or the place of birth of the person or the person's parents or ancestors before their arrival in the United States.

Ancestry data from the 1990 census reflect the diverse ethnic groups that have come to the United States throughout its history.

From what **you told us**, we learned that:

- In 1990, the most frequently reported ancestry in the United States was German (see bar chart). Nearly one-fourth of the American people (58 million) considered themselves to be of German or part-German ancestry.

- The next largest ethnic groups in rank order were Irish, English, Afro-American, and Italian. In all, 33 different ancestry groups had at least 1 million people.

- About 5 percent of respondents reported the general category, "American."

- Most persons reported only one ancestry group; however, a substantial segment reported a mixed background. Nationally, about 60 percent of the population reported only one ancestry; another 30 percent also wrote in a second ancestry. About 10 percent did not report any ancestry.

Nation's Largest Ancestry Group Was Also Tops in Most States

- In over half the States in 1990, more people reported German than any other ancestry (see map).

- Afro-American was the most frequently reported ancestry in the second highest number of States (7), all of which were in the South.

- Irish and English were the largest ancestry groups in five States each, located in the South and Northeast for Irish and Northeast and West for English.

Note: Data on ancestry are based on a sample and are subject to sampling variability.

Top 15 Ancestry Groups: 1990

(In millions. Percent of total population in parentheses)

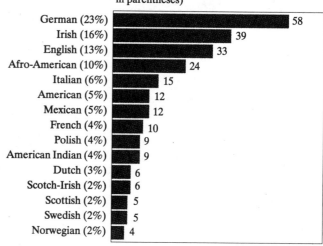

Ancestry Group	Millions
German (23%)	58
Irish (16%)	39
English (13%)	33
Afro-American (10%)	24
Italian (6%)	15
American (5%)	12
Mexican (5%)	12
French (4%)	10
Polish (4%)	9
American Indian (4%)	9
Dutch (3%)	6
Scotch-Irish (2%)	6
Scottish (2%)	5
Swedish (2%)	5
Norwegian (2%)	4

German Was the Largest Ancestry in 29 States

Largest Ancestry Group, by State: 1990

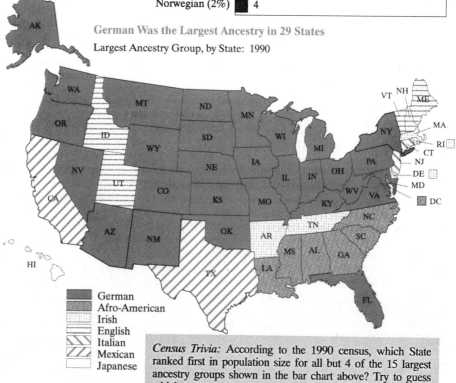

Legend:
- German
- Afro-American
- Irish
- English
- Italian
- Mexican
- Japanese

Census Trivia: According to the 1990 census, which State ranked first in population size for all but 4 of the 15 largest ancestry groups shown in the bar chart above? Try to guess which states ranked first for the other 4 ancestry groups. *(Answer next page)*

Regional Distribution Patterns Varied by Ancestry

- In 1990, individual ancestry groups showed striking variations in their patterns of regional distribution within the United States. These differences often reflected initial settlement patterns, especially for the newer immigrant groups.

- Of the largest European ancestries, French, Scottish, and Welsh were distributed fairly evenly among the four regions. Other large European groups were more concentrated. For example, more than half of the Nation's Italians lived in the Northeast region, and over half of the Norwegians and Czechs were clustered in the Midwest (see chart). About 47 percent of the Scotch-Irish were concentrated in the South, while 45 percent of the Danish lived in the West.

- The regional concentration of persons of Hispanic ancestry depended on their specific country of origin. For instance, the Northeast contained 86 percent of the country's Dominicans, 66 percent of Puerto Ricans, and 63 percent of Ecuadorans. The South was home to 69 percent of Cubans and 51 percent of Nicaraguans. About 62 percent of Salvadorans and Guatemalans and 57 percent of Mexicans lived in the West.

- Persons from the West Indies ancestry groups were concentrated in the Northeast: 59 percent of the Nation's Jamaicans and 55 percent of Haitians lived there.

- Among the larger Southwest Asian ancestry groups, over half of the Armenians and Iranians resided in the West, and 43 percent of the Syrians lived in the Northeast.

- Asian and Pacific Islander ancestry groups were found largely in the West. The West was home to 87 percent of the country's Hawaiians, 72 percent of Japanese, 59 percent of Cambodians, and 55 percent of Chinese and Vietnamese.

Trivia Answer: California—the perennial destination of many migrants—had the largest number of persons of German, Irish, English, Afro-American, Mexican, French, American Indian, Dutch, Scotch-Irish, Scottish, and Swedish ancestry of any State in 1990. New York—the traditional port of entry for large numbers of immigrants—had more Italians and Polish than any other State, and Minnesota ranked first for Norwegians. Texas had the largest number of persons who reported the general ancestry category, "American."

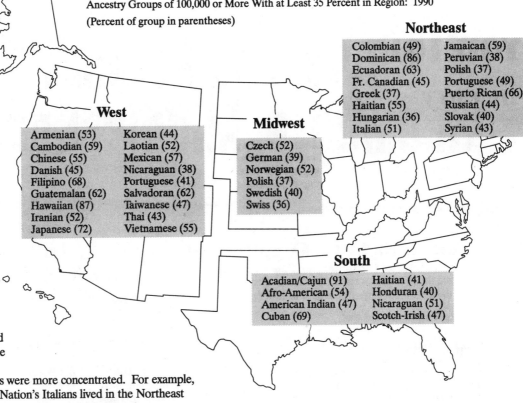

Regional Ethnic Concentrations

Ancestry Groups of 100,000 or More With at Least 35 Percent in Region: 1990

(Percent of group in parentheses)

Northeast

Colombian (49)	Jamaican (59)
Dominican (86)	Peruvian (38)
Ecuadoran (63)	Polish (37)
Fr. Canadian (45)	Portuguese (49)
Greek (37)	Puerto Rican (66)
Haitian (55)	Russian (44)
Hungarian (36)	Slovak (40)
Italian (51)	Syrian (43)

West

Armenian (53)	Korean (44)
Cambodian (59)	Laotian (52)
Chinese (55)	Mexican (57)
Danish (45)	Nicaraguan (38)
Filipino (68)	Portuguese (41)
Guatemalan (62)	Salvadoran (62)
Hawaiian (87)	Taiwanese (47)
Iranian (52)	Thai (43)
Japanese (72)	Vietnamese (55)

Midwest

| Czech (52) |
| German (39) |
| Norwegian (52) |
| Polish (37) |
| Swedish (40) |
| Swiss (36) |

South

Acadian/Cajun (91)	Haitian (41)
Afro-American (54)	Honduran (40)
American Indian (47)	Nicaraguan (51)
Cuban (69)	Scotch-Irish (47)

Who Uses This Information?

Just a few examples:

- Federal agencies to monitor compliance with the anti-discrimination requirements of the Civil Rights Act ■ State and local governments and private social service agencies to assist in providing services to reflect cultural differences ■ Business persons to pinpoint areas of a city for locating new restaurants specializing in particular types of ethnic food

Want to Know More?

Consult the 1990 census report, CP-S-1-2, *Detailed Ancestry Groups for States*, at a large public or university library. Also for sale by Superintendent of Documents, U.S. Government Printing Office (GPO). In addition, ancestry data can be found in the listing, CPH-L-136, *1990 Ethnic Profiles for States*, available for purchase by calling **301-457-2422**. Call:

- Customer Services at the Census Bureau, **301-457-4100**, for ordering information about the GPO reports listed above or to order copies of CQC bulletins or other Census Bureau products ■ Karen Mills or Kim Giesbrecht, **301-457-4008**, for general information on CQC bulletins
- Population Division, **301-457-2403**, for more information on ancestry data

Ethnicity vs. Assimilation: Seeking a Middle Ground

By Lisa Leiter

Since urban flight broke up the old neighborhoods, ethnic enclaves have become less distinct. In many cases, community groups have forged cultural links to supplant geographic ties and share values.

Adam Eterovich relishes memories of his childhood in San Francisco, when his entire family lived close to one another in a downtown neighborhood.

They attended a Croatian Catholic church, the same one where his immigrant parents met and where he was baptized. He and his three sisters spoke English at school, but once the front door slammed at home, Croatian conversation began. "This was a private thing, not a public thing," he recalls.

Since fleeing to the suburb of San Carlos, Eterovich has become more public about his patrimony, attending regular social events organized by Croatian groups and directing the Croatian Genealogical Society, which helps people trace their names and ancestors to Croatian hometowns. He and other urban refugees are trying to continue cultural ties with others of their background living in the ethnically diverse bedroom communities.

Why? Because urban flight, along with intermarriage, transportation improvement, better economic status and scattered family, have combined to weaken the fabric of ethnic belonging and undermine the traditional sense of community and identity. "The suburbs destroyed the family as we know it—of grandma and grandpa watching the kids," says Eterovich, whose 96-year-old mother still lives with him. "If you built a church in a town or a city, then you built a social hall. But when you moved to the suburbs you couldn't take

these structures with you. You destroyed the society at the same time."

The United States is fond of thinking of itself as a melting pot, the only "great and populous world nation-state and world power whose people are not cemented by ties of blood, race or original language," as journalist Dorothy Thompson put it in the October 1954 issue of *Ladies' Home Journal*. But of course the imagined amalgamation doesn't always translate into peaceful coexistence among ethnic groups; this country often has suffered racial and ethnic tensions, particularly in the inner cities. And many immigrants who thought initially that they would sail to America and forsake their origins ultimately have gravitated toward the old culture, explains Susan Rockwell, director of the National Association for Ethnic Studies headquartered at Arizona State University. "The melting pot has always been a myth," she says. "There have always been ethnic enclaves."

Not all of these ethnic enclaves are as visible as the celebrated Chinatowns or Little Italys tucked in major cities across the country. Ethnic sections of suburbia sit buried in strip-mall businesses or recreation centers converted for a night into a replica of some faraway land, like the Croatian dinners Eterovich attends in his neighborhood. He calls it a *drustvo*, the Croatian word for society, club or association, one of the keys to maintaining Old World Traditions. "The societies, outside of the church, are the most important function to express our

ethnicity," he says. "They are the only things that are going to keep us together. If you don't have a cultural center in your area, then it starts to disintegrate."

German-American John Lawrora is another first-generation American trying to hold onto his heritage. He was raised by his maternal grandparents, who taught him both Polish and German in a strict Catholic home. His Italian father died when he was 2. Most of his family—including his 88-year-old mother, have moved to the suburbs from his hometown, Jersey City, N.J., where he still lives. So Lawrora got involved in the German Education Society, which teaches computer-software programs to anyone at a nominal fee; he serves as executive secretary for the German American World Society, a research and historical organization and volunteers as an officer at a retirement home for German-Americans.

Lawrora, like Arizona State's Rockwell, says he believes that many Germans and other ethnic groups are revisiting their cultural roots. Several scholars attribute this reexamination to the social, political and economic situations of the "mother country." For example, between the 1980 and the 1990 census, the number of Americans citing their German origins increased by 10 million, according to John Kromkowski, president of the National Center for Urban Ethnic Affairs and an associate professor of politics at Catholic University in Washington. He attributes the surge to pride resulting from the collapse of the Berlin Wall in 1989, because there were very few German immigrants during that decade. Rockwell adds: "During the second World War, many people lost their ethnicity because they didn't want to be affiliated with the enemy of America. That generation suppressed a lot of stuff. But this generation is saying it is wrong to do that. We have to go back and reclaim it."

Eterovich reports that the number of people seeking information about ancestors in the Balkans has quadrupled as the conflict in Bosnia has escalated during the past four years. "I think it has a lot to do now with the concentrated effort of the youth trying to search deep and find their cultural heritage because they weren't raised with it as much," Rockwell says. "Between being so far removed from their original culture for so many generations plus being immersed in the American culture, they need to do this."

But she insists that these younger generations are more interested in the political links to their heritage rather than the social traditions, which attracted many baby boomers during the 1960s. With the beginning of the civil-rights movement, boomers initially had political intentions. But later, Rockwell says, she and other boomers realized the cultural aspects were important too. The postboomers of generation X, she says, have been drawn to politics because of high-profile issues such as affirmative action, California's Proposition 187 (which denies certain welfare benefits to illegal immigrants) and the current movement to make English America's official language.

It is still unclear whether those in their 20s will choose to repeat the pattern of the baby boomers described by Rockwell. Stephen Steinlight, director of national affairs for the American Jewish Committee, which runs the Institute on Pluralism and Group Identity in Washington, says ethnicity will fail to serve as the primary means of personal identification. Race, if it hasn't

If you are a small group, he said, you will be assimilated. If you don't like it, you shouldn't be living in America. Go back.

done so already, will eclipse it. "Ethnicity is much more attenuated then it was previously," he tells **Insight.** "But its hard to predict a set of circumstances in which it will vanish."

However, he says, its importance increasingly will be diminished as ethnicity is replaced by other categories of identification—such as race, gender, age, social class and sexual orientation. "Some of the old paradigms for defining a person solely on the basis of ethnicity are enormously oversimplified and dated," he says. "Where do we fit ethnicity as a fundamental determinant of who we are when other aspects of who we are emerge?"

In politically correct America, income also seems to be outweighing ethnicity as a primary means of defining a neighborhood. Subdivisions sprout in rapidly growing areas with families of all backgrounds. But the question remains: Will these people feel more comfortable socializing by economic status or ethnic background? Either way, Steinlight says, "Ethnicity is always going to be there, partly because we like it and also because it gives us a handle on who we are."

Major groups—such as Hispanics—will be able to preserve their ethnicity primarily through language, particularly in heavily concentrated areas. But smaller groups such as Croatians must use food, song and dance as the dominant means of conveying the culture to their children, Eterovich says. Intermarriage undoubtedly will escalate assimilation, but most ethnics, such as Eterovich, accept and understand this. "If you are a small group in America, you will be assimilated whether you like it or not," he says. "And if you don't like it, you shouldn't be living in America. If you want to be a purist, go back to your homeland. You can't have it both ways."

Still, if those who want to preserve their culture do not interact with their children and grandchildren, the social, educational and cultural groups such as the ones headed by Eterovich and Lawrora will die. Eterovich, whose daughter (like 95 percent of Croatians) married a man of mixed descent, predicts that ethnicity will disintegrate further, exacerbated by the suburbs and intermarriage. His three grandchildren have yet to explore their ethnic roots. "What are they?" he asks, laughing. "That's America, isn't it?"

Newcomers and Established Residents

Robert L. Bach

Ours is a time of crossing, blurring, and redefining boundaries. Not since the turn of the century have communities throughout America reflected the diversity of cultures, nationalities, languages, and religions brought by immigrants during the last two decades. According to the 1990 census, there are nearly 20 million foreign-born residents in America. As established communities receive these newcomers, diversity is recasting relations among groups, ethnic identities, community associations, and political alliances. Once again, America is changing.

In 1987 a national board of scholars launched a project to examine the interactions of new immigrants and established, long-term residents. Changes in immigration law in the 1960s shifted both the magnitude and composition of new immigrant populations. They opened the gates to immigration from Asia and the Pacific and stabilized flows from Latin America and the Caribbean. The share of European immigrants declined. This new mix of diverse newcomers became an essential ingredient in the transformation of community life. The National Board of the Changing Relations Project sought to identify the ways in which recent immigrants interacted with ethnically diverse established residents, how they organized themselves, in which social institutions they participated, and how host communities were adapting to the newcomers. The board examined, within the context of rapid economic change and frequently deep social divisions, if and how newcomers and established residents crossed social, cultural, and political boundaries to create and to maintain community.

From the outset, the board was concerned with popular reports of dramatic instances of unrest and conflict between members of immigrant and established resident groups. Spectacular incidents, such as conflict between Southeast Asian refugees and Texas shrimp farmers, had been highlighted in the national press and had even become the subject of full-length movies. Similarly dramatic accounts of Korean shopkeepers in conflict with host African-American communities implied unyielding hardship. Invidious comparisons of immigrant success stories with impoverished minorities also fueled a widespread mythology about job competition. Did these incidents suggest what was to become of the nation's increasingly diverse communities?

The Changing Relations Project was launched during a highly charged national debate over reform of U.S. immigration policy. For only the fourth time in U.S. history, the nation sought to change who could immigrate and to reform the rules governing how people could enter. Throughout the debate, undercurrents of concern about the absorptive capacity of U.S. communities remained unsettled. The

From *Changing Relations: Newcomers and Established Residents in U.S. Communities*, a report to the Ford Foundation by the National Board of the Changing Relations Project, 1993, pp. 10-21. © 1993 by the Ford Foundation. Reprinted by permission.

answers found in this study, from the rare and exceptional nature of incidents of open conflict to infrequent but promising efforts at intergroup coalition-building, respond to those undercurrents. The answers are not only about immigrants. They demand that attention be given to community conditions both newcomers and established residents face and struggle to overcome together.

The Changing Economic Background

As a nation, we have been here before. America thrives on its immigrant heritage. Part history, part ideology, immigration embodies the theme of national renewal, rebirth, hope. Uprooted abroad, newcomers become transplants in a land that promises opportunity. Yet America has also become settled. At the turn of the century, the foreign-born accounted for roughly 14 percent of the U.S. population. Today, they make up about one-half. The context of reception, as well as the capacity of immigration to reform community life, has also changed. The story is no longer only that of the uprooted, settled on an open frontier or in industrial cauldrons; it is also the story of subsequent U.S.-born generations that have blossomed or been left behind by the march of American history.

Most Americans today were born when the nation was at its most insular and provincial. In the 1950s few could have foreseen the turnaround in immigration flows that would result from political changes in the 1960s. As America emerged from World War II, the share of the population that was foreign-born was declining. As those who entered the United States in earlier years aged and immigration restrictions excluded entire regions of the world, the proportion of foreign-born dropped from almost 9 percent to 5 percent in the 1950s. In the 1960s, before immigration policy reforms were implemented, the share fell again to historical lows, with less than 5 percent of the total population being foreign-born.

If few could foresee the changes in immigration, even fewer anticipated the transformation of the American political economy that today is popular wisdom. In the last two decades, the U.S. economy lost much of its strength and position in the world. Although it is still the largest economy in the world, it now accounts for only one-fifth of the world's output, compared with one-third during the

1950s and 1960s. The U.S. economy also became increasingly internationalized during that period. Foreign trade grew to become a much larger proportion of the nation's economic activities, but that change brought with it an imbalance that made America not only economically interdependent but financially dependent on foreign capital. In the last decade, rapid increases in foreign investment and foreign ownership of highly visible U.S. property reinforced the image that more and more essential economic decisions were being made abroad.

For many Americans these changes were personal. Manufacturing jobs disappeared and new opportunities were limited primarily to the service sector or to jobs that required higher skills or specialized education. New groups entered the labor market. The proportion of women participating in the labor force increased dramatically, and the share of ethnic minorities working in particular jobs grew rapidly.

Economic restructuring has also realigned the nation's geographical balance. Demographic, economic, and political power has shifted away from the Midwest and Northeast toward high-growth areas in the South and Southwest. The redistribution has been highly uneven, spawning patches of rapid growth alongside pockets of decline. These economic shifts were accompanied by political decentralization, characterized by fierce competition among states, counties, and cities to attract or to hold on to sectors of dynamic economic activity. The result was a redistribution of the nation's political and economic power toward regions and localities. Regional economies, each comprising specific combinations of jobs, markets, and people, became the primary focus of economic vitality. With huge budget deficits handcuffing the federal government, these regions, their political localities, and the unique combinations of people living there assumed the obligations of responding to the social consequences of large-scale political and economic challenges.

Increases in the volume and diversity of immigration were both a response and further stimulus to this restructuring, accentuating the unevenness of regional growth. Immigration has not occurred in all areas of the United States, however. Concentrating in particular areas, newcomers have become inextricable parts of the character and identity of those areas. In New York, Los Angeles, Miami, Chicago, Houston, and other large cities, long-term residents soon lived, worked, and played alongside newcomers.

In the 1950s and 1960s, few observers could have predicted the full implications of this uneven regional concentration and the ways in which it would entangle immigrants and long-established urban populations. The concerns of that earlier period were the increasing concentration and resulting ghettoization of black Americans in urban centers. Successive national commissions warned of the consequences these changes would have for relations between blacks and whites. Yet, few envisioned the emergence of a new generation of ethnically diverse Americans resulting from the increased immigration of diverse peoples to the United States.[1]

The simultaneous concentration of established ethnic minorities and new immigrants in rapidly changing regions sharpened the differences among these groups and reshaped opportunities for interactions among them, heightening awareness and concern for their unequal economic status. In many cities, poverty and wealth grew side by side. As poverty became primarily an urban phenomenon, so did immigration. How was it that some groups were moving into dynamic sectors of the U.S. economy and society, while others were stagnating? How did this unevenness affect opportunities for group interactions and perceptions of common interests and goals as the number of nationalities and ethnic groups multiplied?

Decades of uneven political and economic change have rekindled fundamental arguments over how immigrants adapt to America. Some observers have renewed a traditional interest in assimilation and Americanization by focusing on the potential harmful effects of immigrants' linguistic, political, and social differences, turning public attention to the so-called quality of new immigrants and the different capacities of individuals to move into the dominant culture.

Others have stressed the persistence of ethnic differences and the nation's commitment to pluralism. Rather than individual qualities, this pluralist perspective emphasizes group resources and the limits to social advancement imposed by highly uneven economic and political opportunities. These contrasting views are more than disagreements about immigrant adaptation. They represent fundamentally different conceptions of the role of diversity in American society. As different as these two perspectives are, they share similar shortcomings. Both focus primarily on immigrants themselves, how well they perform economically, and how fast they settle and succeed. As a result, their focus is one-sided, concentrating only on immigrants' individual and group characteristics, or on newcomers' unique positions in U.S. society. They fail to capture the full range of interactions among newcomers and established resident groups and the potential consequences of new, multidimensional relations.

Structure of the Study

In carrying out the research project, the multidisciplinary Changing Relations Board adopted an approach that de-emphasized group characteristics and differences and highlighted interactions and relations. The researchers' goal was to examine the social construction of groups, starting with day-to-day activities, including face-to-face contacts among individuals in daily encounters, group interactions, and relationships between such institutions as community and civic organizations.

The board developed three strategies for studying relations among newcomers and established residents. The first was to capture the diversity of place. Economic and political restructuring, demographic shifts, and immigration have changed the composition of activities in particular localities and have created unique combinations of individuals, groups, and social activities. People understand and act differently within the specific contexts of where they settle.

To reflect the importance of regionalism and to show different segments of the nation's reordered economy, the six sites selected for the study included areas of new growth and capital restructuring in the South and Southwest, deindustrializing rust-belt cities, as well as a range of urban, suburban, and rural areas.

---

1. It should be noted that throughout this report, group labels such as white, black, Hispanic, and Asian have been used according to usage in the research site or for clarity of presentation and comparison. It should also be noted that the board of the Changing Relations Project and the researchers recognize the diversity of the groups that are inappropriately classified by such simple terms. In fact, much of the report's discussion points to the importance of the heterogeneity of immigrant and established minority groups.

The selection also stressed variations in the size of the local immigrant population, and coverage of as many of the largest immigrant and established groups as possible. (For data on the percentages of the foreign-born in the six sites see Table 1.)

The sites selected were:

- *Albany Park, Chicago, Illinois.* An area northwest of downtown Chicago, Albany Park has grown with successive waves of immigrants. The contemporary social mix contains a remarkable degree of diversity, including Southeast Asians, Poles, Koreans, African Americans, Middle Easterners, and Jews, among others. In a city known for immigrant neighborhoods, Albany Park reflects a new pattern of dispersed ethnicity, where members of various groups are distributed within a wide geographical area. Still, most residents confine their relationships to their own ethnic group. Research for this study concentrated on community organizations, including ward-level political organizations and neighborhood civic associations; the use of public space, including streets, sidewalks, bus stops, public schools, libraries, and commercial establishments; and group relationships within a large apartment building.

- *Garden City, Kansas.* For Garden City, a small town caught up in a new round of rural industrialization, the opening of the world's largest meatpacking plant sparked a decade of rapid economic growth and profound social change. During that period, Garden City grew faster than any other town in Kansas. The work attracted immigrants and influenced the community response to them. It turned a community of long-term resident Anglos and Mexican Americans into a diverse town that included Southeast Asian refugees and new immigrants from Mexico and Central America. Faced with rapidly increasing demands on housing, social services, education, and other community services, the residents of Garden City responded with church-led alliances, electoral changes, and increased financial support.

- *Houston, Texas.* Responding to cycles of economic decline and recovery, novel patterns of settlement in Houston have emerged. These include a new settlement of Central American immigrants within an Anglo section of town and an older neighborhood of low-income African American and Latino residents. Community organizations created many of the opportunities for interaction among these groups. By examining a housing complex, an umbrella organization of 30 Hispanic community organizations whose interests were in social issues such as education and employment, and two churches, the study was able to compare efforts that brought people together and also divided people. The effects of the Immigration Reform and Control Act of 1986 were of special interest. The opportunity for undocumented immigrants to legalize and become full social participants changed their relations with established groups and local institutions.

- *Miami, Florida.* The number and concentration of newcomers have made the interplay of immigrants and established residents a central theme of Miami's identity and character. Miami is marked by the contrast of relations among resident Anglos and upper-class Cuban immigrants with relations among working-class Cubans, African Americans, and Haitians. Race plays a dominant role in the control and distribution of resources and in the organization of groups as seen at an apparel factory, a construction site, and two hotels. In the schools, the focus of attention is on relations between Haitian and African-American students.

- *Monterey Park, California.* A middle-class Los Angeles suburb that historically housed the residentially and economically mobile, Monterey Park is feeding off rapid growth throughout the region. It combines Anglos, Latinos, and Asian Americans, and is particularly a magnet for large-scale immigration from Taiwan, Hong Kong, and China. Rapid commercial and residential development, much of it owned and fueled by elite Chinese newcomers, coincided with problems of inflation and congestion. Anglos have retained political power although the city has a Chinese majority. Monterey Park provides a textbook case for the political struggle over language, wealth, community development, and political representation.

- *Philadelphia, Pennsylvania.* Against a backdrop of deeply entrenched black-white relations that have shaped Philadelphia politics and community settlement

Table 1: Percent Foreign Born in Total Population

Research Site	1950	1960	1970	1980	1990
Monterey Park, California	8.0	10.2	13.6	31.2	51.8
Miami, Florida	10.4	12.0	24.2	35.6	45.1
Chicago, Illinois	12.8	9.7	8.1	10.5	13.1
Garden City, Kansas	2.5	2.1	1.4	3.8	–
Philadelphia, Pennsylvania	9.2	7.3	5.4	5.4	5.3
Houston, Texas	2.5	2.3	2.5	7.6	13.3

Sources: United States Department of Commerce. Bureau of the Census.

for decades, immigrants faced an ambivalent reception. They have not dominated any particular locality, but have been incorporated into established struggles over community stability and between neighborhoods and the city government. A city-wide network of social institutions devoted to relations among groups has influenced both coalition-building efforts and the ideology of accommodation. Arenas of interaction, like business strips and schools, bring together not only whites, blacks, and mainland- and island-born Puerto Ricans, but Koreans, recent Polish emigres, Vietnamese, Indians, Portuguese, Chinese, Cambodians, Laotians, Cubans, Guatemalans, Nicaraguans, and Colombians, as well.

The board's second research strategy involved selection of arenas within the local communities in which to observe contact and interaction among newcomers and established residents. Social distance and spatial segregation of groups within these six sites made arenas of interaction rare and special. The arenas presupposed an opportunity for interaction and a particular purpose in bringing people of diverse backgrounds together. The arenas selected included five broad groupings—community organizations, schools, workplaces, places of worship, and neighborhoods. Considerable variation exists within these broad categories. For example, the neighborhood arena includes interactions within three very different housing areas, including a mobile home park, an apartment complex, and an apartment building. (See Table 2.)

The third research strategy incorporated the specificity and uniqueness of local knowledge, history, and perceptions in the national design. The board put together teams of researchers whose members had extensive experience in the localities and arenas of interaction and who represented the groups they were to study. Board members helped craft the local research plans and, from more than 100 initial applications, selected the six that finally constituted this project.

For two years, the research teams spent considerable time in their communities. They interviewed, observed, participated, organized, and lived in the neighborhoods and among those they studied. They recorded detailed descriptions of behavior, activities, and perceptions. They often served as volunteers in organizing community festivals, neighborhood groups, and issue-oriented coalitions, and worked in election campaigns and civic organizations. They were employed in local industries and businesses, shopped in nearby stores, attended neighborhood public events, and became part of everyday interactions among friends and strangers. They complemented these ethnographic techniques with open-ended interviews, formal surveys, and collection of secondary source, statistical information. Each of the six research teams constructed answers to the following five questions that guided the national project.

- What is the nature of relations between native-born or longer-resident Americans and new immigrants? What are the primary settings for interactions among these groups? What situations bring individuals from various groups together or keep them apart?
- What are cultural conceptions of American identity and American life, and how do these take shape through intergroup interactions?

Table 2: Selection of Research Sites and Arenas

Monterey Park	Houston	Garden City	Chicago	Miami	Philadelphia
Neighborhood	Apartment Complex	Trailer Park	Apartment Complex	Neighborhood	
Community Organizations	Community Organizations	Community Organizations	Community Organizations	Community Organizations	Community Organizations
		Workplaces		Workplaces	Workplaces
		Schools		Schools	Schools
City Council			Chamber of Commerce	Chamber of Commerce	

- What sources of conflict, distance, tolerance, accommodation and competition exist among these groups and what factors promote or inhibit their presence?
- To what extent have large-scale, long-term changes in the economy, the population structure, and the polity influenced the way in which immigrants and established residents interact?
- What situations, actions, and strategies promote communication, understanding, accommodation, and accord when multi-group interactions occur?

Board Report and Project Themes

The purpose of this report by the National Board of the Changing Relations Project is to synthesize the findings of the six research teams in a way that addresses questions of national significance.[2]

Chapter 2 examines the influence of economic and political restructuring in the formation of social diversity. In particular, it focuses on the recomposition of the American working class and the subsequent change in opportunities for interaction, tension, separation, and accommodation.

Chapter 3 examines interactions directly. It explores how groups are brought together, organized, and divided. It examines which social institutions are involved in shaping these relations. Part of this analysis involves highlighting the remaking of community in areas deeply influenced historically by racial and class divisions. Chapter 4 focuses on interac-

tions among groups that overcome social divisions and move toward some form of accommodation. It highlights the organizing strategies and attempts of groups and organizers to change community conditions where immigrants and established residents live. It focuses on the processes of inclusion and exclusion and, ultimately, on "membership" in and identity with American society. Finally, Chapter 5 identifies activities, goals, and policies that contribute to cohesion rather than to disintegration, and that promote interaction and accommodation between groups.

Throughout its planning, discussions, and meetings, the board found itself coming back to several consistent themes which reverberate throughout each of the following chapters.

Diversity. The America that immigrants face today is very different from the America of earlier historical periods. The increasing reality of and political commitments to pluralism create a new reference point for adaptation to U.S. society. Notions of Anglo conformity or assimilation to a single culture simply have no immediate relevance in situations in which newcomers and established resident racial and ethnic minorities interact as dominant groups. These mixed settings further legitimize diversity and provide role models that depart from any idealized notion of what America means.

Settlement. Geographical boundaries of settlement have always been important to organizing relations among newcomers and established residents. Traditional notions of

2. Each research team gave the board a site report addressing the five questions of the study. At times, portions of site reports are paraphrased in this book.

community were shaped by relations formed out of the geographical concentration of work and residence. These boundaries are changing. Particularly compelling are persistent issues of segregation, along with the unanticipated consequences of the pressure on the few institutions and places where diverse groups come into contact. Tension and conflict as well as cooperation emerge from these rare contacts.

Conflict.   Dramatic episodes of violent conflict are infrequent throughout the six sites of this study. More prevalent relations include competition, tension, and opposition. Although these relations often deeply divide, their consequences are controlled by social rules created and enforced by a community's own institutions and modes of accommodation. The issue is not simply the infrequency of conflict, but the strength of these rules and institutions.

Class and Gender.   The importance of social class is often ignored in popular commentaries on immigration and social change in America. To some extent this reflects the historical theme of individual opportunity that permeates the nation's immigrant heritage. It also results from a pervasive discourse on race and ethnicity as the primary sources of social divisions. Yet social class, intertwined with race, ethnicity, and gender, remains a cornerstone of the structure of communities and is essential for understanding relations among newcomers and established residents. Women are an essential component of these class-based relations, often serving on the "front lines" of interactions among newcomers and established residents. Service-sector jobs put them there, and participation in community organizations reinforces their involvement. Recognition of common interests also motivates women to organize activities that cross group lines.

Language.   Beyond segregation and social distance, it should come as no surprise that communication—language—stands out as the most important feature of interactions among newcomers and established residents. Language binds and separates. Patterns of language usage often express power relations. But they also reveal individual and collective perceptions of the human experience. Language serves throughout diverse communities as a source of intergroup conflict, tension, and

distance. Creating institutional settings for language acquisition, however, also provides a source of shared interests, an opportunity for interaction and a purpose behind cooperation.

Racial Stratification.   Immigration highlights the social and cultural dimensions of race and ethnicity. The diversity of people and places in this study highlights the blurring and remaking of racial boundaries. It challenges popular conceptions of the so-called browning of America. Immigrants do not simply reflect intermediate colors on a unidimensional scale representing more or less black or white. Rather, they engage in multidimensional relations that form complex interactions crossing several social boundaries simultaneously. Current immigration challenges the traditional correlation of race and ethnicity with class and economic status. The immigration of groups with wealth who are not classified as white is reshaping the intertwining of color, ancestry, and background with class, power, and privilege.

Community Control.   A common experience of crisis in many of America's communities limits interactions and possibilities for cooperation. Yet, these same problems also create shared interests and compatible goals. Many of the most promising signs of leadership and intergroup organization focus on local issues of community standards, including the availability, cost, and value of housing, social services, schools, education, law enforcement, and safety.

Policy

The policy questions raised in this report do not necessarily ask whether America should reduce or increase the volume of immigration or change the national origins or skills of those it admits. These are issues largely settled by recent congressional debate and passage of the Immigration Act of 1990. Rather, the immigrants in which this study is interested have already arrived and have become part of the nation. Our question is how America is absorbing these newcomers and, in turn, how these newcomers are changing America. The nation frequently forgets its responsibility for immigration; movement to America occurs primarily by invitation. What established Americans have never fully understood, but which immigrants never forget, is that America is deeply implicated in the migration flow and its destiny. American employers fuel the immigration, American foreign policy embraces it, and American family values maintain it.

The policy issues addressed in this report concern a framework for action and development. With the increasing diversity of groups becoming social and political actors, the questions for the future will be what effective responses can be developed and by whom? Reshaping community organizations should be a priority. As diversity increases, many current arrangements may not hold. The decentralization of political authority, for instance, has led to gaps between federal policies and regional and local interests. Social distances among groups within communities are reflected in the gap between local and national policy makers. To overcome difficulties encountered by local communities, including financial impasses and politics of disengagement as well as politics of apportioning blame, a new political discourse may be needed that focuses on efforts to organize diversity, to build activities that involve many groups working together.

Contrary to some popular celebrations of pluralism, however, diversity does not mean simple harmony. The challenge for America may be less in harmonizing relations among groups than in mobilizing intergroup cooperation into strategies for economic and political advancement. If the national goal is to create harmony, then the struggle must not be just for social peace but for opportunity and equality.

Indigenous Ethnic Groups

The contemporary issues of Native Americans as well as the descendants of all conquered indigenous peoples add their weight to the claims for cultural justice, equal protection, and due process in our hemisphere, but in fact this is a worldwide phenomenon. Consciousness of indigenous peoples was heightened by attempts to celebrate the 500th anniversary of Christopher Columbus's voyage of discovery. The end of the South African regime also increased awareness of indigenous peoples. The exploration of roots and new remedies for the conquest that turned many into a permanent underclass has awakened indigenous people, and a code of international conduct in protection of cultural rights has entered international law.

The following articles represent a cross section of the current experience of indigenous ethnic groups, their forced accommodation of a high-tech world, the environmental and cultural effects of rapid change, and the challenges to a renewal of their identifying traditions. The indigenous ethnic populations remember and invite us to recall their struggles, to find ways of shaping and sharing the new sense of pluralism offered within the American experience and the spiritual sources of ethnic identity that people encounter as the legitimacy of ancient practices widens.

Indigenous ethnic communities have been plagued by a complex array of historical, social, cultural, and economic factors. As a result, in the late twentieth century, the traditions of indigenous ethnic groups have been renegotiated by yet another generation. The North and South American economies and pluralistic cultures, as well as those of other continents, are a challenging stage for their quest for self-sufficiency as well as their aspirations for the preservation of a unique cultural legacy. Current indigenous ethnic leaders challenge past perceptions. They find it increasingly difficult to strike a balance between traditional values and new demands. Native Americans have increasingly interfaced with the American legal system at the state level on issues of land use and gaming, which represent part of this current redefinition. Finally, however, they are challenging themselves to be themselves, and examples of indigenous self-help reveal insights into how personal leadership and community weave the social fabric of civil society.

Novel approaches toward the peaceful reconciliation of conflict should be explored more thoroughly. For example, unlike conflict among ethnic groups in the United States, conflict between the United States and Native Americans is regulated by treaties. The struggle over claims regarding the rights of nations and the interests of the U.S. government and its citizens is no longer at the margin of public affairs. Does the definition of this conflict as an issue of foreign and not domestic policy provide a meaningful distinction? Should the claims of ethnic groups in defense of culture, territory, and unique institutions be honored and protected by law and public policy?

Ethnicity is built upon the truth and strength of a tradition. Senses of family and community, and an unwillingness to give up, have led to standoffs with many forces within America. From this perspective, this unit details ways in which an ethnic group retrieves its rights and heritage to preserve an ancient culture from amnesia and extinction.

The expansion and profitability of Native American gambling casinos, their attendant impact on state and local economies, and the tax exemptions enjoyed by these ventures appear to be headed toward contentions that may spill over into new issues of public order. On the international level, the discussion of human and cultural rights of peoples guaranteed in the United Nations and the traditional mode of state sovereignty indicates that a fragile accommodation between indigenous people and the mainstream societies at whose margins they exist may be entering a new phase. Their unequal relationship began with the consolidation of large territorial political and economic regimes. Under scrutiny are personal rights and group rights, pluralistic realms that ensure transnational solidarity, and cultural and religious challenges to those in authority fueled by the passion for power at those intersections between modernity and tradition—the large-scale institutional versus the local and culturally specific community.

Looking Ahead: Challenge Questions

How should commitments to the self-determination of people be ensured and enforced? What levels of tolerance are assumed by the UN Working Group? What value conflicts, if any, are beyond compromise? How does gaming affect the work ethic?

What are the most compelling issues that face indigenous ethnic communities? Economy? Culture?

What social, economic, and political conditions will affect the next indigenous ethnic generation?

Because of the strides of the current Native American community, will the next generation enter the middle class of America? Should that be a goal?

What moral guides does the process of the South African Truth and Reconciliation Commission recommend?

What effect would such a process have on public and private bureaucratic systems that have been challenged for their lack of fairness and impartiality? For group claims? For personal claims? For privacy? The presumption of innocence prior to proof of guilt?

12th Session of UN Working Group on Indigenous Peoples

The Declaration Passes and the US Assumes a New Role

GLENN T. MORRIS

Glenn T. Morris is the Executive Director of the Fourth World Center for the Study of Indigenous Law and Politics, at the University of Colorado at Denver. He is also co-editor of the Fourth World Bulletin and Associate Professor of Political Science at CU-Denver.

After nearly nine years of debate, deliberation and revision, the United Nations Working Group on Indigenous Peoples (UNWGIP), at its 12th Session (25-29 July 1994), completed preparation of the Draft Declaration on the Rights of Indigenous Peoples and sent the document on to higher levels in the UN system. Over 160 indigenous peoples' organizations, forty two state members, nine specialized agencies of the United Nations, and dozens of interested nongovernmental organizations, totaling nearly 800 individuals, participated in the 12th Session. The Declaration was forwarded to the UN Sub-Commission on Prevention of Discrimination and Protection of Minorities. At its 46th Session (in August 1994), the Sub-Commission agreed to transmit the Declaration to the UN Commission on Human Rights for discussion at its annual meeting in February 1995. For final adoption as an instrument of emerging international law, the Declaration must be ultimately be accepted by the UN General Assembly.

The 12th Session was notable for several important developments that this article reports in some detail. First, there was a significant debate about the Declaration's treatment of the right to self-determination; the ensuing discussion of the issue left momentous questions unresolved. Second, several other major issues that will have great bearing on the rights of indigenous peoples were postponed to future discussions in which they will be detached from the text of the Declaration. And third, the United States Government assumed a new and decidedly more dynamic role among the states that have actively participated in developing the Draft Declaration.

Self-determination

Discussion of the right to self-determination for indigenous peoples has always provoked passionate and oppositional controversy at Working Group sessions. In the initial drafts of the Declaration, the right was not mentioned explicitly at all. In subsequent drafts, at the insistence of indigenous peoples, the right was expressed, but was often accompanied by limiting language or provisions. At the 11th Session (1993), indigenous delegates proposed that reference to the right to self-determination for indigenous peoples should be modeled after the language already found in the International Covenant on Civil and Political Rights and the International Covenant on Economic, Social and Cultural Rights. That proposal was accepted, and Article 3 of the draft now reads:

> Indigenous peoples have the right of self-determination. By virtue of that right, they freely determine their political status and freely pursue their economic, social and cultural development.

Some states, notably the United States and Canada, have publicly opposed Article 3, and they can be expected to introduce dramatic revisions of it, or try to completely delete it in the future.

The major objection to self-determination stems from the fear by some states that explicit recognition of that right, in the language of the human rights covenants, will allow indigenous peoples and nations to exercise a right of political independence separate from the states that surround them. Through this exercise, states fear the dismemberment of their claimed territories and the emergence of new, independent indigenous states. This fear is especially pronounced in cases where indigenous enclaves are entirely surrounded by states or where indigenous territories contain valuable natural resources.

Most states assert that relations, especially territorial and jurisdictional relations, between themselves and indigenous peoples are internal, domestic matters that are beyond the scope of international law. The inclusion in the Declaration of a right that would allow indigenous peoples to be recognized to possess juridical character, with rights recognized in international forums, is viewed as an attack on the sovereignty and territorial integrity of current UN members.

Conversely, most indigenous peoples argue that they have never given their informed consent to be integrated into the states that came to surround them, that they have not been a party to the establishment of international legal principles to the present, and that they have been (and continue to be) denied the opportunity to decide for themselves their political status. In essence, they argue that they are in a state of internal colonial bondage, and they advocate an extension of international standards of decolonization to apply to their cases. In that regard, indigenous delegates have regularly stated that the right to self-determination is a major cornerstone of the Declaration, upon which other provisions of the document must rest.

Indigenous delegates have consistently argued that under the right to self-determination, complete independence is only one of several available options. They maintain that most indigenous peoples around the world do not aspire towards political independence, and would choose some variation of autonomy, short of independence, within the current state system. However, during the 12th Session, several states (Brazil, India, Myanmar) repeated their steadfast opposition to any recognition of a right to self-determination for indigenous peoples. Others, such as Denmark, expressed support for the self-determination provision.

Upon their arrival at the 12th Session, some indigenous representatives were surprised to find that the Declaration had been altered, without their consultation, from the form that had been concluded at the 11th Session. Of particular concern was the addition of Article 31, which recognizes "autonomy" or "self-government in internal and local affairs" as a specific form of the exercise of self-determination. Miguél Alfonso Martínez, the Latin American regional member of the Working Group and the author of Article 31, had reasoned that Latin American state governments were unlikely to accede to the open-ended interpretation of self-determination expressed in Article 3. He wrote and appended Article 31 to the Declaration in the hope that it would provide essential safeguards for Latin American indigenous peoples but not alarm the state governments of the region.

Serious discussion and disagreement developed over whether Article 31 would limit the right to self-determination expressed in Article 3. Some indigenous delegates (especially some Canadian and United States Indians, Native Hawaiians, Mapuches, Maoris, Nagas, and others) objected that the language of Article 3 was perfectly clear, and any attempt to modify the meaning (as they interpreted the intent of Article 31) might later be contrued as a limitation of the right to self-determination, that "autonomy" might result as the maximum (or at least the preferred) extent of the exercise of the right for indigenous peoples. They argued that Article 31 is therefore superfluous and should be deleted.

The opponents of Article 31 also suggested that certain states, notably the US and Canada, are hostile to Article 3 and can be expected to amend it significantly or even delete it from the Declaration, at future forums. If Article 3 is indeed eventually deleted, Article 31 will remain as the only articulation of what self-determination means. According to the opponents, Article 31, read alone, is an incomplete and inadequate protection of the right of self-determination for indigenous peoples.

The proponents of Article 31, on the other hand, maintained that the article should be read as an extension, not a limitation, of Article 3, and that local and regional autonomy

would result as the *minimum* standard of self-determination that states must recognize for indigenous peoples. They suggested that for many indigenous peoples who must deal with states that fail to provide even minimal recognition of indigenous rights, Article 31 might provide a crucial safeguard against violations of fundamental human rights.

In future deliberations over the draft, the substance of the right to self-determination for indigenous peoples will remain of central importance. In the eyes of many indigenous peoples, the integrity of the entire instrument rests in the willingness of the international community to recognize the right of indigenous peoples to control their political, economic, social and cultural destinies. In contrast, the concerns of states over the freedom of indigenous peoples to exercise their right to self-determination is intimately linked to the belief that states possess a basic right to protect their own sovereignty and territorial integrity from competing indigenous claims. The ultimate success of the Declaration may therefore rest in the ability of the contending sides to assuage the fears of the other, by finding the common ground that satisfies the interests of all concerned.

Future Deliberations over the Declaration

According to modified UN rules of procedure, the discussion of the Draft Declaration at the Working Group level had been open to all UN members, all interested indigenous delegates, and all governmental and non-governmental organizations with an interest and a contribution to make to the efforts of the Working Group. With the conclusion of the Working Group's discussion, however, the Declaration was transmitted to the Sub-Commission and then to the Commission on Human Rights, where the procedures for participation are considerably more restrictive.

To participate at the Sub-Commission or the Commission, delegates must be credentialed by those respective bodies, and the application for credentialing must come through a non-governmental organization (NGO) that possesses consultative status within the UN Economic and Social Council (ECOSOC). To date, only twelve indigenous NGOs, primarily representing indigenous peoples of the Americas, have received consultative status.

During the 12th Session, both indigenous representatives and states expressed doubts that in future forums in which the Draft Declaration is discussed, indigenous peoples who are not affiliated with the recognized NGOs, or who are otherwise not credentialed, will be included in the discussions. This issue is of special concern to peoples from India and other parts of Asia and the Pacific, the Russian Federation, and Africa, because many of them are not currently members of credentialed NGOs.

The issue of who will be able to participate in future discussions becomes especially important when considering the probable course for the Declaration. According to a number of state observers at the 12th Session, once the Draft reaches the Commission on Human Rights, it will be sent to another working group, within the Commission itself. Unlike the discussions at the previous Working Group, which were directed by international legal experts (as opposed to delegates representing the interests of states), the Commission working group may well be directed by appointed delegates whose primary concern will be the protection of their governments' interests.

While the Draft is in the Commission's working group, it will be subject to a comprehensive review and reconsideration. Provisions that might seem problematic to states are susceptible to complete revision or removal. Indigenous representatives expressed concern that a limitation of their participation in this process may endanger the progress that has been made over the past ten years, and it may weaken the most important international legal instrument affecting indigenous peoples ever to appear.

Indigenous delegates have previous experience upon which to base their wariness. In 1989, during the debate over revision of International Labor Organization (ILO) Convention 107, only credentialed indigenous representatives could participate, and then only on a limited basis, while a number of important persons and perspectives were completely excluded. To many indigenous peoples, the ILO rules determining participation were totally arbitrary. Consequently, indigenous delegates now insist on more open participation at the Human Rights Commission and successive fora that deal with the Declaration.

Members of the Working Group itself have also recommended relaxation of the rules of procedure in the Human Rights Commission's discussion of the Draft. The Australian government promised that it would introduce a measure to allow indigenous participation, regardless of consultative status, and it proposed that any meetings of the Commission working group be convened immediately prior to the meeting of the Working Group on Indigenous Peoples, so as to maximize the opportunity for indigenous participation. Australia's proposals were endorsed by a few other countries, particularly Sweden, Denmark and Norway.

The Role of the US at the 12th Session and Beyond

The United States delegation to the 12th Session took a new and decidedly more active role in the deliberations of the Working Group and the discussion of the Draft Declaration. Until the 1994 meeting, the United States has participated mostly as an observer, relying on the lead of countries such as Canada and Australia to fashion and advance the interests of state members at the Working Group.

For several years, some indigenous delegates to the Working Group have become convinced that the most prominent governments from English-speaking countries (Australia, Canada, New Zealand and the United States) have coordinated their participation in international forums concerned with indigenous peoples' rights. Rudolph Rÿser, Director of the Center for World Indigenous Studies, has charted a succession of joint meetings between those governments. According to Rÿser's analysis, Canada has played a particularly active role, one that is considered by many indigenous delegates to be especially hostile toward any expanded recognition of

indigenous rights. Australia, conversely, has played a role that is publicly more sympathetic to indigenous claims, one that has even supported limited usage of terms like "peoples" and "self-determination." New Zealand and the United States, says Rÿser, have taken approaches that vary between those of Canada and Australia, while the US delegation's public posture has ranged from indifference to hostility.

Affirming Rÿser's analysis, the changing agenda of the United States has been revealed in an unclassified internal State Department memorandum of July 1993. In this document, State Department officials acknowledge that for the first dozen years of the Working Group's existence, the US "invested little effort in [it]." By 1993, however, the US attitude toward developments at the Working Group apparently had changed significantly. The memo explains that the Working Group and the Draft Declaration are now at a stage where it is important for the US to "try to shape the text [of the draft] to reflect US interests before it goes to the Commission [on Human Rights]."

Of major concern to the US is the question of what impact the application of the principles of collective rights and self-determination of indigenous peoples might have for the United States and international law. It is clear from the memo that the US opposes extending the right of self-determination, as it has been interpeted in the international human rights covenants, to indigenous peoples. The memo asserts that self-determination "is most commonly understood to mean the right to establish a sovereign and independent state, with separate personality under international law. Like many other countries, the United States could not accept the term in any contexts implying or permitting this meaning."

Addressing an issue closely related to self-determination, the State Department is critical of using the term "peoples" (with an "s" at the end) in conjunction with the word "indigenous." According to the memo, "the term [peoples] implies that such groups have the right to self-determination under international law." The document expresses concern about "the risks and uncertainties of extending the legal concept of self-determination to indigenous groups." It emphasizes that the recognition of indigenous collective rights expressed in the Draft Declaration is troublesome, because as a general rule, "the United States...does not recognize the existence of collective rights under international law..." and "we generally do not think it desirable to incorporate such rights into future legal instruments."

While the memo lends general support to the concept of a declaration for the protection of indigenous peoples, and while it even questions some basic assumptions about generally accepted notions in State Department circles (e.g., "recognizing carefully defined group rights need not *per se* be a BAD THING," and "should we oppose a tightly drawn treaty saying that a defined collective group has a defined legal right to practice their culture or religion opposable against their [sic] government?"), it also makes very clear that the security and integrity of the current state system is of preeminent importance.

The flavor of the 1993 memo was integrated into the US intervention at the 12th Session, where the use of the term "peoples" was deliberately avoided, and instead, the terms "people," "populations," "tribe," and "tribal," were used sixteen times. The delegation (led by Miriam Sapiro, from State's Legal Affairs Office, and John Crook, Counselor for Legal Affairs at the US Mission in Geneva) also provided further insight into the US position regarding indigenous self-determination. The memo suggests that US indigenous policy can be used as a working model for the effective implementation of indigenous rights on an international level, given that the essence and extent of self-determination for indigenous peoples should basically mean "self-governance and autonomy...within an existing state." Of course, this implies that US indigenous policy does not apply to "non-historic" or non-federally-recognized Indian nations, Alaskan or Hawaiian Natives, Chamorros, Samoans, or other indigenous peoples that have never been given any pretense whatsoever in the realm of "self-governance" or "autonomy."

Equally revealing of the true US policy, at unofficial meetings during the 12th Session, Crook and Sapiro made clear that the semantic debates over such terms as "people" versus "peoples" were less important to them than was some resolution of the substance of the right to self-determination itself. Sapiro asked several times, "What does Article 3 mean?" And at one session Crook even called the semantic debate "stupid." However, the term proved important enough that the US delegation has made a conscious, deliberate decision to refuse to use the term "peoples" at all. The apparent implication is that if the term self-determination can be interpreted, in any context, to recognize the right of indigenous peoples to independent political existence, then the United States will oppose it.

The current US position on the Declaration can be identified in a plank of the "Clinton-Gore Plan" (the campaign platform of 1992) and also in a statement by President Clinton on 29 April 1994, both of which affirmed "government-to-government" relationships between indigenous nations and the United States, while placing the treatment of indigenous self-determination solely within the domestic jurisdiction of the United States. Some indigenous delegates have observed that the use of the term "government-to-government" by the United States constitutes an attempt to reduce indigenous issues to "internal" status and to degrade the international (i.e., nation-to-nation) relationship that is embodied in the hundreds of treaties concluded between the US and various Indian nations. Others have observed that the quality of "self-determination" accorded to only the recognized "historic tribes" of the US is truncated by the language of the Indian Self-Determination and Education Act of 1975, which limits the exercise of self-determination to decisions concerning the allocation of appropriations distributed by the federal government.

Sapiro and Crook stated in the Session that the United States plans to play a more active role in the future of both the Draft Declaration and the Working Group. They appeared confident that the Draft would pass through the Sub-Commission in August 1994 (which it did), and that it would then be transmitted to a working group in the Commission on Human Rights, after February 1995. The delegation suggested that in future months very serious discussion and debate of the Draft will take place, especially over such controversial matters as collective rights, self-determination, control of territories and natural resources, and development matters, and that the US will play an active role in both the procedural and substantive aspects of these debates. The inference must be that, because the US and other states disagree with the wording of some key provisions of the Draft Declaration, significant changes might reasonably be expected at the Commission level.

In a briefing held in Washington DC, on 20 January 1995, John Shattuck, Assistant Secretary of State for Human Rights, reiterated that the US position regarding the Draft Declaration, at the February 1995 meeting of the UN Human Rights Commission, will be "supportive," and that the United States will follow Australia's lead in creating an open-ended working group within the Commission. Shattuck and his aides repeated that the US perceives human rights primarily pertaining to individuals, not to groups, that the US wants a clearer definition of "indigenous peoples," in order to determine to whom the rights in the Declaration apply. Shattuck also said that his office was committed to open discussions concerning the Declaration (to be held in the US), in various forums with indigenous groups and other NGOs.

The key features of US policy continue to be: that the US considers individuals and not groups to be the subject of human rights; that questions involving indigenous peoples are basically domestic matters to be negotiated between states and indigenous peoples; that the right to self-determination should be read more narrowly than it was in the past, and should not normally be read as a recognition of the right of independent political existence for indigenous peoples; and that any political and economic sovereignty rights of indigenous peoples are inferior and subordinate to the overarching sovereignty of existing states. Undoubtedly, the basic position of the United States on these questions will play an important and enduring role in the consideration of the Draft Declaration and in the future of the Working Group.

Whatever the role of the US in future deliberations of the Working Group, a serious amount of work remains unfinished and will have to be resolved in the coming years. These issues are, in summary, the scope and substance of the right of indigenous peoples to exercise self-determination, the international legal status of treaties between indigenous peoples and states, and the responsibilities of states and the United Nations in assuring that indigenous peoples and their territories are not sacrificed in the pursuit of national and international economic development.

(continued)

Indigenous Self-Determination and U.S. Policy

Commentary

As explained in the [first part] of this issue article, there has recently been a major shift in the posture of the United States Government regarding the Draft Declaration on the Rights of Indigenous Peoples and the UN Working Group on Indigenous Peoples (UNWGIP). Some have applauded the U.S. awakening in the indigenous-rights arena, replete with its dubious interpretation of the language of "self-determination," as a welcome and positive change. Unfortunately, we are unable to share that optimism.

In our view, the position shift should be viewed cautiously as perhaps the latest reflection of a long tradition in U.S. policy, which is characterized by massive contradictions of legal and moral obligations. American Indians, more than any other indigenous peoples, should understand the implications of U.S. posturing on human rights. The possibility or probability that the U.S. will support or promote the Draft Declaration on the Rights of Indigenous Peoples can and should be measured in relation to the attachment of the U.S. to other, comparable pieces of international legislation on human rights.

It should be understood that the Declaration on Indigenous Rights, even when finally concluded, will not create any immediately binding legal obligation on any state, because it is not a treaty. Subsequent to its adoption by the UN General Assembly, the Declaration may eventually be transformed into a Convention, just as the 1948 Universal Declaration on Human Rights was put into force in the form of two competing (or complementary) human-rights covenants, in 1976, but this development will take many years, if it happens at all. Present U.S. support for the Draft Declaration, therefore, can be understood to be virtually risk-free, as far as immediate legal obligations are concerned.

More importantly, the United States has consistently refused to participate in international human-rights institutions over the past fifty years. The U.S. Senate, which must ratify all treaties to which the country might become state-party, rejected all opportunities for the U.S. to accede to the 1948 Genocide Convention, until 1986. Similarly, it refused to ratify the 1966 International Covenant on Civil and Political Rights (which codifies that set of human rights expressed in the U.S. Bill of Rights itself), until 1992. Only last year, in 1994, did the Senate ratify the 1965 International Convention on the Elimination of All Forms of Racial Discrimination. But did ratification in these very few cases indicate that the United States would actually abide by the terms of the agreements? No, because whenever the Senate has ratified human-rights treaties, it has appended "provisions" and "reservations" that have made international laws subordinate to the laws of the United States. There is little reason to believe that the treatment of the Declaration on Indigenous Rights will be different.

The stated U.S. position should not be regarded as an insignificant policy change in an obscure area of international human-rights discourse, nor should it be viewed in isolation from the evidence of U.S. behavior when indigenous rights are obviously at stake. Rather, the policy statement should be viewed as intimately related to several other important foreign-policy areas that are implicated by past and present indigenous (or "nationality") conflicts around the globe. For example, the U.S. supported a Tibetan rebellion against Chinese occupation in the 1950s and 60s, but when President Nixon decided to play the "China card" against the USSR, in 1972, the Tibetans were abandoned to be slaughtered and exiled by the Chinese Army. Similarly, the U.S. supported Iraqi Kurds in their rebellion against Saddam Hussein, in 1973 (the prelude to the events of the Gulf War in 1991), but when U.S. interests in the region shifted, the Kurds, too, were abandoned to be slaughtered by the thousands. On the other hand, because of the strategic importance of Turkey, the U.S. virtually ignores the fate of Kurds in that country.

In another, similar policy contradiction, the U.S. supported and instigated Ukrainian secessionist rebellion against the USSR until 1991, when President Bush strangely attempted to persuade Ukraine *not* to seek independence, after all (of course, he was too late). Bush's address to the Ukrainians, in which he reversed forty-five years of policy to warn of the "excesses of suicidal nationalism," was labeled his "Chicken Kiev Speech" by *New York Times* columnist William Safire, marking the first evidence of a major dispute within the ranks of U.S. conservatives on indigenous nationality policy generally and the policy applied toward Russia, in particular.

It is difficult to underestimate the cynicism of U.S. policy on human rights. At the Vienna World Conference on Human Rights, in July 1993, President Clinton and Secretary of State Christopher swore before the world that the United States was prepared to join the International Covenant on Economic, Social and Cultural Rights. That promise could not have been less believable, considering the fact that the ESC Covenant has always been understood as the major human-rights statement of socialist regimes, led by the former USSR, and so it hardly could have been expected ever to gain approval in the Senate. Clinton and Christopher also preached human rights to the Chinese government and threatened to withhold Most-Favored Nation (MFN) trading privileges unless China reformed its behavior according to Western precepts of "democracy" -- and then reversed themselves, when China indicated that it was not about to be pressured on human-rights issues.

Meanwhile, within the U.S. itself, indigenous human-rights issues go largely unacknowledged and unaddressed by the public, because of the myth that the U.S. is the world's leader in observance of human rights. This myth probably explains why, though people in western Europe, Russia, and elsewhere are aware that President Clinton has refused to deal with the worldwide campaign to grant clemency to the American Indian political prisoner Leonard Peltier, Americans themselves hardly know his name. The illusion that the U.S. alone is the hegemonic arbiter of good and evil may account for its pursuit of the forced relocation of Diné on the Hopi Partitioned Lands, while it forbids the UNWGIP to discuss that issue, lest the U.S. scuttle that forum.

As a measure of the current U.S. foreign policy on rights of indigenous/nationality peoples, Chechnya is an illustrative case, since Russia remains the "centerpiece" of U.S. foreign policy in the post-Cold War era. U.S. reaction to Russia's most recent invasion of Chechnya (there have been several over the past 300 years) has been typically full of contradictions. Although members of the Clinton Administration have condemned Russia's brutal military *tactics* against the Chechens, there has been virtually no challenge to the legitimacy of the basic Russian claim over Chechen territory. President Clinton is clearly supporting Yeltsin's regime, in its attempt to fend off opponents, including the fascistic Vladimir Zhirinovsky, who has no sympathy for Chechens and wants to re-establish a Russian empire. The Clinton Administration believes that Yeltsin represents the best present hope that Russia will become a pro-Western capitalist enterprise. That hope is contingent on territorial integrity, however, and Chechen secession would probably seal Russia's doom, by tapping the wellspring of endemic separatism in the complex Russian Federation. Such separatism could bring on a period of chaos and, given the genuine possibility of a military coup, precipitate another Cold War.

The absence of official criticism and opposition from the U.S. Government has been matched in the U.S. mainstream media. The *New York Times*, for instance, has repeatedly supported Russia's suppression of Chechen self-determination and encouraged Washington to "quietly counsel [Yeltsin] to apply force carefully," because the Chechen claims "cannot be allowed to stand" (*NYT*, 14 December 1994). This, despite the *Times*' own acknowledgment that the Russians have, in the past, occupied Chechnya but never subdued it — because the Chechens have resisted and rebelled continually against Russian domination, twice earlier in this century.

The U.S. State Department (the agency that is constructing the policy on indigenous peoples' rights) agreed with the *Times*, giving Russian territorial claims and military actions higher legitimacy than those of the Chechens. State Department official Mike McCurry succinctly stated the U.S. position on 14 December 1994 (also later affirmed by President Clinton and Secretary of State Christopher) that "Chechnya is an integral part of Russia, and events in Chechnya, because of that, are largely an internal affair." Vice President Al Gore underlined the Administration's stance by saying that the US is "not going to challenge Russian territorial integrity [on the Chechen question]" (Associated Press, 9 January 1995).

As the *Times* concluded, the U.S. statements gave "Mr. Yeltsin a green light for military intervention" (NYT, 28 December 1994). Apparently, neither the U.S. nor the *Times* will object to the general principle of an established state invading a stateless people's territory. The feeble concern that

they do raise is rather that the invasion was bungled — it was not done quickly or quietly or effectively enough, and it was not executed cleanly out of television camera range.

Ironically, Zbigniew Brezinski (Jimmy Carter's National Security Adviser), recently joined a few Republican members of Congress and a smattering of conservative newpaper editors in condemning U.S. policy for complicity in the denial of Chechen self-determination, in a column in the *Washington Post* (8 January 1995). Brezinski claims that Chechnya "could become the graveyard of America's moral reputation," because the U.S. refuses to come to the assistance of a "freedom-seeking" people that "dared to reach out for independence." His defense of the "helpless Chechens... who are not Russian and do not wish to be Russian," while laudable under normal circumstances, rings hollow when one recalls his lack of defense of the freedom-seeking Tibetans against China, or of the freedom-seeking East Timorese against Indonesia, and the pounding of the freedom-seeking Kurds by Iran, Iraq, and Turkey, during his watch at the White House. His commentary represents the depth of contradictory sentiments within both conservative ranks and the policy community at large.

In a most telling distortion in his column, Brezinski claims that the U.S. vilification of an indigenous or nationality struggle (of the Chechens), and justification of oppression (by the Russians) "has never happened before." In addition to the cases mentioned above, Brezinski seems to have forgotten the decades of U.S. opposition to the African National Congress, the IRA, the Eritreans, the PLO, the Polisario Front in the Western Sahara, and the Naga Nation struggling for its independence from India. The list of freedom-seeking peoples engaged in nationality and indigenous struggles that have been opposed by the United States could fill pages. It is precisely the United States' own history of opposition to self-determination struggles that should give pause to those who are watching the new U.S. agenda unfold on the indigenous-rights stage.

The justification applied by the U.S. to the Chechen case, that the survival of a state (Russia) and its territorial claims are more important than the survival of an indigenous people, can easily be observed in other serious cases at this very moment. The government of Myanmar (Burma) is waging a relentless and brutal military attack against the Karen Nation, killing hundreds and forcing tens of thousands of refugees to flee their homeland into Thailand. Not surprisingly, neither the United States, nor any other major power, has submitted any meaningful challenge to Myanmar's attacks. In November, just three months ago, the State Department claimed that it was taking a "conciliatory approach" toward the Burmese military regime, as far as human rights in general were concerned (especially the imprisonment of Nobel Peace Prize laureate Aung San Suu Kyi), but made no attempt to address the question of indigenous rights in particular. The U.S. maintains extensive trade relations with the Ne Win regime; the petroleum, natural gas, timber, weapons, and narcotics industries are all doing big business in Burma. Meanwhile, the U.S. supports, either actively or tacitly, the open relations between the Ne Win regime and China, Thailand, and Japan.

Rather than support the application of the principle of self-determination to the Chechens or the Karen—lest it set a precedent for other freedom-seeking peoples—the United States and other states of the world would prefer to protect the "sovereignty and territorial integrity" of the chauvinistic and human-rights-abusing governments of Russia and Myanmar out of political or economic expedience. Rather than examine the claims of the Karen or the Chechens, that they have never given their consent to be integrated into the Burmese or the Russian states, and that they have long-standing political and territorial claims of their own, the governments of the world side with the oppressor's invasion in the name of regional stability and order. Similar examples of expedience over principle can be cited from Chiapas to the Western Sahara, from Indonesia to Eritrea.

The self-determination of the peoples of Eritrea was ignored, even actively opposed, for over three decades by the major powers of the world, led alternately by the U.S. and the Soviet Union, in the interests of protecting Ethiopia's sovereignty. At the same time the U.S. was assuaging Israel's fear that the Red Sea might be completely bordered by states hostile to its existence. The Eritrean spirit of freedom prevailed despite prohibitive odds, surviving drought and over thirty years of military oppression from the Ethiopian government that was alternately supported by both the United States and the Soviet Union. Eritrea's seat in the United Nations, which can be celebrated as an enormous monument to the perseverance of the Eritrean people, should also serve as a constant source of shame to the world community that consistently rejected a legitimate claim of self-determination in favor of the territorial integrity claims of a corrupt Ethiopian government. Eritrea would still not be seated at the UN if it had to rely solely on the international community's embrace of high-sounding principles respecting the self-determination of peoples. Eritrea's seat would not exist had the Eritreans not mobilized the military might necessary to liberate their home-land and to defend and protect their claim to self-determination.

The lessons of the Chechens, the Karen, and the Eritreans should serve as important lessons to other indigenous peoples and nationalities. If the international community has a choice between the legitimacy of indigenous peoples' claims for territory, treaty rights, economic sustainability, or self-determination, versus the claims of a state, *any* state, for continued survival, indigenous peoples can be virtually certain that the statist claim will be supported consistently. For the United States, consolidating global hegemony is the preeminent national interest at this time. U.S. hegemony can be managed successfully only with a limited number of sovereign states in the system. The U.S., therefore, judges it imperative to forestall any possibility, real or imagined, of a wave of secessionism.

The United States clearly does not take international human-rights obligations seriously, despite its charade of being the world's bastion of respect for rights. Neither is it ever likely to accept the Declaration of Rights for Indigenous Peoples as a constraint on its own policy towards the indigenous peoples enclosed by its borders. At this point in history, there is no reason to believe that increased U.S. interest in indigenous peoples' rights is anything more than self-serving political posturing. The U.S. has made it clear that it opposes any meaningful recognition of the right to self-determination for indigenous peoples; it opposes any serious assertion of territorial or natural-resource control by indigenous peoples; it opposes recognition of the international standing of treaties between indigenous peoples and states; and its recommendation for the protection of indigenous rights rests solely within the domestic jurisdiction of the very states that have historically attacked, dismembered and sought to destroy indigenous peoples. Does this record bespeak an indigenous-rights policy that should be applauded?

American Indians in the 1990s

The true number of American Indians may be unknowable, but a rapidly growing number of Americans are identifying with Indian culture. The Anglo appetite for Indian products is creating jobs on poverty-plagued reservations. Gambling and tourism are the most lucrative reservation businesses. Meanwhile, the middle-class Indian's urge to "go home" is growing.

Dan Fost

Dan Fost is a contributing editor of American Demographics *in Tiburon, California.*

When Nathan Tsosie was growing up in the Laguna Pueblo in New Mexico, he was not taught the Laguna language. The tribe's goal was to assimilate him into white society.

Today, Tsosie's 9-year-old son Darren learns his ancestral language and culture in the Laguna schools. He speaks Laguna better than either of his parents. "They're trying to bring it back," says Darren's mother, Josephine. "I'm glad he's learning. I just feel bad that we can't reinforce it and really teach it."

The strong bonds American Indians still feel to their native culture are driving a renaissance in Indian communities. This cultural resurrection has not yet erased the poverty, alcoholism, and other ills that affect many Indians. But it has brought educational and economic gains to many Indians living on and off reservations. A college-educated Indian middle class has emerged, American Indian business ownership has increased, and some tribes are creating good jobs for their members.

The census counted 1,878,000 American Indians in 1990, up from fewer than 1.4 million in 1980. This 38 percent leap exceeds the growth rate for blacks (6 percent) and non-Hispanic whites (13 percent), but not the growth of Hispanics (53 percent) or Asians (108 percent).

The increase is not due to an Indian baby boom or to immigration from other countries. Rather, Americans with Indian heritage are increasingly likely to identify their race as Indian on census forms. Also, the Census Bureau is doing a better job of counting American Indians.

Almost 2 million people say that their race is American Indian. But more than 7 million people claim some Indian ancestry, says Jeff Passel at the Urban Institute. That's about 1 American in 35.

"A lot of people have one or more ancestors who are American Indian," says Passel. "There's a clear trend over the last three censuses for increasing numbers of those people to answer the race question as American Indian. But it doesn't tell you how 'Indian' they are in a cultural sense.

"The strength of this identification in places that are not Indian strongholds is transitory. If it becomes unfashionable to be American Indian, it could go down."

People who try to count American Indians employ many different means that often confound demographers. Tribes keep tabs on enrollment, but the rules vary on how much Indian blood makes one a member. Some tribes are not recognized by the federal government. Local health services may keep one set of records, while federal agencies like the Bureau of Indian Affairs will keep another. Some Indians are nomadic; Navajos, for example, may maintain three residences. Rural Indians can be hard to find, and minorities are always more prone to census undercounts. A growing number of mixed marriages blurs the racial boundaries even further.

"I don't know what an Indian is," says Malcolm Margolin, publisher of the

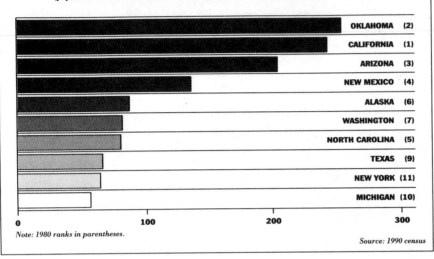

INDIAN STATES

During the 1980s, Oklahoma replaced California as the state with the largest American Indian population. South Dakota dropped off the top ten list as New York moved into ninth place.

(population of the ten states with the largest American Indian populations, in thousands)

OKLAHOMA (2)
CALIFORNIA (1)
ARIZONA (3)
NEW MEXICO (4)
ALASKA (6)
WASHINGTON (7)
NORTH CAROLINA (5)
TEXAS (9)
NEW YORK (11)
MICHIGAN (10)

0   100   200   300

Note: 1980 ranks in parentheses.

Source: 1990 census

monthly *News from Native California.* "Some people are clearly Indian, and some are clearly not. But the U.S. government figures are clearly inadequate for judging how many people are Indian."

Even those who can't agree on the numbers do agree that Indians are returning to their roots. "In the early 1960s, there was a stigma attached to being American Indian," Passel says. These days, even Anglos are proud of Indian heritage.

IDENTIFYING WITH INDIANS

When white patrons at Romo's restaurant in Holbrook, Arizona, learn that their host is half Navajo and half Hopi, they frequently exclaim, "I'm part Cherokee!" The host smiles and secretly rolls his eyes. More *bahanas* (whites) are jumping on the Indian bandwagon.

"In the last three years, interest in Indian beliefs has really taken off," says Marzenda McComb, the former co-owner of a New Age store in Portland, Oregon. To celebrate the sale of her store, a woman performed an Indian smudging ritual with burnt cedar and an eagle feather. Most of McComb's customers were non-Indian.

Controversy often accompanies such practices. Some Indians bristle at the

sharing of their culture and spiritual practices with whites. But others welcome people of any race into their culture. And many tribal leaders recognize that Indian art and tourism are hot markets.

Anglos are not the only ones paying more attention to Indian ways. Indian children are showing a renewed interest in their culture. Jennifer Bates, who owns the Bear and Coyote Gallery in California, says her 9-year-old son has taken an independent interest in Northern Miwok dance. "It's nice, knowing that we're not pushing it on him," she says. "He wanted to dance and make his cape. It's up to us to keep things going, and if we don't, it's gone."

The oldest generation of California Indians "grew up among people who recalled California before the arrival of whites," says Malcolm Margolin. These people have "something in their tone, their mood, their manners—a very Indian quality." Younger generations are more comfortable in the white world, he says, but they sense "something very ominous about the passing of the older generation. It's the sense of the younger generation that it's up to them."

The Zuni tribe is trying to revive an-

cient crafts by opening two tribal-owned craft stores—one in their pueblo in New Mexico, and one on San Francisco's trendy Union Street. The most popular items are fetishes—small stone carvings of animals that serve as good-luck charms. "After *Dances with Wolves* came out, we weren't able to keep the wolf fetishes in stock," says Milford Nahohai, manager of the New Mexico store.

JOBS ON RESERVATIONS

Many Indians on and off the reservation face a well-established litany of problems, from poverty and alcoholism to unemployment. Many tribal leaders say that only jobs can solve the problem. Promoting Indian-owned businesses is their solution.

The number of Indian-owned businesses increased 64 percent between 1982 and 1987, compared with a 14 percent rise for all U.S. firms, according to the Census Bureau. "A whole new system of role models is being established," says Steven Stallings, president of the National Center for American Indian Enterprise Development in Mesa, Arizona. "Indians see self-employment as a viable opportunity."

In boosting reservation-based businesses, Stallings aims to create sustainable, self-reliant economies. In some areas, 92 cents of every dollar earned on a reservation is spent outside the reservation, he says. Non-Indian communities typically retain as much as 85 cents.

Stallings's center hopes to start by attracting employers to Indian country. The next step is to add retail and service businesses that will "create a revolving economy on the reservation."

This strategy is at work in Laguna, New Mexico. The Laguna Indians were hit hard in 1982, when the price of uranium plummeted and the Anaconda Mineral Company closed a mine located on their reservation. But the Lagunas have bounced back with several enterprises, including Laguna Industries, a tribal-owned manufacturing firm that employs 350 people.

Laguna Industries' clients include the Department of Defense, Raytheon, and Martin Marietta. Its flagship product is a communications shelter that U.S. forces

INDIAN INDUSTRIES

*American Indian specialty contractors had receipts of $97 million in 1987.
But automotive and food-store owners may earn higher profits.*

(ten largest industry groups in receipts for firms owned by American Indians and Alaska Natives)

rank	industry group	firms	receipts (in thousands)	receipts per firm (in thousands)
1	Special trade contractors	2,268	$97,400	$43
2	Miscellaneous retail	1,799	85,400	47
3	Agriculture services, forestry, and fishing	3,128	84,000	27
4	Automotive dealers and service stations	222	65,300	294
5	Food stores	301	54,300	180
6	Business services	2,532	48,600	19
7	Eating and drinking places	464	35,300	76
8	Construction	461	34,200	74
9	Trucking and warehousing	590	32,200	55
10	Personal services	1,719	26,500	15

Source: 1987 Economic Censuses, Survey of Minority-Owned Business Enterprises

INDIAN MARKETS

The 1990 census showed rapid increases among American Indians who live in large metropolitan areas. Some of the increases reflect an increasing willingness to declare one's Indian heritage.

(top ten metropolitan areas, ranked by American Indian, Eskimo, and Aleut population in 1990; and percent change in that population, 1980–90)

rank	metropolitan area	1990 population	percent change 1980–90
1	Los Angeles-Anaheim-Riverside, CA	87,500	5%
2	Tulsa, OK	48,200	41
3	New York-Northern New Jersey-Long Island, NY-NJ-CT	46,200	101
4	Oklahoma City, OK	45,700	82
5	San Francisco-Oakland-San Jose, CA	40,800	19
6	Phoenix, AZ	38,000	66
7	Seattle-Tacoma, WA	32,100	42
8	Minneapolis-St. Paul, MN-WI	24,000	49
9	Tucson, AZ	20,300	36
10	San Diego, CA	20,100	37

Source: 1990 census

used in the Gulf War. "It's pretty nice to see your own people getting involved in high-tech stuff," says welding supervisor Phillip Sarracino, 44.

Laguna Indians are given first priority for jobs at the plant, but several middle managers are white. Conrad Lucero, a plant group leader and former tribal governor, says that non-Indian supervisors are often retirees who lend their expertise until Indians can run things on their own.

"I have an 8-year-old daughter," says Sabin Chavez, 26, who works in the quality control division. "I'm hoping to keep this company going, so our kids can live on the reservation. It's a long shot, but we have to believe in long shots."

High morale at Laguna Industries is tempered by the risks of relying on the government. The Lagunas realize that their dependence on military contracts makes them vulnerable to cuts in the de-

fense budget. And in August 1994, the tribe's right to bid on minority set-aside contracts will expire—partly because the business has been so successful.

"We have to be able to meet and beat our competitors on the open market," Lucero says. The Lagunas may succeed: Martin Marietta Corporation has already awarded Laguna Industries a contract based on price and not minority status, says Martin Marietta customer representative Michael King.

Laguna Industries has not solved all the tribe's problems, however. Tribal planner Nathan Tsosie estimates that unemployment runs as high as 35 percent on the reservation. Much of the housing is substandard, water shortages could impede future development, and alcoholism still tears Indian families apart. But Tsosie has an answer: "We just need to develop more. People leave the reservation to get jobs. If there were jobs here, they'd stay."

GAMBLING AND TOURISM

Indians bring some real advantages to the business world. The Lagunas show that a cohesive community can be organized into an efficient production facility. Other reservations have rich natural resources. But the biggest benefit may be "sovereignty," or the suspension of many local, state, and federal laws on Indian territory. Reservations have no sales or property tax, so cigarettes, gasoline, and other items can be sold for low prices. They can also offer activities not permitted off-reservation.

Like gambling.

"Bingo is a way for tribes to amass funds so they can get into other economic development projects," says Frank Collins, a Mescalero Apache from San Jose who specializes in development.

Bingo can be big business. One parlor on the Morongo reservation, just north of Palm Springs, California, draws 5,000 people a week and employs more than 140 people. The Morongo tribe's main objective is to develop as a major resort destination, says bingo general manager Michael Lombardi.

Lombardi won't say how much money bingo generates for the Morongos. He will

THE BEST STATES FOR

Indians in Business

T his table shows how the states rank on the basis of business ownership among American Indians. States in the South may offer the most opportunity for American Indians, while midwestern states may offer the least.

The number of Indian-owned businesses in a state is not closely related to the business ownership rate. Business ownership rates are calculated by dividing the number of Indian-owned businesses by the number of Indians and multiplying by 1,000. The top-ranked state, Alaska, is one of only five states with more than 1,000 Indian-owned firms. But the state that ranks last, Arizona, has the seventh-highest number of Indian-owned businesses.

Statistical analysis also indicates that the pattern of business ownership among American Indians is not driven by the rate of growth in a state's Indian population during the 1980s, or by a state's overall level of business ownership.

There appear to be strong regional biases in patterns of Indian business ownership. The business ownership rate was 12.2 Indian-owned firms per 1,000 Indians in the South, 10.3 in the West, 9.6 in the Northeast, and only 7.4 in the Midwest.

One clue to a state's business ownership rate among Indians could be the share of its Indian population living on reservations. The lowest-ranking state, Arizona, contains seven of the ten most populated reservations in the U.S., including a large share of the huge Navajo reservation (1990 Indian population of 143,400 in Arizona, New Mexico, and Utah). South Dakota, ranking 47th, contains the large and economically troubled Pine Ridge, Rosebud, and Standing Rock reservations. Indians living on a reservation have limited entrepreneurial opportunities. Another factor that may be related to the Indian business rate is the state's general economic health: several states near the bottom of the ranking, Ken-

William O'Hare is Director of Population and Policy Research Program, University of Louisville.

tucky, Nebraska, and Michigan, have experienced weak economic growth during the 1980s.

But the most powerful predictor is probably the business skill of a state's Indian tribes. Third-ranking North Carolina is home to one branch of the Cherokee tribe, which has large investments in lumber and tourism. And Alaska may rank first because its native American, Eskimo, and Aleut population received billions of dollars in a federal land claim settlement. These data do not contain businesses owned by Eskimos or Aleuts. But many of Alaska's Indians live in isolated towns where small businesses have a captive, all-native audience.

— William O'Hare

INDIAN OPPORTUNITY

(states with more than 100 American Indian-owned businesses in 1987, ranked by business ownership rate)

rank	state name	number of firms 1987	American Indian population 1987	business ownership rate*
1	Alaska	1,039	28,700	36.2
2	North Carolina	1,757	75,600	23.2
3	Texas	872	57,500	15.2
4	Virginia	188	13,300	14.1
5	Colorado	343	24,600	13.9
6	California	3,087	225,600	13.7
7	Louisiana	221	16,600	13.3
8	Massachusetts	132	10,700	12.4
9	Kansas	225	20,000	11.3
10	Florida	348	30,900	11.3
11	Maryland	123	11,300	10.9
12	Pennsylvania	139	12,800	10.8
13	Georgia	122	11,400	10.7
14	New Jersey	131	12,800	10.3
15	New Mexico	1,247	126,400	9.9
16	Illinois	182	19,600	9.3
17	Montana	405	44,700	9.1
18	Oklahoma	2,044	229,300	8.9
19	Oregon	306	34,500	8.9
20	North Dakota	208	24,300	8.6
21	Wisconsin	306	36,300	8.4
22	Ohio	149	17,700	8.4
23	Washington	602	72,300	8.3
24	Nevada	146	17,700	8.3
25	New York	425	54,800	7.8
26	Missouri	133	17,500	7.6
27	Minnesota	333	45,400	7.3
28	Michigan	304	50,900	6.0
29	South Dakota	267	49,000	5.5
30	Utah	109	22,700	4.8
31	Arizona	843	189,100	4.5

* Number of American Indian-owned firms per 1,000 Indians.
Source: Bureau of the Census, 1987 economic census, and author's estimates of 1987 Indian population

say that 113 reservations allow some form of gaming, and he attributes bingo's popularity to the effects of Reagan-era cutbacks in the Bureau of Indian Affairs budget. Lombardi says then-Secretary of the Interior James Watt told Indians, "Instead of depending on the Great White Father, why don't you start your own damn business?"

Indian culture also can create unique business opportunities. On the Hopi reservation in northern Arizona, Joe and Janice Day own a small shop on Janice's ancestral property. They swap elk hooves and cottonwood sticks, useful in Indian rituals, for jewelry, and baskets to sell to tourists.

The Days would like to credit their success to their shrewd sense of customer service. But they confess that the difference between profit and loss may be their wildly popular T-shirts, which read "Don't worry, be Hopi."

Not long ago, Hopis had to leave the reservation to go to school or find work. Today, the tribe has its own junior and senior high school and an entrepreneurial spirit. But small schools and small businesses won't keep people on the reservation. The Days still make a two-hour drive to Flagstaff each week to do their banking, laundry, and shopping. "The first Hopi you can get to build a laundromat is going to be a rich man," says Joe Day.

The Days lived in Flagstaff until their children finished high school. At that point, they decided to come "home." Janice's daughter is now an accountant in San Francisco, and she loves the amenities of the big city. "But who knows?" Janice says. "She may also want to come home someday. No matter where you are, you're still going to end up coming home."

THE URGE TO GO HOME

"Going home" may also mean renewing a bond with one's Indian heritage. While the population in 19 "Indian states" grew at predictable levels during the 1980s, the Urban Institute's Jeff Passel says it soared in the non-Indian states.

For example, Passel estimated the 1990 Indian population in Arizona at 202,000 (the 1980 population of 152,700, plus the intervening 58,600 births and minus the intervening 10,300 deaths)—a figure close to the 1990 census number (203,500). But in Alabama, a non-Indian state, Passel found a huge percentage increase that he could not have predicted. Alabama's Indian population grew from 7,600 in 1980 to 16,500 in 1990, a 117 percent increase. Higher birthrates, lower death rates, and migration from other states do not explain the increase.

Passel explains the gap this way: "The people who are Indians always identify themselves as Indians. They tell the census they are Indians, and they register their newborns as Indians." These people are usually found in the Indian states.

"People who are part Indian may not identify themselves as American Indians. But they don't do that consistently over time."

Today, for reasons of ethnic pride, part-Indians may tell the Census Bureau they

> **"Instead of depending on the Great White Father, why don't you start your own damn business?"**

are Indian. At the hospital, they may identify themselves as white to avoid discrimination. This is most common in non-Indian states, which Passel generally defines as having fewer than 3,000 Indians in 1950.

California ranks second only to Oklahoma in its Indian population, but its mixture of tribes is unique in the nation. Some Indian residents trace their roots to native California tribes, says Malcolm Margolin. Others came west as part of a federal relocation program in the 1950s. In California cities, Cherokees, Chippewas, and other out-of-state Indians congregate in clubs.

"What has happened is the formation of an inter-tribal ethic, a pan-Indian ethic," Margolin says. "People feel that America has a lot of problems. That cultural doubt causes them to look for their ethnic roots, for something they can draw strength from. And for Indians, it's right there. It's ready-made."

Canada Pressed on Indian Rights

Commission Urges Self-Rule for Tribes

Howard Schneider

Washington Post Foreign Service

OTTAWA, Nov. 21—Canada's governance of its aboriginal communities has failed and should be replaced by granting self-rule to as many as 80 separate Indian nations that would be provided with extensive land and resource rights, billions of dollars in extra aid and a new branch of Parliament to represent their interests, a blue-ribbon government commission reported today.

In a 4,000-page, $40 million report, the Royal Commission on Aboriginal People concluded that "Euro-Canada" had left the country's more than 800,000 Indians largely destitute, stripped of traditional lands and resources that should have been protected by treaty, and under immense pressure to assimilate into Western culture. The result: widespread poverty, high rates of alcoholism and teen suicide, and a growing potential for violence if Canada does not restructure the relationship with its original residents.

The commission suggested, in essence, that Canada start from scratch, renegotiating virtually every aspect of Indian governance and economics, and even soliciting the Queen of England to embody the new beginning in a royal proclamation. One issued in 1763, Indian leaders say, recognized their rights to independent government and came at a time of cooperation with European settlers, but later it was ignored during decades of domination and mistreatment.

"Some leaders fear that violence is in the wind," the commission stated in its summary. "What aboriginal people need is straightforward, if not simple: control over their lives in place of the well-meaning but ruinous paternalism of past Canadian governments."

The panel was established in 1991 by then-Prime Minister Brian Mulroney following a violent standoff between Mohawks and Quebec security officials. Mulroney appointed four of the commission's seven members from Indian communities and gave it a broad mandate to examine all aspects of Indian life. Its report came two years beyond its deadline, with tens of thousands of pages of testimony and reports collected, and with the distinction of being Canada's most expensive royal commission.

Indian leaders said the government should accept the commission's findings and begin implementing them immediately. "We call upon the government of Canada to deal with aboriginal peoples on a nation-to-nation basis, recognizing and encouraging the emergence of another order of government," said George Erasmus, a co-chairman of the commission.

But the impact of the document is uncertain. Its call for creation of dozens of self-governing nations is bound to echo in a country struggling to keep its European components—English- and French-speakers—unified. Within dozens of local communities, it will touch nerves as well. One recommendation, for example, would give Indian commercial fishermen priority over non-Indians during "times of scarcity"—an explosive issue in the struggling British Columbia salmon industry.

Likewise, the call for increased funding and a redistribution of land, timber, mineral, animal and other resources is likely to cause resentment throughout some parts of Canada; it was promptly criticized today by the Western-based Reform Party as a waste of money.

Indian Affairs Minister Ron Irwin all but ruled out extensive extra spending and many of the more comprehensive ideas included in the study. He said the current Liberal Party government supports Indian self-determination and wants to equitably settle land, resource and other issues in a way that will allow the communities to be economically independent—and is doing so on a case-by-case basis around the country. But that must be done, he said, within the constraints of a government struggling to balance its budget.

"Our aims are the same," he said of the government and the commission. "I don't know if it is going to come out" the way the panel recommended, with changes to the Canadian constitution and perhaps a dozen new independent tribunals established to renegotiate different aspects of Indian self-rule and resource claims.

But commission members and Indian leaders said it was time to abandon what they all a "project-by-project" approach that is neither quick nor comprehensive enough to address the problem. They want Canada to confront and correct an unpleasant part of its past—one they describe as including restrictions on Indian voting rights, prohibitions against free association and forced attendance by Indian children at boarding schools that were often the site of mental and physical abuse.

The price tag is steep in Canada's current fiscal climate—about $27 billion over the next 20 years. The commission contended that will be more than offset as Indian communities become economically successful, develop businesses using their land and resources, and stop having to rely on social services.

"We cannot escape the fact that we have built a great liberal democracy in part through the dispossession of aboriginal people and the imposition of our cultural norms," said Renee Dussault, a co-chairman of the commission. "The . . . sustained denial of this reality—manifested through the violation of agreements, the suppression of cultures and institutions, the refusal to live up to legal obligations—is the core of the problem. . . . Aboriginal people must have the opportunity and resources to exercise responsibility themselves."

The commission's 400 recommendations envision establishment of an extensive set of new institutions: a House of First Peoples to join the Parliament, an aboriginal university, parallel health and justice systems that would employ traditional methods of healing and curbing crime, and a panel, operating at arm's length from the government, to redistribute land and other resources in a way that recognizes historical Indian claims and forms a foundation for economic success. There would be between 60 and 80 such nations, established along historical, cultural and linguistic lines, with rights to establish governing institutions and norms.

Commission executive director Anthony Reynolds said it is a model similar to the one used in the United States, where tribes have developed businesses, including casinos, under their own rules and regulations. The commission report noted also that although Indians make up about 3 percent of Canada's population, they control less than 1 percent of the land, whereas U.S. tribes have land far in excess of the size of their population.

PROFILE: REBECCA ADAMSON

Building entrepreneurship and hope among Native Americans

BY ELENA CABRAL

"Wherever you go across Indian country, if you really listen, you can hear the story of the land and the people."

Rapid City, South Dakota—On a frigid winter morning, Rebecca Adamson revs the engine of her four-wheel drive vehicle, relishing the sound as it shatters the silence blanketing the city. As she drives toward the Pine Ridge reservation, not even subzero temperatures and biting winds can diminish her fascination with the snow-covered Dakota Plains. "Winter brings a stark, brutal beauty to the land out here that just pulls you in," she says. But after a few miles, her mind's eye turns to the spring and she describes in vivid detail the rich hues of green and blue that will soon brighten the landscape. "Wherever you go across Indian country," she says, "if you really listen, you can hear the story of the land and the people."

Here on the Pine Ridge reservation, where 200 Lakota Indians were massacred a century ago at Wounded Knee and where the near-extinction of the buffalo once threatened the end of a people, the story is, in many ways, one of bitter loss that continues to resonate. But it is also a story of the resilience and determination that inspired a young activist years ago.

In her 27-year career as a community organizer and advocate for Native Americans, Adamson has returned again and again to this rugged corner of the country, where poverty is the highest in the nation, to help spur an economic and cultural renewal that is changing lives and strengthening communities. Where others saw desolation, Adamson saw hope.

Born in Akron, Ohio, 47 years ago to a Cherokee mother and a father of Swedish descent, Adamson spent summers as a child in the Smoky Mountains of North Carolina with her maternal grandparents, who introduced her to Indian ways. She first came to Pine Ridge in the early 1970s. After dropping out of the University of Akron and hitchhiking through Indian country, she began working with a movement to help tribes take control of their children's education, which had long been the province of the Bureau of Indian Affairs. Assigned to the Little Wound Elementary School on the reservation, she and others in the movement were determined to reform a system that plucked Indian children from their families, placed them in government-run boarding schools, and forced them to abandon their language and customs. It proved to be a long and contentious effort, and Adamson was arrested three times during protests and demonstrations. Finally, in 1975, Congress passed the Indian Education Self-Determination Act, which gave Indians the legal right to contract for and run their own schools. Considered the most important piece of legislation affecting Native Americans in many years, the law also enabled them to set up a managerial infrastructure that is still used to oversee many other aspects of daily life on the reservations.

Although the new law gave Indian people a measure of educational control, Adamson says, "It became clear that we would not really control anything until we achieved economic independence." Adamson cites the decades of stifling regulation by the Bureau of Indian Affairs and other federal agencies that had denied tribes the right to control their own resources. She recalls the desolate motels and industrial parks that characterized previous attempts to spur economic growth on reservations through large-scale ventures. Since Indians lacked the skills and resources needed to maintain and market them, she says, these projects, though well-intentioned, were destined for failure.

Adamson began to explore the idea of creating smaller-scale income-generating projects and applying to them the marketing techniques of the business world. More broadly, she wanted to find a way to move Indians out of debilitating dependency through development projects that were consistent with their culture and values.

With that in mind, in 1980 Adamson founded First Nations Development Institute in Fredericksburg, Va., and took her ideas to major foundations in New York City. At first, she says, her plan to support "culturally appropriate" ventures was met "with amusement" and some skepticism by many in the economic development field. "At best," she says, "even people who liked me referred to it as a development 'boutique,' kind of cute but not part of the serious stuff." But Adamson kept knocking on doors until one opened. A $25,000 planning grant from the Ford Foundation first set her dream in motion. In less than a decade, the 'boutique' turned into a shopping mall.

Each year since 1980, First Nations has provided business and technical assistance to some 1,500 tribal groups and individual Native-American entrepreneurs. It operates a $400,000 revolving loan fund and a $7 million grants fund that has made 73 grants affecting more than 225 different tribes in 22 states and American Somoa. First Nations also gives marketing advice and holds an annual conference in which Indian people come together to learn how to manage capital and credit and explore new business practices. As a national advocate for Native Americans, First Nations has helped several groups, including the Umatilla tribe of Oregon, regain control of tribal lands. It also helped the Saginaw Chippewa of Michigan recover $10 million in trust funds that were tied up in federal red tape.

Among First Nations' earliest triumphs was the creation of the Lakota Fund, the first microenterprise loan fund in the United States. Established in 1985 on the Pine Ridge reservation, the now independent Lakota Fund has made more than 300 loans—totaling more than $1 million—to Indian entrepreneurs ranging from beadwork artisans to video-store owners. Most had never before had access to bank loans or credit.

Although the fund was modeled in part after the Grameen Bank in Bangladesh, Adamson is quick to point out that the project was first and foremost an affirmation of the Lakota people's ability to solve their own problems. According to Robert Friedman, president of the Corporation for Enterprise Development, "The Lakota Fund showed that in what might look like an economic wasteland to an outsider, there were in fact lots of entrepreneurial activities." The Lakota Fund was one of the pioneering programs that helped shape President Clinton's early legislative effort promoting banking and lending to small enterprises in poor communities. There are now some 250 microenterprise loan funds across the United States.

Today Adamson, who earned a master's degree in economic development at New Hampshire College in 1992 and now teaches a course there on indigenous economics, is regarded as a powerful force in both the development and business communities. Says Friedman, "Rebecca has made people listen to a woman in a male-dominated field, to a Native American in a community where there is a longstanding myth that nothing works, and to a non-economist who probably understands the subject better than most economists." She has done all this, adds Friedman, with a sense of humor that has been one of her greatest assets in an immensely difficult line of work. Last year the Council on Foundations gave Adamson its Robert W. Scrivener Award for creative grant making and the Ms. Foundation named her one of its Women of the Year.

Adamson is especially forceful when contradicting conventional thinking about the poor, particularly the view that traditional cultural values are in conflict with modern economic principles. "There is a myth out there that Indian people can't succeed in business because we aren't competitive enough," she says. "The truth is that Indian people have a different view of economic success."

Adamson believes that economies in the 21st century could learn a great deal from the Native-American world view, which values "prosperity of creation," a different way of looking at the balance between people and nature. "For example," she says, "if you think of energy just in terms of fossil fuels like oil and gas, then yes, we are going to run out of them. But if you consider the ability of humans to create new sources of hydro and solar energy, then all of a sudden you realize that there could be a prosperity of creation that lies within our own ingenuity."

Adamson knows that the country's 2 million Native Americans have a long way to go. According to 1989 statistics of the Bureau of Indian Affairs, only 12 percent earn more than $7,000 annually. Census data in 1990 show unemployment rates of over 50 percent on many reservations, and problems such as alcoholism, drug addiction, and diabetes are rampant.

Just as these ills are linked, Adamson's solutions are broad. "When Rebecca speaks about indigenous economics, she calls it economics with values added," says Gloria Steinem, who profiled Adamson in *Ms. Magazine* last winter. "When she measures success, it's not the bottom line that we're accustomed to. She looks to see if there is less depression, drug addiction, and suicide because people are beginning to feel empowered. She looks to see if the spiritual and cultural values of the group are being preserved and allowed to be part of this advance. It's just a broader and deeper measure of things."

Adamson's vision of economic self-sufficiency is as much about changing attitudes and invigorating the human spirit as it is about banking. "People who have been victims may have the attitude that it was never their fault, so they don't have to take responsibility. That is insidious," she says. "You have to create projects that lock in accountability because the aim is to build a personal efficacy, an 'I-can-do-it' attitude."

First Nations' grant-making vehicle, the Eagle Staff Fund, established in 1993, is designed with these ideas in mind. For example, at the Porcupine Clinic, a community health center on the Pine Ridge reservation, First Nations responded to the clinic's initial proposal for an ambulance with a grant that helped revamp the clinic's financial procedures, which led to a new third-party billing system and a direct-mail fund-raising campaign run jointly with a local public radio station. The campaign, which surpassed projections with more than $100,000 raised in the first year, is building a stream of income that will ease the clinic's dependence on foundation grants and help it become more self-sufficient.

The Inter-Tribal Bison Cooperative (ITBC), a group of 40 plains tribes working to restore the buffalo—once a hallmark of the Native American plains culture and economy—is another example of a project that goes beyond a dollars and cents approach. Rejecting the high-tech practices of the modern cattle industry, the cooperative is using the traditions and knowledge of their tribes to raise free-range buffalo with high protein, low-fat meat for the growing health-food market. With support from First Nations, the cooperative is not only providing jobs and financial assets for families and tribes with herds, it is also restoring endangered prairie grass that once fed wild buffalo herds. Tribal land that had been cut up into hundreds of small allotments and leased to non-Indian cattle ranchers has been reunited into a large common range for the use of ITBC members. Communities have also begun to revive Buffalo ceremonies that once helped connect tribal members to each other and to their environment. So far, the cooperative has increased its holdings from 1,500 buffalo to more than 8,000.

"Indian people are natural systems thinkers," Adamson says. "We understand the interlatedness of problems and can therefore design holistic solutions."

Says Anne Beckett, executive Director of Zuni Publishing, which was launched through a grant from the Eagle Staff Fund and specializes in literature by and about Native American people, "First Nations allows communities to function as they have always functioned by taking tradition and reworking it to be successful in the present. It's a partnership based on two levels of expertise to build something neither could build alone."

Adamson has criss-crossed the United States numerous times. She has worked in all 50 states, advising most of the nation's 234 recognized tribes as well as scores of smaller southwestern pueblos, Alaskan native villages, and non-reservation communities across the country. Today when she visits organizations receiving support from First Nations, Adamson leaves as much information as she takes with her, weaving an ever-wider network of groups to bring tribes closer together and connect them to mainstream foundations and banking institutions.

With major changes expected in the country's economic and social policies in the coming years, First Nations, like many organizations, is feeling the pressure to find creative solutions for those who will be hardest hit. Among the ideas Adamson supports is the creation of individual development accounts (IDAs) for low-income families. Under the IDA plan, families would receive tax incentives or matching funds to set up savings accounts, which they could draw upon for such things as education, health, and home ownership. The idea is in keeping with First Nations' approach to promoting economic stability by focusing on building assets, both financial and otherwise. "What moves people out of poverty are

Adamson has also been trying to help the Khwe and San people of the Kalahari in southern Africa, who are threatened by the Botswana government with removal from their ancestral lands and transferral to remote settlements.

Gathering a group of like-minded people, including Gloria Steinem, to travel to Botswana in the summer of 1995, Adamson organized an effort to suspend the removal, raising money for Kwhe leaders to travel to the United States and Europe to tell their story. Although the outcome in the Kalahari is still uncertain, says Steinem, "Without Rebecca's actions and hard work, it is more than likely that the forced removal would have happened."

"Indian people understand the interrelatedness of problems and can therefore design holistic solutions."

assets not income," Adamson says. "Income can change when a company decides to move somewhere else or when an emergency hits a family. The thing that makes the difference is that cushion to fall back on."

In the past few years, Adamson has broadened the scope of her work to assist indigenous people in other countries who are struggling to hold on to their ancestral lands, develop new systems of self-government, build viable economies, and preserve their cultures. She recently advised aboriginal groups in Australia on how to benefit from the government's use of their culture to market the Olympic games in the year 2000. She notes that corporations in North America have appropriated tribal names like Cherokee, Winnebago, and Oneida, trademarking them for commercial purposes without compensation to the tribes.

On a recent journey to the Dakotas, Adamson stops at a house she has bought just outside the Badlands National Park, a sprawling stretch of jagged rock and wilderness that seems to embody the "brutal beauty" that draws her to the region and to the people who live there. Near the Black Hills, Adamson visits a small herd of wild buffalo belonging to members of the Inter-Tribal Bison Cooperative. As she approaches the burly creatures, she studies them with a quiet reverence. In them she sees both centuries of a tradition that was nearly wiped out and a vibrant promise for the future. "There's a magnificence to the bison," she says, "in the way they fit the land and can stand there through blizzards and wind and survive." Adamson explains that the Lakota people modeled much of their way of life on the buffalo. "It's the old way," she says. "When you see it, you realize it is all still alive."

Cape Town's District Six Rises Again

A museum becomes a rallying point for a dispossessed community

BY DAVID GOODMAN

Cape Town, South Africa—A short, slight middle-aged woman, her head covered in a shawl, walks hesitantly through the door of what was once a church and is now a museum. It is a large, open space with creaking floorboards and an empty pulpit at one end that looks out on dozens of old street signs suspended from the balcony–Balmoral Street, Primrose Street, Eaton Place. A large map in the center of the room locates the streets in a Cape Town neighborhood called District Six.

The woman pauses at the edge of the map, studying it, occasionally nodding her head. Tears run down her face as she leans over to read the handwritten names and addresses scrawled all over the street grid. "Ismail Adams, 68 Williams St." "Yahya Modise, 238 Caledon St., D6." "Maxim's." "Ruth Peterson family."

Along one side of the room are facades of houses and stores. On Horstley Street I peer through a small window into a carpenter's workshop. On Vernon Terrace, I stare into a kitchen that has clothes hanging from a line and food on the stove. It is as if these places were frozen in time, abandoned hurriedly in the wake of some terrible calamity–which indeed they were.

These streets and homes and shops no longer exist. The whole of District Six has vanished, the victim of one of the most notorious forced removals of the apartheid era in South Africa. The neighborhood was supposed to go quietly. Instead, the removal took 15 years to complete. From 1966 to the early 1980s, what had been a richly varied, racially mixed community was systematically destroyed. District Six's 55,000 residents were forced to leave their homes and move into concrete ghettoes on the outskirts of the city.

A sprawling neighborhood in downtown Cape Town, District Six traces its roots to the mid-nineteenth century. It was originally populated by families that worked on the railways and the docks, and derives its name from its early designation as one of six municipal subdivisions, or districts, within the city. By the turn of the 20th century, it was a lively working-class neighborhood, where Jews, Muslims, blacks, whites, Indians, and people of mixed ancestry lived side by side. As Irwin Combrinck, a former resident and political activist observes, "The existence of District Six was the very antithesis of the Nationalist Party's ideology of white superiority and white separateness. It is for that main reason that District Six had to be destroyed."

Forced removals started in South Africa long before 1966 when District Six was designated a "black spot" in an area to be reserved for white people. From 1913, when blacks were first denied the right to own land in most of South Africa, to the introduction of democracy in 1994, some 3.5 million people were forcibly evicted from their lands. In the case of District Six, the South African regime was flexing its muscle, showing that no community–

"In this place we are reclaiming our history, which apartheid tried to erase."

not even this well-known and highly visible urban enclave–would be spared from the apartheid policy of racial separation.

Once the residents and houses of District Six were eliminated, the government appropriated nearly two-thirds of the neighborhood's lands and built a technical college– for whites only. The remaining 50 acres were left barren and rubble-strewn, a

From *The Ford Foundation REPORT*, Spring 1997, pp. 14-17. © 1997 by The Ford Foundation. Reprinted by permission.

stark, ugly monument to apartheid in the beautiful city of Cape Town.

Today, however, as the new South Africa attempts to rectify past injustices, the District Six Museum has emerged as a rallying point for dispossessed people who are fighting to regain some of their previous wealth and status. Although it is housed in an old church in a rundown neighborhood, the museum has become a dynamic cultural institution that has breathed new life into the community it honors.

A grant from the Ford Foundation last year is supporting special projects organized by the museum and assistance to other communities wanting to reclaim their history. One project is an exhibit on the sporting and cultural heritage of the Western Cape. Another is a photographic exhibit of district architecture before the bulldozing. A third is an oral history project.

The museum has had a stunning effect on both visitors and former residents. In the two years since it opened, it has become a national pilgrimage site for thousands of South African and foreign tourists and an obligatory stop for such visiting dignitaries as United States Vice President Al Gore, Irish President Mary Robinson, and Belgium's Queen Beatrix. With little fanfare and almost no publicity, the District Six Museum has become one of South Africa's foremost places of memory.

The museum has also played a leading role in negotiations over the future redevelopment of the District Six neighborhood. Over the next few months, construction of homes will begin on the district's vacant 50 acres, which will enable many former residents to move back to their old neighborhood for the first time in 30 years. Like a phoenix rising from ashes, District Six is coming back to life.

A group of 13- and 14-year-old schoolchildren dressed neatly in navy blue uniforms jostles into the balcony of the District Six Museum. Linda Fortune, a former resident of the area, speaks to the teenagers. "My name is Linda," she says, "and I used to live on Tyne Street in District Six. Those four banners hanging from the ceiling symbolize the Jewish, Muslim, African, and English people. We all lived together here."

"Have any of you seen a 'Europeans Only' sign like that one there?" Fortune asks, pointing to a wooden sign that was common in South Africa until the late 1980s. There is a brief silence until one boy raises his hand. "I saw a picture of it in a book," he says shyly. Their teacher, Riyaad Schroeder, remarks, "For them, apartheid is very abstract." He adds, "I am 31 years old, and even for me lots of things are vague."

As memories of apartheid fade, the District Six Museum is one of the few places in the new South Africa that shows what the old South Africa was like. "In this place," Linda Fortune tells the students, "we are reclaiming our history, which apartheid tried to erase."

In 1988, during the anti-apartheid struggles, former residents formed the Hands Off District Six Committee. HODS aimed to prevent any new development on what was left of the district without the approval of the former residents, and to keep alive the spirit of the community. The following year, HODS proposed mounting temporary exhibitions to commemorate the district. Their idea was not realized, however, until 1992 when the Methodist Church offered the Central Methodist Mission, known as the "Freedom Church" for the role its ministers and people played in fighting apartheid, as a place for the exhibits. Located directly opposite Cape Town's main police station and magistrate's court and on the edge of District Six, the mission seemed a fitting site to honor the people and history of the area.

Following a successful two-week photo exhibit in the church in 1992, the museum committee planned something more ambitious. Old photos and mementos were collected and a map of the old district was drawn up. Then a wonderful discovery was made. The museum's project director, Sandra Prosalendis, learned that the man in charge of the area's demolition in the 1970s had saved the district's street signs. After weeks of gentle coaxing by Prosalendis and Pastor Stan Abrahams of Central Methodist Mission, a museum trustee, the man donated the signs to the museum.

The "Streets Exhibition: Retracing District Six," opened six months after the inauguration of President Nelson Mandela in 1994. The exhibit was scheduled to run for two weeks, but from the first

day, December 10, 1994, people–many of them former residents of District Six–poured into the small church. For veteran anti-apartheid activist and museum trustee Anwah Nagia, it was a stunning affirmation of the struggles of District Six and other dispossessed communities. "The launch of the Streets Exhibition was singly the most moving experience for me," Nagia says. "The first day of that exhibition, the place was completely jammed. People met people they hadn't seen in 20 or 30 years."

The exhibition "became a vindication that all their resistance wasn't for nothing," says Nagia. "The people were so pleased that someone had put this together. They had been relegated to nothing, but now they could say 'I was part of history! My contribution is not forgotten.'"

The museum quickly took on a life of its own. As more and more people flocked to the old Freedom Church, it became apparent that the exhibit could not simply close down. Some said that would be tantamount to another forced removal. So the museum trustees decided to keep it open, and the Methodist Church agreed to give the museum a 10-year lease. Suddenly a community that had vanished had a new town center.

On October 28, 1996, a crowd of about 50 people milled around in a cavernous hearing room in downtown Cape Town. Women clad in skirts, shawls, and saris mingled with men in suits, fezzes, and Nehru jackets; people talked excitedly in the corners. The lively scene was reminiscent of a Friday night outside the Star Bioscope (Cinema) in District Six years ago. But the crowd was gathered for a session of the Land Claims Court. After four black-robed judges entered and took seats on the dais, one rose to announce: "Today, we will consider the land restitution case of the people of District Six." Because of its notoriety, District Six was one of the first cases being heard by South Africa's new Land Claims Court, which decides on restitution for victims of forced removals of the apartheid era.

After several hours of negotiations, the assembled parties, which included representatives of the Cape Town city government, District Six tenants and landlords, local churches, and the trustees of the

District Six Museum, agreed on principles that will in coming years lead to the redevelopment of the neighborhood's vacant lands. Current plans are for approximately 5,000 units of low- and moderate-income housing to be built, which would house about 20,000 former residents. After years in exile, they will finally have the chance to come home.

Behind the scenes, the District Six Museum has played a key role in bringing together the dispersed community and acting as a watchdog for its interests. Because former residents have different views about how best to redevelop the land and compensate victims of the removal, the museum has tried to serve as a catalyst and bridge builder. Besides distributing land-claim forms to former residents, it has provided a central meeting place for the far-flung community. In addition, museum leaders are offering advice and expertise to other forcibly removed South African communities that want to mount similar exhibitions of their history.

"The District Six Museum is part of the political dynamic of the area," observes Andre Odendaal, a museum trustee and the administrator of the Robben Island Museum, the notorious former prison where many opponents of apartheid were held, including President Nelson Mandela. Odendaal rejects the notion that museums should not become involved in political matters. "I think it's healthy for a cultural institution to be a vehicle for political expression," he says, but cautions that it should not "become a political party vehicle."

The activism of the District Six Museum is one of the many ways that it breaks the mold of conventional museums. Irwin Combrinck, now a museum trustee, says that along with former residents like himself who are returning to reclaim their past, some whites have come asking forgiveness. As we stand on the map in the center of the museum, a white-haired man kneels down to write his name where his house used to be. Behind him, a two-story high muslin cloth hangs, with remarks by District Six residents and visitors scrawled across it. I take a swatch of the cloth in my hand and feel, suddenly, the old community coming alive. I read: "Sharifa Nordie. Born 17 Chapel St., daughter of Hadjie Ebrahim Nordien, who taught thousands of Muslim children after full day's work as a street sweeper for more than 50 years. I am looking forward to get back to my roots."

Says Combrinck: "It's not a place where you just come to view artifacts. It's something that you become involved in." Among the projects the museum has undertaken at the behest of community members is a history of sports among South African blacks, and a chronicle of the last days of District Six.

Stan Abrahams notes that the museum stands as both a symbol of hope and a warning. "Maybe people are ashamed that things like this could happen," he says. "Now they are confronting what they might have done to prevent it. We want the museum to be part of the healing, but we don't want this to happen again. We dare not forget."

Abrahams stands in the old church and reflects, "There is a universal message here. Whether you are looking at the Holocaust, or slavery in America, they tell the same story about people not caring for one another. Maybe this place will help people learn that we must care for each other."

David Goodman spent a year in Cape Town near District Six. Now in Vermont, he is writing a book on South Africa's post-apartheid transformation.

A different kind of justice:
Truth and reconciliation in South Africa

by Peter Storey

THE COMMUNITY hall in the dusty township is packed. Most of the people are local black residents, with a small sprinkling of whites from the nearby town. On the platform, under South Africa's bright new flag and a banner proclaiming "Healing Through Truth," the multiracial panel of truth commissioners listens respectfully.

Facing them is a black woman. Hesitatingly, and then with more confidence, this peasant woman speaks of her first-born son, an African National Congress "comrade" who, with other youths of the township, resisted the apartheid regime in the uprising of 1985. She describes his birth and how he was named, and speaks proudly of his performance at school. Then she tells of the night the security police smashed down the door and dragged him away, and about how an anonymous policeman sent for her some days later to come to the mortuary. In horrifying detail she describes the bruised and almost unrecognizable corpse, riddled with 19 bullet wounds, that had once been her son.

The remembrance overwhelms her and affects both panel and audience. Some weep quietly while she struggles with her grief. There is a long pause and the therapist alongside her hugs her close. Then she speaks again: "I do not know if I can forgive," she says. "I must know who did this to my son. When I see the face of the one who killed him, and he tells me why, then perhaps I can forgive."

Another place and a more formal scene, with judges, legal counsel and piles of documents. Arraigned before the judges are three burly Afrikaners, ex-security police whose vicious rule once ran throughout apartheid South Africa. One of them reads from a prepared text: "We blindfolded them and took them to a stone quarry outside the town. We hung Subject Number 1 upside down from a tree branch and lit a fire under him. When his hair burned he screamed a lot and then he told us everything. The other two also confessed. After that, we shot them. Our report said they had resisted arrest."

In the front row, watching and listening, are the families of "Subjects 1, 2 and 3." They are learning for the first time how their sons and brothers died. That night the nation also watches and listens as the proceedings are reported on national television.

> **"Today," said one man after giving his testimony before the commission, "the nation cried my tears with me."**

Over the past 19 months, hearings like these have been held across the length and breadth of South Africa. The nation's Truth and Reconciliation Commission has attracted interest around the world because its attempt to uncover and deal with a brutal past goes further than any similar exercise in history. Furthermore, the TRC's hearings seem to reach beyond the limitations of secular law, exploring new potentials for forgiveness and national reconciliation—themes that are increasingly relevant internationally. Nowhere else has secular legislation produced such an unsecular and almost scriptural understanding of what it takes to heal a nation.

The birth of the TRC, like much else in the recent South African story, was something of a miracle. By 1990, when South African President F. W. de Klerk conceded that apartheid had run out of road and announced negotiations with Nelson Mandela and the

From *The Christian Century*, September 10–17, 1997, pp. 788-791, 793. © 1997 by the Christian Century Foundation. Reprinted by permission.

ANC, small groups of South Africans—nongovernmental organizations, religious leaders and human rights lawyers—had already begun to address the problem of the nation's past. They said there could be no new, united South Africa without a commonly acknowledged history, and that this required honestly facing and dealing with the brutal oppression of the apartheid years.

PRECEDENTS for such an investigation—in postwar Germany or in Central and Latin America—offered more warnings than guidance. They showed that when cruelty becomes national policy, law alone is not enough. Nuremberg dispensed harsh retribution to the top echelon of Nazi butchers, but ignored their victims and allowed ordinary Germans to live in a state of denial. In Chile and Argentina the army and police made general confessions in exchange for blanket amnesties, which permitted the torturers and assassins to evade personal accountability. Their victims, like the mothers of the "disappeared ones," were again overlooked.

The temptation for the privileged class in South Africa was to believe de Klerk's claim that apartheid was a well-intentioned policy that had failed rather than an intrinsically evil program that had succeeded only too tragically. The majority of whites refused to acknowledge the systemic nature of the torture, maiming and assassinations to which individuals had been subjected for more than 30 years by the secret police. Their determined ignorance was aided by years of propaganda and by the fact that even in the worst years of oppression the courts did hold public inquests into the deaths of activists like Steve Biko—inquests that almost always cleared the perpetrators. In the words of Archbishop Desmond Tutu, "It's very difficult to wake up someone who is pretending to be asleep."

A further complication was that the political agreement hammered out at the constitutional talks had to be a delicate balance between victory and compromise. Apartheid may have been defeated, but its minions still dominated the police, army and civil service. Success in the constitutional negotiations depended to a large degree on making a deal with the previous regime, and Nuremberg-type trials were not an option if the country was to reach democratic elections without a coup or chaos.

Any successful attempt to address the past would need to both acknowledge the suffering of apartheid's victims and lead to national reconciliation. It had to steer a delicate course between those who cried "prosecute and punish" and those who demanded "forgive and forget." Negotiators managed to create a process that evokes the biblical paradigm of reconciliation, a process that proceeds according to this rubric: "It is necessary to both remember and judge—and forgive."

Perhaps the birth of the TRC was helped by a remarkable church conference held in Rustenburg in late 1990. Churches that had opposed apartheid, together with the Dutch Reformed Church that gave theological support to the ideology and the Pentecostals who had simply ignored it, released a common confession of sin, acknowledging that even those who had opposed the evil had failed to do enough. The Rustenburg Declaration was the first sign that healing in South Africa was to take an unconventional course.

The TRC's legal roots lie in legislation steered through Parliament by Justice Minister Dullah Omar, a Muslim member of the ANC who himself survived attempts by the security police to poison him. It was Omar who encouraged church and nongovernmental input and resisted all attempts by the previous rulers and his own party to weaken or politicize the process.

Selecting the truth commissioners was also a challenge. They had to be people of proven integrity and capable of impartiality, with a track record of commitment to human rights and the inner strength to cope with the emotional strain of the job. A balance of race, gender, region and vocational or professional background was also crucial.

Some 600 nominations were received from the public. The selection panel, which included a representative of each major political party, two ecumenical church leaders, a trade unionist and two human rights lawyers, picked 45 people to be publicly interviewed. Objections to any name were entertained from any source. A short list of 25 was laid before President Mandela, who consulted his bipartisan cabinet and made the final cut of 18. He appointed Archbishop Tutu as chair and Alex Boraine (an ex-president of the Methodist Church who went into opposition politics and later headed the Institute for Democratic Alternatives in South Africa) as vice-chair.

THE TRC has a number of unique features. First, it gives priority to victims rather than perpetrators. The Gross Human Rights Violations Committee hears the stories of victims across the land. In the words of Father Michael Lapsley, who was half-blinded and maimed by a security police parcel bomb, this committee must ensure that people's suffering is "heard, recognized and reverenced by the nation."

Scores of hearings have been held in city halls and rural community centers. The commission honors the victims by going to them rather than calling them to a central venue. Victims have been empowered by Khulumani ("speak out") groups of fellow victims and assisted by hundreds of volunteer statement-takers. All statements go to the commission's investigation unit. Those who give public evidence represent the range of abuses and types of victim of the apartheid years.

A second unique factor in the work of the TRC is that victims of all sides of the struggle participate. The TRC designers were determined that history would not be sanitized by the victorious side, and so those who suffered at the hands of the liberation forces are also invited to share their experiences. A story of secret police torture may be followed by a white farmer's story of how his wife and children were killed by an ANC land mine, or by an account of abuses and torture in one of the liberation movement's training camps. The scale of these abuses may be minuscule compared to that of apartheid's cruelty, but suffering is a universal language and these stories have touched the mainly black audiences as deeply as any others. They also send the important message that a morally justified struggle does not justify indiscriminate killing and deliberate brutality.

The Amnesty Committee, consisting of Supreme Court judges and lawyers, hears pleas for amnesty. The requirements for amnesty are clear: only individuals—not groups—may apply, there must be full disclosure, the abuses must have been perpetrated to further a political aim, and the principle of "proportionality" must apply, meaning that the degree of violation must bear some relation to the individuals' political goal in the context of that era. If, for instance, a group of young activists was assassinated by the security police, was it for merely distributing antigovernment pamphlets or was it for organizing armed resistance? The first case would fail the test of proportionality; the second, depending on the degree of violence and instability at the time, might not.

The obvious question in designing the Amnesty Committee was how to persuade perpetrators to step forward. What if a perpetrator did so, only to have the application rejected on grounds that it failed to meet these conditions? The Amnesty Committee has been strict in applying its conditions, and at least half the applications heard have been rejected. What would make people risk coming forward?

The TRC's response to this problem has been to balance the carrot and stick. If amnesty is granted, the slate is wiped clean. If not, then disclosures before the commission are not to be used in any subsequent court prosecution. Evidence would have to be independently sought by the attorney general. If the perpetrators didn't come forward by the cut-off date in May 1997, they would live the rest of their lives in fear of being hunted down or fingered by the evidence of a former colleague.

For months there was virtually no response, but as the May deadline loomed, 8,000 applications flooded in.

Vice-President Thabo Mbeki, probable successor to President Mandela, has applied for amnesty, together with the minister of defense in the new government. The actions which they intend to confess are not yet public, but they will be. The most notorious applications from the antiapartheid camp have come from extremist Pan Africanist Congress (PAC) cadres who murdered American exchange student Amy Biehl simply "because she was a white person in the black township that day," and the PAC killers responsible for the massacre of white worshipers in St. James Church in Cape Town.

Most applications, however, come from officers of the police hit squads, whose litany of horrors done in the name of the regime point the finger up the chain of command to the shadowy State Security Council, chaired first by President P. W. Botha and later by de Klerk, neither of whom has applied for amnesty.

A further unique feature of both committees is that all their hearings are public. Provision is made for closed hearings, but the commission has avoided this, which means that perpetrators have to face the individuals they tortured or the families of those they killed.

A THIRD COMMITTEE—on Reparations and Rehabilitation—has received less publicity. South Africa's battered economy, bled by years of apartheid's wars, pillaged by the corruption of the previous regime, and now struggling to overcome the effects of the disinvestment campaign, cannot afford large cash payouts to victims. Other methods of reparation must be fashioned, and the recommendations of this committee have not yet been forwarded to President Mandela.

Thus far victims' requests have been remarkably modest. One prominent victim says: "We have to recognize that our real reward is that we are now a free people." Most of all, the bereaved want the return and proper burial of their relatives' remains, or a memorial in their village, or a small scholarship for orphaned children. All agree that the most important thing is to know the truth. Backing these three TRC committees are research and investigation units. The commission has powers of search and subpoena but has mostly relied on persuasion.

Only time will determine the effectiveness of the TRC process. Its stated aims are to produce a record of the violations of the past and make recommendations to prevent them ever happening again; to acknowledge the suffering of the victims and assist in their rehabilitation; to offer amnesty to past perpetrators; and to facilitate the healing and reconciliation of the nation.

Certainly, South Africans are coming nearer to a common view of the recent past. When the emotional victims' hearings began, hardened whites dismissed them as the "Kleenex Commission" and angry denial was the order of the day. The absence of procedures such as cross-examination was decried. Why should these stories be believed?

But the cumulative effect of hundreds of accounts of horror and human pain has changed this mood. The sheer volume of similar experiences from every corner of the country, rather than accuracy of detail, has proved the veracity of the stories. Denial has given way to defensiveness, and then to the beginnings of what might be called corporate shame, which has deepened as the amnesty hearings have gained pace. Though only a small number of former security police have yet been heard, what has emerged is a horrific picture of deliberate state terrorism. The disclosures are ample proof that the victims' stories are not exaggerated.

Victims do seem to have been helped by telling their stories. Numbers of them have said that they now feel able to move forward with their lives. Most important has been the "reverencing" of their suffering. "Today," said an old black man, "the nation cried my tears with me."

THE ISSUE of amnesty has been more controversial. Some victims' families, including that of Steve Biko, have challenged (unsuccessfully) these provisions in South Africa's highest court. The new constitution guarantees due process and justice for all: amnesty, they say, denies them that justice. Why should those who suffered so much at the hands of the apartheid state be asked to make yet another sacrifice for the sake of the new South Africa? As state assassins have coldly rehearsed their brutalities before the Amnesty Committee, even those most committed to the reconciliation process have felt angry frustration that these men might walk free.

Nevertheless, distasteful as it may be to envisage these brutal men at liberty, most victims seem determined not to become obsessed by their previous tormentors. It is as if, in their disclosures, perpetrators have diminished themselves. The sheer banality of their evil, its moral bankruptcy, stands in glaring contrast to the nobility and courage of the victims. People are coming to see that even with amnesty, their tormentors are judged—that there is a difference between *impunity*, implying escape from accountability, and *amnesty*, which carries profound inward and social consequences.

Some have decried the absence of repentance in many amnesty applications. Apart from the fact that this is a further damning judgment on the distorted morality of these perpetrators, the legislation doesn't require repentance, only the truth. If it did, it would devalue those moments when apparently genuine repentance has been volunteered. In one case, a police officer who masterminded the butchering of a number of families in an attack on a rural village stood and faced his victims: "I can never undo what I have done," he said. "I have no right to ask your forgiveness, but I ask that you will allow me to spend my life helping you to rebuild your village and put your lives together." It is in moments like these that anger at the unrepentant is superseded by a glimpse of something more: out of the horrors of the past, the TRC makes space for grace, and the potential for newness in South Africa shines through.

This potentiality is undoubtedly aided by the person who is chair, Desmond Tutu. He knows the TRC exists not only that the nation should know more, but that it should *feel* more. He has wept with the victims and marked every moment of repentance and forgiveness with awe. Where a jurist would have been logical, he has not hesitated to be theological. He has sensed when to lead the audience in a hymn to help a victim recover composure, and when to call them all to prayer. While some secularists have criticized the God-language he has used, Tutu knows that while the new South Africa may be a secular state, South Africans are not a secular people. He knows that the nation is seeking a deeper healing than mere law can provide.

Rather than denying justice, the TRC process may be exploring justice in a larger, more magnanimous form— what Charles Villa-Vicencio calls restorative justice as opposed to retributive justice. Perhaps this unique exercise points beyond conventional retribution into a realm where justice and mercy coalesce and both victim and perpetrator must know pain if healing is to happen. It is an area more consistent with Calvary than the courtroom. It is the place where the guilty discover the pain of forgiveness because the innocent are willing to bear the greater pain of forgiving.

The TRC must complete its hearings by the end of this year and hand its final report to President Mandela in early 1998. The commissioners will have done all that could fairly be asked of them. But even with the massive exposure given to the hearings, more will be needed for the necessary spirit of repentance to penetrate all levels of the previous ruling class.

Here is a historic challenge to the church. Some church leaders played a significant prophetic role in resisting apartheid, but the majority of the clergy and members failed. Now they can best express their declared repentance by grasping the evangelical and pastoral task of encouraging an ongoing, local process of story-sharing, forgiveness and reconciliation in every congregation, bringing the good news of repentance and healing to those who enjoyed the fruits of apartheid and those who still need their pain to be heard. If they are willing to do this, if the clergy find the courage most of them mislaid during the apartheid years, if they resist the pressure of amnesia themselves, South Africa's experiment in the healing of its memories may truly enter the soul of the nation.

Perhaps other nations with wounded histories may find here a model for hope. As the international community comes to recognize that there is no peace without confronting the hurts of history and without the healing of national and ethnic memories, one nation's imperfect attempt to do so may inspire ways in which God could bring newness in these lands too.

Peter Storey, a columnist for the Sunday Independent, *is past president of the Methodist Church of South Africa and of the South African Council of Churches. He was a member of the selection committee for the Truth and Reconciliation Commission.*

Hispanic/Latino Americans

The following collection of materials on Hispanic/Latino Americans is a composite of findings about ethnicities. The clustering of these ethnicities and nationalities, as well as their relationship to the Spanish and Portuguese languages, seems to be sufficient evidence of the commonalities that constitute the shared expression of this complex of memory and contemporary politics. Yet the use of "Hispanic" and "Latino" that differentiates them from Anglo-American foundations, and their social expression as they search for a cultural and political terrain, are but the surface of the process of intergroup dynamics in the United States.

The articles in this unit propose angles of vision that enable us to view the process of accommodation and change that is articulated in political practice, scholarship, advocacy, and art. The issues presented provocatively shift traditional perspectives from the eastern and Midwestern mindset toward the western and southwestern analysis of the immigration to the United States.

The Immigration Act of 1965 induced a process not unlike the period of large-scale eastern and southern European immigration between 1880 and 1924. This immigration includes scores of various ethnic groups. Cultural/geographic descriptions are not the clearest form of ethnic identity.

Hispanic/Latino Americans are not a single ethnic group. The designation of various ethnic populations whose ancestry is derived from Portuguese- and Spanish-speaking countries by the words "Latino" and "Hispanic" is a relatively recent phenomenon in the United States. The cultural, economic, and political differences and similarities of various Hispanic/Latino communities, as well as the wide dispersal of these communities, suggest the need for care in generalization about Latino and Hispanic American populations.

The realities of these groups—whether they are political refugees, migrant workers, descendants of residents settled prior to territorial incorporation into the United States, long-settled immigrants, recent arrivals, or the children and grandchildren of immigrants—present interesting and varied patterns of enclave community, assimilation, and acculturation as well as isolation and marginalization. Hispanic/Latino American linkages to other Latin countries, the future of their emerging political power, and their contributions to cultural and economic change within the United States are interesting facets of the Hispanic/Latino American experience.

The Hispanic/Latino experience is a composite of groups seeking unity while interacting with the larger arena of ethnic groups that constitute American society.

Convergent issues that bridge differences, as well as those that support ideological and strategic differences, bode a future of both cooperation and conflict.

What issues bind Hispanic or Latino groups together? What values cause cleavages among these populations? What does bilingualism mean? Is bilingualism a freedom-of-speech issue? Is bilingualism a concern of non-Spanish-speaking persons in the United States? What are the implications of establishing an official public language policy?

Competition and conflict over mobility into mainstream leadership positions are aspects of American society that may be exacerbated by the misuse of ethnic indicators. Nonetheless, indicators of social cohesion and traditional family bonds are apparently noncompetitive and nonconflictual dimensions of robust ethnic experiences. Thus, fears that Hispanic/Latino Americans may not relish competitive pressures are assuaged by the capacities of family and community to temper the cost of any such failure. This complex dynamic of personal and group interaction is a fascinating and fruitful topic for a society seeking competitiveness and stronger community bonds. Cast in this fashion, the American dilemma takes on a new and compelling relevance.

Looking Ahead: Challenge Questions

How does attention to historical background and its expression in current culture promote both understanding and tolerance?

When do ethnic and racial issues foster understanding? Tolerance? The appreciation of the particular?

What strengths and weaknesses do strong bonds of ethnic communities possess?

In what respects is Hispanic/Latino American culture becoming part of mainstream American culture?

To what do you attribute the popularity of Mexican, Italian, and Chinese foods in the marketplace?

Specific Hispanics

SUMMARY Los Angeles, New York, Miami, Chicago, and Houston are well-known Hispanic markets. But just below the big five are dozens of smaller Hispanic centers. This first-ever look at 12 Hispanic groups reveals the top towns for Colombians, Brazilians, and others. The rapid growth of specific Hispanic groups is destined to attract attention from marketers.

Morton Winsberg

Morton Winsberg is professor of geography at Florida State University in Tallahassee.

Most marketers are familiar with the three biggest Hispanic-American groups. Since the U.S. census first counted Hispanics in 1970, those who identify Mexico, Puerto Rico, and Cuba as their country of origin have comprised about three-fourths of the total U.S. Hispanic population. Hispanics from other Latin-American nations and cultures are less well-understood, but they constitute one-quarter of an estimated $170 billion consumer market. And because Hispanics of all kinds often live together in small areas, each country of origin can form a visible and desirable target market.

Among all Hispanics, the share of Mexicans has fallen from 62 percent of all U.S. Hispanics in 1970 to 61 percent in 1990.

The Puerto Rican and Cuban shares have remained at about 12 percent and 5 percent, respectively. Hispanic Americans who don't have origins in these three countries are a small share of the nation's total Hispanic population, but they have been growing. Their numbers grew by slightly more than 2 million between 1970 and 1990. Immigrants of the new wave have been fleeing civil wars in Nicaragua, El Salvador, Guatemala, and Colombia. Others come for jobs or to rejoin family members already here.

The 1970 and 1980 censuses identified just four categories of Hispanics: Mexican, Puerto Rican, Cuban, and "other." The 1990 census provides much more detailed information, identifying 12 nations of Hispanic origin, as well as "other" Central Americans and "other" South Americans. These data provide the first opportunity to understand where specific Hispanic groups live.

Many of the smaller Hispanic subgroups never show up on marketers' computer screens. Language barriers and the lack of large ethnic neighborhoods can make it hard to reach them with specially designed messages. Also, many Hispanic immigrants do not plan to become U.S.

> **Immigrants have always settled in America's largest cities, and today's immigrants are not much different.**

citizens or permanent residents. But rapid growth will inevitably lead more businesses to target Hispanic diversity. In ten years, America's Little Havanas will get a lot bigger.

BELOW THE BIG FIVE

Immigrants have always settled in America's largest cities, and today's immigrants are not much different. Six of the 12 Hispanic subgroups identified in the 1990 census have more than 80 percent of their populations in the nation's 20 largest cities, and 3 others have between 70 and 79 percent.

Mexican Americans are the only exception to the urban rule, because many of their ancestors never immigrated. Many Mexicans became U.S. citizens in the 19th century following the acquisition of Mexican territory by the United States. Almost all of this land was and still is rural or small cities. Many Mexicans who immigrated to the U.S. in recent years have settled in these same southwestern states. Here they normally reside in cities both large and small, as well as in rural areas.

Hispanics, like immigrants who came earlier, tend to concentrate in one or two major urban areas. New York City and Los Angeles early became a popular destination for Hispanics, but more recently, many have chosen Miami, Washington, D.C., and San Francisco. An example of an unusually high concentration of a Hispanic group in one city is the 77 percent concentration of people of Dominican origin in the New York urbanized area. Greater New York also has 60 percent of the nation's Ecuadorians and 44 percent of Puerto Ricans. Los Angeles has 49 percent of the nation's Guatemalans and 47 percent of its Salvadoreans. Miami is home to 53 percent of Cuban Americans.

Several U.S. places have Hispanic populations that rival or even surpass the largest cities in their countries of origin. New York's Puerto Rican population is now more than double that of San Juan. New York also has the second-largest urban population of Dominicans in the world, and the third-largest Ecuadorian population. The Mexican, Salvadorean, and Guatemalan populations of urban Los Angeles are surpassed only by those of their respective capitals: Mexico City, San Salvador, and Guatemala City.

Eighteen percent of all Hispanic Ameri-

> **The most exotic place where Mexicans cluster may be Bay City-Saginaw, Michigan.**

cans live in Los Angeles, and 12 percent live in New York. These two urban areas rank among the top-5 for 11 of the 12 Hispanic groups. Miami is on the top-5 list for 9 Hispanic groups, Washington, D.C., for 6, San Francisco for 5, and Houston and Chicago for 4.

The census also reveals many smaller areas with large and growing populations of specific Hispanics. For example, San Antonio and San Diego have the fourth- and fifth-largest Mexican-American communities in the nation, and Philadelphia has the third-largest Puerto Rican population. Tampa and Fort Lauderdale have the fourth- and fifth-largest concentrations of Cubans, and the Massachusetts areas of Boston and Lawrence have the third- and fourth-largest Dominican groups.

Chicago is the only midwestern urban area to come up on any of the top-5 lists, but it comes up a lot. Chicago has the country's second-largest Puerto Rican population, the second-largest Mexican population, and the third-largest Guatemalan and Ecuadorian populations. As a whole, Chicago has the fourth-largest Hispanic population of any urban area, at 4 percent of the national total.

TWELVE HISPANIC GROUPS

Laredo, Texas, is not big as urban areas go, with 99,258 people in 1990. But 94 percent of Laredo residents are Hispanic, and the overwhelming majority are of Mexican origin. The census count of Hispanics, also mainly Mexican, is 90 percent in Brownsville and 83 percent in McAllen, two other Texas border towns. Several border towns in other states have equally high shares of Mexican Americans.

Perhaps the most exotic place where Mexicans congregate in large numbers is in the Bay City-Saginaw metropolitan area in Michigan. Mexicans first came to Bay City-Saginaw to work on the local cu-

cumber farms. The descendants of these farm laborers now hold urban jobs, many in the local foundries.

Puerto Ricans began immigrating to the U.S. after World War II, and now they are a significant presence in the industrial cities of New York and southern New England. When older residents of these cities had achieved middle-class status and moved to the suburbs, they left behind entry-level jobs in manufacturing and service, and low-cost housing. The Puerto Ricans who took those jobs established the barrios of New York City.

While less affluent Puerto Ricans came to the U.S. for jobs, many middle-class Cubans fled their native country for political reasons. Cubans soon became closely identified with southeastern Florida, but now they are found in several other Florida towns. In the university towns of Gainesville and Tallahassee, for example, many second-generation Cuban Americans live as students.

Dominicans are a major Hispanic force in New York City and several New England industrial towns. They are only 2 percent of the nation's 1990 Hispanic population, but they are 15 percent of Hispanics in New York, 22 percent in Providence, and 35 percent in Lawrence, Massachusetts. Dominicans are flocking to the Northeast for the same reason Puerto Ricans did several decades ago: jobs. Hondurans and Nicaraguans, who have also immigrated largely for economic reasons, are settling in more bilingual areas on the Gulf of Mexico.

Hondurans are most numerous in New York, Los Angeles, and Miami, and Nicaraguans are most common in Miami, Los Angeles, and San Francisco. But both groups are dwarfed by the enormous numbers of other Hispanics in these large urban areas, so their largest concentrations emerge in unexpected places. Although Hondurans are less than 1 percent of the nation's Hispanic population, they are 20 percent of Hispanics in New Orleans. Nicaraguans are also well-represented among New Orleans Hispanics, and they are visible in nearby Baton Rouge and Port Arthur. Salvadoreans are just 3 percent of the

TWELVE FLAGS

Hispanics of all types cluster in New York a
Central Americans in San Francisco, Colomb

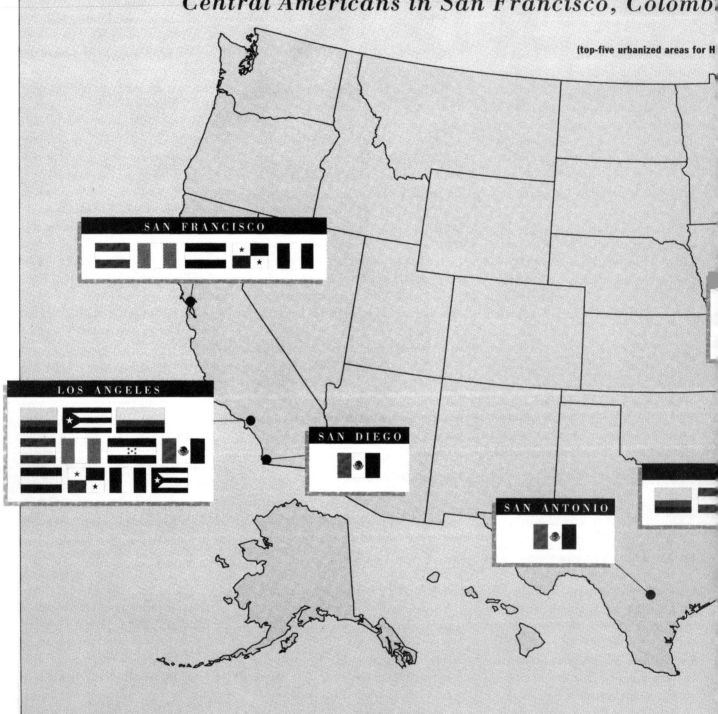

(top-five urbanized areas for H

SAN FRANCISCO

LOS ANGELES

SAN DIEGO

SAN ANTONIO

OVER AMERICA

*l Los Angeles. But you can also find lots of
ns in Chicago, and Peruvians in Washington.*

ics by country of origin, 1990)

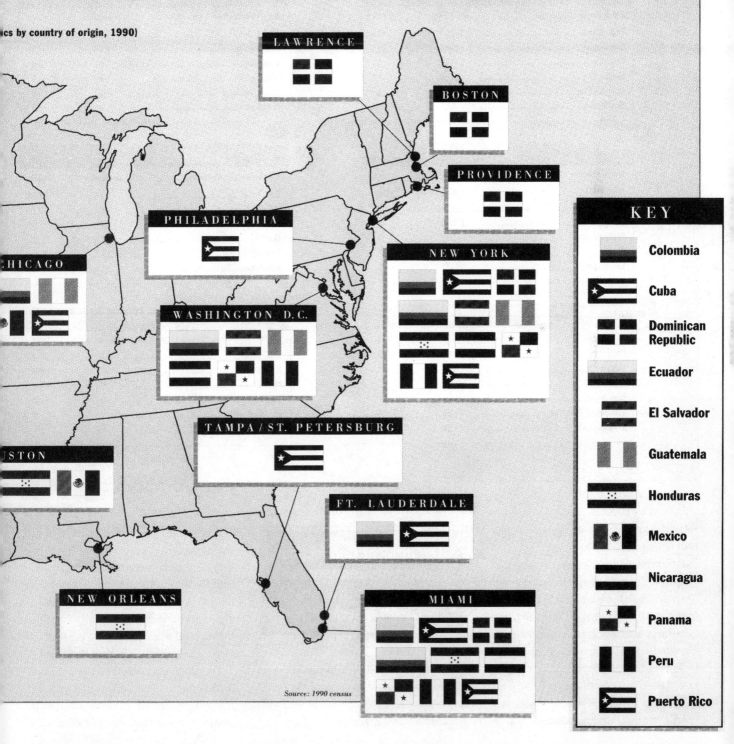

LAWRENCE

BOSTON

PROVIDENCE

PHILADELPHIA

CHICAGO

NEW YORK

WASHINGTON D.C.

TAMPA/ST. PETERSBURG

STON

FT. LAUDERDALE

NEW ORLEANS

MIAMI

Source: 1990 census

KEY

	Colombia
	Cuba
	Dominican Republic
	Ecuador
	El Salvador
	Guatemala
	Honduras
	Mexico
	Nicaragua
	Panama
	Peru
	Puerto Rico

Little Quitos and Little

Mexico

top-five urbanized areas	population	share
U.S. total	13,393	100%
Los Angeles	3,066	23
Chicago	538	4
Houston	528	4
San Antonio	524	4
San Diego	414	3

El Salvador

top-five urbanized areas	population	share
U.S. total	565	100%
Los Angeles	265	47
New York	62	11
Washington, DC	52	9
San Francisco	43	8
Houston	39	7

Puerto Rico

top-five urbanized areas	population	share
U.S. total	2,652	100%
New York	1,178	44
Chicago	1,464	6
Philadelphia	107	4
Miami	68	3
Los Angeles	51	2

Dominican Republic

top-five urbanized areas	population	share
U.S. total	520	100%
New York	403	77
Miami	23	5
Boston	16	3
Lawrence, MA	12	2
Providence, RI	9	2

Cuba

top-five urbanized areas	population	share
U.S. total	1,053	100%
Miami	559	53
New York	154	15
Los Angeles	55	5
Tampa-St. Petersburg	32	3
Ft. Lauderdale	24	2

Colombia

top-five urbanized areas	population	share
U.S. total	379	100%
New York	152	40
Miami	53	14
Los Angeles	27	7
Ft. Lauderdale	12	3
Houston	10	3

nation's Hispanic population, but 25 percent of Hispanics in Washington, D.C.

Panamanians are perhaps the most geographically diverse of any Hispanic group. They are disproportionately represented in the local Hispanic population in towns near large military installations such as Fayetteville, North Carolina (Fort Bragg); Columbus, Georgia (Fort Benning); Clarksville, Tennessee (Fort Campbell); Killeen, Texas (Fort Hood); Seaside, California (Fort Ord); and naval installations in Nor-

> **The affluent Connecticut town of Stamford is particularly attractive to South Americans.**

folk, Virginia; and Tacoma, Washington. Many who identified their ethnic origin as Panamanian in the 1990 census were military personnel once stationed in the former Panama Canal Zone.

People of South-American origin began moving in large numbers from New York City or coming directly from their homelands to coastal Connecticut towns during the 1980s, attracted to a growing number of service jobs that were not being filled by the local population. Housing was also more affordable than in New York City.

The affluent Connecticut town of Stamford is particularly attractive to South Americans. Its Hispanic population includes large proportions of Colombians,

San Juans

Mexicans are by far the largest Hispanic-American group, but 77 percent of Dominican Americans live in one urban area.

(top-five urbanized areas for Hispanics by country of origin, population in thousands; and share of segment, 1990)

Guatemala

top-five urbanized areas	population	share
U.S. total	269	100%
Los Angeles	133	49
New York	27	10
Chicago	15	6
San Francisco	11	4
Washington, DC	9	4

Peru

top-five urbanized areas	population	share
U.S. total	175	100%
New York	54	31
Los Angeles	27	15
Miami	16	9
Washington, DC	11	7
San Francisco	9	5

Nicaragua

top-five urbanized areas	population	share
U.S. total	203	100%
Miami	74	37
Los Angeles	37	18
San Francisco	25	12
New York	14	7
Washington, DC	8	4

Honduras

top-five urbanized areas	population	share
U.S. total	131	100%
New York	33	25
Los Angeles	24	18
Miami	18	14
New Orleans	9	7
Houston	5	4

Ecuador

top-five urbanized areas	population	share
U.S. total	191	100%
New York	115	60
Los Angeles	21	11
Chicago	8	4
Miami	8	4
Washington, DC	5	3

Panama

top-five urbanized areas	population	share
U.S. total	92	100%
New York	27	29
Miami	7	7
Los Angeles	6	6
Washington, DC	4	4
San Francisco	2	2

Source: 1990 census

Ecuadorians, and Peruvians. In nearby Norwalk, Colombians are 20 percent of the city's Hispanic population.

MARKETING ATTENTION

So far, few U.S. corporations have paid attention to the special needs of "other" Hispanics. Mainstream marketers "are resistant enough to work with Hispanic marketing in total," says Nilda Anderson, president of Hispanic Market Research in New York City. "They are not going to do focused marketing."

One problem is a lack of marketing information. Recent census results and private research have improved the data on smaller Hispanic groups, says Gary Berman, president of Market Segment Research in Coral Gables, Florida, but few data were available until the 1990s.

Another problem is that Hispanic immigrants are less likely than previous generations of immigrants to live in ethnic-specific neighborhoods. In Miami, for example, newly arrived Cubans are often neighbors to Nicaraguans, and Nicaraguans may live next to Venezuelans. The city's celebrated "Little Havana" neighborhood is defined by its Cuban-owned businesses, but census data do not show an extreme overrepresentation of Cubans living in the area adjacent to those businesses.

Whatever their nation of origin, most Hispanic immigrants quickly acquire two basic American tools: a car and a telephone. Miami's Cubans may go to Little Havana to shop, socialize, and eat, just as Miami's Nicaraguans go to the Sweetwater district to buy copies of *El Diario La Prensa* and loaves of *pan Nicaraguense*. But when the trip is over, they return to homes scattered all over the city.

Another problem is that many Hispanic immigrants are not interested in owning a home, buying a new car, or otherwise participating as full-fledged American consumers. New York City is home to about 10,000 foreign-born Brazilians, for example. But "most Brazilians are in New York only to save money for the return to Brazil," says Maxine L. Margolis, an anthropology professor at the University of Florida in Gainesville. In her book *Little Brazil*, Margolis tells the story of a local television news program called "TV Bra-

> **Whatever their nation of origin, most Hispanic immigrants quickly acquire two basic American tools: a car and a telephone.**

sil." When it began, Brazilian-owned businesses were eager to sponsor it. But the ads failed to attract new customers, she says, because many Brazilians spend only what they must and save everything else.

Perhaps the biggest problem is the size of "other" Hispanic groups. "TV Brasil's" producers tried to persuade the Coors Brewing Company to advertise by claiming that 200,000 Brazilians lived in New York City, according to Margolis. But Coors turned them down anyway, claiming that the market was too small.

These obstacles may scare most businesses away, but the few that do target "other" Hispanics are rewarded with a growing source of loyal customers. As the airline of Colombia, Avianca focuses its U.S. advertising on Colombians, says Alberto Gil, a marketing analyst for the airline in New York City. The city's five boroughs are home to about 86,000 Colombians, according to demographer Frank Vardy at the Department of City Planning.

Avianca advertising runs primarily on Spanish-language television, radio, and in newspapers circulated in New York. "We don't care so much about whether the [medium] has a high rating for all Hispanics, but for Colombians," he says. The airline gauges Colombians' interests by asking its customers to name their favorite publications, radio stations, and TV shows.

The airline also focuses on a 20-block area in North Queens that is the geographic heart of Colombian settlement in New York City. Travel agents in that neighborhood receive special attention from the airline, says Gil. "We are a sym-

bol for [Colombians]," he says. "We are Colombia in the United States."

Colombian politicians are well aware that New York-based expatriates form a powerful voting bloc. In past elections, polling places for Colombian elections have been established at the Colombian consulate and in Queens, says Javier Castano, a reporter for the Spanish-language newspaper *El Diario*. Colombian presidential candidates occasionally travel to New York City at election time, and politicians from many countries buy advertising in *El Diario* and other New York media.

Immigrants follow well-worn paths when they come to the United States, and these paths do not change rapidly. If immigration from Latin America continues at its current rapid pace, America's Little Havanas, Little San Juans, and other Hispanic enclaves will eventually grow to the point where targeting "other" Hispanics makes sense to mainstream marketers. Investing small amounts of time and money on specific Hispanics today could yield big payoffs tomorrow.

—*Additional reporting by Patricia Braus*

Behind the Numbers This study examines 1990 Hispanic populations in urbanized areas, defined by the U.S. Census Bureau as "one or more places (central place) and the adjacent densely settled surrounding territory (urban fringe) that together have a minimum of 50,000 persons." In 1990, the census identified 397 urbanized areas. For more information, contact the author at (904) 644-8377 or the Census Bureau at (301) 763-4040.

There's More to Racism Than Black and White

Elizabeth Martinez

The small brown woman with a serious face stood on the curb almost motionless as thousands of people marched by her in a line that stretched 22 blocks. Amidst huge banners and hundreds of big colorful signs, her hand-lettered words on corrugated paper had a haunting simplicity:

> *We were here*
> *We are here*
> *This was our land*
> *is still our land*
> *Stand up for your rights.*

It was August 25, 1990, in Los Angeles and people—mostly Mexican American—were marking the 20th anniversary of the Chicano Moratorium against the war in Vietnam. We assembled at the same park as we did two decades ago and marched the same route to the same park for a rally. As the *señora*'s sign indicated, the struggle goes on and in many ways conditions have worsened for Latinos—La Raza-over the past 20 years. At the same time, the Moratorium reflected important, complex, and often positive new developments. Finally, for the U.S. left in general, the event carried a message that cannot be ignored.

On August 29, 1970, some 20,000 mostly Chicano people came from all over the country to protest the Vietnam war and especially the fact that our casualties were running at a much higher rate than the Mexican American proportion of the U.S. population. As the rally began around midday, a minor scuffle near the edge of the park served as the excuse for a massive police attack. Tear gas filled the air as 500 officers charged the youth, families, and elderly who had been sitting on the grass and drove out the panicked crowd. I remember running with a dozen other people into a nearby house to get away from the tear gas. Friends and relatives were scattered; my daughter, for one, could not be located until ten o'clock in the evening.

Three Chicanos died that day as a result of the police repression: Angel Diaz, Ruben Salazar and Lynn Ward. The best-known was journalist Salazar, who had been investigating and writing a series of articles on recent cases of police brutality for *The Los Angeles Times;* he had reportedly become radicalized in the process. After the attack in the park he had stopped with a friend at the nearby Silver Dollar cafe and was sitting at the bar. From the sidewalk outside, a sheriff's deputy fired a 10-inch tear-gas projectile into the cafe, which almost blew off Salazar's head. Later claiming they had received reports of an armed man in the bar, police said that before firing they had told all occupants to leave; witnesses said they heard no such warning.

That evening the sky over East Los Angeles turned black with smoke as protesters selectively torched many buildings. Sirens wailed for hours; barricades everywhere made "East Los," as it's called, look like an occupied territory. In the weeks that followed, the District Attorney refused to prosecute Salazar's killer despite an inquest damaging to the Sheriff's Department. Protesters demonstrated over the next few months; at one event, when officers again fired on the crowd with tear gas, some people hurled objects at them. Police killed one man, an Austrian student who looked Chicano, and left 19 wounded by buck-shot.

At this year's Moratorium police seemed to keep a relatively low profile. News reports said 6,000 people came, mostly from the Southwest with a sprinkling of Chicago and New York participants. It looked like more, and it certainly felt like more because of the high spirits and energized mood. Was it yet another Day of Nostalgia in the current era of 1960s anniversaries? Yes, but mostly no.

Moratorium organizers had said the day's goal was not just to commemorate a historic event but to protest conditions now facing the overwhelming majority of La Raza. The excellent, thoughtful tabloid *L.A. Moratorium,* published by the organizing committee, pointed to the elimination of Chicano studies, attacks on bilingual education, "English Only" laws, terror from police and immigration officers, attacks by the Klan and skinheads, youth killing one another, the dumping of toxic wastes in Raza communities, and CIA/FBI imported drugs. (One might add a recent statistic: the infant mortality rate among Latinos in Los Angeles County has risen by over a third since 1987.) At the same time, the tabloid said, "the ability of the Movement to defend its people's rights is extremely limited or nonexistent" and the lack of organization also prevents effective support for Native American struggles and against U.S. colonialism in Central America.

The rally program sustained these themes. Although activists with long histories of struggle were featured, like Dolores Huerta of the United Farm Workers and Professor Rudy Acuña, they never lingered on "the wonderful 1960s." This was no mere pep rally. Instead they and other speakers talked eloquently about domestic issues as well as U.S. militarism and intervention, democracy in Mexico, and opposition to the 1992 quincentenary to "celebrate" Christopher Columbus's arrival in 1492.

What about lessons to be drawn from the past, or a long-range strategy and developed vision for the future? The rally itself did not go much beyond calling for greater activism. Still something was being born, something new and very young was in the air.

About half the Moratorium participants seemed to be under 25, including many college as well as high school students. A major force in mobilizing the youth was MEChA (Movimiento Estudiantil Chicano de Aztlan, the Chicano Student Movement of Aztlan). Born in 1969, its strength ebbed in later years. By 1985, according to one MEChA leader, much of the organization was splintered by ideological debate; activism revived in response to worsening socioeconomic conditions. Today divisions still exist on such issues as a strictly Chicano vs. broader Latino focus, and the merits of affiliation with nonstudent, left organizations. Still, MEChA has lasted far longer than most student groups and retains a certain moral authority.

Many of the Chicano youth marching on August 25 were not even born when the first Moratorium took place, and most schools teach little about the extraordinary struggles of the 1960s worldwide. At its best MEChA helps to fill this void, serving as a transmission belt from past to present, with faculty members who were 1960s activists sometimes providing continuity as well as inspiration. The youth on the march seemed to be learning their history and respecting it. You could feel a thrill ripple through the crowd when one speaker said: "20 years ago they tried to destroy the Chicano movement. 20 years later we are here to tell them that they failed!"

All that week and through September, events related to the Moratorium took place in Los Angeles: several days of extensive TV coverage; a photo exhibit; two plays, one of them a re-enactment of the killing of Salazar staged in the Silver Dollar itself and another called "August 29." A major exhibition, "Chicano Art: Resistance and Affirmation" (CARA) from 1965–1985 opened at the University of California, with many special cultural events scheduled around it.

"We want to pass on our history," said one student at the Moratorium and the spirit that visibly animated the youth that day was indeed nationalist. Dozens of times the 1960s cry of "Chicano Power!" rang out. But the words seem to have a different meaning today— more concrete and more complex than yesterday's generalized rhetoric.

"'Chicano Power' is different now because people realize we will be the majority in a few years," said a young Chicana from Fresno. "The next step will be to turn those numbers into political and economic power, to take over our communities. For example, in the valley in Fresno the people are 80 percent Chicano and Mexicano. The mayor and the school board should reflect that. When it happens, it will be a real affirmation of Chicano Power."

A second meaning of Chicano Power today lies in its implicit rejection of "Hispanic" as a label imposed by the dominant society and adopted by many Latinos themselves—specially those sometimes called Chuppies or Buppies—Chicano or Brown yuppies. "Hispanic" is a fundamentally racist term which obliterates the Native American and African American heritages of La Raza in favor of the white European component from Spain. The August 25 march countered this distortion with a contingent of Native Americans at the head of the line. Others carried signs rejecting "Hispanic" and affirming "Chicano."

That message also came across while people assembled to march, when the group Culture Clash performed and "Slick Rick" did his bilingual Chicano rap songs. He chided: "Chicanos who are wearing blue contact lenses today—forget it, you're Chicano. Don't try to be white, they do it better!" And: "The 1980s were supposed to be the 'Decade of the Hispanic' but that turned out to be an event sponsored by Coors beer." In other words: the concept "Hispanic" emerged as a marketing tool to conveniently target all Spanish-speaking cultures at once.

The Chicano/Latino/Raza versus "Hispanic" debate is about more than terminology or even racism. It also concerns values, politics, and class: the Raza tradition of collectivity and sharing versus the individualism and consumerism that intensified during the 1980s. In that decade, for example, we saw one "Hispanic" art exhibit after another, often with corporate sponsors and usually apolitical in content. But the new exhibit, CARA, is consciously entitled "Chicano Art" and is not by chance much more political than its predecessors. CARA organizers also say they sought to avoid commercialization and cultural homogeneity. Further, the show was organized by means of an unusually collective approach—regional committees rather than a single curator—so as to promote the empowerment of community people rather than professional elitism.

In these and other ways, the nationalism that ran strong on August 25 has an implicitly or overtly anticapitalist thrust. Any denunciation of capitalist exploitation brought strong cheers from the rally audience. The presence of organized labor at this year's Moratorium also seemed stronger than 20 years ago, in part because of militant struggles that have been recently waged by workers like Janitors for Justice. Mostly Central Americans, they have attracted wide support from many groups with their courage, determination, imaginative tactics – and by winning a major victory. The extremely brutal police attack on their peaceful demonstration at Century Plaza earlier this year further generated solidarity.

A NEW INTERNATIONALISM

Above all, the Moratorium emanated an internationalism much stronger than 20 years ago. Some of us had wondered if it would address current U.S. policy in the Persian Gulf. We need not have doubted. Signs everywhere, and not just from predominantly white left formations, called for an end to U.S. militarism in the Middle East. "The oil belongs to the people, not Texaco!" got some of the loudest applause at the rally.

There was also a much stronger Mexican presence than in 1970, which speaks to the ever-growing Mexican population. Their numbers are rising so rapidly that formerly Chicano neighborhoods are now Mexican (the different terms here meaning, simplistically, born in the U.S. as opposed to born in Mexico). A well-known Mexican socialist leader, Heberto Castillo of the Democratic Revolutionary Party (PRD), spoke eloquently at the rally, stressing the crucial links between today's struggle for democracy in Mexico and action by Mexican-origin people here.

In another kind of internationalism not seen 20 years ago, a group from the Nation of Islam attended the rally and one of the best-received speakers came from the African People's Socialist Party. This spirit may be drawing encouragement from cross-cultural developments like the black-inspired Chicano rap music from Culture Clash, Kid Frost's *Hispanic Causing Panic* album, and other singers. Finally, a small Korean contingent marched in the Moratorium – a welcome sight.

The National Chicano Moratorium Committee, which worked on the event for many months at the national and regional levels, deserves much credit for its success. "The most democratic mobilization effort in my memory," Professor Rudy Acuña called it, despite having disagreed with members at times. Its commitment to combat sectarianism paid off well, judging by the wide variety of politics represented. The banner of the Mothers of East Los Angeles, a strong community organization, could be seen not far from a small sign proclaiming "Mao – hoy mas que nunca" (Mao, today more than ever). Although the "Principles of Unity" limited membership on the organizing committee to Chicano/Mexican organizations, anti-white feeling seemed absent.

When it came to gender roles, the committee showed little progress over 20 years ago. Women held the posts of – guess what – secretary and treasurer, plus one youth coordinator. All four media liaisons were men. Rally speakers had a better balance: far from equal but solid, and women's participation in the movement was not trivialized by tokenistic recognition. In addition to Dolores Huerta, Nita Gonzales of Denver (longtime community organizer and daughter of "Corky" Gonzales) spoke as did Juana Gutierrez of the Mothers of East Los Angeles and Patricia Marin of Orange County MEChA.

On the march itself you could see a Chicana women's consciousness that was absent 20 years ago. Signs like "Vote Chicano – Vote Chicana" may not have been numerous, but they wouldn't have been seen at all before. Activist women agree it's time for the decline of the "CPMG," a species identified by several Chicanas talking in the Silver Dollar after the Moratorium: the Chicano Person Movement Guy. The generation of women now in college may bring major changes. In recent years, for example, it has not been unusual to find a woman heading a MEChA chapter or women outnumbering the men on a MEChA board. A future Moratorium organizing committee should find more women with experience, in their 30s and 40s like much of the current committee, and ready at least to run more of the show.

HOW SHALL WHITE LEFTISTS RELATE TO A NEW MOVIMIENTO?

Some of us felt a new Chicano movement being born last Aug. 25. The day made it clear that sooner or later this will happen – a Latino movement, I would hope. An old question then arises: how will leftists relate to it? Past experience has been so poor that for many Latinos – not to mention other people of color in the U.S. – "the left" has often come to mean white folks. In the next era, will so much of the Anglo left continue to minimize the Mexican American struggle?

At the heart of the problem is a tendency to see race relations and the struggle against racism primarily or exclusively in terms of black and white. Every week articles or books appear that claim to address racial issues like Affirmative Action but contain not a single word about any population except the African American. In the histories of the 1960s by white authors, although the treatment of black struggle is never adequate one can at least find Martin Luther King, the Black Panthers, and a few other references. But in 25 such books reviewed by this writer, the massive Chicano movement of the 1960s and early 1970s might never have happened. (See "That Old White (Male) Magic," Z, July–August 1989.)

To criticize this blindness is not to deny the primacy of African American struggle: the genocidal nature of enslavement, the constant resistance by slaves, the "Second Reconstruction" of the 1960s and its extraordinary leaders, and today's destruction of black youth if not black males in general. Also, African Americans up to now remain the largest population of color in this country. I began my own political work in the black civil rights movement because it was so obviously on the cutting edge of history for all people of color, for the whole society. Many white progressives also gave support, sometimes even their lives, to that movement. But somehow, while combating the symbolism of blacks as "the Invisible Man" they overlooked new "invisible" men—and women—of other colors.

One apparent exception to the left's myopia about Mexican Americans surfaced during the party-building movement of the 1970s. A flurry of Marxist-Leninist position papers about Chicanos descended, telling us that we were a nation and should secede from the U.S. (wha?), or that we were a national minority whose goal should be regional autonomy (wha?), or that we were nothing more than part of the U.S. working-class (wha?), or that we were a racial but not a national minority (hunh?!). Those we called the Alphabet Soup came to visit Chicano groups in New Mexico at different times. Their organizational positions were unrelated to the realities we knew, concoctions that seemed to have sprung full-grown from their heads, nourished by theory alone. This could only leave us feeling a lack of respect for our history, culture, and struggle.

Earlier the Communist Party had done better and provided courageous leadership to labor struggles involving Mexican or Chicano workers. But here too Raza who were in the party have their stories to tell of an alienating chauvinism. All in all, left organizations too often use that demeaning stock phrase: "African Americans and other minorities" or "African Americans and other Third World people" or "African Americans and other people of color."

Even when Anglo leftists do study Raza culture and history, the problem remains of demonstrating support for Latinos abroad rather than at home. Many Anglos have worked hard on solidarity with Central America and against U.S. intervention. They learn Spanish, embrace the culture, pass hard and often dangerous time in Central American countries. But, except for the issue of refugees and sanctuary, this has rarely translated into support for domestic struggles by Latino peoples—for example, Chicanos/Mexicans or Puerto Ricans in the U.S. Intentions aside, a romanticized and in the end paternalistic view of Latinos tends to prevail all too often.

Anglos are not alone in showing little effort to understand the history, culture, and struggles of Mexican Americans. Peoples of color can also be blind. Among blacks, for example, author Manning Marable is one of the few who regularly brings Latinos into his

worldview. Even within the same population, class differences make some Chicanos want racism exposed, while others prefer to maintain a pretense of "No problem." Some will affirm their brownness proudly while others prefer to pass for white if possible.

Up to now the dominant society has had no interest in teaching our unknown histories to anyone and preferred to leave in place the melting-pot model. The burden then falls on the rest of us to work for internationalism inside—not just outside—U.S. borders. We have to teach and learn from each other, we have to develop mutual knowledge of and respect for all our cultures. A new kind of U.S. left will not be born otherwise, as activist/author Carlos Muñoz emphasized in a recent hard-hitting *Crossroads* article.

1992: A CHANCE TO SING "DE COLORES" AS NEVER BEFORE

The upcoming quincentenary offers a once-in-500-years chance to pull our colors together in common protest. Christopher Columbus's arrival on this continent has meaning, usually deadly, for all people of color and many others. In the face of what will be constant, repugnant official celebrations of 1492, we can together mount educational events and demonstrations of all kinds with great scope and impact. The symbolism begs for sweeping protest, a protest that will not merely say "No" to what happened 500 years ago but affirm the infinite treasure-house of non-European cultures and histories, then and now.

For Native Americans, of course, Columbus's arrival meant instant genocide. Today indigenous peoples all over the continent are already planning domestic and international actions. Europe's colonization also paved the way for the enslavement of Africans by the million, brought here to build vast wealth for others with their blood and sweat. At the same time, colonialism launched the birth—by conquest and rape—of a whole new people, La Raza, who combine the red, white, and black in what we may still call a bronze people.

On the backs of all these colors was constructed the greatest wealth ever seen in the world, a wealth that soon came to need more slaves of one kind or another. This time it drew them from the East: Chinese, Japanese, Filipino, Pacific peoples, and many others. Ultimately the whites failed to protect many of their own children from an inhuman poverty and contempt.

So we can come together on this, if we choose. We can make 1992 a year that THEY will remember. We can, in gentler terms, make it the year of "De Colores," of new alliances, in the spirit of the old song by that name: *"Y por eso los grandes amores de muchos colores me gustan a mi"* ("And so the loves of many colors are pleasing to me.")

A Place of Our Own

Despite strong ties to the Catholic faith, Hispanics have not always felt comfortable in the U.S. church. In some places that's changing.

Kevin Coyne

Kevin Coyne is a freelance writer in New Jersey and the author of DOMERS: A Year at Notre Dame, *published by Viking Penguin. Senia Torres Fix assisted with this article as a translator.*

As the 11:15 Mass at Saint Rose of Lima is about to begin, the last few worshipers slip quietly into the back of church, pushing through the heavy oak doors, stepping lightly past the baptismal font, finding a place in the last pew. The Sunday-morning sun slants sharply through the stained-glass windows high up on the wall of the nave. The altar table is draped with a red cloth in honor of the day's feast, Christ the King. The priest and the altar boys enter the sanctuary from the sacristy door, and the congregation stands to pray—just as congregations have been standing to pray in this sturdy, simple church for more than a century.

From the outside, Saint Rose looks much the same today as it did when it was consecrated in 1882 — a single-tower, carpenter-Gothic edifice of red brick and yellow terra cotta, surrounded by a web of close-packed, wood-frame houses, physically tied to the neighborhood by the kind of intimate proximity that zoning laws no longer allow. Inside, though, much has changed. As the priest offers the greeting this morning, a large, sunburst-colored mosaic of the risen Christ fills the wall behind him. The high and ornate white altar that once dominated the sanctuary is long since gone, a casualty of some post-Vatican-II house-cleaning. The dark, brooding ceiling murals are gone too, replaced by a stark, nubbly coat of cream-colored plaster that lends a vaguely Southwestern air to the church's interior. The vaulted sanctuary rises around the priest at the altar table now like a sparse desert cavern filled with light.

And when the congregation begins to recite the penitential rite, it becomes apparent that the changes aren't exclusively architectural. "*Yo confieso ante Dios todopoderoso,*" they say together in Spanish, "*y ante ustedes, hermanos, que he pacado. . . .*"

* * *

In stately old Catholic churches all over America — most of them built, like Saint Rose, to accommodate the waves of European immigrants and shaped to echo the ancient rhythms of the Latin Mass — the pews are now filling with more recent immigrants, and the language of worship is shifting to Spanish. More than a quarter of all the Catholics in the United States today are of Hispanic descent, and their numbers are rising faster than those of any other ethnic group; before long, some demographers estimate, they will account for almost half of American Catholics.

After decades of quiet growth, Hispanics are now beginning to assume a role within the church that more accurately reflects their numbers, and their influence can be felt in every corner of Catholic America—from huge Southwestern dioceses like San Antonio to small Northeastern towns like Freehold, New Jersey, the home of Saint Rose of Lima. If the last century belonged to the Irish, who now account for just 13 percent of American Catholics, the next century belongs to the Hispanics.

As the one parish in a one-parish town, Saint Rose has always been home to a variety of ethnic groups: Irish who came to work in the potato fields, Eastern Europeans who came to work in the factories, Italians who migrated down from Northern New Jersey and New York City. Mexicans are the most recent addition, a large and quick influx that, when added to the small, longstanding Puerto Rican population, has created a significant Hispanic minority in the parish. More than a decade ago, Saint Rose started offering

one Mass in Spanish each Sunday, relying on the services of a patchwork network of visiting priests. By last year, the Hispanic population had grown large enough to warrant a Spanish-speaking priest of its own — and to start making ambitious plans for the future.

"*El Señor este con ustedes,*" Father Oran Ramirez says from the pulpit now, introducing the Gospel.

"*Y con tu espiritu,*" the congregation responds.

"*Lectura del santo Evangelio segun San Juan,*" intones the Colombian-born priest, who was sent here by the diocese to build a new and separate parish in town, a Spanish-speaking parish for Spanish-speaking Catholics.

"*Gloria a ti, Señor,*" the congregation answers. "*Glory to you, O Lord.*"

* * *

Each new Mexican immigrant welcomed into the parish, each new baby baptized, each new call for more Spanish services has confronted Saint Rose with the same basic question that, on a larger scale, confronts the Catholic Church across America: How best to serve a population it has sometimes served poorly.

Some of the first Catholics in America, of course, were Spanish — missionaries who evangelized the Southwest. Eventually overshadowed by immigrants from Europe, the Hispanics were relegated to the uncertain status of a small, foreign-tongued minority searching for a home in a church that neither spoke their language nor understood the trappings of their faith.

When European Catholics came to America they brought their own priests with them, priests who spoke German or Italian or Polish, who shared their culture and history, who built national parishes in ethnic neighborhoods, who helped ease the passage from the old world to the new. Hispanics, by contrast, came mostly alone and found few Spanish-speaking priests awaiting them. Even now there are only 2,000 Hispanic priests in America, just 3 percent of the total, stretched thin to serve 25 percent of the Catholic population.

What Hispanics did bring with them was a distinct tradition of Catholicism that didn't always mesh with the European-shaped American tradition. Many Hispanic immigrants — especially those from Mexico, with its long history of anticlericalism and its chronic shortage of priests — were used to a more personal kind of religion, centered less on the church than on the family. In villages without priests or regular Masses, they developed a sort of informal, lay-run church, mixing Catholic practices with folk customs. They might not go to Mass on Sunday (there might not be any Mass on Sunday) but they would devotedly join in the house-to-house procession on the Feast of Our Lady of Guadalupe, stage passion plays and celebrate saints' festivals. And they baptized, married and buried each other without the aid of clergy.

But in America, they soon learned, the priests were in charge. There were no processions and the Masses seemed colder and more distant than the worship rituals back home. The parishes were large, often forbidding, and the rules were rigid. Rather than bend to fit this unfamiliar form of Catholicism, many Hispanic Americans simply abandoned it, some for Protestant churches, some for no church at all.

As the defection rate among Hispanic Catholics climbed to alarming heights — 60,000 a year, according to Rev. Andrew Greeley, who calls it a "catastrophe" and "an ecclesiastical failure of unprecedented proportions"—church leaders finally came to realize that maybe it was the shepherd who should bend, not the flock.

* * *

The pulpit at Saint Rose, scaled to a taller man, accentuates Father Oran Ramirez's short stature, but as he thunders through his homily this morning, raising his arms and gesticulating toward heaven, he seems to grow to the size of his voice. He speaks in fiery, rhythmic cadences. His message is the primacy of Christ the King, the eternal leader who has outlasted so many temporal empires, and he delivers it with such force that the congregation, standing to recite the Profession of Faith when he finishes, is moved to raise its volume to match his.

"Creo en un solo Dios, Padre todopoderoso," their voices swell.

In the years before Father Ramirez's arrival, the average attendance at the Spanish Mass on Sundays hovered around 100. Some Hispanics were attending the local evangelical Protestant churches, where the religious practices seemed more welcoming: more Spanish-speaking ministers, more lay participation, a less rigid hierarchy and services that stressed emotion over structure. But Ramirez, with his passionate preaching, his knowledge of their culture and customs, his vision of an autonomous community, has lured them back. On this morning, maybe 300 worshipers are in the church.

"When he came, many people started coming, many new people," says Antonio Huerta, who sits with his family today in a pew near the front of the church. He, for one, comes to the Mass more now than he ever did in Mexico. "Many people want to help now."

Although he is just 42, Huerta is the elder statesmen of the Mexican community in Freehold. He arrived in 1976, a full decade ahead of the big wave, and worked for a tree nursery, as a dishwasher and finally as a mason earning paychecks large enough to make plans for buying a permanent home in America. He has also served as an unofficial, one-man resource agency for the Mexicans who followed him in the sudden migration, part of a huge influx all over the New York metropolitan area that started in the mid-1980s. "They all come to me," he says modestly, "for information, for work, for transportation, for anything."

He encouraged them to go to church too, but not many followed the advice. The weekly Spanish Mass alone, it turned out, was not enough to establish a lasting bond between the parish and the Hispanic community.

Like most parishes, Saint Rose has long since been assimilated into America, and it's had little recent experience in dealing with immigrants. Its intentions were good but the results were spotty. The main problem was a lack of stability, in both the congregation and the pulpit: The Mexicans often moved on to new jobs and new towns, and the Spanish-speaking priests shuttled through the parish like the itinerant pastors who served Saint Rose in the mid-19th century. There were priests from Ecuador, Colombia, Argentina, but none of them stayed very long and none of them lived in town.

As the Hispanic population in Freehold continued to grow but attendance at the Spanish Mass didn't, the diocese decided to take the next step. Last August it bought a five-acre wooded lot on the edge of town for $180,000. When Ramirez moved into the small house on the property, it was a significant milestone on the path to stability.

"We had to fix it up in a hurry, because Father was coming fast," says Antonio Huerta, who took a week off from work to help clean and paint the house. He is eager to volunteer his labor again on behalf of a church building. "It's not only for me, it's for my people. We need to go to church. When people don't, you see a lot of drinking and trouble."

When the early waves of Catholic immigrants arrived in America from Europe, one effective way to minister to their needs was to establish national parishes. When the more recent wave of Catholic immigrants arrived from Central and South America and the Caribbean, the church at first tried, with less success, a more assimilationist approach. Eventually it circled back toward the older strategy: establishing a new round of national parishes.

"When Italians moved into a neighborhood," says Notre Dame history professor Jay Dolan of earlier immigrant groups, "there would be special Masses for them in the basement of the church, and they really resented that to no end because the Irish were having their Masses upstairs." An expert on the national-parish phenomenon in America, Dolan is a former director of Notre Dame's Cushwa Center for the Study of American Catholicism and the editor of a three volume study, *Notre Dame History of Hispanic Catholics in the United States,* published last October by Notre Dame Press. " What's clear now," he says, "is that most Hispanic pastoral ministers want national churches."

Assimilation works well with some groups of Hispanics, especially English-speaking Puerto Ricans, and in some kinds of institutions, especially schools. Notre Dame, for instance, has seen a surge in Hispanic enrollment in recent years: from 10 Hispanic-American students in the 1970 freshman class to 130 in 1994. Notre Dame now appeals to first-generation American children of Mexican immigrants in much the same way it once did to first-generation children of Irish immigrants. "When you look at the natural evolution of Hispanics in America," says admissions director Kevin Rooney, "and the natural evolution of the church in America, then this is what should be Notre Dame's natural evolution as well."

But in parishes like Saint Rose of Lima, assimilation has been less successful. "Most of them who come here, they come to be richer, not to become better

Catholics," says Father Manuel Fernandez, the director of the Hispanic Apostolate for the Diocese of Trenton. "They may be Protestant for a while, but then they go back to the church they belong to."

What helps most, Fernandez has learned, is if their church also belongs to them. When he came to New Jersey in 1970 from his native Spain, after a brief detour to Texas, the Diocese of Trenton had only one Hispanic parish, the one he was assigned to. There are now 13, including one Fernandez built from scratch in a rehabbed old garment factory in the small coastal city of Long Branch.

Says Fernandez, "I'm not here to Americanize them." In describing the absorption of immigrants into American society, his preferred metaphor is the tossed salad, not the melting pot: "Every culture has value, and it would be a tremendous loss if they lose their ancestry and traditions."

* * *

When Father Ramirez steps out the back door of his small house to survey his new domain — the big yellow concrete block-garage, an auto repair shop in a previous life; the five acres reaching back to a high clearing surrounded by trees — he carries with him a plan for the future and a vision of the sort of transformation Father Fernandez wrought in that old garment factory in Long Branch.

"Maybe we could make this a small chapel now," says Ramirez. The flat ceiling of the garage, supported by a naked steel I-beam, rises tall and grimy above him. Lying jumbled in the rear corner are the disassembled pieces of an altar, salvaged from a nearby church renovation. He has a second altar stashed in the basement of the house. "then later maybe we could build something new and expand."

It requires a strong act of will, an act of faith really, to imagine this rough and worn property as the seat of a new parish, but Ramirez is accustomed to thinking in such terms. Born 50 years ago on a coffee farm in Colombia, he spent 16 years as a Redemptorist missionary shuttling from parish to parish in Venezuela. He was on vacation in New York when he met Father Fernandez and accepted his latest challenge.

Saint Rose has been generous in lending its church and some space in the grammar school, but it remains somebody else's parish, not the home Ramirez is looking for. In his view, a new church would be the center of a new community, a place where Hispanics could worship in their own way more than just once a week, a place that would be theirs alone.

But in America, he has found, it takes more than just faith to build a church. Standing in the way are questions about zoning variances, unhappy neighbors, site improvements, frontage requirements and other regulatory issues.

The new parish has a name already (Our Lady of Guadalupe), but for now its home is wherever Ramirez happens to be, whether at Saint Rose or at one of the churches in nearby towns where he also says Mass regularly. Although the proposed site of the new parish is just a mile from Saint Rose and a few blocks from the Mexican neighborhood, its jurisdiction will extend in a wide arc around Freehold and it will be open to any Hispanics in the region who don't find what they need in their own parishes.

While he waits for answers about the future, Ramirez spends almost as much time on the road as he did back in Venezuela. He visits other parishes, hospitals and the county jail just around the corner from his house. He is much in demand at Cursillo retreats. He takes every opportunity he can to make his presence known among the Hispanic community, but he lacks one forum here that proved particularly effective for spreading the word back in South America: the long novenas and wakes and funerals that accompany all deaths there.

"You can use that as a means of evangelization," he says. "You can reach more people that way." In Freehold, the Hispanic community is so young that death is still a stranger: In his first year here, Ramirez presided at only two funerals.

Baptisms are another story: He did 23 of those that year.

* * *

"Puedan ir en paz," Father Ramirez says from the altar of Saint Rose. *"Go in peace."*

Standing on the aisle in the first pew, Phil Martinez joins the congregation in answering, *"Demos gracias a Dios."*

As he turns to leave, Martinez holds in his hand his regular offering envelope for Saint Rose de Lima, which he plans to slip through the mail slot at the rectory next door. When the basket came around this morning on behalf of the new parish, he dug some money out of his pocket; but he wants also to make sure that the old parish doesn't get shortchanged. One of the original stalwarts of the local Hispanic community, a native of Puerto Rico who came to Freehold in the late 1950s and opened a small grocery store, Martinez and his wife lobbied for years to have a Spanish-speaking priest assigned here.

Now that their hopes have been realized, he finds his loyalties, like his offertory gifts, split. "I'd like to see it all together," he says. "We started as part of Saint Rose, and I'd like to continue that way."

Over four decades, Phil and Carmen Martinez have forged a strong bond with Saint Rose — they have buried one daughter, a young car-accident victim, seen another daughter married, and bought a burial plot for themselves in the parish cemetery. Their ties to the Hispanic community in the parish are equally strong: Through raffles, bake sales and dances, they have helped raise $25,000 over the years. On Sundays now, they alternate between the Hispanic Mass and what they call "the American Mass," at which Carmen sings in the choir.

"We really needed a full-time priest, because you found that people got sick and there was no one to give them last rites," says Carmen, who was asked by a priest at Saint Rose, back in 1965, to find out how many parishioners would be interested in a Spanish-language Mass. Going door-to-door, she compiled a list of 50 families. "Then I said, 'Where will we have these Masses?' and he said, 'Your house?' and I got mad. I figured, such a big church, why my house? I took the list and threw it away."

Within the Hispanic community, opinions about the proposed new parish range from enthusiastic to ambivalent. Some members, especially among the longer-settled, more assimilated Puerto Ricans, remain unconvinced of the need for a new parish, a view shared by the pastor of Saint Rose.

"The tendency in the community here is to be separate, and I'm not sure that's such a good idea," says Father Gerard McCarron, who holds a Ph.D. from Princeton Theological Seminary. He has earned high marks from the Hispanic community for the parish facilities he has made available to them and the respectful autonomy he has offered. "This is a decision they've made, and I'm helping them to the extent I can, but I don't want to be paternalistic about it. I support the decision, but now I've faded out of the picture and let them take a larger role."

* * *

For a long time after Mass, people linger in the church, chatting and mingling, swapping information about jobs and apartments. Children chase each other through the pews, their laughter a reminder of how young the congregation is and how fast it is growing. One girl runs her hand along the cool marble surface of the old communion rail, which is inscribed in memory of Saint Rose's first pastor, Monsignor Federick Kivelitz, the German-born priest who built the parish and anchored it for 58 years.

When Monsignor Kivelitz died in 1930, the mourners waiting to enter the church to view his body looked up at the cross atop the steeple and saw it glowing against the dusk sky — a strange, shimmering rose hue that some believers immediately took as a sign. The church itself, it seemed, was mourning its beloved pastor.

Thousands of people flocked to Saint Rose on subsequent nights to see the glowing cross, their pilgrimage halted only when a volunteer climbed the steeple for a closer look. The rose-colored hue, he found, was caused by nothing more miraculous than the copper surface of the cross itself, exposed when the gold leaf peeled away in several places.

This morning, a young Mexican woman leading her children to the back of the church stops to take a loaf of bread from the boxes of donated food that are placed there each week, a welcome gift in a hard season when jobs grow tight. She pushes out through the heavy oak doors.

As she starts walking toward home, leading her children and carrying her bread, the cross on the steeple above her is outlined starkly against the pale, cold sky, illuminated only by the small miracle of a peaceful Sunday in America.

A Balancing Act

By Jerry Berrios

Latinas are making great strides in corporate America, leading divisions, implementing important policies, sharing their creativity, and reaching out to the Hispanic community. It doesn't take long for a Latina to show she is invaluable. And although the route to the pinnacle of the corporate America mountain can be rocky, Latinas are getting there with their tireless work ethic and resolve.

LATINA *Style* interviewed six women from various fields in corporate America—all highly motivated executives who bring a great deal of skill to their respective companies.

One of the overriding themes they all sounded was the need to find the perfect fit and balance in one's personal and professional life. As society strives to fit round pegs into square holes, these individuals emphatically stress the need for balance, confidence, flexibility, and diversity. They are reaching the upper echelons of their corporations, one step at a time.

Cuban-born Yvonne Chang, Director of Corporate Affairs for AT&T in Basking Ridge, New Jersey, is a nine-year veteran of the telecommunications giant. Her responsibilities include public relations and policy, community affairs, and constituency relations with Hispanic leaders. Chang controls a program budget which includes special projects and event sponsorship relating to the Hispanic community.

She began her career on the technology side, receiving a degree in electrical engineering and starting off with a Department of Defense contractor in Washington, D.C. "[When I was] in that company for a couple of years, I realized [that no matter] how good I was, I was never going to move up because I was female in a very male-oriented [area]," says Chang. "Secondly, I was a minority. I am half-Asian, half-Hispanic. To [have] climbed up that ladder would [have been] very difficult."

From there she took an entry-level management job at AT&T and was later transferred to Miami, Florida. As Managing Director for Wireless Business Development, she involved herself in every aspect of the business, including its multi-billion dollar projects.

"[To] succeed in corporate America, [you have to] be flexible, and have many different skills," says Chang. "You can't be very good at one thing; you have to be good at a lot of different things. The most important things to have are diversity of knowledge, interpersonal skills, and an understanding of technology."

Of corporate America's challenges, Chang feels that competition is the biggest. "No matter how good you are, there is always someone who has more education," she says. "[You are] constantly in an environment of doing more with less. You have to have a positive attitude: if there isn't a way, then find a way. From a female and minority perspective, you tend to work harder. The whole nine-to-five thing is non-existent."

According to Chang, the pro for working for a large corporation is resources and the con is the size. "You can be a very small fish in a very large ocean," she says.

In the corporate world, there aren't many oceans larger than the Coca-Cola Company, which has become almost synonymous with the city of Atlanta. The company reaches out to the Hispanic community through the work of Beatriz Perez, Associate Manager of Consumer Segment Marketing. Her responsibilities include carrying out marketing for Hispanic and blue-collar consumers, including controlling the budget for those areas throughout the United States.

Perez began her career at the U.S. Hispanic Chamber of Commerce and then joined Sosa, the Hispanic advertising agency based in San Antonio, Texas. She initially worked as an account executive on the Coca-Cola account, developing marketing strategies for the Hispanic segment.

"I was very fortunate," says Perez. "I actually helped develop a new strategy for the Hispanic consumer marketing group and brought in what Coca-Cola was doing against that segment. From that, I was pretty much recognized here throughout the company."

Perez was then promoted to account supervisor on the Coca-Cola account, and won the Aguila Dedication Award for the agency. Within a few months, Coca-Cola offered her a position as Hispanic consumer marketer, and expanded her responsibilities.

"I took it on as a great challenge," says Perez. "I've been so happy ever since. It really is an exciting company to work for. This place treats their employees so well. Coca-Cola topped Fortune magazine's annual list of 'America's Most Admired Companies' two years in a row, in 1996 and 1997. [They] believe in balance and quality of life."

According to Perez, one of the most fun and worthwhile programs she has implemented was the recent "Selena" movie campaign. The nationwide program hosted "Selena" premieres for Coca-Cola consumers in 36 markets, including Los Angeles, New York, Chicago, and San Antonio. Four hundred consumer winners in each market had the opportunity to see the movie before it was released to the public.

"It was really rewarding," says Perez. "[The movie] did a great job of portraying someone who was so critical to being a role model. She broke the tradition of what a Tejano singer was."

Perez feels the challenges posed by corporate America include not getting lost, and making your skills and qualities known to other people. "I think to really be a success you need to get out there and show people what you are doing."

Perez says that Coca-Cola helps develop its employees' objectives and goals. "People help you develop your career; the company will identify ventures for you and help you get to know other people," she says. "Recently, I won the Most Promising Manager of the Year honor from the National Hispanic Employee Association. I would not have been recognized if it weren't for Coca-Cola supporting the Hispanic community and allowing me to get out there and really shine."

According to Perez, the pros of a career at Coca-Cola are many, and include the benefit of working for a company that is giving back to the community. "That's a big pro for me, because I'm a Latina. I grew up in a very Latin household and I don't want to just do anything for anybody. I want to make sure what I'm doing is giving back to my people and my culture. To me that's critical."

Giving back to the community is a common theme among the corporate Latinas we spoke to. And one area of corporate America that is constantly providing for those less fortunate is foundation work.

Gloria De Necochea is Manager of the Mattel Foundation in El Segundo, California, where she oversees direct grant programs and local, national, international, arts, and social welfare programs. De Necochea also directs the foundation's employee volunteer program in the United States, which includes volunteer grants as well as an employee matching gift and scholarship program. She has been with Mattel for two years, and currently controls a budget of approximately $4 million.

Prior to joining Mattel, De Necochea worked with the ARCO Foundation managing education and arts/humanities funding. She started in the philanthropy field ten years ago at the Carnegie Foundation of New York. "I've been fortunate to work in a range of foundations, [both] local and national, that serve [those with] low income," says De Necochea. "One of the exciting parts of philanthropy is being a referral resource to the community.

She feels that working for a company's foundation is different than laboring in traditional corporate America. "It's the best of both worlds," says De Necochea. "[You] distribute the company's profits and give back to children. The other rewarding part is helping employees give back to the community. [You have] an opportunity to be a link."

De Necochea sees the challenge of corporate America as finding opportunities to be effective while developing as a human being. She uses a phrase from Girls, Inc., a nationwide organization that supports girls, to explain her philosophy: "'Strong, smart, and bold'. I have always learned. I always encourage younger Latinas to face every obstacle as a learning and growing opportunity."

De Necochea feels that Latinas are unique in their contributions to corporations. "It's difficult to assess each corporate culture and find thoughtful ways that you can contribute to the company's goals. But it's extremely rewarding [to give] our unique perspective as women and Latinas to management's knowledge base and help a company succeed. Companies succeed because of diversity."

She advises Latinas, no matter how busy, to make time to mentor or be guest speakers. "We benefit more than the women we speak to," says De Necochea. "[It] energizes me, and [helps me] refocus on my own needs to practice what I'm teaching. By sharing our stories with younger women, we will accelerate the speed in which they recognize themselves by providing role models."

De Necochea has come a long way from the Southern California border town of Calexico, and has overcome many obstacles. Spanish is her native language. She worked her way through school. She has also been a single mother for most of her career "[I've had] so many jobs that my friends laugh about it," says De Necochea. "But the breadth of my experience has helped me succeed in my [current] job."

Juanita Hawkins, Vice President of Quality Assurance for Johnson & Johnson's Janssen Pharmaceutica division in Titusville, New Jersey, has been in the right place at the right time. She has had opportunities and experiences during her career that others can only imagine. Currently, she ensures that all products produced by and for Johnson & Johnson meet all federal and local regulations and customer needs.

Hawkins has been with Johnson & Johnson for 29 years, and with her division since October 1994. There she oversees products produced in Puerto Rico, Europe, and the United States, controlling a huge budget and a staff of 150 in various locations. She also supports new development and production for products that will be on the market in a few years.

Hawkins began her career as a microbiologist, working first as a junior chemist at American Cyanamid, and then joining Johnson & Johnson's Ethicon division. She moved through the ranks of supervisor and manager before going into operations.

"At Ethicon, I reviewed the sterilization of moon bags to collect moon rocks on the first space walk," says Hawkins. "[It was a] wonderful opportunity. We also tested the sutures for the first heart transplant in South Africa."

She has worked in many different divisions within corporate Johnson & Johnson, including overseeing Latin American and U.S. quality. "I've had so many wonderful experiences meeting technical people and their families all over the world," says Hawkins. "I really can't explain, but it gets in your heart. You are building business and personal relationships."

Through her experience in corporate America, Hawkins feels the challenges are "primarily doing more with less. You have to do that to be competitive." She also states the need to "balance work and family and continue to focus on building the leaders of tomorrow while managing the chaos of today."

She feels that women in the technical field need to master assertiveness and team-building, as opposed to aggressiveness and exclusionary tactics. Among the pros of corporate America, according to Hawkins, is the opportunity to broaden your career in many areas of the business, learning about the various divisions and franchises and how they improve the customer's quality of life. The negative is that corporate America prohibits you from focusing and becoming a master in one particular area.

Hawkins says she couldn't have achieved all of her accomplishments without marrying a man of the '90s in the '60s, and having her family's support. Her husband, Bill Hawkins, says that being married to a Latina in corporate America is extremely positive. "We work together as a team and we make decisions together." He says the pros are the economic benefits but the cons are the long hours and travel. "I miss her when she's gone," he says.

Finding your fit can be difficult, especially in predominantly male-dominated industries. Puerto Rican Carmen Sciackitano works in those areas on a daily basis. She is the Senior Real Estate/Energy Counsel at Kraft Foods, Inc., in Northfield, Illinois. Sciackitano handles Kraft's real estate, energy, and construction matters, and manages the outside counsel budget for her three areas.

Before her tenure at Kraft, Sciackitano had been a trial lawyer at United Airlines. She joined Kraft ten years ago doing commercial contract work, and was soon given responsibility for handling real estate and construction issues. "I always felt that I could do whatever," she says. "I never turned down anything new and interesting—that's how you get ahead."

Sciackitano sees the biggest challenge in corporate America as continuing the advancement and promotion of qualified Hispanic women to the top managerial side of companies. "In order to really succeed in a company, you need a mentor," says Sciackitano. "Somebody who is in the highest ranks of the company, recognizes you, and can promote you from within. They know the ropes."

"[I] really believe if you have confidence in yourself, work hard, and apply yourself to know the area [you are working in], clients will respect you," says Sciackitano. "If you have the client's confidence, [that's] how you succeed in corporate America. I think everybody has to take ownership over their own careers. If you are in a rut you accept that."

Sciackitano stresses the importance of balance in achieving success. "If you don't have something else other than the job to focus on, then you are in trouble," she says. "Life is brutal. Work cannot be the primary motivater."

Family support has been an important factor in Michelle Vasquez's success. Vasquez, Advertising Manager for Levi Strauss & Co., in San Francisco, California, is responsible for developing and implementing marketing strategies for the Hispanic segment. Vasquez describes herself as a motivated individual. She grew up in Uvalde, a town near San Antonio, Texas, within a community "that didn't always

think Latinas could achieve." She felt she had something to prove, graduating from Stanford University and launching her career in New York. All along, her family was supportive of her achievements and drive to succeed.

"There were a lot of small hurdles along the way," says Vasquez. "[But if] you are doing things that you really like and feel passionate about, there isn't anything you can't achieve. The hurdles are more opportunities, [and they] become something positive."

Prior to her current job Vasquez worked in the banking industry in New York, then proceeded to AT&T in Hispanic marketing and then sales. She moved to the West Coast and did freelance work for two years before joining Levi Strauss & Co., six months ago.

Corporate America's challenges, Vasquez says, include understanding the formal and informal structures and the written and unwritten rules, finding mentors, choosing your priorities, and finding a comfortable way of communicating. "At the end of the day [you have to be] comfortable with how you express yourself," says Vasquez.

"[The] things you can learn in a corporate environment are equal to a different kind of education," she says. "It provides you with a paradigm of thinking [which is] useful throughout your career."

Although these Latinas are making giant strides in their respective industries, there is still room for improvement in corporate America. According to a November 6, 1996, *New York Times* article, women hold just two percent of the power positions, no matter how you define them by title, paycheck, or responsibility for the bottom line. Of the nation's 500 largest companies, only 61 can count a woman among their top 5 earners, or can say that 25 percent or more of their officers are women (only 13 companies do both).

The Hispanic Association on Corporate Responsibility has identified 38 Hispanic women who are executives in the 1996 listing of Fortune's 1000 companies. More women need to be in high-level management positions. Society and young girls need role models to emulate to succeed and *echar para adelante*—go forward.

TICKLED BROWN

Nationwide, emerging Latino comedians draw material from the culture

BY VALERIE MENARD

Dramedy—that's how comedian Jeff Valdez describes the Latino sense of humor—as a mix of drama and comedy. It's this kind of humor that producer-writer Valdez has tried to expose on television since his first show, *Comedy Compadres*, which aired in the early nineties on cable. Since then, Latino comedic talent, from standup to sketch comedy troupes, has emerged. "It used to be I'd go to a Latino showcase in L.A. and I'd go [down the list]: 'Know 'em, know 'em, seen 'em," said Valdez. "Now I go out, and I'm like, 'Who's this person? I've never heard of them.' " Encouraged but not satisfied with the degree of growth, Valdez and other Latino Hollywood veterans continue to groom future comedic stars.

One of the significant venues for new talent, the American Airlines Latino Laugh Festival, debuted last year in San Antonio. The Alamo City will again play host to the festival this year, on August 14 through 17, and Valdez will again coproduce it with his partner, Paul Block. Last year the festival format consisted of thirteen 30-minute episodes that were aired on Showtime from September through October. Made up of four different segments—Latinologues, comedy sketches written by Valdez and performed by Latino celebrities like Maria Conchita Alonso and Geraldo Rivera; Diamonds in the Rough, standup routines from undiscovered Latino comics; film clips and novelty acts like Elvis imitator El Vez; and standup routines by comedians like Paul Rodriguez, John Mendoza, and Valdez—the show was hosted by veteran comic actor Cheech Marin, with Rodriguez and MTV personality Daisy Fuentes filling in as co-hosts.

Marin returns as host this year, as do most of the show's components, but in a more abbreviated form. Featured celebrities like *Access Hollywood* co-host Giselle Fernandez, will perform a new set of comedic monologues but rather than thirteen episodes, only one 90-minute show will air, first in September on pay-per-view

and later will be rebroadcast on Showtime. This format is much more to Valdez's liking. "Our original idea was to do one 90-minute show," he explained. "It was the format of the network to do thirteen at the time, and we said, 'Okay.' Believe me, it was a production challenge. I had grown people crying. But we pulled it off. That was the great thing." Impressed with the effort and ratings, Showtime renewed the show. "They see the future," said Valdez. "They also understand that it's something that takes time too—it's a blossoming arena."

What most impressed Marin about last year's festival was the diversity of talent he witnessed. "I was so impressed with the range of comedy," he said. "It ran the gamut from suburban to urban voices, from family humor to political satire." The festival also produced tangible results for some of its participants. New comedians like Freddy Soto and Pablo Francisco (who has now joined the cast of *Mad TV*) were approached by agents after the festival, and veteran comic Rodriguez found his career reenergized, asserted Valdez. This year, with only one episode, the number of young comics performing will be limited to three. But because launching new talent is his overriding concern, Valdez also plans to tape thirteen half-hour episodes featuring young comedians, to be packaged and sold as an additional television concept. Another measure of the event's success is that this year American Airlines came on board as the title sponsor.

> "**M**y brothers' names are Alfonso, Lorenzo, Ramon ... [and me], Jeff. I guess that was right about the time my parents assimilated ... right there."
>
> —**Jeff Valdez**

The airline will also be making a donation toward the renovation of San Antonio's historic Alameda Theater, which was built in 1949 and was the first stop in the international touring circuit for Latin America's brightest stars.

Latino comedy has been blossoming for several years, spurred by a combination of factors beginning with the efforts of leading Latinos to expand the pool of Latino actors, writers, and comics. Valdez began in Colorado by opening his own comedy club, and after moving to Los Angeles and working as a writer and producer, he developed the concept for the television show *Comedy Compadres*, a predecessor of the Laugh Festival that introduced young comics like Carlos Mencia and Jackie Guerra. *Comedy Compadres* did have early competition

from the comedy troupe Culture Clash, who starred in their own groundbreaking show. Both shows introduced viewers to Latino comedy. "You've never seen a lot of Latino comics on TV," said Valdez. "When I did the show *Comedy Compadres*, I was thrilled to use them. Shortly after that, a lot of people started putting Latino comics on. I was thrilled to see that."

Mencia confirms that when he decided to pursue comedy, there were very few Latino standup comics performing in comedy clubs. There were a few pioneers on television comedy shows—Desi Arnaz, Freddie Prinze, and Rodriguez—but they were so scarce that Mencia, a child of the eighties, emulated comedians like Sam Kinison and Richard Pryor. "Before *Comedy Compadres*,

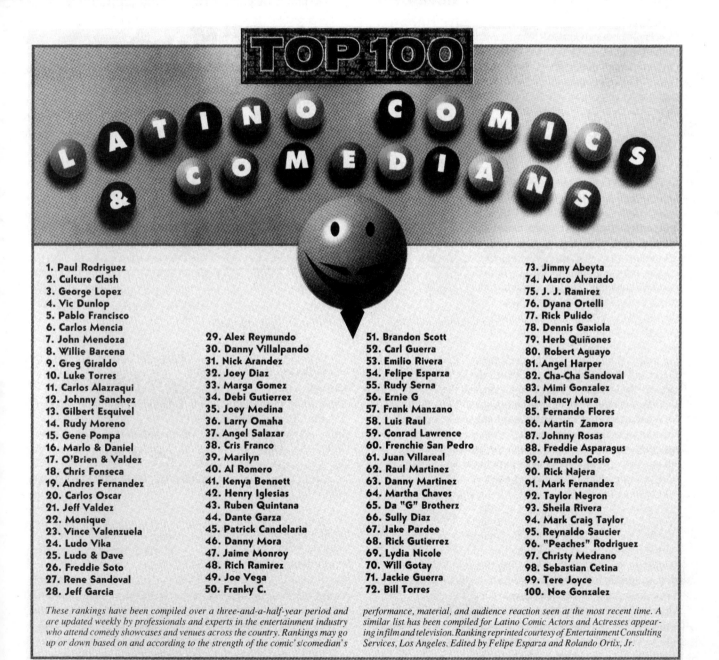

TOP 100 LATINO COMICS & COMEDIANS

1. Paul Rodriguez
2. Culture Clash
3. George Lopez
4. Vic Dunlop
5. Pablo Francisco
6. Carlos Mencia
7. John Mendoza
8. Willie Barcena
9. Greg Giraldo
10. Luke Torres
11. Carlos Alazraqui
12. Johnny Sanchez
13. Gilbert Esquivel
14. Rudy Moreno
15. Gene Pompa
16. Marlo & Daniel
17. O'Brien & Valdez
18. Chris Fonseca
19. Andres Fernandez
20. Carlos Oscar
21. Jeff Valdez
22. Monique
23. Vince Valenzuela
24. Ludo Vika
25. Ludo & Dave
26. Freddie Soto
27. Rene Sandoval
28. Jeff Garcia

29. Alex Reymundo
30. Danny Villalpando
31. Nick Arandez
32. Joey Diaz
33. Marga Gomez
34. Debi Gutierrez
35. Joey Medina
36. Larry Omaha
37. Angel Salazar
38. Cris Franco
39. Marilyn
40. Al Romero
41. Kenya Bennett
42. Henry Iglesias
43. Ruben Quintana
44. Dante Garza
45. Patrick Candelaria
46. Danny Mora
47. Jaime Monroy
48. Rich Ramirez
49. Joe Vega
50. Franky C.

51. Brandon Scott
52. Carl Guerra
53. Emilio Rivera
54. Felipe Esparza
55. Rudy Serna
56. Ernie G
57. Frank Manzano
58. Luis Raul
59. Conrad Lawrence
60. Frenchie San Pedro
61. Juan Villareal
62. Raul Martinez
63. Danny Martinez
64. Martha Chaves
65. Da "G" Brotherz
66. Sully Diaz
67. Jake Pardee
68. Rick Gutierrez
69. Lydia Nicole
70. Will Gotay
71. Jackie Guerra
72. Bill Torres

73. Jimmy Abeyta
74. Marco Alvarado
75. J. J. Ramirez
76. Dyana Ortelli
77. Rick Pulido
78. Dennis Gaxiola
79. Herb Quiñones
80. Robert Aguayo
81. Angel Harper
82. Cha-Cha Sandoval
83. Mimi Gonzalez
84. Nancy Mura
85. Fernando Flores
86. Martin Zamora
87. Johnny Rosas
88. Freddie Asparagus
89. Armando Cosio
90. Rick Najera
91. Mark Fernandez
92. Taylor Negron
93. Sheila Rivera
94. Mark Craig Taylor
95. Reynaldo Saucier
96. "Peaches" Rodriguez
97. Christy Medrano
98. Sebastian Cetina
99. Tere Joyce
100. Noe Gonzalez

These rankings have been compiled over a three-and-a-half-year period and are updated weekly by professionals and experts in the entertainment industry who attend comedy showcases and venues across the country. Rankings may go up or down based on and according to the strength of the comic's/comedian's performance, material, and audience reaction seen at the most recent time. A similar list has been compiled for Latino Comic Actors and Actresses appearing in film and television. Ranking reprinted courtesy of Entertainment Consulting Services, Los Angeles. Edited by Felipe Esparza and Rolando Ortix, Jr.

young Latino comics were stuck without a venue, and successful Latinos in standup were practically nonexistent," said Mencia. "Paul Rodriguez was the only one I knew about. He was our entire army." Broadcast by Superstation KTLA from 1993 through 1994, *Comedy Compadres* televised twenty episodes in its one-year run and featured about 60 different comics.

Valdez has not been alone in his efforts to encourage young Latino comics. Last year Hollywood veteran writer-producer Jon Mercedes III also tackled the lack of Latinos on television sitcoms by instigating his own talent search—the Latino Comedy Olympics. A year-round competition that took place at the Improv in Los Angeles and will culminate in a taping for television of the championship round (very likely in Las Vegas but not yet confirmed), the Latino Comedy Olympics is modeled after the Olympic Games, with preliminary, semifinal, and final rounds. It also includes several comedy disciplines—sketch, standup, group, clowns, improvisation, impressionists, and ventriloquists. Contestants are judged by a panel of experts in each discipline. "Three years ago, I saw that television had left out the Latino voice. I started scouting Latino comics. I saw the pool coming from two areas: standup and comedic actors," said Mercedes. To illustrate to Hollywood executives the depth of the Latino comedic talent pool, he has compiled a list of more than 300 performers, and every three months he, in conjunction with Entertainment Consulting Services, releases a ranking of the top 100 Latino comics [see previous].

Valdez sees a two-pronged approach to increasing the Latino presence on TV. First, to simply include Latinos in the cast. A sitcom script may call for three friends, but they don't all have to be the same ethnic group—one could be Hispanic. Once Latinos have been cast on television, the second step, according to Valdez, becomes more viable—developing shows with Latino themes. By that time, he said, "Americans will have become more comfortable with seeing our faces, and not just our faces but the diversity of our faces, and [they will] understand the true diversity of our culture."

Although efforts by Valdez and Mercedes have contributed to the Latino comedy boom, another factor is the changing dynamic of comedy audiences. With three of the top comedy clubs in Los Angeles—the Comedy Store, the Improv, and the Laugh Factory—featuring La-

> "I liked the original Batman because the Joker was Latino—Cesar Romero—but I thought Batman should have been Mexican because that car was too nice for a white man to be driving."
> —George Lopez

tino comedy nights, it's obvious that there's a market for Latino comedy. At the same time, Latino audiences have become more relaxed and less sensitive to exposing our cultural foibles, and non-Hispanic audiences find the Latino sense of humor refreshing and new. As more Latino comics gain visibility, the Latino community is embracing comedy as an artistic outlet and form of self-expression to an unprecedented degree. Contends Valdez: "As a community, [we've] never seen a lot of Latino comics. It's very new to a lot of our community, and it's very fresh—and so our people are coming to shows. Shows in L.A. sell out all the time. So the demand of the market is showing itself."

Searching for a venue for the Latina perspective, the group Hot and Spicy Mamitas formed three years ago. It consists of five Los Angles-based comedians: Dyana Ortelli, Marilyn Martinez, Sully Diaz, Lydia Nicole, and Ludo Vika. "The guys had taken over [comedy]. The Mamitas talk about things that we've always wanted to talk about but didn't dare to," said Vika, also a *Comedy Compadres* alumna. As part of the show, each comedian tackles a topic by sharing personal experiences or creating fictional ones. Diaz discusses her life as a single mom; Martinez satirizes sexual foibles by enacting a phone sex conversation; Nicole, whose mother was a prostitute and father was a pimp, shares moments from her childhood; and Ortelli relates her experiences as a Latina actress in Hollywood. Vika attributes the new surge of comedic activity to increased self-confidence. Audiences seem more open to the Latino perspective, and Latino comics have also matured, she said. "It used to be that Latinos used to just laugh about sex—now we laugh about ourselves," Vika explained. "I once told a joke about Puerto Rico and my mother got calls from people saying, 'How dare she say that about our country?' Latino audiences as well as comics are learning how to joke about themselves."

Comedy as a discipline offers a powerful form of communication and self-expression. What began as a need to ventilate her frustrations was quickly transformed into a form of expression for Guerra. She distinctly remembers taking the stage at an open-mike

> "The guys had taken over [comedy]. The Mamitas talk about things that we've always wanted to talk about but didn't dare to."
> —Ludo Vika, of the Hot and Spicy Mamitas

competition at a West Hollywood club in 1993, exhausted from years of work as a labor organizer for the Hotel Employees and Restaurant Employees Union. On a dare, she went onstage, and that moment changed her life. Her routine was simply a monologue about her day as a labor organizer, once again using the formula of finding the comedic lining in an otherwise dreary topic. "It was like, when you hear other people talking about having a great religious experience. . . . It was the first time I could relate to any of these stories," she recounted. "It was so sexy. People were laughing and clapping and cheering. There were, like, 400 people crammed into this club, and they were all listening to what I was saying, laughing, and getting off on it."

Although he feels too young to be a grandfather of comedy, Rodriguez admitted that he enjoys watching young Latino comedians take the stage, and he also understands the attraction: "It was very lonely out there when I started, but laughter is dangerous, it's very addictive. Once you get that first laugh, you want another, and another, and another. I've known professionals—doctors, lawyers, firemen—that put their careers on hold to pursue comedy."

Coast to coast, Latino comics and comedy groups have emerged. In New York, a cable access show, *Comedy Rhumba,* has made news. Hosted by local standup comedian Mike Robles, the show features a man-in-the-street interview segment conducted by Robles, who asks Latino passersby to comment, usually on a fictitious topic. One of the more creative subjects was the "Chubacca fish," which was developed after reports on the local news that fish with mysterious bite marks had washed ashore. Robles sets up his victims by describing the fish in eerie detail and then asks them to comment. One man simply admits, "I don't swim in that water," to which Robles asks, "Why not? Because it's mysterious?" The man responds confidently, "No, because I only swim in the Caribbean, where the water's blue."

In Austin, Texas, the director of a ballet folklorico group, Roén Salinas, and the director of a theater company, Rodney Garza, joined forces to form the Chicano Inteligencia Agency (CIA). The group debuted at the first annual Chupacabra Chupafest last September, which also included the California-based comedy team of Lalo Lopez (formerly with Chicano Secret Service) and Esteban Zul as headliners. A CIA performance features original comedy sketches—one involves the talk show host Crustino (the brother of psychic Walter Mercado) whose regular guest is Juan El Sancho del Rancho; a news update from Station KAKA; and sketches written by recruited talent, like the "Chicano Dating Game," by Adrian Villegas. The group has performed three times since then, each time pulling in local talent. "That was the real intent of forming the CIA," said Salinas. "We not only had a message to convey, we also wanted to bring [in] the local community as participants in a performance, and the most accessible form for that seemed to be comedy." Austin also saw the premiere of the Mojado Brothers Comedy Festival, courtesy of television producer Samm Peña. The show featured established standup comics, and Peña hopes to sell the tape to a network as the nucleus for more Latino programming from Texas that targets English-speaking Hispanics.

It may seem like a win-win situation for Latinos in comedy, but some say there is room for criticism. Without efforts like the American Airlines Latino Laugh Festival and the Latino Comedy Olympics, venues for Latino comedians would still be limited, yet some Latino comics relish an opportunity to share the stage with mainstream comedians and not be forever relegated to what several comedians call "beaner shows." One young comic said that although he appreciates Latino comedy projects, he thinks Latino comics focus too much on appealing to Latino audiences and not enough on appealing to mainstream audiences. "I want people to come to my show because they like my work and because I make them laugh—not because I'm Latino," he said. Mercedes responded, "There are a certain [number] of culturally ignorant comedians who will say that the bottom line is that mainstream audiences only accept their own voice. But Richard Pryor didn't make white jokes. He talked about his own very black experience, but more importantly it was a human experience."

Even Valdez admits that responses from audiences can be great, but because very few venues for Latino comics exist, he has become Noah and the festival is the Ark. He had only so many slots available, so of course those comics who were not included in the first voyage tend to be resentful. "I've had comics launch into me," admitted Valdez. "Coming from a standup background, I really understand their desperation. I tell them, 'Even though you didn't get it this year, you should hope for next year and be thrilled that there's a vehicle out there. Would you rather be pissed at me for not getting on the show or be pissed at me for never even trying to get a show on the air?' The alternatives are much worse."

The process of breaking new ground for Latinos in Hollywood has been compared to a spring-loaded door: as soon as someone gets in, the door slams shut. Not so in comedy. The massive influx of Latino comedians has swung the door off its hinges, and it will have to translate into more Latinos on television.

African Americans

A 1988 *New York Times* editorial suggests an appropriate introductory focus for the following collection of articles about an ethnic group that traces its American ancestry to initial participation as "three-fifths" persons in the U.S. Constitution and to its later exclusion from the polity altogether by the U.S. Supreme Court's *Dred Scott* decision. The editors of the *Times* wrote in the article "Negro, Black and African American" (December 22, 1988):

> The archaeology is dramatically plain to older adults who, in one lifetime, have already heard preferred usage shift from *colored* to *Negro* to *black*. The four lingual layers provide an abbreviated history of civil rights in this century.

Renaming this ethnic group "African American" may produce the fresh vision needed to understand and transcend the deep racism that infects society. The following glimpses of the African American reality, its struggles for freedom, its tradition and community, its achievements, and the stresses of building bridges between worlds reveal a dense set of problems. More importantly, they suggest pieces of authentic identity rather than stereotype. Becoming a healthy ethnic society involves more than the end of ethnic stereotyping. The basis of ethnic identity is sustained by authentic portrayal of positive personal and group identity. The cultivation of ethnicity that does not encourage disdain for and self-hatred among members and groups is an important psychological and social artifice.

Progress on issues of race involves examination of a complex of historical, social, cultural, and economic factors. Analysis of this sort requires assessment of the deep racism in the American mentality—that is, the cultural consciousness and the institutions whose images and practices shape social reality.

Discrimination and prejudice based on skin color are issues rarely broached in mainstream journals of opinion. Ethnic and racial intermarriage and the influence and impact of skin hue within the African American community raise attendant issues of discrimination and consciousness of color. This concern began in eighteenth- and nineteenth-century laws and practices of defining race that shaped the mentalities of color consciousness, prejudice, and racism in America. Other dimensions of the African American experience can be found in this unit's accounts of African American traditions and experiences of self-help and the family. New perspectives on the civil rights era can be gained from reflective accounts of the leaders who

influenced the direction of social change that reconfigured race and ethnic relations in America.

As this debate continues, patterns of change within African American populations compel discussion of the emerging black middle class. The purpose and influence of the historically black university, the reopening of the discussion of the separate-but-equal issue in the courts, and the renewed attention to Afrocentric education are clear evidence of the ambivalence and ambiguity inherent in the challenges of a multicultural society. Earlier dichotomies—slave/free, black/white, poor/rich—are still evident, but a variety of group relations based on historical and regional as well as institutional agendas to preserve cultural and racial consciousness have complicated the simple hope for liberty and justice that was shared by many Americans. Issues of race and class are addressed in this section. Various approaches to Afrocentrism are explained and contrasted.

Questions on the future state of American ethnic groups raise profound issues. For example, understanding of the changing structure of the African American family has stubbornly eluded researchers and parents who confront the realities of pride and prejudice. Does the continual discovery of prejudice and discrimination in corporations have implications for public policy? Should public policy sustain an ethnic model of family or direct the formation of family life that is consonant with public purposes and goals?

The civil rights movement has been over for more than 20 years, but many African Americans still face challenges in housing, employment, and education. Changing circumstances within the larger American society and the civil rights agenda itself have been affected by success and failure, and once-clear issues and solutions have taken on more complex structural, economic, and philosophical dimensions. The growing gap between blacks and whites in terms of education, financial status, and class and the growing crime and death rates of young black men paint a daunting picture of past policies and of this population's future. According to scales of mortality, health, income, education, and marital status, African Americans have emerged as one of the most troubled segments of American society. These problems also foreshadow grave difficulties for the African American family in the years ahead.

To be sure, African Americans have made advances since the civil rights movement of the 1960s. They have made dramatic gains in education, employment, and financial status. Unfortunately, they still are portrayed as

both the public and the private sectors in areas of education, employment, and training. Suggestions for meeting future needs of this population and pragmatic policy responses also will help the general population.

Patent historical distortion and various forms of statistical evidence have been included in interpretations and rearticulations of race and ethnicity. The issues of race in the workplace and remedies for discriminating practices have been raised in the debate regarding the Civil Rights Act of 1991. Exploring ethnic and racial mobility and developing strategies that foster the breakdown of discrimination engage us in a web of baffling arguments and social, political, and institutional procedures.

Looking Ahead: Challenge Questions

What are the most compelling issues that face African American communities? Is location an important variable in the formulation of your answer?

What role will new African immigrants play in the African American community?

What social, economic, and political conditions have supported the expansion of an African American middle class?

What explains the persistence of an African American underclass? In what respect is this question related to integration?

Does the impact of the O. J. Simpson trial have long-term consequences for shaping consciousness of ethnic group identity? The Million Man/Million Woman Marches?

In what respect is attention to education an answer to economic and social integration of African Americans?

Does the name "African Americans" augment the development of pluralism? Discuss in terms of Afrocentrism and integration.

Discuss the influence of religion on the civil rights movement.

What effect will the Supreme Court's deemphasis on remedies for segregation and on other initiatives that use racial preferences have on race and ethnic relations?

What relevance does the Nation of Islam have to the public dialogue that shapes relationships among racial and ethnic populations?

Comment on the idea that attitudinal change founded on achieving middle-class status could extend to the diminishing of interest in and the relevance of being an African American.

being part of an urban underclass when only one-third of their population is considered part of this group. While not all African Americans are poor, those who are poor are in desperate situations. Will help come from the African American population that now constitutes part of the middle and upper classes of American society?

Scholarly differences of opinion concerning the composition of the urban underclass do not minimize the hardships that many endure. The growth of the underclass, its isolation from society, and society's inability to help it are tremendous obstacles that face our nation. Concrete strategies for improving this situation call upon

10 Most Dramatic Events In African-American History

Lerone Bennett Jr.

1. The Black Coming

A YEAR before the arrival of the celebrated *Mayflower*, 244 years before the signing of the Emancipation Proclamation, 335 years before *Brown* vs. *Board of Education*, a big, bluff-bowed ship sailed up the river James and landed the first generation of African-Americans at Jamestown, Va.

Nobody knows the hour or the date of the official Black coming. But there is not the slightest doubt about the month. John Rolfe, who betrayed Pochohontas and experimented with tobacco, was there, and he said in a letter that the ship arrived "about the latter end of August" in 1619 and that it "brought not anything but 20 and odd Negroes." Concerning which the most charitable thing to say is that John Rolfe was probably pulling his boss' leg. For no ship ever called at an American port with a more important cargo. In the hold of that ship, in a manner of speaking, was the whole gorgeous panorama of Black America, was jazz and the spirituals and the black gold that made American capitalism possible.* Bird was there and Bigger and King and Malcolm and millions of other Xs and crosses, along with Mahalia singing, Duke Ellington composing, Gwendolyn Brooks rhyming and Michael Jordan slam-dunking. It was all there, illegible and inevitable, on that day. A man with eyes would have seen it and would have announced to his contemporaries that this ship heralds the beginning of the first Civil War and the second.

As befitting a herald of fate, the ship was nameless, and mystery surrounds it to this day. Where did this ship come from? From the high seas, where the

The Shaping of Black America

crew robbed a Spanish vessel of a cargo of Africans bound for the West Indies. The captain "ptended," John Rolfe noted, that he needed food, and he offered to exchange his cargo for "victualle." The deal was arranged. Antoney, Pedro, Isabella and 17 other Africans with Spanish names stepped ashore, and the history of Africans in America began.

And it began, contrary to what almost all texts say, not in slavery but in freedom. For there is indisputable evidence that most of the first Black immigrants, like most of the first White immigrants, were held in indentured servitude for a number of years and then freed. During a transitional period of some 40 years, the first Black immigrants held real property, sued in court and accumulated pounds and plantations.

This changed drastically in the sixth decade of the century when the White founding fathers, spurred on by greed and the unprotected status of African immigrants, enacted laws that reduced most Africans to slavery. And so, some 40 years after the Black coming, Black and White crossed a fatal threshold, and the echo of that decision will reverberate in the corridors of Black and White history forever.

2. The Founding of Black America

WHEN, on a Sunday in November 1786, the little band of Black Christians arrived at Philadelphia's St. George's Methodist Episcopal Church, the sexton pointed to the gallery. The Blacks paused and then started up the rickety stairs with downcast eyes and heavy hearts. To the leaders of this group, Richard Allen and Absalom Jones, this was the ultimate indignity—to be shunted from the first floor to the gallery in a church Black men had helped build.

The group had barely reached the top of the stairs when a voice from the pulpit said, "Let us pray." Without thinking, the men plopped down where they were—in the *front* of the gallery. Allen was praying as hard as he could when he heard loud voices. He opened his eyes and saw a white sexton trying to pull Absalom Jones from his knees.

"You must get up; you must not kneel down here!" the White sexton said.

"Wait until the prayer is over," Jones replied.

The voices echoed through the church, and people looked up and beheld the incredible scene of a Black Christian and a White Christian wrestling in the house of the Lord over the color of God's word.

"Get up!" the sexton said. "Get up!"

"Wait until the prayer is over," Jones replied wearily, "and I will not trouble you any more."

Four or five White Christians rushed to the sexton's aid, and the struggle spread over the gallery. Before the issue was resolved, the prayer ended. The Black men stood up then and, without a word, streamed out of the church in the first mass demonstration in Black American history.

Richard Allen added a mournful postscript:

". . . And they were no more plagued by us in the church."

They were no more plagued by Blacks in a lot of places. For the Philadelphia demonstration was the focal point of a national movement that created the foundations of Black America. On April 12, 1787, Richard Allen and Absalom

Jones created the Free African Society which DuBois called "the first wavering step of a people toward a more organized social life."

Similar societies were formed in most major Northern cities. And on this foundation rose an intricate structure of independent Black churches, schools and cultural organizations. The movement climaxed in the 1820s and 1830s with the founding of Freedom's Journal, the first Black newspaper, and the convening of the first national Black convention.

3. *Nat Turner's War*

GOD was speaking, Nat Turner said later.

There was, he remembered, thunder and lightning and a "loud voice" in the sky. And the voice spoke to him, telling him to take up the yoke and fight against the serpent "for the time was fast approaching when the first should be last and the last should be first."

Nat Turner was numbered among the last. And although he was a slave in Southampton County, Va., it would be said of him later that he "made an impact upon the people of his section as great as that of John C. Calhoun or Jefferson Davis." A mystic with blood on his mind and a preacher with vengeance on his lips, he was an implacable foe of slaveholders. He had believed since he was a child that God had set him aside for some great purpose. And he decided now that God was calling him to rise up and "slay my enemies with their own weapons."

To this end, Turner, who was about 30 years old, chose four disciples and set his face towards Jerusalem, the county seat of Southampton.

On Sunday morning, Aug. 21, 1831, the disciples gathered on the banks of Cabin Pond on the property of Joseph Travis, who had married the widow of Turner's last master and who had therefore inherited Turner and death. Nat, who appreciated the value of a delayed and dramatic entrance, appeared suddenly late in the afternoon and announced that they would strike that night, beginning at the home of his master and proceeding from house to house, killing every man, woman and child.

At 1 a.m., Nat Turner and his army crept through the woods to the home of the luckless Joseph Travis. They were seven men, armed with one hatchet and a broadax. Twenty-four hours later, they

would be seventy and at least fifty-seven Whites would be dead.

When, on Monday morning, the first bodies were discovered, a nameless dread seized the citizens. Men, women and children fled to the woods and hid under the leaves until soldiers and sailors arrived from Richmond and Norfolk. Some Whites left the county; others left the state.

Defeated in an engagement near Jerusalem, Turner went into hiding and was not captured until six weeks later. On Nov. 11, 1831, the short Black man called the Prophet was hanged in a field near the courthouse. Before climbing the gallows, he made one last prophecy, saying there would be a storm after his execution and that the sun would refuse to shine. There was, in fact, a storm in Jerusalem on that day, but Turner was not talking about the weather—he was predicting a major disturbance in the American psyche. The storm he saw came in the generation of crisis that his act helped precipitate.

4. *Free at Last!*

TO Felix Haywood, who was there, it was the Time of Glory when men and women walked "on golden clouds."

To Frederick Douglass, it was a downpayment on the redemption of the American soul.

To Sister Winny in Virginia, to Jane Montgomery in Louisiana, to Ed Bluff in Mississippi, to Black people all over the South and all over America, it was the Time of Jubilee, the wild, happy, sad, mocking, tearful, fearful time of the unchaining of the bodies of Black folks. And the air was sweet with song.

Free at last!
Free at last!
Thank God Almighty!
We're free at last.

W.E.B. Dubois was not there, but he summed the whole thing up in phrases worthy of the ages. It was all, he said, "foolish, bizarre, and tawdry. Gangs of dirty Negroes howling and dancing; poverty-stricken ignorant laborers mistaking war, destruction, and revolution for the mystery of the free human soul; and yet to these Black folk it was the Apocalypse." And he added:

"All that was Beauty, all that was Love, all that was Truth, stood on the top of these mad mornings and sang with the stars. A great human sob shrieked in the

wind, and tossed its tears upon the sea—free, free, free."

Contrary to the common view, the emancipation of Blacks didn't happen at one time or even in one place. It started with the first shot fired at Fort Sumter. It continued during the war and in the Jubilee summer of 1865, *and it has not been completed.* For the slaves, who created the foundation of American wealth, never received the 40 acres of land that would have made freedom meaningful.

It was in this milieu that African-Americans embarked on a road called freedom. As the road twisted and turned, doubling back on itself, their enemies and their problems multiplied. But they endured, and endure.

5. *Booker T. Washington vs. W. E. B. DuBois*

THERE was a big parade in Atlanta on Wednesday, Sept. 18, 1895, and a huge crowd gathered in the Exposition Building at the Cotton States Exposition for the opening speeches. Several Whites spoke and then former Gov. Rufus Bullock introduced "Professor Booker T. Washington." The 39-year-old president of Tuskegee Institute moved to the front of the platform and started speaking to the segregated audience. Within 10 minutes, reporter James Creelman wrote, "the multitude was in an uproar of enthusiasm — handkerchiefs were waved . . . hats were tossed into the air. The fairest women of Georgia stood up and cheered."

What was the cheering about?

Metaphors mostly—and words millions of Whites wanted to hear. Washington told Blacks: "Cast down your buckets where you are." To Whites, he offered the same advice: "Cast down your bucket [among] the most patient, faithful, law-abiding and unresentful people the world has seen . . . ."

Suddenly, he flung his hand aloft, with the fingers held wide apart.

"In all things purely social," he said, "we can be as separate as the fingers, yet [he balled the fingers into a fist] one as the hand in all things essential to mutual progress."

The crowd came to its feet, yelling.

Washington's "Atlanta Compromise" speech made him famous and set the tone for race relations for some 20 years. One year after his speech, the Supreme Court rounded a fateful fork, endorsing in *Plessy* vs. *Ferguson* the principle of "separate but equal."

Washington's refusal to make a direct and open attack on Jim Crow and his implicit acceptance of segregation brought him into conflict with W.E.B. DuBois and a group of Black militants who organized the germinal Niagara Movement. At its first national meeting at Harpers Ferry in 1906, the Niagara militants said, "We claim for ourselves every single right that belongs to a freeborn American, political, civil, and social; and until we get these rights we will never cease to protest and assail the ears of America."

So saying, the Niagara militants laid the foundation for the National Association for the Advancement of Colored People which merged the forces of Black militancy and White liberalism.

6. The Great Migration

HISTORY does not always come with drums beating and flags flying.

Sometimes it comes in on a wave of silence.

Sometimes it whispers.

It was like that in the terrible days of despair that preceded the unprecedented explosion of hope and movement that is called The Great Migration.

This event, which was the largest internal migration in American history and one of the central events of African-American history, started in the cracks of history, in the minds and moods of the masses of Blacks, who were reduced to the status of semi-slaves in the post-Reconstruction period. Pushed back toward slavery by lynchings, segregation and the sharecropping systems, they turned around within themselves and decided that there had to be another way and another and better place. The feeling moved, became a mood, an imperative, a command. Without preamble, without a plan, without leadership, the people began to move, going from the plantation to Southern cities, going from there to the big cities of the North. There, they found jobs in wartime industries and sent letters to a cousin or an aunt or sister or brother, saying: Come! And they came, hundreds and hundreds of thousands. The first wave (300,000) came between 1910 and 1920, followed by a second wave (1,300,000) between 1920 and 1930, and

third (500,000) and fourth (2,500,000) waves, even larger, in the '30s and '40s.

In the big cities of the North, Blacks emancipated themselves politically and economically and created the foundation of contemporary Black America.

7. Brown vs. Board of Education

THE marshal's voice was loud and clear.

"Oyez! Oyez! Oyez! All persons having business before the Honorable, the Supreme Court of the United States, are admonished to draw near and give their attention, for the Court is now sitting."

The marshal paused and intoned the traditional words:

"God save the United States and this Honorable Court!"

It was high noon on Monday, May 17, 1954, and the Supreme Court was crammed to capacity with spectators. Among the dozen or so Blacks present was Thurgood Marshall, chief counsel of the NAACP, who leaned forward in expectation.

Cases from four states (South Carolina, Virginia, Delaware, Kansas) and the District of Columbia were before the Court, which had been asked by Marshall and his associates to overturn the *Plessy* vs. *Ferguson* decision and declare segregation in public schools unconstitutional. All America awaited the long-expected decision which would come on a Monday. But which Monday? No one knew, and there was no sign on the faces of the justices that the issue was going to be settled on this day.

The Court disposed of routine business and announced decisions in several boring cases involving the sale of milk and the picketing of retail stores. Then Chief Justice Earl Warren picked up a document and said in a firm, quiet voice: "I have for announcement the judgment and opinion of the Court in No. 1—*Oliver Brown et al. v. Board of Education of Topeka*. It was 12:52 p.m. A shiver ran through the courtroom, and bells started ringing in press rooms all over the world.

Warren held the crowd in suspense, reviewing the history of the cases. Then, abruptly, he came to the heart of the matter:

"Does segregation of children in public schools solely on the basis of race, even though the physical facilities and

other "tangible" factors may be equal, deprive the children of the minority group of equal educational opportunities?" Warren paused and said: "We believe that it does." The decision was unanimous: 9-0.

The words raced across the country and were received by different people according to their different lights. Southern diehards like Herman Talmadge issued statements of defiance and promised a generation of litigation, but the implications of the decision were so enormous that many Americans were shocked into silence and wonder. In Farmville, Va., a 16-year-old student named Barbara Trent burst into tears when her teacher announced the decision. "We went on studying history," she said later, "but things weren't the same and will never be the same again."

8. Montgomery and the Freedom Movement

IT was a quiet, peaceful day in Montgomery, Ala., the Cradle of the Confederacy—but it was unseasonably hot for December 1.

The Cleveland Avenue bus rolled through Court Square, where Blacks were auctioned in the days of the Confederacy, and braked to a halt in front of the Empire Theater. There was nothing special about the bus or the day; neither the driver nor the passengers realized that a revolution was about to begin that would turn America and the South upside down.

Six Whites boarded the bus at the Empire Theater, and the driver stormed to the rear and ordered the foremost Blacks to get up and give their seats to the White citizens. This was an ancient custom, sanctioned by the peculiar mores of the South, and it excited no undue comment. Three Blacks got up immediately, but Rosa Parks, a mild-mannered seamstress in rimless glasses, kept her seat. For this act of defiance, she was arrested. Local leaders called a one-day bus boycott on Monday, Dec. 5, 1955, to protest the arrest. The one-day boycott stretched out to 381 days; the 381 days changed the face and heart of Black America, creating a new leader (Martin Luther King Jr.), and a new movement. There then followed in quick succession a series of movements (the Sit-ins and Freedom Rides) and dramatic events (Birmingham, Selma, Watts, the March on Washington) that constituted Black America's finest hour and one of the greatest moments in the history of the Republic.

9. Little Rock

THE GIANT C-119 flying boxcars circled the field, like grim birds.

One by one, they glided into the Little Rock, Ark., airport and debouched paratroopers in full battle gear. There were, in all, more than 1,000 soldiers, Black and White; and they were in Little Rock to enforce the orders of a federal court. For the first time since the Reconstruction era, the United States of America was deploying federal troops to defend the rights of Black Americans.

Escorted by city police cars, a convoy of olive-drab jeeps and trucks sped to Central High School where a howling mob had prevented the enrollment of nine Black students. The troops deployed on the double to block all entrances to the schools, and signalmen strung telephone lines and set up command posts.

Wednesday morning, Sept. 25, 1957, dawned bright and clear, and nine Black teenagers gathered at the ranch-style home of Daisy Bates, president of the Arkansas NAACP. At 8:50 a.m., there was a rumble of heavy wheels. The teenagers rushed to the window.

"The streets were blocked off," Daisy Bates recalled later. "The soldiers closed ranks . . . Oh! It was beautiful. And the attitude of the children at that moment: the respect they had. I could hear them saying, 'For the first time in my life I truly feel like an American.' I could see it in their faces: Somebody cares for me—*America cares*."

At 9:45, U.S. soldiers with drawn bayonets escorted six Black females and three Black males into Central High School, and the Rev. Dunbar H. Ogden, president of the Greater Little Rock Ministerial Association, said: "This may be looked back upon by future historians as the turning point—for good—of race relations in this country."

10. Memphis and the Triumph of the Spirit

THERE had never been a moment like this one.

Time stopped.
Everything stopped.

And every man and woman living at that terrible time would be able to tell you until the end of their time what they were doing and where they were on Thursday, April 4, 1968, when word came that Martin Luther King Jr. had been assassinated on the balcony of the Lorraine Motel in Memphis, Tenn.

The response in Black and White America was tumultuous. Performances, plays, meetings, baseball games were cancelled, and men and women walked aimlessly through the streets, weeping.

There were tears, rivers of tears, and there was also blood. For Black communities exploded, one after another, like firecrackers on a string. Some 46 persons were killed in uprisings in 126 cities, and federal troops were mobilized to put down rebellions in Chicago, Baltimore and Washington, D.C.

To counteract this fury, and to express their sorrow, Americans of all races and creeds joined forces in an unprecedented tribute to a Black American. President Lyndon B. Johnson declared a national day of mourning and ordered U.S. flags to fly at half-mast over U.S. installations at home and abroad. On the day of the funeral—Tuesday, April 9— more than 200,000 mourners followed King's coffin, which was carried through the streets of Atlanta on a wagon, borne by two Georgia mules.

Eighteen years later, the spirit and the truth of Martin Luther King Jr. triumphed when he became the second American citizen (with George Washington) to be celebrated in a personal national holiday.

Black Politics, the 1996 Elections, and the End of the Second Reconstruction

Dean E. Robinson

In reviewing the 1996 election, we should not be surprised that Bill Clinton received 83 percent of the black vote, and that Bob Dole, who received 12 percent of his votes from blacks, did not manage to secure more. Indeed, blacks of all age groups and regions of the country voted solidly for Clinton, though there was a gender gap (89 percent of black women to 78 percent of men). Despite the fact that the GOP enjoyed 18 percent of the black vote in House elections, the same pattern held: blacks remain solidly Democratic.[1]

What might be surprising is that despite these statistics, it is unlikely that this "race gap" will mean that American government will be more responsive to the issues that concern black voters. What issues? In a general sense, black interests are the same as everyone else's: employment, education, housing, health care, and so on. However, because of their historical and current experiences as a racial minority, their more particular concerns as a group involve ensuring that discrimination does not limit their access to employment, housing, and education, and that the government maintains its commitment to substantive equality. Despite the fact that black Americans are not monolithic—they work in different occupations, live in different parts of the country, have different ideas about religion, and so on—certain objective circumstances and subjective orientations separate them from white Americans.[2]

Consider objective measures. The relative economic position of most black families with respect to whites has deteriorated in recent times, especially during the decade of the 1980s. By 1989 the median white family had 20 times the wealth of the median nonwhite family.[3] This is not helped by a black male unemployment rate of 11.5 percent, compared to 5.3 for white males. Further, despite an expanded middle class, one-third of all blacks remain impoverished and nearly half of black children under the age of six live in poverty.[4] These statistics result from the fact that discrimination, inferior education, inadequate health care, and crippling unemployment are still the rule for black communities across the country. Perhaps not so surprisingly, blacks are considerably more supportive of government efforts to help the disadvantaged in general and Afro-Americans in particular. Blacks and whites differ sharply over this issue. Blacks overwhelmingly think the government can do things to help. They also overwhelmingly (76 to 36 percent for whites) favor affirmative action for racial minorities.[5]

Despite these trends, and despite black voter loyalty, it is unlikely that President Clinton and the Democratic Party will respond to these sorts of concerns. Clinton's strategy has been to pursue centrist goals, divorced from any strong commitment to policies targeted toward racial minorities and the poor. Centrist goals have meant less rhetorical and substantive support for the programs and policies that seek to address some of the problems mentioned above.

Black voters are "stuck" in ways reminiscent of a century ago. Then and now, politics has swung to the right. At the end of the nineteenth century, the party backing civil rights retreated in the face of white opposition, and the Supreme Court undercut civil rights legislation. Then, as now, black voters voted solidly for one particular party, only to be sacrificed in the game of national politics. And liberals abandoned racial equality on the grounds of political pragmatism. Finally, in the face of a rightward turn, many blacks themselves adopted conservative (accommodationist) stands.

THE FIRST RECONSTRUCTION

One hundred years ago, black people threw their weight to the Republican Party—when they could. Because, of course, by then the political ground was crumbling beneath them. Well before the *Plessy v. Ferguson* (1896) decision sanctioned Jim Crow in national law, whites had begun to purge blacks from the mainstream. The mainstream was, in fact, where blacks had been—in the middle of political action. Throughout the Reconstruction South, blacks voted and held political office at local, state, and national levels. They had the greatest influence in South Carolina, where, in the first state legislature, they outnumbered whites 87 to 40. The first legislature in Mississippi had 40 blacks, some of whom had been slaves. And Louisiana, as a final example, had 133 black legislators between 1868 and 1896.[6] The first black representatives to Congress came from the states with high black populations. Between 1869 and 1901, 20 blacks served in the House of Representatives and 2 in the Senate.[7] The two senators, Hiram R. Revels and Blanche K. Bruce, both represented Mississippi.[8]

This political success—limited from our contemporary vantage point—was the direct result of Republican Party support. The party of Lincoln was determined to strengthen its position following the war, and they did so with the help of the freedmen. Republicans established the Freedmen's Bureau in 1865 in order to distribute clothing, food, and fuel to destitute freedmen and oversee all policies related to their condition.[9] The Bureau also fostered political activity. Many Freedmen's Bureau officials were interested as much in expanding the Republican Party as they were in the welfare of ex-slaves. Another benevolent group, the Union League of America, also encouraged political activity among blacks in chapters throughout the South. And other organizations like the Lincoln Brotherhood and the Red Strings "delivered the black vote to the Republican party in national as well as state and local elections."[10]

These political efforts, in turn, had been facilitated by three amendments to the Constitution and an array of legislation. The Thirteenth Amendment abolished slavery. The Fourteenth Amendment made Americans citizens of *both* the United States and the states in which they resided. And the Fifteenth Amendment gave black men the right to vote. The 1866 Civil Rights Act "gave all U.S. citizens equal rights to inherit, purchase, lease, hold, or convey real or personal property."[11] The Reconstruction Act of 1867 disenfranchised vast numbers of white southerners, allowing whites and blacks who had been loyal to the Union access to the ballot. It also divided the Confederate states, except Tennessee, into five military districts under commanders authorized to protect the peace.[12] The Civil Rights Act of 1875 prohibited racial discrimination in public accommodations.

CONSERVATIVE BACKLASH

The momentum of integration had already started to wane well before the Compromise of 1877 effectively ended Reconstruction. From the beginning, Republicans had confronted the open hostility many white northerners felt toward the granting of rights to black Americans. Most white Americans, northerners as well as southerners, thought blacks unfit for political life, and support for black suffrage depended upon the support of the small radical block of the Republican Party. As the leadership of the party changed, and as political elites, North and South, worked to buttress economic links between regions, southern whites pushed blacks to the political, economic, and social margins.

As early as 1870, the border states began to go Democratic. "The issue of white supremacy, low taxes, and control of the black labor force dominated the Democratic campaigns of the mid-1870s," and to great effect.[13] "Redeemers" took control in North Carolina and Virginia and, in 1871, Georgia gave way to Democratic control. In 1874 and 1875 Texas, Arkansas, and Alabama did the same.[14] This reflected the fact that many white southerners resisted efforts to transform the South's system of racial castes. Such stalling foreshadowed a similar resistance to federally imposed civil rights policy in the 1960s.

Southern "Redeemers" benefited from a number of Supreme Court rulings that effectively undercut civil rights enforcement. In the *Slaughter-House Cases* (1873), the Supreme Court ruled that the Fourteenth Amendment "protected only those rights that owed their existence to the federal government."[15] In *U.S. v. Cruikshank* (1876), the Supreme Court overturned the convictions obtained under the Enforcement Act of 1870. Remarkably, the Court argued that the postwar amendments could only prohibit the violation of black rights by states. When individual whites violated black rights, they were subject to state, not federal, laws. This ruling effectively ended federal protection against acts of terror from blacks in the South.

Jim Crow was aided by Supreme Court rulings. In the *Civil Rights Cases* (1883), the Court took the position that the Reconstruction Amendments did not apply to private accommodations and that the federal government could not interfere with "social rights." And, of course, *Plessy* (1896) established the "separate but equal" doctrine. The Court argued, "If one race be inferior to the other socially, the Constitution of the United States cannot put them on the same plane."[16]

LIBERAL CAPITULATION AND BLACK POLITICS: PHASE I

As blacks' gains were rolled back, the "liberals" in the North increasingly offered opinions regarding racial policies that mirrored the South's. First, with sights set on economic development, commentators in journals like *Harper's* and the *Atlantic Monthly* argued that black rights had to be subordinated on the grounds of the South's need for "home rule"—a first step toward regional prosperity. In the 1880s and 1890s it was common in journals like the *Nation* and *Harper's* to hear accounts of black people's innate inferiority and inability to meet the requirements of citizenship. These attitudes were helped along by Social Darwinian studies like Frederick L. Hoffman's influential *Race Traits and Tendencies of the American Negro* (1896). Hoffman argued, among other things, that black poverty "was not the result of white discrimination or lack of opportunity but stemmed directly from an innate tendency toward 'crime and immorality.' "[17]

Blacks played an increasingly marginal role in politics after the Compromise of 1877 because of procedural barriers like "literacy" and "grandfather" clauses, as well as intimidation and violence. By the last decade of the nineteenth century, black politics had accommodated to white supremacy and Jim Crow. Indeed, Booker T. Washington seized the mantle of Afro-American leadership in 1895 by promising that black people would not agitate for civil rights or make demands on the federal government; rather, black people would be self-reliant, patient, disciplined, and morally upright citizens. Washington's vision of industrialization and accommodation to Jim Crow placed him squarely within "mainstream" racial policy. This was clear when he remarked a year before *Plessy*:

> The wisest among my race understand that the agitation of questions of social equality is the extremest folly. . . . It is important and right that the privileges of the law be ours, but it is vastly more important that we be prepared for the exercises of these privileges.[18]

THE SECOND (DE)CONSTRUCTION

Developments in national politics suggest that we may be witnessing the end of the second reconstruction. The second reconstruction began with the Civil Rights Act of 1964 and the Voting Rights Act of 1965—the culmination of more than a decade of struggle by blacks and their allies for civil rights. The Civil Rights Act forbade discrimination in most public places. It increased the power of the attorney general to protect citizens against segregation and discrimination in voting, education, and public facilities. It established a federal Community Relations Service and the more significant Equal Employment Opportunity Commission (EEOC). And, among its more controversial provisions, the Civil Rights Act required the elimination of discrimination in federally assisted programs. The Voting Rights Act of 1965 gave teeth to the Fifteenth Amendment. This act stationed federal examiners in those individual southern counties with the worst histories of abuse. The act also required states with a history of low black participation to submit all proposed changes in election procedure to the U.S. Department of Justice for "preclearance." The Voting Rights Act had a profound impact on black voter participation. In three decades—1940–1970—black registration in southern states increased from 3.1 to 66.9 percent. Over roughly the same period of time, the number of black elected officials—city, state, and national—increased from 33 to 1,469.[19]

The late 1960s and early 1970s were periods of federal activism geared toward expanding opportunity for black Americans specifically and poor Americans generally. President Lyndon B. Johnson's Great Society began with the Economic Opportunity Act of 1964. This act created the Office of Economic Opportunity (OEO), which oversaw the establishment of new programs geared toward community development. The Economic Opportunity Act also provided day care in conjunction with other programs. Operation Head Start, for instance, had its origins in the community action programs administered by the OEO.

Affirmative action evolved through a series of executive orders, administrative policies, and court decisions. As opposed to "non-discrimination" policies that "merely enjoined employers from practicing discrimination," "affirmative action committed employers to go a step beyond non-discrimination and to *actively* seek out protected groups in employment." Historically, "good-faith efforts to increase minority representation were generally ineffective until they were backed up by specific 'goals and timetables' that, in effect, gave preference to minority applicants who met basic qualifications."[20] AT&T and the former Bell System offer a good example of the ways in which companies enacted affirmative action policies. In 1973, AT&T employed 351,000 persons nationwide in low-paying operator or clerical classifications, 95 percent of whom were women. The overwhelming majority of higher-paid craft workers (95 percent) were male, and only 6 percent of these were black. Few women or blacks were in management positions. Only after the federal government investigated the Bell System's employment practices did the company agree to raise salaries for women and blacks and to meet employment targets for these groups.

Affirmative action propelled millions of Afro-Americans into all levels of the labor force. Studies demonstrate that companies subject to EEOC requirements have higher levels of black employment than do companies not under scrutiny. Furthermore, the occupational spheres where blacks are now best represented—"in government service, major blue-collar occupations, corporate management, and the professions—are all areas where vigorous affirmative action programs have been in place over the past two decades."[21]

In a reversal of political momentum similar in some ways to that of the late part of last century, the Supreme Court under Chief Justice William Rehnquist began to pull the teeth out of laws designed to achieve racial equality. The Court first narrowed the terms under which affirmative action programs could legitimately exist. The *Bakke* (1978) decision outlawed the use of quotas. And in *Richmond v. Croson* (1989), the Court found that a set-aside program was deficient on the grounds that (1) there was no direct evidence that the city's contractors had discriminated against minority-owned subcontractors; and (2) it was inappropriate to use national statistics of racial discrimination in the construction industry as a basis for establishing the set-aside program.

The Court has also made it more difficult for blacks to elect representatives by challenging the constitutionality of black or minority-majority districts designed to promote minority representation in Congress. *Shaw v. Reno* (1993) was perhaps the most significant decision regarding black-majority districts. Writing for the majority, Justice Sandra Day O'Connor argued that appellants had stated a claim under the Equal Protection clause by alleging that the North Carolina General Assembly adopted a reapportionment scheme so irrational on its face that it could be understood only as an effort to segregate voters into separate voting districts because of their race.[22] The majority rejected the idea that "race" can be an appropriate criterion in a context of historical inequity.

Regarding employment discrimination, the Court has also shifted to the right. In *Wards Cove Packing Company, Inc. v. Frank Antonio* (1989), the Court rejected statistics used by minority employees that hiring and promotion practices had accounted for their disparate positions in relation to white employees. The Court also argued that the burden of proof should not shift to the employer but should remain with the plaintiff.

In these decisions, the Rehnquist Court has chipped away at the concrete methods that minority-majority districting and affirmative action laws used to achieve representation and parity. And, in so doing, the Court has responded to broader trends in national politics, particularly the civil rights orientation of the Bush and Reagan administrations.

Indeed, Ronald Reagan did not wish simply to ignore civil rights programs; he sought to *reduce* government's role in the enforcement and administration of them. For instance, "almost immediately upon assuming office in January 1981, Reagan suspended Carter's affirmative action guidelines and reduced their enforcement."[23] That same year, Reagan also decreased the number of contractors that were required to have affirmative action plans. Small firms, Reagan argued, did not need to comply. Reagan's Omnibus Budget Reconciliation Act removed 400,000 individuals from the food stamp program. It reduced or eliminated welfare and Medicaid benefits for the working poor. It also eliminated the entire "public service jobs program, and the minimum benefit for low-income Social Security recipients, ended the modest death benefit, and phased out benefits for older children of deceased workers."[24]

Between 1981 and 1992 the federal budget dropped steeply in almost all issue areas: 40 percent for community development, 63 percent for job training, and 82 percent for subsidized housing.[25] The cuts disproportionately affected black Americans.

A RACIAL REALIGNMENT

This reversal toward conservatism was fueled by a "conversion" of some traditional supporters of the Democratic Party based on a backlash against programs of Johnson's Great Society and more race-specific efforts like affirmative action and busing. Democrats had long understood the potential costs of supporting civil rights. In fact, the New Deal's origins had depended upon a number of agreements that would not upset the racial caste system of the South.[26] President Franklin D. Roosevelt needed southern congressmen to move his programs through key House and Senate committees. Southern congressmen, however, opposed *any* program "that would grant cash directly to black workers, because direct cash could undermine the entire foundation of the plantation economy." Hence the core programs of the Social Security Act left out agricultural workers and domestic servants, the occupational spheres where most black men and women worked.[27]

The Civil Rights and Voting Rights Acts and Johnson's War on Poverty were, in effect, the Freedmen's Bureaus of the 1960s. And, where "the New Deal had excluded African Americans, the War on Poverty would favor them." The War on Poverty sought to integrate blacks into local politics, local job markets, and

local housing markets.[28] Under the OEO, Community Action Agencies channeled resources into civil rights organizations, job and educational programs, and similar efforts. By so doing, the War on Poverty bypassed the traditional political elites that had effectively locked blacks out.

Hence, the Johnson administration's support of the civil rights cause in 1964 and the Republicans' support of "home rule" started the process in which white southern Democrats turned Republican, and the Republican Party essentially abandoned liberalism. By 1972, with George McGovern's nomination, the process of racial realignment was complete. Table 10.1 shows the percentage of whites who have supported Democratic presidential candidates from 1972 to 1996. During this same period, whites have consistently thrown their weight to Republican candidates, as shown in Table 10.2.

And, of course, over the same period of time, blacks have represented the most solidly Democratic constituency.

LIBERAL CAPITULATION AND BLACK POLITICS: PHASE II

The defeat in 1984 and 1988 of the Democratic Party's nominees for president, Walter Mondale and Michael Dukakis, led many analysts and Democratic Party strategists to the conclusion that the party's "liberalism" and association with "special interest groups"—blacks in particular—was no longer good strategy. A study conducted by Stanley Greenberg in 1985 concluded that the party's identification with blacks was a problem:

> These white Democratic defectors express a profound distaste for blacks, a sentiment that pervades almost everything they think about government and politics. . . . Blacks constitute the explanation for their [white defectors'] vulnerability for almost everything that has gone wrong in their lives; not being black is what constitutes being middle class; not living with blacks is what makes a neighborhood a decent place to live. . . . Ronald Reagan's image [was] formed against this backdrop. . . . Reagan represented a determined consistency and an aspiration to unity and pride.[29]

Subsequent analyses built upon this idea to reach one conclusion: the Democratic Party needed to distance itself from blacks and their interests and recast itself as the party of the white middle class. A 1989 study by the Pro-

Table 10.1

Democratic Percentage of White Vote in the Presidential Election by Ethnicity and Region, 1972–1996

	1972	1976	1980	1984	1988	1992	1996
All Whites	31%	47%	36%	35%	40%	39%	43%
Protestants	22	41	31	27	33	33	36
Catholics	44	54	42	45	47	44	53
Jews	64	64	45	67	64	80	78
From the East	34	49	38	42	45	36	51
From the Midwest	32	46	37	35	42	40	45
From the South	23	47	35	28	32	34	36
From the West	36	44	32	33	41	39	43

Table 10.2

Republican Percentage of White Vote in the Presidential Election by Ethnicity and Region, 1972–1996

	1972	1976	1980	1984	1988	1992	1996
All Whites	67%	52%	56%	64%	59%	40%	46%
Protestants	76	58	63	72	66	47	53
Catholics	54	44	50	54	52	35	37
Jews	34	34	39	31	35	11	16
From the East	65	50	52	57	54	36	37
From the Midwest	65	52	55	64	57	39	43
From the South	76	52	61	71	67	49	56
From the West	60	54	55	66	58	37	44

Source: "Portrait of the Electorate," *New York Times,* November 10, 1996.

gressive Policy Institute, the research arm of the Democratic Leadership Council, also argued that the party needed to reconnect with the middle class.[30]

President Clinton has relied on this strategy. Clinton's domestic policy agenda has not, and probably will not, tackle issues of pressing concern to the black poor. As a "New Democrat," Clinton has distanced himself from the tradition of New Deal liberalism, declaring that the "era of big government is over." In his first term, Clinton managed to combine this neoliberal posture with appeals to egalitarian commitments. But he is clearly a centrist. His health care reform proposal, support for NAFTA and GATT, his anticrime and antiterrorism legislation, and his signing of the welfare bill solidified his centrist credentials.

Furthermore, black Americans may interpret several of Clinton's gestures as racially coded. He "got tough on crime" in 1992 when he oversaw the execution of the black, mentally impaired convict Ricky Ray Rector. And he signed the welfare reform bill while being flanked by two black women. This act can be seen as drawing on a racist stereotype—that black women make up the majority of welfare recipients. In the 1996 election, Clinton gave tepid support to affirmative action through his pledge to "mend it, not end it." Ironically, it took GOP vice presidential candidate Jack Kemp to bring racial policies to the fore, specifically affirmative action and "empowerment zones" for inner cities.

Robert Smith notes that in post–civil rights opinion poll data, the majority of whites consistently, and wrongly, view blacks as more prone to crime and violence than whites, more lazy, more sexually promiscuous, and lacking in family values.[31] This is a picture of black America that the Right has painted in literally thousands of forms—from *Wall Street Journal* editorials to the columns of George Will and the speeches of Rush Limbaugh.[32]

There is, in fact, a liberal tradition arguing that aberrant black behavior is an independent cause of black poverty. The most significant for-mulation of this sort appeared in Daniel Patrick Moynihan's controversial "The Negro Family: The Case for National Action" (1965). This report offered mountains of evidence showing high rates of divorce, illegitimacy, and female-headed households. More importantly, Moynihan suggested that this "pathology" had a dynamic all its own—based on "the disintegration of the Negro family"—independent of job-lessness and poverty. The implication of Moynihan's study was the view of "inner-city poverty as driven by behavior defects and social pathology among the poor themselves, and explicitly in ways linked to black women's reproductive activity."[33] Even before Moynihan's report, he and Nathan Glazer had reached similar conclusions about black Americans' lack of comparative success. "It was the heritage of two hundred years of slavery" that deformed family and community life, making it more difficult for blacks to "make use of a free educational system to advance into higher occupations."[34] In a more recent article, Glazer remarked that policy cannot solve "the social and personal problems of people who . . . are engaged in self-destructive behavior—resisting schools, [and] taking to drugs and crime."[35]

The same focus has cohered around analyses of the so-called "underclass" that began during the Reagan era. The underclass is said to comprise between 10 and 20 percent of the poor. Furthermore, according to liberal analysts like Isabel Sawhill and former Clinton appointee David Ellwood, this group suffers in part because their values differ from those of the mainstream.[36] Joe Klein offered the latest spin on the underclass in an October issue of the *New Republic*. Here Klein criticized liberals like William Julius Wilson for denying the fact that poor black people's bad behavior and attitudes, not lack of jobs, are the real cause of inner-city poverty. Klein argued, "They are isolated from us; they have different values. And it seems very clear that their problems were neither entirely caused by the loss of work, nor will they be entirely solved by government action." He notes at another point that, in inner cities across America, "the rudiments of civilization have vanished like cellophane on fire."[37] Such theories have deep roots in American policy discourse. A similar focus on "deviance" and family "disorganization" can be seen in sociological studies beginning in the early decades of this century.

Ironically, the only recent and significant stirring in black politics—the October 1995 Million Man March—was most noteworthy because of the liberal/conservative view of black problems and their solutions that it apparently adopted. The Million Man March may explain the upsurge in black male voting from 1992 (roughly 3 million to 4.8 million) as well as relatively high-level support for the GOP in House races.[38]

Indeed, Louis Farrakhan's rise to power follows the latter-day version of the deconstruction of Reconstruction. As conservatives have undermined black political gains of the 1960s, and as conditions have worsened for large portions of the Afro-American population, Farrakhan has risen as the lone "radical" voice, champion of the oppressed and marginalized. Yet, as many have noted, Farrakhan's ascension is also connected to his social vision—his political and economic agenda blends smoothly into contemporary conservative political thought. When black men pledged to take greater responsibility for their lives, the words echoed the accommodationism of Booker T. Washington and his supporters 100 years ago. Like Washington, Farrakhan is not bothered by racial segregation. Instead, he invites political acquiescence while promoting moral rehabilitation and strict discipline. His anti-Semitism and his unorthodox version of Islam are perhaps the obstacles that prevent Farrakhan from becoming a Booker T. Washington–like power broker.

Conclusion: Lessons Past and Present

Historically, the only times that national parties have confronted the legacy of racism have come in the aftermath of enormous social upheavals: the Civil War and the civil rights movement. During the first Reconstruction, Republicans realized that they needed the political participation of the freedmen to maintain their hegemony. After 1877, however, the Republican Party adopted schemes that would attract southern white men to Republicanism.[39] This, Republicans knew, was the only way they could hope to win power over Democrats.

The civil rights movement triggered the second reconstruction in the 1960s, and for both Presidents Kennedy and Johnson the Afro-American vote was key. But at least since the New Deal, Democratic calculations have been not unlike those of Republicans at the end of the last century. The argument runs like this: Since America is too racist to support programs targeted specifically for blacks, highlighting racial issues drives whites out of the Democratic Party. From the New Deal forward, Democrats seem to have defended their wavering commitments to racial equality on these grounds.

Black voters may feel they have too few choices now, but that need not remain true. They could consider a third-party alternative—such as the Labor Party, the New Party, or an independent black party—that would work toward policies that address their concerns. Easier registration and campaign finance reform could also further their cause.

Endnotes

1. "Portrait of the Electorate," *New York Times*, November 10, 1996.

2. Carol M. Swain, *Black Faces, Black Interests: The Representation of African Americans in Congress* (Cambridge, MA: Harvard University Press, 1993), p. 7.

3. Edward N. Wolff, *Top Heavy: The Increasing Inequality of Wealth in America and What Can Be Done about It* (New York: New Press, 1996), pp. 1–3.

4. Figures come from the Bureau of Labor Statistics and are cited in Holly Sklar, *Chaos or Community? Seeking Solutions, Not Scapegoats for Bad Economics* (Boston: South End Press, 1995), p. 62.

5. See "Race in the United States: It's Not a Matter of Black and White," *The Public Perspective*, Volume 7, Number 2, February/March 1996, pp. 26–27.

6. John Hope Franklin and Alfred A. Moss Jr., *From Slavery to Freedom: A History of African Americans*, 7th ed. (New York: McGraw-Hill, 1994), p. 239.

7. Swain, *Black Faces, Black Interests*, pp. 21–23.

8. Franklin and Moss, *From Slavery to Freedom*, p. 242. In 1874 Bruce was elected to a full term. It wasn't until the election of Edward Brooke in 1966 that another black would be elected again.

9. Eric Foner, *A Short History of Reconstruction: 1863–1877* (New York: Harper & Row, 1990), p. 31.

10. Franklin and Moss, *From Slavery to Freedom*, p. 249.

11. Steven A. Shull, *A Kinder Gentler Racism? The Reagan-Bush Civil Rights Legacy* (Armonk, NY: M. E. Sharpe, 1993), pp. 32–33.

12. Foner, *A Short History of Reconstruction*, p. 122.

13. Foner, *A Short History of Reconstruction*, p. 251.

14. Franklin and Moss, *From Slavery to Freedom*, p. 251.

15. Foner, *A Short History of Reconstruction*, p. 224.

16. Taken from Sheldon Goldman, *Constitutional Law: Cases and Essays* (New York: Harper & Row, 1987), p. 794.

17. George M. Fredrickson, *The Black Image in the White Mind: The Debate on Afro-American Character and Destiny, 1817–1914* (Middletown, CT: Wesleyan University Press, 1971), p. 251.

18. Booker T. Washington, *Up from Slavery* (New York: Oxford University Press, 1995), p. 131.

19. *A Common Destiny: Blacks and American Society* (Washington, DC: National Academy Press, 1989), pp. 225–238.

20. Stephen Steinberg, *Turning Back: The Retreat from Racial Justice in American Thought and Policy* (Boston: Beacon Press, 1995), p. 165.

21. Steinberg, *Turning Back*, p. 167.

22. Quoted in Michael W. Combs, "The Supreme Court, African Americans, and Public Policy: Changes and Transformations," in Huey L. Perry and Wayne Parent (eds.), *Blacks and the American Political System* (Miami, FL: University Press of Florida, 1995), p. 193.

23. Shull, *A Kinder Gentler Racism*, p. 183.

24. Jill Quadagno, *The Color of Welfare: How Racism Undermined the War on Poverty* (New York: Oxford University Press, 1994), p. 162.

25. Shull, *A Kinder Gentler Racism*, p. 191.

26. Charles Hamilton, "Minority Politics and 'Political Realities' in American Politics," in *The Democrats Must Lead* (San Francisco: Westview Press, 1992), p. 149.

27. Quadagno, *The Color of Welfare*, p. 21.

28. Quadagno, *The Color of Welfare*, p. 31.

29. Quoted in Thomas Byrne Edsall and Mary D. Edsall, *Chain Reaction: The Impact of Race, Rights, and Taxes on American Politics* (New York: W. W. Norton, 1991), p. 182.

30. Robert C. Smith, *We Have No Leaders: African Americans in the Post–Civil Rights Era* (Albany, NY: State University of Albany Press, 1996), p. 256.

31. Smith, *We Have No Leaders*, p. 264.

32. Lewis Lapham, "Reactionary Chic: How the Nineties Right Recycles the Bombast of the Sixties Left," *Harper's Magazine*, March 1995, pp. 39–42.

33. Adolph Reed Jr., "Dissing the Underclass," *The Progressive*, December 1996, p. 21.

34. Quoted in Steinberg, *Turning Back*, p. 105.

35. Quoted in Steinberg, *Turning Back*, p. 239.

36. Adolph Reed Jr., "The Underclass as Myth and Symbol: The Poverty of Discourse about Poverty," in *Radical America*, vol. 24, January 1992.

37. Joe Klein, "The True Disadvantage," *The New Republic*, October 28, 1996, p. 33.

38. David A. Bositis, "Blacks and the 1996 Elections: A Preliminary Analysis," November 13, 1996.

39. Stanley P. Hirshon, *Farewell to the Bloody Shirt: Northern Republicans and the Southern Negro, 1877–1893* (Bloomington, IN: Indiana University Press, 1962), p. 253.

UNDERSTANDING AFROCENTRISM

WHY BLACKS DREAM OF A WORLD WITHOUT WHITES

GERALD EARLY

Gerald Early is director of the African and Afro-American Studies Program at Washington University in St. Louis.

The White man will never admit his real references. He will steal everything you have and still call you those names.

—Ishmael Reed,
Mumbo Jumbo (1972)

Furthermore, no one can be thoroughly educated until he learns as much about the Negro as he knows about other people.

—Carter G. Woodson,
The Mis-Education of the Negro (1933)

[Alexander] Crummell's black nationalism was marked by certain inconsistencies, but they derived from the inconsistencies and hypocrisy of American racism, rather than from any intellectual shortcomings on his part. It was impossible to create an ideology that responded rationally to an irrational system.

—Wilson Jeremiah Moses,
Alexander Crummell: A Study of Civilization and Discontent
(1989)

I N A SPAN OF THREE WEEKS DURING THE EARLY SPRING semester of 1995, Angela Davis and bell hooks, two notable black leftist, feminist thinkers, visited the campus of Washington University in St. Louis, invited by different student groups. They were generally well received, indeed, enthusiastically so. But there was, for each of them during these visits, something of a jarring note, both involving black students.

Professor Davis, entertaining questions during a panel session after having spoken earlier on the subject of prison reform, was asked by a black woman student what she had to offer black people as a solution to their problems. The student went on to explain that she did not consider herself an African-American. She was simply an African, wishing to have nothing to do with being an American or with America itself. She wanted black people to separate themselves entirely from "Europeans," as she called white Americans, and wanted to know what Davis could suggest to further that aim.

Davis answered that she was not inclined to such stringent race separation. She was proud of being of African descent but wished to be around a variety of people, not just people like herself. Davis felt further that blacks should not isolate themselves but accept in partnership anyone who was sincerely interested in the cause of overthrowing capitalism, a standard and reasonable Marxist response to the "essentializing" of race in a way that would divert true political engagement "against the system." The student was visibly annoyed with the answer, which presumably smacked of "white" intellectualism.

Professor bell hooks, after her address on ending racism and sexism in America—love, I think, was the answer—was asked by a black woman student how feminism was relevant to black women. Hooks explained that feminism was not only for white women, that black women needed to read more feminist texts. even if some of them were racist. After all, Karl Marx was racist but he did give the world a brilliant analysis of capitalism. She had said in her speech how disappointed she was that her black women students at City College of New York were not inclined to embrace feminism, rejecting it as something white. She felt that these black women were unduly influenced by black male rappers who bashed feminism. The answer did not persuade or please the student.

From *Civilization*, July/August 1995, pp. 31-39. © 1995 by Gerald Early. Reprinted by permission.

Later that day, I heard many black undergraduates dismiss hooks's talk as not addressing the needs of black people, as being too geared to the white feminists in the audience. Some were disturbed that hooks would feel that they formed their opinions on the basis of listening to rap records. None of this was said, necessarily, with hostility, but rather with regret and a shade of condescension that only the young can so keenly and innocently express when speaking about the foolishness of their elders.

I recall a fairly recent incident where a black student, a very bright young woman, asked if, when doing research, one had to acknowledge racist books. I told her that a certain amount of objectivity was part of the discipline of being a scholar. Anger at unjust or inaccurate statements and assessments was understandable, but personalizing everything often caused a kind of tunnel vision where crude self-affirmation seemed to be the only fit end of scholarship. She responded that she would refuse to acknowledge racist sources, that if the book was racist, then everything it said was tainted and should be disregarded.

The attitudes of these students have been shaped by Afrocentrism, an insistence by a growing number of black Americans to see the world from an "African-centered" perspective in response to the dominant "European-centered" perspective to which they feel they have been subjected throughout their lives. Afrocentrism is many things and has many degrees of advocacy. It can range from the commercialism and pretense of the shallow holiday called Kwanza (no shallower, it should be said, than the commercialized celebration of Christmas) to the kente-cloth ads and nationalist talk that one finds in most black publications these days; from talk about racist European scholarship to a view that world culture is essentially African in origin and that Europeans are usurpers, thieves, and generally inferior. On the one hand, we have the recent cover story "Is Jesus Black?" in *Emerge*, an Afrocentric-tinged news magazine for the black middle class. The answer in this instance, of course, is clearly yes. (Obviously, this is grounds for competing claims between blacks and Jews; whatever can be said about Jesus' skin color or the religious movement that bears his name, there is no question that he was a Jew.) On the other hand, we have the first explicitly Afrocentric Hollywood Western in Mario Van Peebles's 1993 film *Posse*, a jumbled multicultural critique of white *fin de siècle* imperialism and the myth of how the West was won.

No doubt, Afrocentrists specifically and black folk generally found it to be a signal victory that in the recent television dramatization of the love affair between Solomon and Sheba, Sheba was played by a black actress and Solomon by a swarthy Hispanic. In the 1959 Hollywood film version of *Solomon and Sheba*, directed by King Vidor—who, incidentally, made the first all-black Hollywood film—Solomon was played by Yul Brynner and Sheba by Gina Lollobrigida. It is safe to say that the real Solomon and the real Sheba, if they ever existed, did not look remotely like any of the actors who ever played them. But whom we want them to look like is very important. The Afrocentrists will feel their triumph to be complete when black actors portray Beethoven, Joseph Haydn, Warren G. Harding, Alexander Hamilton, Han-

nibal, Abraham Lincoln, Dwight Eisenhower, Cleopatra, Moses, Jesus Christ and Saint Augustine. Many African-Americans are inclined to believe that any noted white with ambiguous ancestry must be black. They are also inclined to believe that any white with dark skin tones, one who hangs around blacks or who "acts black" in some way is truly black. At various times in my life, I have heard blacks argue vehemently that Madonna, Phoebe Snow, Keith Jarrett, Mae West, Ava Gardner and Dorothy Parker were black, even though they did not have a shred of evidence to support the claims. Blacks have always been fascinated by "passing," by the possibility that some whites are really black— "fooling old massa," so to speak.

AFROCENTRISM IS AN INTELLECTUAL MOVEMENT, a political view, a historically traceable evolution, a religious orthodoxy. It derives, in part, from Negritude and Pan-Africanism, which stressed the culture and achievements of Africans. Both movements were started by Africans, West Indians and African-Americans in response to European colonialism and the worldwide oppression of African-descended people. But Afrocentrism is also a direct offshoot of earlier forms of black nationalism, in which blacks around the world believed they had a special destiny to fulfill and a special consciousness to redeem. More important, Afrocentrism is a mood that has largely erupted in the last 10 to 15 years in response to integration or, perhaps more precisely, to the failure of integration. Many blacks who have succeeded in the white world tend to feel most Afrocentric, although I think it would be a mistake to see Afrocentrism purely as middle-class, since significant numbers of working-class blacks are attracted to some elements of it. The bourgeois, "midcult" element of Afrocentrism, nonetheless, is very strong. "Integrated" middle-class blacks see it as a demonstration of their race loyalty and solidarity with their brothers and sisters throughout the world, whether in American cities or on African farms. (It is worth noting the economic clout of the black middle class, which can be seen in the growing number of black Hollywood films and filmmakers, in new black magazines ranging from *Body and Soul* to *The Source* to *Upscale*, and in the larger audience for black books. It is the market power of this class that has given Afrocentrism its force as a consumer ideology.)

So the middle-class black, having had more contact with whites and their institutions, is expected to speak for and to other blacks. Afrocentrism, like Negritude and Pan-Africanism, is meant to be an ideological glue to bring black people together, not just on the basis of color but as the expression of a cultural and spiritual will that crosses class and geographical lines. As W.E.B. Du Bois wrote in 1940: "Since the fifteenth century these ancestors of mine and their other descendants have had a common history; have suffered a common disaster and have one long memory.... The real essence of this kinship is its social heritage of slavery; the discrimination and insults; and this heritage binds together not simply the children of Africa, but extends through yellow Asia and into the South Seas. It is this unity that draws me to Africa."

Louis H. Farrakhan, the head of the Nation of Islam, is probably the most familiar figure associated with Afrocentrism. (Muhammad Ali introduced Islamic conversion to an even bigger public, suffering greatly for his religious and political beliefs and becoming the most noted and charismatic dissident of his era. Ali's prodigious athletic abilities and his genial temperament succeeded in endearing him to the American public despite his religion. He never became a member of Farrakhan's sect.) Farrakhan is a fiery preacher, prone to making extreme statements, with a militant flair and a racist edge, that have the conviction of truth among some blacks. He especially exploits the idea that he is a heroic black man at grave risk for daring to tell the truth about the white man. (Malcolm X used this device effectively, too.) He is also a master demagogue who exploits the paranoia of his audience. But then, as a friend once said to me, "What black person isn't justified in being at least half-paranoid?"

Farrakhan has found three effective lines of entry among blacks, particularly young blacks, that draw on the Afrocentric impulse: First, that Islam is the true religion of black people. (This has led to a move among black Christian leaders to point out with great vehemence the African origins of Christianity, to make it, in effect, a black religion.) Second, that black people need business enterprise in their community in order to liberate themselves (an old belief among blacks, going back to at least the early part of the 19th century). And third, that Jews of European descent (what he calls "false Jews") are not to be trusted, a charge that exploits the current tension between blacks and Jews—and that Farrakhan has used to move into the black civil-rights establishment. All three positions enjoy remarkable support within the black middle class, a situation that has helped Farrakhan tap people's insecurities for his own purposes. The Nation of Islam may be famous for converting addicts and criminals, but above all, it wants, as all religions do, to win over the middle class, with its money, its respectability and its organizational know-how.

Whatever might be said of Farrakhan's importance as a political figure in the black community or in the United States, he is a minor figure in the development of Afrocentrism. His position in the history of Afrocentrism is similar to that of, say, Rush Limbaugh in the development of American conservatism. He is, like Limbaugh, a figure the media can use to give a sellable face and voice to a unique temper among a group of people. For both Limbaugh and Farrakhan represent an intense sentimentality in American life, a yearning for a fantasized, idealized past of racial grandeur and simplicity. This sentimentality appeals powerfully to the black middle class, which yearns for a usable, untainted past. This partly explains why Farrakhan and the Muslims can often be found speaking to black college students.

In thinking about the connection between class and nationalistic feelings, it should be recalled that in Harriet Beecher Stowe's 1852 novel, *Uncle Tom's Cabin*, the most light-complexioned blacks, the ones with the greatest skills, George, Eliza and Cassy, return to Africa at the novel's end to retrieve their degraded patrimony. It might be said that this is purely Stowe's own perverse vision, since some of the fiercest advocates for returning to Africa have been Martin Delany, Alexander Crummell and Marcus Garvey, all very dark men. Yet there is more than a little truth to the idea that class, caste and race consciousness are closely interwoven. Nationalism of whatever sort has almost always been an

affair of a disaffected middle class. And until the 1920s, the black middle class in America was disproportionately made up of light-skinned people.

The paradox of the bourgeois aspect of Afrocentrism is that it rejects cosmopolitanism as being "white" or "Eurocentric." Yet Afrocentrism has no other way of seeing cosmopolitanism except on the "Eurocentric" model, so it tries to make Africa for black Americans the equivalent of what Europe is for white Americans: the source of civilization. Indeed, by trying to argue that Africa is the source of Western civilization, the Afrocentric sees the African, symbolically, as the mother of white Europe (just as the black mother, the mammy, is the mythic progenitor of the white South, or so Langston Hughes seemed to believe in his famous short story "Father and Son," which became his even more famous play, *Mulatto)*. The African becomes, in this view, the most deeply cultured person on the planet, which matches his status as the oldest person on the planet, with the longest and deepest genetic history. In short, Afrocentrism becomes another form of the American apologizing for being American to people he imagines are his cultural superiors. Afrocentrism tries to mask a quest for American filiopiety behind a facade of African ancestor and culture worship.

IT WOULD BE EASY, ON ONE LEVEL, TO DISMISS AFROCENtrism as an expression, in white workplaces and white colleges, of intimidated black folk who are desperately trying to find a space for themselves in what they feel to be alien, unsympathetic environments. Seen this way, Afrocentrism becomes an expression of the low self-esteem and inferiority that blacks feel most intensely when they are around whites; their response is to become more "black," estranged from the environment that they find so unaccepting of them. The greatest psychic burden of the African-American is that he must not only think constantly about being different but about what his difference means. And it might be suggested that Afrocentrism does not solve this problem but merely reflects it in a different mirror. There is a certain amount of truth to this, especially at a time when affirmative action, which promotes group identification and group difference, tends to intensify black self-consciousness. And black people, through no fault of their own, are afflicted with a debilitating sense of self-consciousness when around whites. When whites are in the rare situation of being a minority in a sea of blacks, they often exhibit an abject self-consciousness as well, but the source of that self-consciousness is quite different. The white is used to traveling anywhere in the world and having his cultural inclinations accommodated. The black is neither used to this nor does he realistically expect it. The European exults in his culture while the African is utterly degraded by his. That blacks should want to free themselves from the white gaze seems not merely normal but essential to the project of reconstructing themselves as a people on their own terms. And the history of blacks in the United States has been an ongoing project—tragic, pathetic, noble, heroic, misguided, sublime—of self-reconstruction.

NOT JUST ON THE BASIS OF COLOR BUT AS AN EXPRESSION OF CULTURAL WILL

When it comes to black folk in America, the white man wants to say that if you have one-thirty-second portion of black blood, a mere drop of black blood, then you are black, no matter what your skin color. But when it comes to the ancient Egyptians, it doesn't matter if they have a drop of black blood, and we know that they had at least one-thirty-second portion of African blood. It doesn't matter how much African blood they have, they are still white. The white man wants to have his cake and eat it too. When it's convenient, he wants you to be black and when it's convenient, he wants you to be white. Either you're a nigger, because he thinks you're nothing. Or you're white, if you have done anything he's bound to respect. The white man wants to control all the definitions of blackness.

—A conversation with an Afrocentric friend

Afrocentrism, like a good many nationalistic ideologies, might be called the orthodoxy of the book, or more precisely, the orthodoxy of the books. Afrocentrism is an attempt to wed knowledge and ideology. Movements like Afrocentrism, which feels both its mission and its authority hinge on the revelation of a denied and buried truth, promote a fervent scholasticism, a hermeneutical ardor among true believers for compilations of historical minutiae on the one hand, and for grand philosophical tracts on the other. The former might be best represented by George G.M. James's *Stolen Legacy*, published in 1954, the latter by Mustafa El-Amin's *Al-Islam, Christianity, and Freemasonry* and *Freemasonry, Ancient Egypt, and the Islamic Destiny*. These books were not written by professional historians or by college professors. The fact that several classic Afrocentric texts have been written by amateurs gives Afrocentrism its powerful populist appeal, its legitimacy as an expression of "truth" that white institutional forces hide or obscure. At the same time, this leaves it vulnerable to charges of being homemade, unprofessional, theoretically immature and the like. It is one of the striking aspects of Afrocentrism that within the last 20 years it has developed a cadre of academics to speak for it, to professionalize it, to make it a considerable insurgency movement on the college campus.

There are several texts that might be considered the literary and intellectual cornerstones of the Afrocentrism movement. Molefi K. Asante, professor and chair of African-American studies at Temple University in Philadelphia, is credited with inventing the name "Afrocentrism" or "Afrocentricity" (although currently the term "Africentrism" is on the rise in certain quarters, probably because there is a group of black folk who, for some reason, despise the prefix "Afro," as if the word "Africa" itself were created by the people of the continent rather than by Europeans). Asante's very short books, including *The Afrocentric Idea*, published in 1987, and *Afrocentricity: The Theory of Social Change*, published in 1980, are frequently the starting points for people seeking a basic explanation of this ideology. As defined by Asante, Afrocentrism seems to take the terms and values of Eurocentrism—intense individualism, crass greed, lack of spirituality, warlike inclinations, dominance and racism, dishonesty and hypocrisy—and color their opposites black, giving us a view of black people not terribly different from the romantic racism of Harriet Beecher Stowe and other whites like her in the 19th and 20th centuries. I cannot recount the number of "race sensitivity" meetings I have attended where blacks begin to describe themselves (or those they perceive to be Africans) as more spiritual, more family-oriented, more community-oriented, more rhythmic, more natural and less combative than whites. All of which is, of course, a crock of nonsense, largely the expression of wishes for qualities that blacks see as absent from their community life now. But, thanks to Asante, this has become the profile of the African in the Afrocentric vision.

Martin Bernal's massively researched two-volume *Black Athena* (published in 1987 and 1991) is a popular title in Afrocentric circles, in large measure because Bernal, a professor at Cornell, is one of the few white scholars to take Afrocentrism seriously—William Piersen, Robert Farris Thompson and Andrew Hacker, in decidedly different ways, are others—and one of the few to write an academic treatise in its defense that forces whites to take it seriously too. (The irony that blacks still need whites, in some measure, to sell their ideas and themselves to other whites is not entirely lost on those who have thought about this.)

Black Athena supports three major contentions of the Afrocentrists: 1) ancient Egypt was a black civilization; 2) the Greeks derived a good deal, if not all, of their philosophy and religion from the Egyptians; 3) European historiography has tried strenuously and with clear political objectives to deny both. Bernal's book provoked a scathing attack by Mary R. Lefkowitz, a professor at Wellesley, who characterizes Afrocentrism as a perversion of the historiography of antiquity and a degradation of academic standards for political ends. Lefkowitz has also battled with Tony Martin, a cultural historian, barrister and Marcus Garvey specialist, who began using and endorsing the Nation of Islam's anti-Semitic *The Secret Relationship Between Blacks and Jews* (Vol. 1) in his classes on slavery at Wellesley. Martin responded in 1993 with his own account of the dispute, *The Jewish Onslaught: Despatches from the Wellesley Battlefront*, which elaborates his claims of Jewish racism and the hypocrisy of academic freedom.

Maulana Karenga, professor and chair of black studies at California State University at Long Beach, created the black philosophical code called the Kawaida, which was the inspiration for Kwanza and the seven principles (Nguzo Saba) that the holiday celebrates. The code contains a bit of Marxism to create a "theoretical" ambiance. Karenga is also author of the popular *Introduction to Black Studies*, used by many colleges in their introductory courses, despite its rather tendentious manner, which he tries to pass off as sharp-minded Marxism, and the fact that the book is weak on a good many aspects of African-American life and culture.

Perhaps the most popular Afrocentric text is Chancellor Williams's *The Destruction of Black Civilization: Great Issues of a Race from 4500 B.C. to 2000 A.D.* (published in 1987), an account of his exhaustive research trips to Africa. Although not directly trained in the study of African history, Williams studied under William Leo Hansberry, a history professor at Howard University and probably the leading black American authority on Africa during the 1930s, 1940s and 1950s. Hansberry did path-breaking work in an utterly neglected field, eventually becoming known as "the father of African studies" in the United States. (Scholars, until recently, did not think Africa had a "history." The continent, especially its sub-Saharan regions, had an "anthropology" and an "archaeology," folkways to be discovered and remains to be unearthed, but never a record of institutions, traditions, political ideologies and complex societies.) Williams also did research on African history at Oxford and at the University of London, where, because of colonialism, interest in the nature of African societies was far keener than in the United States. His book *The Re-Birth of African Civilization,* an account of his 1953–1957 research project investigating the nature of education in Europe and Africa, calls for Pan-African education of blacks in Africa and around the world. Williams concluded that "European" and "Eurocentric" education was antithetical, both politically and intellectually, to African interests, a common refrain in Afrocentrist thought.

Most Afrocentric scholars at universities today genuflect at the intellectual altar of Cheikh Anta Diop, a Senegalese humanist and scientist who began his research into African history in 1946, as the battle against European colonialism in Africa was beginning. Diop saw his mission as undermining European colonialism by destroying the European's claim to a superior history. He was tenacious in demonstrating that Africa had a "real" history that showed that Africans were the product of civilizations and not of the jungle. This claim to history was a sign to the African that he was an equal player in the family of man, and was essential to any demand for independence.

For Diop, it was not enough to reconstruct African history; it was also necessary to depict a unified Africa, an idea that, whether myth or fact, was considered ideologically crucial by the Pan-African movement to overthrow European imperialism. Like every other oppressed people, the African could face the future only if he could hark back to some version of his past, preferably a past touched with greatness. This could be done only by running African history and civilization through Egypt, the only African civilization that impressed European intellectuals. As jazz and cultural critic Stanley Crouch suggested, Egypt is the only African civilization that has monuments, a physical legacy that indicates history as understood in European terms. Thus, for black people in Africa to be unified, for black people around the world to feel unified, ancient Egypt has to be a "black" civilization and serve as the origin of all blackness and, even more important, all whiteness. We know from scientific evidence that Africa is the place of origin for human life. If it is also true that Egypt is the oldest civilization from which Europeans borrowed freely (Bernal makes a persuasive argument for the influence of Egypt on European intellectuals through the 19th century), then Africans helped shape Western culture and were major actors in history, not bit players in the unfolding drama of European dominance.

Diop's doctoral dissertation, based on the idea that Egypt was African and that European civilization was largely built on Egyptian ideas, was rejected at the University of Paris in 1951. The story goes that he was able to defend his dissertation successfully only in 1960 when he was accompanied into the examination room by an army of historians, sociologists and anthropologists who supported his views, or at least his right as a responsible scholar to express them. By then, with African independence in full swing, his ideas had a political currency in Africa as an expression of Pan-Africanism. And no one supported the idea of a unified Africa

more than Egypt's then-president, Gamal Abdel Nasser, probably the most powerful independent leader on the continent. Like Gandhi, Nasser called himself a black man, and he envisioned an Africa united in opposition to Israel and South Africa. It was a good moment for Diop to be saying what he was saying. At the 1956 Conference of Negro-African Writers and Artists in Paris, Diop was one of the most popular speakers, although black American James Baldwin was not much impressed with his thesis. (Admittedly, for Baldwin this was pretty new stuff.) For his part, Diop, a Marxist, thought the American delegation was blindly anticommunist and naively committed to the integrationist policies of the civil-rights movement.

Diop produced a number of volumes translated into English, some based on his dissertation. They include *The African Origin of Civilization: Myth or Reality, Civilization or Barbarism: An Authentic Anthropology* and *The Cultural Unity of Negro Africa.* For Diop, everything turned on establishing that ancient Egypt was a black civilization: "The history of Black Africa will remain suspended in air and cannot be written correctly until African historians dare to connect it with the history of Egypt." Moreover, Diop felt that the African could not remove the chains of colonialism from his psyche until he had a fully reconstructed history—in other words, until he had an unusual past. Diop was brilliant and clearly obsessed. His importance in the formation of African-American intellectual history does not depend on whether his historical theories are correct. (Although there is considerable debate about ancient Egypt—not surprising, since there is no documentation of the claim in the language of the people who lived there at the time—it is now conceded by virtually everyone that the Egyptians were a mixed-race people.) Diop's work transcends questions of historical accuracy and enters the realm of "belief." Much of what Diop wrote may be true (he had vast amounts of evidence to support his claims) but, as a Marxist, he was not motivated simply by the quest for positivistic, objective "truth." He wanted to use the supposed objectivity of scientific research for political ends.

DIOP BROUGHT TOGETHER THREE IMPORTANT elements in understanding the origins of Afrocentrism: first, the tradition of professional, politically motivated historical research that buttresses the claims of untrained, amateur historians; second, the explicit connection between knowledge of one's "proper" history and one's psychological and spiritual well-being; third, the connection between "proper" knowledge of one's history and the realization of a political mission and purpose. If European history functioned as an ideological and political justification for Europe's place in the world and its hope for its future, why shouldn't African history function in the same manner? This is the reasoning of the Pan-Africanists and Afrocentrists who see "proper" history as the version that is most ideologically and politically useful to their group. Diop's research supports the idea of a conspiracy among white historians to discredit or ignore black civilization. Without a "proper" knowledge of African history, Diop argues, blacks will remain politically impotent and psychologically crippled. These ideas have become the uncritical dogma of Afrocentrism. By the time Diop died in 1986, he had been virtually canonized by an important set of black American scholars who identified themselves as Afrocentric.

Diop is useful for Afrocentrism today not only because of his monumental research but because he was an African, thus linking Afrocentrism to Africa itself and permitting the black American to kneel before the perfect intellect of the "purer" African. But Diop's ideas about ancient black civilization in Egypt and the importance of fuller knowledge of its history had been advanced earlier by several African-American intellectuals, including W.E.B. Du Bois in his momentous book *Black Folk, Then and Now: An Essay in the History and Sociology of the Negro Race*, which appeared in 1939. Du Bois said he was inspired to write about the glories of the Negro past after hearing a lecture in 1906 at Atlanta University by the preeminent white anthropologist Franz Boas, debunker of racism and mentor of Zora Neale Hurston. Du Bois's work remains, despite the more richly researched efforts of Diop, Bernal and St. Clair Drake in *Black Folk Here and There* (published in two volumes in 1987 and 1990), the best and most readable examination of the subject. Indeed, his work must be seen in a larger historical context, dating back to the founding of the American Negro Academy in 1897, when he and other black intellectuals tried to organize themselves for the purpose of producing scholarship that defended the race and promoted race consciousness. Yet Du Bois's book is not the central work of the Afrocentric movement by a black American writer.

That book would be Carter G. Woodson's *The Mis-Education of the Negro*, originally published in 1933. Woodson, a Harvard Ph.D. in history who launched both the Association for the Study of Negro Life and History (1915) and Negro History Week (1926), was as obsessed with the reconstruction of the Negro past as Diop or Du Bois. He churned out dozens of books on virtually every aspect of African and African-American history. Some were wooden, opaque or just plain sloppy, and several are unreadable (even in the opinion of his assistant, the late, brilliant black historian Lorenzo Greene), indicating the haste with which they were composed. Even so, Woodson was a serious and demanding scholar. Greene thought of him, at times, as having the pious devotion of a Franciscan friar and the crotchety temper of an eccentric intellectual consumed by his work.

The Mis-Education of the Negro, although written by a man who endorsed Booker T. Washington and the Tuskegee method, was generally critical of black education. Black people, Woodson argued, were not being educated in a way that would encourage them to press their own political and economic interests or make them a viable social group in the United States. They were, in fact, being educated against their own interests, largely because their education was controlled by whites who saw advantage in giving blacks an inferior education. Moreover, Woodson made the explicit connection between "improper" education, including a lack of knowledge about the black past, and the psychological degradation of the Negro, his internalized sense of inferiority. In short, a white-controlled education led to Uncle Tomism and black sellouts, to a defective Negro who suffered from false consciousness, or, more precisely, "white" conscious-

ness. Some of this argument was restated in black sociologist E. Franklin Frazier's seminal 1957 work, *Black Bourgeoisie*. The black middle class was almost exclusively the target of this indictment—a fact that prompted that class to romanticize certain aspects of black lower-class life, particularly its antisocial and criminal elements, in an effort to demonstrate its solidarity with "authentic" black experience. This was true with the Black Panthers in the late 1960s and it continues with rap music today. Another consequence is that the black middle class insists on a degree of race loyalty that sometimes thwarts any critical inquiry that does not promote race unity.

Much of Woodson's argument resonates with blacks today because it seems to endorse the idea of Afrocentric schools and especially the idea that knowledge of a glorious African past would give black youngsters self-esteem, reduce violence and criminality in black neighborhoods, and lead to the spiritual and political uplift of black people. This is why history is actually a less important discipline to the rise of Afrocentrism than psychology. After all, the reconstruction of black history was always connected with the reconstruction of the black mind, a mind that existed before the coming of the white man—or at least a mind that could be free of the white man and his image of what black people were.

In some ways, the rise of Afrocentrism is related to the rise of "black psychology" as a discipline. The Association of Black Psychologists was organized in 1968, a time when a number of black professional offshoots were formed in political and ideological protest against the mainstream, white-dominated versions of their organizations. Somewhat later came the *Journal of Black Psychology*, given impetus by the initial assaults against black intelligence or pointed suggestions of black genetic inferiority by Richard Herrnstein, Arthur Jensen and others in the early 1970s; this was also the time of the first wave of court challenges against affirmative action. The black psychology movement argued for new modes of treatment for black mental illness, the medical efficacy of using black history to repair a collectively damaged black psyche, and the destruction of "Eurocentrism" and the values it spawned—from the idealization of white standards of beauty to the scientific measurement of intelligence—as totally inimical to the political and psychological interests of black people. Rationality, order, individualism, dominance, sexual repression as well as sexual license, aggression, warmaking, moneymaking, capitalism itself—all soon became "white values."

That all of this happened during the era of Vietnam War protests, when white Western civilization was coming under withering intellectual attack from the radical left, is not without significance. Radical white intellectuals, who otherwise had no more use for a black epic history than a white one, found the black version useful as a weapon against "Eurocentrism," which, as a result of the Vietnam War, they held in utter contempt. In short, Jean-Paul Sartre and Susan Sontag were as instrumental, albeit indirectly, in the formation of Afrocentrism as, say, the Black Power movement of the late 1960s or the writings of African psychiatrist Franz Fanon, whose *The Wretched of the Earth* became the revolutionary psychological profile of the oppressed black diaspora. Also occurring at this time was the movement on white college campuses to establish black studies programs, which provided a black intellectual wedge into the white academy. These programs, largely multidisciplinary, required an ideological purpose and mission to bind together the various disciplines, which is why many began to articulate some kind of Afrocentrism or, as it was called in the 1970s, "black aesthetic"—in other words, an ideological framework to give black studies a reason for being. When used to challenge the dominance of Western thought, Afrocentrism becomes part of a multicultural wave of complaint and resentment against the white man by a number of groups that feel they have been oppressed.

In an age of dysfunction and psychotherapy, no one can have greater claim to having been made dysfunctional by political oppression than the African-American, who was literally a slave; and no one can have a greater need for recourse to psychotherapy in the form of Afrocentrism. But what made the black psychology movement possible was the rise of the Nation of Islam, particularly the rise of Malcolm X.

The charismatic Muslim minister did two things. First, he forced the white mainstream press to take notice of black nationalism, Pan Africanism and the concept of African unity. Previously these ideas had been marginalized as ridiculous or even comic expressions of black nationalism, to be read by blacks in black barbershops and beauty salons as they thumbed through the Ripley's-Believe-It-or-Not-type work of the self-taught black historian J. A. Rogers (*One Hundred Amazing Facts About the Negro*, *Five Negro Presidents* and the like). Malcolm X revitalized the ideas of Marcus Garvey, the great black nationalist leader of the 1910s and 1920s, whose Universal Negro Improvement Association became, for a time, one of the most popular black political groups in America. Malcolm, like Garvey, felt that the Negro still needed to be "improved" but, unlike Garveyites, the Muslims did not offer costumes and parades but sober suits, puritanical religion, dietary discipline and no-nonsense business practices. Malcolm himself was also, by his physical appearance alone, a figure who would not be dismissed as a buffoon, as Garvey often was by both blacks and whites. According to Malcolm's *Autobiography*, his father had been a Garveyite as well as a wife beater who favored his lighter-skinned children. Malcolm's Islamic-based black nationalism, his sexual abstinence, which lasted from his religious conversion until his marriage a decade later, and his triumph over his own preference for lighter-skinned blacks and whites were all meant to demonstrate, vividly, how he superseded his father as a nationalist and how the Nation of Islam has superseded Garveyism.

Malcolm enlisted a body of enforcers, the feared Fruit of Islam, grim-faced men who, one imagines, were supposed to personify the essence of an unbowed yet disciplined black manhood. In this way, he dramatically associated black nationalism with a new type of regenerated black male. It was said in the black community, and may still be, that no one bothers a Muslim for fear of retribution from the Fruit of Islam. Certainly, there was a point in the development of the Fruit of Islam and the Nation itself in the 1960s and early 1970s (Malcolm was assassinated in 1965) when both were closely associated with racketeering and gangster activity. During this period, many East Coast mosques were among the most terrifying organizations in the black community.

Second, Malcolm, in his *Autobiography*, also managed to link the psychological redemption of the Negro with his reacquaintance with his history. The prison chapters of the *Autobiography* have become nearly mythic as a paradigm of black reawakening. Malcolm's religious conversion became, in a sense, the redemption of the black male and the rehabilitation of black masculinity itself. Lately, we have seen two major black male public figures who were incarcerated for serious crimes, Marion Barry and Mike Tyson, use the Malcolm paradigm to resuscitate their standing with the black public. The martyrdom of Malcolm gave this paradigm a blood-endorsed political heroism that has virtually foreclosed any serious criticism of either its origins or its meaning.

It is extraordinary to contemplate how highly regarded Malcolm X is in the black community today, especially in comparison with Martin Luther King. (When I wrote an article for *Harper's* that was critical of Malcolm X, I received three death threats.) Despite the fact that King's achievements were enormous—and that Malcolm left really nothing behind other than a book—King's association with integration, with nonviolence, even with Christianity has reduced him in the eyes of many blacks. When blacks in major cities, inspired by figures like Malcolm X and the romanticization of Africa that Malcolm's nationalism wrought, began to organize African-oriented celebrations, such as my aunts did in Philadelphia with the creation of the Yoruba-inspired Odunde festival in 1975, then Afrocentrism has succeeded not only in intellectual spheres but on the grass-roots level as well. Its triumph as the legitimation of the black mind and the black aesthetic vision was complete.

Afrocentrism may eventually wane in the black community but probably not very soon. Moreover, a certain type of nationalistic mood, a kind of racial preoccupation, will always exist among blacks. It always has, in varying degrees. Homesickness is strong among black Americans, although it is difficult to point to a homeland. What Afrocentrism reflects is the inability of a large number of black people to deal with the reality of being American and with the meaning of their American experience.

Stanley Crouch is right in pointing out that the Afrocentrist is similar to the white Southerner after the Civil War. To black nationalists, the lost war was the "war of liberation" led by black "revolutionaries" in the late 1960s, which in their imagination was modeled on the struggles against colonialism then taking place around the world. (The enslavement of the Africans, of course, was an earlier lost war, and it also weighs heavily on the Afrocentrist. He, like the white Southerner, hates the idea of belonging to a defeated people.) This imaginative vision of a restored and indomitable ethnicity is not to be taken lightly. In a culture as driven by the idea of redemption and as corrupted by racism as this one, race war is our Armageddon. It can be seen in works as various as Thomas Jefferson's *Notes on the State of Virginia*, David Walker's *Appeal to the Colored Citizens of the World*, Joseph Smith's *Book of Mormon*, D.W. Griffith's *Birth of a Nation* and Mario Van Peebles's *Posse*.

WHAT BLACKS DESIRE DURING THESE TURBULENT TIMES IS EXACTLY WHAT

WHITES WANT: THE SECURITY OF A GOLDEN PAST THAT NEVER EXISTED

TODAY, AFROCENTRISM IS NOT A MATURE POLITICAL movement but rather a cultural style and a moral stance. There is a deep, almost lyrical poignancy in the fantasy of the Afrocentrist, as there is in the white Southerner's. What would I have been had I not lost the war? The Afrocentrist is devoted to his ancestry and his blood, fixated on the set of traditions that define his nobility, preoccupied with an imagined lost way of life. What drives the Afrocentrist and the white Southerner is not the expression of a group self-interest but concern with pride and honor. One group's myth is built on the surfeit of honor and pride, the other on the total absence of them.

Like the white Southerner, the Afrocentrist is in revolt against liberalism itself, against the idea of individual liberty. In a way, the Afrocentrist is right to rage against it, because liberalism set free the individual but did not encourage the development of a community within which the individual could flower. This is what the Afrocentrist wishes to retrieve, a place for himself in his own community. Wilson Jeremiah Moses, a black historian, is right: Afrocentrism is a historiography of decline, like the mythic epic of the South. The tragedy is that black people fail to see their "Americanization" as one of the great human triumphs of the past 500 years. The United States is virtually the only country where the ex-masters and the ex-slaves try to live together as equals, not only by consent of the ex-masters but by the demand of the ex-slaves. Ironically, what the Afrocentrist can best hope for is precisely what multiculturalism offers: the idea that American culture is a blend of many white and nonwhite cultures. In the end, although many Afrocentrists claim they want this blending, multiculturalism will not satisfy. For if the Euro-American is reminded through this that he is not European or wholly white, the African-American will surely be reminded that he is not African or wholly black. The Afrocentrist does not wish to be a mongrel. He wants, like the Southerner, to be pure.

Afrocentrism is intense now because blacks are in a special period of social development in a nation going through a period of fearsome transition. Social development, by its nature, is ambivalent, characterized by a sense of exchange, of gaining and losing. Afrocentrism, in its conservatism, is opposed to this ambivalence and to this sense of exchange. What blacks desire during these turbulent times is exactly what whites want: the security of a golden past that never existed. A significant number of both blacks and whites want, strangely, to go back to an era of segregation, a fantasy time between 1920 and 1955, when whites felt secure in a stable culture and when blacks felt unified and strong because black people were forced to live together. Afrocentrism wants social change without having to pay the psychic price for it. Perhaps many black folk feel that they have paid too much already, and who is to say they are not right.

The issue raised by Afrocentrism is the meaning and formation of identity, which is the major fixation of the American, especially the black American. In a country that relentlessly promotes the myth of self-reliance because it is unable to provide any sense of security in a cauldron of capitalistic change, identity struggle is so acute because so much is at stake. Afrocentrism may be wrong in many respects, and it certainly can be stifling and restrictive, but some of its impulses are right. In a culture where information and resources of knowledge are the main levers for social and economic advancement, psychological well-being has become increasingly important as, in the words of one scholar, "a social resource," just as "social networks of care and community support [have become] central features of a dynamic economy." Black folk know, and rightly so, that their individual identities are tied to the strength of their community. The struggle over black identity in the United States has been the struggle over the creation of a true black community here. What integration has done to the individual black mind in the United States is directly related to what it has done to the black community. This is the first lesson we must learn. The second is that perhaps many black folk cling to Afrocentrism because the black *American* experience still costs more, requires more courage, than white Americans—and black Americans—are willing to admit.

UNDERSTANDING INTEGRATION

By GERALD EARLY

Why blacks and whites must come together as Americans

There is a new race in America. I am a member of this new race. It is neither white nor black nor in-between. It is the American race, differing as much from white and black as white and black differ from each other.

—Jean Toomer, author of the
Harlem Renaissance masterpiece *Cane* (1923)

THE AGE OF RACIAL INTEGRATION AS AN OFFICIAL aim of American democracy was launched on April 15, 1947, when the Brooklyn Dodgers opened the baseball season at Ebbets Field against the Boston Braves. The crowd of 25,623 was relatively small, but more than half were African-American, probably the largest number of blacks ever to attend an official big-league ball game and certainly the first time that the majority of those in attendance were black. They came to see the debut of Jackie Robinson, the first African-American to play major-league baseball in the 20th century. Although hitless that day, Robinson went on to become the National League Rookie of the Year and led the Dodgers to the National League championship. Attendance at National League games in 1947 rose from 8,902,107 to 10,388,470, with Robinson drawing record crowds everywhere he went. The Dodgers attracted 1.8 million to their home games, a record for the franchise while it was in Brooklyn. Most of this increase, surely, was due to blacks buying tickets in record numbers, although many whites came to the ballpark out of curiosity, perverse interest or even sheer hostility.

Until then, ironically, big-league owners had excluded black players on economic grounds, arguing that the increased black crowds would scare off whites. The truth of the matter was that white owners did not want integrated teams because they feared a threat to America's social order: Integrated audiences might lead to sexual mingling between blacks and whites. (Both Norman Mailer and James Baldwin, the two young literary lions of this era, thought that whites supported segregation in order to prevent miscegenation.) Whites knew that

segregation cost them economically, but they were quite willing to pay the price in order to preserve their superior racial status.

Blacks responded to their exclusion from the major leagues by forming the first of the Negro leagues in 1920. (Blacks, of course, had professional "nines" much earlier, but they could not organize a league, as was chronicled in *Sol White's History of Colored Base Ball,* published in 1907). Both white and black baseball owners believed that segregation served their interests. Big-league owners saw professional baseball as white man's preserve with a nearly all-white fan base that protected the racial status quo; Negro-league owners saw baseball as an economic and social institution that gave blacks a sense of cohesion beyond the bond of unrelenting oppression.

When integration came to professional baseball, it was a one-way street. The major leagues could steal black players from the Negro leagues (few black players had enforceable contracts, and there was no "reserve clause" binding them to their teams), but the Negro leagues could not steal white players because they lacked the economic resources, the organizational strength and the prestige to do so. In the end, owners of black baseball clubs had no choice but to endorse integration because it was what both the black players and the black public wanted, strenuously so with the onset of World War II and the increasing urbanization of the black population.

Today, both blacks and whites are showing renewed interest in Negro-league baseball, which had been largely forgotten, probably because both groups viewed it with shame and regret. The Negro leagues existed, after all, because whites felt that blacks were inferior beings and incapable of playing on the same fields with them in day-to-day competition. Blacks could not help but see the Negro leagues, no matter how well the players played or how much they enjoyed the game, as a reminder that they were not equal to whites. Separate clearly meant "inherently unequal," to borrow the phrase the Supreme Court used in the 1954 *Brown* decision that elevated integration to public policy. Both groups are now attracted to Negro-league

From *Civilization*, October/November 1996, pp. 51-59. © 1996 by Gerald Early. Reprinted by permission.

baseball because it helps them understand what racial separation means by understanding what it meant before the *Brown* decision. Both sentimentalize, even romanticize, the communal power of black life before integration, in large measure because they feel that integration has been a disappointment and has run its course.

A T THIS CRITICAL MOMENT IN AMERICAN RACE relations, it is time to reinvent integration by revisiting segregation. For starters, we should recall how black people lived under segregation and how we, both black and white, feel about it now and felt about it then. Martin Luther King Jr. spoke of an integrated America as "the beloved community," but now both races perceive that our sense of community is deteriorating, and neither seems to feel that the other has much to offer. It is not surprising, then, that blacks and whites are nostalgic about a time when segregation at least gave meaning to each of their communities. In the microcosm of professional baseball, blacks and whites find commonly understood heritages and legacies. Perhaps nowhere else can one see so vividly the tangled loom of integration in the United States.

Racial integration—or the ideal of blacks and whites living as social equals—has always drawn its greatest power from symbols, and perhaps for that reason its greatest impact has always been symbolic. Integration naturally involves the economic and political relations between blacks and whites, but it is largely an enactment of a preoccupation with status. It is the act of elevating the status of blacks, a group that carries the stigma of having been slaves in a democratic society and having been considered biologically inferior (why else would they have been enslaved?), by placing them in situations where it is clearly announced that they are the equals of whites, where the

---

The tokenism of integration gave it its drama and made it a compelling moral lever against white racial exclusion

---

stigma of their race is erased by saying, in effect, that race does not matter.

As the civil-rights movement became more militant during the 1950s and 1960s, there were frequent complaints about "token" integration. This concern about tokenism and about blacks having to be exceptional in order to be able to integrate laid the groundwork for affirmative action, the institution of the idea that blacks should be represented in jobs, universities and other activities in numbers at least equal to their proportion of the general population. (Affirmative action is also meant to serve as a form of reparations.)

But it was precisely the tokenism of integration that gave it its drama, that made it such a compelling moral lever against white racial exclusion. The White House dinner in 1901 where Booker T. Washington was the guest of Theodore Roosevelt; the 1924 dinner party of black and white literati announcing the publication of Jessie Fauset's *There Is Confusion*; Bill "Bojangles" Robinson's dance routines with Shirley Temple in *The Little Colonel*, *The Littlest Rebel*, *Just Around the Corner* and *Rebecca of*

Sunnybrook Farm; the 1936 Olympics where Jesse Owens represented American democratic values against Nazism; Benny Goodman's Carnegie Hall concert in 1938, which featured an integrated jazz band and paid tribute to both white and black musicians of the past; Joe Louis's victory over the German boxer Max Schmeling in 1938, when Louis represented American democracy and Schmeling European fascism; Hattie McDaniel's winning of the 1939 Academy Award for Best Supporting Actress for *Gone with the Wind*—what makes these examples of integration memorable is the explicitly symbolic, "token" nature of each event. The idea of being "the first Negro" in any area, especially after the example of Jackie Robinson, fascinated and moved both the black and the white public. And it enabled both groups to throw off the antique racial etiquette that had governed their relationship. It endowed blacks with a sense of dignity, even martyrdom, while forcing whites to examine the shoddy premises upon which they built the myth of their superiority.

Robinson's impact was so pronounced because he performed so brilliantly, easily becoming the best-known black person in America, supplanting Joe Louis and far exceeding the fame of black political leaders like W.E.B. Du Bois, Walter White, Mary McLeod Bethune, A. Philip Randolph and Adam Clayton Powell Jr. Robinson was even more renowned than any black entertainer, including Duke Ellington, Charlie Parker, Billie Holiday, Lena Horne, Hattie McDaniel and Paul Robeson. Robinson's preeminence lasted until the rise of Martin Luther King Jr., who was the first black political leader to become a true charismatic media star.

Robinson's power as a cultural icon owed something to timing: He integrated the most deeply felt American game at the end of a world war that revealed the pathological horrors of racist ideas, and at the beginning of the Cold War, when the U.S. was fighting an ideological battle against the tyranny of Communism. Robinson emerged at a time when colonized countries, most of them controlled by European powers, were demanding and fighting for independence. There was clearly a growing sense of "color" consciousness in international affairs. Indeed, in 1955, one year after the *Brown* decision, the so-called "colored" nations of the world met in Bandung, Indonesia, at the first Afro-Asian unity conference—much to the chagrin of the State Department, which thought the meeting was simply a showcase for Communist China. (Adam Clayton Powell was one of the American observers.) In the war against Communism, racism in the U.S. impeded efforts to export democratic ideals to these rapidly decolonizing nations. Indeed, in the 1950s, when black authors like Richard Wright, Jay Saunders Redding, Carl Rowan and Louis Lomax wrote books about their travels in formerly colonized countries, race was a constant theme, and the U.S. was often depicted by the people interviewed as intractably racist and oppressive. (With an increasing number of blacks becoming expatriates after the war, African-Americans generally had more exposure to international opinions and affairs than ever before. Certainly, the black intelligentsia and elite were becoming far less provincial than they had been.)

It may be that Robinson's remarkable stoicism during his first three years in professional baseball, his decision to turn the other cheek to taunts and insults, was entirely the result of an agreement he made with Dodgers president Branch Rickey, who engineered Robinson's entry into white professional baseball. But other influences might well have been at work. Mahatma Gandhi, long engaged in the battle for India's independence, was the best-known Third World leader in the West at the time. His tactic of nonviolent resistance, of converting one's enemy through love and peaceful protest rather than subduing him by violent means, had an enormous impact on the imaginations of blacks and whites in America. Gandhi seemed to offer the oppressed enormous dignity while giving the oppressor an avenue to change not simply his actions but the way he thought of both himself and his instruments of power. In 1948, for instance, Du Bois called for "a Negro Gandhi and a host of earnest followers." Sportswriters had been calling Rickey "the Mahatma" for years. Since Rickey read books like Frank Tannenbaum's *Slave and Citizen* (1946), about the difference in slavery in Protestant and Catholic countries in the Americas, he was certainly capable of thinking about race on a serious level. Therefore, it is conceivable that Rickey was influenced as much by Gandhi as he was by his own Methodist upbringing in asking Robinson, in effect, to practice nonviolent resistance for three years. (Gandhi was himself an integrationist, believing that Muslims and Hindus should live together in one society and that the Indian caste system should be abolished.)

Racial integration was meant to produce a new race, an American prototype that transcended all previous racial groupings

---

In the film *The Jackie Robinson Story*, made in 1950 and starring Robinson as himself, Branch Rickey's character emphasizes to Robinson on several occasions that he must not fight back against provocation. Rickey had to know or sense that the first black man to break the color line in professional baseball had to be someone who, while he did not fight, had to look as though he could. Robinson was a tough, competitive, fairly irascible man who did not brook insult and was likely to defend his dignity at the least hint of a slight. He had been court-martialed for refusing to sit in the back of an Army base bus, a fact that was not mentioned in *The Jackie Robinson Story*—perhaps because he was acquitted. As a former football and track star at UCLA, Robinson was also used to competing with whites. He was no whiz with the books, never graduating from college, but he was still more educated than many men, both black and white, who played professional baseball in the 1940s (although several Negro-league players had degrees from black colleges). This meant that he would not be intimidated by the white press and would handle himself well in interviews. Rickey knew all of this when he chose Robinson for "the noble experiment."

It is worth noting that once the agreement ended and Robinson began to react more aggressively to insult of all sort, white sportswriters and the white public generally no longer saw him quite as sympathetically as they had during those first years. But the expression of Robinson's anger was an important cultural act and surely contributed, for instance, to the popular acceptance of jazz trumpeter Miles Davis in the mid- and late 1950s. Davis had transformed his skittish anger and crackling rudeness into a marketable persona: He was known as "the Prince of Darkness," the kind of romantic image that the white jazz-loving public craved.

By the time Robinson took the field in Brooklyn, blacks had been demanding for years that professional baseball integrate its teams. Paul Robeson, one of the most famous and accomplished black men — actor, singer and writer — of his generation, was at the forefront of this movement. Ironically, Robeson's Marxism later made him the target of Jackie Robinson's testimony before the House Un-American Activities Committee on July 18, 1949. At a conference in Paris, Robeson had said that it was unthinkable for "American Negroes [to] go to war on behalf of those who have oppressed us … against [the Soviet Union] which in one generation has raised our people to the full dignity of mankind." Responding to Robeson's statement, Robinson denounced racism, but assured the committee that black Americans were nevertheless loyal to the American ideal and eager to pursue the American Dream.

Gunnar Myrdal's *An American Dilemma*, published in 1944, was the major sociological treatise on race relations and the bible for integration. The appearance of the book was epochal, as Ralph Ellison describes it: "The whole setting is dramatic. A young scholar-scientist of international reputation, a banker, economic adviser to the Swedish Government and a member of the Swedish Senate [Myrdal], is invited by one of the wealthiest groups in the United States [the Carnegie Corporation] to come in and publicly air its soiled democratic linen." The book argued, in the main, that racism had compromised the American creed of equal opportunity, fair play and justice for all. Racism was seen not only as wrong but also as an irrational pathology. The book also argued that the Negro was himself pathological as a result of his oppression; he was the product of an insufficient, degraded subculture. It was only through integration that one could hope to end the Negro's pathologies, restore his self-esteem and make him a fully functioning citizen. *An American Dilemma* was cited by the Supreme Court as one of the sociological authorities on which it based its 1954 *Brown* decision.

Americans, of course, had always believed that this country was the land of opportunity, where one succeeded on one's own talents and hustle, and where citizenship was based on consent, not descent. In *The Jackie Robinson Story*, Branch Rickey's character berates a Dodger player who has signed a petition threatening to refuse to play with Robinson by reminding him that he wishes to deny Robinson the same chance that the country offered his immigrant Italian parents. It effectively shames the player. The entire Robinson episode in professional baseball served to repudiate American pluralism or the idea that we are a culture made up of many distinct groups and ethnic identities. Jackie Robinson returned us to the earlier idea of a melting pot of discrete individuals. Robinson did not bring with him an African memory or claim to be anything other than an American. It was not expected that he or any black would. It was not a matter of the black choosing whether he wanted to be an American or something else, as other immigrants had, but rather recognizing that he had been unjustly denied becoming the only thing he could be: a full-fledged American.

The essence of the black American's experience has been characterized by separation from whites and the absence of opportunity. (Martin Luther King Jr. used this thesis to great effect. Black Power advocates, frustrated by the apparently slow rate of change, and wanting an alternative to being American, rejected these interpretations, creating the fictive heroic African of the black American mind as a relief from being a construct of the white liberal's mind. King had been a sociology major at Morehouse and believed that the future of black Americans was in becoming *American,* not some foreign ethnic group.) As a consequence, the goal of integration was not just a matter of assimilating the Negro. Integration also meant understanding the pathologies that result from oppression and giving the Negro a chance to liberate himself from his defects. In effect, racial integration was meant to produce a new race, an American prototype that transcended all previous racial groupings. It was the zenith of the American century, and nothing could better demonstrate the power of national creed than the total integration of the Negro—the quintessential marginalized being—into the mainstream of American life. That we are now mired by multiculturalism with more rigid racial classifications than ever is due to the failure to consider the evolution of black communal life and how aspects of it could enrich the nation. Blacks were simply expected to be whites of a different color.

Jackie Robinson became the cultural paradigm for racial integration. His story—roughly the embodiment of the integrationist ideal—was replayed again and again by Hollywood, beginning with *Home of the Brave* in 1949, produced by Stanley Kramer, with James Edwards as a black GI who suffers a nervous breakdown while on a reconnaissance mission with four white soldiers. Three of the whites—one of whom is a rabid racist—are unsure if the black has the ability to do the job or to fit in as a team member. The other white is a high-school friend who is killed during the mission. The story is told in flashbacks, as a psychiatrist tries to "cure" the black soldier's trauma. Eventually he convinces the soldier that he is "the same as anybody else." "I'm colored," responds the black soldier. "That sensitivity," says the psychiatrist, "that's the disease you've got…. You've had that feeling of difference pounded into you when you were a child." In the end, the black soldier and one of his white comrades decide to become partners and open a bar, breaking the taboo of blacks and whites eating and drinking together, one supposes. (In 1962, reversing the polarities, Kramer produced a film called *Pressure Point*, in which a black psychiatrist tries to cure the racism of his Nazi patient.)

Edwards played a hard-bitten, experienced medic in Sam Fuller's tribute to the infantry, *The Steel Helmet* (1951), a Korean War combat film. After a fierce battle against the enemy from inside a Buddhist temple, only four Americans survive: a war-scarred, nearly psychotic sergeant, a Japanese-American weapons expert, Edwards's stoic medic, and a young white soldier who lost all of his hair as a youth because of scarlet fever. The power of this team—ordinary men whose ordinariness is emphasized throughout the film—is its dedication to the democratic teamwork that its diversity symbolizes. Race is twice introduced in the film. In the first instance, the sergeant encounters a Korean boy and refers to him as a "gook." The boy insists upon being called Korean. The sergeant never again refers to the boy or any other Koreans as gooks. Indeed, he eventually forms a gruff but deep attachment to the boy. The second time race is mentioned is when the American company captures a North Korean officer. The North Korean tries with both the Japanese-American soldier and the black medic to make a racial appeal, asking how they can fight for a country that treats their groups so poorly. He reminds the black about public discrimination, the Japanese-American about the internment camps. Neither man is swayed by this appeal to "color" consciousness, and the North Korean dismisses them both as oppressed men who have accepted the terms of their oppression. But the underlying message is that while a democratic white American (like the sergeant) can be cured of his narrow racist beliefs, the North Korean Communist cannot escape his ideology of color and self-consciousness. *The Steel Helmet* was the first American film to broach the subject of race in quite this way, and it vividly shows the impact of Robinson on the American mind.

King understood that many Americans feared continued tensions between blacks and whites would lead to a race war

---

Even more striking was Joseph Mankiewicz's 1950 film *No Way Out*, which featured Sidney Poitier in his first film role. The bookish, sophisticated Mankiewicz, who loved psychoanalysis, was an important screenwriter and director, whose *All About Eve*, released the same year, would win him Oscars for Best Director, Best Screenplay and Best Picture. He had won Oscars for Best Screenplay and Best Director the previous year for *A Letter to Three Wives*, making him the hottest filmmaker in Hollywood. In *No Way Out*, Poitier plays a doctor at a white county hospital accused by a white racist, played by Richard Widmark, of killing his brother through misdiagnosis. Poitier tries to clear his name with the help of his liberal white superior and the widow of the man he treated. In the final scene, when Poitier is nearly killed by Widmark's character, he refuses to take revenge by killing the man, instead treating him for his wounds. The film was hailed by the NAACP and most black newspapers as a hard-hitting drama about race. Up to then, Hollywood had never made a film about race relations that was so honest or that took black middle-class and working-class characters so seriously. The controversial film was not shown in the South, not surprising for the time, and played in Chicago and Boston only with difficulty and after blacks demanded to see it. *No Way Out* had two elements that made white theater owners in Chicago and Boston uncomfortable: First, the film depicts a race riot where the blacks win, up until that time an almost unheard-of occurrence in American film. Second, the film depicts the white working class in an uncharitable light, and both Chicago and Boston had huge enclaves of whites very much like those represented in the film's "Beaver Canal."

Whatever else can be said about the virtues and flaws of *No Way Out*, it probably would not have been made without the example of Robinson. Poitier is a young black man, unsure of himself, placed in a pressure-filled environment where no black had ever worked before as an equal to the whites. He is a very dark-skinned black man, like Robinson, and he wears white a great deal in his profession (as did Robinson), further accenting the blackness of his skin. In effect, the film is Mankiewicz's interpretation of the Jackie Robinson paradigm of integration: Racism is a sickness, a pathology, mostly associated with the lower class; the black who enters the white professional world may be competent but often must rely on the patronage of white liberals in power to protect him, because he brings little from his black communal experience that can help him, other than his determination to prove himself.

Poitier, of course, went on to become a significant actor in the 1950s and 1960s, appearing mainly in dramas about integration or race relations, culminating one stage of his career with his portrayal of the ambitious but frustrated Walter Lee Younger in Lorraine Hansberry's famous 1959 play about integration and black social aspirations, *A Raisin in the Sun*. Among Poitier's most striking films about integration was *All the Young Men*, made in 1960 and starring Alan Ladd, an actor whose star was dimming as Poitier's was growing ever brighter. The film is about a young black soldier in Korea who becomes the head of a small combat unit after the death of the commanding officer. Although technically he should have the command, he is less experienced than Alan Ladd's character and less sure of himself. The men also have little confidence in him at first both because he is untested and because he is black. Poitier, in the end, wins the men over and saves Ladd's life through a blood transfusion—an obvious bit of symbolism. The difference between this integration film and earlier ones is that *All the Young Men* is not about working as an equal among whites but about leading them. It also anticipates some of the issues surrounding affirmative action because a less qualified black was selected over a seemingly more qualified white. The film, a relatively minor effort in Poitier's career, shows how integration was accelerating and growing more urgent in America by 1960, and

---

The consequence of stressing differences as the multicultural movement does today, is to make difference the only reality

---

how the optimism surrounding it was intensifying. The acceleration, the urgency, the unstoppable optimism—all largely coalesced around one man: Martin Luther King Jr.

WHAT IS MOST REMARKABLE ABOUT KING IS that he managed to make integration the philosophical goal of a mass movement of civil disobedience that very much resembled a series of religious revivals. That is, King was able to take a social ideal or, more precisely, a theory about how American pluralism or American heterogeneity is supposed to work—a theory, in essence, about what it means to be an American—and not only invest it with the real possibility of achievement but with messianic fervor. Integration became the new Great Awakening of the United States.

Integration, of course, did not have to be the result or even the aim of the assault against segregation and Jim Crow, much less the instrument of an even larger ideological assault against racism. Nationalistic aspirations have long had a grip on the African-American imagination, probably longer than integration or assimilation, although the majority of African-Americans, especially since the Civil War, have wanted to be a part of American life and have seen themselves unquestionably as Americans. Even the Communists, before and during the days of the popular front in the 1930s, were unsure whether blacks should be treated as a nation-within-a-nation or as simply a minority group whose classes correspond to those of the larger society. Moreover, assimilation can be a hard idea to sell. As Eric Hoffer pointed out in *The True Believer* (1951), the marginalized person who fails when playing by the rules of the majority is likely to feel even more alienated—the marginalized generally are apt to feel excessively paranoid and cynical about

what they perceive as majority values in any case—and the marginalized person who succeeds is likely to "resent the admission of inferiority implied in the process of assimilation." On a strictly emotional basis, it is easier to sell nationalism, which says, in effect, if you can't join 'em, beat 'em.

Thus, the rise of Malcolm X and black nationalism in the 1960s was not an aberration but an inevitable result of the mass movement created around the idea of integration. There were two reasons for this nationalistic movement: First, as Hoffer and others argued, nationalism was the most powerful idea to arise in colonial countries during the Cold War, and black Americans, as another oppressed group, were particularly susceptible to it because it already existed in their historical imagination. Second, the nationalistic impulse had been strong throughout American history. The U.S., after all, was a country founded by "separatists." As America grew, so did the myth of separation: immigrants separating themselves from their countries of origin, and various groups separating themselves within the geography of the country in pursuit of greater freedom—witness the Shakers, Mormons, Father Divine's followers, and today's homeschoolers, militiamen, neo-Luddites, vegans and environmentalists, and various ethnic and religious groups. Indeed, the most mythologized group of Americans, Southerners, are the arch-separatists. Is *I'll Take My Stand* (1930), a brilliant but often reactionary collection of essays by the Nashville Agrarians (a group of a dozen writers, including John Crowe Ransom, Allen Tate and Robert Penn Warren), any less a separatist-inspired tract than anything written by the most ardent Afrocentrist? Democracy can be frustrating and deeply unsatisfying for a significant number of people; the U.S., in order to survive as a union, has always had to fight the urge of some of its citizens to separate. So it should come as no surprise that blacks, a largely pariah, alienated community, might also want to separate.

King's genius for selling the idea of integration hinged on his understanding of three important characteristics of Cold War American culture. First, as David Riesman astutely observed in his classic study, *The Lonely Crowd* (1950), the change in emphasis from production to consumption made Americans less inner-directed and goal-fixated and more outer-directed and relationship-oriented. As Riesman wrote, "The problem for people in America today is other people." This change signified a willingness to examine racism and segregation because they were such essential aspects of American social relations. King relied heavily on sociology, which had become a very influential discipline after the war; since the Holocaust could not be attributed solely to innate human qualities, scholars set out to explain human behavior by examining social and political environments. Human beings were seen as social and economic outcomes that could be shaped by external conditions. King also relied on the rise of the welfare state. Like white liberals, he believed that an active, well-intentioned government could correct economic inequalities and perfect social arrangements. (Hooking integration to the star of the welfare state was probably a dubious strategy. The power of the Robinson story was that it had nothing to do with government intervention.)

Second, as a religious leader operating in the political realm, King knew the power of symbolism; he understood that integration, in symbolic terms, was an extraordinary evocation of idealized community. That was what the 1963 march on Washington was about, an evocation of idealized community, an evocation, more concretely, of a new popular front, a new assemblage of America's progressive and liberal-left forces. Most of the activities of the civil-rights movement, whether led by King or by others, were symbolic: the Montgomery bus boycott; the integration of Central High School in Little Rock; the student sit-ins; the integration of the Universities of Mississippi, Alabama and Georgia; the freedom rides; the campaigns in Birmingham, Albany (Georgia) and other locations. Indeed, King ran into his greatest problems when he tried to use the same tactics in the North, where dramatic symbolic gestures had little impact on black-white relations, because the region lacked the intricate history of symbols and codes that characterized the relationship between the two groups in the South. The emergence of television as a mass medium only emphasized the need for powerful, emotional symbolism as a way to make a deep political impact on the society. In the 1950s, King knew this better than anyone else: The television footage of the Montgomery bus boycott in 1955-1956 had made him a media star.

Third, King understood that many Americans feared that continued tensions between blacks and whites would lead to a race war. This fear is at least as old as Jefferson's *Notes on Virginia* (1785) and David Walker's *Appeal* (1829). Many prominent Americans, including James Madison, Abraham Lincoln and Henry Clay believed some version of the race-war idea because they were convinced that blacks and whites couldn't live together as equals in this society. As Jefferson wrote: "Deep-rooted prejudices entertained by the whites; ten thousand recollections, by the blacks, of the injuries they have sustained; new provocations; the real distinctions which nature has made; and many other circumstances, will divide us into parties, and produce convulsions, which will probably never end but in the extermination of the one or the other race."

The cry of nationalism among nonwhite nations during the '50s and '60s and the rising militancy of African-Americans intensified the idea of race war as the American Armageddon. The violent showdowns King forced in various Southern communities were meant to resemble race wars but with some significant differences. Blacks, because they were nonviolent and nonaggressive, were seen as heroic, noble, self-sacrificing people who were willing to die for a cause but not kill for it. The whites were made to seem irrational, unreasonable, cowardly. Racism and segregation were made out to be illnesses. In effect, King's tactic was to make race war impossible by providing his own manipulated version of it. Integration was the only reasonable way out of the dilemma. Who would not want to integrate with these brave marchers? Who would try to defend the murderous oppression of those who opposed it? The end of history was not a victory of white over black or black over white, but rather it was black and white lying down side by side as equals.

THE UNDOING OF INTEGRATION AS A SOCIAL IDEAL and a realizable social goal can be traced to three main causes. First, of course, was the naive optimism of the movement. Many civil-rights leaders, including King himself, at least for a time, thought that by the late '60s the race problem would be solved in America. When integration met with fierce resistance and scorn from both whites and blacks in increasing numbers, its adherents were nonplussed, unable to think through the implications of its failures. They either became institutionalized moralizers when civil rights became a branch of the federal bureaucracy or succumbed to the new mood of racial separatism. At a certain point, the critics of integration were able to argue against it better than its proponents could argue for it, especially as it seemed to be producing a great deal of nihilism (as "liberation" itself became chic) and violence but little racial understanding. School busing, for instance, turned into an exorbitant absurdity.

Second, other mass movements, generated from the left, began to compete with the civil-rights movement: the women's liberation movement, the anti-Vietnam War movement, the student movement, the American Indian movement, the environmental movement. (Eric Hoffer was right: Mass movements are competitive and often interchangeable.) None of these movements was exactly concerned with the meaning of American pluralism and none had integration as its aim. Ralph Ellison reflected the view of most blacks when he wrote about the rise of "liberation" as a movement in the 1960s: "I think [the antiwar movement] led to a diffusion of interests and it allowed a lot of nonblack people who were part of [King's] support to focus their energies elsewhere. It let them off the hook when the going got hot in the racial arena. I trace some of the defection of energies to ecology and antiwar protest back to people who realized when blacks started moving into their neighborhoods and their schools that they were dealing with something more difficult than just taking a high moral position as they looked toward the South." In short, whites found "liberation" to be a convenient retreat from the rigorous implications of integration in their own ways of living.

Third, the seeds for the dissolution of integration were embedded in the very concept of it. For instance, Ellison, who in 1953 became the first black man to win the National Book Award with *The Invisible Man*, wrote: "Whence all this passion toward conformity anyway? — diversity is the word. Let man keep his many parts and you'll have no tyrant states. Why, if they follow this conformity business they'll end up by forcing me, an invisible man, to become white, which is not a color but the lack of one. Must I strive toward colorlessness?... America is woven of many strands; I would recognize them and let it so remain." Ellison's words were composed when the greatest fear among American intellectuals like himself was conformity, especially in the witch-hunt atmosphere generated by Joe McCarthy. But Ellison sounds almost exactly like any garden-variety multiculturalist today. It is not a big leap from viewing anti-Communism as an instrument of conformity to viewing integration in the same light or, to use the current term, to think of integration as "cultural genocide." Du Bois expressed such a fear back in 1903 when he wrote about black double-consciousness: "[The Negro] would not bleach his Negro soul in a flood of white Americanism, for he knows that Negro blood has a message for the world." Integration could only work as an ideal if people respected what they had in common, not simply the ways in which they were different.

The consequence of continuously emphasizing difference, as the multicultural movement does today, is to make difference the only reality. It now seems old-fashioned or even reactionary to talk about what Americans have in common. As David Hollinger recently suggested in *Postethnic America*, multiculturalism denies choice because it suggests that the sociological difference you represent is your only identity. In the laudable effort to make racism a socially disreputable belief, multiculturalism has made it nearly impossible to talk about human difference except to deplore any discomfort we have with it. The effect of multiculturalism is to make people feel more different than they actually are. The triumph of the civil-rights movement, it turned out, was not the realization of integration but the ascendancy of the sociological imagination.

Even in the heyday of the civil-rights movement, blacks questioned aspects of integration. Hansberry's *A Raisin in the Sun*, which endorses integration, poses a key issue: What of the black American's African heritage? In the play, Beneatha, the sister, winds up rejecting the middle-class George Murchison, who has all the philistine traits of his class as described in E. Franklin Frazier's 1957 classic treatise, *Black Bourgeoisie*. Her decision to consider marriage to the African, Asagai, who wishes to free his people from colonialism, is symbolized by her new Afro hairstyle. Hansberry uses Beneatha's dilemma to suggest that the African-American is freighted with both an African past and an American present that somehow must be reconciled. But the play also asserts that the black American has an American past that both he and his white oppressor must face. Walter Lee Younger (Poitier's character) acknowledges this past when he announces at the end of the play that he and his family will move into a house in a white neighborhood because Walter's father, a common laborer, "earned it." The play also raises the question of what the African-American, from the life he or she was forced to forge in segregation, brings to the melting pot of integration. And it questions the fate of black manhood—an unavoidable concern in a play with an absent patriarch and a young father who seems dominated by women, by his limited circumstances, and by his enormous sense of frustration. It is a crucial point because it focuses attention on the fate of the race itself. Integration as a social goal never answered those questions. It was never equipped to.

These considerations lead inexorably to the Million Man March. For if Jackie Robinson's breakthrough was the symbolic beginning of the age of integration, then the Million Man March in October 1995 was the symbolic end of that age. The march was the brainchild of Benjamin Chavis, former political revolutionary of the 1960s and later executive director of the NAACP, and Louis Farrakhan, leader of the Nation of Islam and former singer and instrumentalist. In its quest for "unity," the march was completely about separation: blacks from whites, men from women. Farrakhan, particularly, is obsessed with separation, which he sees as the only rational solution for all questions of difference. The march was an expression of frustration at the inability of blacks to come up with a compelling political or social idea to replace integration and to deal with the breakdown of their own communities. It was a populist complaint against the entrenched bureaucratic elitism of the civil-rights movement and its leaders, who seem totally disconnected from the day-to-day life of the average black person.

This impressive and moving gathering of black men was a clear repudiation of integration as it was dramatized in the 1963 march on Washington, surely one of Farrakhan's aims. As he recognizes, many black people today view the crisis in their communities as the direct result of integration, which weakened black solidarity and undermined black communal life. In their nostalgia for a mythical way of life, Jackie Robinson becomes a symbol for the failure of integration: He succeeds as an individual but destroys the Negro leagues in the process. The Million Man March was an expression of black community, a statement that black life is to be rescued from within, without white help or intervention. In this evocation of a newly revitalized black community, integration seems beside the point. But the Million Man March sidestepped some pivotal questions: What

is the aim and goal of black community? Why should it survive as a desire, an intention, a set of expressions, a memory? Unless Chavis, Farrakhan and their followers address these issues, and unless they are able to transform the symbolic power of the march into concrete benefits for blacks, it may end up.as a historical footnote, successful only as a publicity stunt.

Integration should be criticized for its failure to recognize what black people had to tell, from their own experience, about what it means to be an American. But this does not mean that the idea of integration is wrong. Integration should be repaired, not blamed for the failures of the black community. It has become a commonplace for many black intellectuals to romanticize the black community under segregation. In hindsight, our schools were havens of black self-esteem, caring and wholeness; in truth they were marred by social pettiness and cruelty, pedagogical tyranny, and frustration. Our churches are remembered as havens of love and saintliness, not (as they so often were) places for social climbing, anti-intellectual preaching, and ritualized escapes for frustrated men and women from their unfulfilling lives. This is not to say that those institutions have not been important sources of strength and creativity for blacks, but merely to point out that idealizing them is as much a mistake as diminishing them. It is true that these institutions have produced some extraordinary leaders, but integration has produced far more. Black people have more money now, more access to power now, more influence in society now. These gains have put them in a position to strengthen their communities in substantial ways. Because integration has made black people a more effective pressure group, it paved the way for Martin Luther King Jr. Day, Kwanzaa, black publishing houses, black consumerism and Afrocentrism itself. The problems with black urban communities today are a result of unforeseen economic forces and bad public-policy moves that have almost nothing to do with integration. The inner city is largely the creation of the federal government, which built expressways that allowed employees to relocate to the suburbs, destroyed neighborhoods with festering public housing, and created a welfare system that discouraged enterprise and disrupted family life.

Black people are right to see their individual redemption linked to the redemption of their communal experience. But the strength of any community is its willingness to absorb things outside itself. Black people have always struggled to have community because, since the days of slavery, whites have never allowed them to function as a true community; instead, blacks were kept in a condition more closely resembling state-enforced isolation. It was this isolation that was terrible then, just as it is terrible now for the black underclass. Jackie Robinson did not destroy the Negro leagues; they should never have existed at all, and it is much to the shame of whites that they did. Integration, rightly understood not as becoming "white" but as a true engagement with what this country and culture have to offer, is the only way to have a vital black community.

The issue of black community aside, integration has come under scrutiny along with the liberalism that brought it into existence. Liberalism says that beneath our differences is a core of common humanity and common history. This liberalism is the essence of American experience, of democratic living. Whites have criticized it because it is often inconvenient or threatening to their status as a majority. Blacks have criticized it because it has failed to deliver on its implicit promise to make recompense for the past. But multiculturalism is not the antidote. It does not provide relief through transcendence but only through social category. In this way, it is an expression of group narcissism. The Million Man March might have been partly right in its skepticism about government intervention, but it was wholly wrong in its exclusion of so many people who are concerned with the problems of blacks today.

Doubtless, many whites are still deeply racist, but the ideal of integration dramatically changed the thinking of many others. Doubtless, too, being black in America still has its severe trials and difficulties, but no black today faces the limitations imposed on previous generations. Integration has opened doors that our parents could only dream about. It is an interesting irony that Martin Luther King, the ardent integrationist, grew up in an extraordinarily vibrant all-black community, was shaped by all-black churches and schools, had a loving black family, and never had any uneasiness about being black. I believe he succeeded in selling the idea to other blacks because of where and how he grew up. Malcolm X, on the other hand, grew up spending a great deal of time with whites, felt uneasy about his race, never experienced a strong black family life, and never had positive experiences at a black church or a black school. He became a nationalist and a separatist, perhaps because he was seeking something he needed, something in the black experience. King, too, was seeking a sort of completion, which was probably why he preached integration.

I think, in the end, we know which man had the more profound idea, judging by who has had the bigger impact on America. As my colleague Wayne Fields has pointed out, Malcolm X had a ready-made constituency of resentful, frustrated blacks. King had to create his integrated audience. Moreover, he had to sustain his followers instead of being sustained by them. This extraordinary feat will not be undone or "revised" by "X" hats and Afrocentrism. But both men's lives tell us much: We need strong black communities in America because that is, after all, for better and for worse, part of being an American, with a redeemed ethnic past and a sense of ethnic consensus.

But we need integration even more, for that is what America is supposed to be, a place where everyone partakes of our unique mixture, where everyone is part of a greater consensus. I need white experience to understand what it means to be an American, just as whites need mine. The failure of integration has been a failure of nerve, a failure to pursue a utopian ideal simply because it demands much from both sides, especially unwavering good faith. Perhaps we might learn much about "good faith" from the Shakers who sang:

In yonder valley there flows sweet union
Let us arise and drink our fill.

It is, in our great American resolve, only a matter of going.

America's Caste System: Will It Change?

George M. Fredrickson

Liberal Racism
by Jim Sleeper.
Viking, 195 pp., $21.95

**America in Black and White:
One Nation, Indivisible**
by Stephan Thernstrom and
Abigail Thernstrom.
Simon and Schuster, 704 pp., $32.50

**A Country of Strangers:
Blacks and Whites in America**
by David K. Shipler.
Knopf, 640 pp., $30.00

**The Ordeal of Integration:
Progress and Resentment in
America's "Racial" Crisis**[1]
by Orlando Patterson.
Civitas, distributed by Counterpoint,
240 pp., $24.50

1.

President Clinton's recent call for a "national conversation on race" and his appointment of a commission headed by the historian John Hope Franklin to report on the current state of race relations are strong indications that there is once again an upsurge of concern about America's oldest and most persistent problem. Unfortunately, the conversation could easily become a debate that will further polarize rather than unify Americans.

There are several questions that have to be asked and answered honestly and objectively before a productive conversation can begin. The first is to inquire what we mean by the term "race," so that we know what we are talking about. The word has strong historical associations with a theory of biological determinism that has been shown to have no scientific validity. But if we substitute a term such as "ethnicity," which normally refers to culture rather than biology, we risk underestimating the historical and contemporary significance of racism as an ideology or set of beliefs and attitudes.

Sociologists have long recognized that race is a social rather than a biological phenomenon, and recently the proposition that race is "a social and cultural construction" has become an academic cliché. But social and cultural constructions can justify the enslavement, forced segregation, or even the extermination of people designated as having inferior ancestry or bad genes. When such attitudes are influential, or have been influential for extended periods in the past with effects that persist, a race problem may be said to exist. As a practical matter, therefore, it is difficult to avoid using the term.

In the history of the United States only one minority has been consistently thought of as a "race" in the full and invidious sense—African-Americans. Hostilities toward other groups, such as American Indians, Asians, Mexicans, Irish, Italians, and Jews, have often been intense and have led in some cases to widespread violence and deplorable injustices. But cultural intolerance has usually played a greater role in provoking their mistreatment than a strong belief in their natural incapacities. Most other persecuted minorities were eventually considered candidates for assimilation and were denounced and abused when they chose to remain culturally distinctive. Blacks, on the other hand, were regarded for centuries as inherently unassimilable because, as subhuman, they lacked a developed or refined human culture and were deemed incapable of having one. Consequently, every effort was made to keep them from taking a full part in American society. John Hope Franklin, therefore, has historical justification when he argues, against the multiculturalist approach of President Clinton, that his commission on race should be primarily concerned with the basic enduring problem of black–white relations rather than with the full American mosaic that has complicated the classic race question but not eliminated it.

If race in America is still mainly a matter of black and white, then the next question that needs attention is the very contentious one of how well African-Americans are doing. Scarcely anyone denies that their situation is better in some ways than it was before the civil rights legislation of the 1960s ended legalized segregation, gave Southern blacks access to the ballot box, and provided African-Americans with legal remedies against employment discrimination which came to include affirmative action policies. But many believe that progress since the 1970s has slowed or stalled and that there are current signs of regression toward greater segregation and economic or cultural deprivation. Almost everyone agrees that there is both good news and bad news; the debate is over which should be in the headlines.

Relatively uncontroversial is the proposition that African-Americans as a group have not been as successfully integrated into the mainstream of American life as the architects of the civil rights reforms hoped and expected that they would be. What accounts for the disappointment of these hopes? The answer of many liberals and of most African-American leaders and intellectuals is the persistence of white racism, prejudice, and discrimination—the belief that the traditional American caste system has adapted to the new legal and political equality by finding subtler ways of keeping blacks "in their place" at the bottom of the nation's status hierarchy. But others, including some liberals, argue that the evidence from opinion surveys and other data show that white racism has declined so substantially that the cause of black poverty, resentment, and demoralization must be sought elsewhere.

Alleged deficiencies of culture and leadership among blacks themselves—especially their tendency to blame racism for self-inflicted wounds and to short-circuit the integration process by practicing self-segregation—are the most popular explanations of those who deny the force of persistent racism.[2] Also blamed for recent setbacks are misguided governmental policies, especially affirmative action and the welfare system, that have allegedly lowered group standards of conduct and achievement, creating feelings of depend-

ency and entitlement that have sapped the initiative and capacity for sustained effort on the part of a substantial segment of the black population.[3]

Disagreement on the causes of black underachievement, poverty, crime, and family disintegration point to radically different remedies. Many white liberals and most black leaders favor an expansion of governmental activity—more effective affirmative action, WPA-type job programs for the ghetto unemployed, a social safety net for children and the unemployable, and universal health care. Libertarian conservatives would go in the opposite direction—ending welfare, affirmative action, and all other programs that protect people from the "discipline" of the free market and the need to "stand on their own two feet." Centrists like President Clinton try to split the difference by reducing but not ending government programs to help the disadvantaged.

The books under review are all serious efforts to address these basic questions concerning the state of black–white relations in 1997. They approach the problem from the same starting point—a commitment to the liberal ideal of equality of rights and opportunities for all Americans. The authors all claim to share the integrationist dream of Martin Luther King, Jr., and seek in differing ways to recapture the hopeful "black and white together" spirit of the civil rights movement. Unrepresented and generally disdained in these works are the views of black nationalists and pessimistic social scientists who regard antiblack racism as so deep-seated among whites that there is little or no hope of overcoming it; but also repudiated are those who would deny or forget the terrible racist past of the United States and fail to see its relevance to the present.

Despite this measure of ideological agreement among the authors, each of whom claims to speak for liberal values, they end up disagreeing sharply on the wisdom and legitimacy of race-conscious public policies, especially affirmative action. Two of the books, those by David Shipler and Orlando Patterson, present the case for affirmative action, while the works by Jim Sleeper and Stephan and Abigail Thernstrom argue against it. This quarrel among analysts of race relations who draw on the liberal integrationist tradition reflects a deep division among Americans who consider themselves liberal in some sense. Survey data show that those who describe themselves as both liberals and Democrats are almost equally split on whether remedies for black disadvantage should take account of race or be colorblind.[4]

The most polemical and least substantial of the books is Jim Sleeper's *Liberal Racism*. But it is useful because of the forthright way that it presents the case against race-conscious policies and more broadly against what the author takes to be the current gospel of "multiculturalism." Sleeper, a former columnist for the New York *Daily News*, considers himself a man of the left and frequently contributes to liberal periodicals. His principal argument is that liberals have betrayed the colorblind, race-transcending values that inspired their support of the civil rights movement. He excoriates race-conscious liberals for endorsing multiculturalism, "identity politics," and affirmative action, as well as condoning black separatism on college campuses and elsewhere. Sleeper especially deplores the extent to which liberals have accepted the self-serving contention of black demagogues that white racism is worse than ever, when in fact it has declined markedly in recent years.

In my opinion, Sleeper is on relatively firm ground in his criticisms of racial gerrymandering to increase black representation in the South. Its unintended effect has been to increase the power of conservatives in Congress; it has substituted symbolic representation—more black faces in Congress—for the greater influence that would have come from having more racially mixed districts in which blacks would hold the balance of power. His provocative title means that, for him, using racial classifications for the professed purpose of overcoming racism is actually racist in itself and deepens the divisions between black and white rather than overcoming them. With views that sometimes recall those of Arthur Schlesinger, Jr., in *The Disuniting of America*, he argues that liberal concessions to racial and ethnic particularism endanger the civic unity on which the cohesiveness of the nation depends.[5]

The problem with his book is that it overstates its case and wastes much of its heavy artillery on straw targets. Who exactly are the "racist liberals" whom Sleeper is attacking? Andrew Hacker and Derrick Bell are his most frequent, indeed virtually his only, examples of pessimistic liberals who argue seriously that white supremacy is so central to American values and institutions that there is virtually no hope of overcoming it.[6] Most liberals that I know and whose books I have read are more hopeful. Some, like William Julius Wilson and Martin Carnoy, put much of their faith in traditional liberal policies of the New Deal type that are aimed at class disadvantages rather than specifically racial ones, although they find that there is still need for some race-specific remedies.[7] Others, like Lani Guinier and the Princeton political philosopher Amy Gutmann, believe that affirmative action is not only consistent with liberal values but, if properly conceived and implemented, can unify rather than divide America.[8] Although there may be such persons in New York City, I do not personally know anyone I would consider a liberal who is sympathetic to Al Sharpton's demagoguery in the Tawana Brawley case or to militant Afrocentrism in education and scholarship.

The liberal policy of multicultural higher education, as it works at my own university and most others I know of, does not, as Sleeper claims, intentionally condone or encourage racial and ethnic separatism and has nothing whatever to do with Afrocentrism, which is obviously a form of monoculturalism. Multicultural education, properly conceived, is a serious effort to achieve what historian John Higham calls "pluralistic integration," a search for common ground and mutual tolerance among people of diverse cultural backgrounds.[9] It should encourage a cosmopolitan respect for different cultures rather than an ethnocentric preoccupation with one's own and is therefore consistent with the highest aims of a liberal education. By describing liberals who favor multiculturalism and some race-conscious policies as "racists," Sleeper is giving credence to misleading right-wing propaganda and muddying the issues rather than clarifying them.

A more scholarly and extensively documented presentation of a similar perspective is *America in Black and White* by Stephan and Abigail Thernstrom. He is a distinguished Harvard historian; more than anyone else he led the movement for quantitative social history in the 1960s and 1970s. She is a political scientist who has specialized in voting rights issues. Because of its extensive and seemingly authoritative use of statistical data, *America in Black and White* is a challenging book. Not being a statistician, I have to accept most of its data on faith, as I am quite prepared to do in view of Stephan Thernstrom's well-established reputation for statistical analysis. Sometimes, however, the analysis of data that, on the face of it, do not support the general argument seems forced and unpersuasive. For example, the authors criticize a research project on employment discrimination in Washing-

ton, D.C., in which equally qualified blacks and whites were asked to apply for the same jobs. Although the results showed that the employers had a significant preference for whites, the Thernstroms argue that the study should be discredited because it did not include the federal government. But it was, after all, a study of discrimination in the private sector. One expects the federal government, where affirmative action has long been in effect, to be "an equal opportunity employer."

The book first seeks to demonstrate that at least some blacks have had substantial gains during the last half-century; it then argues that the current racial "crisis" is caused by a combination of ignorance about how far blacks have come and misguided race-conscious policies, such as affirmative action, that have been based on a false assumption that the persistence of white racism is at the core of the problems that remain.

The long historical section at the beginning tells the story of black–white relations through the 1960s in a generally accurate and effective way. It is unsparing in its account of the horrors of the Jim Crow system in the South and strongly appreciative of the heroism and achievements of the nonviolent civil rights movement of the 1950s and early 1960s. But the Thernstroms may draw too sharp a contrast between the integrationist struggle personified by Martin Luther King, Jr., and the Black Power or black nationalist phase that followed and scuttled King's dream of racial togetherness. We sometimes forget that the Southern civil rights movement was in many ways an expression of black autonomy and self-determination. Led by blacks, premised on black solidarity, and drawing on the distinctive traditions of the black church, it was in its own way a manifestation of African-American ethnic identity and assertiveness. King won crucial national support from whites by stressing the compatibility of the movement's goals with universalist American values.

But he was also aware, as were most of his black followers, that they were seeking liberation as a people from a species of colonial domination by another people. (King often likened his struggle to anti-colonial movements in the third world.) Group consciousness as a basis for black identity politics was as much a legacy of the Southern civil rights movement as the ideal of a colorblind America.

Contrary to the prevailing assumption that King would have been opposed to affirmative action if he were living today, he clearly endorsed its basic principle in 1964: "Whenever this issue of compensatory or preferential treatment for the Negro is raised," he wrote in *Why We Can't Wait*,

> some of our friends recoil in horror. The Negro should be granted equality, they agree; but he should ask nothing more. On the surface, this appears reasonable, but it is not realistic. For it is obvious that if a man is entered at the starting line in a race three hundred years after another man, the first man would have to perform some impossible feat in order to catch up with his fellow runner.[10]

It is high time that contemporary advocates of "colorblind" policies stop claiming King's authority and recognize that he was strongly in favor of "doing something special" for the Negro "in order to balance the equation and equip him to compete on a just and equal basis."

The second section of *America in Black and White* records and analyzes recent trends and concludes that blacks have made great gains since the 1960s. The Thernstroms summarize the current situation as follows:

> Blacks participate—often decisively—in elections: had Colin Powell chosen to run, we might well have inaugurated our first African-American president in January 1997. The black underclass often seems to define black America, but less than one-fifth of

African-Americans are actually poverty-stricken residents of central cities, and (contrary to conventional wisdom) almost all [black students] get a high school diploma. Median family income for married black couples is now only 13 percent below that of white couples; half of all black families have incomes that are at least double the poverty line. Almost no adult men with full-time jobs are destitute, and the substantial black middle class that has emerged since 1940 is passing on its status to the next generation.... Not only has residential segregation declined in most big cities; 30 percent of the black population lived in suburbs by 1994....

> There is, of course, bad news as well as good.... Most blacks are not poor, and most of America's poor are not black. Nevertheless, nearly a third of African-Americans are still impoverished, a consequence in large measure of the number of single-parent black households. A social pattern with devastating economic consequences has become the norm in the black community; in 1995, 85 percent of black children in poverty lived in households with no father present. In addition, since the 1960s, crime rates have been surging in the black community, particularly among young black males.

It would seem that the good news outweighs the bad, but not by much. The success of married and middle-class blacks appears to be in some danger of being overshadowed or undercut by the disintegration of the black family and the poverty associated with it. Not noted here but discussed elsewhere in the book are the appalling rates of unemployment among black males: only 52 percent of those eighteen to sixty-four "have full-time, year round jobs, as compared with two-thirds of white males."

But the Thernstroms deny the connection often made between male joblessness and family disintegration. The unemployment rate does not correlate statistically, they show, with the rise of unwed motherhood. In the past unemployed young men were much more likely to marry than they are now. They

blame persistent black poverty mainly on the breakdown of the black family and they hint, but do not show, that there is a cultural explanation for the rise of single-parent households. At this point Dinesh D'Souza would rush in and talk about black cultural pathology; but it is worth noting that unwed motherhood is rising at a faster rate among whites than among blacks, although it remains at a lower level, and that single-parent households are becoming much more common, especially among poorer citizens, in other modern industrial nations. Something has been happening here that we do not fully understand and, until we do, we should perhaps reserve judgment about the causes.[11]

The undeniable good news is that the black middle class has expanded greatly since the 1960s—to the point where 40 percent of all blacks consider themselves to be middle class and about 30 percent actually qualify according to standards used by social demographers. How was this gain achieved? The Thernstroms deny that affirmative action has had much to do with it. They argue that the black middle class was growing as rapidly before the beginnings of affirmative action as it has since. This strikes me as one of their weaker contentions. As they themselves demonstrate, the substantial gains in per capita black income relative to that of whites between the 1940s and 1960s, which laid a foundation for expansion of the middle class, occurred because of favorable circumstances that were unique to that period—a booming economy, a tight labor market, and a mass migration of blacks from rural poverty in the South to relatively well-paying industrial jobs in the North.

Since the 1970s, very different conditions have prevailed. Deindustrialization and decline or stagnation in real income for most workers have made it more difficult for blacks, as for other members of the working class, to attain middle-class status. But the solid black middle class of professionals, executives, managers, business owners, military officers, and civil servants has nonetheless continued to grow, notwithstanding downsizing in the private sector and cutbacks in the government spending that sustains a high level of public employment. Affirmative action must have contributed to this growth. The effects of the large increase in the proportion of blacks in higher education since the 1960s and the race-conscious hiring policies that many corporations have instituted since the 1970s can scarcely be denied. Many blacks with high achievements (including Colin Powell, federal judges, presidents of corporations or foundations, and provosts, deans, and professors at prestigious universities) have candidly expressed their debt to affirmative action—without, in most cases, being the least bit embarrassed by it. For it should be obvious to everyone that they have proved themselves more than competent to shoulder the responsibilities they were asked to assume.

It might be argued, however, that affirmative action has served its purpose and is no longer needed because racial prejudice is no longer a significant barrier to the advancement of qualified blacks. From a variety of polling and survey data the Thernstroms provide evidence of a steady decline in white prejudice over the past thirty years to the point where, they argue, it is no longer a significant cause of black disadvantage. For them, affirmative action was never a legitimate remedy, because it was in conflict with the principle stated in Justice John Harlan's classic dissent in *Plessy v. Ferguson* that the Constitution is "color-blind." They even fault *Brown v. Board of Education* for not clearly stating this principle, a failure that made it possible later on for some race-conscious policies to pass judicial scrutiny. But even if one believes, as Martin Luther King, Jr., did

and as the Supreme Court has held, that race must sometimes be taken into account in order to insure equal opportunity for the victims of racism, do we still need to do it if racism has declined to the extent that the Thernstroms claim?

The results of surveys and studies of white racial opinion are actually mixed or ambiguous, and differing conclusions can be drawn. It is true that fewer and fewer whites give blatantly racist answers to the questions asked them by opinion researchers, but a significant minority still do. Orlando Patterson, looking at the same evidence as the Thernstroms in his provocative book, *The Ordeal of Integration*, estimates that roughly a quarter of all white Americans are hardcore, unabashed racists. That many bigots can give blacks a lot of trouble; they outnumber blacks in the total American population by about two-to-one and are likely to be overrepresented among whites with whom blacks have frequent (and often unpleasant) contact, such as policemen, store clerks, and taxi drivers. And how strongly committed to racial equality are the whites who do not share these attitudes? Would they actively intervene on behalf of an African-American who they observed was being subjected to insulting or discriminatory treatment by another white? Some would, but I suspect that many would not. Good Samaritanism is always a rare virtue.

The Thernstroms do not mention the 1990 University of Chicago study cited by David Shipler in *A Country of Strangers* to support his view that prejudice has been persistent. Instead of simply asking people to agree or disagree with flat statements to the effect that blacks are less intelligent or more lazy than whites—questions of the type that other surveys had used over the years to reveal a steady decline in racist attitudes—the university's National Opinion Research Center asked

people to rank various ethnic groups in intelligence, industriousness, and willingness to be self-supporting instead of living on welfare. In response, 53.2 percent of a cross section of Americans said blacks were less intelligent than whites; 62.2 percent thought they were lazier; and 77.7 percent believed they were more likely to prefer welfare to work. If surveys of this type had been taken thirty years ago, they would undoubtedly have revealed even higher percentages of people with negative stereotypes of blacks. But it would be hard to deny, on the basis of such data, that low expectations of black abilities are still prevalent in this society and are bound to make many employers more reluctant to hire and promote blacks over equally—or even less—qualified whites, unless some kind of affirmative action program is in operation.

2.

Although it draws support from the University of Chicago study and other efforts to quantify racial attitudes, David K. Shipler's *A Country of Strangers* tries to get behind the statistical evidence and describe how actual human beings confront the race issue on a day-to-day basis. A former *New York Times* reporter and Pulitzer Prize–winning author of a book about the Arab–Israeli conflict, Shipler traveled around the country and interviewed in some depth hundreds of people about their perceptions and experiences of the division between black and white. He found that many whites believe blacks are much better off than they actually are; a majority think that African-Americans have the edge over whites in jobs and education. This gross exaggeration of black well-being and achievement reinforces opposition to affirmative action and other policies in which blacks are beneficiaries of special government programs.

Shipler also talked to African-Americans and believed them when they complained about constantly being devalued and suspected of incompetence, or worse, by the whites whom they encounter, work for, or are taught by. Low expectations of achievement can be self-fulfilling prophecies, as in the educational tracking systems that are the new face of separate-but-unequal education in supposedly integrated schools. When most blacks are excluded, sometimes arbitrarily, from the honors courses that prepare students for college, they tend to internalize a belief in their own incapacity or, worse, they come to devalue educational achievement as a "white thing" that they want no part of. If employers, like many teachers, expect little of blacks, they are either reluctant to hire them in the first place or to give them the respect and responsibility that would put them in line for promotion. The stereotypes that persist in the minds of many whites that African-Americans are lazy, dishonest, or lacking in leadership qualities create a vicious circle that may encourage such inadequacies and make discrimination appear "rational" and non-racist.

The belief of many whites—an overwhelming majority according to most polls—that affirmative action gives preferences to unqualified blacks over qualified whites is compatible with the stereotype of black incompetence and may cause its black beneficiaries to doubt themselves and fail to perform as well as they are capable of doing. "When African-Americans are excluded," Shipler notes, "it is because they are less capable. When they are accepted, they are still less capable, but their deficiencies have been unjustly ignored in favor of the color of their skin. The virus of bigotry mutates and survives."

Despite such negative results of affirmative action, Shipler believes that it is a just and necessary policy. The current problem is not the blatant kind of racism that allows blacks to be excluded or discriminated against purely on the grounds

of race; public attitudes no longer tolerate this kind of bigotry. It is the "subtle" prejudice that apparently denies opportunity to blacks on grounds other than race but is in reality influenced by racial stereotypes.

> Whites who discriminate subtly may not even be aware of what they are doing; almost all would deny being racists [and, one might add, would probably not be counted as racists in most opinion polls]. They can fool themselves into honestly thinking that what they are seeing is one characteristic (lack of leadership ability) when their perception is actually triggered by another (blackness).

Going to the heart of opposition to affirmative action in admission to higher education—the willingness to admit blacks with lower test scores than whites—Shipler argues that standardized tests are an imperfect and unreliable measure of ability and potential achievements. College admissions officers also look for ambition, perseverance, and energy, as shown by the extent to which an applicant has been relatively successful in school despite a disadvantaged environment or background. SATs are good predictors of freshman grades, he writes, but not of later academic or professional success. He points to a study showing a high success rate among Harvard alumni from blue-collar backgrounds who were admitted with low SAT scores under an earlier form of affirmative action.

It is therefore quite possible that admitting blacks or minority students with lower test scores than is required of others is not really reverse discrimination at all. It may be a matter of admitting people who are fully qualified to do the work on the basis of a better mode of evaluation than test scores alone can provide. The Thernstroms cite the claim of the president of Williams College that black students admitted under affirmative action do on the average

as well over four years as other students. They are skeptical of the claim, and their faith in the predictive quality of test scores leads them to believe that it cannot be generally true of other elite institutions that admit blacks with lower scores. I strongly suspect that it is. In more than thirty years of teaching at Northwestern and Stanford, both of which have had vigorous affirmative action programs, I have never had the sense that blacks in my classes were performing less well and getting lower grades than whites. The Thernstroms cite no studies demonstrating black underachievement in such institutions.

Recognizing that affirmative action in hiring or admissions does not guarantee an environment conducive to fair treatment once one is employed or enrolled, Shipler also advocates "diversity management" and "sensitivity training"—that is, some combination of workshops and courses designed to change white attitudes by exposing and refuting the prejudices that prevent them from treating blacks fairly. But the notion that white prejudice and its effects on blacks can be significantly reduced by cleverly designed diversity classes and similar measures is doubtful on several grounds. For one thing, it would seem to contradict Shipler's recognition of the role of "power" in race relations. In a chapter showing that many whites instinctively feel that a social order that gives them power and precedence over blacks is normal and natural, Shipler raises the possibility that the rewards of caste superiority are so central to the self-esteem of many whites that they would be unwilling to surrender them no matter how strong the evidence that blacks are unfairly treated. Power and privilege are like valued material possessions; people do not readily give them up even if they cannot justify them on rational grounds.

It is also difficult to see how affirmative action and diversity management will help poor blacks who lack the education and motivation to take the first step up the ladder to educational or occupational success. If the problem of white racism and black disadvantage is as serious as Shipler claims, more radical remedies would seem to be called for. Is the responsibility of corporate executives and their affluent shareholders toward African-Americans fully discharged when they provide for affirmative action and diversity management (which in fact cost them little and may even be good for business)? Or should they be taxed more heavily to provide good schools, decent housing, job subsidies, guaranteed medical care, and other government programs that would enable larger numbers of disadvantaged blacks and others to meet the minimum qualifications that they need to benefit from any kind of affirmative action program?

Orlando Patterson in *The Ordeal of Integration* agrees with Shipler on the need for affirmative action and in fact provides an argument for it that is broader and bolder in its historical and philosophical implications. But he emphatically disagrees with Shipler on the desirability of diversity management and sensitivity training, methods that he finds manipulative, condescending, and likely to do more harm than good.

Patterson is a Harvard sociologist of West Indian origin and British education who has written brilliantly on slavery and freedom as social and philosophical issues in world history. He is a resolutely independent thinker whose take on "America's 'racial' crisis" is thoroughly original, and his is the most profound and thought-provoking of the books under review. But a great many people—black and white alike—would have to change their way of thinking about "race," and other matters as well, for his views to receive the attention they deserve.

Patterson, first of all, wants to deracialize the terminology we use, substituting "ethnicity" for "race" and "Afro-Americans" and "Euro-Americans" for "black" and "white." In international or comparative terms, it is in fact often hard to distinguish the practical effects of what we call "race" in one context and "ethnicity" in another. People have been enslaved, segregated, and massacred as readily on the basis of differences in religion and culture as because they had varying pigmentation. An alternative would be to divorce the terms "race" and "racism" from a strict association with discredited biological theories and apply them to all situations where the members of one ethnic group (defined by their solidarity on the basis of a belief that they share a common ancestry) seek to dominate or exterminate those of another. Under this reformulation there would be race and racism in nations throughout the world, as well as in the United States and South Africa. But the relationship between "Afro-Americans" and the various "Euro-American" ethnic groups that became "whites" in the United States is one of the most intense and long-lasting examples of ethnic domination or applied racism to be found in the annals of human iniquity.

Unlike most African-American intellectuals, Patterson is an optimist in his views on how blacks have been doing in the past thirty or forty years. Almost as strongly as the Thernstroms, he makes a case that life has gotten much better for most blacks since the civil rights movement, and he sharply criticizes those who insist that nothing has changed or that matters have gotten worse. He accepts the proposition that white prejudice has declined drastically and he celebrates the growth of the black middle class. He admits that there is an "underclass" that creates serious problems, but he insists that it makes up "only a small fraction, at most 10 percent of the Afro-American poor—or a total of about 900,000 persons." He notes that there is also a Euro-American underclass, slightly less numerous perhaps, that exhibits the same traits of violence, criminality, sexual predation, and "moral nihilism."

In general therefore, Patterson supports the view of Sleeper and the Thernstroms that there has been great improvement in African-American circumstances and in race (or ethnic) relations in recent decades. He also shares with them an opposition to racially gerrymandered congressional districts. In contrast to Shipler, as already noted, he has no use for diversity management in integrated settings. Integration, he contends, is bound to be painful, with frequent conflict and misunderstandings; people just have to work their way through it. There is "no need," he argues,

> for any special set of sensitivities in our interactions with people from different ethnic backgrounds. Any attempt to do so will be folly, for it will lead down the path of patronizing contempt or relativistic social and political chaos.

Patterson also criticizes the social or environmental determinism that attributes the poverty of a third of the black population and the criminality of a much smaller segment entirely to circumstances beyond their control. He rejects such heavy emphasis on victimization and asserts that even the most disadvantaged young men and women have the capacity and freedom to avoid crime and improve the conditions under which they live. Most poor people, he points out, do not deal drugs or commit violent crimes.

Careless readers of the first half or so of his book might conclude that Patterson is an African-American conservative, like Thomas Sowell, for example, who believes that blacks have little to complain about: they should make their way in the market economy and expect no help from government. How wrong such readers would be! As he reveals in his ingenious and original defense of affirmative action, he is more radical than most liberal defenders of race-conscious policies. By broadening the concept of social responsibility to include corporations and other organizations as well as individuals, he directly challenges market conservatism and gives affirmative action something that it has generally lacked, a well-grounded moral and philosophical rationale.

Using polling data, Patterson shows that the overwhelming white opposition to affirmative action does not reflect a sense of being personally damaged by the policy. Only 7 percent of respondents actually claim to have been victims of "reverse discrimination," and only 16 percent know of someone else who has. More strikingly, most whites have no complaints about the affirmative action policies that are in effect where they actually work. Why then do eight out of ten oppose such policies in the abstract?

The reason, according to Patterson, is that they have been manipulated by politicians and the press and television into believing that affirmative action is unfair to whites because it violates the principle of equal opportunity that is central to the American value system. Furthermore, some of the defenders of affirmative action have encouraged this belief by presenting it as a kind of group entitlement based simply on race. He accepts the findings of the political scientist Paul Sniderman and his associates that the heavy white opposition to affirmative action is not based primarily on race prejudice but on moral and political beliefs about fairness and equity.[12]

For Patterson, affirmative action can be justified on general principles that meet the objections of its principled opponents. There is, he writes, widespread agreement that individuals should be held morally responsible for their actions, but the ideologues of free market capitalism have managed to obscure the principle that corporate bodies enjoying the same rights as individuals are similarly responsible. Patterson's essentially social democratic position is that government is the agent that acts on behalf of the people to ensure that both individuals and corporations act responsibly and in the interest of the society as a whole. In the case of natural disasters, or "Acts of God," everyone agrees that the government should be the agent that provides relief for those who have suffered through no fault of their own. Patterson sees no reason why it should not act similarly in the case of man-made disasters or "Acts of Man," such as the closing of a factory on which a whole community depends for employment.

His expansive concept of the government's "representational agency" extends to "Acts of Degradation" of the natural and social environment, which again require a collective rather than individual response. The same concept of agency emphatically includes the righting of injustices or inequities produced by historical developments ("Acts of History"), such as the growth of monopolies and the loss of educational and economic opportunities because of extended service in one of the nation's wars. Social welfare programs, as well as law enforcement, are collective responses to "the horrendous social and physical blight of the inner cities and the nihilistic violence and other behavior of Afro-American and Euro-American underclasses." They are an effort to deal with "Acts of Degradation to the social and cultural environment . . . with dire consequences for all members of society."

Affirmative action is, in Patterson's view, a collective response to the history of enslavement, segregation, discrimination, and exclusion from mainstream culture that have left many African-Americans with such an accumulation of disadvantages that they need special help, just as the victims of floods, hurricanes, and earthquakes do. "Whatever its flaws, this policy is one of the finest examples of a nation recognizing and attempting to remedy the collective impact of Acts of History on a specially disadvantaged group."

Patterson nevertheless acknowledges that such a moral and philosophical justification of affirmative action does not prevent the policy being challenged on ideological grounds; Americans venerate individual self-reliance and scarcely realize when they are departing from it, even though they often do. He concedes that "affirmative action does come into conflict with some of the moral presuppositions of American society and any defense of it must take account of these tensions." Patterson realizes that his conception that groups as well as individuals have claims and responsibilities is not a popular one, despite the precedent of veterans' preferences and other implicit acknowledgements that entire classes of citizens deserve special help from government. He is also aware that affirmative action, especially in education, has led some blacks to engage in forms of racial separatism–such as demands for separate dormitories and commencement ceremonies—that negate the integrationist purpose of the policy and encourage the belief that it leads to Balkanization.

He therefore concludes his case for affirmative action by showing how, in its absence, African-Americans will be denied true equality of opportunity. He puts great emphasis on what he calls the principle of "homophyly," which means that "people who share common attributes tend to marry each other, tend to play more together, and in general tend to get along better and form more effective work teams." It follows that an employer or personnel officer who is completely devoid of prejudice may find it more "organizationally rational to choose a Euro-American for promotion."

It is also true that in the real world prejudices based on stereotypes about black incompetence are unlikely to be completely absent, further stacking the deck against a black job applicant or candidate for promotion. Patterson's response to the colorblind approach recommended by Sleeper and the Thernstroms is pointed:

> To argue that we should begin to solve the problem of ethno-cultural exclusion by assuming a color-blind world is to assume away the very problem that we are trying to solve.... The simple truth, the simple reality, is that ethno-racial categorization is a fact of American life, one that we can only do away with by first acknowledging.

I find Patterson's thoughtful defense of affirmative action as an arguable but necessary step toward the transcendence of race more persuasive than the leap to colorblindness advocated by Sleeper and the Thernstroms. His willingness to engage with basic principles seems to me preferable to the reliance on "diversity" specialists that characterizes Shipler's otherwise useful and informative account of what Americans are currently thinking and feeling about race. Patterson's efforts to arrive at a synthesis of what is most persuasive in liberal, conservative, and socialist views may help those who think seriously about race to break out of what has tended to become a sterile debate between fixed positions.

The problem, as Patterson is quite aware, is that affirmative action is very unpopular among whites, some because they dislike blacks but a larger number because they think that "racial preferences" are inherently unfair and a legitimate cause of resentment. In California, we are embarking on an experiment to see what life will be like without affirmative action. The result so far is extremely disheartening: African- and Mexican-Americans have virtually disappeared from the entering classes of the top University of California medical and law schools.

Proponents of affirmative action who have defended the policy as re-quiring group entitlements based strictly on the race of the beneficiaries have played into the hands of their opponents. The only way that affirmative action can be revived in California and preserved elsewhere is for the terms of the debate to be changed. The defenders of such a policy must base their claims convincingly on the principles of fairness. They should banish the terms "racial preferences" and "reverse discrimination" from their vocabulary and make it clear that they are advocating equality of opportunity and not special privileges for the unqualified or undeserving. They should draw the public's attention to the situations in which affirmative action has worked fairly and effectively.[13] If whites realize that the beneficiaries of affirmative action have made good use of their opportunities and have, for the most part, shown themselves to be competent, white opposition may diminish.

Still, it will be difficult for many whites to support a controversial policy that may conceivably harm them, or, at best, provides them with no obvious benefits. What, then, of a program that would achieve the goals of affirmative action while also offering expanded opportunities to some whites? Might this broaden the constituency of its supporters? (It would not actually require a large shift of white opinion in California; only 54 percent of the electorate supported the referendum doing away with "racial preferences.") Using class, as well as race, as a basis for special consideration—as is already being done to some extent—would certainly help. And putting less emphasis on standardized tests—as opposed to high school grades and evidence of sustained effort to overcome initial disadvantages—can be defended as a fairer way to determine qualifications. It would also benefit whites who have had to attend bad schools and come from impoverished environments.

We would no longer have affirmative action in any meaningful sense if race were to be disregarded as one important source of disadvantage; but other factors—which often in fact coincide with race—need to be emphasized more than they have been. "Equal opportunity" should be the basic claim of those who would seek to open the doors to all of those who have been excluded, not because of lack of ambition, natural ability, and willingness to work, but because of social circumstances that they were powerless to prevent but have been struggling to overcome.

In an increasingly diverse society, we need ethnic diversity at every social and occupational level, not just at the bottom. Otherwise we will become, even more than we are now, a society stratified by race and ethnicity, as well as by class. If that were to happen, the resulting racial tensions might make today's "crisis" between blacks and whites seem relatively minor in comparison. What kind of America will we have if, by the mid-twenty-first century, a privileged white minority or bare majority is pitted against an aggrieved black and brown majority or near majority? A carefully formulated and cogently defended policy of affirmative action, one that unifies rather than divides, is needed now to avert that catastrophe.

Notes

1. To be published in November, 1997.
2. For a strong statement of this position, see Dinesh D'Souza, *The End of Racism* (The Free Press, 1995), and my review of it in *The New York Review*, October 19, 1995.
3. Charles Murray's *Losing Ground* (Basic Books, 1984) remains the most influential work arguing in this vein.
4. Another new book, Paul M. Sniderman and Edward G. Carmines, *Reaching Beyond Race* (Harvard University Press, 1997), reveals, on the basis of carefully designed surveys of public opinion, that such respondents are "divided more or less up the middle" on the subject of affirmative action (see p. 143).
5. Norton, 1992.
6. The pessimistic liberal view that Sleeper, Stephan and Abigail Thernstrom, and

Orlando Patterson all criticize in the books under review is best represented in Andrew Hacker, *Two Nations: Blacks and White, Separate, Hostile, Unequal* (Scribners, 1992). Hacker, of course, was not necessarily wrong simply because he brought bad news; his book was a wake-up call that was badly needed to counter the complacency about race relations that had developed among whites since the 1970s. But the books under review have helped to strengthen my own conviction that progress has been made and that the struggle for black equality is not hopeless.

7. See William Julius Wilson, *When Work Disappears* (Knopf, 1996); and Martin Carnoy, *Faded Dreams* (Cambridge University Press, 1994).

8. I heard them make this argument in public lectures given at Stanford University during the past two years.

9. See the last chapter of Higham's *Send These To Me* (Johns Hopkins University Press, 1984).

10. Signet Books, 1964, p. 134.

11. Shipler notes that out-of-wedlock births among whites grew from 1.7 percent of the total in 1950 to 25.4 percent in 1994 and that the percentage of such births among blacks declined from 9.4 times the white rate in 1960 to 2.8 times in 1994 (p. 330).

12. He cites Paul M. Sniderman and Thomas Piazza, *The Scar of Race* (Harvard University Press, 1993), which makes many of the same arguments as Sniderman and Carmines, *Reaching Beyond Race,* cited earlier. My only problem with the work of Sniderman and his associates is the way they define affirmative action. The majority of whites polled by Harris in 1988, Sniderman and Piazza acknowledge, came out in favor of affirmative action when it was described as not involving "rigid quotas." Since the Bakke decision rigid quotas have been outlawed. What we have actually had in most parts of the US is an affirmative action of the kind that takes race into account but does not make it absolutely determinative. To say that affirmative action is a racial quota system is to accept the propaganda of its opponents.

13. I am tempted here to brag a little about my own institution, Stanford University, partly to counter the dated and generally distorted picture that the Thernstroms have derived from the exaggerated accounts of right-wing ideologues about the controversy over multicultural curriculum reform at Stanford almost a decade ago. In 1996 the Stanford Faculty Senate voted unanimously to continue affirmative action—a pointed response to the decision of the University of California Board of Regents to end it in state institutions. The drive to make the curriculum more multicultural has led to the development of a program on Comparative Studies in Race and Ethnicity that has brought various ethnic studies programs, including both Jewish and African-American studies, together in the same interdepartmental program, with the aim of stimulating group interactions and the search for common perspectives.

Asian Americans

The following collection of articles on Asian Americans invites us to reflect on the fact that the United States is related to Asia in ways that would seem utterly amazing to the worldview of the American founders. The expansion of the American regime across the continent, the importation of Asian workers, and the subsequent exclusion of Asians from the American polity are signs of the tarnished image and broken promise of refuge that America extended and then revoked. The Asian world is a composite of ethnicities and traditions ranging from the Indian subcontinent northeastward to China and Japan. The engagement of the United States beyond its continental limits brought American and Asian interests into a common arena now called the Pacific Rim. The most recent and perhaps most traumatic episode of this encounter was the conflict that erupted in 1941 at Pearl Harbor in Hawaii. Thus, examining the Asian relationship to America begins with the dual burdens of domestic exclusion and war.

The cultural roots and current interaction between the United States and Asia form a complex of concerns explored in this unit's articles. Understanding the cultural matrices of Asian nations and their ethnicities and languages initiates the process of learning about the Asian emigrants who for many reasons decided to leave Asia to seek a fresh beginning in the United States.

The Asian American population growth since the immigration reform of 1965, the emergence of Japan and other Asian nations as international fiscal players, and the image of Asian American intellectual and financial success have heightened interest in this ethnic group in the United States. The variety of religious traditions that Asian immigrants bring to America is another dimension of cultural and moral importance. In what respect are non-Judeo-Christian-Islamic faith traditions issues of consequence? This aftermath of conflict and resulting analysis have riveted attention on the ethnic factor.

The details of familial and cultural development within Asian American communities compose worlds of meaning that are a rich source of material from which both insights and troubling questions of personal and group identity emerge. Pivotal periods of conflict in the drama of the American experience provide an occasion for learning as much about ourselves as about one of the newest clusters of ethnicities—the Asian Americans.

One of the first large-scale interactions between the United States and Asia was with the Philippine Islands and its population. This experience of war and empire and the attendant century-long process of military and defense relationships as well as the exportation of institutions and cultural change have forged a unique international-intercultural symbiosis. The role of the ethnic Chinese diaspora and the emergence of economic strength and political change in Asia suggest the globalization of the ethnic factor. Even the name of this American ethnic population has changed, as has its relationship to the islands and its ancestry. There is new politicization of the future of both an Asian homeland and the diasporic remnant. Its aspiring leaders are fashioning a new consciousness that is meaningful for its time and is inspiring actions that will articulate a most worthy future.

Looking Ahead: Challenge Questions

The public passions generated during World War II have subsided, and anti-Japanese sentiment is no longer heard. Is this statement true or false? Why?

Under what circumstances and toward which nations could the snarls of ethnic hatred be renewed?

What impact did Asian Americans have on the presidential elections? Are attitudinal and institutional obstacles to inclusion such as contributions from people associated with foreign interests and corporations simply matters of law or are they symptoms of prejudices and fears of ethnic politics?

Has campaign finance reform become an anti-Asian crusade?

How can inclusiveness as an American value be taught? What approaches are most promising?

Misperceived Minorities

'Good' and 'bad' stereotypes saddle Hispanics and Asian Americans

Pamela Constable

Washington Post Staff Writer

Richard Lopez, 29, a fourth-generation Mexican American businessman from San Bernardino, Calif., grew up in what he called a "Brady Bunch" suburb, and learned Spanish only to communicate with his great-grandmother. He is mystified when Hispanic newcomers complain of discrimination and angry when whites assume he needed special help to move up in American society.

"Nobody ever put a roadblock in front of me. I earned my way into college, and it offended me when people asked if I was receiving affirmative action," he says in a telephone interview. "I think a lot of the whining about discrimination is blown out of proportion. The biggest thing holding a lot of Mexicans back here is their resentment against those who succeed."

Ray Chin, 46, an insurance agent in New York's Chinatown, spent his teenage years washing bathrooms and delivering groceries in the city after his parents fled Communist China in the 1950s. Today he has earned the stature that often leads Asian Americans to be called the "model minority," a phrase he views as more curse than compliment.

"Yes, we can successfully join the mainstream, but once we reach a certain level, we're stifled by that glass ceiling," Chin says amid the din of a crowded Chinese restaurant. "People think we Asians can take care of ourselves, and they don't see the need to help us. But it's not true. We are still not included in things and we have to work three times harder to get to the same level as our co-workers."

No matter how much personal success they achieve, Hispanics and Asian Americans say they must fight stereotypes that can undermine their confidence or limit their potential. Whether "negative" or "positive"—the lazy, welfare-dependent Hispanic or the shy, technically oriented Asian American— such perceptions can be equally harmful and unfair, members of both groups say.

Worse, they say, is that ethnic minorities in the United States sometimes come to accept others' stereotypes about them, even when the facts and their experiences do not support those biases. For that reason, they may remain extremely sensitive to discrimination even when they have matched or surpassed white Americans in income and education.

Such contradictions—both in the views of other Americans toward Hispanics and Asian Americans and, at times, in the views of those groups about themselves—appeared throughout a nationwide telephone poll of 1,970 people conducted by The Washington Post, the Kaiser Family Foundation and Harvard University.

Yet there is also enormous diversity of opinion and experience within these two ethnic categories, other surveys and interviews show. The perceptions of Hispanics and Asian Americans about their opportunities and obstacles vary dramatically depending on their class, community and country of origin.

"It's very misleading to talk about the views of whites versus the views of minority groups like Latinos, because you cannot assume commonalty within those groups at all," says Rodolfo de la Garza, a professor of government at the University of Texas in Austin. He says it is crucial to know what language people speak, where they were born and how long they had been in the United States to accurately assess their views.

In a recent nationwide survey of 1,600 Hispanics by the Tomas Rivera Center in Claremont, Calif., for example, 71 percent of Hispanics from Central America said they believe that U.S. society discriminates against Hispanics, but only 42 percent of Cuban Americans agreed. Just over half of Mexican American respondents, by far the largest group of Hispanics in the United States, shared that view.

Poverty rates vary widely within both the Hispanic and Asian American communities, often depending on when, and from what country, members emigrated. In Los Angeles, unemployment is only 4 percent among Korean Americans, who flocked to the United States in the 1960s, but it is 21 percent among newly arrived Cambodian refugees. In New York, 32 percent of Dominican Americans are poor, but only 11 percent of Colombian Americans are.

For Hispanics or Asian Americans who live in the cocoon of urban ethnic enclaves, it may take a foray into other regions to make them appreciate the prejudice faced by others. Juan Santiago, 30, an office manager in the Bronx, N.Y., whose parents emigrated from the Dominican Republic, says he never experienced discrimination growing up in his heavily Dominican neighborhood. Then he went out to New Mexico as a foreman on a construction job.

"All the workers were Mexican, and the white owners had no respect for them. The work was very hard, the pay was

Poll

HOW HISPANICS, ASIANS SEE THEMSELVES AND HOW OTHERS SEE THEM

Poll respondents were given a list of things some people have mentioned as reasons for the economic and social problems that some Hispanics and Asian Americans face today and were asked if each one is a major reason for those problems.

Is this a major reason for Hispanics' problems?	Hispanics who said 'yes'	Whites who said 'yes'	Blacks who said 'yes'	Asians who said 'yes'
Lack of jobs	68%	42%	74%	53%
Language difficulties	66%	56%	59%	59%
Lack of educational opportunities	51%	46%	63%	53%
Breakup of the Hispanic family	45%	28%	38%	22%
Past and present discrimination	43%	31%	58%	29%
Lack of motivation and an unwillingness to work hard	41%	25%	19%	32%

Those polled were asked the same question about Asians:

Is this a major reason for Asians' problems?	Asians who said 'yes'	Whites who said 'yes'	Blacks who said 'yes'	Hispanics who said 'yes'
Language difficulties	44%	44%	52%	37%
Lack of jobs	34%	31%	46%	43%
Past and present discrimination	20%	24%	41%	31%
Lack of educational opportunities	17%	18%	31%	31%
Breakup of the Asian family	14%	16%	27%	35%
Lack of motivation and an unwillingness to work hard	10%	22%	23%	20%

Polling data comes from a survey of 1,970 randomly selected adults interviewed in August and September, including 802 whites, 474 blacks, 352 Asian Americans and 252 Hispanics. The minority groups were oversampled to obtain large enough subsamples to analyze reliably. Margin of sampling error for the overall results is plus or minus 3 percentage points. The margins of sampling error for the four subsamples ranged from 4 percentage points for the white subsample to 7 percentage points for the Hispanic subsample. Sampling error is only one of many potential sources of error in public opinion polls.

SOURCES: Washington Post/Kaiser Family Foundation/Harvard University survey

THE WASHINGTON POST

very low, and there was no overtime," he recounts. "They tried to exploit me, too, but I knew my rights and I wouldn't let them. Until, then, I never really understood what discrimination was."

BUT LIFE INSIDE ETHNIC GHETTOS ALSO CAN CONFINE and isolate, discouraging immigrants from joining American society at large and reinforcing others' misperceptions about them. In interviews, many foreign-born Hispanics and Asian

Americans said they cling to immigrant communities, speaking to bosses and salesclerks in their native tongues and rarely meeting white Americans.

Yu Hui Chang, 35, a waitress in lower Manhattan, N.Y., says she and her husband work 12 hours a day in Chinese restaurants and rarely see their young son. Speaking through an interpreter in the cramped office of a Chinatown labor union, the Shanghai-born woman says she feels trapped in her community but is determined to succeed in her new country.

"It is very hard to be a woman in Chinatown," says Chang, who emigrated in 1982. "My life is nothing but working, working all the time. In China, I thought America was full of gold, and I still have the dream of taking that gold back home, but I can never save any."

Like Chang, the great majority of Asian Americans and Hispanics who responded to the Post/Kaiser/Harvard poll said they believe strongly in the American dream, but 46 percent of Asian Americans and 55 percent of Hispanics said they are farther from achieving it than they were a decade ago.

Both groups singled out hard work and family unity as keys to success here, and both singled out the same major obstacles: lack of good jobs, crime and violence, high taxes and the gap between their incomes and the rising cost of living. All agreed that learning English is crucial.

"You have to learn the language of the enemy to survive," says Juan Garcia, a Dominican-born man who manages a discount clothing shop in Washington Heights, a largely Hispanic section of Manhattan. "I've been here 13 years and my English is still poor, so I can't always defend myself," he adds in Spanish, describing his humiliation at being turned away from a fast-food counter when he could not explain his order.

Nonetheless, Garcia says he would not want to give up the comforts of American life. His son, 16, is studying computers and dreams of becoming a doctor. "Once you become civilized, you don't want to go back to a village with no lights or running water," he says.

Nationwide, the poll suggested that Asian Americans as a group think they have done much better economically than Hispanics think they have done. Asian Americans also have a far more optimistic view of their chances for success. Eighty-four percent of Asian Americans guessed that the average Asian American is at least as well off as the average white American, and 58 percent said they have the same or better chance of becoming wealthy.

Hispanics, on the other hand, tended to be more pessimistic and to believe others' critical views of them. In the poll, 74 percent of Hispanics said the average Hispanic is worse off than the average white, and 41 percent cited low motivation and unwillingness to work as a reason for their lack of advancement. Yet studies show that Hispanics have an unusually high level of participation in the work force.

"We are very susceptible to what others think about us, so we absorb those negative stereotypes in defiance of the facts," says Cecilia Munoz, Washington director of the National Council of La Raza, a Hispanic advocacy group. A 1994 survey by the council found that Hispanics have been most often depicted on TV and in films as "poor, of low status, lazy, deceptive, and criminals."

In the Post/Kaiser/Harvard poll, only one-quarter of white Americans cited unwillingness to work as a major obstacle for Hispanics; many more agreed with Hispanics that language problems and lack of educational opportunities are their biggest problems. In assessing the status of Asian Americans, whites cited only language difficulties as a major problem, suggesting that whites believe that Asian Americans face fewer barriers than Hispanics face.

More Hispanics say they thought they face the most discrimination as a group, but despite their relative economic success, more Asian Americans say they and their relatives and friends had experienced prejudice personally.

A majority of both groups agree that minorities should work their way up without special government help but also insist that government should protect their rights, for example by enacting tougher laws against workplace discrimination. And in interviews, many Hispanics and Asian Americans expressed deep concerns about a rising tide of anti-immigrant feeling.

Some specialists say the recent political furor over illegal immigrants has exacerbated a false impression that hordes of foreigners are arriving on U.S. shores. In the poll, the respondents guessed that 65 percent of Hispanics in the United States were born in foreign countries. According to the National Council of La Raza, only 33 percent of Hispanics were born in foreign countries.

"I see many Latinos trying to distance themselves from their roots as they react to the wave of anti-immigrant sentiment," says Harry Pachon, who directs the Tomas Rivera Center. "But I keep asking, how does an Anglo driving down the street pick out which Latino is native-born, which is a refugee, which is undocumented?"

IN OTHER WAYS, THE POLL SUGGESTED THAT MOST respondents are not especially hostile to either ethnic minority. Three-quarters said it "wouldn't make much difference" to the country if the number of Hispanics or Asian Americans were to increase significantly. Less than one-quarter said it would be a "bad thing" if either group were to grow substantially.

Yet the perception of growing xenophobia has created tensions between foreign-born and more established Hispanics and Asian Americans. Even in a community such as Jackson Heights, in Queens, N.Y., where Korean, Cuban, Vietnamese and Colombian immigrants live in tolerant proximity, second-generation residents expressed concern in interviews that illiterate or illegal newcomers are creating a negative image of all ethnic minorities.

"People have this idea that we are coming here in industrial quantities to invade America and go on welfare. The truth is that most of us were born here, we are working hard or going to school," says Mario Vargas, 22, a college student whose parents emigrated from Colombia. "But these days, the stereotypes are making it harder for the rest of us."

NEIGHBORING FAITHS

HOW WILL AMERICANS COPE WITH INCREASING RELIGIOUS DIVERSITY?

DIANA L. ECK

Diana L. Eck, Ph.D. '76, professor of comparative religion and Indian studies, chairs the Committee on the Study of Religion in the Faculty of Arts and Sciences and is also director of the Pluralism Project. The project's multimedia CD-ROM, On Common Ground: World Religions in America, *will be published in early 1997 by Columbia University Press. Eck's most recent book is* Encountering God: A Spiritual Journey from Bozeman to Banaras *(Beacon Press, 1993). This article is slightly adapted from Eck's 1996 Phi Beta Kappa Oration, delivered during Commencement week.*

I first came to Harvard as a student of the culture and religions of India. I was fascinated by India's many religious traditions—the interrelations, tensions, and movements of Hindu, Buddhist, Jain, Muslim, and Sikh traditions over many centuries in a complex culture. But never did I imagine as I began teaching here in the late 1970s that the very interests

counter in a world shaped by a new geopolitical and a new "georeligious" reality.

For me, this journey began in the academic year 1989–90. Suddenly the contextual ground under my own feet as a scholar and teacher began to shift. In the past, I had always had several students from India in my classes on India, but in that year, their numbers increased. Only now, they were not from India, but were Indian Americans, born and raised in San Antonio, Baltimore, or Cleveland. They were, as I discovered, the children of the first generation of immigrants who had settled in America after the passage of the 1965 immigration act. That historic event finally removed the legal legacy of racism that had been built into immigration legislation from the first Chinese exclusion act in 1882 to the Johnson Reed Act in 1924, which effectively barred Asian immigrants for four decades. The 1965 policy opened the door again for immigration from Asia and from other parts of the world.

There were Muslims from Providence, Hindus from Baltimore, Sikhs from Chicago, Jains from New Jersey. They represented the emergence in America of a new cultural and religious reality.

that drew me to India would lead me in the 1990s to the study of the United States. So how is it that a scholar of comparative religion and Indian studies has spent the past five years studying America—furtively at first, fearful to be treading on the territory of some of Harvard's most distinguished scholars, then unapologetically, flagrantly, even zealously?

That intellectual passage from India to America began here at Harvard. The circumstances that drove me to study America raise important issues—for Harvard, for the United States, and perhaps for the world. They are issues all of us will en-

As a scholar of India, I had taken note of the effects of the new immigration on that country, the so-called "brain drain," as thousands of Indian professionals, doctors, and scientists left India for the United States. I have to admit, however, that I had never stopped to think what this would mean for the United States until the children of this first generation of Indian immigrants reached college age and enrolled in my classes at Harvard that year. There were Muslims from Providence, Hindus from Baltimore, Sikhs from Chicago, Jains from New Jersey. They represented the emergence in America of a new cultural and religious reality.

Some came from very secular families and knew little of their Indian heritage. Others had grown up in the new Hindu or Muslim culture of temples and Islamic centers their parents had begun to establish here in the United States. Some had been to Muslim youth leadership camps, organized by the Islamic Society of North America. Some had been to a Hindu summer camp at Rajarajeswari Pitha in the Poconos, or to a family Vedanta camp at Arsha Vidya Gurukulam in Saylorsburg, Pennsylvania. Some were involved as founding members of the Jain Youth of North America. Straddling two worlds, critically appropriating two cultures, they lived in perpetual inner dialogue between the distinctive cultures of their parents and grandparents and the forceful, multiple currents of American culture. In their own struggles with identity lay the very issues that were beginning to torment the soul of the United States.

The new questions that arose were not only those that underlay the foreign cultures requirement of the Core Curriculum—how we might understand some "other" civilization so different from our own. Other questions pushed themselves to the fore: What does it mean to speak of "our own" culture? Who do "we" mean when we say "we?" How are "difference" and "otherness" defined, and by whom? The word "multicultural" signaled the fact that every dimension of American culture had become more complex. Racial issues became multisided, with Hispanic and Latino, Korean and Filipino, Chinese and Indian perspectives. Religious diversity shattered the paradigm of an America the sociologist Will Herberg had confidently described as a "three religion country"—Protestant, Catholic, and Jewish. By the 1990s, there were Hindus and Sikhs, Buddhists and Jains. There were more Muslims than Episcopalians, more Muslims than Presbyterians, perhaps soon more Muslims than Jews.

The sons and daughters of the first generation from South Asia rose at Harvard to become some 5 percent of the Harvard undergraduate population. In the spring of 1993, when that first class graduated, I slipped into the balcony at Memorial Church for the Baccalaureate service and sat with the families of Mukesh Prasad and Maitri Chowdhury, the first marshals of the Harvard and Radcliffe graduating classes that year—both Hindus. Maitri recited a hymn from the Rig-Veda in ancient Sanskrit. It was a new Harvard. It had happened in four years.

The Puritans founded Harvard College to provide an educated Christian ministry for the churches. Before Judah Monis, a Sephardic Jew, was hired to teach Hebrew in 1722, he publically converted to Christianity. But both Judah Monis and Cotton Mather would be astounded at Harvard in the 1990s—its Chinese and Korean Christian fellowships, its diverse and vibrant Jewish community, its rapidly growing Islamic Society. In December 1994, the newly founded Harvard Buddhist Community observed the Buddha's Enlightenment Day for the first time ever at Harvard. There in the Divinity School's Braun Room, beneath the august portraits of a long lineage of divinity deans, some 50 Harvard students from a dozen Buddhist lineages sat on rows of square zabutons, listening to Pali, Tibetan, and Vietnamese chanting and rising, one by one, to make offerings of incense.

What has happened at Harvard has happened at major universities throughout the country. In the 1990s, universities have become the microcosms and laboratories of a new multicultural and multireligious America. It is not uncommon to have Hindu and Jew, Muslim and Christian in a single rooming group. These changes in university demographics have come not from abroad, but from the rapidly changing cultural and religious landscape of the United States. Harvard's issues, America's issues, have become, increasingly, a fresh recasting of many of India's issues, the world's issues: race, culture, religion, difference, diversity, and whether it is possible to move from diversity to pluralism.

I knew in 1990 that my own teaching context had radically changed and the scope of my academic work would have to change, too. Increasingly, it became clear to me that the very shape of traditional fields of study was inadequate to this new world. In my field, those of us who study Buddhism, Islam, or Hinduism all earn our academic stripes, so to speak, by intensive study in Japan, Egypt, or India, doing language studies, textual editions and translations, fieldwork. And those who study religion in America focus largely on the Protestant mainstream, or perhaps on Catholics, or American Judaism—but not on American Buddhism, not on the Muslims of America, not on the Sikhs of America. And those historians who focus their work on what has become known as ethnic studies are curiously silent about the religious traditions of America's ethnic minorities—the old Islamic traditions of the African slaves, the old Chinese temples in Montana and Idaho, or the early Sikh communities in California's Imperial Valley.

The Muslim Community Center on New Hampshire Avenue in Silver Spring, Maryland.

IN 1991, THE PLURALISM PROJECT AT HARVARD SET OUT TO STUDY multireligious America, beginning right here in Boston. Our research seminar visited the mosque in Quincy built in the shadow of the great cranes of the shipyards by Lebanese immigrants who came early in the century, and we found that there were some 20 other mosques and Islamic centers that are part of the Islamic Council of New England—in Dorchester, Wayland, Cambridge. We went to the spectacular new Sri Lakshmi temple in Ashland, a temple designed by Hindu ritual architects with tall towers decorated with the images of the gods and consecrated with the waters of the Ganges mingled with the waters of the Mississippi, the Colorado, and the Merrimack rivers. We visited half a dozen other Hindu communities in Boston, and two Sikh gurdwaras in Millis and Milford, and a Jain temple in Norwood, housed in a former Swedish Lutheran church. We found a dozen Buddhist meditation centers, with their respective Tibetan, Burmese, Korean, and Japanese lineages of instruction. And we visited the temples of the Cambodian Buddhists in Lowell and Lynn, the Vietnamese in Roslindale and Revere, the Chinese in Quincy and Lexington. Eventually, we published *World Religions in Boston*, a documentary guide to a city whose Asian population had doubled in 10 years, now a multireligious city.

It was clear that what was true of Boston might well be true of many other American cities. So the Pluralism Project sent a research team of students, multiethnic and multire-

Stupa containing relics of the Buddha, presented as a gift from Thailand to the Jodo Shinshu Buddhist Mission of North America in 1935. The stupa is built on the roof of the Buddhist Church of San Francisco on Pine Street.

ligious, to study "hometown" America, fanning out across the United States every summer for three years. We were guided by three kinds of questions. First, who is here now in the 1990s? How many Hindu temples are there in Chicago? How many mosques in Oklahoma City? How many Buddhist temples in Houston? Second, how are these traditions changing as they take root in American soil? And third, how is America changing as Americans of many religions begin to appropriate this new multireligious reality and come to terms once again with our foundational commitment to religious freedom and, consequently, religious pluralism?

We found many remarkable developments. For example, Buddhist communities widely separated in Asia are now neighbors in Los Angeles, Seattle, and Chicago—Vietnamese, Cambodian, Thai, Chinese, Japanese, Korean, and Tibetan Buddhists. Here in America, these Buddhist communities are just beginning to know one another and to meet the distinctive communities of "new Buddhists"—Americans of all races who have come to Buddhism through its meditation practices and its ethics. The Buddhist Sangha Council of Southern California, the Buddhist Council of the Midwest, the Texas Buddhist Association are evidence of the beginning of a new "ecumenical" Buddhism. There are American Buddhist newspapers and magazines, feminist Zen sitting groups, exemplary Buddhist AIDS hospice projects. Today Buddhism is an American religion.

We visited communities that represent the entire spectrum of Islam in America: African American communities, Muslim immigrants from Syria and Lebanon whose forebears came in the early 1900s, and new immigrant Muslims from Africa and South Asia. All of them are in the process of working out what it is to be both Muslim and American. They gather in huge annual conventions in Dayton or in Kansas City to discuss the Muslim family in America or the American public schools. The Islamic Medical Association tackles ethical issues in medical practice, while the Washington-based American Muslim Council facilitates Islamic participation in the American political process.

We found that most of the new religious institutions are invisible. The first generation of American mosques could be found in places like a former watch factory in Queens, a U-Haul dealership in Pawtucket, Rhode Island, a gymnasium in Oklahoma City, and a former mattress showroom in Northridge, California. There were Hindu temples in a huge warehouse in Queens, a former YMCA in New Jersey, or a former Methodist church in Minneapolis. Most of the Vietnamese Buddhist temples of Denver, Houston, and Orange County were in ranch-style homes. Because of the invisibility of these first-generation religious institutions, many Americans, understandably, have remained quite unaware of these new communities.

The past decades, however, have also seen the beginnings of a striking new visible landscape. There are new mosques and Islamic centers in Manhattan and Phoenix, rising from the cornfields outside Toledo and from the suburbs of Chicago and Houston. There are multimillion-dollar Hindu temples, like the Sri Venkateswara temple in Pittsburgh, the Bharatiya Temple in the northern suburbs of Detroit, the spectacular Sri Meenakshi Temple south of Houston, the Ganesha temple in Nashville, and dozens of others. The Buddhists have made a striking architectural imprint, with, for example, the huge Hsi Lai temple in Hacienda Heights, California, and the Jade Temple in Houston. In the western Chicago suburb of Bartlett, the Jains have built a large new temple. To the north in Palatine is a striking new hexagonal gurdwara of the Sikhs.

There are some neighborhoods where all this is visible in short compass. For example, driving out New Hampshire Avenue, one of the great spokes of Washington, D.C., into Silver Spring, Maryland, just beyond the Beltway there is a stretch of road a few miles long where one passes the new Cambodian Buddhist temple with its graceful, sloping tiled roof, the Ukrainian Orthodox Church, the Muslim Community Center with its new copper-domed mosque. Farther along is the new Gujarati Hindu temple called Mangal Mandir. The many churches along the way also reveal the new dimensions of America's Christian landscape: Hispanic Pentecostal, Vietnamese Catholic, and Korean evangelical congregations sharing facilities with more traditional English-speaking "mainline" churches.

THE DIVERSITY OF NEW HAMPSHIRE AVENUE, HOWEVER, IS NOT simply a curiosity for a Sunday drive. What it represents has profound implications for *every* aspect of American public life. What is happening to America as all of us begin to renegotiate the "we" of "We, the people"? That "we" in the United States is increasingly complex, not only culturally and racially, but also religiously What will this religious diversity mean for American electoral politics, for the continuing interpretation of "church-state" issues by the Supreme Court, for American public education and the controversies of school boards, for hospitals and health-care programs with an increasingly diverse patient population, and for colleges and universities with an increasingly multireligious student body? While many Americans are only dimly aware of the changing religious landscape, the issues this new diversity has raised are already on the agenda of virtually every public institution, including Harvard.

New Hampshire Avenue dramatizes the new diversity, but building a pluralist society from that diversity is no easy matter in a world in which the "politics of identity" is busy minting our identities in smaller and smaller coins, and in a world in which religious markers of identity are often presumed to be the most divisive of all differences. American public debate is charged with the power of these issues. Some say such a multicultural and multireligious society is impossible. Their voices have been raised at each and every stage of American immigration—too many Catholics, too many Jews, too many Chinese and Japanese. Those voices are present today, and some of the most extreme have called for the repeal of the 1965 immigration act. Others have insisted there is simply too much *pluribus* and not enough *unum*. And still others would insist that this is a secular society, so why make a point of looking at religious differences at all?

But to ascertain how we—all of us—are doing in this new struggle for America's soul, we have to look not only at race, not only at ethnicity, but at religion. The history of prejudice and stereotype demonstrates that religious insignia and institutions often become key markers of "difference." The persistent attacks on synagogues and Jewish graveyards provide ample testimony to the tactics of hatred. So does the long and continuing history of racist attacks on black churches. Religious insignia, religious markers of identity, and religious institutions come to stand in a public way for the very heart of the community and often become the most visible targets for bigotry and violence.

And so it is as America's new immigrants become increasingly visible as religious minorities. In New Jersey, the dot or *bindi* on the forehead, worn by many Hindu women, stood for the strangeness of the whole Indian immigrant community in the eyes of a racist group calling themselves the "Dotbus-

Above: The Hindu Sri Lakshmi temple in Ashland, Massachusetts. Above left: Priests circle the temple with water to be used in the consecration ceremony, the "mahakumbhabhishekam," in May 1990.

ters." Those who beat Navroze Mody to death in 1987, shouting "Hindu, Hindu, Hindu," did not know or care whether he was a Hindu, but conflated race, religion, and culture in one cry of hatred.

The Pluralism Project has documented the ways in which today's minority religious communities have experienced the violence of attacks on their visible religious institutions. In February 1983, for example, vandals broke into the newly constructed Hindu-Jain Temple in Pittsburgh and smashed all the white marble images of the Hindu deities. The sacred scripture of the Sikhs, housed on a side altar, was torn to pieces. "Leave!" was written across the main altar. In 1993, the temple of a tiny Cambodian Buddhist community in Portland, Maine, was vandalized with an axe, its doorjambs hacked, its doors broken, the contents of the Buddha hall strewn in the front yard, and the words "Dirty Asian Chink, Go Home!" written

while serving as policemen. The Interfaith Conference of Metropolitan Washington, D.C., brought people of all religious communities together in March 1994 in the wake of the Hebron massacre. Because of new relationships of trust, the head of the Washington board of rabbis offered prayers right there on New Hampshire Avenue at the Muslim Community Center.

The public symbolic acknowledgment of America's diversity is also becoming more visible. In April 1990, for example, the city council of Savannah, Georgia, issued a proclamation in which Islam was recognized as having been "a vital part of the development of the United States of America and the city of Savannah." On June 25, 1991, for the first time in history, a Muslim imam, Siraj Wahaj of Brooklyn, opened a session of the U.S. House of Representatives with prayer. On February 20, 1996, at the end of the month of Ramadan, Hillary Clinton welcomed Muslims to the White House for the

There on a hillside overlooking farm fields, rabbis and priests, imams and Muslim leaders each turned a shovel of earth for the new Islamic Center of New England.

on the walls. In September 1994, a nearly completed mosque in Yuba City, California, was burned to the ground, leaving its dome and minaret in the ashes of a fire that the sheriff deemed to be arson. There are dozens of these incidents every year, some of them now documented by such groups as the Council on American-Islamic Relations, but most of them noted only in the pages of local newspapers.

The documentary register of acts of violence is easier to assemble than the register of new initiatives of cooperation and understanding, for violence is still deemed more "newsworthy" than cooperation. Yet assembling the evidence of new patterns of interreligious encounter, cooperation, and relationship is also important in discerning how the "we" is being reconfigured in multireligious America. For example, on April 2, 1993, a groundbreaking in Sharon, Massachusetts, brought Jews, Christians, and Muslims together from the Greater Boston area. There on a hillside overlooking the fields of a former horse farm, rabbis and priests, imams and Muslim leaders each turned a shovel of earth for the new Islamic Center of New England. Two weeks later, across the country in Fremont, California, Saint Paul's United Methodist Church and the Islamic Society of the East Bay broke ground together for a new church and a new mosque, to be built side by side on the same property. They named their common access road "Peace Terrace," and they are now next-door neighbors. "We want to set an example for the world," said one of the Muslim leaders.

All across America, there are new interreligious councils—in cities like Tulsa, Oklahoma, and Lincoln, Nebraska. The Interreligious Council of Southern California supported the appointment of a Buddhist chaplain in the California State Senate and backed the Sikhs in their petition to the Los Angeles Police Department to be allowed to wear the turban

first Eid celebration ever to take place there. She said, "This celebration is an American event. We are a nation of immigrants who have long drawn on our diverse religious traditions and faiths for the strength and courage that make America great."

The sacred Hindu thread ceremony, the "upanayana," at Sri Venkateswara Temple, Bridgewater, New Jersey.

A FEW YEARS AGO, MY HARVARD COLLEAGUE SAMUEL HUNTINGTON, a distinguished political scientist, wrote of the deep religious currents that so profoundly shape the great civilizations of the world.* In the new post-Cold War era, he predicted that "civilizational identity" will have a major role in the coming political realignment. He contended that the Confucian, Islamic, and Hindu worlds will be forces to reckon with in the geopolitical arena and he foresees a "clash of civilizations." But where exactly are these worlds and civilizations, we might ask, with Hindus in Leicester, Durban, Toronto, and Houston? With huge mosques in Paris, London, Chicago, and Toledo? One of the decisive facts of the 1980s and 1990s has been the tremendous migration of peoples from one nation to another, both as immigrants and as refugees. Every part of the globe is experiencing the demographic changes of these migrations. Today, the Islamic world is no longer somewhere

---

*Samuel P. Huntington, "The Clash of Civilizations?" *Foreign Affairs*, volume 72, number 3 (summer, 1993).

Today, the Islamic world is no longer somewhere else, in some other part of the world; instead Chicago, with its 50 mosques and nearly half a million Muslims, is part of the Islamic world.

else, in some other part of the world; instead Chicago, with its 50 mosques and nearly half a million Muslims, is part of the Islamic world. America today is part of the Islamic, the Hindu, the Confucian world. It is precisely the interpenetration of ancient civilizations and cultures that is the hallmark of the late twentieth century. *This* is our new georeligious reality. The map of the world in which we now live cannot be color-coded as to its Christian, Muslim, or Hindu identity, but each part of the world is marbled with the colors and textures of the whole.

The plurality of religious traditions and cultures challenges people in every part of the world today, including the United States, which is now the most religiously diverse country on earth. Diversity we have—here in America and here at Harvard. It is not an ideology invented by the multicultural enthusiasts of the left. It is the new reality of our society. Diversity we have. But what is pluralism? First, pluralism is not diversity alone, but the energetic engagement with that diversity. Diversity can and has meant the creation of religious ghettoes with little traffic between or among them. In this new world of religious diversity, pluralism is not a given, but an achievement. In the world into which we now move, diversity without engagement, without a fabric of relationship, will be increasingly difficult and increasingly dangerous.

Second, pluralism will require not just tolerance, but the active seeking of understanding. Tolerance is a necessary public virtue, but it does not require Christians and Muslims, Hindus, Jews, and ardent secularists to know anything about one another. Tolerance is simply too thin a foundation for a world of religious differences. It does nothing to remove our ignorance of one another, and leaves in place the stereotype, the half-truth, the fear that underlie old patterns of division and violence. In the world into which we now move, our ignorance of one another will be increasingly costly.

And finally, pluralism is not simply relativism. The new paradigm of pluralism does not require us to leave our identities and our commitments behind, for pluralism is the encounter of commitments. It means holding our deepest differences, even our religious differences, not in isolation, but in relationship to one another. The language of pluralism is that of dialogue and encounter, give and take, criticism and self-criticism. In the world into which we now move, it is a language we will have to learn.

Whether in India or America, whether on New Hampshire Avenue or at Harvard University, the challenge for all of us today is how to shape societies, nations, neighborhoods, and universities that now replicate and potentially may reconfigure the differences that have long divided humankind.

Above: Masjid Al-Khair in Youngstown, Ohio. Above left: New construction supervised by Phramaha Prasert Kavissaro, abbot at Wat Buddhanusorn, a Thai Buddhist temple in Fremont, California.

THE
CHINESE
DIASPORA

PETER KWONG

Hundreds of years before there was any talk of an "Asian miracle," vast numbers of Chinese left their homeland in search of fortune abroad. Most, from southern China, traveled first to the area that is now Laos, Myanmar, and Vietnam, then farther afield, into what is now Thailand, Indonesia, and Malaysia. The California gold rush lured some, while economic growth in Latin America beckoned others. Often they left China out of desperation—because of land shortages, wars, famines, or intrusive governments. Many left home with little except their dreams of returning as wealthy men.

Now the wealth created by the ethnic Chinese consists of a great deal more than the Chinatowns of major cities. The Chinese businessmen who live across Southeast Asia have been the driving force behind the region's economic explosion. In Thailand ethnic Chinese make up 10 percent of the population but control 81 percent of the market value of listed companies. In Indonesia they compose 3.5 percent of the population but control 73 percent of such capital. Most of Asia's estimated one hundred billionaires are ethnic Chinese.

Some of these tycoons have also transformed parts of North America. For example, the moneyed elite from Hong Kong own sizable portions of San Francisco's downtown area and reside in large Mediterranean-style mansions in the hills surrounding the city. In the mid-1980s, they began investing in Canada, where the government has promised permanent residence to people who have a net worth of at least a half-million Canadian dollars and who are willing to invest significant sums in the Canadian economy. From 1985 to 1994, a little over 9.7 percent of all immigrants to Canada were businesspeople, and by 1994 more than half of those usually affluent immigrants came from either Taiwan or Hong Kong. By the end of 1994, according to one estimate, ethnic Chinese had added a net worth of $15 billion to Canada's economy. Toronto and Montreal both benefited from this movement of overseas Chinese capital, and Vancouver, partly because of its location and climate, has been particularly blessed by some of East Asia's wealthiest investors, who now control 25 percent of its most expensive and prestigious neighborhood, the West End.

When the totals are added up, overseas Chinese are said to control more than $2.5 trillion of wealth. For perspective, compare that with the 1995 gross domestic product in Japan of $5.1 trillion, or the figure for the United States of $7.2 trillion.

In a sense, many of these Chinese have fulfilled their ancestors' dreams of coming home rich. The entrepreneurs who fared so well in Asia and North America have been fueling mainland China's double-digit growth since free-market reforms opened its economy in 1979. By 1993, 69 percent of direct foreign investment in China, totaling $47.5 billion, came from ethnic Chinese in Hong Kong. Taiwan, according to China, had by 1993 put up $6.4 billion, or 9.3 percent of total foreign investment in the mainland economy. (The true figure is likely to be much higher.)

The recent success of Chinese expatriates has been so stunning that businesspeople everywhere are searching for explanations, much like when pundits speculated on the successes of Japan in the 1970s and 1980s. Was the secret ingredient teamwork? Company loyalty? A stronger work ethic? Now economic theorists are studying Chinese culture and history, and Confucius has become the patron saint of entrepreneurs and developing economies worldwide. The overseas Chinese,

Powerful overseas Chinese are investing in China, to be sure. But it's not just out of love of ancient homeland. It's business.

Reprinted with permission from *Worldbusiness*, May/June 1996, pp. 26-31. © 1996 by KPMG Peat Marwick LLP, 767 Fifth Avenue, New York, NY 10153 long the outcasts of Asia, are now the international business community's model citizens.

———————

Ask Casey K. C. Foung why the majority of investors who fueled and have capitalized on the Asian boom are of Chinese descent, and he has a simple answer. "When Asian countries sought foreign investment to develop, Western capital was not there," says Foung, a New York resident who is the founder of Arch Associates, a medium-size quilt-making firm with extensive operations in China. "When China decided to open, the only capital came from the overseas Chinese. China would have preferred infusion from high-tech American and European corporations, but the West was reluctant to venture in without legal guarantees: property rights, tax laws, price deregulation, international arbitration. Overseas Chinese capital took the risk."

Members of the Chinese "diaspora" come from a 600-year tradition of enterprising fortune seekers who escaped China's strict government controls in order to ply their trades. Most of them came from two southeastern provinces, Guangdong and Fujian, on the cultural periphery of the Chinese empire. Operating in their new homelands without the protection of China's government, they readily adapted to different trading systems and governing styles and established import-export businesses through commercial networks, often made up of Chinese who spoke the same dialect.

For more than 300 years, ethnic Chinese around Asia controlled rice mills, light manufacturing, and money lending. They owned plantations, oil mills, timber industries, manufacturing concerns, and the bulk of small retail shops selling staples. They thereby made themselves indispensable to the various indigenous populations and later to the imperialists who ruled them. "The Chinese," wrote T. M. Ward, a British physician stationed in Malacca in 1827, "are the most enterprising, the most opulent, the most industrious and the most determined in pursuit of wealth."

British, Dutch, and French colonial rulers recognized this indispensability and capitalized on it, giving the ethnic Chinese throughout Asia special status as go-betweens, especially during the nineteenth century, colonialism's peak. Their businesses also provided the most reliable and readily available tax revenue for colonial governments, and because of that these governments barred the Chinese from all but their traditional trading occupations.

Understandably, the non-Chinese who lagged behind economically were often resentful, accusing their Chinese residents of dominating their economies by dubious means and unfair practices. After World War II, postcolonial nationalist governments in the region generally became hostile to Chinese residents, and after the fall of the nationalists in 1949, suspected them of having ties to the communists. Almost without exception, the ethnic Chinese experienced severe persecution and restrictions. In Thailand and Indonesia, they were forced to assimilate by adopting local names. In Malaysia, the government set up impediments through occupational, educational, and other quotas favoring ethnic *bumiputras*, or "sons of the soil." There have been periods of intense racial violence, such as in Malaysia in the 1960s and 1970s, and in Indonesia in 1965.

Because of the centuries of persecution, overseas Chinese have developed a deep-

---

FOLLOW THE MONEY

Foreign direct investment in China, 1979–1994, in billions of dollars

Hong Kong	**$67.3**
Taiwan*	9.8
United States	6.1
Japan	5.3
Singapore	2.7

*Analysts estimate that the Chinese government may underreport Taiwanese investment in China by as much as 50 percent because a large percentage of Taiwanese money is invested in China via Hong Kong companies.

Source: *Statistical Yearbook of China 1995* and *Overseas Chinese Business Networks in Asia*

---

rooted sense of insecurity and impermanence. "We'll be here as long as there's money to be made," is a frequent refrain of theirs throughout Asia. This outlook, not unlike that of an illegal street vendor ready to roll up his merchandise and disappear before the police arrive, is reflected in the way in which many smaller overseas Chinese businesses operate. They favor gutsy investments in industries such as garment manufacturing, shoes, toys, textiles, plastics, and electronics, while spreading their investments around the world in order to minimize risks from political or economic collapse in their own fields. Deals are often marked by access to reliable, timely information and quick action, both of which are made possible by far-flung business networks forged along the lines of kinship and common dialects—as well as by the family structure of the businesses themselves.

"When it's all in the family, things are more flexible; there is more trust," says the director of a publicly traded real estate company in Hong Kong. (Like many overseas Chinese business executives, the executive shuns publicity, asking to remain anonymous.) "There isn't so much of a corporate hierarchy. People genuinely work for the family's interests, not to prove themselves and climb the corporate ladder. Traditionally, decisions are made more quickly. There's no need to jump through the hoops of board meetings and shareholders' meetings."

Of course, there is nothing peculiarly *Chinese* about these networks or patriarchal family businesses. "Just look at the Rockefeller family," says a Chinese American with a master's degree in business from Columbia University who once worked for a major United States corporation. He is now helping to restructure his family's manufacturing business, which has operations in Asia, North America, and Latin America. "There is nothing ethnic about it. American businesses start out small, too, and they have the same family-oriented structure. But as the business grows, accountability and reporting become more and more important. Westerners don't know much about the Chinese, so they like to romanticize them. And they are wrong!"

Says Peter Li, a Hong Kong–born sociology professor at the University of Saskatchewan: "The West has not been paying attention [to ethnic Chinese business development], and when it finally did, it was surprised and felt locked out. When you don't know what's going on, you look for all sorts of cultural explanations. This happened to the Jews as well."

The crudest, most commonly expressed cultural explanation is that Chinese people succeed because of their work ethic: Chinese entrepreneurs are the very embodiment of diligence and thrift. Herman Kahn, the founder of a United States think tank, the Hudson Institute, observed as early as 1979 that so-called neo-Confucian societies create dedicated, motivated, responsible, and educated individuals with an enhanced sense of commitment, organizational identity, and loyalty to various institutions. These societies, Kahn argued, are superior to those of the West in the pursuit of industrialization, affluence, and modernization.

There are overseas Chinese who promote this characterization as well. Wang Gungwu, a prominent Indonesian-born historian and a retired vice chancellor of the University of Hong Kong, has observed many ethnic Chinese striving to embrace their historic culture. For example, dozens of conferences on the overseas Chinese have been held in Hong Kong, Taiwan, Singapore, the United States, France, and the Netherlands, with numerous panels discussing such matters as the role of Chinese culture in business.

Mainland China too invites overseas experts to seminars and conferences, on such topics as "Socialism with Chinese Characteristics," or on the capitalist reforms instituted by Deng Xiaoping. Overseas Chinese parents previously uninterested in Chinese

AT HOME ABROAD

Population and percentage of ethnic Chinese in selected countries

Country	Chinese population	% of total population
Taiwan	20,370,000	97.0%
Myanmar	7,805,000	17.5
Indonesia	6,552,000	3.5
Hong Kong	6,174,000	98.0
Thailand	5,800,000	10.0
Malaysia	5,510,000	29.0
Singapore	2,079,000	77.0
United States	1,645,500	0.7
Philippines	1,200,000	2.0
Vietnam	1,000,000	1.4
Canada	587,000	2.2
Macao	446,200	97.0
Cambodia	250,000	2.5
Japan	110,000	0.9
Laos	50,000	1.3

Sources: *Overseas Chinese Business Networks in Asia*, by the East Asia Analytical Unit of the Australian Department of Foreign Affairs and Trade; 1990 United States Census; 1991 Canadian Census; United States State Department; World Bank

culture are now pushing their children to learn the Chinese language and study their heritage in order to be in a better position to exploit the new opportunities proliferating through ethnic ties. For example, during a 1989 conference on Confucianism held in China, China's president, Jiang Zemin, appealed to overseas Chinese to show support for China's precious cultural heritage. The overseas Chinese have, at times, answered such calls, such as when they donated $700,000 for the reconstruction of a shrine to the Yellow Emperor (the mythical ancestor of all Chinese people) in central China.

One of neo-Confucianism's top promoters is Singapore's senior minister, Lee Kuan Yew. Lee is a former Anglophile, who is proud of his Cambridge University education. His is a well-ordered society, buttressed by Lee's interpretation of neo-Confucianism. He has been outspoken among those attributing Asian successes to "Asian values," often a euphemism for strong rulers, obedient citizens, and hard work. Lee argues that democracy as understood and practiced in the West, is not conducive to rapid economic growth and that Asians strongly desire that kind of growth.

This new love of Confucianism—by people in business, no less—is strange. In the Confucian world, merchants were always frowned upon because their main motivation was profit instead of learning. And although China's ruling bureaucracies historically colluded with merchants to control the peasant population, and merchants were sometimes allowed to elevate their status by paying off officials, merchants were generally kept at the very bottom of the Confucian social ladder.

Starting in the late nineteenth century, every Chinese leader who attempted to pull China out of the backwardness and misery of the feudal age saw Confucianism as a curse. Getting rid of its pervasive, stultifying influence was critical, they thought, if China was to emerge as a modern nation in the twentieth century.

Coastal traders from southern China in the 1700s and 1800s sailed across the South China Sea to escape the restrictions placed on them by the Confucian state. They went as far as they could from the seat of Confucian authority—Beijing—in pursuit of the freedom to trade and make a profit. All the Asian economic miracles have so far occurred on the periphery of China's Confucian civilization: Japan, South Korea, Taiwan, Hong Kong, Singapore, and now the special economic zones in coastal China. These booming areas are very much heirs to the old colonial treaty ports, areas that were the most exposed to the influences of Western civilization in the nineteenth and twentieth centuries.

I'm successful not because I'm Chinese," says Casey Foung, the New York–based executive. "I'm not Chinese. I grew up an American in the United States, and had to learn Chinese late in life. I am successful precisely because I am American, bringing American know-how to the Chinese. Americans can be helpful in Chinese economic development, and they can take advantage of their knowledge of marketing, advertising, international finance. The Chinese are so new to this that they can use any help they can get. That's precisely what I did."

Foung's vision contrasts dramatically with other theories about why members of the Chinese diaspora have been so successful and in turn what it takes to be successful in China and the rest of Asia. If success is implicitly attributed to membership in an exclusive group, doesn't that mean that competition is unfairly stacked against people who aren't of that group? Overseas Chinese businesses *do* help one another, pool their resources, and feed one another information within their business networks. But too frequently, all that is distilled into a simple cultural explanation: To do business with the Chinese, you have to be Chinese. At the very least, Westerners feel they need *guanxi*, connections to break into the networks of this alien culture, or a Chinese mediator who can provide such connections.

"Old-boy" networks based on college affiliation, club memberships, or ethnicity are common in the United States and elsewhere, but knowing the right people can be even more important in an environment where the legal system is weak, as in China. In this sense, men such as Singapore's Lee cannot claim to share in China's socialist values, so Confucian culture becomes a form of *guanxi*. For example, at the Second World Chinese Entrepreneurs Convention in Hong Kong in 1993, Lee enthusiastically hobnobbed with some of the top overseas Chinese businesspeople, such as Hong Kong's Li Ka-shing, the head of Hutchison Whampoa, and Malaysia's Robert Kuok, who controls Shangri-La Hotels and Resorts, stressing that *guanxi* is an important advantage of the overseas Chinese that they should put to use as they compete against Western rivals for business opportunities in China. *Guanxi*, Lee said, will be useful for about twenty years, until China develops a legal system that will assuage foreign investors.

One businessman, who as a college student in the United States in the 1960s was a Maoist but is now an investor in chemical factories in China, doesn't underestimate the importance of having an understanding of language and culture that overseas Chinese might bring to the negotiating table. But their expertise often boils down to something far more vulgar than a deep knowledge of China's history, language, or literature. "When you operate in Asia, you are talking about doing business in areas where there are no written laws," he says. "Doing business means dealing with officials and bureaucrats at all levels and bribing them to leave you alone. The real advantage for Chinese expatriates is that the officials expect you to understand that. They find it easier to open their mouth to ask for bribes openly."

The overheated economy of the mainland is still hobbled by a myriad of bureaucratic restraints. All new ventures there require commercial permits; licenses to buy, own, sell, or lease property; land-use permits; construction permits; licenses to import raw materials; permission to exchange currency—the list goes on and on. "Doing business in China is a constant problem," says a manufacturer from Taiwan who recently set up a factory in the city of Changchun, in the northern province of Jilin. "First you spend a lot of money to obtain licenses. Then you entertain local officials. You pay high rents, you bribe [your way] around housing regulations—it cost us a mint just to wine and dine the officials in charge. It took six months to get the operating license, then another three months to get the land permit to build the factory. Doing business in China is not just about the business operation: You are really dealing with people. Without a legal system, you have to satisfy all the people in charge. And although they won't let you do business unless their palms are greased, the officials in charge find it difficult to tell you exactly what they want with people they don't know."

Overseas Chinese entrepreneurs in Asia are accustomed to this kind of bribery, which is prevalent throughout the region. Executives from United States companies, on the other hand, are not. In fact, the Foreign Corrupt Practices Act makes bribery illegal. One Chinese American consultant was hired by a major United States telecommunications company to make a bid for a cable television channel license in China's Sichuan province. Unable to offer any sweet deals, he didn't get the contract. Most of the mainland contracts go to overseas Chinese companies from Hong Kong and Taiwan, although the Japanese and the Germans have been quick to catch on to the realities of doing business in China. The only reason the Japanese don't get more business deals in China is that many Chinese still hate them on account of the Japanese occupation of China more than fifty years ago.

There may be advantages for ethnic Chinese, but businesspeople don't *have* to be Chinese to be successful in China. Westerners can succeed if they understand the bribery system there and are willing to cultivate personal trust with officials. "It's really no big deal for most businesses," the ex-Maoist chemical executive says. "You are only asked to do double accounting. If the cost of a product is $1,000, your invoice should say $1,100. Once the bill is paid, you and the official split the $100. It's no skin off your back. The poor Chinese people are paying for it anyway." After a pause, he adds, "I wish that capitalism would eliminate this corrupt feudal Chinese system—though I feel funny saying this."

Western observers have noted, with a dose of derision, Hong Kong's obsession with the cellular telephone. But the standard phone greeting in Hong Kong these days shows that there is more going on than just idle chatter. Instead of the traditional Chinese "Have you eaten?" comes the rather more modern "What's your game these days?" That constant, obsessive search for the latest business opportunity fits perfectly with the ever-shifting nature of global business. Globalization has meant that, more often than not, goods are not produced in single factories but in several places around the world. For example, a computer's parts may be constructed in various cities around Asia, assembled in Shenzhen, tested and packaged near Boston, and sold in Paris.

The traditional, family-based system is remarkably well suited for fast movement within these subcontracting setups, constantly taking advantage of shifting labor costs, while in a typical Western corporation the hierarchical chain of command makes major changes difficult. "For the Americans, every contract is scrutinized by hundreds of lawyers and bickered over by various departments," says the Hong Kong real estate executive. By the time the cumbersome decision-making machinery reacts, the opportunities in the flexible new markets have already been detected by smaller, more agile firms, and are long gone.

In the 1970s and 1980s, for example, while the West focused its attention on competition from Japan, other parts of Asia presented a host of new business opportunities. Though many Southeast Asian national economies were enjoying an even faster rate of growth than Japan's, Western firms were reluctant to venture into what they considered to be risky markets. Overseas Chinese businesses were already there, however: They detected the new opportunities and took full advantage of them.

The global marketplace has also seen these ethnic Chinese family businesses begin to modify the age-old structures based on family, clan, and home village, in favor of the same rational business organizations that businesspeople of any other ethnic group would establish. Deals such as the one in which Li Ka-shing bought Canada-based Husky Oil in 1987 and the one in which Thailand's Chinese-owned Charoen Pokphand teamed up for a time with the United States giant Wal-Mart to open discount stores throughout China are examples of how business for the diaspora has evolved.

As China has tried to become a modern, industrialized country, the various reformers and revolutionaries have lobbied the overseas Chinese communities for material support. Attributing their mistreatment in foreign lands at least partly to China's backwardness and degraded international status, the overseas Chinese wanted to help transform China, and a few of them became very nationalistic and patriotic. The father of Chinese nationalism and the founder of the Republic of China, Sun Yat-sen, was himself a scion of an overseas Chinese family. In the 1940s the overseas Chinese became heavily embroiled in the civil war, as both the communists and the nationalists competed for their loyalty. Their involvement culminated in 1949 when many returned to China to help the revolutionary government's cause; among them were hundreds of Chinese Americans and some 250,000 Chinese Indonesians. Unfortunately, many encountered a miserable fate because of their bourgeois Western backgrounds. Branded traitors and capitalists because of their relatives still abroad, their family property was confiscated during the Cultural Revolution, and they were imprisoned. Some tried to escape, and many died.

Those who survived joked bitterly about their predicament by calling themselves the "dead *huaqiao*" [the dead overseas Chinese] in contrast to the "living *huaqiao*," their compatriots who had remained abroad and prospered.

Ever since the mainland Chinese government began to allow capitalism to flower in the 1980s in an effort to modernize, it has tried to enlist the help of the overseas Chinese. In doing so it has even been willing to admit that some excesses were made during the Cultural Revolution, and as a gesture of goodwill it has returned confiscated property to expatriate families and praised them copiously for their patriotism and their contributions to the betterment of China.

Although they may be enjoying some of the benefits, the overseas Chinese have learned to keep their distance from the mainland. Their loyalties do not lie with the Chinese nation-state but rather with the profits that can be made there, through special economic zones where their investments are protected and they are free to move their capital. At the same time, ethnic Chinese around the world are watching how China deals with Taiwan and Hong Kong. For many of them who might have been sold on the "We are all Chinese" pitch, the saber rattling of recent months has been sobering. Many Hong Kong and Taiwan residents hold foreign passports, obtained either through investment in Canada, the United States, or Australia or through their children's foreign citizenship abroad. Although overseas Chinese claim that all they need is freedom to make money, they like to send their children to Western universities and establish a foothold in an English-speaking country. They regard their assets in countries such as the United States as an insurance policy against potential instability in Southeast Asia or on mainland China.

"In the United States there really is a respect for law," says Andrew Kwan, a United States citizen who owns an insecticide factory near Beijing. "That's very attractive for us. My family is here; we have a house. A lot of us would not be willing to give up our foreign passport to go back to China."

Overseas Chinese businesspeople whose professional and private interests are truly global are called astronauts by their less fortunate compatriots because, for example, they live in California and do business in Asia. They will invest in China if that is where the money is to be made, but if the labor costs there increase and productivity levels off, they are just as likely to turn to Vietnam to set up fertilizer plants, to India to set up joint ventures in electronics, or to Bangladesh, Fiji, Mauritius, or Guatemala to set up garment factories. Increasingly, they are joining the transnational world of capitalism developed under European domination, where national borders lose meaning and national identity is neither a hindrance nor an asset. It is increasingly a world in which "Chineseness" also means very little. As Ien Ang, a Chinese scholar born in Indonesia to Chinese parents and raised in Holland, says: "I am inescapably Chinese by descent. I am only sometimes Chinese by consent. When and how is a matter of politics."

It is ultimately political questions such as whether China attacks Taiwan or crushes the spirit and laws of Hong Kong that will determine if overseas Chinese continue to invest in China and profit from its seemingly boundless opportunities. Even Singapore's Lee Kuan Yew, a great champion of the cultural pull of Confucianism, admits that ethnicity will take a backseat to the pressures of realpolitik. "We are ethnic Chinese," Lee has said, "but we must be honest with ourselves and recognize that at the end of the day, our fundamental loyalties are to our home, not to our ancestral country. To think otherwise is not realistic. It will only lead to grief when our interests fail to coincide."

Peter Kwong, the director of Asian American Studies at Hunter College in New York City, is the author of The New Chinatown. *Dusanka Miscevic, a writer and historian, also contributed to this article.*

The challenge for U.S. Asians in the year 2000

By E. San Juan, Jr.

Part I

E. San Juan, Jr. is emeritus professor of English and Comparative Literature at the University of Connecticut, Storrs. He was 1993 Fellow at the Institute for the Advanced Studies in Humanities, University of Edinburgh, Scotland, and currently teaches Ethnic Studies and American Culture at Bowling Green State University, Ohio. He received graduate degrees from the University of the Philippines and Harvard University. His book Racial Formation/Critical Transformations *won awards from the Association for Asian American Studies and the Gustavus Myers Center for Human Rights.*

In this age of postality (postCold War, postmodern), one would expect that the public perception of Asian Americans—I prefer the term "U.S. Asians" to avoid any hint of unqualified acculturation or assimilation—would now be past stereotypes, myths, clichés. Not so. One textbook easily splices the narrative of the European "immigrant's quest for the American dream" with "the racial minority's" victimization by "discriminating laws and attitudes." In a revealing analysis of Judge Karlin's sentencing colloquy in the 1992 trial of Du Soon Ja, Neil Gotanda found that old paradigms are alive and well amid the reconfiguration of the planet's geopolitical map and the passing of the "American Century."

By the year 2020, the population labelled "Asian Americans" in this country will number 20.2 million. Filipinos now constitute the largest group (more than 2 million, up from 1,406,770 in the 1990 Census). And yet they still are considered pariahs: in the University of California at Berkeley, the treatment of Filipinos may be conceived as a symptom of benign "ethnic cleansing."

Given the heterogeneity of the histories, economic stratification, and cultural composition of the post-1965 immigrants and refugees, all talk of Asian pan-ethnicity should now be abandoned as useless, and even harmful, speculation. Not so long ago, Professor Roger Daniels stated the obvious: "The conglomerate image of Asian Americans is a chimera." This is more true today. No longer sharing the common pre-World War II experience of being hounded by exclusion acts, antimiscegenation laws, and other disciplinary apparatuses of racialization, Vietnamese, Kampucheans, and Hmongs have now diverged from the once dominant pattern of settlement, occupation, education, family structure, and other modes of ethnic identification. (We don't even reckon with the presence of Thais, Malaysians, Indonesians, Bangladeshis, not to mention the Pacific Islanders.) After 1965, one can no longer postulate a homogeneous "Asian American" bloc—except in fantasy. To use current jargon, the bureaucratic and totalizing category "Asian American" has been decentered by systemic contingencies to the point where today a cult of multiple and indeterminate subject-positions is flourishing. However, I have yet to meet a cyborg or borderland denizen of confirmed U.S. Asian genealogy.

Despite such changes, versions of the "melting pot" theory are still recycled to flatten out the politically significant mutations within a patriotic dogma of pluralism. A recent textbook entitled *Asian Americans* has no hesitation predicting that Asians will be easily assimilated in time. The trick is the promotion of toleration via consumerist "multi-culturalism," backed by the economic power of Japan and the Asian "Tigers." This accommodationism refuses to take seriously what I call the Vincent Chin syndrome: political demagoguery in times of social crisis can shift the target of scapegoating onto any Asian-looking "object" that can reactivate the sedimented persona of the wily, inscrutable, shifty-eyed foreigner in our midst. And multiculturalism is for the most part a refurbished version of white supremacy, the enshrined cooptative formula for peacefully managing differences among the subalterns.

In his 1972 pathbreaking book *Racial Oppression in America*, Robert Blauner repudiated the fallacy of subsuming the diverse experiences of subjugation of people of color under the immigrant model that privileges the teleology of Eurocentric assimilation in defining the character of the U.S. nation-state. But the specter of "American exceptionalism" has a way of being resurrected, especially in periods of crisis and neoconservative resurgence. Asian American panethnicity falls within this conjuncture. It is one specimen of the ideological recuperation of what I would call the Myrdal complex (the presumed schizoid nature of U.S. democracy preaching equality but institutionalizing exclusionary and oppressive practices) that plagues all utilitarian thought, including its radical and pragmatic variants.

Despite its reflection of a need for principled unity against institutional racism, pan-Asianism concealed the ethnic chauvinisms and class cleavages, hierarchy, and conflicts generated by the operation of U.S. racializing politics and its divide-and-rule policies. As Glenn Omatsu has pointed out, the "cultural entrepreneurs" of pan-Asianism turned out to be agents for opportunist electoral politics and brokers for the "get rich quick" ethos even while Asians (associated with the competitive power of Pacific Rim nations) are collectively perceived as a threat by blacks and other minority groups. They begot the post-1980s Asian neo-conservatives who glorify the "model minority" stereo-

From *Philippine News*, January 22–28, 1997, and January 29–February 4, 1997. © 1997 by E. San Juan, Jr. Reprinted by permission.

type while nurturing the seeds for the Los Angeles explosion of April 1992.

The more profound motivation for pan-Asianism is the historically specific racism of white supremacy towards Asians. The historian Sucheng Chan notes: "In their relationship to the host society, well-to-do merchants and poor servants, landowning farmers and propertyless farm workers, exploitative labor contractors and exploited laborers alike were considered inferior to all Euro-Americans, regardless of the internal ethnic and socio-economic divisions among the latter." Instead of valorizing ethnicity or cultural difference per se, we need to concentrate on the "racialization" process, its ideological and institutional articulations, within the framework of the capitalist world system.

Part II

We need to attend to the national/international division of labor which provides the context to understand ethnicization as, in Immanuel Wallerstein's view, "the distinctive cultural socialization of the work force that enables the complex occupational hierarchy of labor (marked by differential allocation of surplus value, class/status antagonisms, etc.) to be legitimized without contradicting the formal equality of citizens before the law in liberal-democratic polities." Wallerstein points out that capitalism gains flexibility in restructuring itself to preserve its legitimacy, hence the unconscionable exploitation of the multicultural workforce in the Los Angeles garment industry, in the "free trade" zones of Mexico, the Philippines, South Korea, Malaysia and elsewhere. Ethnicity, then, is not a primordial category that testifies to the virtue of a pluralist market-centered system, but a means utilized to legitimize the contradictions of a plural society premised on racial hierarchy, also called a *Herrenvolk* democracy. What I would stress is precisely the need to analyze the racialization of ethnicized, class/gendered identities (initially enslaved, conquered, and colonized) to avoid the trap of multiculturalism as a discussion of formalistically reconciling cultural differences.

Recent scholarship on the ideological construction of "whiteness" in U.S. history should illuminate also the invention of the "Asian American" as a monolithic, standardizing rubric. It is clear that the diverse collectivities classified as "Asian American" manifest more discordant features than affinities and commonalities. The argument that they share similar values (e.g., Confucian ethics), ascribed "racial" characteristics, and kindred interests in politics, education, social services, etc. cannot be justified by the historical experiences of the peoples involved, especially those who came after World War II.

This does not mean that U.S. Asians did not and do not now engage in coalitions and alliances to support certain causes or cooperate for mutual benefit; examples are numerous. In fact, the insistence on pan-Asianism can only obscure if not obfuscate the enduring problems of underemployment and unequal reward ("glass ceiling"), occupational segregation, underrepresentation, and class polarization obscured by the "model minority" orthodoxy that props up the American Dream of Success.

Faced with the racial politics of the eighties and nineties, all talk about fashioning or searching for an "authentic Asian American identity" and "reclaiming" our history can only sound fatuous. More culpable is the view that in order to transcend the Frank Chin-Maxine Hong Kingston misrecognition of each other, U.S. Asian artists should utilize their "ethnic sensibility to describe aspects of the Asian American experience that appeal to a common humanity"—a plea for commodifying the formerly "exotic" into plain American pie. The ubiquitous troupe of reconfigured "Lotus Blossoms" and "Gunga Dins," now of course sporting more fashionable trappings, still dominate the travelling roadshows of "Asian American" cultural production today.

Incalculable damage has been inflicted by a postmodernist skepticism that sometimes has claimed to be more revolutionary than rigorous research into internal colonialism, labor segmentation, national self-determination, and so on. One example of postmodernist chic is the notion of transnational subjectivity. It doesn't require Superman's x-ray vision for us to tell that the paragon of the diasporic subject as a postcolonial "hybrid" often masks the working of a dominant "common culture" premised on differences, not contradictions. Heterogeneity can then be a ruse for recuperative patriotism. The latest version is the theory of "multiple identities" and "fluid" positions of immigrants (for example, Filipino Americans) straddling two nation-states assumed to be of equal status and ranking in the world system; such identities are unique because they allegedly participate in the political economies of both worlds. This is obviously a paradigm based on the dynamics of market exchange-value whereby all goods and values can be made equivalent. The status of the transnational migrant, however, remains parasitic on the superior nation-state (the United States), belying its claim to autonomy and integrity. The fatal mistake of the transnational model is analogous to that of panethnicity: despite its gesture of acknowledging political and ideological differences, it assumes the parity of colonized/dominated peoples and the U.S. nation-state in contemporary global capitalism.

It is a truism that for all neocolonized subjects in the Western metropoles, the process of survival involves constant renegotiation of cultural spaces, revision of inherited folkways, reappropriation of dominant practices, and invention of new patterns of adjustment. All these embody the resistance habitus of peoples attempting to transcend subalternity. What is crucial is how and why a specific repertoire of practices is enabled by the structures of civil society, the state, and the disposition of the agents themselves. When Filipinos, for example, construct the meaning of their lives, they don't simultaneously conform to and resist the

> *The argument that they share similar values (e.g., Confucian ethics), ascribed 'racial' characteristics, and kindred interests in politics, education, social services, etc. cannot be justified by the historical experiences of the peoples involved, especially those who came after World War II.*

hegemonic "free enterprise" ideology. This implies a reservoir of free choices that doesn't exist for most subjugated communities. Indeed the construction of Filipino identity as a dynamic, complex phenomenon defies both assimilationist and pluralist models when it affirms its anti-racist, counterhegemonic antecedent: the long-lived revolutionary opposition of the Filipino people to U.S. imperial domination.

New postCold War realignments compel us to return to a historical materialist analysis of political economy and its overdeterminations in order to grasp the new racial politics of transnationality and multiculturalism. With respect to the Asian/Pacific Rim countries whose destinies now seem more closely tied to the vicissitudes of unequal exchange as well as indebtedness to the World Bank-IMF, the reconfiguring of corporate capital's strategy in dealing with this area requires more astute analysis of the flow of migrant labor, capital investments, media manipulation, tourism, and so on.

There are over a million Filipinos (chiefly women) employed as domestics and low-skilled workers in Hong Kong, Singapore, Japan, Taiwan, Korea, and Malaysia. Their exploitation is worsened by the racializing process of inferiorization imposed by the Asian nation-states, the Asian "tigers," competing for their share in global capital accumulation. The Western press then reconfigures the Asian as neoSocial Darwinist denizen of booty capitalism in the "New World Order."

All these recent developments inevitably resonate in the image of the Asian—its foreignness, malleability, affinities with the West, etc.—that in turn determines a complex of contradictory and variable attitudes toward U.S.-domiciled Asians. Such attitudes can be read from the drift of the following questions: Is Japan always going to be portrayed as the scapegoat for the loss of U.S. jobs? Is China obdurately refusing to conform to Western standards in upholding human rights and opening the country to the seductions of market in-

dividualism? What about "mail order brides" from the Philippines and Thailand as possible carriers of AIDS virus? Are the Singaporeans that barbaric? And despite the end of history in this postCold War milieu, will the North Koreans continue to be the paragons of communist barbarism? Are Korean and Indian merchants really that greedy and clannish?

In effect, given the demographic and sociopolitical re-articulation of U.S. Asian collectivities, we have not even begun to address what Nancy Fraser calls the redistribution-recognition dilemma, that is, how political-economic justice and cultural justice can be realized together by transformative means instead of repackaging liberal nostrums so popular among people of color in the mainstream academy. In short, the challenge of a radical democratic critique still needs to be taken up as we confront the disintegration of panAsian metaphysics and transnationalist discourse amid the postCold War realignments of nation-states and North/South power blocs.

The Ethnic Legacy

Ethnicity is often associated with immigrants and with importation of culture, language, stories, and foods from foreign shores. Appalachian, western, and other regional ethnicities are evidence of multigenerational ethnic cultural development within the American reality. The persistent, ongoing process of humanity expressed in unique and intriguing folkways, dialect languages, myths, festivals, and food displays another enduring and public dimension of ethnicity. As this unit's articles illustrate, ethnic experiences may be less foreign and alien than most imagine them to be.

The contributions and concerns of various ethnic immigrant groups over many generations provided a deep weave and pattern to the material and social history of America. Today we see a consciousness of ethnic tradition, exasperation and anger about stereotypes, and efforts to institutionalize attention to groups. Change and ethnicity are not contradictory, for each generation creates anew its ethnicity, which, alongside other affinities, affiliations, and loyalties, helps to guide our interactions. Present concerns of ethnic groups include language, preservation of neighborhoods, ethnic studies, and the rearticulation of historical claims to fairness, justice, and equity.

Perhaps the most obvious oscillation between celebration of achievement and concern about fairness is seen in the legacies of ancestry-conscious persons and groups. Should such populations be denied their distinctiveness through absorption into the mass of modernity, or can their distinctiveness accompany them into mainstream modern American identities? Their ethnicity is not a form of diminished existence; they are "Americans Plus"—Americans with a multicultural affinity and competencies in more than one culture.

The winds of political change in Ireland and England, the Middle East, and Eastern and Central Europe reveal the saliency of ethnicity and the varied textures of group relations. In America the ongoing affinity of ethnic populations to the nations of their origin is expressed in subtle as well as obvious ways. These articles explain the transmission of ethnic tradition in music and suggest linkages between religion and ethnicity. The story of the interaction of ethnicity and religion is curiously exposed in the etymology of the Greek word *ethnikos* (i.e., the rural, Gentile, or pagan people of the ancient Mediterranean world). Though such philological roots no longer drive our principal understanding of ethnicity, the experience of social affinity and cultural affiliation elaborated in the following articles about ethnics deepens our awareness and understanding of ethnicity—a changing yet persistent aspect of human identity and social cohesiveness.

Looking Ahead: Challenge Questions

How does ethnicity of an earlier era suggest the tension between worlds of meaning discussed in this section?

Comment on the idea that the legacy of multiple ancestral origins and ethnic identities of European Americans from an earlier era in America argues for the passing relevancy and their marginality to the central ethnic issues of our time.

What is a central ethnic issue? By what criteria do we decide the importance and preferential protection of one ethnic group vis-à-vis another group?

What lessons can be learned from the immigration and settlement experiences of Eastern and Southern Europeans?

Migrations to the Thirteen British North American Colonies, 1700–1775: New Estimates

Aaron Fogleman

Mainstream historians have finally begun to study the long-neglected, yet extremely important topic of eighteenth-century immigration. Bailyn and DeWolfe's study, *Voyagers to the West*, and other monographs and articles on this subject appeared with increasing frequency during the 1980s.[1] Accurate statistics for immigration during the eighteenth century as a whole are lacking, however, and this gap has forced historians to rely on approximations which are sometimes sketchy and do not reveal much about the varied and complex nature of immigration during that century.

Although it is difficult to compile immigration statistics for the eighteenth century, it is still possible to update the work of previous historians, and for many reasons it is important to do so. With better information on immigration available, historians can compare the relative effects of immigration and natural increase in causing the phenomenal population growth of the colonies in the eighteenth century and of the United States during the early national period. Also, if one simply wants to know approximately how many people of each ethnic or racial group arrived and helped to shape early American society, a single reference with this information would be valuable. In this article, I review some recent estimates of eighteenth-century immigration, showing their accomplishments and problems, and then present an alternative method which corroborates some earlier estimates and provides more information for reference purposes than was heretofore available.

It is impossible to establish definitively the volume of eighteenth-century immigration to America. The only records kept over a long period of time for any ethnic group are the ship lists maintained in Philadelphia for German-speaking passengers arriving from 1727 to 1808.[2] Still, there is enough demographic and other data available for eighteenth-century America to allow historians cautiously to estimate the levels of immigration (and other demographic measures)—not crude, "ballpark" guesses, but cautious estimates which can illuminate a great deal about life in early America. Historians will continually correct and hopefully improve these estimates as they rework old data, discover new data, and develop new methods. But what we have now is suggestive.

Whereas in the past historians relied on rough guesses of the levels of eighteenth-century immigration, they have recently begun to use sophisticated residual methods which may be more accurate. Twenty-five years ago, Potter estimated that 350,000 whites immigrated from 1700 to 1790—an estimate which was, in his own words, "little more than a shot in the dark." About ten years later, Henretta concluded that "nearly 400,000" whites arrived between 1700 and 1775. Higham suggested that about 450,000 came in the eighteenth century, over half of whom were Irish. More recently, Fogel and several of his colleagues used a simulation model of generational progression and an estimated set of mortality, net reproduction, and gross reproduction rates to measure net migration as a residual, concluding that 822,000 more whites arrived in the colony-states from 1607 to 1790

Aaron Fogleman is Assistant Professor of History at the University of South Alabama.

The author thanks John Shy, Kenneth Lockridge, and Rosalind Remer for their helpful comments on this article.

1. See Bernard Bailyn, with the assistance of Barbara DeWolfe, *Voyagers to the West: A Passage in the Peopling of America on the Eve of the Revolution* (New York, 1986). This book, along with Bailyn's companion volume, *The Peopling of British North America: An Introduction* (New York, 1986), provide important bibliographic material on the subject.

2. The most comprehensive and best-edited publication of these lists is Ralph B. Strassburger and William J. Hinke (eds.), *Pennsylvania German Pioneers. A Publication of the Original Lists of Arrivals in the Port of Philadelphia from 1727–1808*, (Norristown, Pa., 1934), 3 v. They list all males sixteen years and older (and some women and children) well enough to disembark upon arrival and sign oaths of loyalty to the British king. Because the large majority of Germans landed in Philadelphia after 1726, these lists are the starting point for any estimation of German immigration into all ports during the colonial period.

From *Journal of Interdisciplinary History*, Spring 1992, pp. 691-709. © 1992 by the Massachusetts Institute of Technology and the editors of *The Journal of Interdisciplinary History*. Reprinted by permission.

than migrated out of this region. For the period 1700 to 1790 their figure was 663,000 whites. Yet in 1981 Galenson, using a different residual method, in which he took into account the high mortality of immigrants shortly after their arrival, as they adjusted to the new disease environment, concluded that a net migration of 435,694 whites and 220,839 blacks took place between 1650 and 1780, and that 346,099 whites and 196,411 blacks arrived from 1700 to 1780, a figure close to Potter's.[3]

Still more recently, Gemery has provided the best summation of all these estimates, as well as many older ones, and pointed out some problems with their sources and methodologies. Given the scarcity of appropriate statistics for the eighteenth century, it is not surprising that the range for net migration calculated by the previously mentioned historians is fairly substantial—from 350,000 to 663,000 for 1700 to 1790. Realizing that estimates of early mortality and fertility rates were tenuous at best, Gemery opted to present a set of plausible immigration estimates from 1700 to 1820, rather than making a single estimate. Using a scale of annual rates of natural increase based on various estimates by historians measuring fertility and mortality, along with his own estimates for mortality during the overseas passage and the period of adjustment by migrants thereafter, Gemery concludes that the "New England pattern" was the most favorable for demographic growth and all other regions were moving in that direction during the eighteenth century. He calculates net migration as a residual, with the results being a plausible range of 765,000 to 1,300,000 white immigrants for the period 1700 to 1820 and a more precise one of 278,400 to 485,300 for the period 1700 to 1780. Allowing for the fact that this estimate does not cover the decade 1780 to 1790, his range runs only somewhat below that established by previous estimates. Gemery understands the difficulties in measuring and generalizing from mortality and fertility rates in early America. He concludes his article with a call for more research—more precise demographic data—so that the range of migration estimates can be narrowed.[4]

This note suggests an alternative method for measuring eighteenth-century migration—one that avoids the impasse created by relying too heavily on fertility and mortality rates, which are difficult to establish for the colonial period. My method is also somewhat simpler,

yet corroborates the results of residual methods, especially Gemery's, while yielding more detailed information. The method relies on three sources of information for estimating the volume and timing of eighteenth-century immigration, all of which yield strong estimates for some ethnic groups and time periods, and somewhat weaker estimates for others. The first source is the work of ethnic-group historians who have produced plausible estimates of immigration for their respective groups. The second source (most important for the British and Irish immigration) is the more qualitative aspects of the ethnic-group historians' work on the timing, flow, and general conditions of the various migrations. The last source is an improved surname analysis of the first federal census in 1790, which, when used in conjunction with the above two sources, allows one to infer what the levels of migration may have been in previous decades, producing what Gemery calls "quasi-numbers."

The first source produces the strongest estimates. Ethnic-group historians have used information on ship departures and arrivals, as well as samples of how many immigrants could be carried by different kinds of ships, to arrive at reasonable estimates of total immigration of Germans, northern and southern Irish, Scots, African slaves, and others. Grouping the best of these estimates by decade and ethnic group into an estimate of overall immigration in the eighteenth century conveys a clear sense of how immigration varied over time and between ethnic groups, something other estimates have not done.

In the past, relying heavily on the estimates of ethnic-group historians would have been a risky enterprise. However, the recent trend among historians has been to lower the estimates of their perhaps more filiopietistic predecessors. Since Dunaway's calculation of at least 250,000 Scots-Irish immigrants in the eighteenth century, Leyburn estimated 200,000 from 1717 to 1775. Still later, Dickson found approximately 109,000 to 129,000 for the years 1718 to 1775. And very recently, Wokeck has found even Dickson's estimates to be too high. For Germans, older estimates of 200,000 to North America before 1800 by both Mönckmeier, along with 225,000 to 250,000 before 1770 by Clarence Ver Steeg, have been revised downward by Fenske (125,000 for the entire century) and Wokeck (about 100,000 in the years 1683 to 1776). Butler has drastically revised the immigration estimates for French Huguenots by Higonnet from 14,000 to about 1,500 (or at most 2,000)—all before 1700. On the other hand, Bailyn and DeWolfe conclude that 100,000 to 150,000 Scots-Irish came before 1760 and over 55,000 Protestant Irish arrived from 1760 to 1775. Furthermore, they raise Graham's estimate for Scots from less than 25,000 for 1763–1775 to approximately 40,000 for 1760–1775. And Doyle has recently emphasized that there was a large southern Irish immigration into the colonies, which Dickson may have overlooked. Extreme accuracy will never be possible, given the nature of eighteenth-century statistics, but given such re-

3. See James Potter, "The Growth of Population in America, 1700–1860," in David V. Glass and D.E.C. Eversley (eds.), *Population in History: Essays in Historical Demography* (London, 1965), 645; James A. Henretta, *The Evolution of American Society, 1700–1815: An Interdisciplinary Analysis* (Lexington, Mass., 1973), 11; John Higham, *Send These to Me. Immigrants in Urban America* (Baltimore, 1984; rev. ed.), 18; Robert W. Fogel et al., "The Economics of Mortality in North America, 1650–1910: A Description of a Research Project," *Historical Methods*, XI (1978), 100; David W. Galenson, *White Servitude in Colonial America: An Economic Analysis* (Cambridge, 1981), 212–218.
4. Henry A. Gemery, "European Immigration to North America, 1700–1820: Numbers and Quasi-Numbers," *Perspectives in American History*, I (1984), 318, 320.

cent work, we can make significantly better estimates of the volume of immigration of some ethnic groups than was previously possible.[5]

The second source of information for this method, the discussions by the ethnic-group historians of the more qualitative aspects of migration, helps give one a sense of when peaks and valleys in immigration occurred, even when no actual data on volume are available. Population pressure, famine, unemployment, rack-renting (the doubling or tripling of rents after the expiration of long-term leases in order to accelerate the removal of tenants from the land), and active recruitment by colonials were major causes of the British and Irish emigration to the colonies. Extended discussions of these developments throughout the eighteenth century give a rough indication of how the total estimated immigration for each group should be distributed over the decades.

The third source of information, Purvis' recent surname analysis of the 1790 federal census, serves as a check and a supplement to estimates of immigration of each ethnic group by indicating to some extent the plausible proportions of the total immigration one could expect from various groups. Purvis calculated the percentage distribution of each white ethnic group (immigrants and their descendants) in the total population of 1790. His work contains some problems, but represents a marked improvement over Hansen and Barker, and the McDonalds, who did not include non-British ethnic groups.[6]

The method allows one to make use of the expertise of those who best understand the history of immigration. Using conservative estimates for each group tends to correct any bias toward inflation of numbers for filiopietistic or other reasons. This method essentially represents a trade-off: instead of the residual methods using decennial population figures from *Historical Statistics* and the sketchy fertility and mortality data compiled by other historians, my method relies on an improved surname analysis of the 1790 census as a check for the increasing expertise of ethnic-group historians who, in turn, rely on

actual data regarding immigrants—ship and passenger lists. The results are presented in Tables 1, 2, and 3.

The quality of the estimates varies by time and ethnic group, but the tables as a whole are useful. The "most accurate" estimates are based on solid information produced by the ethnic-group historians. The "less accurate" estimates should be used with care, but the sum totals for these ethnic groups, especially Africans, Germans, northern and southern Irish, and to some extent the Scots, and Welsh, are plausible and the distribution by decade probably reflects a small margin of error in most cases. It is only the "least accurate" estimates that are dubious, and for this reason they should be used with the greatest care, if at all.

In spite of the problem with filling in the gaps which ethnic-group historians have not yet thoroughly covered, this method as a whole produces enlightening results for most ethnic groups during most of the period in question. The sum total of 585,800 immigrants—278,400 blacks and 307,400 whites—is consistent with Gemery's findings (from 278,400 to 485,300 whites). Indeed, the two methods, one using fertility and mortality data calculating immigration as a residual, and the other relying on actual estimates of immigration by the ethnic-group historians, tend to provide a check for each other. Yet the second method provides much more reference information, listing immigration by decade and ethnic group instead of merely the sum total.

Further study of individual ethnic groups will surely require that adjustments be made to these tables, but

5. Wayland F. Dunaway, *The Scotch-Irish of Colonial Pennsylvania* (Chapel Hill, 1944), 41; James G. Leyburn, *The Scotch-Irish: A Social History* (Chapel Hill, 1962), 180–181; R.J. Dickson, *Ulster Emigration to Colonial America, 1718–1775* (London, 1966), 20–64; Marianne Wokeck, "Irish Immigration to the Delaware Valley before the American Revolution," forthcoming in David B. Quinn (ed.), *Ireland and America, 1500–1800;* Wilhelm Mönckmeier, *Die deutsche uberseeische Auswanderung. Ein Beitrag zur deutschen Wanderungsgeschichte* (Jena, 1912), 13; Clarence Ver Steeg, *The Formative Years, 1607–1763* (New York, 1964), 167; Hans Fenske, "International Migration: Germany in the Eighteenth Century," *Central European History,* (1980), 344; Marianne Wokeck, "German Immigration to Colonial America: Prototype of a Transatlantic Mass Migration," in Frank Trommler and Joseph McVeigh (eds.), *America and the Germans: An Assessment of a Three-Hundred-Year History* (Philadelphia, 1985), I, 12; Jon Butler, *The Huguenots in America: A Refugee People in New World Society* (Cambridge, Mass., 1983), 49; Patrice L. R. Higonnet, "French," in Stephan Thernstrom, Ann Orlov, and Oscar Handlin (eds.), *Harvard Encyclopedia of American Ethnic Groups* (Cambridge, Mass., 1980), 381; Bailyn and DeWolfe, *Voyagers to the West,* 25–26; Ian C.C. Graham, *Colonists from Scotland: Emigration to North America, 1707–1783* (Ithaca, 1956), 185–189; David N. Doyle, *Ireland, Irishmen and Revolutionary America, 1760–1820* (Dublin, 1981), 51–76.

6. The oft-quoted figures from U.S. Bureau of the Census, *Historical Statistics of the United States, Colonial Times to 1970, Bicentennial Edition, Part 2* (Washington, D.C., 1975), Series Z 20–23, 1168 originate from a study conducted primarily by Howard F. Barker and Marcus L. Hansen, "Report of the Committee on Linguistic and National Stocks in the Population of the United States," American Historical Association, *Annual Report for the Year 1931,* (Washington, D.C., 1932), I, 107–441. Forrest McDonald and Ellen Shapiro McDonald recently revised these estimates, "The Ethnic Origins of the American People, 1790," *William and Mary Quarterly,* XXXVII (1980), 179–199. See Thomas L. Purvis, "The European Ancestry of the United States Population, 1790," *William and Mary Quarterly,* XLI (1984), 98. A symposium in that volume contains an enlightening discussion between Purvis, Donald H. Akensen, and the McDonalds on the problems and merits of the various estimates available for the 1790 population.

Purvis improves upon previous work by more carefully analyzing distinctive surnames known to be borne by a certain percentage of a European group and then calculating an arithmetical coefficient sufficiently accurate to allow computation of the proportion of people belonging to that nationality within the United States in 1790. The number of individuals with the same surnames, multiplied by the appropriate numerical constant, equals the approximate size of the group in the United States. The problem with this method is that the surnames from the base population with which Purvis initially worked was not always representative of the actual immigrant population. For immigrants from the European continent he found sufficient passenger lists and other information which adequately reflect the actual population of immigrants. For British and Irish immigrants, however, the dearth of seventeenth- and eighteenth-century passenger lists and censuses forced Purvis to rely on nineteenth-century surname lists from Britain and Ireland, rather than surname lists from the actual immigrant population. Another problem with Purvis' method is that he was unable to distinguish between Scots-Irish and Scottish surnames, which forced him to assume that the number of Scots-Irish was twice the number of Scots in 1790.

In spite of these problems, Purvis' work is the best available, and significantly better than the much older research on which historians have often relied. He completed it diligently and without any apparent bias.

Table 1   Estimated Decennial Immigration by Ethnic Group into the Thirteen Colonies, 1700–1775

DECADE	AFRICANS	GERMANS	NORTHERN IRISH	SOUTHERN IRISH	SCOTS	ENGLISH	WELSH	OTHER	TOTAL
1700–09	9,000	(100)	(600)	(800)	(200)	<400>	<300>	<100>	(11,500)
1710–19	10,800	(3,700)	(1,200)	(1,700)	(500)	<1,300>	<900>	<200>	(20,300)
1720–29	9,900	(2,300)	(2,100)	(3,000)	(800)	<2,200>	<1,500>	<200>	(22,000)
1730–39	40,500	13,000	4,400	7,400	(2,000)	<4,900>	<3,200>	<800>	(76,200)
1740–49	58,500	16,600	9,200	9,100	(3,100)	<7,500>	<4,900>	<1,100>	(110,000)
1750–59	49,600	29,100	14,200	8,100	(3,700)	<8,800>	<5,800>	<1,200>	(120,500)
1760–69	82,300	14,500	21,200	8,500	10,000	<11,900>	<7,800>	<1,600>	157,800
1770–75	17,800	5,200	13,200	3,900	15,000	7,100	<4,600>	<700>	67,500
Total	278,400	84,500	66,100	42,500	35,300	<44,100>	<29,000>	<5,900>	(585,800)

NOTE   Figures were rounded to the nearest 100 immigrants. Estimates are divided into three categories: most accurate—no demarcation, less accurate—( ), and least accurate—< >.

SOURCES   See Appendix.

Table 2   Estimated Proportional Distribution of Ethnic-Group Immigrants in the Thirteen Colonies by Decade, 1700–1775

DECADE	AFRICANS	GERMANS	NORTHERN IRISH	SOUTHERN IRISH	SCOTS	ENGLISH	WELSH	OTHER	TOTAL
1700–09	.03	(.00)	(.01)	(.02)	(.01)	<.01>	<.01>	<.02>	(.02)
1710–19	.04	(.04)	(.02)	(.04)	(.01)	<.03>	<.03>	<.03>	(.03)
1720–29	.04	(.03)	(.03)	(.07)	(.02)	<.05>	<.05>	<.03>	(.04)
1730–39	.14	.15	.07	.17	(.06)	<.11>	<.11>	<.14>	(.13)
1740–49	.21	.20	.14	.22	(.09)	<.17>	<.17>	<.19>	(.19)
1750–59	.18	.35	.21	.19	(.11)	<.20>	<.20>	<.20>	(.20)
1760–69	.30	.17	.32	.20	.28	(.27)	<.27>	<.27>	.27
1770–75	.06	.06	.20	.09	.42	.16	<.16>	<.12>	.12
Total	1.00	1.00	1.00	1.00	1.00	1.00	1.00	1.00	1.00

NOTE   The estimates are divided into three categories: most accurate—no demarkation, less accurate—( ), and least accurate—< >. Slight adjustments were made to account for rounding errors.

SOURCE   From Table 1.

Table 3   Estimated Proportional Distribution of Immigration per Decade in the Thirteen Colonies by Ethnic Group, 1700–1775

	1700–09	1710–19	1720–29	1730–39	1740–49	1750–59	1760–69	1770–75	TOTAL 1700–75
Africans	.78	.53	.45	.53	.53	.41	.52	.26	.48
Germans	(.01)	(.18)	(.10)	.17	.15	.24	.09	.08	.14
Northern Irish	(.05)	(.06)	(.09)	.06	.08	.12	.14	.20	.11
Southern Irish	(.07)	(.08)	(.14)	.10	.08	.07	.05	.06	.07
Scots	(.02)	(.03)	(.04)	(.03)	(.03)	(.03)	.06	.22	(.06)
English	<.03>	<.06>	<.10>	<.06>	<.07>	<.07>	(.08)	.10	<.08>
Welsh	<.03>	<.05>	<.07>	<.04>	<.05>	<.05>	<.05>	<.07>	<.05>
Other	<.01>	<.01>	<.01>	<.01>	<.01>	<.01>	<.01>	<.01>	<.01>
Total	1.00	1.00	1.00	1.00	1.00	1.00	1.00	1.00	1.00

NOTE   The estimates are divided into three categories: most accurate—no demarkation, less accurate—( ), and least accurate—< >. Slight adjustments were made to account for rounding errors.

SOURCE   From Table 1.

they do reflect in a simpler and more usable way the approximate magnitude of colonial immigration in the eighteenth century. I do not mean to evoke the old, filiopietistic practice of inflating numbers (I have used conservative estimates for each ethnic group), but it is ironic that the work of ethnic-group historians, once looked upon with disdain by many, may have provided the beginning of a methodology which yields important and usable results that corroborate the work of more sophisticated techniques.

APPENDIX

AFRICANS If immigrants are people who voluntarily leave their homeland to find a better life elsewhere, then African slaves are not immigrants. But in strictly demographic terms immigrants are people who came from somewhere else, as opposed to being a product of the natural increase in the indigenous population. In this sense everyone who came from elsewhere was an immigrant, including slaves, transported convicts, and so forth. I have included Africans in these tables of immigration by "ethnic" group because they contributed to early American demographic growth in the same ways as the other groups in the tables. The Africans actually came from a variety of different ethnic backgrounds, but taken together, their numbers more than triple those of the largest European group, the Germans. (On the importance of ethnicity among African slaves in the American colonies see, for example, Ira Berlin, "Time, Space, and the Evolution of Afro-American Society," *American Historical Review*, LXXXV [1980], 44–78.)

Since the appearance of Philip D. Curtin, *The Atlantic Slave Trade, A Census* (Madison, 1969), a bitter debate has arisen on the volume of the Atlantic slave trade and Curtin's figures are no longer acceptable without qualification. (For a good summary of the debate see David Henige, "Measuring the Immeasurable: The Atlantic Slave Trade, West African Population and the Pyrrhonian Critic," *Journal of African History*, XXVII [1986], 295–313.) I have used Curtin's figures for North America (137) as modified by Paul E. Lovejoy in "The Volume of the Atlantic Slave Trade: A Synthesis," *Journal of African History*, XXIII (1982), 487.

GERMANS I have used my own method to calculate the volume and distribution of colonial German immigration. The large majority of Germans came through the port of Philadelphia, for which there are good records (passenger lists), especially for the period after 1726. The greatest difficulty occurs when one tries to measure the volume and distribution for other ports. To do this I divided the ethnic-German population of 1790 into two geographical groups—one settled overwhelmingly by immigrants through the port of Philadelphia, the other settled by immigrants through all other ports. Next, a ratio of immigrants to 1790 population was calculated for the first, or Philadelphia, group which was then extended to the second group to estimate the number of immigrants necessary to produce the known 1790 population for that group.

Using Purvis' surname analysis of the ethnic-German population in 1790 ("European Ancestry," 98), the following two geographical groups were created. The German population of some states had to be divided because its roots were in the immigration through Philadelphia and other ports:

GROUP I

State	1790 white population	% German	Total Germans
Tennessee	31,913	6.6	2,106
Kentucky	61,913	4.9	2,996
New Jersey	169,954	6.5	11,047
Pennsylvania	424,049	38.0	161,139
Delaware	46,310	2.6	1,204
2/3 Maryland	139,099	12.7	17,666
2/3 Virginia	294,745	4.5	13,264
7/8 North Carolina	252,179	5.1	12,861
TOTAL	1,420,162	15.7	222,283

GROUP 2

State	1790 white population	% German	Total Germans
Maine	96,002	1.2	1,152
New Hampshire	141,097	0.1	141
Vermont	85,268	0.2	171
Massachusetts	373,324	0.3	1,120
Rhode Island	64,470	0.1	64
Connecticut	232,374	0.4	929
New York	314,142	9.1	28,587
1/3 Maryland	69,550	12.7	8,833
1/3 Virginia	147,372	4.5	6,632
South Carolina	140,178	5.5	7,710
1/8 North Carolina	36,025	5.1	1,837
Georgia	52,886	3.5	1,851
TOTAL	1,752,688	3.4	59,027

To measure the immigration through Philadelphia I used a variety of sources. For the early period (1700–1726) these included the text from Strassburger and Hinke, *Pennsylvania German Pioneers*; Julius F. Sachse, *The German Pietists of Provincial Pennsylvania* (Philadelphia, 1895), 1–10; Martin G. Brumbaugh, *A History of the German Baptist Brethren in Europe and America* (Morris, Ill., 1899), 54–70. Also, I estimated that approximately 500 Germans, who were part of the large migration to New York beginning in 1709, eventually moved to Pennsylvania and contributed to the growth of the population in Group 1—see Walter A. Knittle, *Early Eighteenth Century Palatine Emigration* (Philadelphia, 1937); Henry Z. Jones, *The Palatine Families of New York* (Universal City, Calif., 1985).

For the period 1727–1775 I used the passenger lists in Strassburger and Hinke, which are not entirely comprehensive, but do represent the best collection of immigrant lists for any ethnic group in the eighteenth century. They include all male passengers sixteen years and older well enough to disembark at Philadelphia and sign an oath of allegiance to the king. Further, many of the more than 300 ship lists for this period also contain lists of women and children, or list a total number of passengers and/or "freights" (children were counted as half freights or not at all). This allows one to calculate the ratio of total passengers to adult males, a figure that changed over the decades. After controlling for these changes, the difference between "passengers" and "freights," and adding the Moravian immigrants, who settled in Pennsylvania but immigrated primarily through New York (see John W. Jordan, "Moravian Immigration to Pennsylvania, 1734–1765," *Pennsylvania Magazine of History and Biography*, III [1909], 228–248; *idem*, "Moravian Immigration to America, 1734–1800," unpub. ms. [Historical Society of Pennsylvania, Philadelphia, n.d.]), a fairly complete picture of German immigration through Philadelphia for the years 1700–1775 can be compiled.

Records for other ports are incomplete, although historians and genealogists constantly make new discoveries. I have reproduced data from several sources here to give an idea of the distribution through other ports which produced the ethnic-German population for Group 2 in 1790. These sources include Knittle, *Early Eighteenth Century Palatine Emigration*; Jones, *Palatine Families in New York*; Daniel I. Rupp, *Thirty Thousand Names of German, Swiss, Dutch, French, and Other Immigrants in Pennsylvania from 1727 to 1776* (Philadelphia, 1875); newspaper and other accounts located in the research files of the Museum of Early Southern Decorative Arts in Winston-Salem, N.C.; Jane Revill, (ed.), *A Compilation of the Original Lists of Protestant Immigrants to South Carolina, 1763–1773* (Columbia, 1939).

The following is the estimated distribution by decade for all known immigrants by port of entry (Group 1—Philadelphia, Group 2—other ports). Group 1 is fairly complete, but Group 2 is incomplete:

	GROUP 1		GROUP 2	
	N	%	N	%
1700–09	0	0	50	0
1710–19	1,000	2	2,548	41
1720–29	2,161	3	0	0
1730–39	12,477	19	138	2
1740–49	14,201	21	594	9
1750–59	24,971	37	1,033	16
1760–69	7,712	12	1,690	27
1770–75	4,211	6	242	4
TOTAL:	66,733	100%	6,295	100%

Because the data in Group 2 is so incomplete, I have extended the ratio of immigrants-to-1790 population for Group 1 to Group 2, for whom the 1790 population is known. The following results were achieved:

$$\begin{array}{cc} & \text{GROUP 1} \quad \text{GROUP 2} \\ \frac{\text{1700–75 immigration:}}{\text{1790 population:}} & \frac{66,700}{222,300} = \frac{x}{59,000} \quad x \approx 17,700 \end{array}$$

Total immigration through 1770–75: 66,700 + 17,700 = 84,400. (All figures were rounded to the nearest 100 persons.)

About 17,700 Germans (21 percent of the total) immigrated through ports other than Philadelphia, and 84,400 immigrated through all ports of the thirteen colonies during the period 1700–1775. (The final estimate in Table 1 was adjusted to account for rounding errors.)

The validity of this calculation rests on two assumptions (in addition to the assumption that Purvis' surname analysis is reasonably accurate). The first is that the fertility/mortality experience, or rate of natural increase, was the same for both groups. The second is that the time pattern of arrival was the same for both groups, or that the differences were such that the net effect was the same.

To deal with the first assumption, the work of Gemery must be addressed ("European Immigration to North America"). He found that the widest discrepancies in the rate of natural increase during the colonial period occurred between northern and southern colonies in the seventeenth century. By the eighteenth century the fertility/mortality experience for whites in all regions was becoming similar. This, along with the fact that both Group 1 and Group 2 contain inhabitants from northern and southern colonies, tends to make this assumption reasonable, although there is some error introduced in the final estimates because of it.

The second assumption is more difficult to make, since the above table clearly shows a discrepancy in the distribution of known immigrants in the two groups.

There are many factors which could have contributed to the same number of immigrants from 1700 to 1775 producing differing numbers of inhabitants in 1790. These include when they arrived, their age, and to what degree they came as families (early or late in the reproductive period), or single individuals. Group 2 contains more earlier immigrants, which means they had time to produce more descendants by 1790 than their counterparts in Group 1. On the other hand, there were also more immigrants in Group 2 in the 1760s and 1770s (relative to the middle decades of the century) than were in Group 1, which means that more of Group 2 had relatively less time to reproduce by 1790 than was true for Group 1. These two characteristics tend to cancel one another out, at least to a degree. There is no doubt some error was introduced by assuming equal growth rates and timing of immigration for both groups, but the reasons outlined above and the fact that a large majority clearly emigrated to Philadelphia tends to indicate that the margin of error in the final estimates of Tables 1–3 is small.

Lastly, German immigration from 1775 to 1790 did have some effect on the population of 1790, but it was very slight. During the war years, 1775–1783, German immigration ceased almost completely, except for some 3,000 "Hessian" deserters (see Rodney Atwood, *The Hessians: Mercenaries from Hessen-Kassel in the American Revolution* [Cambridge, 1980], 254). Immigration into Philadelphia resumed in 1785, and by 1790 only 1,467 persons had arrived (calculated from Strassburger and Hinke, III. 3–44).

The final estimate in Table 1—84,500—is lower than Wokeck's generally accepted figure of 100,000 German-speaking persons immigrating through all ports before 1776 (see "German Immigration to Colonial America," 12). I distributed the final total, including the "unknown" immigrant figure arrived at by the above calculation, according to that of the known immigrants listed above. Some adjustments were made for the early decades, however, because there are fairly complete records for the large emigration from 1709 to 1714 to New York and North Carolina (represented in Group 2). Therefore few "unknown" immigrants in Group 2 were added to the period before 1720.

NORTHERN AND SOUTHERN IRISH Estimates of the volume of northern Irish, which includes primarily people of Scottish descent ("Scots-Irish"), but also native Irish from the northern counties, have fluctuated wildly through the years. Dunaway estimated 250,000 Scots-Irish arrived in the eighteenth century (*The Scotch-Irish of Colonial Pennsylvania*, 41) and Maldwyn A. Jones calculated the same number for the entire colonial period ("Scotch-Irish," in Thernstrom, *Harvard Encyclopedia of American Ethnic Groups*, 896). Further, Leyburn concluded that 200,000 Scots-Irish immigrants arrived from 1717 to 1775 (*The Scotch-Irish*, 180–181). Until recently, Dickson was the only historian to present some quanti-

tative evidence justifying his calculations, and to show how the flow of immigration varied over time. He concluded that 109,000 to 129,000 Ulster Irish immigrated into the colonies from 1718 to 1775.

On the other hand, the immigration of Catholic, "southern," or non-Ulster Irish was largely ignored until the work of Audrey Lockhart, *Some Aspects of Emigration from Ireland to the North American Colonies between 1660 and 1775* (New York, 1976) and David N. Doyle, *Ireland, Irishmen and Revolutionary America, 1760–1820* (Dublin, 1981) appeared. Although Lockhart does not attempt to estimate the numbers of immigrants arriving, she does present important evidence on the volume of immigrant-carrying ships, which, when used with other evidence, allows one to make an estimate of the total number of immigrants arriving and to show how this migration varied over time. Doyle's work has helped alert historians to this large immigration. He also showed with qualitative evidence how southern Irish emigration varied over the decades, paralleling to a large degree Ulster Irish emigration.

But Doyle has overestimated the numbers of this emigrant group. He states that about 90,000 southern Catholic Irish came before 1776 (almost all in the eighteenth century), up to 30,000 native (that is, Catholic) Ulster Irish, and 10,000 southern Anglo-Irish (Protestant), even though there were only 156,000 to 166,000 inhabitants in the United States in 1790 who descended from all these groups. He attributes their slow natural growth rate to the large number of single men emigrating, who had to marry non-Irish women in America (51–76, especially 61 and 70–71). They did marry and have children, however, and even if all "Irish" found by surname analysis in the 1790 census were not really "100 percent" Irish (due to marriage migration), the number of immigrants from which they descended must have been much lower than Doyle indicates.

My estimates of 66,100 northern and 42,500 southern Irish in Table 1 are based upon Lockhart, Dickson, and the very recent work of Wokeck, who has found passenger lists for the Delaware ports which allowed her to calculate approximate passenger-per-ship ratios for both northern and southern Irish and extend them to the number of ships arriving from 1729 to 1774. See "Irish Immigration to the Delaware Valley." Wokeck calculated 17,296 southern Irish and 35,399 northern Irish arriving in the Delaware ports from 1729 to 1774. I have grouped them by decade as follows:

DECADE	SOUTHERN	NORTHERN	TOTAL
1729	723	296	1,019
1730–39	3,328	2,510	5,838
1740–49	4,106	5,225	9,331
1750–59	3,639	8,099	11,738
1760–69	3,811	12,067	15,878
1770–74	1,689	7,202	8,891
TOTAL	17,296	35,399	52,695

According to Lockhart's tables, 45 percent of all the immigrant-carrying ships went to the Delaware ports during this same time period (calculated from Appendix C, 175–208). From Dickson's tables (Appendix E, 282–287) one can calculate that 57 percent of immigrant-carrying ships from northern Ireland went to Delaware Valley ports, although this data only reflects the situation in the years 1750 to 1775. If one extends Dickson's figure to the entire period 1729–1774, the following calculations can be made for total Irish immigration into all ports of the thirteen colonies in the years 1729 to 1774:

SOUTHERN IRISH

			TOTAL
1729	723	÷ .45 =	1,607
1730–39	3,328	÷ .45 =	7,396
1740–49	4,106	÷ .45 =	9,124
1750–59	3,639	÷ .45 =	8,087
1760–69	3,811	÷ .45 =	8,469
1770–74	1,689	÷ .45 =	3,753
TOTAL	17,296	÷ .45 =	38,436

NORTHERN IRISH

			TOTAL
1729	296	÷ .57 =	519
1730–39	2,510	÷ .57 =	4,404
1740–49	5,225	÷ .57 =	9,167
1750–59	8,099	÷ .57 =	14,209
1760–69	12,067	÷ .57 =	21,170
1770–74	7,202	÷ .57 =	12,635
TOTAL	35,399	÷ .57 =	62,104

To estimate immigration for the remaining years, 1700–1728 and 1775, the following steps were taken. According to Lockhart's tables, 13 percent of all immigrant-carrying ships from southern Ireland from 1700 to 1775 arrived in the first three decades of the eighteenth century—2 percent from 1700 to 1709, 4 percent from 1710 to 1719, and 7 percent from 1720 to 1729. Thus 87 percent arrived in the years 1730 to 1775. Subtracting the 1,903 that Wokeck found for 1729, and extending her passenger-per-ship ratio for 1770–1774 to the nine ships Lockhart found arriving in the colonies in 1775, one can calculate total southern Irish immigration from 1700 to 1775 as follows:

$$38,436 - 1,903 + 180 = .87x$$

$$x = 42,199 \text{ immigrants}$$

This total number is distributed as follows for 1700–1729:

1700–09	.02 × 42,199 =	844
1710–19	.04 × 42,199 =	1,688
1720–29	.07 × 42,199 =	2,954

In Table 1, I inflated the figure for the 1720s to 3,500 because of the higher passenger-per-ship ratio prevalent for that decade in the few instances in Lockhart's tables where this information was given.

Since Dickson's tables do not include the number of ships arriving before 1750, and since Wokeck has shown that Dickson's method consistently overestimated the number of immigrants per ship, the only option remaining for calculating northern Irish immigration from 1700 to 1728 is to make use of the proportion of southern Irish to total Irish for the period closest to 1700–1728. From 1729 to 1739 southern Irish immigration equaled 58 percent of the total. Thus one can calculate:

	SOUTHERN		TOTAL			NORTHERN
1700–09	844 ÷ .58 =		1,455	1,455 −	844 =	611
1710–19	1,688 ÷ .58 =		2,910	2,910 −	1,688 =	1,222
1720–29	2,954 ÷ .58 =		5,093	5,093 −	2,954 =	2,139

All these calculations can be summarized as follows:

Total Irish Immigration Through All Ports, 1700–1775

DECADE	SOUTHERN	NORTHERN	TOTAL
1700–09	844	611	1,455
1710–19	1,688	1,222	2,910
1720–29	2,954	2,139	5,093
1730–39	7,396	4,404	11,800
1740–49	9,124	9,167	18,291
1750–59	8,087	14,209	22,296
1760–69	8,469	21,170	29,639
1770–75	3,933	13,185	17,118
TOTAL	42,495	66,107	108,602

In Table 1 all figures were rounded to the nearest 100 immigrants. Purvis found 16.3 percent (c. 520,000 persons) of the white population in 1790 to be of Scots-Irish and Irish descent, or northern and southern Irish (see "European Ancestry," 98). The ratio of immigrants 1700–1775 to the total population in 1790 was thus .21 (108,600 ÷ 520,000), a factor which will be used to help calculate immigration for other ethnic groups with less quantitative evidence available than the Irish.

SCOTS   It is difficult to get a sense of the overall number of Scottish immigrants in eighteenth-century America. Graham estimates that emigration to America was "sporadic" from 1707 to 1763. From 1763 to 1775 less than 25,000 departed. Emigration was truly massive only in the years 1768 to 1775, when 20,245 left Scotland for America, see Colonists from Scotland, 185–189. Graham's figures, however, are probably too low. Using the same ratio of immigrants to 1790 population as existed for the northern and southern Irish (.21), combined with Purvis' finding that 5.3 percent (or c. 168,000) of the white population in 1790 was of Scottish descent ("European Ancestry," 98) allows an estimate of 35,300 Scottish immigrants from 1700 to 1775.

The lack of good data for pre-1760 immigration prohibits the labeling of these estimates as "most accurate."

Nevertheless, because of the similarities between the Scottish and Irish emigration experience to America—both began in the early eighteenth century, and were caused by population pressure, rack-renting, and agricultural dislocations which occurred in both places at about the same time—I have opted to distribute the total immigration for the period 1700–60 in the same manner as the Irish (both northern and southern combined). It is only in the late 1760s and 1770s that Scottish emigration to the North American colonies noticeably differs form the Irish. The Irish emigration was larger in real numbers, but the Scottish emigration became relatively more intense (compared to the earlier Scottish migrations) as Graham has shown. For these reasons I have labeled the pre-1760 estimates as "less accurate" and the post-1760 estimates, based on Graham's work, as "most accurate."

ENGLISH Estimates of English immigrants are even scarcer than those for Scottish. Furthermore, the English are the only ethnic group for which significant immigration occurred in both the seventeenth and eighteenth centuries, which makes it impossible to use Purvis' surname analysis of the 1790 census to assist in calculating eighteenth-century immigration. E. Anthony Wrigley and Roger S. Schofield, *Population History of England, 1541–1871: A Reconstruction* (Cambridge, Mass., 1981) found net migration in England from 1701 to 1775 to be 423,162 (calculated from Table 7.11, 219), but the only period for which there are statistics available for arrivals in the thirteen colonies is the 1770s. Here Bailyn and DeWolfe found about 4,500 English emigrants bound for America during the years 1773–1776 in the Register maintained in London, as opposed to 3,600 Scottish emigrants (*Voyagers to the West*, 92). In the absence of any other data I have made the assumption that the ratio of English to Scottish emigrants in the 1770s extended back to 1700, which would mean about 44,100 English immigrants arrived in the colonies during the period in question. This is not to say that the emigration history of Scotland and England are exactly parallel and there is little reason to accept this figure as being very accurate, but it does compare well with Richard S. Dunn's estimate of 25,000 English servants arriving in the colonies during these years, see "Servants and Slaves: The Recruitment and Employment of Labor," in Jack P. Greene and J.R. Pole (eds.), *Colonial British America: Essays in the New History of the Early Modern Era* (Baltimore, 1984), 159. Similar to the Scottish and Irish emigrants, the English, too, were plagued by population pressure and agricultural dislo-

cations that coincided with these developments elsewhere in the realm. Thus I have distributed the total figure throughout the decades in the same manner as the southern and northern Irish. My figures for English immigrants are no doubt the weakest in Table 1 and for this reason I have labeled them "least accurate."

WELSH There is little literature on Welsh immigration in eighteenth-century America and quantitative estimates are virtually nonexistent. Rowland Berthoff found the first "sizable" Welsh immigration to have taken place in the years 1680 to 1720, when a few hundred arrived in Pennsylvania. But he does not discuss any other Welsh immigration before the nineteenth century. See "Welsh," in Thernstrom, *Harvard Encyclopedia*, 1011–1012. Yet Arthur H. Dodd did find Welsh settlements in Maryland (1703), North Carolina (1733), South Carolina (1737 and 1780), and Virginia (1740 and 1762), although he made no estimate of their numbers. See *The Character of Early Welsh Emigration to the United States* (Cardiff, 1953), 2. In contrast to the English, most Welsh emigration to the colonies appears to have taken place in the eighteenth century, making it possible to use Purvis' work in this calculation. My estimate of 29,000 Welsh immigrants is based upon his estimate of 4.3 percent of the white population being of Welsh descent in 1790 (Purvis, 98), or about 138,000 people, and the same ratio of immigrants to 1790 population used for the Irish (.21). The 29,000 figure is distributed over the decades in the same manner as the Irish. The advantage of being able to use Purvis' work is offset, however, by the lack of discussion in the literature of the causes, conditions, and timing of the Welsh emigration in the eighteenth century, which has led me to label all these estimates "least accurate."

OTHERS Purvis ("European Ancestry," 98) gives the following percentages for white ethnic distribution in 1790: Dutch 3.1, French 2.1, and Swedish 0.3. Most of these groups arrived before 1700, but there were occasional immigrations of these and other groups during the eighteenth century. For example, over 200 French-speaking passengers arrived in Charleston from 1763 to 1773 (calculated from Revill, *Protestant Immigrants to South Carolina*, [Columbia, 1939], 18, 112, 127). I have placed "other" immigration at a minimal 1 percent of the total per decade to cover this and other such scattered examples during this period and labeled them "least accurate."

THE SETTLEMENT OF THE OLD NORTHWEST: ETHNIC PLURALISM IN A FEATURELESS PLAIN

Robert P. Swierenga

Migration created the Old Northwest. In 1787 there were almost no permanent American settlements in the "Ohio country," but by 1860 nearly a quarter of the United States population (seven million persons) lived there and the population center of the nation was located near Chillicothe, Ohio.[1] Before 1840 most of the newcomers came from the older states but thereafter large families and foreign immigration boosted the total. Foreigners accounted for 79 percent of the net migration into the Old Northwest in the 1840s and a whopping 88 percent in the 1850s.[2]

This explosive settlement of the Old Northwest, America's first landed empire, was stimulated and shaped by the Land Ordinance of 1785 and the Northwest Ordinance of 1787. The land act and its numerous permutations encouraged rapid settlement by providing secure land titles for unlimited purchases of blocs of land. The land laws were also sufficiently flexible to allow for individual and group settlements. Immigrants who had for centuries clustered in their European farm villages could settle in compact groups and transplant their communal institutions.

The Northwest Ordinance ensured a uniform governmental system and guaranteed eventual statehood, although the territorial governments were more authoritarian than

most settlers wanted. Congress put the territories on a short leash because easterners held a jaundiced view of early settlers; they were, in Jefferson's words, "halfway between savages and tractable people." The French Canadians who were scattered throughout the region, it was thought, preferred their traditional autocracy. Thus, both American and Canadian pioneer settlers required an indeterminate apprenticeship into the mysteries of republican government.[3]

The ordinance also encouraged settlement because it provided some of the features of a bill of rights, including freedom of religion, sanctity of private contracts, and partible inheritance (in place of primogeniture); it encouraged education; it promised to apply the Golden Rule in Indian relations; it guaranteed freedom of transit on the Mississippi, Ohio, and St. Lawrence river systems; and, most importantly, it prohibited slavery.[4] All of the provisions, but particularly the ban on slavery which was carried over into the state constitutions, were critically important in attracting European immigrants to the Old Northwest.[5]

For many years the common perception of the Old Northwest was that its population, although initially diverse, melded into a homogeneous society. A Federal Writers Project pamphlet published by the Northwest Territory Celebration Commission in 1937, on the 150th anniversary of the ordinance, said it best:

> The name "Old Northwest" implies that the five states included in it share a common historical and social background.... [T]here are

Mr. Swierenga is co-editor of *Social Science History* and a member of the Department of History at Kent State University. He wishes to thank Dr. Douglas K. Meyer of the Geography Department at Eastern Illinois University for reading the manuscript and offering several valuable suggestions.

From *Journal of the Early Republic*, Spring 1989, pp. 73-105. © 1989 by the Society for Historians of the Early Republic. Reprinted by permission.

wide variations of geographic and economic conditions; yet the teeming millions who now inhabit this region are conscious of an identity of interests, and of a common outlook upon life, which gives to this section an individuality as distinct as that possessed by the people of New England, or of the Old South. Any explanation of this individuality [the authors concluded] leads inevitably to the Ordinance of 1787.[6]

The noted historian Joseph Schafer, editor of the *Wisconsin Magazine of History,* stated in 1937 that the grandchildren of immigrants in Wisconsin were "thoroughly indoctrinated and permanently habituated Americans" who were "for the most part indistinguishable from old-line Americans."[7] William N. Parker, a leading American economic historian, described the frontier population of the Old Northwest as living under conditions that were "remarkably homogeneous."[8]

In the 1970s, however, Americans rediscovered ethnicity. No longer do scholars assume a homogeneous society, especially in urban America. Nevertheless, the foreign-born in rural society are yet largely overlooked, on the mistaken notion that they assimilated more rapidly into the dominant Anglo-American society than did their city cousins.[9]

Although the agricultural frontier of the Old Northwest may have had a prosaic sameness, the peopling of that frontier is a fascinating story of cultural variety and conflict. A closer look reveals "intricately meshed mosaics," in the words of cultural geographer Wilbur Zelinsky.[10] Sprinkled throughout the Old Northwest in the nineteenth century were transplanted communities of people from states to the east and from Europe. Each settlement had its matching locales of origin or "culture hearths."[11] Over time, particular families from particular staging areas migrated over particular paths to particular destinations, bringing with them as part of their cultural baggage their particular values and folkways. Clustered settlements were the norm on the midwestern frontier. Families migrated to places where kith and kin had already settled and were able to help them with finding work and housing.

The spatial zonation of ethnic groups in the Old Northwest was on a smaller scale than in colonial America, and this has caused scholars to overlook it. Single ethnic groups imprinted their culture widely, such as the English in

New England, Germans in Pennsylvania, and Dutch in New Netherlands and early New York. But in the Midwest of the nineteenth century, rural immigrant groups seldom prevailed beyond a single township or two and, in the cities, distinct ethnic neighborhoods existed side by side. Scholars, many with a social science bent, in the past fifteen years have identified and begun mapping systematically the various sources of the population and culture of the Old Northwest.[12] Census and land records, linguistic and religious atlases, and even architectural artifacts, foodways, folkways, and agricultural practices have been used as sources.

A body of theory has also been developed to explain the causes of the territorial clustering of cultural groups.[13] One theory is that migration was latitude-specific (the law of "environmental affinity") and moved along east-west lines, thus resulting in settlements stratified by place of birth. It was most cost-effective, particularly for farmers, to move to nearby frontier areas with similar climate, soils, and terrain, so that they could continue to use customary cropping and animal husbandry practices.[14] Another theory is the "distance-decay effect," or the law of relative proximity. Migrants moved the shortest distance possible and frequently settled along points of entry or passage inland before reaching their intended destination. Third is the theory of chain migration.[15] Once a viable ethnic community took hold in a new locale, letters back home induced more and more relatives and friends to come in an extended migration chain.

The Ezra Olin tribe of Connecticut Yankees exemplifies all three theories. Over three generations the Olin clan migrated in a series of short east-west moves through western New York, Ohio, Michigan, and points west. In 1816 the oldest son, John, and several cousins set out for the Genesee country of New York where they joined relatives. Within a decade thirteen of John's fourteen siblings, all married, had relocated in the Genesee Valley with their families. By 1834 one of John's younger brothers, Arvin Olin, began another migration by moving with his wife and eleven children to Ohio's Western Reserve, where Arvin's uncle had previously settled. Over the next five years, eight of Arvin's siblings, plus his parents, left New York for Ohio. In 1850 several Olins moved to the Kalamazoo, Michigan, area and a third migration stage began. In the end, the first and second generation families made a combined total of three hundred moves, but always clustering in the three core homestead areas.[16]

The Kellog family of Canaan, Connecticut, provides a similar example.[17] Austin Kellog migrated to Kenosha, Wisconsin, in 1835 and a year later his brother Thaddeus and his family followed. Within a year more Kellogs left Connecticut for Kellog's Corners, as the new settlement in Racine County was named. There were Uncle Seth and Uncle Chauncey, with their families, plus the four grandparents of the Kellog and Howe lines. The extended clan customarily gathered for prayers in each other's homes each evening after the dishes were cleaned.

Charting these in-migration streams is no small task, but it is a greater challenge to follow the complex cultural developments in the new country resulting from the interactions of the various cultural groups. Some of the cultural conflicts in the Old Northwest are legendary: the Yankee-southern rivalry in the Indiana-Illinois cornbelt, the Yankee-German struggle for supremacy in Wisconsin, and the Yankee-French Canadian conflict in Michigan.[18] In all areas, traditionalists tried to ward off modernizers and immigrants struggled to preserve their identity. The major immigrant groups truly sought after and held on to land. Germans and Scandinavians were greatly over-represented in agriculture in 1910—the Germans by 50 percent and the Scandinavians by more than 100 percent. The degree to which the varying cultural backgrounds of the immigrants actually affected their farming and land inheritance practices has only recently been systematically studied. While farming practices apparently differed little from native-born farmers in the same area, there were cultural "survivals," especially among strongly church-centered ethnic groups.[19]

Linguists and cultural geographers have found that the first settlers imprinted an indelible stamp on frontier communities that latecomers, even in large numbers, displaced only partially after many generations. Given that fact, it is necessary to describe the migration fields of the Old Northwest pioneers. Since the region was open for settlement before European immigration began in earnest in the 1840s, the first wave of settlers were Americans from the older states.

The predominant native-born settlers of the Old Northwest hailed from three of the four major cultural-linguistic regions in the United States in 1790: New England, Midland, and Upland Southern. Lowland southerners stayed below the Mason-Dixon line. The New England or Yankee cultural region included nuclear New England plus the zone of primary expansion into New York. The Midland subculture, based in the Delaware and Susquehanna valleys, included the Mid-Atlantic states. The Upland South included the Piedmont, Blue Ridge, and Shenandoah Valley, as well as the Appalachian and Interior Low plateaus.[20]

The general migration paths of the native-born into the Old Northwest are quite distinct and follow the three principal western entryways.[21] Upland southerners crossed the Cumberland Gap and traveled the Wilderness Road and Nashville-Saline Trail or the southern tributaries of the Ohio River (the Tennessee, Cumberland, and Kentucky rivers) into southern Ohio, Indiana, and Illinois. Midlanders entered the central region via the National Road and Ohio River. Yankees reached the northernmost parts by following the Erie Canal and Great Lakes. Yankees also settled northeastern Ohio and the southern portions of Michigan and Wisconsin by the same routes (see Figure 1).

In addition to the four culture zones of the native-born in 1790, there were five major (white) foreign-born nationalities in the thirteen original states.[22] The English, who comprised over eighty percent of all foreign-born, were interspersed from Massachusetts to North Carolina; the Scotch-Irish preferred Pennsylvania, Virginia, and North Carolina; Germans were concentrated in Pennsylvania; the Dutch settled in New York; and the Irish were widely scattered. Of these foreign-born groups, the English, Scotch-Irish, and Germans had the greatest influence in the Old Northwest.

The population influx into each of the five states of the Old Northwest differed, although each followed the customary pattern of latitude-specific migration and selective settlement. Ohio, the first settled, set the pattern. In the first decade of settlement, upland southerners from the Virginia Panhandle and Kentucky crossed the Ohio River into southern Ohio.[23] Uplanders became the most numerous and influential element in early Ohio. But soon southern Pennsylvania became the beehive of Ohio's midsection. By 1850, over 200,000 Pennsylvanians, mainly Germans and Scotch-Irish, had swarmed into Ohio, where they comprised 43 percent of all migrants.

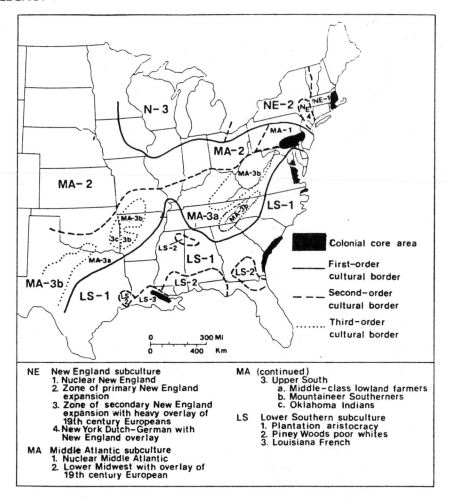

Figure 1

Traditional Rural Culture Regions of the Eastern and Central United States. This regionalization of the eastern half of the United States is concerned solely with rural populations and their cultural configurations. The date would seem to be the early twentieth century.
Source: John F. Rooney, Jr., Wilbur Zelinsky, and Dean R. Louder, eds., *This Remarkable Continent: An Atlas of United States and Canadian Society and Cultures* (College Station, Tex. 1982), 10. Reprinted by permission of Harper & Row Publishers.

This was twice as many as any other state and three times those of New Englanders.[24] The Pennsylvania influence in Ohio was even greater before 1850, since many of the Ohio-born were children of Pennsylvania migrants. The primary zone of Pennsylvania Germans was the north-central "Backbone" area while the Scotch-Irish were more attracted to the Miami Valley of southwestern Ohio.[25] The Old German region of central Ohio is marked by Pennsylvania Dutch barns with their familiar overhang construction and spires of the Evangelical United Brethren churches.

Unlike the midlanders and southerners, New Englanders in Ohio became concentrated in one area—the Connecticut Western Reserve and the Erie Firelands on the north coast, where nearly sixty percent of all Yankees in the state lived in 1850.[26] This was the most homogeneous New England settlement in the Old Northwest and it enabled the Ohio Yankees to achieve a greater cultural and political influence in the Buckeye State than their numbers warranted. Yankees were also better educated and wealthier than southerners.

Antebellum Ohio never became a prime receiving area for foreigners. In 1850 only ten percent of Ohioans were foreign-born. Those who came were widely dispersed in isolated, spatially distinct settlements, although some were contiguous to or overlapped with other groups. Wilhelm's 1850 population census map of Ohio (Figure 2) identified more than one hundred ethnic and cultural enclaves.[27] Half of the foreign-born in Ohio were German, a quarter Irish, an eighth English, and the rest were French, Canadian, Welsh, Scotch, and Dutch. Nearly one third of Ohio immi-

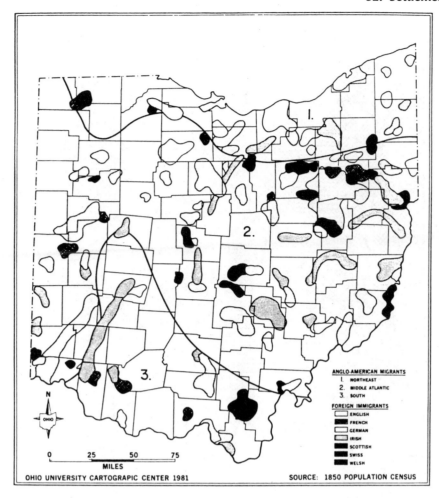

Figure 2

Origin of Settlement Groups in Rural Ohio, 1850
Source: Hubert G. H. Wilhelm, *The Origin and Distribution of Settlement Groups: Ohio, 1850* (Athens, Ohio 1982), 94. Reprinted by permission of Hubert G. H. Wilhelm.

grants in 1850 lived in Cincinnati and Hamilton County, but by 1880 Cleveland and Cuyahoga County became the leading immigrant center with 35 percent of the population foreign-born.[28] Only eight Ohio counties ranked above the average of foreign-born in the entire Old Northwest in 1880; five of these bordered Lake Erie from Cleveland to Toledo, one was Hamilton County (Cincinnati), and two were mainly British-born counties on the Pennsylvania border at Warren and Youngstown (Figure 3).

The German and Irish Immigrants came initially in the 1830s to hire on with the Ohio and Miami canal projects and then they settled along the canal routes. But over time Germans settled mainly among their Pennsylvania Dutch ancestors in east-central Ohio, from which they opened the fertile flat lands of the northwestern and west-central counties that had been avoided because of drainage

problems. The noted German immigrant towns in Ohio were New Bremen and Minster in Auglaize County (interestingly, the former was entirely Protestant and the latter was Catholic). Among large cities, Cincinnati became synonymous with German settlement. Between 1830 and 1900, the proportion of Germans in the Queen City grew from 5 to 40 percent.[29]

Indiana, like Ohio, had an even stronger southern heritage as well as the smallest immigrant population. Only 6 percent were foreign-born in 1850, compared to 11 percent in Ohio, 13 percent in Illinois, 14 percent in Michigan, and 36 percent in Wisconsin (Table 1). Indiana's proportion of foreign-born peaked in 1860 at 9 percent and declined gradually thereafter. Ohio similarly peaked in 1860 and 1870 at a low 14 percent. Illinois and Michigan were in the 19–24 percent range and

179

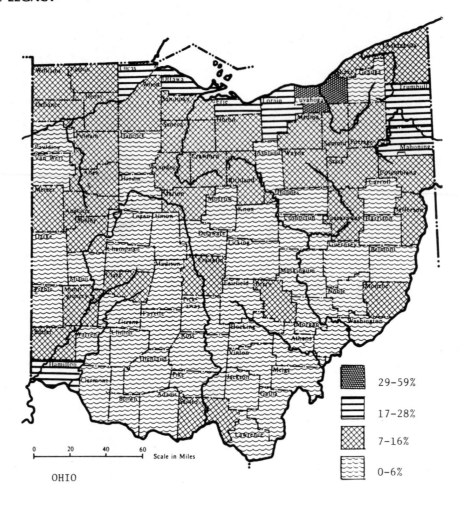

Figure 3

Percentage of Foreign-Born in Ohio, 1880
Source: U.S. Bureau of the Census, *Tenth Census of the United States, 1880,* Vol. 1: *Population* (Washington 1883), 524–526.

Wisconsin was highest at 31–36 percent. Inhabitants with foreign parentage were also sparse in Indiana and Ohio; in 1870 one in five residents of Indiana and one in three of Ohio had one or both parents of foreign birth. This compares with foreign parentage of 39, 41, and 68 percent, respectively, in Illinois, Michigan, and Wisconsin. Indiana's proportion was thus only half as large as Ohio's and only one fifth as large as Wisconsin's.

Early Indiana was also strikingly different because its frontier expanded diagonally from southeast to northwest.[30] Upland southerners, the original Hoosiers, entirely dominated the southern half of the state and they controlled Indiana's government for several generations. Yankees moved into the northernmost tier of counties, but not in large numbers. In 1850 fewer than 3 percent of non-native Indiana residents were of New England-New York

stock compared to 10 percent in the Old Northwest as a whole. Midlanders settled in the northern third and the southeastern corner of the state, but again not in large numbers. In 1850 fewer than 20 percent of non-natives in Indiana were midlanders, compared with 42 percent for the entire Northwest. Hence, Yankees were underrepresented by one third and midlanders by one half, whereas southerners were overrepresented by more than one half. They comprised 44 percent of Indiana non-natives, compared to 28 percent in the whole Northwest.[31]

Because of the early southern dominance in Indiana, Yankees and midlanders as well as European immigrants largely bypassed the state. In 1880, only four counties had more immigrants than the average of 17 percent for the entire Northwest. Three of the counties skirted the shore of Lake Michigan and one

Table 1

Native and Foreign-born Population in the Old Northwest, 1850–1880 (in 1,000s)

| | 1850 | | | 1860 | | | 1870 | | | 1880 | | |
	Native Born	Foreign Born	%FB	Native Born	Foreign Born	%FB	Native Born*	Foreign Born	%FB	Native Born+	Foreign Born	%FB
Ohio	1,733	218	11	2,011	328	14	2,239	372	14	2,803	394	12
Indiana	920	56	6	1,232	118	9	1,539	141	8	1,834	144	7
Illinois	731	112	13	1,387	324	19	2,025	515	20	2,494	584	19
Michigan	340	55	14	600	149	20	916	268	23	1,248	389	24
Wisconsin	193	110	36	499	277	36	690	364	35	910	405	31
Totals	3,917	551	12	5,729	1,196	17	7,409	1,660	18	9,289	1,916	27

* Inhabitants with foreign parentage (either father, mother, or both), which are included in these totals, are: Ohio 850, 32%; Ind. 341, 20%, Ill. 986, 39%; Mich. 488, 41%; Wisc. 718, 68%.

+ The 1880 census report provides data on foreign parentage for a sample of 35 states, which includes only Wisconsin for the states of the Old Northwest. The number of children of foreign immigrants in Wisconsin in 1880 was 450,000, or 49 percent of the native-born.

Sources: J. B. D. DeBow, comp., *Statistical View of the United States... Being a compendium of the Seventh Census* (Washington 1854), Table XL, 61; U.S. Bureau of the Census, *Compendium of the Tenth Census* (Washington 1884), Table XXI, 332–333; U.S. Bureau of the Census, *Tenth*

(Vanderburgh) was on the Ohio River at Evansville (Figure 4). Germans dominated these counties and statewide over half of Indiana's foreign-born were Germans in 1880 (Table 2). Upland southerners thus remained culturally dominant and their impact even exceeded their numbers because of the law of "first effective settlement." Southerners created an entrenched Hoosier culture that predominated in speech and dialect patterns, religious affiliation, house and barn architecture, and farming practices. Despite their energy, the later arriving Yankees and midlanders could not obliterate that imprint, as they did in much of Ohio.

Indiana's center was the most interesting cultural area. It was a transitional zone where southerners and midlanders both intermingled. The traditional view was that Pennsylvanians entered the area via the National Road after uplanders were well established there, and that the two cultures were intermixed. But new linguistic evidence and studies of folkways indicate that the upland southerners had already acquired a mixed culture *before* settling in central Indiana. Before entering Indiana, these Kentucky and Virginia natives had used Cincinnati's hinterland in the Miami and Whitewater valleys as a staging area. Here they had intermingled with midland settlers, especially Pennsylvanians, and created a unique Ohio Valley culture in the years 1800–1815. This cultural amalgam blended southern subsistence farming and northern commercial agriculture into the fa-

bled corn-hog economy. Since Cincinnati was the jumping off point for the expansion of uplanders into central Indiana, the hybrid Ohio Valley culture became the mother culture there.[32]

Southern Illinois, like southern Indiana, was at the end of the Ohio River corridor by which upland southerners from Kentucky and Tennessee advanced northward in large numbers. When Illinois entered the Union in 1818, two thirds of its residents were southern, and the ratio did not change until after 1830.[33] As late as 1850, 90 percent of all native-born (excluding Illinois-born) in the eleven-county Shawnee Hills region of southern Illinois were southerners. Upland southerners also penetrated farther northward and in greater numbers than is commonly recognized. Figure 5 indicates that the sphere of influence of uplanders, who were the core group in southern Illinois and the dominant group in the central counties, even reached into north-central Illinois by 1850. But uplanders avoided the northern region, which became a Yankee core zone centering in Chicago. Hence, Illinois had a very distinct north-south dichotomy between upland southern and New England clusters. Midlanders from Ohio and Pennsylvania formed a wedge in central Illinois between the two core areas. In this transitional zone, midlanders and southerners intermingled, especially in the south-central counties, but to the north the boundary was very abrupt between midlanders and Yankees.[34]

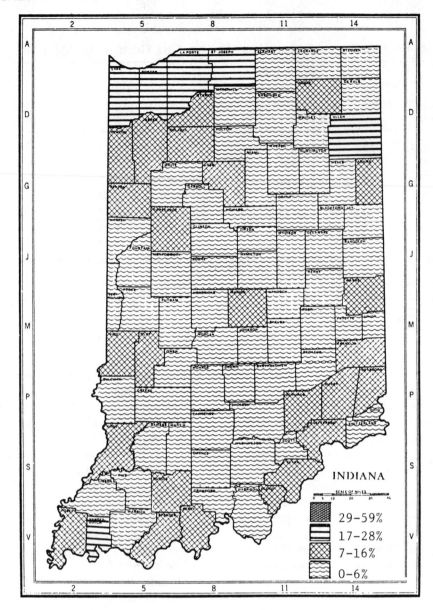

Figure 4

Percentage of Foreign-Born in Indiana, 1880
Source: U.S. Bureau of the Census, *Tenth Census of the United States, 1880,* Vol. 1: *Population* (Washington 1883), 501–503.

Microscopic analyses of the Illinois settlement patterns at the regional and county level reveal the usual channelized population flows and spatial clustering that migration scholars have come to expect. Certain Illinois counties or blocks of counties attracted a disproportionate number of immigrants from particular southern source areas. Tennessee and Kentucky links were very pronounced in southern Illinois; and New England, New York, and Ohio migration fields can be found in the Illinois Military Tract and elsewhere. Even long-distance channels existed. For example, Germans from two North Carolina counties were concentrated in Union County, Illinois, in the 1820s and 1830s.[35]

Given these initial settlement patterns, Illinois, like Indiana and Ohio, for generations was polarized culturally between southern traditionalists and Yankee modernizers. The southerners practiced subsistence agriculture and "rejected reform or innovation of any sort," according to Richard Jensen, but the Yankees engaged in commercial farming and, through their "ambition, hard work, and shrewd bargains," became the leading industrial and financial entrepreneurs of the state. By 1870, Yankee farmers were worth fifty per-

Table 2

Foreign-Born Population in the Old Northwest, 1880, by State

Nativity	Ohio	%	Ind.	%	Ill.	%	Mich.	%	Wisc.	%	United States
Austria	1,681 (0.4)	4.3	511 (0.4)	1.3	2,608 (0.4)	6.7	1,025 (0.3)	2.6	4,601 (1.1)	11.9	38,663 (0.5)
Belgium	754 (0.2)	4.5	503 (0.4)	3.2	1,464 (0.2)	9.4	979 (0.2)	6.3	5,267 (1.3)	34.6	15,535 (0.2)
Bohemia	6,232 (1.6)	7.3	306 (0.2)	0.4	13,408 (2.3)	15.7	1,789 (0.5)	2.1	13,848 (3.4)	16.2	95,361 1.3
Canada	16,146 (4.1)	2.2	5,569 (3.9)	0.8	34,043 (5.8)	4.7	148,866 (38.3)	20.8	28,965 (7.1)	4.0	717,157 (10.7)
Denmark	642 (0.1)	1.0	583 (0.4)	0.9	6,029 (1.0)	9.4	3,513 (0.9)	5.5	8,797 (2.2)	13.7	64,196 (1.0)
France	10,136 (2.6)	9.5	4,473 (3.1)	4.2	8,524 (1.5)	8.0	3,203 (0.8)	3.0	2,412 (0l6)	2.2	106,971 (1.6)
Germany	192,597 (48.8)	9.8	80,756 (56.0)	4.1	235,786 (40.4)	12.0	89,085 (22.9)	4.5	184,328 (45.5)	9.4	1,966,742 (29.4)
Gr. Britain	64,340 (16.3)	7.0	14,767 (10.8)	1.6	75,859 (13.0)	8.3	54,827 (14.1)	6.0	36,150 (8.9)	3.9	917,598 (13.7)
Holland	2,455 (0.6)	4.2	1,368 (1.0)	2.3	5,012 (0.8)	8.6	17,197 (4.4)	29.6	5,698 (1.4)	9.8	58,090 (0.9)
Hungary	1,477 (0.4)	12.8	77 (0.0)	0.7	691 (0.1)	6.0	193 (0.0)	1.7	447 (0.1)	3.9	11,526 (0.2)
Ireland	78,927 (10.0)	4.3	25,741 (17.8)	1.4	117,343 (10.1)	6.3	43,413 (11.2)	2.3	41,907 (10.3)	2.3	1,854,571 (27.8)
Italy	1,064 (0.3)	8.3	198 (0.1)	0.4	1,764 (0.3)	4.0	555 (0.1)	1.2	253 (0.6)	0.6	44,230 (0.7)
Luxemb.	484 (0.1)	3.8	130 (0.1)	1.0	1,610 (0.3)	12.5	450 (0.1)	3.5	2,232 (1.6)	17.4	12,836 (0.2)
Norway	178 (0.0)	0.1	182 (0.1)	0.1	16,770 (0.3)	9.2	3,520 (0.1)	1.9	49,349 (12.2)	27.2	181,729 (2.7)
Poland	2,039 (0.5)	4.2	917 (0.6)	1.9	6,962 (1.2)	14.3	5,421 (1.4)	11.2	5,263 (1.3)	10.8	48,557 (0.7)
Russia	610 (0.2)	1.7	370 (0.3)	1.0	1,276 (0.2)	3.6	1,560 (0.4)	4.4	312 (0.1)	0.9	35,722 (0.5)
Sweden	1,186 (0.3)	0.6	3,121 (2.2)	1.6	42,415 (7.3)	21.8	9,412 (2.4)	4.8	8,138 (2.0)	4.2	194,337 (2.9)
Sweitzer	11,989 (3.0)	13.5	3,695 (2.6)	4.2	8,881 (1.5)	10.0	2,474 (0.6)	2.8	6,283 (1.6)	7.1	88,621 (1.3)
Other	2,006 (0.5)	0.8	911 (0.6)	0.4	3,131 (0.5)	1.3	1,046 (0.3)	0.4	1.175 (0.3)	0.5	237,501 (3.6)
Totals	394,943 (5.9)		144,178 (2.1)		583,576 (8.7)		388,528 (5.8)		405,425 (6.1)		6,679,943

Source: U.S. Bureau of the Census, *Compendium of the Tenth Census* (Washington 1884), I, Table XXI, 332–333; Table XXX, 482–487; Table XXXI, 499–540.

cent more than other farmers, and the wealth of southern farmers was only half the state average.[36] Yankees not only preferred Illinois above all the states in the Old Northwest, but they came to dominate the state culturally, economically, and politically. In Stewart Holbrook's words: "For every Yankee who stopped in Indiana, approximately four Yankees passed into Michigan, eight into Illinois, six into Wisconsin, half a dozen more into Minnesota."[37]

Illinois was also hospitable to foreigners, who comprised one fifth of the population between 1860 and 1880. Another two fifths were children of foreign immigrants (Table 1). As Figure 6 shows, the foreign-born were concentrated in the northern third of the state,

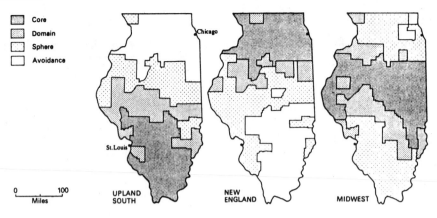

Figure 5

Native-Born Cultural Regions in Illinois, 1850
Source: Douglas K. Meyer, "Native-Born Immigrant Clusters on the Illinois Frontier," *Proceedings of the Association of American Geographers*, 8 (1976), 42. Reprinted by permission of the Association of American Geographers.

particularly in Cook, Will, and surrounding counties. Forty percent of Cook County inhabitants in 1880 were foreign-born, led by Germans (93,000) and Irish (50,000), with lesser numbers of Scandinavians, English, and Canadians. A secondary immigrant region was a five-county area around St. Louis, which was also heavily German. German farmers were dispersed along a diagonal corridor between St. Louis and Chicago. Illinois thus became the center for German-American culture, anchored in Chicago and St. Louis.[38] In 1880, Germans comprised 40 percent of the foreign-born in Illinois, Irish were 20 percent, British 13 percent, and Scandinavians (Denmark, Norway, Sweden) 11 percent (Table 2).

While the southern half of Michigan and Wisconsin became Yankeeland, the dominant settlers of the northern reaches, initially called the "Siberia of Michigan," were French Canadians from the St. Lawrence River valley. The Canadians also penetrated into the mid-sections of both states where they intermingled with Yankees. French Canadians particularly dominated the Detroit area of southeastern Michigan. As a result, a deep antagonism developed in Michigan between Yankees and Canadians. The French Catholic culture was traditional, land rooted, and convivial; the Yankee Protestants were modern, rationalist, and ascetic.[39] So Michigan had competing traditional and modern-oriented cultures that resembled the Yankee-southern rift in Illinois.

Wisconsin also had a cultural conflict between moderns and traditionals. Joseph Schafer, director of the Wisconsin Historical Society and the father of Wisconsin history, in a famous series of articles in the 1920s entitled "The Yankee and the Teuton in Wisconsin," described how the Yankees, "imaginative and space-free," were risk takers and highly mobile, eager to open large, mechanized wheat farms in the interior and to welcome new transportation improvements. The Germans, by contrast, huddled in the forests near Lake Michigan ports where they slowly "cleared" their modest-sized farms, always cautious about debt and averse to speculation. "His land was his home," said Schafer, and his ancestral estate was a "sacred trust" to be expanded but never sold. When Wisconsin wheat farming failed, Yankee farmers moved west in search of new wheat lands, but German farmers with their diversified, intensive cropping hung on and carried the state's economy until dairying cooperatives developed. The plodding turtle saved the hare from disaster.[40]

Cultural dividing lines in Michigan and Wisconsin ran along longitudinal as well as latitudinal lines. Michigan's Lake Huron region to the east was Canadian while the Lake Michigan region to the west was Yankee. In southern Wisconsin, Yankees dominated the region east of Madison to Lake Michigan while midlanders settled to the west in the Mississippi River Valley.[41] The latter was an expansion of the midland zone in northwestern Illinois stretching west across central Iowa into Kansas.[42]

Another distinct phenomenon of settlement in the northland was the higher number of foreign immigrants in the upper Great Lakes.

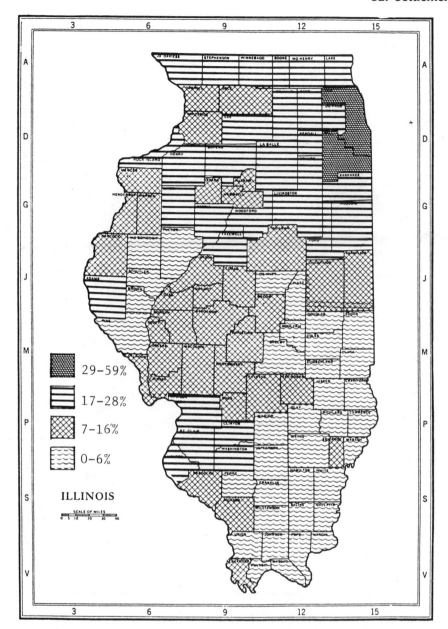

Figure 6

Percentage of Foreign-Born in Illinois, 1880
Source: U.S. Bureau of the Census, *Tenth Census of the United States, 1880,* Vol. 1: *Population* (Washington 1883), 499–501.

The frontier ran northward after 1840 because that was the cheap land area. Between 1860 and 1880 one third of Wisconsin's population and nearly one quarter of Michigan's was foreign-born. If the second generation is included, Michigan had 41 percent and Wisconsin a whopping 68 percent of its population of foreign stock (Table 1). The foreign-born in Wisconsin were spread evenly throughout the state (Figure 7). Only four counties in 1880 recorded fewer than 20 percent foreign-born. They were in the south-western corner and in the extreme north, which regions generally had fewer immigrants than in the eastern half of the state. In Michigan the foreign-born were concentrated in the "thumb area" of Lake Huron, along Saginaw Bay and the northeastern quarter, and in the Upper Peninsula (Figure 8). Germans were the dominant group in Wisconsin, as were French Canadians (and later English Canadians) in Michigan. In Wisconsin in 1880, 45 percent of all foreign-born were Germans, mainly Prussians, and in Michigan 39 percent

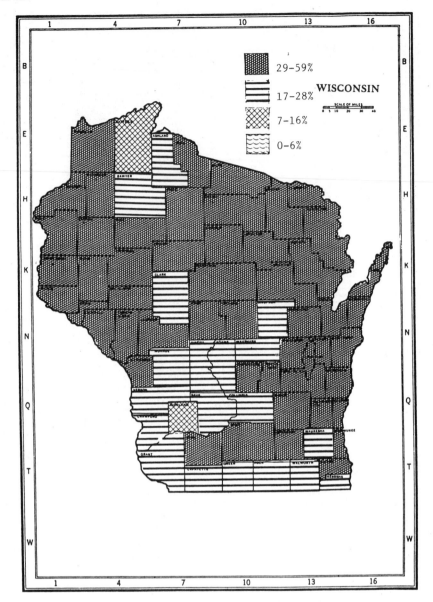

Figure 7

Percentage of Foreign-Born in Wisconsin, 1880
Source: U.S. Bureau of the Census, *Tenth Census of the United States, 1880,* Vol. 1: *Population* (Washington 1883), 537–540.

of foreigners were Canadians. Scandinavians made up the second largest group in Wisconsin at 16 percent followed by Irish at 10 percent. In Michigan, Germans ranked second (23 percent) followed by English at 14 percent and Irish at 11 percent (Table 2).

The spatial distribution of the immigrant population at the subcounty level has not been mapped over time in much of the Old Northwest.[43] In the few systematic microstudies that have been done, however, clustered ethnic settlements are readily identified. The Ohio picture, which revealed numerous little

Germanies and little Switzerlands, has already been noted (Figure 2). William Bowen's map of the dominant migrant group in each Wisconsin county, according to the 1880 census, shows Germans dominated the eastern half of the state and Scandinavians the western half.[44] Merle Curti's census analysis of Trempealeau County on the Mississippi River in southwestern Wisconsin in the mid-nineteenth century uncovered, among others, Scotch, Polish, and Norwegian communities.[45] Ronald Formisano, in his ethnocultural analyses of Michigan voting behavior in the mid-

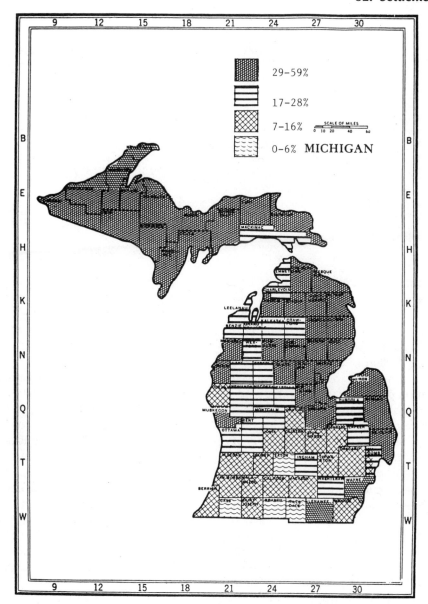

Figure 8

Percentage of Foreign-Born in Michigan, 1880
Source: U.S. Bureau of the Census, *Tenth Census of the United States, 1880,* Vol. 1: *Population* (Washington 1883), 511–512.

nineteenth century, also identified numerous ethnic settlements. Pennsylvania Germans were prominent in Addison (Oakland County), Noble (Branch County), and Bertrand (Berrien County). Old Dutch Reformed from New York were concentrated in Ridgeway and Macon (Lenawee County). Vermontville (Eaton County) was a "pure" Yankee New England town of Vermonters, while French Canadian communities were in Mendon (St. Joseph County), Ignace and Moran townships (Mackinac County), Hamtramck and Frenchtown (Monroe County), Ecorse (Wayne County),

and Ira Township (St. Clair County). The latter two were over fifty percent French Canadian.[46] George Fuller, an early Michigan historian, surveyed the population of frontier Michigan and noted numerous ethnic communities. There was a Scotch colony in Bruce township and a German colony just outside of Mt. Clemens, both in Macomb County; other Scotch colonies were at West Bloomfield and Highland and a Canadian center in Avon township, all in Lenawee County; an English colony was in Independence township (Oakland County), a Quaker colony at Penn town-

Table 3

Dutch-Born in the Old Northwest by State, 1850–1880

Year	Ill.	%	Ind.	%	Mich.	%	Ohio	%	Wisc.	%
1850	269	5.1	43	0.8	3114	59.0	398	6.6	1502	28.5
1860	1416	9.5	450	3.0	6335	42.6	1756	11.7	4906	33.0
1870	4180	16.3	837	3.3	12559	49.1	2018	7.9	5990	23.4
1880	5012	15.8	1368	4.3	17177	54.2	2455	7.7	5698	18.0

Source: Decennial U.S. population censuses, 1850–1880. The published figures for 1850 for Illinois (226), Michigan (2,542), and Wisconsin (1,157) undercount the Dutch-born by 966. The table uses figures compiled by the author from the manuscript population censuses in Robert P. Swierenga, comp., *Dutch Households in the U.S. Population Censuese, 1850, 1860, and 1870: An Alphabetical Listing by Family Heads and Singles* (Wilmington, Del., 1987).

ship (Cass County), a German Catholic village of Westphalia township (Clinton County), and others at White Pigeon and just west of Ann Arbor.[47] This recital could continue indefinitely. The Old Northwest, like so much of the northern United States, was a polyglot of transplanted communities. So regular was the inland migration process that, says John Hudson, "it is possible to predict with specified accuracy where a typical pioneer settler of a given county was born simply on the basis of the county's location."[48]

The settlement patterns of the Dutch, a group that I have studied extensively, exemplify the process of transplanting.[49] The Dutch are a relatively small group. Only 300,000 Netherlanders came to the United States in the great century of migration, 1820–1925, where they favored the Old Northwest; three times as many settled in this region as in the nation as a whole between 1870 and 1910. More than half (55 percent) of the Dutch in the United States in these years lived in the Old Northwest—their numbers increased to 60,000 in 1910. Michigan, with 33,000 Dutch-born in 1910, had almost three times more than any other state; Illinois was second with 14,000.

The Dutch were more rural than other immigrant nationalities, except Norwegians, Finns, and Danes. (The percentage rural in 1920 was, respectively, Norwegians 53, Finns and Danes 47, and Dutch 44). Grand Rapids and Chicago were the primary Dutch urban centers. Nearly 12 percent of all Dutch in the United States in 1900 lived in Grand Rapids (another 5 percent lived in nearby Muskegon and Kalamazoo), and 9 percent were in Chicago.

The Dutch immigrants in the Midwest were from the lower rungs of society who had the most to gain by leaving their homeland.

They were almost all peasant folk—rural laborers, farmers, village craftsmen, and mechanics in rural industry—who moved with their families in the hope of becoming independent farmers in America. These were people of low to middling economic status in the Netherlands; a fifth had actually been on the public dole. Religiously, 80 percent were Protestant Calvinists and 20 percent were Roman Catholics. Among the Protestants, nearly a quarter were ultra-Calvinists—Seceders from the national Reformed church who suffered bitter government suppression and social and economic discrimination. Beginning in 1846, thousands of Seceders immigrated to America for religious freedom, led by their dominies. Frequently, entire congregations migrated together. More than ten times as many Seceders departed the fatherland as their share of the population.

The Netherlanders lived mostly in clustered settlements. In 1870, 25 years after immigration began in earnest, 60 percent of all the Dutch in America lived in only 22 counties in seven midwestern and two mid-Atlantic states. The primary settlement field was within a 50-mile radius of Lake Michigan—from Muskegon, Grand Rapids, Holland, and Kalamazoo on the east shore to Chicago, Milwaukee, Sheboygan, and Green Bay on the west shore. The major colony was in southwestern Michigan, centering around the village of Holland in Ottawa County on Lake Michigan, but it soon expanded into adjacent Allegan, Kent, and Muskegon counties, as well as south to Kalamazoo County.

Because persons from the same Old Country villages preferred to settle together in order to lessen the emotional shock of leaving the homeland and to facilitate the adjustment to a new environment, provincial or local loy-

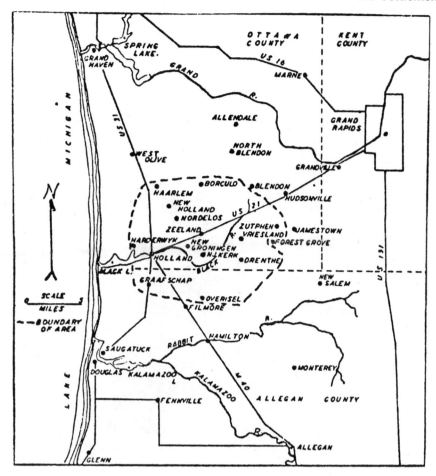

Figure 9

Area of Dutch Place Names in Kent, Allegan, and Ottawa Counties, Michigan
Source: Roger A. Leestma, "Origin of Dutch Place Names in Allegan and Ottawa Counties, Michigan," *Papers of the Michigan Academy of Science, Arts, and Letters,* 34 (1948), 147–151.

alties remained strong, at least in the early settlements. In the classic example of this phenomenon, nearly every village and town in half a dozen townships surrounding the central city of Holland boasted a Dutch place-name from the province or town where most of the first settlers originated (Figure 9). Here they spoke the local dialect, established their churches and schools, and perpetuated dress and food customs. The entire settlement was known as *de Kolonie,* but it required the passing of the first generation before the colony became a community. Dutch Reformed cultural features remain strong in this region to the present day and scholars have mapped them (see Figure 10).

In American cities and villages that predated Dutch occupancy, the new immigrants likewise clustered in neighborhoods with family and friends. In Grand Rapids, the quintessential Dutch-American large city, 40 percent of the population was of Dutch birth or ancestry in 1900—the largest proportion of Dutch in any American city over 25,000 population. Here the Dutch isolated themselves not only from the west-side Poles but even from their fellow countrymen. In the period 1850–1900, twelve distinct neighborhoods have been identified, each composed mainly of immigrants from the same villages and regions in the Netherlands. Thus, "even though each Dutch neighborhood . . . could easily be characterized as a 'little Holland' . . . it would be more precise to identify each cluster as a 'little Zeeland,' 'little Groningen,' or 'little Overijssee,'" thereby affirming the provinciality of the particular settlements."[50] Even later moves within the city were often dictated by these connections; only one fourth of the families that moved within the city left their own neighborhoods. The magnet at the center of each locality, of course, was a church where

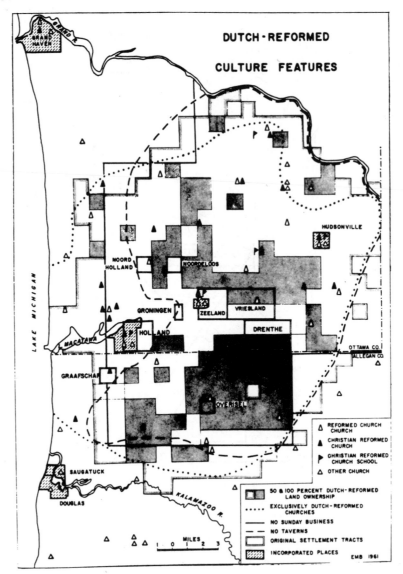

Figure 10

Dutch Reformed Cultural Features in Ottawa and Allegan Counties, 1961
Source: Elaine M. Bjorklund, "Ideology and Culture Exemplified in Southwestern Michigan," *Annals of the Association of American Geographers,* 54 (June 1964), 235. Reprinted by permission of the Association of American Geographers.

the people could worship in the old way in the Dutch language, and even be served in many instances by pastors called from their home villages in the Old Country.

The implications of this fragmentation and localism within immigrant groups such as the Dutch are only dimly perceived today. It affected political and economic as well as church life. Paul Kleppner, the noted ethnocultural political historian, discovered that in the nineteenth century Calvinist Dutch immigrants in western Michigan who were members of the Reformed church in America supported the Republican party more strongly than did Chris-

tian Reformed adherents.[51] In a full-scale furniture strike in Grand Rapids in 1911, the furniture workers, many Dutch and Polish, failed to outlast the manufacturers because they were fragmented by conflicting loyalties and thus were unable to organize themselves.[52]

The Grand Rapids pattern of voluntary fragmentation along localistic lines occurred in many other places in the 1840s and 1850s. In Chicago, immigrants from the province of Zuid-Holland located their community in the Calumet district of south Chicago, calling their village *Lage* (Low) Prairie and later South Holland. Meanwhile, other immigrants from the province of Noord-Holland planted their settlement six miles north in *Hooge* (High) Prairie (later called Roseland), while yet another group from Groningen Province established themselves nine miles away and near to the center of Chicago in a neighborhood popularly known as the *Groningsche Hoek* (Groningen Quarter). In Cleveland, where the Cuyahoga River bisects the city, Zeelanders settled in the east side and Gelderlanders on the west side. Sometimes, immigrants from only one Dutch province could be found in a given city. Milwaukee's "Dutch Hill" was populated with Gelderlanders. In Wisconsin, Frisians founded the towns of Friesland in Columbia County and New Amsterdam in LaCrosse County, Zeelanders dominated the cities of Sheboygan and Oostburg, Gelderlanders in Alto, Groningers in Gibbsville, and Catholic Noord Brabanters in Little Chute.

There was also a religious "fault line" among Dutch immigrants. Over one third of the Catholic immigrants went to the cities and larger towns along the established transportation routes to the Midwest: Cincinnati and St. Louis from the South, and Rochester, Buffalo, Cleveland, Detroit, Bay City, Chicago, Milwaukee, and Green Bay from the East.[53] These places were all Catholic centers with institutional infrastructures in place. As a result, Dutch Catholics readily worshipped and intermarried with Catholics of other nationalities, especially Germans, Belgians, and Irish. Only the cities of Cincinnati, Chicago, and Grand Rapids had parishes served by a Dutch-speaking priest in the mid to late nineteenth century. By contrast, the Dutch Calvinists maintained five hundred congregations and Dutch-language worship services were still common in the 1920s. Thus, the Dutch Catholics established only a few immigrant colonies, whereas the Calvinists, and especially the Seceders, formed enclaves wherever they settled. In short, religion helped assimilate Dutch Catholics but confirmed Dutch Calvinists in their Dutchness.

As this survey has shown, the Northwest immigrants, both foreign- and American-born, settled in clusters. The norm was homogeneous groups with traditional values and an ethnoreligious "glue" provided by their churches and schools. The more traditional the values, the more they sought to preserve the group. Fathers kept married children "close" by providing farms for sons or sons-in-law and by keeping the homestead "in the family." German, Dutch, and Scandinavian farm settlements, for example, always expanded geographically because fathers were willing to pay premium prices for nearby farms put on the market by native-born neighbors. As the adage said: "When the German comes in, the Yankee goes out." Similarly, fathers bequeathed their farms intact to one of their sons in exchange for parental care and support in retirement.[54] Thus did Old Stock farmers cling to their cherished clans. But the historical forces were against them. The remorseless rectangularity of the Land Ordinance militated against communal living in the Old World style, in favor of individual farmsteads strung out along the section-line roads. The Northwest Ordinance and Constitution recognized persons and their rights but groups are invisible in American jurisprudence. Above all, the forces of urbanization and industrial growth, with their promises of higher living standards off the farm, proved irresistible.

Migrants who settled in colonies were also pressured to intermingle and diffuse, especially by their American neighbors. As one early Illinois leader, George Flower, wrote in an 1830s tract, *The Error of Emigrants:* "The idea of forming exclusive settlements of Germans, English, or Irish is very erroneous and highly prejudicial to the interests of the settlers themselves."[55] Flower thought immigrants needed to intermix in order to learn the best ways of living on the frontier; group settlement hindered rather than enhanced their chances of success. The editors of the *Illinois Journal* (Springfield) in 1849 expressed the prevailing wisdom: "When foreigners come to our country . . . they should become Americanized as soon as possible and this can never be done if they are located in isolated communities."[56]

Despite these admonitions, the European immigrants, like the New England Yankees and Pennsylvania Germans, preferred transplanting their "covenanted communities" centered around church, schoolhouse, and meeting house.[57] Eventually individualism triumphed over communalism, but even today, after 150 years, many ethnoreligious communities proudly cling to their traditions. The Old Northwest, despite its monotonous topography, never was a featureless cultural plain. Rather it was an ethnic mosaic of amazing richness and diversity, created under the institutional umbrella of the "Trinity of Revolutionary Testaments" of 1785 and 1787.[58] This is one of the bicentennial legacies we celebrate.

Notes

1. Jeremy Atack and Fred Bateman, *To Their Own Soil: Agriculture in the Antebellum North* (Ames, Iowa 1987), 72.
2. Richard K. Vedder and Lowell E. Gallaway estimate migration rates as follows: 1800–1810, 382%; 1810–1820, 148%; 1820–1830, 43%; 1830–1840, 58%; 1840–1850, 17%; 1850–1860, 19%. See Vedder and Gallaway, "Migration and the Old Northwest" in David C. Klingaman and Richard K. Vedder, eds., *Essays in Nineteenth Century Economic History: The Old Northwest* (Athens, Ohio 1975), 161 (Table 1), 166.
3. Jack Ericson Eblen, *The First and Second United States Empires: Governors and Territorial Government, 1784–1912* (Pittsburgh 1968); Robert F. Berkhofer, Jr., "The Northwest Ordinance and the Principle of Territorial Evolution," in John Porter Bloom, ed., *The American Territorial System* (Athens, Ohio 1973), 45–55 (the Jefferson quotation is at page 50). Reginald Horsman offers a more positive view in "Thomas Jefferson and the Ordinance of 1784," *Illinois Historical Journal*, 79 (Summer 1986), 99–112, esp. 111–112.
4. A fresh interpretation is Peter S. Onuf, *Statehood and Union: A History of the Northwest Ordinance* (Bloomington and Indianapolis 1987); and Onuf, *The Origins of the Federal Republic: Jurisdictional Controversies in the United States, 1775–1787* (Philadelphia 1983). As Paul Finkelman has argued, the slavery ban was not iron-clad during the territorial period, especially in Illinois Territory. See Finkelman, "Slavery and the Northwest Ordinance: A Study in Ambiguity," *Journal of the Early Republic*, 6 (Winter 1986), 343–370. For a contrasting view that stresses the ideological consequences of the free soil proviso, see David Brion Davis, "The Significance of Excluding Slavery from the Old Northwest in 1787," *Indiana Magazine of History*, 84 (Mar. 1988), 75–89, esp. 83–87. This entire issue is devoted to articles analyzing the Northwest Ordinance.
5. Other factors were climate, fertile soils, and the prominence of the New York port of entry and the Erie Canal route inland.
6. Northwest Territory Celebration Commission, *History of the Ordinance of 1787 and the Old Northwest Territory* (Marietta, Ohio 1937), 75.
7. Joseph Schafer, "Editorial Comment: Peopling the Middle West," *Wisconsin Magazine of History*, 21 (Sept. 1937), 100.
8. William N. Parker, "From Northwest to Midwest: Social Bases of a Regional History," in Klingaman and Vedder, eds., *Essays in Nineteenth Century Economic History*, 3–34.
9. Kathleen Neils Conzen, "Historical Approaches to the Study of Rural Ethnic Communities," in Frederick C. Luebke, ed., *Ethnicity on the Great Plains* (Lincoln, Neb. 1980), 1–18; Frederick C. Luebke, "Ethnic Group Settlement on the Great Plains," *Western Historical Quarterly*, 8 (Oct. 1977), 405–430.
10. Wilbur Zelinsky, *The Cultural Geography of the United States* (Englewood Cliffs, N. J. 1973), 26.
11. Geographer Robert D. Mitchell developed the theory of seaboard culture hearths and traced their interior expansion into the trans-Appalachian west in "The Formation of Early American Cultural Regions: An Interpretation" in James R. Gibson, ed., *European Settlement and Development in North America: Essays in Honour and Memory of Andrew Hill Clark* (Toronto and Buffalo 1978), 66–90.
12. James M. Bergquist, "Tracing the Origins of a Midwestern Culture: The Case of Central Indiana," *Indiana Magazine of History*, 77 (Mar. 1981), 1–32; William A. Bowen, "American Ethnic Regions, 1880," *Proceedings of the Association of American Geographers*, 8 (1976), 44–46; Edwin Scott Gaustad, *Historical Atlas of Religion in America* (New York 1976); Henry Glassie, *Pattern in the Material Folk Culture of the Eastern United States* (Philadelphia 1968); John C. Hudson, "North American Origins of Middlewestern Frontier Populations," *Annals of the Association of American Geographers*, 78 (Sept. 1988), 395–413; John C. Hudson, "Yankeeland in the Middle West," *Journal of Geography*, 85 (Sept./Oct. 1986), 195–205; John C. Hudson, "Cultural Geography and the Upper Great Lakes Region," *Journal of Cultural Geography*, 5 (Fall/Winter 1984), 19–32; Elfrieda Lang, "An Analysis of Northern Indiana's Population in 1850," *Indiana Magazine of History*, 49 (Mar. 1953), 17–60; Elfrieda Lang, "Ohioans in Northern Indiana before 1850," *Indiana Magazine of History*, 49 (Dec. 1953), 392–404; Elfrieda Lang, "Southern Migration to Northern Indiana Before 1850," *Indiana Magazine of History*, 50 (Dec. 1954), 349–356; Douglas K. Meyer, "Illinois Culture Regions at Mid-Nineteenth Century," *Bulletin of the Illinois Geographical Society*, 18 (Dec. 1976), 3–13; Douglas K. Meyer, "Native-Born Immigrant Clusters on the Illinois Frontier," *Proceedings of the Association of American Geographers*, 8 (1976), 41–44; Douglas K. Meyer, "Southern Illinois Migration Fields: The Shawnee Hills in 1850," *The Professional Geographer*, 28 (May 1976), 151–160; Douglas K. Meyer, "Immigrant Clusters in the Illinois Military Tract," *Pioneer America: The Journal of Historic American Material Culture*, 12 (May 1980), 97–112; Gregory S. Rose, "Hoosier Origins: The Nativity of Indiana's United States-Born Population in 1850," *Indiana Magazine of History*, 81 (Sept. 1985), 201–232; Gregory S. Rose, "Information Sources for Nineteenth Century Midwestern Migration," *The Professional Geographer*, 37 (Feb. 1985), 66–72; Gregory S. Rose, "Upland Southerners: The County Origins of Southern Migrants to Indiana by 1850," *Indiana Magazine of History*, 82 (Sept. 1986), 242–263; Hubert G.H. Wilhelm, *The Origin and Distribution of Settlement Groups: Ohio, 1850* (Athens, Ohio 1982).
13. Zelinsky, *Cultural Geography*, 28–33.
14. Richard H. Steckel, "The Economic Foundations of East-West Migration during the 19th Century," *Explorations in Economic History*, 20 (Jan. 1983), 14–36; Atack and Bateman, *To Their Own Soil*, 73–76.
15. John S. Macdonald and Leatrice D. Macdonald, "Chain Migration, Ethnic Neighborhood Formation and Social Networks," *Milbank Memorial Fund Quarterly*, 42 (Jan. 1964), 82–97; Atack and Bateman, *To Their Own Soil*, 75–76.
16. Robert M. Taylor, Jr., "The Olin Tribe: Migration, Mutual Aid, and Solidarity of a Nineteenth Century Rural American Kin Group" (Ph.D. diss., Kent State University 1979), 24–86.
17. Stewart H. Holbrook, *The Yankee Exodus: An Account of Migration from New England* (New York 1950), 119. Another example is the Union colony of twenty-two Vermont farm families who settled in Vermontville, Branch County, Michigan, in 1836. *Ibid.*, 79–81.
18. Richard Lyle Power, *Planting Corn Belt Culture: The Impress of the Upland Southerner and Yankee in the Old Northwest* (Indianapolis 1953); Joseph Schafer, "The Yankee and the Teuton in Wisconsin," *Wisconsin Magazine of History*, 6 (1922), 125–145; 6 (1923), 261–279, 386–402; 7 (1923), 3–19, 148–171; Ronald P. Formisano, *The Birth of Mass Political Parties: Michigan, 1827–1861* (Princeton 1971); George Newman Fuller, *Economic and Social Beginnings of Michigan: A Study of the Settlement of the Lower Peninsula During the Territorial Period, 1805–1837* (Lansing 1916), 95–183.
19. Robert P. Swierenga, "Ethnicity and American Agriculture," *Ohio History*, 89 (Summer 1980), 323–344.
20. John F. Rooney, Jr., Wilbur Zelinsky, and Dean R. Louder, eds., *This Remarkable Continent: An Atlas of United States and Canadian Society and Cultures* (College Station, Tex. 1982), 10–11; Zelinsky, *Cultural Geography*, 117–129. See also Mitchell, "Formation of

Early American Cultural Regions" 72–74, who developed the concept of regional "way stations" or intermediate areas in the earliest trans-Appalachian frontiers after 1776, where pioneer settlers experienced cultural fusions which they later brought into the Ohio country. Such way stations are the "Burned Over" District of western New York and northeastern Ohio and the Middle Ohio Valley of southwestern Ohio.

21. A detailed map showing the major transportation routes to frontier Indiana is in Rose, "Hoosier Origins," 227.
22. I deliberately omit Afro-Americans, who comprised a major immigrant group that dominated several southern states and had a sizable presence in the mid-Atlantic states.
23. Wilhelm, *Settlement Groups: Ohio*, 13–15, 56–66.
24. Robert E. Chaddock, *Ohio Before 1850: A Study of the Early Influence of Pennsylvania and Southern Populations in Ohio*, vol. 31, no. 2 of *Columbia University Studies in History, Economics and Public Law* (New York 1908), 46, 40.
25. Hudson, "Middlewestern Frontier Populations," 403.
26. Wilhelm, *Settlement Groups: Ohio*, 47–48.
27. *Ibid.*, 93–94.
28. Eugene H. Roseboom and Francis P. Weisenburger, eds., *A History of Ohio* (Columbus 1967), 115; Chaddock, *Ohio Before 1850*, 41.
29. Wilhelm, *Settlement Groups: Ohio*, 80.
30. Rose, "Hoosier Origins," 205.
31. *Ibid.*, 212, 214.
32. Bergquist, "Tracing the Origins of a Midwestern Culture," 10–11.
33. Meyer, "Southern Illinois Migration Fields," 151, citing Solon J. Buck, *Illinois in 1818* (Springfield, Ill. 1918), who based his estimate on data in county histories.
34. Meyer, "Southern Illinois Migration Fields," 153; John Hudson, "Yankeeland in the Middle West," 195–205.
35. Meyer, "Illinois Culture Regions," 7–9; Meyer, "Southern Illinois Migration Fields," 154–157; Meyer, "Immigrant Clusters in the Illinois Military Tract," 106–109.
36. Richard J. Jensen, *Illinois: A Bicentennial History* (New York 1978), 51, 48.
37. Holbrook, *Yankee Exodus*, 64, but unfortunately there is no documentation.
38. Jensen, *Illinois*, 49–50.
39. Formisano, *Birth of Mass Political Parties*, 179; Fuller, *Economic and Social Beginnings of Michigan*, 95–183.
40. Schafer, "The Yankee and the Teuton," 6 (1922–1923), 142–145, 276–277.
41. R. Carlyle Buley, *The Old Northwest: Pioneer Period, 1815–1840* (2 vols., Indianapolis 1950), II, 92, 142; Hudson, "Cultural Geography and the Upper Great Lakes Region," 22–30.
42. Hudson, "Yankeeland in the Middle West," 196 (Figure 1).
43. Zelinsky, *Cultural Geography*, 32–33, 133–134. Mapping the rural ethnic neighborhoods, says Zelinsky (134), "remains an imposing agenda of unfinished business." But John Hudson's innovative "isothermic" statistical mapping of birthplace data derived from a large sample of midwestern county histories and biographical directories holds out the promise of such

detailed mapping. See Hudson, "North American Origins," for the most extensive application of this technique.
44. Bowen, "American Ethnic Regions, 1880," 45 (Figure 1).
45. Merle Curti, *The Making of an American Community: A Case Study of Democracy in a Frontier County* (Stanford 1959), 91–96.
46. Formisano, *Birth of Mass Political Parties*, 168–173.
47. Fuller, *Economic and Social Beginnings in Michigan*, 183–185, 238–242, 301–304, 362–363.
48. Hudson, "Middlewestern Frontier Populations," 412.
49. Robert P. Swierenga, "Exodus Netherlands, Promised Land America: Dutch Immigration and Settlement in the United States," in J. W. Schulte Nordholt and Robert P. Swierenga, eds., *A Bilateral Bicentennial: A History of Dutch-American Relations, 1782–1982* (New York and Amsterdam 1982), 127–147; Swierenga, "Dutch Immigration Patterns in the Nineteenth and Twentieth Centuries," in Swierenga, ed., *The Dutch in America: Immigration, Settlement, and Cultural Change* (New Brunswick, N. J. 1985), 15–42; Swierenga, "Religion and Immigration Patterns: A Comparative Analysis of Dutch Protestants and Catholics, 1835–1880," *Journal of American Ethnic History*, 5 (Spring 1986), 23–45; Henry S. Lucas, *Netherlanders in America: Dutch Immigration to the United States and Canada, 1789–1950* (Ann Arbor 1955); Jacob Van Hinte, *Netherlanders in America: A Study of Emigration and Settlement in the Nineteenth and Twentieth Centuries in the United States of America*, ed. Robert P. Swierenga (Grand Rapids, Mich. 1985).
50. David G. Vanderstel, "Dutch Immigrant Neighborhood Development in Grand Rapids, 1850–1900," in Swierenga, ed., *The Dutch in America*, 131.
51. Paul Kleppner, *The Cross of Culture: A Social Analysis of Midwestern Politics, 1850–1900* (New York 1970), 58–61; Kleppner, *The Third Electoral System, 1853–1892: Parties, Voters, and Political Cultures* (Chapel Hill 1979), 166–170.
52. Jeffrey D. Kleiman, "The Great Strike: Religion, Labor and Reform in Grand Rapids, Michigan, 1890–1916" (Ph.D. diss., Michigan State University 1985). The Dutch also divided over political reform. When the city adopted a commission-city manager form of government in 1916, the first generation Dutch on the southwest side strongly opposed it, but the second generation Dutch on the southeast side supported it.
53. Swierenga, "Religion and Immigration Patterns," 36–40.
54. Mark Friedberger, "The Farm Family and the Inheritance Process: Evidence from the Corn Belt, 1870–1950," *Agricultural History*, 57 (Jan. 1983), 1–13.
55. Cited in Buley, *Old Northwest*, II, 105.
56. Quoted in Don Harrison Doyle, *The Social Order of a Frontier Community: Jacksonville, Illinois, 1825–70* (Urbana 1978), 119.
57. Page Smith develops this concept of "covenanted communities" in *As a City Upon a Hill: The Town in American History* (New York 1966).
58. John P. Bloom, "The Continental Nation—Our Trinity of Revolutionary Testaments," *Western Historical Quarterly*, 6 (Jan. 1975), 5.

Italian Americans as a Cognizable Racial Group

Dominic R. Massaro

Dominic Massaro is a Justice of the Supreme Court of New York. A "Grande Ufficiale della Repubblica Italiana," he is chairman emeritus of The Conference of Presidents of Major Italian-American Organizations. In 1991 his treatise, Cesare Beccaria—The Father of Criminal Justice: His Impact on Anglo-American Jurisprudence *(Prescia: International UP, 1991), garnered Italy's International Dorso Prize. Justice Massaro is the representative of the American Judges Association to the United Nations.*

Italian Americans are a cognizable racial group for purposes of the scope and application of civil rights laws. This view is confirmed by the sophistication of sociological definition and historical evidence, which is grounded in legal analysis and judicial interpretation. There are a number of citations, quotes, and references to which I will allude, including a limited amount of previous scholarship. Let me note at the onset that Italian Americans, more often than not, take umbrage at being defined as a minority group. Yet, a review of the relevant case law suggests that in no other manner can they hope for success in advancing legal claims that allege discrimination on the basis of national origin. Traditionally, civil rights legislation has provided virtually no protection against this form of discrimination. But the decision in *Scelsa v. the City University of New York* (CUNY) decided last November in Federal District Court in Manhattan— hereinafter referred to as *Scelsa*—accents the slow but steady erosion of the artificial distinction between "race" and "national origin" that has heretofore given rise to ethnic minorities, including Italian Americans, receiving "different treatment under the law, as written or applied."

As an aside, you should be aware of what lies behind my view of *Scelsa*. In my position [as] Human Rights Commissioner, and in response to a growing number of complaints, I threatened mandamus against CUNY in November 1971; that is, I mandated that it release a statistical breakdown of Americans of Italian descent employed throughout the university system. Twenty years later, while on the bench as a non-partisan choice, I

was invited to chair the Legislative Advisory Committee on Urban Public Higher Education. The Committee's central charge was to investigate and suggest redress for discrimination against Italian Americans at CUNY. Its final report, rendered 12 September 1991, contained a series of recommendations utilizing the special expertise of CUNY's Italian American Institute aimed at "underscor[ing] the University's commitment to the richness of diversity." Within a year, as the *Scelsa* Court observed that CUNY sought "to sever the outreach, counseling and research aspects of the Institute . . . [and] shunt aside its Director."

However, what I found particularly disturbing was that, despite two intervening decades, only negligible changes had been made to remedy the woeful underrepresentation of Italian Americans in the work force. The release of these earlier statistics became the underpinning for critical reportage, academic study, the designation of Italian Americans as an affirmative action category by CUNY (the so-called Kibbee Memorandum), and legislative inquiry. The latter culminated in public hearings and provided the backdrop for the establishment of the John D. Calandra Italian American Institute of CUNY in 1979.

From a purely legal perspective, *Scelsa* presents us with a precedent-making judicial grant of extraordinary relief to Italian Americans; not only did the case galvanize Italian-American organizations, it placed the Italian American Legal Defense and Higher Education Fund that handled the action in the forefront of civil rights activity. By its very nature, injunctive relief is an extraordinary remedy; it is grounded in equity; that is, it is responsive to the demands of justice and right conscience. The manner in which it was granted and the fact that it was granted by the *Scelsa* Court is significant. A colleague stated it rather succinctly; namely, that the decision "is a delight to those who are sympathetic to the plaintiffs' position and a nightmare to those favoring the defendants."

The petitioner, Dr. Joseph V. Scelsa, filed the action in both an individual and representative capacity (as director of the Calandra Institute). As dual plaintiff, he sought to bar CUNY from accomplishing three things: (1) "from employment discrimination against Italian Americans";

(2) "from relocating the Institute and transferring its operations to several different units of CUNY"; and (3) from removing him as the Institute's director. At the heart of his brief was the averment of discrimination in employment on the basis of national origin. The statutory prohibition against this type of discrimination is specifically proscribed by Title VII of the Civil Rights Act of 1964. Notwithstanding, the prohibition has been largely ignored by the courts and rarely used with success by plaintiffs seeking redress on this ground.

The *Scelsa* Court granted all three requests (or prayers as we say) by way of a preliminary injunction *pendente lite*; that is, pending trial, it barred CUNY from acting so as to prevent the further perpetration of a perceived wrong(s) until such time as the underlying issues are resolved. It concluded that the plaintiffs (Dr. Scelsa and the Institute) had "shown a balance of hardships tipping decidedly in their favor" and "irreparable harm" would otherwise follow. Significantly, the Court allowed Dr. Scelsa, equating his position as director of the Calandra Institute with representation of the Italian-American community of New York City, to cross the litigation threshold to test the merits of the case. In doing so, the Court relied not only on the so-called "disparate impact" theory of Title VII, wherein a discriminatory effect may be shown vis-à-vis employment patterns, but, *sua sponte*: by its own initiative, it also invoked Section 1981 of the Civil Rights Act of 1866, our nation's first civil rights statute for jurisdictional purposes.

This Reconstruction era statute is far wider in scope than Title VII. It concerns the right to make and enforce both private and public contracts and provides broad federal remedies for the enjoyment of all benefits of a contractual relationship. The Court noted that "in grant-[ing injunctive] relief to which the party in whose favor it is rendered is entitled," it may do so on such grounds "even if the party has not [specifically] demanded such relief in the party's pleading." Section 1981 was not pleaded in the moving papers. But the Court raised CUNY's two-decade-old awareness of Italian-American nonrepresentation and the university's pledge(s) to address and seek to correct this imbalance to the level of a contractual relationship with the Italian-American community. It noted:

A Section 1981 violation may be established not only via presentation of evidence regarding defendant's affirmative acts but also by evidence regarding defendant's omission where defendant is under some duty to act. . . . The Court must find that CUNY's current policy represents either an attempt to renege on the promises of the past or, by denying that such promises were ever made or intended to be kept, a reaffirmation of the original findings of discrimination against an under-representation of Italian Americans that motivated the original Kibbee Memorandum. . . .

Cited by the *Scelsa* Court is a case entitled *St. Francis College v. Al-Khazraj*, which was decided by the United States Supreme Court five years earlier in 1987. This also

is significant. Due to the representative conferral granted to Dr. Scelsa because of the Calandra Institute's wider purposes, the citation espouses, on a stage even larger than employment, an opportunity for Italian Americans as a group to redress harms arising out of national origin discrimination. Discrimination on the basis of national origin has always been, and sadly continues to be, a destructive force in American society. As such, it is indistinguishable from racial discrimination. Notwithstanding, modern day civil rights legislation expressly prohibiting discrimination based on "race, color, religion, sex or national origin," has not been interpreted either administratively or judicially to afford protection to these victims of national origin discrimination. The clear and unambiguous language set forth in Title VII as advanced in *Scelsa* states that failure by an employer because of national origin "to hire . . . or otherwise to discriminate against any individual with respect to his compensation, terms, conditions, or privileges of employment" is an unlawful employment practice. Yet the Act has a history of selective enforcement and it would appear that claims of national origin discrimination—either dismissed on procedural grounds or on the merits—have met with failure. A review of the regulations charting compliance with Title VII reveal that, notwithstanding the clear reference to "national origin," redress has primarily been defined within the context of racial classification for governmental purposes. Neither racial minorities nor ethnic minorities (including Italian Americans) have "melted" into Anglo conformity. Sociologists generally agree that thus far in the American saga, "acculturation" and not "structural assimilation" has proven to be the norm; and the diversity inherent in "cultural pluralism" has persisted well into the third, even the fourth generation. Public policy misconception of the process continues to ignore this reality, and the legal definition of minority continues for practical purposes to be synonymous with skin color.

In light of this, no governmental compilation of ethnic data is either required or taken; thus, legal writers rightly contend that is all but impossible to prove the existence of discrimination based on national origin. Therefore, Italian Americans who are victims of discrimination must try to prove their case without the benefit of officially compiled statistics—an overwhelming task given essential Title VII procedural requirements. The need for statistical analysis in order to fulfill the initial legal burden of going forward to establish what we term a *prima facie* case was noted in *Scelsa*; nor did CUNY, despite good faith promises extracted in the 1970s to do so, maintain ongoing data on Italian-American recruitment and employment for affirmative action purposes. However, and in view of this failure, two statistical studies compiled by the plaintiff, Calandra Institute, were deemed "the best available evidence" by the Court. The *Scelsa* Court went further. By adopting the conception of race set forth in *St. Francis College* under the 1866 law, it eased the way toward addressing not only employment but an array of civil rights violations alleging national origin discrimination against Italian Americans by CUNY.

The Civil Rights Act of 1866 was an enabling statute for the Thirteenth Amendment. This post-Civil War enactment intended to confer the equality "enjoyed by white citizens" of the time—the white majoritarian Anglo or Nordic "race" then populating the country, the standard control group, if you will—upon all other persons and in all respects. The Supreme Court's decision in *St. Francis College*, relying on the 1866 Act, significantly expanded the definition of "race" for purposes that can find and have found expression in the modern day search for equal protection under the law by those claiming national origin discrimination.

In *St. Francis College*, the Court held that a white person may be protected from racial discrimination. It based its holding on a broad construction of the original intent of Section 1981 of the 1866 Act. Section 1981 of the Act states: "All Persons . . . shall have the same right . . . to make and enforce contracts . . . and to the full and equal benefit of all laws and proceedings. . . ." The Court rejected the counter argument that a Caucasian was barred from suing other Caucasians under the statute. Instead, relying heavily on the legislative history of Section 1981 and on the general conception of race during the nineteenth century when the statute was enacted, it observed:

> [It] may be that a variety of ethnic groups . . . are now considered to be within the Caucasian race. The understanding of "race" in the nineteenth century, however was different. Plainly, all those who might be deemed Caucasian today were not thought to be of the same race at the time Section 1981 became law.

In support of this reasoning, the Court examined two strands of evidence from the nineteenth century: dictionary and encyclopedia definitions of "race" and the legislative history of Section 1981. In considering nineteenth-century definitions of race, Webster's dictionary of 1877 proved insightful: "[t]he descendants of a common ancestor; a family, tribe, people or nation, believed or presumed to belong to the same stock." The Court also listed "races" found in nineteenth-century encyclopedias: the *Encyclopedia Americana* (1858) and the *Encyclopedia Britannica* (1878) that *inter alia* referred to "Italians" and various other ethnic "races." Similarly, a review of the legislative history of Section 1981 proved convincing to the Court. It too was "replete with references to the universality of its application"; that is, to all ethnic "races." This, combined with the nineteenth-century concept of race as illustrated by reference materials of the period, formed the foundation for the Court's holding:

> Based on the history of Section 1981, we have little trouble in concluding that Congress intended to protect from discrimination identifiable classes of persons who are subjected to intentional discrimination solely because of their ancestry or ethnic characteristics. Such discrimination is racial discrimination that Congress intended Sec-

tion 1981 to forbid, whether or not it would be classified as racial in terms of modern scientific theory.

The Court's opinion specifically rejected reliance on genetics and/or physical characteristics:

> It is clear from our holding that a distinctive physiognomy is not essential to qualify for Section 1981 protection.

In making this finding, the Court defined the word "race" in its sociological, perhaps sociopolitical, rather than biological sense. "Race" in the sociological sense considers the concept that people differ from each other not primarily because of physical attributes, but because of differences rooted in culture. A review of the legislative history of the Act reveals that its supporters intended that its protection be liberally construed, encompassing the civil liberties of all persons without distinction as between race and national origin. Interestingly, the Court's research disclosed that only in this century have "races" been divided physiognomically, that is, "Caucasoid," "Mongoloid" and "Negroid," footnoting that many modern biologists and anthropologists . . . criticize [these] classifications as arbitrary and of little use in understanding the viability of human beings."

The *Scelsa* Court found that "[d]iscrimination on the basis of national origin is encompassed within the scope of activities prohibited by Section 1981." Italian Americans have benefited from this revised standard on a number of occasions prior to *Scelsa*, although not with the same potential for a sweeping remedy. The District of Maine in *DeSalle v. Key Bank of Southern Maine* in 1988 was the first Court to hold that Italian Americans are an identifiable class entitled to maintain an action under Section 1981 for purposes of discrimination. In *DeSalle*, the plaintiff had sued his former employer, alleging breach of contract and violation of civil rights on the basis of his Italian heritage. In accordance with *St. Francis College*, the Court held that discrimination based on a plaintiffs ancestry was actionable as a civil rights claim under Section 1981. The Court highlighted the references in *St. Francis College* to various ethnic "races." It concluded:

> The definition of race in the nineteenth century, when the legislative sources for Section 1981 were enacted, differed from the definition prevalent today; not all Caucasians were considered of the same race. . . . Section 1981 was designed to protect identifiable classes of persons, such as Italo-Americans, "who are subjected to intentional discrimination solely because of their ancestry or ethnic characteristics. . . ."

In one of the few cases where a plaintiff prevailed on the merits is a 1989 national origin discrimination case. The Ninth Circuit, which is based in San Francisco, held in *Benigni v. City of Hemet* that Italian Americans are protected against discrimination for purposes of a companion Section 1982 of the 1866 Act, which concerns the right to hold property. The plaintiff, an owner of a restaurant, had obtained a jury verdict claiming that the defendant's police officers had discriminatorily harassed his business and customers forcing him to sell his business at a loss. The Court of appeals, in upholding the verdict, agreed:

> Elements of an intentional discrimination claim . . . are present in this case because the evidence tends to show the discriminatory effect of greater law enforcement activity at [the plaintiffs business] than at other bars, and the discriminatory intent of singling out Benigni based on his Italian ancestry.

The Court cited *St. Francis College* for the interrelated proposition: "targets of race discrimination for purposes of Section 1981 include groups that today are considered merely different ethnic or national groups.

In another context, the Supreme Court has ruled that peremptory challenges in jury selection may not be used to further racially discriminatory motives. Under existing case law, a defendant must establish that he is "a member of a cognizable racial group" to make a *prima facie* or initial showing of discriminatory peremptory challenges. In 1989, *United States v. Biaggi* treated the issue. A motion to set aside a verdict on the ground that the prosecution had used its peremptory challenges discriminatorily to exclude Italian Americans from the jury was brought. In his moment of defeat, Mario Biaggi, the senior United States Congressman from New York City, provided yet another service to an Italian-American constituency that extended well beyond the confines of his congressional district. Relying on characteristic Italian names ending in vowels to make the claim, it was argued that the prosecution had exercised certain peremptory challenges solely to strike potential Italian-American jurors. The Court held that Italian Americans constitute a "cognizable racial group" for purposes of raising objections to this form of challenge. The *Biaggi* decision followed two strands of reasoning: The first traced the meaning of "racially cognizable group"; the second traced the meaning of this term in light of *St. Francis College*. As to the first strand, the Court found:

> Italian Americans are "recognizable" and "distinct." and appear to have been "singled out for different treatment under the laws, as written or applied. . . ." Italian Americans share a common ancestry in Italy, a common cultural and religious heritage here and there, and they often still share a common language. They are identifiable, in part, by their characteristic last names. The Court takes judicial notice that Italian Americans are considered in this district to be a recognizable and distinct ethnic group, commonly identified by their last names and by their neighborhoods. These qualities are sufficient to render Italian Americans no less cognizable than the other groups who have already been recognized for equal protection purposes.

The Court referred to three criteria useful in finding Italian Americans a cognizable racial group. They "(1) are definable and limited by some clearly identifiable factor; (2) share a common thread of attitudes, ideas or experiences; and (3) share a community of interests, such that the group's interests cannot be adequately represented if the group is excluded from the jury selection process."

Limiting its holding to the Eastern District of New York, which is based in Brooklyn, the Court held that Italian Americans satisfy these criteria to make "a sufficient showing to categorize [themselves] as cognizable." Moreover, it provided a detailed and illuminating discussion of its reasons for taking judicial notice of Italian Americans' cognizability:

> These observable, distinguishable names constitute a clearly identifiable factor separating Italian Americans from most other ethnic groups. These names emanate from Italian ancestors who immigrated to this country and who constitute a discrete resource from which Italian-American heritage has been passed down.
>
> Italian Americans share a common experience and background in their links to Italian families, Italian culture, and Italian group loyalties, and often share the same religious and culinary practices. The Court takes judicial notice that Italians have been subject to stereotyping, invidious ethnic humor and discrimination. (" . . . Italians . . . continue to be excluded from executive, middle-management, and other job levels because of discrimination based upon their religion and/or national origin"). . . . Like any group recently emigrated from a cohesive nation, Italian Americans share numerous common *threads* of attitudes, ideas, and experiences, often including largely intertwined family relations in the country of origin. Finally, Italian Americans have a community of interest; they generally share certain cherished values received through generations of Italian civilization and religion, including values relevant to moral culpability. Across the board exclusion of this group could not but impair the representation of these interests in juries.

Having concluded that Italian Americans are a cognizable racial group, the Court recounted *St. Francis College's* review of the nineteenth-century scholarly definitions of race and the legislative history of the 1866 Act. As to this second strand of reasoning, it found that the [l]egislative history of post-Civil War statutes provides corroborative support for the view that, at that time, "races" included "immigrant groups" coming from each foreign nation and, further, "[i]t can therefore be confidently concluded that . . . *cognizable racial groups* include[s] a variety of ethnic and ancestral groups subject to intentional discrimination, including Italian Americans."

The *Biaggi* decision has since been cited with approval. Although the Court did accept the prosecution's racially neutral explanations for exercising the peremptory challenges, and denied the motion to set aside the guilty verdict, the decision is still crucial. It admirably recognizes discrimination against Italian Americans in various aspects of American society. Additionally, it highlights for us that as an ethnic group, "Italian Americans are also shielded by the [Fourteenth Amendment's] equal protection clause's prohibition against discrimination because of ancestry."

In sum, Section 1981 grounds for seeking relief in cases of national origin discrimination illustrate a definite trend; namely, an expanded equal protection jurisprudence where race can be and, in fact, has been equated with ethnicity, or national origin. The Section provides an effective vehicle where injustice or inequity prevails against ethnic minorities. Moreover, Section 1981 filings are neither limited to the employment arena nor burdened with detailed procedural requirements that are a prerequisite to filings under modern-day civil rights legislation. Ethnics who have suffered discrimination as a result of their national origin in any area, would be well served in seeking judicial solicitude by alleging discrimination based on "race" under this statute—either alone or in conjunction with other statutory remedies.

In seeking social justice where right or entitlement within a sphere of cultural pluralism is denied, servitude in any form is alien to the espousal of a philosophy based on mutual respect and tolerance for differences. Indeed, it has been argued that the theory of Anglo conformity is inherently discriminatory: it requires assimilation into a majoritarian culture and inferentially emarginates other legitimate forms of cultural expression. Section 1981 relief, as we have seen from a reading of *Scelsa*, provides a wide avenue to redress this form of coercion. At the very least, it should suffice to assist plaintiffs who allege national origin discrimination in crossing the litigation threshold to test the merits of their cause before the Courts.

WORK CITED

Scelsa v the City University of New York, 806 F.Supp. 1126 (S.D.N.Y., 1992).
St. Francis College v. Al-Kharaj, 481 U.S. 604 (1987).
DeSalle v Key Bank of Southern Maine, 685 F. Supp. 282 (D. Me., 1988).
Benigni v. City of Hemet, 879 F. 2d 472 (9th Cir., 1989).
United States v. Biaggi, 673 F. Supp. 96 (E.D.N.Y., 1989).

If Names Could Kill

My Name May Be Gambino, But a Notorious Mobster I'm Not

By Erica-Lynn Gambino

Erica-Lynn Gambino is a writer in Providence, R.I.

MY FRIENDS and I are watching a B-movie of the vampire genre. In one scene, the modern-day vampires are suddenly involved in a crime even more serious than neck biting. Concerned about being discovered, one vampire exclaims, "How should I know who knows? It could be anybody—the feds, the police, the Gambinos!" My friends all laugh heartily. It is the first real laugh this movie has given us, myself included.

The first time I can remember my name making people suspicious of me was in junior high school. One morning I arrived late and ran into the principal's office to get a pass.

"Name?" the secretary asked.

"Erica-Lynn Gambino."

"Gambino?" she enunciated slowly, a slight gleam in her eye.

"Um . . . yes," I stammered uncomfortably. I wasn't that late, was I?

The secretary leaned forward, lowering her voice. "C'mon, you can tell me."

"Tell you what?" I asked, leaning in too.

"You're one of . . . them. *The* Gambinos."

I thought a moment. "Well, my mom is the music teacher at the elementary school and. . . ."

"Uh-huh. Shuo-uh [Long Island for 'sure']." The gleam in her eye intensified. Her blue-gray bouffant was prickly with excitement, fear, repulsion and horror

that she was actually in the presence of one of . . . them.

Who were they, those other Gambinos? What had they done that she was speaking to me so accusingly? Already, I was conjuring up wild criminal scenarios in my 12-year-old mind; they robbed banks like Patty Hearst or roamed huge dark mansions in search of victims like Dracula. When I came home that day and told my parents what had happened, their immediate response was, "Ignore it."

I've learned a lot about those other Gambinos since my days at John Philip Sousa Junior High. Like that they are a notorious crime family from Long Island and that people believe that if you cross them, you could end up buried somewhere in New Jersey.

Now, 15 years later, I am on the phone reserving an Amtrak ticket from Providence to New York. "G-a-m-b-i-n-o," I spell, waiting for the wisecrack. The operator indeed snickers. Instead of asking me for my Visa number, he asks, "Know where Jimmy Hoffa is?"

"You'll have to ask the Kennedys about that," I say curtly.

I was in a bad mood. I had sent out articles and essays to various local New England publications and was subsequently scolded by my Rhode Island friends: "You sent it under your *real* name? Are you crazy?"

Almost everybody I know seems to be under the impression that the Mafia owns and/or runs Providence, so you might wonder why a woman who has

been mistaken for the heiress to a legacy of murder and drug-peddling chose to move here. The answer is ridiculously simple: It seemed like a nice place to live.

Back when I was an NYU undergraduate, I had to scrounge Avenue B for a cheap hole in the wall to live and study in. Landlord after landlord would ask, as he assured me I could squeeze my twin futon into the studio and still avoid the cockroaches that lived in the sink in the junior kitchen, "So, Gambino—as in . . . ?"

As in what? As in someone who could afford to live on Sutton Place but actually longs to spend her nights with a view of a crack house? Oh, yes, that must be me.

I then moved to the picturesque mind-your-own-beeswax state of Vermont, where I obtained my master's degree at Bennington. I spent three blissful years with interesting, unusual people who never judged books by their covers. Recently, one of my Bennington friends admitted that "of course we just assumed you were Erica Gambino of the Gambino Family. We thought it was great." Great. Bret Easton Ellis couldn't have dreamed up a better character. Artsy Mafia princess goes to small, elite, liberal arts college, discreetly driving a bottom-of-the-line Honda Civic and living in a small, nondescript apartment. What a fabulous cover!

Every time I think I am at the point where I can finally laugh off people's reactions and insinuations—I mean, it could be worse, my name could be Manson—something happens to remind me that my name is no laughing matter. This spring I was in London, thousands of miles away, I thought, from the American ethnic stereotyping I had always experienced. I was visiting my half-sister, whose blissfully Irish last name—Beatty—suggests gorgeous Hollywood actors to most. In Portobello market, we stood at a currency exchange booth as a friendly Pakistani man patiently counted my traveler's checks. He looked up at me with eyes wide, a grin of sheer fascination—and fear?—spread across his face. "Gambino!" he exclaimed. *"The Mafia. . . ."*

Instead of smirking awkwardly, making a snide comeback or cowering helplessly when I get this reaction, perhaps someday I'll be more like my mother, a Jew from the Upper West Side of Manhattan who revels in the proclamation of our last name. Being madly in love with my father has always made her madly in love with his name, without regard to its connotations. A sweet sentiment, but for me it is nevertheless disconcerting to hear her proudly bellow, in the projecting New York Schubert Alley way, "Gam-BEE-Nooo" when asked who our dinner reservation is for.

The son of a poor, hard-working immigrant, my father has chosen to plow through the barriers of ignorance with academic zeal. He is the founder of the first university-level Italian American studies program in the United States and is the author of several best-selling books on Italian American ethnicity. In short, he has become an expert at being himself—a Gambino.

Since my junior high school induction into the Crime Lords Hall of Fame, I have become an expert myself at those little tricks that help me avoid having to say my last name at all. I have a secret career as a historical romance writer named Veronica Stephens. And, like my wonderfully unselfconscious mother, I prefer to make dinner reservations under my beloved's name. He, on the other hand, thinks it's thoroughly amusing and interesting to use *my* last name. (His own, Huberty, causes people to become suddenly hard of hearing and very embarrassed.)

The word "gambino," incidentally, means shrimp fisherman in Italian. Not every name is what it seems, after all. I went to Bennington with people named Mohammed Ali, Matt Dillon, Amy Fisher and Mark Spitz. Perhaps it's the Bennington Curse—destined to be associated, by one's birth-given name, with celebrities. Maybe I should start a club for people like me. I might call it People With Societally and Ethnically Challenged Last Names.

THE END OF THE RAINBOW

The poverty of racial politics and the future of liberalism

BY MICHAEL LIND

IN THE CONCLUSION OF GOETHE'S EPIC *FAUST,* THE great magician who has made a pact with the devil hears the clinking of shovels. Faust, who is blind, believes he is listening to the sound of workers on a project he is promoting to reclaim land from the sea for the benefit of mankind. In fact, the shovels are in the hands of demons, who are digging Faust's own grave.

American liberalism faces a similar irony. For the past generation, the left has been identified with the strategy of what Jesse Jackson calls the Rainbow Coalition. Where the old left assigned the vanguard role in history to factory workers, the New Left assigns it to people of color. The assumption has been that policies such as affirmative action and racial redistricting would unite blacks, Hispanics, and Asian-Americans politically. Sympathetic whites would be permitted to join the coalition, but white concerns about reverse discrimination would be dismissed as racist. In time, many on the left assumed, "rainbow liberalism" would triumph purely as a result of demographic trends, as California, Texas, New York, and eventually the whole country acquired nonwhite majorities.

The strategy of rainbow liberalism has rested on two assumptions. The first is that conservatism would not appeal to nonwhite Americans. The second is that the very policies that promote the rainbow strategy—affirmative action and high immigration—would not produce tensions among the multiracial rainbow's constituent bands. If these assumptions are wrong, then rainbow liberalism is digging its own grave.

They are, and it is.

Already mainstream leaders in the GOP are rejecting white nativism. Some are even supporting affirmative action and immigration in the hope of appealing to socially or economically conservative blacks, Hispanics, or Asian-Americans. At the same time, affirmative action in higher education divides blacks and Hispanics from Asian-Ameri-

cans, while high levels of immigration hurt black workers in some parts of the country. The rise of a multicultural right, though it may doom rainbow liberalism, provides an opening for a new liberalism that stresses social equality and national integration.

DOES RIGHT EQUAL WHITE?

In the past generation, conservatives have offered two incompatible responses to rainbow liberalism. One is a conservative-populist nativism, or white nationalism, whose spokesmen are Patrick Buchanan and Peter Brimelow. Reminiscent of the white supremacist populist of the Old South, this new nativism holds that nonwhite immigration is a racial and cultural threat to the country's diminishing white Euro-American "core." When combined with eugenics theory, as in the work of Charles Murray, this kind of white nationalism becomes even more sinister. For strategic reasons, liberals might hope that the nativist version prevails among conservatives. Already, nativist agitation (particularly in California) has arrested the drift of Hispanics toward the GOP and pushed many back into the Democratic Party. White racism is the perfect mortar for uniting the colors of the rainbow.

But the other conservative answer to the rainbow strategy has not been so conveniently stupid. Most mainstream Republicans have reacted to Buchananism with horror and have rejected white national populism. Contrary to the propaganda of the left, the members of the dominant business-class wing of the GOP are not more racist on average than elite white liberals. During his tenure as executive director of the Christian Coalition, Ralph Reed worked to reach out to conservative black, Hispanic, and Asian-American Christians. And Republicans count more prominent leaders who are partners in interracial marriages—Jeb

Reprinted with permission from *Mother Jones,* September/October 1997, pp. 39-43, 75. © 1997 by the Foundation for National Progress.

Bush, Phil Gramm, Clarence Thomas—than do the Democrats. This is not tokenism.

Even if it were consistently bigoted, the conservative white elite, unlike the white working class, would not compete with nonwhites for jobs or feel culturally threatened by blacks or Latin American or Asian immigrants. Indeed, members of the white professional elite may feel they have more in common with successful Asian-Americans, and perhaps affluent Hispanics and blacks as well, than with working-class whites. The country club Republicans, while they are sometimes both, are more classist than racist. They rail against "class war" while finding kind things to say about high immigration (which is good for business) and even affirmative action (which makes corporate America look more diverse to a diverse public).

The present danger liberals face is less a "fascist right" in America—our neo-Nazis hate the military and the police, and they have trouble taking over a ranch, much less a country—than a "Creole right" oligarchy that does not care what color your skin is, as long as you are wealthy. As the Latin American saying has it, "Money whitens." (For most white Americans, O. J. Simpson was just a rich celebrity.)

A "rainbow right" is possible, perhaps even likely. Black voters remain committed to the Democratic Party, despite Republican proselytizing. But Asian and Hispanic allegiances are in play. A majority of Asian-Americans voted for Bush in 1992. They could play a role in the Republican Party comparable to that of academically and economically successful Jews in the Democratic Party. In the 1992 elections, Hispanics gave the Democrats only about 60 percent of the vote. If close to half of American Hispanics sided against Democrats then, it is quite possible that a majority will follow white ethnic voters into the GOP in the future as they move up the socioeconomic scale. A moderately conservative white-Asian-Hispanic coalition, based in the growing South and West, could be a formidable opponent of the liberal white-Protestant-Jewish-black coalition, concentrated in the demographically declining Northeast.

This racially mixed conservative coalition might be reinforced by the large number of working-class whites who have been leaving states with high immigration, such as California, for the interior and the Rocky Mountain states. Such whites, who might have competed for jobs with Hispanic immigrants back in their home states, might become their political allies once they have moved to more or less lily-white states where white-Hispanic tensions are insignificant. What would hold this multiracial conservative coalition together? The answer is: (a) conservative social values (shared by many whites, East Asian immigrants, and Hispanics); (b) redistribution (the coalition's partisans in Congress would tax the Northeast and subsidize Republican defense contractors and agribusiness in the South and West); (c) a live-and-let-live states' rights compromise (for example, different affirmative action policies for the white-majority states and the nonwhite-majority states); and, last but not least, (d) a common hostility to the black urban poor, everybody's favorite scapegoat.

RACIALISM BREAKS UP THE RAINBOW

The assumption that right equals white, then, is no longer realistic. Equally flawed is the other premise of the rainbow liberal strategy—the belief that programs such as high immigration and affirmative action will unite rather than divide blacks, Hispanics, and Asian-Americans.

The high number of blacks who supported Proposition 187, California's anti-immigration referendum, should have sent a signal to liberal strategists. The tensions between blacks and Hispanic and Asian immigrants are deep. According to a recent Roger Poll, non-Hispanic blacks favor deep cuts in immigration by a ratio of 11-to-1 (even Hispanic Americans favored such cuts by 7-to-1). The continued immigration of poor workers (many of whom make up a significant percentage of the nearly 1 million *legal* immigrants we now have a year) may keep wages down and make union organizing more difficult. Three Harvard economists, George Borjas, Richard Freeman, and Lawrence Katz, have estimated that immigrant competition accounts for 44 to 60 percent of the drop in relative earnings high school dropouts suffered between 1979 and 1995. From the perspective of employers, of course, wages can never be too low. Little wonder, then, that the pro-immigration wing of the Republican Party, bolstered by the *Wall Street Journal's* editorial page, has beaten back the immigration restrictions favored by the nativist wing of the GOP.

Affirmative action, like immigration, divides rather than unites the rainbow. Ensuring the proportional representation of blacks and Hispanics in universities means discriminating against academically gifted Asian-Americans. The evolution of nonwhite-majority states such as California and Texas may not have the optimistic result rainbow liberals expect. As the percentage of whites diminishes, blacks and Hispanics and Asians will likely turn on one another, with representatives at each category demanding a "fair share" of political offices, jobs, and opportunities for higher education. Strict proportional representation, however, means overall racial numbers won't be a floor, but a *cap*. Blacks, who tend to be overrepresented in civil service jobs, would have *no more* than 12.5 percent of the positions in, say, the post office. Black representation in government jobs and politics would become directly threatened by the rainbow liberals' own policies. Indeed, in absolute numbers most of the beneficiaries of affirmative action (if it is not abolished) will soon be white women and immigrants from Latin America—not the black Americans for whom the program was intended in the first place. (By 1993, 74.9 percent of legal immigrants were eligible for affirmative action on the basis of race.)

Of course, in recent years the right has lost few chances to hammer a wedge between the bands of the rainbow, contrasting "hardworking" immigrants with the native black and white poor.

What's Your Favorite Statistic About Race?

These leading thinkers prove that questions of race rarely have simple—or numerical—answers.

C. ERIC LINCOLN, author of *Coming Through the Fire*
"By 2050, more than **half of the people** in the United States will be nonwhite. And the Tiger Woods syndrome is upon us."

GLENN C. LOURY, director of the Institute of Race and Social Division at Boston University.
"Between 1977 and 1994 the number of first professional degrees (law, business, and medical school, mainly) awarded to African-American women increased by 219 percent (from 776 to 2,477). That number grew by only 5.1 percent for African-American men (from 1,761 to 1,851)."

RON TAKAKI, professor of ethnic studies, University of California at Berkeley
"Bob Dole announced his support for **Proposition 209** in a speech at Little Saigon, in Orange County, Calif. There was a public perception that identified Asian-Americans with the eventually successful assault on affirmative action. But, according to the *Los Angeles Times,* **The Asian-American vote was 61 percent** against Prop. 209."

JOHN B. JUDIS, senior editor at the *New Republic*
"I live in Silver Spring, Md., a racially mixed, middle-class suburb of Washington, D. C., and my daughters go to public school there. They have always had black friends, but by the beginning of middle or high school, these friends had **departed for predominantly white private schools.** The reason, we learned, was that their parents feared that if they stayed in public schools, they would fall under the spell of other blacks who identified success in school with being white."

LINDA CHAVEZ, president, Center for Equal Opportunity
"According to a recent survey conducted by Lou Harris for the National Conference, 46 percent of Latinos and 42 percent of African-Americans agreed with the statement that Asians are '**unscrupulous, crafty, and devious in business,**' while only 27 percent of whites agreed; 68 percent of Asian-Americans and 49 percent of African-Americans agreed with the statement that Latinos '**tend to have bigger families than they are able to support,**' as did 50 percent of whites; 33 percent of Latinos and 22 percent of Asian-Americans agreed with the statement that African-Americans '**even if given a chance, aren't capable of getting ahead,**' yet only 12 percent of whites agreed."

JAMES McBRIDE, author of *The Color of Water*
"**There are 60,000 black children** waiting to be adopted in the United States, while every week newspapers and magazines across the country are graced with ads by parents who are willing to pay huge bucks for a baby. Unspoken, of course, is their willingness to **pay for white babies,** which are apparently in short supply. As a black man raised by a white Jewish mother and black American father; I don't fault these folks for trying to obtain a baby who 'looks like them.' But I'm glad I'm not that baby."

TROY DUSTER, professor of sociology, University of California at Berkeley
"Cheryl Hopwood, a white female, sued the University of Texas Law School, claiming she had been the victim of racial discrimination because she was **not admitted even though she had higher test scores** than students of color who were admitted. The appellate court directed the lower court to consider damages to Hopwood, and she is seeking more than **$1** million from the state. In all these decades of racial exclusion, **no court in this nation has ever been directed to consider damages** for a single student of color."

PAUL BEGALA, advisor to President Clinton
"This year's incoming class at the University of Texas Law School—which once produced more African-American and Hispanic lawyers than nearly any other law school in the country—includes a **grand total of four African-Americans.**"

RUY TEIXEIRA, director, Politics and Public Opinion Program, Economic Policy Institute
"In 1958, **44 percent of whites said they would move out** if a black person moved next door. In 1997, the figure is 1 percent. Yet the economic problems of blacks persist. This suggests that: (a) the problem is no longer racism or discrimination, but broader economic arrangements that intersect with race; or (b) racism has simply become covert."

JIM SLEEPER, author of *Liberal Racism*
"Almost all polling data reveal that **the closer black Americans get to middle-class life,** the more unhappy and untrusting toward whites they feel. Never mind that the indices of two-parent homes, education, mortality, and career mobility are improving among blacks; liberals still encourage thousands of diversity trainers and racial gatekeepers to create an industry for which **no good racial news can be real news.** Conservatives spent centuries telling blacks how different they were. Why have so many liberals replaced that historic racism with an elaborate thicket of treatments that prolong the disease?"

RUBÉN ORTIZ-TORRES, artist and photographer
"My favorite fact of the month is that **Che Guevara's car in Havana** was an emerald-green 1960 Chevy Impala with a V-8 engine, automatic transmission, white upholstery, and an AM radio. Another interesting fact is that **the largest sombrero in the world** is the Sombrero Tower in a theme park called South of the Border next to North and South Carolina's border. The Sombrero Tower is 200 feet high and has an elevator that takes you to the top."

THE LEFT'S ACCIDENTAL SUICIDE

If a multicultural right threatens to kill rainbow liberalism, the left unwittingly may be acting as its own Dr. Kevorkian. We are so used to the routinized debate between the multicultural left and the unicultural right that we can hardly imagine a contest for the future of America between a multicultural right and a class-based, nationalist left. Throughout history, however, it has generally been the left that has favored more inclusive identities—class, nation, humanity—over the parochialisms of race, region, religion, and ethnicity. In the early 20th century, it should be recalled, the idea of the melting pot was progressive, if not radical. It has been conservatives and reactionaries who defended the parochial and the particular. Today, of course, it is the left that tends to insist on the permanence and inviolability of racial categories (misdescribed as "cultures") and to be hostile to the idea of a melting pot.

Liberals long before now should have seen that in many cases economics creates a community of interest between blacks and whites against immigration. The reason low-income whites have no prominent role in the left-liberal rainbow has to do with the evolution of the Democratic Party in the 1960s and the 1970s. During and after the civil rights revolution, black Americans found many allies among affluent whites (who did not compete with urban blacks for jobs and housing) and many of their political opponents among working-class whites (who often saw blacks as rivals). In taking over the Democratic Party, however, the civil rights coalition drove enough white Southerners and working-class Northern Catholics into the GOP to permit the Republicans to dominate first the presidency and now Congress.

Yet the New Deal coalition might have been kept intact while promoting the goals of the civil rights revolution. A white ethnic/white populist/black alliance against the bicoastal white overclass would not have been any more bizarre than the alliance of black Americans with wealthy white feminists against working-class white Catholics. A majority of liberal thinkers and activists, however, opted for rainbow liberalism. Instead of treating blacks as "ethnics" and "immigrants" who were owed an informal share in the spoils system, the liberal leadership has treated immigrant ethnic groups from Latin America and Asia, and even white women (whom it regards as members of a quasi-minority group), as "races," defined against a white power structure.

ONE NATION UNDER ELVIS

What is now needed is an alternative American liberalism; or liberal populism, that rejects the rainbow strategy in order to concentrate on the interests of working Americans from all backgrounds. Call it "one-nation liberalism." This would draw the lines differently. For example, affirmative action would be replaced by programs based on the horizontal line between classes, rather than the vertical lines between races.

One-nation liberals would not take it for granted that black Americans belong with immigrants from Latin America and Asia in a coalition opposed to native white Americans. The two largest groups of Americans living below the poverty level, in absolute numbers, are low-income whites and blacks. If immigration policy is considered as it should be—a form of labor policy—then the "liberal" approach ought to be to minimize the immigration of low-wage workers who might compete with the American working poor (including naturalized immigrants). A pro-labor immigration policy would not be xenophobic or racist; its logic would disfavor low-income white immigrants from postcommunist Europe.

If race is strategy, so is culture. To unite working-class and poor whites with working-class and poor blacks (at the expense, if necessary, of high levels of low-wage immigrants), a one-nation liberal coalition needs to be reinforced by a common identity. Such a superordinate community shared by whites and blacks, along with Americans of other backgrounds, cannot be defined by race (given the legacy of America's bipolar caste system); it might, just might, be provided by culture—the disproportionately black vernacular culture shared by American whites and blacks alike. That common national culture is Judeo-Christian, not Black Muslim; its holidays are Thanksgiving and Christmas and the Fourth of July, not Yul or Kwanza; its common institutions include sports and the military; its mythic homeland is not Europe or Africa, but North America; and it can find symbols in vernacular-culture heroes like Elvis Presley, the mixed-race, white/Cherokee prole who sang like a black man.

Many thinkers and artists on the left envisioned such an eclectic vernacular culture after the 1930s, when they rejected both European high culture and commercial kitsch in favor of the folk-influenced high art epitomized by Woody Guthrie, Aaron Copland, Jacob Lawrence, and Martha Graham. Today, Bruce Springsteen is one of the rare artists who recognizes the political as well as the artistic promise of this venerable and rich tradition.

Does one-nation liberalism slight the cultures of immigrants who arrived a week ago? Don't they represent the destiny of American culture? What about that fabled symbol of our supposed cosmopolitan future, the sushi burrito?

The radical transformation of American culture by the influx of new immigrants is unlikely. Historians have long recognized that later immigrant groups tend to assimilate to the founding cultures in an area. Americans of German and Irish descent today outnumber Americans of English and African descent. Nevertheless, the German and Irish elements of the common culture are minuscule by comparison. The same may occur with today's Asian and Latin American immigrants (though Mexican culture, because of Mexico's proximity, may prove more enduring and influential). Within a generation, outside of the most homogeneous ethnic enclaves, these immigrants—even the

Table 1. *Comparison of US census classifications of race or colour, 1890–1990*[a]

1890	1900	1910	1920	1930	1940	1950	1960	1970[g]	1980[h]	1990[i]
White	White	White	White	White	White[e]	White[e]	White[f]	White	White	White
Black	Black	Black	Black	Negro	Negro	Negro	Negro	Negro or	Black or	Black or
Mulatto	Chinese	Mulatto	Mulatto	Mexican	Indian	American	American	Black	Negro	Negro
Quadroon	Japanese	Chinese	Chinese	Indian[d]	Chinese	Indian	Indian	Indian	Japanese	Indian
Octoroon	Indian[b]	Japanese	Japanese	Chinese	Japanese	Japanese	Japanese	(Amer.)	Chinese	(Amer.)
Chinese		Indian[b]	Indian[b]	Japanese	Filipino	Chinese	Chinese	Japanese	Filipino	Eskimo
Japanese		Other[c]	Other	Filipino	Hindu	Filipino	Filipino	Chinese	Korean	Aleut
Indian[b]				Hindu	Korean	Other	Hawaiian	Filipino	Vietnamese	*Asian or*
				Korean	Other		Part	Hawaiian	Indian	*Pacific*
				Other			Hawaiian	Korean	(Amer.)	*Islander*
							Aleut	Other	Asian Indian	(API)
							Eskimo		Hawaiian	Chinese
							Other, etc.[f]		Guamanian	Filipino
									Samoan	Hawaiian
									Eskimo	Korean
									Aleut	Vietnamese
									Other	Japanese
										Asian
										Indian
										Samoan
										Guamanian
										Other

Notes:

[a] The racial classifications are from the question on race or colour in each decennial population schedule. The source for Table 1 is US Bureau of the Census (1989).

[b] Separate enumerations of the Indian population on reservations were carried out in these years, in addition to the enumeration of Indians who lived among the 'general' population. The proportion of 'Indian blood' (whether 'full' or 'mixed blood') and type of mixture (with white or black) were also noted on the separate Indian schedules.

[c] The category, 'other,' included groups that varied in number and characteristics over time. The Census Bureau routinely instructed enumerators to assign these responses to one of the given classifications but sometimes retained a classification for 'other' (for example, Asian Indians in 1960.

[d] Beginning in 1930 there were no more separate schedules for enumerating Indians who live on reservations. Instead, a supplement was attached to the general population schedule in order to collect additional information on Indians who live on reservations.

[e] Mexicans were included in the white category, beginning in 1940.

[f] Enumerators were instructed to classify (by observation) Puerto Ricans, Mexicans, and other persons of Latin descent as 'white' when they were definitely not Negro, Indian, or some other race. Southern European and Near Eastern people were also to be considered 'white,' but Asian Indians were to be classified as 'other'.

[g] Respondents self-identified themselves on the race question but enumerators were instructed to change responses such as 'Chicano', 'La Raza', 'Mexican American', 'Moslem' or 'Brown' to 'White' and 'Brown (Negro)' to 'Negro' or 'Black'.

[h] In 1980, the lead-in to the question on race dropped any mention of race, Instead, the question read: 'Is this person —?'

[i] In 1990, the question on race read: 'What is —'s race?'

Source: "Racial Classifications in the US Census: 1890–1990," Sharon M. Lee, *Ethnic and Racial Studies*, January 1993, p. 78.

Mexican-Americans—will only speak English, and with the loss of their native languages will go all but a few nonpolitical foreign traditions.

Among other things, this means that if conservatives appeal to Mexican-Americans by waving the U.S. flag and invoking Abraham Lincoln, while the left waves the red, white, and green and invokes Quetzalcoatl and Father Hidalgo, the right is likely to win. The left too often forgets that voluntary immigrants have come here—whether from Germany, Ireland, Mexico, or China—because they want to become Americans, to join a huge, diffuse nationality that, though far from cosmopolitan, is much more inclusive than most nations in the world. Liberals who generally favor personal choice have no business condemning, as "inauthentic," immigrants who choose to adopt America's mongrel culture as their own.

Some veterans of the left, having retreated from the political battlefield to campuses and editorial offices, may find all of this incomprehensible. A transracial populist liberalism, uniting non-elite whites and blacks, and encouraging the assimilation of immigrants to America's historic mulatto culture? Please—we'd rather wax rhapsodic about the dissolution of the nation-state thanks to the Internet, and ponder the significance of that sushi burrito.

It is easy to stick with the old rainbow strategy and hope that in time nonwhite majorities will bring about the repeatedly deferred revolution, just as it is easy to continue to treat inherited racial categories and alliances as facts of nature, rather than as constructs serving time-bound (and perhaps obsolete) strategies. Easy, but disastrous—for the rejection of strategy is itself a strategy for defeat.

Michael Lind is the author of The Next American Nation *(Free Press, 1995) and* Up From Conservatism *(Free Press, 1996).*

The Ethnic Factor:
International Challenges
for the 1990s

The process of better understanding the multiethnic character of America and the world involves the coordinated efforts of formal and informal education, which are influenced by public and private institutions and the community-based voluntary associations that are the building blocks of society. This collection of articles addresses resistance to the challenges that are embedded in passionately held and politically potent traditions of ethnic opposition. The persistence of confusion, uncertainty, insensitivity, and violence toward and among ethnic groups is sobering and stunning fact. Strategies for dealing with the tension and reality of bias are examined in this unit. Hatred and prejudice are frequently based on conscious manipulation of powerful images that profoundly shape personal and group identity. Exploring other societies is often a way of gaining fresh perspective on the American reality; differences and commonalities of the situations described in this unit are worth pondering.

Examination, for example, of the legacy of the civil rights laws crafted during the 1960s and the process of shaping a society grounded in exclusionary habits and institutions involves assessment on many levels—the social, the political, the ideological, and the economic. Even on the most basic level of public perception, most agree that progress has been made toward a society of equality and social justice, with increased hopes for decreased segregation in schools and neighborhoods. Yet disparities of these views among ethnic and racial groups indicate that uniformity and a shared sense of the past and present are not generally common. Attempting to overcome such gulfs of misunderstanding before they lead to more serious forms of conflict is among the great challenges of the present.

Since the breakup of the Soviet empire, ethnicity has reoriented the international arena. New national claims as well as the revival of ancient antagonisms are fragmenting Europe. War, the systematic expression of conflict, and its aftermath are also occasions for the use and misuse of ethnically charged political rhetoric. The presence of a politically relevant past and the invocation of religious warrants for group conflict have indicated the need for new approaches to peacekeeping and educational strategies for meeting and transcending group differences. The critiques challenging multiculturalism, the educational controversy regarding which should be the dominant expressions of our human commonality, and the various values and virtues found in all ethnic traditions pose challenges for economically and socially turbulent times. Whether these moments are crises of growth or decline will be measured by a host of indicators. Which of these indicators are the most salient is, of course, another question, whose answer depends on our selective invocation of historical materials and ethnic symbols as guides for contemporary analysis.

Ethnic relations have erupted into warfare in Africa, where conflicts have shattered emerging states and thus challenged the hopeful myth of postcolonial renewal as well as the racial/ethnic myth of black solidarity. But Africa's emerging countries are not alone: The Middle East, Central Europe, Canada, and the Balkans are additional venues of destructive conflict. Each of these simmering cauldrons—not melting pots—illustrates the stakes and consequences of unresolved conflict and distrust concerning land, religion, culture, leadership, and economic production and distribution. Each also shows the rewards and recognitions that fuel human passions, ambitions, and the will to dominate and to govern the affairs and destinies of various peoples that cohabit contiguous regions. Thus, the dramas of regional ethnic struggle and the growth of worldwide ethnic challenges to the constitution of human order itself are increasingly marked by episodes of blatant bigotry and intolerance. Fanaticism and zealotry impose themselves on the stage of history, which is rushing toward a new millennium. The threshold of hope that it promises for those who can recover and embrace the mystery of diversity waits to define the human condition in the twenty-first century.

Looking Ahead: Challenge Questions

International events frequently affect the United States. In what ways can such events affect ethnic populations?

Explain how the relationship of ethnic Americans to changes and challenges in the world arena provides strength or liability to American interests. Does conflict between ethnic interests and national interests present real or imaginary fears about our activities in international affairs? Explain.

How will increased immigration, technological advances, and a more competitive world market affect the relationships between ethnic groups?

Is the American military becoming a society unto itself? Has the end of the military draft isolated military society from the American mainstream? Is national service a duty of citizenship?

Should the claims of ethnic groups in the United States in defense of culture, territory, and unique institutions be honored and protected by law and public policy?

POLISH AMERICANS AND THE HOLOCAUST

Rev. John T. Pawlikowski, O.S.M., PhD.

I am most grateful for the opportunity to present the 1994 Fierdorczyk lecture. The topic suggested to me, Polish Americans and the Holocaust, is one surrounded with great possibilities for enhanced understanding but considerable controversy as well. Since I have found members of Polonia, as well as the general American community, fairly unacquainted with the details of the Polish story of victimization during the Nazi era I shall begin my narrative with a brief account of that story. Following that I would like to turn my attention, and yours, to some contemporary implications of the Holocaust for Polish Americans, in particular for their relations with Jewish Americans with whom they share a patrimony of victimization.

The Nazi Invasion of Poland: Its Goals and Impact

On September 1, 1939, Poland was invaded by one of the world's strongest and most modern armies. Over 1,800,000 soldiers, representing the elite of the German army, took part in the campaign against it. The German army was vastly superior to any counter-force Poland could mount in its defense because of its tremendous fire-power and mobility enhanced by its motorization. On September 3, 1939, in fulfillment of their treaty obligations to Poland, Great Britain and France declared war on Nazi Germany. The war had been transformed into an allied effort. Though this Franco-British declaration was of great political significance, it had little immediate impact on the military situation. Fighting alone and basically unaided, Poland had to confront more than two thirds of the combined German forces.

From the very outset of the German invasion of Poland, it was apparent that the Nazis were not engaged in a conventional war to defeat the Polish military nor even to subdue the state politically. Instead, as the contemporary Polish-American historian Richard Lukas puts it, " . . . the Germans waged war against the Polish people, intent on de-stroying the Polish nation."[1] This is an extremely crucial point, one that is often overlooked in writings on Polish victimization under the Nazis. Poles were not killed first and foremost as individual dissenters, whether religious or political. Nor did the Nazi leadership wish only to conquer Poland in a military or political sense. Rather, the Polish nation as nation fell victim to the same basic ideology which eventually turned its attention with even greater fury to the annihilation of the entire Jewish population of Europe.

The Nazi theory of racial superiority totally dehumanized the Polish people. In the Nazi perspective, Poles were considered untermenschen (subhumans) who lived on land coveted by the superior German race. Poland was not simply to be defeated and occupied, the primary goal of the subsequent Nazi invasions of other Western European countries. "The aim is not the arrival at a certain line," declared Hitler, "but the annihilation of living forces."[2]

Even prior to the actual invasion of Poland, Hitler had authorized on August 22, 1939, killing, "without pity or mercy all men, women, and children of Polish descent or language. Only in this way," he insisted, "can we obtain the living space we need."[3] And the person placed in charge of implementing Hitler's Polish "plan," Heinrich Himmler, said outright that "all Poles will disappear from the world. . . . It is essential that the great German people should consider it as its major task to destroy all Poles."[4]

From the above quotations it becomes amply evident that key Nazi operatives, including Hitler himself, seriously contemplated the total extermination of the Polish population in due time. Whether they would have carried out this plan fully if they had been given the opportunity is a matter of conjecture at best. The annihilation of Jews is a fact, not merely a possibility. But on the level of theory, in trying to understand where the Poles fit into the Nazi victimization scheme, no other conclusion can be drawn except that they belong with Jews, Gypsies, and the mentally and physically incapacitated

From *Occasional Papers in Polish and Polish American Studies*, Number 1, 1996, "Perspectives in Polish History." © 1996 by the Polish Studies Program, Central Connecticut State University. Reprinted by permission.

as candidates for eventual total extinction in the gradual emergence of the new Aryan humanity.[5]

Once Poland was firmly under Nazi control, the country was divided into two separate zones. All of western Poland, including the regions of Poznania, Pomerania and Silesia, and sections of central and southern Poland were formally annexed to the Reich. The remaining Polish territories not annexed outright into Germany were set up for administrative purposes as an occupation region and assigned the name "General Government."

The Nazi policy of imposed "Germanization" in the annexed territories relied upon four strategies: a campaign of wide-spread and unmitigated terror; expropriation of land and possessions; deportations; and enslavement. The terror, designed to be harsh enough to mute all possible resistance, began immediately after the invasion in 1939. Virtually every city, town and village in western Poland witnessed wholesale massacres and executions of the leading citizenry. In the city of Bydgoszcz, for example, some 10,000 people perished, out of a population of 140,000, during the first four months of occupation. But even the regions designated as falling under the "General Government" were subjected to much the same treatment.

The terror employed by the Nazis to pacify the Polish population included an extensive use of torture. One of the most notorious sites was the training school for the Gestapo at Fort VII in Poznan. Famous as an institute of sadism, Fort VII drew its victims from the ranks of the clergy, university professors and politicians. It experimented with every conceivable form of torture, from massive beatings to the inflation of prisoners' intestines to the point of bursting.

The Nazi policy of destroying the Polish nations focused strongly, but not exclusively, upon eliminating anyone with even the least political and cultural prominence. But the Nazis had a wide definition of those falling under the rubric of "elite." The category included teachers, physicians, priests, officers, people in business, landowners, writers and extended even to anyone who had completed secondary school. As a result, millions of Poles qualified for liquidation in the Nazi effort to reduce Poland to a nation of indentured servants in the first instance and, perhaps in due time, to wipe it off the map completely.

Hitler gave the initial approval and then turned over direction of the Polish campaign to Himler's SS and the police forces. The SS lost little time in implementing his order. In November, 1939, they arrested almost two hundred professors and fellows of the Jagiellonian University in Cracow, one of Europe's oldest centers of higher learning, as well as the faculty of the Polytechnic. Those seized were

all sent to Sachsenhausen, where many perished. The incident caused great concern throughout Europe. The Nazis thus decided to speed up the process of removing the Polish professors from the scene. Taking advantage of the preoccupation of world opinion with military operations in the West in the Spring of 1940, the Nazis launched a massive program to exterminate the Polish intelligentsia living in the General Government region under the code name of "extraordinary purification action." At least six thousand were murdered on the spot; several thousand others were arrested and sent to the newly established Auschwitz concentration camp.

It is important to underline at this point the centrality of the Auschwitz camp in the Nazi plan to destroy Poland and why, as a result, it retains such central symbolic value for contemporary Poles. Originally opened as a camp for German prisoners of war, Auschwitz was quickly transformed into the principal camp for Polish victims even though Poles were also sent to Stutthof, Dachau, Ravensbruck, Sachsenhausen, Mauthausen and Neuengamme. Poles remained the majority of the inmates at Auschwitz until 1942, when Jews assumed that dubious distinction. For Poles, the Auschwitz camp remains a vital link in their collective memory of facing the threat of national, not just political, extinction.

In the course of the controversy over the Carmelite convent at the Auschwitz site, significant mistakes were made on all sides.[6] Surely the first critical misstep was taken on the Catholic side when approval was granted for the erection of the Carmelite convent at the camp without any consultation with the Jewish community. Intended or not, this unilateral move left the distinct impression within the Jewish community that Catholics considered Auschwitz their sacred shrine alone. This was bound to provoke deep and quite understandable feelings of hostility among Jews, especially the survivor community and the members of families whose relatives had perished at Auschwitz. But as the controversy became public and grew more intense, some European Jewish leaders in particular spoke about Auschwitz as though it was the exclusive domain of their community. Some seemed to lack any basic information about the historical origins of the camp as a place of incarceration for German political prisoners and its early role as the central execution site in the Nazi plan to annihilate the elite of Polish society.[7] Mr. Stanislaw Krajewski, a Polish Jew who serves as the American Jewish Committee's representative in Warsaw, has written of the problem of mutual misunderstanding. He admits that "most Poles do not recognize the exceptional character of the project to wipe out the Jewish people and either poorly understand or altogether ignore the Jewish significance of Auschwitz." But he likewise insists that people in the West, including Jews, simply do not appreciate the depth of Polish suffering at Auschwitz: "The historical fact is that the Nazis tried to crush the Polish nation; they not only introduced bloody terror but began to murder Polish elites and destroy Polish culture. The Auschwitz camp was used also for this purpose, and during its first two years of existence, this was its main function."[8] I might add at this point that even Western Christians, with extensive experience in Christian-Jewish dialogue, frequently reveal insufficient awareness of the profound (and enduring) impact of the Nazi era on Polish national life.

Returning to the narrative of the Nazi attack on the Polish nation, we find various tactical shifts in the campaign of extermination against the Polish elite. But the main thrust of the campaign, reduction of the nation to a condition of servitude, continued unabated throughout the war, even when personnel and equipment were needed much more urgently on the war front itself. This took a heavy toll on the Polish people, not only physically but psychologically as well. The Nazis, for example, committed troops to the work of museum destruction in Poland at a time when the absence of reserves on the frontlines was beginning to impinge upon the Nazi war machine. Such activities clearly show that the Nazis envisioned far more than merely the military defeat of Poland. They literally wished to wipe out its cultural identity, preparing perhaps for the time in the future when the people itself might vanish as well.

By the time the war had ended and the Nazis defeated, Poland had suffered the loss of forty-five percent of its physicians and dentists, fifty-seven percent of its attorneys, over fifteen percent of its teachers, forty percent of its professors, thirty percent of its technicians, and nearly twenty percent of its clergy. The majority of its journalists also disappeared. While these statistics are considerably lower than the ones for the Jewish community, and probably lower than those for the Gypsy community as well (though not all categories would be applicable to this community), it still represents a substantial destruction of the "carriers" of the Polish cultural, intellectual, political and religious traditions.

The Nazi effort to annihilate the Polish intelligentsia was part of a systematic program to destroy Polish culture. Education was a particular focus of the Nazi plan. The Nazis hoped eventually to transform Poland into an "intellectual desert." The Nazis denied Polish young people the right to a secondary and university education. Most primary schools were forced to use German as their language of instruction. Polish universities were often occupied by military and civil authorities, and their libraries and laboratories were pillaged. State, municipal, and ecclesiastical archives suffered the same fate.

Polish art and history also became the targets of the Nazi effort to eradicate Polish national self-identity. Major art museums were generally stripped of their collections, with many going to Germany (including some to Hitler himself). After the war only thirty-three of the one hundred seventy-five pre-war art museums had sufficient collections remaining to reopen for public viewing. Museums that were left untouched usually were used by the Nazis to demonstrate alleged German influences on Polish culture. History books were largely confiscated by the Nazis and teachers forbidden to make reference to the nation's past and the persons who shaped it. Monuments, busts, memorials, and inscriptions of Polish heroes, including Kosciuszko, Chopin, and Piłsudski were removed. In Warsaw the Nazis even planned to erect a monument to the victory of the Third Reich in the exact place where the monument to King Zygmunt III was located. This was thus a plan of total national annihilation, *a plan the Nazis enacted in Poland alone of all their occupied territories.*

Hitler understood that the attack on Polish culture would remain incomplete unless Poland's cities took on a German character. The change in this direction began with a change of names—Gdynia became Gotenhafen, Lódz was called Litzmannstadt, Rzeszów was renamed Reichshof. Street names were also Germanized. Hitler hoped eventually to reduce Warsaw to a German provincial town of 100,000–200,000 people. This plan was never realized, however, because of the increasing drain on Nazi resources as the war went on. Cracow, however, which became the center of the General Government, did take on a very German flavor with a large transplanted German population.

Himmler and his chief assistant in the Polish campaign, General Hans Frank, launched a program to expel Poles from certain areas of the country (e.g., the Lublin region) and replace them with German peasants. By and large, these programs proved unsuccessful. But they were very painful for the affected people, sometimes involving the abductions of children from their parents who in some instances were sent to the Reich to be raised as "Germans" and in others were assigned to medical experimentation centers. Racial factors played an important role in determining where a person, especially a child, was sent. Auschwitz and other camps were the lot of many of those displaced.

Because of the close ties between the Catholic church and Polish nationalism over the centuries, the Nazis realized they would have to break the back of the church if their plan of national annihilation was to succeed. When the Nazis partitioned Poland after the invasion, they seriously undercut the church's own territorial structures by dividing up historic dioceses. Thus weakened, the Polish church, especially in the annexed areas, lost most of its hierarchy and clergy: Wrocław, 49.2 percent; Chełmo, 47.8 percent; Lódz, 36.8 percent; and in Poznan, 31.1 percent. Overall 1,811 Polish diocesan priests perished under the Nazis out of the total of 10,017 in 1939. Many church buildings were also destroyed. In Poznan, for example, only two out of the pre-war thirty churches remained at the end of the war.

Polish Catholics, in addition to suffering the internal destruction of their church, also felt abandoned by the Catholic leadership. The Holy See basically followed a policy of reserve even after it received strong appeals from Polish bishops to denounce Nazi atrocities against Polish Catholics as well as in the case of the Third Reich's "euthanasia campaign" and the Italian attack against Greece. The London-based Polish government-in-exile also frequently expressed discontent with the Vatican's unwillingness to denounce the Nazi atrocities against the Polish nation in a more public and detailed fashion.

Richard Lukas addresses this issue in his writings on the Nazi era. He recognizes the practical difficulties the Vatican faced with respect to Poland, in part due to the flight of Cardinal Hlond from the country which caused great disruption in the Polish church. He likewise acknowledges that Pius XII's rather cold reception of Hlond in Rome is considered by Poles one saving feature of the overall papal approach to their national suffering under the Nazis. Yet, for Lukas, the balance sheet does not read well, an evaluation he supports with references to concrete reactions by Poles during the period.

"In the face of the persecution of the church of Poland," says Lukas, "the Vatican pursued a timid, reserved attitude."[9] This was likely the result of a constellation of forces—a sentimentality about Poland on Pius' part, a tinge of Germanophilism, and fears that public denunciations would make matters worse for the Poles. It was not until June 2, 1943, that the Pope finally issued the long awaited statement denouncing the attack against Poland. Just as in the case of the Jews, Pius XII shied away from explicit condemnation of the Nazis.

The 1943 statement, which admittedly did ease Polish-Vatican tensions to some degree, was an effort to counteract the wide-spread criticism that had grown up within clerical ranks because of the Vatican's seeming hesitancy on the Polish question. There were even Polish voices calling for the severing of ties with the Vatican. Some Poles, according

to Lukas, were so upset at Rome that they left church at the mention of Pius' name. The Jesuits of Warsaw were so concerned about the situation that they published a defense of Vatican activities in behalf of Poland. And Catholic historian Fr. John Morley, who also raises the Polish question and sees Vatican inaction as resulting from the primacy accorded by the Holy See to its relations with Germany, relates how Rome explicitly instructed its nuncios on ways to counter the mounting dissatisfaction with its approach to Poland.[10]

The political opposition forces in Poland were also highly critical of Pius' stance. An underground organ published by the Polish Socialists accused the Pope of "walking hand in hand with the Hitlerite . . . Fascists." *Glos Pracy*, another underground newspaper, declared that the Pope had shut himself up in the Vatican without bothering to defend his own people. And the Polish Minister of Interior said that "the people would be relieved by official news about the protest of the Holy See and the Polish government, given the flagrant and never hitherto-experienced persecution of the church in Poland."[11]

Contemporary Implications of Polish Victimization Under the Nazis

As we reflect today on the continuing significance of the determined effort by the Nazis to reduce Poland to perpetual servitude by totally destroying its national identity, and perhaps even, if the possibility had presented itself, to eradicate the population as such, the first responsibility that looms large is remembrance. Nobel prize author Elie Wiesel has said that to forget the victims of the Holocaust is to kill them a second time. Yet, I must candidly say, that in working on Holocaust-related issues in scholarly and public circles for well over two decades my judgment must be that both Polonia and Poland itself has fared poorly up till now in this duty of remembrance. We have been far more vocal in criticizing Jews for not including remembrance of Polish victims in programs under their auspices than we have been active as a community in organizing our own. My own efforts over the years to generate interest within Polish organizations in this regard has generally met no response. While it may be quite proper to criticize the exclusion of Polish victims in public Holocaust ceremonies in particular, such criticism will inevitably lose its force unless it is accompanied by internal efforts from within Polonia and within Poland. For that reason I was pleased to read several months ago in *Zgoda*, a call by PNA President Edward J. Moskal for enhanced commemoration of the Polish victims of the Nazis coupled with a willingness to extend blame for the failures in this regard to the Polish community as well.[12] My fervent hope is that this plea by President Moskal will be taken seriously and implemented by Polish religious groups, fraternal organizations, and academic associations.

Let me add here that in addition to remembering the Polish victims, we must also pay greater honor to the Polish righteous, especially the heroic members of *Zegota,* the only group in Nazi occupied Europe dedicated specifically to saving Jews. I am well aware of some of the political complications with respect to certain members of this movement. But we must put that aside and honor them here in North America as well as in Poland for their courage during the war itself. So far the only film or video that I know of on *Zegota* was produced by a Jewish film maker from Washington, Sy Rotter. Where are the Polish efforts in this regard?

At this point let me introduce an issue which has produced considerable controversy within Polonia, namely, the presentation of Polish victimization and the Polish righteousness in the new U.S. Holocaust Memorial Museum in Washington, D.C. As a member of the federal Holocaust Commission since its creation by Congress in 1980, I feel quite justified in standing before you and saying that the initial goals for this museum with respect to Poland have been realized to a significant extent. The stories of Polish victimization, as well as of Polish rescue efforts, have been fully integrated into the museum's main exhibit. They are not just off somewhere in a side room. And the stories are told with fundamental accuracy. While some legitimate questions have been raised about certain portions of the text, and while I certainly believe the exhibit needs amplification and expansion, the museum graphically portrays the Nazi attack on the Polish nation, depicts the incarceration and extermination of the "elites," and even includes (prominently displayed) one of the key texts regarding future Nazi plans for mass annihilation of Poles. And the special exhibit on Zegota, as well as the official lists of Righteous from Yad Vashem in Israel, clearly give visitors (the vast majority of whom are non-Jewish) an understanding of the extent to which Poles attempted to rescue Jews under the most trying of conditions.

Clearly there are issues in the Museum (e.g. the Kielce pogrom) that need further review. I am committed to such an effort, along with additional Polish representatives on the Council who President Clinton will hopefully soon appoint. I look forward to continued collaboration with interested Polish academics and groups, such as the Holocaust Education Committee of the Kosciuszko Foundation in New York, who have proven so helpful in generating materials and testimonies from Polish survivors. The witness of Joseph Wardzala of Derby, CT, for example, in recording his personal testimony of prison life under the Nazis for the Museum is vital for preserving the story of Polish victimization for future generations. So is the witness of Ambassador Władysław Bartoszewski, a leading figure in *Zegota* and now Polish Ambassador in Vienna, who was honored along with *Zegota* at a public ceremony at the Holocaust Museum on March 22nd.

All is not perfect in terms of the Polish story at the Holocaust Museum. But it is far better than many have made it out to be in public comments in the press. I might add that a recent professional poll of Museum visitors which included a question on attitudes towards Poles and Poland revealed little or no "anti-Polish" feeling among such visitors.

The second major implication I see for Polonia and Poland today from a reflection on the Holocaust is the importance of cultural preservation and enhancement. This does not mean that I advocate cultural isolationism on the part of Poles or Polish Americans. Quite the contrary. I am totally in support of my colleague Dr. Thaddeus Gromada, Director of the Polish Institute of Arts and Sciences, who insisted, in a major address at the Shrine in Doylestown, PA in September 1992, on efforts to integrate the authentic Polish and Polish-American experience into the mainstream of American culture.[13] But we have seen from the example of the Nazi period that destruction of a culture goes hand-in-hand with the physical disappearance of a people. Polish culture served during the Nazi era, as well as the subsequent Communist era, as a powerful bulwark against annihilation by extermination or assimilation. Neither Poles nor Polish Americans today can afford to enter new partnerships in an increasingly pluralistic Europe and America without firm roots in our own culture. We must be prepared to bring something substantial to these new partnerships.

The third implication of the Holocaust concerns the much-debated issue of Church-State relations. This remains a central constitutional question for Poland today and we are facing it anew, albeit in somewhat different ways, here in the United States. Considerable study has been done by Protestant and Catholic scholars on this issue. Some, such as Professor Gordan Zahn, have emphasized how the desire on the part of the German Catholic Church to maintain its Concordat with Hitler muffled its original prophetic critique of Nazism developed by the German Bishops at their Fulde meeting in 1934. For Zahn, one lesson of the Holocaust for the churches is the importance of maintaining a distance from the state for the sake of the church's own integrity.

As Poles and Polish Americans continue to weigh the complex issues involved in church-state relations today in both our countries, the Holocaust can teach us that it seems in the best interests of the Church itself to keep a distance from the state. Official recognition may well mean official cooperation which can easily degenerate into co-option by the state authorities for their own ends, thereby muting the Church's prophetic mandate in any society. In light of the Holocaust experience it is important for Poles to listen to such voices as Jerzy Turowicz, Józef Tischner and Bishop Józef Zycinski, who in varied ways have urged restraint with respect to the Church's direct role in public affairs.[14] And Polish Americans should support such a perspective in Poland rather than giving encouragement to the forces of excessive religio-nationalism. The Polish American community can also assist Poles in better understanding the American experience in Church-State separation, even though they recognize that no simple transfer of perspective is possible or desirable. As in other central areas of Polish national life, Poland must be allowed to be Poland even though it can surely profit from contact with the U.S. experience. I have in fact found many Poles significantly interested in such interchange on the Church-State question, as a number of recent colloquia, including one sponsored by the Marshall Foundation to which I was invited, bear witness.

The final implication of the Polish experience of the Holocaust that I would like to raise this evening is that of *solidarity*. On one of the walls of the Holocaust Museum in Washington we have a portion of the famous quote attributed to Lutheran Pastor Niemoller who eventually died for his opposition to Hitler. Pastor Niemoller said, if I may paraphrase his remarks, that when the Nazis came for the trade unionists, the homosexuals, the Communists, the Jews, and the Catholics, he did not protest because he was not identified with any of these groups. And when the Nazis finally came for him, there was no one left to protest.

Niemoller's statement serves as a powerful reminder for all peoples today, including Polish Americans, of two basic realities. The first is the critical importance of establishing networks of intergroup bonding and support in times of relative social tranquility. There is little hope of developing such ties in times of acute social crisis if they have not been nurtured in more peaceful moments. And we never know when and where such can suddenly become vital. Only recently two U.S. cities, Billings, Montana and Eugene, Oregon have experienced sudden challenges from neo-Nazi elements. Both have responded in exemplary fashion. One lesson that emerges from a study of the Holocaust for Polish Americans (and I dare say for Poles as well) is that the Polish nation stood pretty much alone when it was attacked by the Nazis in 1939. The

nation was more or less abandoned by the Western countries, despite certain military alliances that existed on paper, and even to a significant degree by the Vatican.

This abandonment has generated decades of anger within Polonia. I do not wish to suggest that this anger has been without any foundation. But I do want to urge Polish Americans to take a second look at the matter, to see whether a certain exaggerated nationalism which in turn bred isolationism might not have contributed to the relative lack of effective alliances in the inter-war period.

Poles in Poland will need to re-examine the nation's set of alliances in this new hopeful, yet potentially threatening, era in Europe. It is not my role to enter into that discussion here. But Polish Americans will also need to seriously re-examine their ties to other groups in our society. Clearly, establishing effective relationships with key minority groups, especially Hispanics and African Americans with whom Polish Americans often share the urban landscape, becomes an important priority. Equally so do ties with American Jewry given the historic linkage between the two communities stemming from Poland itself. While Polish-Jewish relations have been marked by tensions on numerous occasions here in America,[15] we have also witnessed reasonably successful efforts to build lasting coalitions, both in several local communities such as New York, Chicago, Buffalo and Milwaukee and through the National Polish American-Jewish American Council based in Chicago. Through these channels Poles and Jews have begun not merely to discuss and study our past mutual history, but, as we continue this process, to work cooperatively for mutual support of each other's social agendas as well as joint action on issues of importance to both our communities (e.g. foreign aid legislation). Such efforts need expanded support both from the leadership of American Polonia as well as from the grass roots. The Holocaust has taught both Poles and Polish Americans that safety exists only in solidarity with others.

The second implication emerging from the more general notion of solidarity is the importance of standing up for the basic rights of all people. Poles must answer the challenge of discrimination whether directed against them or others. When any one group is singled out for attack, the poison inevitably enters the bloodstream of society and begins to claim other victims as well. This is crystal clear in the Holocaust. The experience of victimization under the Nazis, then, should place Polish Americans in the forefront of the struggle for human rights and human equality for all. The day on which Polonia becomes identified with opposition to human rights and human equality is the day on which it has lost all sense of its own victimization under the Nazis.

Responding to the Holocaust in the constructive ways I have suggested above, particularly the commitment to improve bonding with the Jewish community with whom we share a history of Nazi victimization, will not prove easy. But I know from my own experience of my grandmother's very human and personal interaction with Polish Jews in the Logan Square neighborhood of Chicago where I was reared, as well as from my experience of seeing firsthand the profound welcome accorded the first group of Israelis to revisit Poland in twenty years (a professional dance company), Jews and Poles both have roots in the soil of Poland that can never be totally erased. It will take the courage and tenacity of the soldiers who tried to defend Poland against impossible military odds and the partisans who kept the spirit of freedom alive; it will take the resolve of the courageous men and women of Zegota. We should not expect it to be otherwise. Nothing worthwhile ever is.

Notes

1. Richard C. Lukas, *Forgotten Holocaust: The Poles Under German Occupation 1939–1944.* Lexington, KY: The University Press of Kentucky. 1986.
2. Cf. Eugeniusz Duraczynski, *Wojna i Okupacja: Wrzesien 1939–Kwiecien 1943.* Warsaw: Wiedza Powszechna, 1974, 17. Also Jewry 1933–1945. New York: Schocken, 1973, 163; 193 and Leon Poliakov, *Harvest of Hate: The Nazi Program for the Destruction of the Jews of Europe* (New York: Holocaust Library, 1979), 263.
3. Cf. Janusz Gumkowski and Kazimierz Leszczynski, *Poland under Nazi Occupation.* (Warsaw: Polonia Publishing House, 1961), 59.
4. Cf. Karol Pospieszalski, *Polska pod Niemieckim Prawem.* (Poznan: Wydawnictwo Instytutu Zachodniego, 1946), 189.
5. For a discussion of the elimination of the handicapped and the Gypsies relative to the extermination of the Jews, cf. Sybil Milton, "The Context of the Holocaust," *German Studies Review,* 13:2 (May 1990), 269–283.
6. Cf. John T. Pawlikowski, "The Auschwitz Convent Controversy: Mutual Misperceptions," in Carol Rittner and John K. Roth (eds.), *Memory Offended: The Auschwitz Convent Controversy.* (New York, Westport, CT., London: Praeger, 1991), 63–73. Also cf. Wladyslaw T. Bartoszewski, *The Convent at Auschwitz.* (New York: George Braziller, 1990).
7. John T. Pawlikowski, "The Auschwitz Convent Controversy," 65.
8. Cf. Stanislaw Krajewski, "Carmel at Auschwitz: on the Recent Polish Church Document and Its Background," *SIDIC* 22 (1989), 16.
9. Richard Lukas, *Forgotten Holocaust,* 16.
10. John Morely, *Vatican Diplomacy and the Jews During the Holocaust: 1939–1943.* (New York: Ktav, 1980), 140; 146.
11. Cited in Richard Lukas, *Forgotten Holocaust,* 16–17.
12. Edward J. Moskal, "The Polish Victims of the Holocaust," *Zgoda* (February 15, 1994), 5.
13. Thaddeus V. Gromada, "Polish Americans and Mainstream America," unpublished lecture, Polish Apostolate Seminar, Our Lady of Czestochowa Shrine, Doylestown, PA, September 27, 1992, 4.
14. Cf. John T. Pawlikowski, "The Holocaust: Its Implications for Contemporary Church-State Relations in Poland," *Religion in Eastern Europe,* XIII:2 (April 1993), 1–13 and "Katolicyzm a zycie publiczne najnowsze doswiadczenia amerykanskie," *WIEZ* 35:2 (Luty 1992), 93–110. Also cf. Part IV, "The Church," in Janine R. Wedel, (ed.), *The Unplanned Society: Poland During and After Communism.* New York: Columbia University Press, 1992, 188–219.
15. The tension over the Auschwitz convent situation is certainly not the first instance of Polish-Jewish controversy in the United States. For an earlier example, cf. Andrzej Kapiszewski, "Polish-Jewish Conflicts in America During the Paris Peace Conference: Milwaukee as a Case Study," *Polish American Studies,* XLIX:2 (Autumn 1992), 5–18.

BELONGING IN THE WEST

Multiple challenges and concerns arise from the presence of ever-growing Muslim communities within Western society.

YVONNE YAZBECK HADDAD

When Daniel Pipes sounded the alarm: "The Muslims Are Coming! The Muslims Are Coming!" in the November 19, 1990, issue of *National Review*, it was clear that Muslims were already here. Indeed, they had become an integral part of the West. Since that time, Islam, particularly Islamic fundamentalism, has continually been depicted as the next enemy: as a force replacing communism as a challenge to the West.

Consequently, Muslims have often suffered from considerable prejudice. They have been accused of adhering to a religion that is devoid of integrity, that encourages violent passions in its adherents, that

menaces civil society and is a threat to our way of life. Muslims are stereotyped as potentially bloodthirsty terrorists whose loyalty as citizens must be questioned. Not one promoter of political correctness has put them on a list of communities to be protected. But Muslims have been victims of hate crimes that include assault, murder, and the burning of mosques in both Europe and North America. As a result, their apprehension about their security and future in Western society has increased.

The Muslim encounter with the West dates back to the beginning of Islam. As Muslims spread into Byzantium and North Africa, they established their hegemony over large areas inhabited by Christian populations. While their expansion into western Europe was halted at Poitiers in 731, Muslims created a thriving civilization in different parts of Spain, Portugal, Sicily, and southern France between the eighth and fifteenth centuries. In the East, Ottoman expansion into Europe was not halted until the failure of the siege of

This article first appeared in *The World & I*, September 1997, pp. 50-59. Reprinted by permission of *The World & I*, a publication of The Washington Times Corporation. © 1997.

Vienna in 1683. While a significant number of Muslims continued to live in eastern Europe, in Bulgaria, Romania, Albania, and Serbia, the fall of Grenada in 1492 and the Inquisition (which gave Muslims the options of conversion to Christianity, expulsion, or death) all but eliminated a Muslim presence in western Europe. Thus, the recent growth of the Muslim community in Europe and North America has been called the "new Islamic presence."

Indeed, since the sixteenth century, Muslims have encountered Western cultures as conquering and imperial powers, competing in their quest to subjugate Muslims and monopolize their economic resources. Consequently, some Muslims depict the West as bent on combating Islam not only through colonial conquest but through armies of missionaries. They perceive a West that is and ever has been eager to displace or eradicate Muslims. They find evidence in the Reconquista, the Crusades, and, more recently, in Palestine and Bosnia.

Living beyond the Islamic state

Muslim jurists have offered various opinions about whether it is permissible for Muslims to live outside the jurisdiction of an Islamic state. This issue has been raised during the last two decades, as some Muslim scholars have admonished Muslims to leave the West lest they lose their soul amid its wayward ways. Other jurists have insisted that as long as Muslims are free to practice their faith, they are allowed to live outside the house of Islam, while still others have said that it is Muslims' duty to propagate the faith in their new abode. Thus they not only have the opportunity to share the salvific teachings of Islam but must try to redeem Western society from its evil ways and restore it to the worship of God.

The question then is often asked: "Given their experience of the West, why do they come?" Surveys show that Muslims move to Europe and North America for the same reasons that other populations have chosen to come: for higher education, better economic opportunities, and political and religious freedom. Others are refugees, the by-product of Euro-

Here Yet Apart

❧ *Though an integral part of twentieth-century Western society, Muslims have lately been targets of considerable prejudice.*

❧ *Many argue that it may not be possible to lead a Muslim lifestyle beyond the borders of an Islamic state.*

❧ *Both Islamic and European governments have helped build mosques and Muslim centers in the West, in the hopes of blunting the rise of fundamentalism and aiding the assimilation of Muslim immigrants.*

❧ *Muslims ask whether Western society, which prides itself on liberal democracy, pluralism, and multiculturalism, will be flexible enough to provide for Islamic input into the shaping of its future.*

American adventures in the world. Thus the first significant group of Muslims to come to France were North Africans and Senegalese who were recruited to fight in French colonial wars. Immigrants to Britain are from its former colonies and from the ranks of its Asian (Bangladeshi, Indian, and Pakistani) colonial civil servants expelled from Africa by the leaders of newly independent nations. In the Netherlands, the initial Muslim population came from the colonies of Indonesia and Suriname.

The majority of Muslims in Europe were recruited as temporary guest workers to relieve the shortage of labor in the post–World War II reconstruction. The host countries of Germany, the Netherlands, Austria, Britain, Switzerland, and France expected them to leave when their contracts expired. In the 1970s, a recession and growing unemployment prompted European governments to reduce imported labor. Some even provided financial incentives for the laborers to return to their homelands. This policy led to an unintended growth of the Muslim community, as many opted to bring their families and settle for fear that they would not have another opportunity.

In European nations with an official

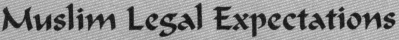

Muslim Legal Expectations

Kathleen Moore

When a truck bomb shattered the Murrah Federal Building in downtown Oklahoma City on April 19, 1995—the worst terrorist act ever on American soil—many in the media and federal law enforcement jumped to the conclusion that an "Islamic fundamentalist" was responsible. Similarly, the downing of TWA Flight 800 and the Olympic Park explosion in Atlanta set off allegations that "Middle Eastern–looking" terrorists were to blame. Those hasty conclusions have proved groundless. However, Muslim defendants have been convicted for the 1993 bombing of the World Trade Center, and a Muslim suspect has been arrested in connection with the attack on traffic near the CIA headquarters in January of that year.

Instantly attributing blame to unknown Muslim terrorists was not just the result of the media and law enforcement officials letting their imaginations run amok. Such images were also conjured up—and in some instances acted upon—by the general public. Some 200 incidents of anti-Muslim harassment were reported in the days immediately following the tragedy in Oklahoma.

Consequently, American Muslim communities mobilized to an unprecedented degree. Existing organizations, such as the American Muslim Council and the Islamic Society of North America, were joined by newly formed groups such as the Council on American-Islamic Relations (CAIR) to defend Muslims' civil rights. Public relations and lobbying efforts and press conferences highlighted not merely the Muslim presence in the United States but also the American Muslims' experiences as targets of discrimination. Thus the rights consciousness of this growing segment of the American population is largely being shaped by Muslims' responses to media distortions and perceived demonization of Islam.

The fears that motivate anti-Islamic sentiment appear to derive from a sense of insecurity that has lurked just beneath the surface of our national life since the fall of the Berlin Wall in 1989. The prospects for world peace would seem to be greater than at any other time in this century, but our doubts about the future seem nevertheless to escalate. This post–Cold War malaise has its consequences for those who fear they may come to take the unenviable place of the "Red menace" in the public mind. Of great concern to many Muslims is the prospect that they will be increasingly subjected to various forms of discrimination in Western countries as negative portrayals of Islam and Muslims take their toll.

The visible effects of these concerns and experiences of mistreatment can be seen in the emergence of rights-advocacy groups that have used a variety of legal strategies to assert Muslim rights. For instance, in the United States, CAIR has conducted media campaigns over the last two years or so to bring to public attention instances where women have been prohibited from wearing the traditional Islamic *hijab* (head scarf) at work. Cases of harassment involving Muslims who have been taunted with epithets relating to prevalent prejudicial stereotypes have been documented and financially sup-

(Continued)

ported through the legal process by these advocacy groups. In Britain, a few Muslim activists have (so far, unsuccessfully) pressed the government for greater autonomy, particularly allowing Islamic courts to adjudicate issues of family law separate from the civil court system.

We are now witnessing the emergence of a distinctive Western Muslim identity, carved out of the secular social environment of the West. It would not be accurate, however, to assume that the Muslim identity being forged is uniform or monolithic. In fact, significant distinctions and disagreements exist within Muslim communities that are differentiated by sectarian, ethnic, regional, or generational traits. But it is meaningful to note that there are shared experiences and to recognize that the formulation of this identity is taking place under constraints imposed by the host societies. Muslim legal expectations and interpretations are thus voiced within particular contexts, in response to specific events, cultural characteristics, and historical pressures.

In an idealized sense, Muslims migrated to the United States and Britain with a centuries-old legal tradition in hand. In this legal framework are the classical traditions of Islamic jurisprudence that offer models for minority living. Historically, these models focus on three essential questions: First, under what conditions are Muslims allowed to live outside Muslim territory? In essence, the answer is only where religious freedom prevails. Second, what responsibilities do Muslim minorities have with respect to their host society? Here, answers are varied. Third, what is the relationship of Muslim minorities, living in places like the United States and Britain, to the global Muslim community as a whole? Again, answers are varied and problematic.

In general, the classical models suggest that if a Muslim minority does not encounter religious freedom and is unable to practice its faith, then it has the options of fighting back (*jihad*) or emigration (*hijrah*).

Yet many see these traditions as out of touch with Muslim minorities' realities and in need of revision to fit today's circumstances. Recent calls have been made for the formulation of a "new" jurisprudence in light of changing conditions. A variety of issues have been singled out by the British and American Muslim communities as being crucial.

Some issues are the product of the secular environment in which Muslims live. Do they have rights to religious freedom that require accommodation of their specific needs in the workplace, at school, or in the military? How will Muslims survive as a vibrant religious community in the West? Will they be able to freely and fully participate in its religious landscape and in defining the future as a pluralistic society? How can Muslim children be successfully integrated into the larger society, to function as hyphenated Americans or Britons without abandoning the faith? Can Muslims vote or run for political office in a secular society where the institutions of government are not based on Islamic values? What roles are women permitted to play in public life?

Attendance at mosques and Islamic centers (in the West) has gone up over the last decade or so. Mosques are now not only for prayer at the five prescribed times: They have become community centers and provide facilities for tutoring students in their school subjects, Qur'anic studies, marriage ceremonies, free counseling and mediation, and legal services.

In some of these places, Muslims are listening to those who warn from the pulpit that the encounter with the secular West is destructive and that the only option for Mus-

(Continued)

lim survival is to remain marginal to public life. From this isolationist perspective, the Muslim minority should reaffirm a Muslim identity in isolation, untainted by the materialistic values of the West. This, it is thought, will have the effect of inviting others to Islam by providing an example of an incorruptible "city on a hill" in the midst of moral decay.

On the other side of the debate are the "accommodationists," who struggle to feel at home in the United States and Britain. Muhammad Abduh, an early twentieth-century reformer in Egypt, provides some insight into the accommodationists' position. Abduh gave a *fatwa* (religious legal opinion) permitting Muslims in South Africa to consume meat butchered for People of the Book (i.e., Christians and Jews) when no *halal* meat (i.e., food prepared or butchered in the Islamically prescribed way, similar to the Jewish tradition of kosher) was available.

Accommodationists advise cooperation with non-Muslims, provided that it benefits the Muslim community. As long as the Muslim who lives as a minority is at liberty to maintain the "core" of the religion, he may adjust to the host society. Accommodationists argue that diet, as long as it is nourishing, need not comply with stringent Islamic strictures; attire, as long as it is clean and modest, need not be restricting (such as the so-called veil or head scarf is); and the architecture of mosques and Islamic centers need not slavishly imitate Middle Eastern styles as long as the buildings are accessible and functional.

In the last two decades the circumstances of Muslim minorities have come to the attention of various international Islamic organizations, such as the Muslim World League, which has established a Fiqh Council, a body that engages in the interpretation of Islamic law to address minority concerns. The council represents a wide variety of Islamic legal schools and advocates what is being called the "jurisprudence of necessity" (*fiqh al-darurah*) and "jurisprudence of minority" (*fiqh al-aqalliyah*) to respond to issues of Muslim life in a non-Islamic environment.

Some critics within Islam, though, see this as an effort to impose a "top-down" understanding of Muslim contingencies and reject it in favor of a "bottom-up" approach. Efforts at using American legal rules and then sanctifying them as "Islamic" because they are fair and just can be seen at the local level. For instance, American laws governing marriage, divorce, and child custody, where the woman would, arguably, have greater rights than Islam affords, have been sanctified in places where the *imam* (leader of the mosque) has sanctioned a civil marriage license or divorce decree obtained by a member of his mosque.

The secular legal system has had its effect on Muslim legal consciousness. For example, one leader of a large mosque community in an urban area in the western United States asserts that the process of working out a set of rules to govern Muslim life must be thought of as a jurisprudence of "minority," not because of any specific Islamic tradition but because Muslims are living in the United States, where a significant body of case law on minority relations already exists. To be labeled a minority entitles one to rights. The word *minority* may connote weakness or vulnerability, but it is also a recognized basis for making claims to resources and privilege in America. Thus, it is imperative to accommodate Islamic practices to fit the opportunities provided by the local customs and laws of the community in which they are now a permanent part.

Kathleen Moore is assistant professor of political science at the University of Connecticut.

state religion, such as Britain and the Netherlands, Muslims have sought parity with Jews and Catholics who have been given special privileges. But to no avail. Thus, during the Salman Rushdie affair, Muslims sought implementation of the blasphemy law, only to find out that it operates only to protect Anglicanism. In Britain, for example, the school day starts with a Christian prayer. In courts, the oath is taken on the Bible. Town council meetings start with a prayer. Anglican clergy celebrate marriage that is automatically legal without having to go to the registrar. While Catholic and Jewish marriages are recognized, those performed by imams are not. Catholics and Jews obtain state funding to support their parochial schools, but Muslim requests for parity have been denied.

Muslims have fared differently in nations that have historically welcomed immigrants—the United States, Canada, Latin America, and Australia. Muslim migrant laborers began coming to America in the nineteenth century. While many returned, a few settled permanently and formed the nucleus of what is now the fourth and fifth American-born generation of Muslims. The largest number of Muslims came in the 1970s on a preference visa and were accepted as citizens and given voting rights. Predominantly members of the educated elite, they are doctors, professors, and engineers.

Islam is the second- or third-largest religion in various European nations. It is estimated that there are five million Muslims in France, organized in over 1,000 mosques and prayer halls. They constitute about 10 percent of the population, making Islam the largest religion after Catholicism and with more active adherents than either Protestants or Jews. In Britain, the Muslim population is estimated at about two million, organized in over 600 mosques. The Muslim community of the United States is estimated at five million, about 10 percent of whom are involved in organized religion in over 1,250 mosques and Islamic centers. Canada has about half a million.

It is expected that Muslims will outnumber Jews in Canada and the United States by the first decade of the next century. The North American community is noted for its ethnic, national, linguistic,

and sectarian diversity. It includes over a million converts, mostly African Americans. While it is estimated that up to 18 percent of the slaves brought to America were Muslims, most had converted to Christianity by the beginning of this century. The conversion of African Americans to Islam is a twentieth-century phenomenon.

The Muslim experience in the West

The Muslim experience in the West varies according to the immigrants' background, the nations they came from, their reasons for leaving, and their educational attainments. The host country's policies are also influential: whether it

Some Muslim scholars have admonished Muslims to leave the West, lest they lose their souls.

welcomes foreigners and/or grants them citizenship rights, its perceptions of Islam, and its laws governing the relationship between religion and state.

During the eighties, various Muslim countries began laying Islamic foundations in the West by providing funds for the construction of mosques and schools and the teaching of Arabic and Islam. For example, in a two-year period, Saudi Arabia spent $10 million to construct mosques in North America. In Germany, Sweden, and the Netherlands—where there are large Turkish and Moroccan communities—the fear of the potential for growth of Islamic fundamentalism among the marginalized guest workers led to arrangements with the Turkish and Moroccan governments to supervise the religious affairs of the community. Both governments welcomed the opportunity to blunt the growth of fundamentalism and curtail its dissemination in their countries. The European governments paid for construction of Islamic centers and mosques and imported the religious leaders to lead prayers and provide religious instruction.

Two issues are of paramount importance for both the immigrants and host countries: security and cultural coherence. All nation-states have developed a myth of national identity that has been inculcated in schoolchildren through literature, art, music, assumptions, legends, and a particular understanding of history. These myths have shaped several generations of Europeans and Americans through the cauldron of two wars and created distinctive identities marking the way the West sees itself and what it takes for granted, as well as what it identifies as alien, strange, and weird.

Educated Muslims who emigrated in the postwar period also have a preformed understanding of Western culture based on the experience of colonialism and neocolonialism. Their perceptions have been shaped by watching Western movies and television, which they perceive as imbued with drugs, violence, racism, and pornography. Muslims are repelled by what they see as a degenerate society with weak family values. They condemn premarital or extramarital sex and having children out of wedlock, both of which increase the fragility of marriage and hence the family bond. They believe that Western values concerning parents and children's duties toward one another are lacking. There is too much emphasis on individual freedom and not enough on corporate responsibility.

A primary concern for Muslim immigrants is surviving in what they experience as a hostile environment and safeguarding the welfare of their children. They are fully aware that Europe and the Americas have been shaped by secular Christianity. They seek to maintain the right to practice their faith according to its tenets as revealed to them by God. They are concerned about perpetuation of the faith among their children and preservation of Islamic values. In this context they have sought to have employers provide them with time off to fulfill their religious duties during the day, to attend the Friday prayer at the mosque, fast during the month of Ramadan, and celebrate the two major holidays (Eid al-Fitr and Eid al-Adha). Many are concerned about properly slaughtered meat (*halal*), while others seek the right to have their children excused from coed athletics and sex education (which they believe promotes promiscuity). They believe that religious freedom should provide the right to wear the head scarf (*hijab*) for women.

Muslims are repelled by what they see as a degenerate Western society with weak family values

In France, the issue of wearing the hijab took on national significance when several female students were banned from wearing it on the grounds that such behavior is tantamount to proselytizing, a proscribed activity in the secular schools of France. For Muslims, the ban was seen as an anti-Muslim act, since Christians are allowed to wear a cross and Jews a yarmulke, both of which could then be interpreted as an act of propagating a faith.

The issue of the hijab has surfaced in other Western nations under different rubrics. For example, in Canada, feminists championed the banning of head scarfs, which they depicted as a symbol of oppression. Muslim girls who put them on insisted that it was an act of obedience to a divine injunction and therefore protected under the freedom of religion. More important, they viewed it as an instrument of liberation from being a sex object. In the United States, the Council on American-Islamic Relations reported that there was a 50 percent increase in 1996 in the number of incidents of discrimination against women who wear the hijab.

Islam in a plural society

The Western experience is also shaping new forms of Islamic organization and administration. The imam not only leads prayer and worship but acts as an ambassador to the host culture, attempting to build bridges to other faith communities and representing Muslims in interfaith events. Moreover, the mosque, besides being a place of congregational prayer, has become a social center where the community meets for a variety of events that help cement relationships and provide for community celebrations. In this center for Islamic knowledge and education Islam is taught to the next generation, which reflects on its meaning in the new environment. The mosque has become an island of security and a venue for the sharing of one's experiences. It is not unusual to see people clothed in their ethnic dress for Sunday services, taking advantage of a chance to affirm primary identity in an environment where individuals can be themselves without being under constant scrutiny for conformity.

Some Muslims contemplate the option of returning to their homeland, should conditions of life in the West continue to be unacceptable. Their children, however, have been reared and educated in the West. The West is their homeland. They are bicultural and possess an intimate experience and knowledge of Western society, as well as a knowledge about the culture of the parents as remembered and reinvented in the West. While immigrants struggle to maintain their identity, they are increasingly being challenged and changed as their children become more indigenized into the surrounding culture.

Some Western authors have continued to question whether Muslims are worthy of citizenship in a democratic nation or whether their presence will alter the place where they settle. While some continue to debate whether they belong *in* the West, it is evident that Muslims are part and parcel *of* the West. An estimated ten thousand Muslims currently serve in the armed services of the United States,

> While immigrants struggle to maintain their identity, they are increasingly challenged as their children become indigenized into the surrounding culture.

for example. There are two Muslim chaplains, one in the Navy and one in the Army, and plans have been made to appoint one in the Air Force.

Muslims in the West generally favor keeping a low profile for security reasons. They are the latest victims of chauvinism and xenophobia. Events such as the oil embargo of 1973, the Iranian revolution, the holding of American hostages for 444 days, and the Pan Am bombing have created concern among many westerners. Irresponsible and irrational actions such as the bombing of the World Trade Center have heightened fears of Islamic fundamentalism. This has exacerbated the fear of Islam and tapped into a history of misunderstanding and vilification. Thus, Muslims fear they are becoming the new villains on the block, replacing Jews, Gypsies, Italians, and African Americans as objects of odium.

Muslims continue to ask whether Western democracies are liberal enough to include Islamic input into the national consensus, or if they will insist on an exclusively Judeo-Christian culture. Will Western pluralism or multiculturalism be flexible enough to provide for Islamic input into the shaping of the future of Western society? Or will Muslims continue to be marginalized, ostracized, studied, and evaluated, always judged as lacking, always the "other"?

Yvonne Yazbeck Haddad is professor of the history of Islam and Christian-Muslim relations at Georgetown University.

istory has stripped Africa's people of the dignity of building their nations on their own indigenous values, institutions, and heritage. The modern African state is the product of Europe, not Africa. To attempt at this late date to return to ancestral identities and resources as bases for building the modern African nation would risk the collapse of many countries. At the same time, to disregard ethnic realities would be to build on loose sand, also a high-risk exercise. Is it possible to consolidate the framework of the modern African state while giving recognition and maximum utility to the component elements of ethnicities, cultures, and aspirations for self-determination?

THE CHALLENGE OF ETHNICITY IN AFRICA

Ethnicity is more than skin color or physical characteristics, more than language, song, and dance. It is the embodiment of values, institutions, and patterns of behavior, a composite whole

ultimately rested on police and military force, the tools of authoritarian rule. This crude force was, however, softened by making use of traditional leaders as extended arms of state control over the tribes or the local communities, giving this externally imposed system a semblance of legitimacy for the masses. Adding to this appearance of legitimacy was the introduction of a welfare system by which the state provided meager social services and limited development opportunities to privileged sectors. National resources were otherwise extracted and exported as raw materials to feed the metropolitan industries of the colonial masters.

This new system undermined the people's indigenous system, which provided them with the means for pursuing their modest but sustainable life objectives, and replaced it with centrally controlled resources that were in short supply and subject to severely competitive demands. Development was conceived as a means of receiving basic services from the state, rather than as a process of growth and collective accumulation of wealth that could in turn be invested in further growth. The

Ethnicity

AN AFRICAN PREDICAMENT

BY FRANCIS M. DENG

representing a people's historical experience, aspirations, and world view. Deprive a people of their ethnicity, their culture, and you deprive them of their sense of direction or purpose.

Traditionally, African societies and even states functioned through an elaborate system based on the family, the lineage, the clan, the tribe, and ultimately a confederation of groups with ethnic, cultural, and linguistic characteristics in common. These were the units of social, economic, and political organizations and inter-communal relations.

In the process of colonial state-formation, groups were divided or brought together with little or no regard to their common characteristics or distinctive attributes. They were placed in new administrative frameworks, governed by new values, new institutions, and new operational principles and techniques. The autonomous local outlook of the old order was replaced by the control mechanisms of the state, in which the ultimate authority was an outsider, a foreigner. This mechanism functioned through the centralization of power, which

localized, broad-based, low-risk, self-sustaining subsistence activities gave way to high-risk, stratifying competition for state power and scarce resources, a zero-sum conflict of identities based on tribalism or ethnicity. Independence removed the common enemy, the colonial oppressor, but actually sharpened the conflict over centralized power and control over national resources.

Today, virtually every African conflict has some ethno-regional dimension to it. Even those conflicts that may appear to be free of ethnic concerns involve factions and alliances built around ethnic loyalties. Analysts have tended to have one of two views of the role of ethnicity in these conflicts. Some see ethnicity as a source of conflict; others see it as a tool used by political entrepreneurs to promote their ambitions. In reality, it is both. Ethnicity, especially when combined with terri-

Francis M. Deng is a senior fellow in the Brookings Foreign Policy Studies program.

torial identity, is a reality that exists independently of political maneuvers. To argue that ethnic groups are unwitting tools of political manipulation is to underestimate a fundamental social reality. On the other hand, ethnicity is clearly a resource for political manipulation and entrepreneurship.

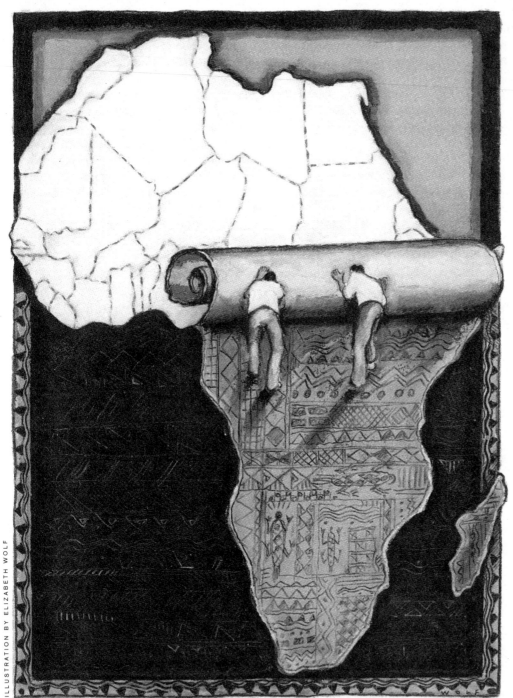

ILLUSTRATION BY ELIZABETH WOLF

through shrewd distribution of ministerial posts, civil service jobs, social services, and development projects. Julius Nyerere, a scion of tribal chieftaincy, stamped out tribalism by fostering nationalistic pride in Tanganyika and later, Tanzania, born out of the union with Zanzibar. Jommo Kenyatta of Kenya forged a delicate alliance of ethnic groups behind the dominance of his Kenyan African National Union party. In South Africa, apartheid recognized and stratified races and ethnicities to an unsustainable degree. Post-apartheid South Africa, however, remains poised between a racially, ethnically, and tribally blind democratic system and a proud ethnic self-assertiveness, represented and exploited by Zulu nationalists, spearheaded by the emotive leadership of Chief Buthelezi.

Throughout Africa, the goal of safeguarding unity within the colonial state has preserved the stability of colonial borders while generating ethnic tensions and violence within those borders. Sudan offers an extreme example. The dominant North, a hybrid of Arab and African racial, cultural, and religious elements, is trying to resolve its identity crisis by being more Arab and Islamic than its prototypes. Worse, this distorted self-perception, heightened by the agendas of political elites, is projected as the framework for unifying and integrating the country, generating a devastating zero-sum conflict between the Arab-Muslim North and the indigenously African South, whose modern leadership is predominantly Christian.

The decision of the Founding Fathers of the Organization of African Unity to respect the colonial borders established a normative principle that has been followed with remarkable success. Secession movements have met with strong resistance from the OAU. Katanga tried to break away from the Congo (which became Zaire, now back to the Democratic Republic of the Congo) but failed. The secessionist Biafran war in Nigeria also failed. Somalia's attempt to take

AFRICA'S RESPONSE TO THE CHALLENGE

After independence Africans were eager to disavow tribalism as divisive. Unity was postulated in a way that assumed a mythical homogeneity amidst diversity. Kwame Nkrumah of Ghana outlawed parties organized on tribal or ethnic bases. Houphouet-Boigny of Côte d'Ivoire coopted ethnic groups the Ogaden from Ethiopia was decisively thwarted. Southern Sudan struggled for 17 years to break away from the North and in the end settled for autonomy in 1972. When the fighting resumed in 1983, the stated goal was and remains the creation of a new Sudan that would be free from any discrimination based on race, ethnicity, culture, or religion.

Eritrea's breakaway from Ethiopia is seen not as a case of violating colonial borders, but of upholding them, since Eritrea had been a colony under Italian rule. Likewise, the de facto breakaway of Northern Somalia is seen as a restoration of colonial borders, since the North had been governed separately by the British. Even in the Sudan, often said to be a good candidate for partition, should the country be divided, the division might be rationalized as an extension of the British colonial policy that governed the Sudan as two separate entities, one Arab-Islamic and the other indigenous African with rudiments of Christian Western influences.

In most African countries, the determination to preserve national unity following independence provided the motivation behind one-party rule, excessive centralization of power, oppressive authoritarian regimes, and systematic violation of human rights and fundamental liberties. These in turn have generated a reaction, manifested in heightened tension and the demand for a

the public. But these upheavals involved only a rotation of like-minded elites, or worse, military dictators, intent on occupying the seat of power vacated by the colonial masters. Such leaders soon became their colonial masters' images.

At the moment, for the overwhelming majority of African countries the quest for unity underscores the intensity of disunity. As long as the Africans avoid confronting the issue of ethnicity and fail to develop norms and means for managing diversity within the framework of unity, peace and stability will continue to elude the pluralistic state.

MODELS OF ETHNIC CONFIGURATION

African governments have responded to the challenge in varying ways, ranging from pragmatic management to blind neglect and catastrophic mismanagement. The particular form the ethnic policies of a country take may in large measure be dictated by the characteristics of its identity configuration.

A few states in Africa enjoy a high degree of homogeneity or, at least, a relatively inconsequential diversity. Botswana, for example, reflects exemplary cohesiveness, democracy, stability, and sustained growth.

Most African countries, particularly those in West Africa (possibly excepting Nigeria), Kenya, and southern African coun-

DEPRIVE A PEOPLE OF THEIR ETHNICITY, THEIR CULTURE, AND YOU DEPRIVE THEM OF THEIR SENSE OF DIRECTION OR PURPOSE.

second liberation. Managing ethnic diversity within the unity of the colonial borders is a challenge that African states are reluctant to face, but cannot wish away.

Ethiopia, after Eritrea's breakaway, can claim credit for being the only African country trying to confront head-on the challenge of tribalism or ethnicity by recognizing territorially based ethnic groups, granting them not only a large measure of autonomy, but also the constitutional right of self-determination, even to the extent of secession. Ethiopia's leaders assert emphatically that they are committed to the right of self-determination, wherever it leads. Less idealistically, it can be argued that giving the people the right to determine their destiny leads them to believe that their interests will be provided for, if only to give them a reason to opt for unity.

The only sustainable unity is that based on mutual understanding and agreement. Unfortunately, the normative framework for national unity in modern Africa is not the result of consensus. Except for post-apartheid South Africa, Africans won their independence without negotiating an internal social contract that would win and sustain national consensus. The constitutions for independence were laden with idealistic principles developed outside the continent. The regimes built on them lacked legitimacy and in most cases were soon overthrown with no remorse or regrets from

tries (exclusive of South Africa), fall into a second category. These countries face significant ethnic pluralism that is nevertheless containable through an effective system of distribution that upholds the integrity and legitimacy of the state. The way the nations in this group perceive themselves is consonant with the self-perceptions of their component groups.

A third group of countries, including Zimbabwe, Namibia, and modern-day South Africa, suffers racial, ethnic, religious, or cultural divisions severe enough to require special arrangements to be mutually accommodating in an ambivalent form of unity in diversity. Burundi and Rwanda, as well as Sudan, are candidates for this category, though all also have aspects of the fourth, and final, category.

The fourth category, the zero-sum conflict situation, consists of states embroiled in acute crisis with no collective sense of identification, no shared values, and no common vision for the nation. The framework of the nation-state is perceived as an imposition by the colonial invaders, now perpetuated by the dominant group whose identity defines the national character. Such definition might be explicit, as in apartheid South Africa, where race and ethnicity were factors in allocating or denying the rights of citizenship, or in the Sudan, where the identification of the country as Arab and Islamic carries inherent stratification and discrimination on racial, ethnic, and religious grounds. These conflicts are the most difficult to manage within the unity framework; depending on the particular circumstance of the case, they may call for fundamental restructuring and perhaps partition.

POLICY IMPLICATIONS FOR NATIONBUILDING

At present, most African countries are addressing the racial and ethnic identity issues through a pacifying system of distribution and allocation—a form of ad hoc pragmatic management rather than a strategic approach. What makes the issue of identity particularly acute for the continent is that it touches not only on politics, but also on economics and the organizational capacity for a self-generating and sustainable development from within.

There are four policy options for managing pluralistic identities. One is to create a national framework with which all can identify without any distinction based on race, ethnicity, tribe, or religion. This option, of course, best suits those countries that are highly homogeneous. The second option is to create a pluralistic framework to accommodate nations that are racially, ethnically, culturally, or religiously diverse. Under this option, probably a federal arrangement, groups would accommodate each other on the basis of the principle of live and let live, but with a more uniting commitment to the common purpose of national identification. In the third case, for more seriously divided countries, some form of power sharing combined with decentralization, with identities being geographically defined, may be the answer. In the zero-sum conflict situations, federalism would expand into confederalism, paradoxically trying to reconcile unity with separation. Where even this degree of accommodation is not workable, and where territorial configurations permit, partition ought to be accepted.

THE ROLE OF THE INTERNATIONAL COMMUNITY

How are these options to be brought about? Deciding which option to adopt is, of course, in the first place part of the sovereign right of the people of the country. But regional and international actors also have a responsibility that cannot be abdicated in the name of national sovereignty. By its very nature, sovereignty implies a tension between the demand for internal solutions and the need for corrective remedies from the outside. In other words, the responsibilities of sovereignty require both internal and external accountability, which are inherently at odds, especially since the need for external involvement is commensurate with the failure of internal systems. Given the ambivalence of the international system about intervention, this responsibility should belong first to the subregional and regional actors, with the international community, through the United Nations, as the ultimate resort.

The interconnectedness of the conflicts of neighboring countries means that preventing, managing, or resolving conflicts is becoming recognized as a matter of interest and concern not only to the countries directly involved, but also to the region as a whole. Regional awakening to the common threat of internal conflict is still nascent, but the importance of the shared threat is being increasingly realized, especially in view of the tendency toward isolationism in Europe and the United States, the only powers still capable of effectively intervening for humanitarian reasons or for the cause of peace, security, and stability in other parts of the world.

RECONCILING TWO CONFLICTING PATHS

Final accountability for the responsibilities of sovereignty must ultimately fall on the international community, more specifically the United Nations. The intervention of international financial institutions in the affairs of sovereign countries to ensure more efficient management of their economies has now become a truism. International concern with issues of governance, such as democracy and respect for fundamental human rights, has also become widely accepted, despite the lingering resistance of vulnerable regimes. Beyond the issue of protection of minorities, long recognized as a legitimate concern for the international community, the politics and conflicts of identity and their impact on the prospects for peace, stability, development, and nation building must also be recognized as critical items on the agenda of a responsible and accountable sovereignty.

Insofar as the modern African state is the creation of European conquest, restructuring the continent, linking it to the international system, and reconceptualizing and reconstituting the state will require the cooperation of Africa's global partners. Outside actors can offer an objective and impartial perspective that can be pivotal to balancing the concerns of the internal actors. In addition, the international legitimacy of any new arrangements, which is necessary for building support from outside sources, can best be ensured by enlisting international partners in the search for effective solutions to these internal crises.

Post-colonial Africa stands poised between rediscovering its roots—its indigenous values, institutions, and experiences—and pursuing the logic of the colonial state in the context of universalizing modernity, primarily based on Western experience. The resulting tensions cannot be easily resolved. But an eclectic process that fashions a system in which ethnic groups can play a constructive role in the modern African state could significantly reduce the tension, foster cooperation, and facilitate the process of nation building.

Gypsies in Canada:

Outcasts Once Again

■ *Gypsies have suffered discrimination for centuries, and hundreds of thousands of them died in Hitler's death camps. After the war, they lived in uneasy coexistence with the communist regimes of Eastern Europe. But now Gypsies have become targets again. The following articles describe their search for a land where they can live undisturbed.*

THE GLOBE AND MAIL

In a dingy bar in downtown Toronto, a dozen Gypsy men from the Czech Republic talk mournfully about life in the homeland they have left behind—a homeland where people like them are routinely described as "black," whatever the color of their skin. It is a land where in older times, Gypsy women had an ear cut off merely because they were Gypsy. The stories spill out about beatings by skinheads with big black boots, brass knuckles, and knives. They are the kind of stories told everywhere in Europe, because in many places hostility to Gypsies is as casual a fact of life as anti-Semitism was a few generations ago.

For the several hundred Gypsy men, women, and children who have made their way to Canada in search of refuge in the past few months, their arrival is just the latest stop in a history of persecution that has pursued them in Europe and around the world for centuries.

Since the collapse of communism, it has again become open season on Gypsies. John Murray, coordinator of activities on Roma-Gypsies at the Council of Europe in Strasbourg, says, "Everywhere in Europe, they are among the victims of racism and discrimination."

Veronika Szente, a researcher at the European Roma Rights Center, a Budapest-based pro-Gypsy lobbying group, says the situation of Gypsies in the Czech Republic is particularly bad. The center has documented harassment and violence against Gypsies in the Czech Republic and says the courts have failed to provide redress to the victims. It says Gypsies "face a daunting array of discriminatory practices and hindrances to their ability to live with dignity."

Listening to those who have made it to Canada in recent weeks, that judgment seems a discreet understatement. Michal Tokar, 45, a short, dark-skinned man with spiky black hair and a big smile, talks of an attack in June that made him decide to leave the Czech Republic. He distracted the skinheads long enough to allow his wife, Ruzena, and his daughter Sylvinka, who is blind and afflicted with a learning disability, to get away. The skinheads got Michal Tokar instead. Armed with baseball bats, they cracked a rib, cut his

> "Stories spill out of beatings by skinheads with brass knuckles and knives."

head, broke a cheekbone, and blackened both his eyes.

Tokar had long heard about Canada. He has a cousin living there, and even in communist times, he says, people said that Canada was a democratic country. His cousin had urged him to pack up and leave the skinheads behind. So Tokar was not expecting what awaited him in Toronto.

"The interpreter was looking into our eyes and laughing," he says. Officials made him and his family, including a pregnant daughter and three children under the age of five, wait for seven hours. The family was given a piece of paper with names and addresses on it and shown the door. One bag, the one with their best clothes in it, was gone, either lost or stolen. The family slept at the airport that night, Tokar keeping awake most of the night.

"I was crying like a little baby at the airport on the floor while everyone was sleeping," he says. Finally, a man helped them get taxis—at a cost of $129—to take the whole family to a Toronto shelter.

For the past few months, the Tokar family—Michal and nine others—have been living in a Toronto hostel in one room so crammed with people and belongings that the door cannot fully open. They are waiting to see whether their request for refugee status will be accepted.

Tokar's tale of apparent indifference or hostility by Canadian authorities is not unique. Milos Rezi, 38, who arrived from the Czech Republic in August, tells much the same story: "They told me they're not going to give me anything, that I should go with my children onto the street, that they won't give me any food but if I decide to steal any food, I will be punished for that, and that I am to take care of myself." When Rezi tried to plead his case, the immigration officer refused to listen: "When I wanted to explain my case . . . she immediately jumped into my speech and said this [racism] does not exist."

Vincent Banda, who arrived in Canada in August, tells much the same kind of story. "We wanted to explain exactly what the problems were in the Czech Republic," he says. "The immigration lady, when I started to say my story, said, no, no, no, that she's not interested in that. She said, 'I don't want to hear about racism, and I won't give you anything,' that we should take care of ourselves on the street and that we should pick up our bags and go home."

There are echoes of disillusionment across the Atlantic in Prague, where a trickle of Czech Gypsies have returned from an unsuccessful trip to Canada. In just one week in August, more than 30 flew back to Prague, Czech immigration officials say. Several of those who returned speak of intimidation by Canadian immigration officials. Milan Skuka, 24, says he did not want financial support but that, from what had been reported in the Czech Republic, he did expect accommodations in Canada. His next surprise came when he was told he would have to give up his passport for three months; Skuka did not understand how he would get a place to stay if he didn't have a passport.

Some Czech Gypsies were inspired to come to Canada by a recent program about life in the country on the Czech station Nova TV. The Prague newspaper *Mladá Fronta Dnes* has reported that unsigned fliers were appearing on the streets inviting Gypsies to leave the Czech Republic and head for Canada. According to the newspaper, the flier promised a place to stay and an income of $1,000 a month until the applicant's refugee status was settled. It urged prospective refugees: "Do not lose your chance. Canada is waiting for you."

Discrimination has followed the Gypsies to Canada. George Kubes, a Toronto lawyer who is handling refugee applications for many of the Gypsies, has come under attack from expatriate Czechs who accuse him of "shaming the community" by helping "these dirty people."

None of this seems to be surprising to the people who call themselves Roma, after the word *rom*, which means man in the Romany language. Where they have not suffered outright persecution and discrimination, they have encountered suspicion, whether they are permanent city dwellers or pursue the traditional life that their ancestors have followed since they left India in the 14th century.

King Frederick William of Prussia decreed in 1725 that any Gypsy older than 18, man or woman, should be hanged. In the Holy Roman Empire it was decreed in that same year

that Gypsy men were to be put to death. In Silesia and Moravia, Gypsy women were to have their left ears cut off. In Bohemia, which is now part of the Czech Republic, the right ears of Gypsy women were to be severed.

In his quest for an Aryan Europe, Adolf Hitler exterminated 500,000 Gypsies. In the aftermath of the Holocaust there was a brief respite. Communist authorities who ruled Eastern and Central Europe wanted no ethnic agitation that would disturb the social order.

But now, many believe, the tide has turned. Isabel Fonseca spent almost five years in Eastern Europe researching her 1995 book about Gypsies called *Bury Me Standing*. In her travels, she witnessed even educated, so-called liberal Europeans discriminating against Gypsies. "These people have always been on the fringes," she says. "The question is: Are they nomadic because of their profession or because they have been kicked out of every place they went?"

Why the Gypsies have been persecuted through the centuries is a complex issue, she says. They're the blacks of Eastern Europe, no doubt, but "the reason why they're such an easy scapegoat is because they don't have a home state." Fonseca disagrees with the official Czech Republic position that discrimination and prejudice against Gypsies is not institutional. She also believes the fall of communism has had an adverse effect on Gypsies, that discrimination and harassment have bloomed along with the burgeoning economic and democratic possibilities.

"In some ways it was easier for them [under communism]," she says. "There were jobs. Now they're the last to be hired and the first to be fired." There's no question, she adds, that Gypsies shun regimented wage labor. Most of them would rather gather scrap metal and be independent than answer to a boss. For "not falling into line," as she calls it, they are relegated to the fringes of society.

—John Gray, Kim Honey, Alan Freeman, and Michele Legge, "Globe and Mail" (centrist), Toronto, Aug. 23, 1977.

Paradise Found—And Then Lost

RZECZPOSPOLITA

Within a week of the airing of the program *Gypsies Go to Heaven*, produced for Nova TV, about 16,000 people requested information about emigrating from the Czech Republic to Canada. The program presented the life of Gypsy immigrants in Canada in extremely rosy hues, saying that a Gypsy need only present a petition for political asylum in order to receive assistance from Canadian officials. "The report created unre-

alistic and dangerous illusions, giving the impression that it was an invitation for the Gypsies to come to Canada," says Czech Ambassador to Canada Stanislav Chylek.

The Gypsies' enthusiasm was further fueled by an offer from Liana Janaczkova, a politician from the eastern city of Ostrava, to pay for a plane ticket to Canada for any Gypsies willing to forfeit their rights to an apartment in the Czech Republic. And so it began. Thousands of Gypsies started feverishly to calculate how they could leave as quickly as possible, to the dismay of Canadian officials in Prague.

The first Gypsy families returned from Canada in August. They had been unable to communicate in either English or French; they were not assured of instant care; and no guarantees were given that their requests for political refugee status would be granted. This was enough to send the five members of Dezider Gini's family (with another child on the way) back to Prague after a 48-hour stay in Canada. When Gini heard that his family would have to fend for itself until political asylum proceedings were concluded and that the birth of his new child would cost $12,000, he decided to return to the Czech Republic.

Gini has not completely given up on the idea of emigrating. But next time he will make better preparations. He will go alone, make some money, and then bring his family over.

Why does he want to leave the Czech Republic? "This is difficult to explain to someone who has not gone through it," he says. "We have problems with the skinheads, broken windows. But the worst is the way the 'white' Czechs look at us. No one looked at us that way in Canada. We were treated like other people."

Gypsy representatives consult almost daily with Czech politicians, who are trying to talk them out of emigrating. Some want to downplay the issue, while others, such as Interior Minister Jan Rumi, believe that the government must establish a program for peaceful coexistence with this minority. Others say that an exodus of Gypsies would taint the Czechs in the eyes of the world, which might accuse the Czech Republic of racism at a time when it is applying for admission to the European Union.

A scandal erupted last year over a sign banning Gypsies from a provincial hotel, causing a candidate for the 1996 parliamentary elections to be taken off the voting list. Nationalist Republican Party chief Miroslav Sladek said he wanted to send the Gypsies to Spain or to the gas chamber. The slightly less extreme Prague Senator Zdenek Klausner suggested simply exiling the "problem minority" to other towns. More original was Janaczkova's proposal to buy tickets to Canada for Gypsies. A statement by Klausner's and Janaczkova's Citizens' Democratic Party condemns racism in its ranks, but it does not specifically mention Klausner and Janaczkova or order them to make an official apology.

Signs of xenophobia and intolerance exist at all levels in the Czech Republic. People of many nationalities feel its weight: Vietnamese, Romanians, Ukrainians, Poles. The Gypsy minority feels this discrimination most painfully, and several Gypsies have been murdered by skinheads.

Yet the Gypsies themselves are not entirely without fault. They must find a way to make their representatives hold talks with the democratic Czech authorities about integration with the Czech majority. The exodus to Canada has made both sides aware that there is much to be done.

—Barbara Sierszula, "Rzeczpospolita"
(independent), Warsaw, Aug. 20, 1997.

Eugenics, Anyone?

William Pfaff

Until recently it has been, not a secret, but a fact kept carefully closeted, that the countries that consider themselves the most advanced and civilized had for many years been sterilizing "undesirable" people, or taking their children away from them, in order to improve the "race." This was going on in the United States until 1973.

The matter gained renewed public attention in August when the Swedish press revealed that between 1935 and 1976 more than 60,000 people in Sweden were sterilized against their will, or in ignorance of what was being done to them. These were mentally or physically handicapped people, or those congenitally ill, or socially "undesirable" women who had "too many" children and were considered to be living "bad lives." Among them, at least in the earlier years of the program, were Gypsies, vagabonds, and people who were not "of pure Swedish race" (as that race was supposed to look, according to a series of engraved plates produced at the Institute of Racial Biology in Uppsala in 1922).

However, Sweden should not be singled out. The same thing was going on in other Nordic countries, as well as in Switzerland, France, Britain, Japan, the United States, and elsewhere. In the United States, the American Eugenics Society, founded in 1921, called for sterilization of 10 percent of the American population in order to prevent "the suicide of the white race." In 1927, in rejecting a suit against the state of Virginia on behalf of a white woman of eighteen who had been forcibly sterilized in a Virginia asylum, the Supreme Court ruled that rather than eventually having to execute criminals born of the mentally defective, or see their children die of want, it was better for the state to prevent their birth.

Forcible sterilizations were banned by the US Department of Health, Education and Welfare only in 1973, following Senate hearings chaired by Senator Ted Kennedy, which revealed that in 1972 alone some sixteen thousand men and eight thousand women had been sterilized under existing federal programs.

There have been two rationales for such policies. One claims to protect the well-being of the sterilized person and his or her offspring. Sterilization is requested by the person's family or by doctors or institutional authorities who find that the person is incapable of responsible choice with respect to bearing children, or would be incapable of caring for offspring. In Britain, France, and most other countries, these interventions have been made under some system of ethical and legal oversight, at least in principle. In France this September a weekly magazine caused a stir with an article estimating that some fifteen thousand mentally handicapped people had been sterilized in recent years. Senior ministers promised an inquiry and asked the inspector general of social services to ascertain whether new measures were needed to protect people's rights in such matters.

The other rationale is the theory for improving mankind proposed by a cousin of Charles Darwin, Francis Galton (1822–1911), and based on Darwin's observations of natural selection in the plant and animal kingdoms. The theory of eugenics held that factors under social control could improve or impair future generations of humanity. In its early and radical versions eugenic theory held that human beings should be "bred" in order to eliminate the unfit or "degenerate," and to promote the propagation of the allegedly superior.

Eugenics first became a popular social cause in Britain after the Boer War, stimulated by the fear that Britain's troubles were the result of "degeneration" of the British "race." Later it seemed to offer a response to manpower losses in World War I. From that period until the 1950s, some British children's charities sent large numbers of poor or illegitimate children confided to them—some orphans, some the children of people who could not afford to support them—to institutions in Australia, where a number of them ended in more or less the condition of indentured servants, totally cut off from their origins.

All of this was based on clear assumptions about which "races" are superior and which inferior. Bitterly remembered in Australia is a comment made by Winston Churchill in 1942, when he diverted Australian troops to doomed Singapore, in place of British divisions, revealed in official documents released under the fifty-year rule. He said the Australians could be sacrificed because they were "bad blood."

 Reprinted with permission from *The New York Review of Books,* October 23, 1997, pp. 23-24. © 1997 by NYREV, Inc.

The United States at the same time was drafting black citizens mainly to serve in segregated Army labor and transport battalions. Blacks weren't allowed in the Navy or Marines. The Navy Department believed they didn't have what it takes for combat, and that white Americans would not share quarters with them on ships.

That is the way people thought, including some who might seem the least likely to have done so. A scandal recently erupted in Israel concerning the treatment of Yemeni Jews in the late 1940s, when the Israeli state had barely been established. It was revealed that hundreds of children of immigrant Yemeni Jews were literally stolen from their Arabic-speaking parents for adoption by families of European Jewish origin, in an attempt to meld the Yemenis into what then was the European mainstream. The blood of Ethiopian Jews was for a time segregated in Israel's blood banks. The entire relationship between Jews and Arabs, from the time of Mandate Palestine to the present day, has been influenced on both sides by racist stereotypes.

One must judge all this in historical perspective. The Darwinian analogy with plant and animal kingdoms seemed convincing. Programs to "improve" the race seemed progressive, which is why Social Democratic leaders in Scandinavia were particularly attracted to them, as well as "progressive" thinkers elsewhere. They were ideas congenial to a generation of intellectuals in the United States and Europe given to larger theories of social engineering and social planning. Eugenic programs resulted from the "best" scientific opinion of the time, the "best" medical opinion, and many were ordered and carried out in the democracies with the best of intentions. If some individuals suffered, that simply was the price of progress.

Nazism carried eugenics to a demented climax, not only in the death camps themselves but in the eugenically inspired murders of insane, handicapped, or congenitally ill individuals begun in Germany in 1939, and in the experiments on living humans conducted by Nazi doctors during the war. Church protests against the early euthanasia program in Germany caused it to be for the most part abandoned by the end of 1941, although a similar program for killing handicapped and "antisocial" children at Vienna's Steinhof Psychiatric Hospital continued until 1945, eliminating what Hitler called "lives unworthy of life." The brains of the murdered children, preserved for research purposes, are only now to be given burial, after recent publicity in Austria concerning what were described at the time as "death accelerations."

Nazism gave eugenics a bad name. As a result there now is a nervous refusal to admit that any differences at all exist between groups of people. It is all but impossible to talk about "race," whatever race is. Probably this is a good thing. Possibly it is not, since there could eventually be a cost to be paid for the claim that there are no distinctions to be discussed.

The obvious lesson is not only that theories, even ostensibly progressive theories, can be deadly, which we knew, but also that when a theory requires that people be made to suffer here and now in the cause of some grand future project, we should just say no.

Another lesson concerns the consequences of professedly value-free science, when closed to criticisms founded on philosophical or religious considerations. The record of eugenics is pertinent to the debate over new developments in genetic research and engineering, which, some claim, now offer us an opportunity vastly to improve mankind by remaking men.

Understanding Cultural Pluralism

The increase in racial violence and hatred on campuses across the country is manifested in acts ranging from hateful speech to physical violence. Strategies for dealing with this problem on a campus include increased awareness through mandatory ethnic studies, the empowerment of targets of violence, and fostering social and cultural interaction in festivals, folk-arts fairs, and literary and political forums. Systematic knowledge about ethnic groups has not been a central scholarly concern. In fact, mainstream literary, humanistic, and historical disciplines have only recently begun to displace sociological attention to the pathologies of urban ethnicity as the primary contact and source of information and interpretation of ethnic traditions. The historic role that voluntary groups have played in the reduction of bias and bigotry also needs to be revalued and revitalized. Voluntary associations can take part in a host of state and local initiatives to improve intergroup relations. Schools and parents can help children understand commonalities and differences among and within ethnic traditions and groups. The incorporation of everyday experiences of families and a formal pedagogy rooted in accurate and locally relevant resources are essential building blocks for understanding diversity.

The reemergence of the discussion of race, ethnicity, and intelligence that is included in the selections found in this unit reveals the embeddedness of interpretive categories that frame the discussion and analysis of race and ethnic relations. The enormity of the educational effort that is required as we attempt to move beyond the ethnocentrism and racism that bred hatred and destructive relationships between persons and communities is revealed in a variety of ways. Philosophic reflection on the epistemological issues associated with explaining human variety is rarely invited. However, it is precisely at this intersection of social philosophy and science that the crucial breakthroughs in understanding are likely to appear. The continual mismeasures of intelligence and misreading of meaning indicate the long-term need for critical reformulation of the very idea of race.

At this time a variety of ways of measuring the development of race and ethnic relations are imposing the accuracy of their claims. Evidence cited by claimants to such authoritative knowledge and the attendant public criterion of credibility point to the expectation of a spirited debate. This unit challenges us to rethink the assumptions, contradictions, and aspirations of social development models.

Looking Ahead: Challenge Questions

What signs have you seen of an increase in racist, anti-Semitic, anti-immigrant, and antiminority group acts that recent studies apparently confirm?

What explains the fact that large population studies confirm that in the areas of ethnic, racial, and religious differences, Americans are more tolerant than ever?

Why do teenagers commit 80 percent of all bias-related acts?

What problems does conflict in ethnic and race relations pose for corporate and governmental institutions?

What media images of race and ethnicity are dominant?

What avenues are available for the authentic cultural resources of ethnic communities and traditions?

How can multiethnic expressions of traditions intersect with the breakdown of community and the isolationist tendencies related to individual and personal achievement?

How can the promotion of positive prototypes of ethnicity ever become as powerful as negative stereotypes?

How can dialogue among conflicting parties about dilemmas that are essential to technological and economic change enable us to share and shape the burden of social change?

Contrast local knowledge with national and local media as sources of information on race and ethnicity.

Why should advocates of multicultural development and diversity argue for the following: (1) Fair and equal protection under the law; (2) The compilation of full and accurate data on the ethnic composition of the American population; (3) Corporate and governmental leaders who are focused on issues that do not exacerbate relations among persons because of ethnicity and race.

What are the benefits of ethnic groups meeting regularly with other ethnic groups and engaging in friendly "what's your agenda" meetings?

In the eighteenth century a disastrous shift occurred in the way Westerners perceived races. The man responsible was Johann Friedrich Blumenbach, one of the least racist thinkers of his day.

the Geometer of Race

STEPHEN JAY GOULD

Stephen Jay Gould, a contributing editor of Discover, *is a professor of zoology at Harvard who also teaches geology, biology, and the history of science. His writing on evolution has won many prizes, including a National Book Award, a National Magazine Award, and the Phi Beta Kappa Science Award. For* Discover*'s November 1993 special section on ten great science museums, Gould wrote about the glass flowers at Harvard's Botanical Museum.*

INTERESTING STORIES often lie encoded in names that seem either capricious or misconstrued. Why, for example, are political radicals called "left" and their conservative counterparts "right"? In many European legislatures, the most distinguished members sat at the chairman's right, following a custom of courtesy as old as our prejudices for favoring the dominant hand of most people. (These biases run deep, extending well beyond can openers and scissors to language itself, where *dexterous* stems from the Latin for "right," and *sinister* from the word for "left.") Since these distinguished nobles and moguls tended to espouse conservative views, the right and left wings of the legislature came to define a geometry of political views.

Among such apparently capricious names in my own field of biology and evolution, none seems more curious, and none elicits more questions after lectures, than the official designation of light-skinned people in Europe, western Asia, and North Africa as Caucasian. Why should the most common racial group of the Western world be named for a mountain range that straddles Russia and Georgia? Johann Friedrich Blumenbach (1752–1840), the German anatomist and naturalist who established the most influential of all racial classifications, invented this name in 1795, in the third edition of his seminal work, *De Generis Humani Varietate Nativa* (On the Natural Variety of Mankind). Blumenbach's definition cites two reasons for his choice—the maximal beauty of people from this small region, and the probability that humans were first created in this area.

> *Caucasian variety.* I have taken the name of this variety from Mount Caucasus, both because its neighborhood, and especially its southern slope, produces the most beautiful race of men, I mean the Georgian; and because . . . in that region, if anywhere, it seems we ought with the greatest probability to place the autochthones [original forms] of mankind.

Blumenbach, one of the greatest and most honored scientists of the Enlightenment, spent his entire career as a professor at the University of Göttingen in Germany. He first presented *De Generis Humani Varietate Nativa* as a doctoral dissertation to the medical faculty of Göttingen in 1775, as the minutemen of Lexington and Concord began the American Revolution. He then republished the text for general distribution in 1776, as a fateful meeting in Philadelphia proclaimed our independence. The coincidence of three great documents in 1776—Jefferson's Declaration of Independence (on the politics of liberty), Adam Smith's *Wealth of Nations* (on the economics of individualism), and Blumenbach's treatise on racial classification (on the science of human diversity)—records the social ferment of these decades and sets the wider context that makes Blumenbach's taxonomy, and his subsequent decision to call the European race Caucasian, so important for our history and current concerns.

The solution to big puzzles often hinges upon tiny curiosities, easy to miss or to pass over. I suggest that the key to understanding Blumenbach's classification, the foundation of much that continues to influence and disturb us today, lies in the peculiar criterion he used to name the European race Caucasian—the supposed superior beauty of people from this region. Why, first of all, should a scientist attach such importance to an evidently subjective assessment; and why, secondly, should an aesthetic criterion become the basis of a scientific judgment about place of origin? To answer these questions, we must compare Blumenbach's original 1775 text with the later edition of 1795, when Caucasians received their name.

Blumenbach's final taxonomy of 1795 divided all humans into five groups, defined both by geography and appearance—in his order, the Caucasian variety, for the light-skinned people of Europe and adjacent parts of Asia and Africa; the Mongolian variety, for most other inhabitants of Asia, including China and Japan; the Ethiopian variety, for the dark-skinned people of Africa; the American variety, for most native populations of the New World; and the Malay variety, for the Polynesians and Melanesians of the Pacific and for the aborigines of Australia. But Blumenbach's original classification of 1775 recognized only the first four of these five, and united members of the Malay variety with the other people of Asia whom Blumenbach came to name Mongolian.

We now encounter the paradox of Blumenbach's reputation as the inventor of modern racial classification. The original four-race system, as I shall illustrate in a moment, did not arise from Blumenbach's observations but only represents, as Blumenbach readily admits, the classification promoted by his guru Carolus Linnaeus in the founding document of taxonomy, the *Systema Naturae* of 1758. Therefore, Blumenbach's only original contribution to racial classification lies in the later addition of a Malay variety for some Pacific peoples first included in a broader Asian group.

This change seems so minor. Why, then, do we credit Blumenbach, rather than Linnaeus, as the founder of racial classification? (One might prefer to say "discredit," as the enterprise does not, for good reason, enjoy high repute these days.) But Blumenbach's apparently small change actually records a theoretical shift that could not have been broader, or more portentous, in scope. This change has been missed or misconstrued because later scientists have not grasped the vital historical and philosophical principle that theories are models subject to visual representation, usually in clearly definable geometric terms.

By moving from the Linnaean four-race system to his own five-race scheme, Blumenbach radically changed the geometry of human order from a geographically based model without explicit ranking to a hierarchy of worth, oddly based upon perceived beauty, and fanning out in two directions from a Caucasian ideal. The addition of a Malay category was crucial to this geometric reformulation—and therefore becomes the key to the conceptual transformation rather than a simple refinement of factual information within an old scheme. (For the insight that scientific revolutions embody such geometric shifts, I am grateful to my friend Rhonda Roland Shearer, who portrays these themes in a forthcoming book, *The Flatland Hypothesis*.)

BLUMENBACH IDOLIZED his teacher Linnaeus and acknowledged him as the source of his original fourfold racial classification: "I have followed Linnaeus in the number, but have defined my varieties by other boundaries" (1775 edition). Later, in adding his Malay variety, Blumenbach identified his change as a departure from his old mentor in the most respectful terms: "It became very clear that the Linnaean division of mankind could no longer be adhered to; for which reason I, in this little work, ceased like others to follow that illustrious man."

Linnaeus divided the species *Homo sapiens* into four basic varieties, defined primarily by geography and, interestingly, not in the ranked order favored by most Europeans in the racist tradition—*Americanus, Europaeus, Asiaticus,* and *Afer,* or African. (He also alluded to two other fanciful categories: *ferus* for "wild boys," occasionally discovered in the woods and possibly raised by animals—most turned out to be retarded or mentally ill youngsters abandoned by their parents—and *monstrosus* for hairy men with tails, and other travelers' confabulations.) In so doing, Linnaeus presented nothing original; he merely mapped humans onto the four geographic regions of conventional cartography.

Linnaeus then characterized each of these groups by noting color, humor, and posture, in that order. Again, none of these categories explicitly implies ranking by worth. Once again, Linnaeus was simply bowing to classical taxonomic theories in making these decisions. For example, his use of the four humors reflects the ancient and medieval theory that a person's temperament arises from a balance of four fluids (*humor* is Latin for "moisture")—blood, phlegm, choler (yellow bile), and melancholy (black bile). Depending on which of the four substances dominated, a person would be sanguine (the cheerful realm of blood), phlegmatic (sluggish), choleric (prone to anger), or melancholic (sad). Four geographic regions, four humors, four races.

For the American variety, Linnaeus wrote "*rufus, cholericus, rectus*" (red, choleric, upright); for the European, "*albus, sanguineus, torosus*" (white, sanguine, muscular); for the Asian, "*luridus, melancholicus, rigidus*" (pale yellow, melancholy, stiff); and for the African, "*niger, phlegmaticus, laxus*" (black, phlegmatic, relaxed).

I don't mean to deny that Linnaeus held conventional beliefs about the superiority of his own European variety over others. Being a sanguine, muscular European surely sounds better than being a melancholy, stiff Asian. Indeed, Linnaeus ended each group's description with a more overtly racist label, an attempt to epitomize behavior in just two words. Thus the American was *regitur consuetudine* (ruled by habit); the European, *regitur ritibus* (ruled by custom); the Asian, *regitur opinionibus* (ruled by belief); and the African, *regitur arbitrio* (ruled by caprice). Surely regulation by established and considered custom beats the unthinking rule of habit or belief, and all of these are superior to caprice—thus leading to the implied and conventional racist ranking of Europeans first, Asians and Americans in the middle, and Africans at the bottom.

Nonetheless, and despite these implications, the overt geometry of Linnaeus's model is not linear or hierarchical. When

Scientists assume that their own shifts in interpretation record only their better understanding of newly discovered facts. They tend to be unaware of their own mental impositions upon the world's messy and ambiguous factuality.

we visualize his scheme as an essential picture in our mind, we see a map of the world divided into four regions, with the people in each region characterized by a list of different traits. In short, Linnaeus's primary ordering principle is cartographic; if he had wished to push hierarchy as the essential picture of human variety, he would surely have listed Europeans first and Africans last, but he started with native Americans instead.

The shift from a geographic to a hierarchical ordering of human diversity must stand as one of the most fateful transitions in the history of Western science—for what, short of railroads and nuclear bombs, has had more practical impact, in this case almost entirely negative, upon our collective lives? Ironically, Blumenbach is the focus of this shift, for his five-race scheme became canonical and changed the geometry of human order from Linnaean cartography to linear ranking—in short, to a system based on putative worth.

I say ironic because Blumenbach was the least racist and most genial of all Enlightenment thinkers. How peculiar that the man most committed to human unity, and to inconsequential moral and intellectual differences among groups, should have changed the mental geometry of human order to a scheme that has served racism ever since. Yet on second thought, this situation is really not so odd—for most scientists have been quite unaware of the mental machinery, and particularly of the visual or geometric implications, lying behind all their theorizing.

An old tradition in science proclaims that changes in theory must be driven by observation. Since most scientists believe this simplistic formula, they assume that their own shifts in interpretation record only their better understanding of newly discovered facts. Scientists therefore tend to be unaware of their own mental impositions upon the world's messy and ambiguous factuality. Such mental impositions arise from a variety of sources, including psychological predisposition and social context. Blumenbach lived in an age when ideas of progress, and the cultural superiority of European ways, dominated political and social life. Implicit, loosely formulated, or even unconscious notions of racial ranking fit well with such a worldview—indeed, almost any other organizational scheme would have seemed anomalous. I doubt that Blumenbach was actively encouraging racism by redrawing the mental diagram of human groups. He was only, and largely passively, recording the social view of his time. But ideas have consequences, whatever the motives or intentions of their promoters.

Blumenbach certainly thought that his switch from the Linnaean four-race system to his own five-race scheme arose only from his improved understanding of nature's factuality. He said as much when he announced his change in the second (1781) edition of his treatise: "Formerly in the first edition of this work, I divided all mankind into four varieties; but after I had more actively investigated the different nations of Eastern Asia and America, and, so to speak, looked at them more closely, I was compelled to give up that division, and to place in its stead the following five varieties, as more consonant to nature." And in the preface to the third edition, of 1795, Blumenbach states

that he gave up the Linnaean scheme in order to arrange "the varieties of man according to the truth of nature." When scientists adopt the myth that theories arise solely from observation, and do not grasp the personal and social influences acting on their thinking, they not only miss the causes of their changed opinions; they may even fail to comprehend the deep mental shift encoded by the new theory.

Blumenbach strongly upheld the unity of the human species against an alternative view, then growing in popularity (and surely more conducive to conventional forms of racism), that each major race had been separately created. He ended his third edition by writing: "No doubt can any longer remain but that we are with great probability right in referring all . . . varieties of man . . . to one and the same species."

AS HIS MAJOR ARGUMENT for unity, Blumenbach noted that all supposed racial characteristics grade continuously from one people to another and cannot define any separate and bounded group. "For although there seems to be so great a difference between widely separate nations, that you might easily take the inhabitants of the Cape of Good Hope, the Greenlanders, and the Circassians for so many different species of man, yet when the matter is thoroughly considered, you see that all do so run into one another, and that one variety of mankind does so sensibly pass into the other, that you cannot mark out the limits between them." He particularly refuted the common racist claim that black Africans bore unique features of their inferiority: "There is no single character so peculiar and so universal among the Ethiopians, but what it may be observed on the one hand everywhere in other varieties of men."

Blumenbach, writing 80 years before Darwin, believed that *Homo sapiens* had been created in a single region and had then spread over the globe. Our racial diversity, he then argued, arose as a result of this spread to other climates and topographies, and to our adoption of different modes of life in these various regions. Following the terminology of his time, Blumenbach referred to these changes as "degenerations"—not intending the modern sense of deterioration, but the literal meaning of departure from an initial form of humanity at the creation (*de* means "from," and *genus* refers to our original stock).

Most of these degenerations, Blumenbach argued, arose directly from differences in climate and habitat—ranging from such broad patterns as the correlation of dark skin with tropical environments, to more particular (and fanciful) attributions, including a speculation that the narrow eye slits of some Australian aborigines may have arisen in response to "constant clouds of gnats . . . contracting the natural face of the inhabitants." Other changes, he maintained, arose as a consequence of customs adopted in different regions. For example, nations that compressed the heads of babies by swaddling boards or papoose carriers ended up with relatively long skulls. Blumenbach held that "almost all the diversity of the form of the head in different nations is to be attributed to the mode of life and to art."

Blumenbach believed that such changes, promoted over many generations, could eventually become hereditary. "With

Blumenbach upheld the unity of the human species against an alternative view, then growing in popularity (and surely more conducive to conventional racism), that each race had been separately created.

the progress of time," Blumenbach wrote, "art may degenerate into a second nature." But he also argued that most racial variations, as superficial impositions of climate and custom, could be easily altered or reversed by moving to a new region or by adopting new behavior. White Europeans living for generations in the tropics could become dark-skinned, while Africans transported as slaves to high latitudes could eventually become white: "Color, whatever be its cause, be it bile, or the influence of the sun, the air, or the climate, is, at all events, an adventitious and easily changeable thing, and can never constitute a diversity of species," he wrote.

Convinced of the superficiality of racial variation, Blumenbach defended the mental and moral unity of all peoples. He held particularly strong opinions on the equal status of black Africans and white Europeans. He may have been patronizing in praising "the good disposition and faculties of these our black brethren," but better paternalism than malign contempt. He campaigned for the abolition of slavery and asserted the moral superiority of slaves to their captors, speaking of a "natural tenderness of heart, which has never been benumbed or extirpated on board the transport vessels or on the West India sugar plantations by the brutality of their white executioners."

Blumenbach established a special library in his house devoted exclusively to black authors, singling out for special praise the poetry of Phillis Wheatley, a Boston slave whose writings have only recently been rediscovered: "I possess English, Dutch, and Latin poems by several [black authors], amongst which however above all, those of Phillis Wheatley of Boston, who is justly famous for them, deserves mention here." Finally, Blumenbach noted that many Caucasian nations could not boast so fine a set of authors and scholars as black Africa has produced under the most depressing circumstances of prejudice and slavery: "It would not be difficult to mention entire well-known provinces of Europe, from out of which you would not easily expect to obtain off-hand such good authors, poets, philosophers, and correspondents of the Paris Academy."

Nonetheless, when Blumenbach presented his mental picture of human diversity in his fateful shift away from Linnaean geography, he singled out a particular group as closest to the created ideal and then characterized all other groups by relative degrees of departure from this archetypal standard. He ended up with a system that placed a single race at the pinnacle, and then envisioned two symmetrical lines of departure away from this ideal toward greater and greater degeneration.

WE MAY NOW RETURN to the riddle of the name Caucasian, and to the significance of Blumenbach's addition of a fifth race, the Malay variety. Blumenbach chose to regard his own European variety as closest to the created ideal and then searched for the subset of Europeans with greatest perfection—the highest of the high, so to speak. As we have seen, he identified the people around Mount Caucasus as the closest embodiments of the original ideal and proceeded to name the entire European race for its finest representatives.

But Blumenbach now faced a dilemma. He had already affirmed the mental and moral equality of all peoples. He therefore could not use these conventional criteria of racist ranking to establish degrees of relative departure from the Caucasian ideal. Instead, and however subjective (and even risible) we view the criterion today, Blumenbach chose physical beauty as his guide to ranking. He simply affirmed that Europeans were most beautiful, with Caucasians as the most comely of all. This explains why Blumenbach, in the first quote cited in this article, linked the maximal beauty of the Caucasians to the place of human origin. Blumenbach viewed all subsequent variation as departures from the originally created ideal—therefore, the most beautiful people must live closest to our primal home.

Blumenbach's descriptions are pervaded by his subjective sense of relative beauty, presented as though he were discussing an objective and quantifiable property, not subject to doubt or disagreement. He describes a Georgian female skull (found close to Mount Caucasus) as "really the most beautiful form of skull which . . . always of itself attracts every eye, however little observant." He then defends his European standard on aesthetic grounds: "In the first place, that stock displays . . . the most beautiful form of the skull, from which, as from a mean and primeval type, the others diverge by most easy gradations. . . . Besides, it is white in color, which we may fairly assume to have been the primitive color of mankind, since . . . it is very easy for that to degenerate into brown, but very much more difficult for dark to become white."

Blumenbach then presented all human variety on two lines of successive departure from this Caucasian ideal, ending in the two most degenerate (least attractive, not least morally unworthy or mentally obtuse) forms of humanity—Asians on one side, and Africans on the other. But Blumenbach also wanted to designate intermediary forms between ideal and most degenerate, especially since even gradation formed his primary argument for human unity. In his original four-race system, he could identify native Americans as intermediary between Europeans and Asians, but who would serve as the transitional form between Europeans and Africans?

The four-race system contained no appropriate group. But inventing a fifth racial category as an intermediary between Europeans and Africans would complete the new symmetrical geometry. Blumenbach therefore added the Malay race, not as a minor, factual refinement but as a device for reformulating an entire theory of human diversity. With this one stroke, he produced the geometric transformation from Linnaeus's unranked geographic model to the conventional hierarchy of implied worth that has fostered so much social grief ever since.

I have allotted the first place to the Caucasian . . . which makes me esteem it the primeval one. This diverges in both directions into two, most remote and very different from each other; on the one side, namely, into the Ethiopian, and on the other into the Mongolian. The remaining two occupy the intermediate positions between that primeval one and these two extreme varieties; that is, the American between the Caucasian and Mongolian; the Malay between the same Caucasian and Ethiopian. [From Blumenbach's third edition.]

With one stroke, Blumenbach produced the geometric transformation from Linnaeus's unranked geographic model to the conventional hierarchy of implied worth that has fostered so much social grief ever since.

Scholars often think that academic ideas must remain at worst, harmless, and at best, mildly amusing or even instructive. But ideas do not reside in the ivory tower of our usual metaphor about academic irrelevance. We are, as Pascal said, a thinking reed, and ideas motivate human history. Where would Hitler have been without racism, Jefferson without liberty? Blumenbach lived as a cloistered professor all his life, but his ideas have reverberated in ways that he never could have anticipated, through our wars, our social upheavals, our sufferings, and our hopes.

I therefore end by returning once more to the extraordinary coincidences of 1776—as Jefferson wrote the Declaration of Independence while Blumenbach was publishing the first edition of his treatise in Latin. We should remember the words of the nineteenth-century British historian and moralist Lord Acton, on the power of ideas to propel history:

It was from America that . . . ideas long locked in the breast of solitary thinkers, and hidden among Latin folios, burst forth like a conqueror upon the world they were destined to transform, under the title of the Rights of Man.

FOR FURTHER READING

Daughters of Africa. Margaret Busby, editor. Pantheon, 1992. A comprehensive anthology of prose and poetry written by women of African descent, from ancient Egyptian love songs to the work of contemporary Americans. The collection features the work of Phillis Wheatley, the first black to publish a book of poetry in the United States.

BRED IN THE BONE?

For all their claims about the usefulness of race, physicians and forensic experts leave a trail of misdiagnoses and misidentifications in their wake

BY ALAN H. GOODMAN

ON THE MORNING OF MAY 30, 1995, REScue workers in Oklahoma City made a final, melancholy sweep through the ruins of the Alfred P. Murrah Federal Building. In the weeks after the building was bombed, 165 victims had been discovered and removed, but three more bodies had been lodged in places too unstable to reach. Rather than risk more lives in a futile rescue—any survivors of the blast would have long since died of starvation or suffocation—workers simply had marked the three locations with Day-Glo orange paint, before bringing down the rest of the building with dynamite. Now they picked methodically through the rubble, searching for glimpses of orange.

Clyde Snow, a forensic anthropologist with a long history of identifying victims of war crimes, was stationed in the state morgue at the time, listening to reports from the bomb site. "Everything was going swimmingly," he later recalled. "When they got down to level zero, people could hear them talking on their mobile phones: 'Okay, we have one, two, three bodies. . . . Fine, wrap it up, we can all go home.'" The rescue team, events soon showed, was jumping the gun just a bit. Two or three minutes after the third body had been found, a voice suddenly broke back over the airwaves: "Hey wait a minute! We've got a leg down here. A left leg."

During the explosion and its aftermath, about twenty-five of the victims had been dismembered. Snow assumed, at first, that the leg must belong to one of those. "In all the confusion, with bodies going back and forth for X rays, I thought somebody just overlooked that one body had a left leg missing," he said. "So we'll just match it up." But one recount after another yielded the same number: 168 right legs, 168 left legs; none of the survivors was missing a leg. "We went through autopsy records, pathology reports, body diagrams, and photographs. I did it twice, the pathologist did it twice," Snow said. "It was just a mathematical paradox."

Baffled, Snow took a closer look at the leg itself. Sheared off just above the knee by the blast, it still wore the remains of a black, military-style boot, two socks and an olive-drab blousing strap. Its skin, Snow said, suggested "a darkly complected Caucasoid." By measuring the lower leg and plugging the numbers into computer programs that categorize bones by race and sex, Snow confirmed his hunch: the leg probably came from a white male. An attorney for the prime suspect in the bombing, Timothy J. McVeigh, pounced on the news, suggesting that the leg belonged to the "real bomber." Snow wondered if it might belong to one of the transients who hung out on the first floor of the building. Fred B. Jordan, the Chief Medical Examiner for the state of Oklahoma, guessed that the leg belonged to a person walking alongside the truck carrying explosives.

As it turned out, the leg belonged to none of the above. Its owner was one Lakesha R. Levy of New Orleans, an Airman First Class, stationed at Tinker Air Force Base in Midwest City, Oklahoma. On April 19 Levy had gone to the Murrah building to get a Social Security card and gotten caught near the epicenter of the blast. Levy was five feet, five inches tall, twenty-one years old and female. She was also, in the words of one forensics expert, "obviously black." With that disclosure, McVeigh's attorney declared, "no one can have confidence in any of the forensic work in this case."

Just a few weeks before the leg was found, in the pages of this magazine, Snow had said that he could accurately discern a victim's race from its skull 90 percent of the time [see "Murder Most Foul," by Clyde Snow, May/June 1995]. True, a skull provides more clues to its owner's identity than a leg does, and Levy's leg was discovered and examined under extremely trying conditions. But the leg was still covered in skin, only partly decomposed, and skin is the most common indicator of "race."

In fact, numerous examples suggest that mistakes like the one in Oklahoma City are common. They are common not because forensics experts do shoddy work—they don't, the errors in Oklahoma City notwithstanding—but because their conclusions are based on a deeply flawed premise. As long as race is used as a shorthand to describe human biological variations—

variations that blur from one race into the next, and are greatest *within* so-called races rather than among them—misidentifications are inevitable. Whether it is used in police work, medical studies or countless everyday situations where people are grouped biologically, the answer is the same: race science is bad science.

THIRTY YEARS AGO, THE AMERICAN paleontologist George Gaylord Simpson declared all pre-Darwinian definitions of humanity worthless. "We will be better off," he wrote, "if we ignore them completely." The scientific concept of race—an outgrowth of the Greek idea of a great chain of being and the Platonic notion of ideal types—is anti-evolutionary to its core. It should therefore have been the first relic consigned to the scrap heap.

Race should have been discarded at the turn of the century, when the American anthropologist Franz Boas showed that race, language and culture do not go hand-in-hand, as raciologists had contended. But race persisted. It should have vanished in the 1930s, when the "new evolutionary synthesis" helped explain subtle human variations. Yet between 1899, when William Z. Ripley published *Races of Europe,* and 1939, when the American anthropologist Carleton S. Coon published a book by the same name, the concept of race as type persisted almost unchanged. (Coon, on the eve of the Second World War, went to some lengths to ponder the essence of Jewishness. "There is a quality of looking Jewish," he wrote "and its existence cannot be denied.") Race should have disappeared in the 1950s and 1960s, when physical anthropologists switched from studying types to studying variations as responses to evolutionary forces. But race lived on. To Coon, for instance, races just became populations with distinct adaptive problems.

Most anthropologists today acknowledge that biological races are a myth. Yet the idea survives, in a variety of forms. A crude typology of world views goes something like this. At one end of the spectrum are the true believers: At the University of Western Ontario in London, for example, the psychologist J. Philippe Rushton asserts that there are three main races—Mongoloid, Negroid and Caucasoid—and he ranks them according to intelligence and procreative ability. Here, sure enough, the old racial stereotypes leak out: the two traits allegedly appear in inverse proportion. You can have either a large brain or a large . . . (insert sexual organ of choice). Rushton's Mongoloids rank as the most intelligent; Negroids allegedly have the strongest sexual drive; Caucasoids fit into the comfortable middle.

At the other end of the spectrum are two groups who agree that races are a myth, but draw radically different conclusions from that premise. The politically conservative group, known for proclaiming a "color-free society," argues that if races do not exist, sociopolitical policies such as affirmative action ought not to be based on race. Social constructionists, on the other hand, realize that race-as-bad-biol-ogy has nothing to do with race-as-lived-experience. Social policy does not need a biological basis, especially when a dark-skinned American is still roughly twice as likely to be denied a mortgage as is a light-skinned person with an equivalent income. True races may not exist, but racism does.

A fourth group, the confused, occupies the middle ground. Some do not understand why race biology is such bad science, yet they avoid any appeal to race because they do not want to be politically incorrect. Others apply race as a quasi-biological, quasi-genetic category and cannot figure out what is wrong with it. Still others think the stance against racial biology is political rather than scientific.

That middle category of the confused is huge. It includes nearly all public health and medical professionals, as well as most physical anthropologists. Moreover, the continued "soft" use of race by that well-meaning group acts to legitimize the "hard" use by true believers and scientific racists. And if most professionals are confused about race, most of the public is both dazed and confused. There is no single, stable or monolithic public perception about race, but races are generally thought to be about genes (or blood) and (only slightly less permanent) cultural ties. Regardless, race is considered to be deep, primordial and constant: in short, indistinguishable from its nineteenth-century definition.

IN 1992 THE FORENSIC ANTHROPOLOGIST NORman J. Sauer of Michigan State University in East Lansing published an article in the journal *Social Science and Medicine* provocatively titled, "Forensic Anthropology and the Concept of Race: If Races Don't Exist, Why Are Forensic Anthropologists So Good at Identifying Them?" Race may be unscientific, Sauer argued, but people of one socially constructed racial category still tend to look alike—and different from the people of another "race." The biological anthropologist C. Loring Brace of the University of Michigan in Ann Arbor explains Sauer's paradox in a slightly different way. Forensic scientists are good at estimating race, Brace says, because so-called racial variations are statistically confounded with real regional differences. People do vary in a systematic way depending on their environment.

Both arguments make sense, and forensic anthropologists do important work. But how good are they, really, at identifying race? Like Snow, the authors of forensic texts and review articles typically maintain that the race of a skull can be correctly identified between 85 and 90 percent of the time. The scientific reference for those estimates—if cited as anything other than common knowledge—is a single, groundbreaking study by the physical anthropologists Eugene Giles, at the University of Illinois in Urbana-Champaign, and Orville S. Elliot, at the University of Victoria in British Columbia. In the early 1960s Giles and Elliot measured the skulls of modern, adult blacks and whites who had died in Missouri and Ohio, many of them at the turn of the century, as well as Native American skulls from a prehistoric site in Indian Knoll, Kentucky. Using a statistical equation known as a discriminant function, they then identified a combination of eight measurements that could determine a skull's "race" once its sex was known.

When Giles and Elliot applied the formula to additional skulls from the same collections, it agreed with the race assigned to the deceased at death between 80 and 90 percent of the time. To be useful, however, the formula has to work in places other than Missouri, Ohio and prehistoric Kentucky. I have found four retests of the Giles and Elliot method, and their results do not inspire confidence. Two of the retests restricted themselves to Native American skulls: in one of them almost two-thirds of the skulls were correctly classified as Native Americans; in the second, only 31 percent were correctly classified. For the two other studies, in which the skulls were of mixed race, skulls were correctly identified as Native American just 18.2 percent and 14.3 percent of the time. Thus in three of the four tests, the formula proved less accurate than a random assignment of races to skulls—not even good enough for government work.

Contemporary Native American skulls may be particularly hard to classify because the formula is based on a very old sample. But the four retests were carried out on complete crania that had already been sexed, a necessary prerequisite to determining race. Forensic anthropologists often have much less to go on. Moreover, Native Americans are easier to classify than Hispanics or Southeast Asians, not to mention infants, children or adolescents of any race. At best, in other words, racial identifications are depressingly inaccurate. At worst, they are completely haphazard. How many bodies and body parts, like Lakesha Levy's leg, are sending investigators down wrong paths because the wrong box was checked off?

Forensic anthropologists usually blame such mistakes on the melting pot. Yet distinct racial types have never existed. What changes are social definitions of race—the color line—and human biology. Whites in Cleveland in 1897 were different from whites in Amarillo, Texas, in 1997. Science 101: generalizations ought not be based on an ill-defined, constantly changing and contextually loaded variable.

SKULLS AND CORPSES, ONE COULD ARGUE, HAVE ceased to care to which race they belong—though their families and friends might disagree. But when physicians base their actions on perceived racial categories, their patients ought to care a great deal. Does race, however imperfect a category, help physicians diagnose, treat, prevent or understand the etiology of a disease?

Before the Second World War, physicians were often blinded by the conviction that certain races suffered from certain diseases. People who had sickle-cell anemia, for instance, were assumed to have "African blood." In 1927 the American physician J. S. Lawrence discovered a case of the disease in a "white" person. "Special attention was paid to the question of racial admixture of negro blood in the family but no evidence could be obtained," Lawrence wrote in the *Journal of Clinical Investigation*. "There must be some caution in calling this sickle-cell anemia because no evidence of negro blood could be found."

Evelynn M. Hammonds, a historian of science at the Massachusetts Institute of Technology, has brought to my attention some early diagnoses of ovarian cysts that express the same logic. In 1899 the American physician Thomas R. Brown reported that he often heard surgeons say that tumors found in black women had all the features of ovarian cysts, "but inasmuch as the patient is a negress it is certainly not so, as multilocular cysts are unknown in the negress." The following year Daniel H. Williams, the eminent African-American physician and the first American to perform successful heart surgery, quoted a physician from Alabama speculating that: "Possibly the Alabama negro has not evolved to the cyst-bearing age." Williams went on to show unambiguously, in a study, that ovarian cysts are common in black women including women from Alabama. He noted that white physicians have a history of ignoring black women, then offered examples of black women whose cysts swelled to 100 pounds or more before they were diagnosed.

TODAY THE PARADIGM OF RACIALLY DISTINCT diseases has been replaced by the more flexible idea of race as disease risk factor. Yet the medical effects are the same. Some 25 million Americans are said to suffer from osteoporosis, a progressive loss of bone mass that leads to 1.5 million fractures a year. Since the nineteenth century, blacks have been thought to have thicker bones than whites have and to lose bone mass more slowly with age. (A few years ago, when a dentist visited my laboratory, he was shocked to find that neither one of us could tell a black jaw from a white one.) In the journal *Seminars in Nuclear Medicine,* a review titled "Osteoporosis: The State of the Art in 1987" listed race as a major risk factor. The section on race begins: "It is a well-known fact that blacks do not suffer from osteoporosis."

That "fact" is backed by a single reference, a seminal paper by the American physical anthropologist Mildred Trotter and her colleagues titled "Densities of Bones of White and Negro Skeletons." Trotter and her colleagues evaluated the bone densities of skeletons from forty adult blacks and forty adult whites. They excluded skeletons with obvious bone diseases, but they did not describe how they chose the cadavers or whether the samples were matched for causes of death, diet or other known risk factors for osteoporosis. Of the ten bones they studied in each skeleton, Trotter and her colleagues found that six tended to be denser in blacks than in whites; the other four showed no differences by race. Furthermore, the authors wrote, the decline in density took place at "approximately the same rate" for each sex-race group.

Trotter and her colleagues may have realized that their data could be overinterpreted. In later publications they present scatterplots with age on one axis and bone density on the other. The scatterplots confirm that bone densities tend to decline with age: the clusters of data points slope downward. It is a challenge, however, to discern any difference between the densities of bones from blacks and those from whites. The six lowest radius densities, for example, were found in bones of blacks.

Let me be clear: I am only following citations to see if the data say what the references say they say. But my conclusion is dismaying. If the "well-known fact that blacks do not suffer from osteoporosis" is based on poorly interpreted data, then black women may not be getting enough preventive care, are not targeted in the media and are underdiagnosed as osteoporotic.

In every instance I have cited, a double leap of scientific faith seems to have taken place. First, a serious medical condition (sickle-cell anemia, ovarian cysts, osteoporosis) is regarded as genetic, even though environmental factors have not been adequately examined. Second, anything genetic is assumed to imply a panracial phenomenon. Thus, what might be true in a statistical sense is assumed true for all members of a so-called race. All blacks are protected from osteoporosis. All blacks are less prone to heart disease. By the same logic, Native Americans have some special predisposition to obesity and diabetes, though, in truth, rates vary wildly among groups and regions.

"RACE" DOES NOT determine skin color, nor does skin color determine "race."

WHY ARE MY FINDINGS MORE THAN IDIOsyncratic examples? Why does race not work as a shorthand for biological variation? The answer lies in the structure of human variation and in the chameleon-like concept of race.

• Most traits vary in small increments, or clines, across geographic areas. Imagine a merchant walking from Stockholm, Sweden, to Cape Town, South Africa, in the year 1400. He would notice that the skin colors of local people darkened until he reached the equator, then slowly turned lighter again. If he took a different route, perhaps starting in Siberia and wandering all the way to Singapore, he would observe the same phenomenon, though none of the people he passed on this second route would be classified as white or black today: all of them would be "Asian." Race, in other words, does not determine skin color, nor does skin color determine race. As Frank B. Livingstone, an anthropological geneticist at the University of Michigan in Ann Arbor, put it more than thirty years ago: "There are no races, there are only clines."

• Most traits are nonconcordant. That is, traits tend to vary in different and entirely independent ways. If you know a person's height, you can guess weight and shoe size because tall people tend to be heavier and have bigger feet than short people. Those traits are concordant. By the same

token, however, you could guess nothing about the person's skin color, facial features or most genes. Height is nonconcordant with nearly every other trait. If you know skin color, you might be able to guess eye color and perhaps (but surprisingly inaccurately) hair color and form. But that is all. Race, for that reason, is only skin deep.

• As I mentioned earlier, nearly all variations in genetic traits occur within so-called races rather than among them. Some thirty years ago the population geneticist Richard C. Lewontin of Harvard University conducted a statistical study of blood groups with two of the more common forms. On average, he found about 94 percent of the variation in blood forms occurred within perceived races; fewer than 6 percent could be explained by variations among races. Extrapolating from race to individuals is hardly more accurate than extrapolating from the human species to an individual.

One could argue that such classifications, however crude, are still useful as first approximations. Here is where one needs to see race as something more than the equivalent of shoe size.

• Racial differences are interpreted differently. Sometimes people consider them genetic, sometimes ethnic or cultural, and sometimes they use the term "race" to mean differences in lived experience. When race is assigned as a risk factor, the meaning is often unclear, and that ambiguity dramatically affects medical treatment. Sometimes race is a proxy for socioeconomic status or even for the effects of racism. If so, a particular racial classification suggests a possible set of actions. But if a racial classification is intended to signal a panracial genetic difference, as in osteoporosis, an entirely different set of actions should be undertaken. The conflation of genetics with culture, class and lived experience may be the most serious flaw in racial analysis.

• Race is impossible to define in a stable, repeatable way because, to repeat, race as biology varies with time and place, as do social classifications. Color lines change. When the skeletons studied by Giles and Elliot began to be collected in Cleveland at the turn of the century, the United States Census Bureau classified people not only as white or black, but as mulatto, quadroon or octoroon. Europe at the time was thought to be home to a dozen or so distinct races. One cannot do predictive science based on a changing and undefinable cause.

In studies such as those on osteoporosis—or any other disease—race is either undefined or assigned on the basis of the patient's own self-identification. "Since self-assignments to racial categories are commonly used," the authors of a review of race and nutritional status wrote in 1976, "the problem of racial identification is minimal." Compare that statement with the finding of a recent infant-mortality study by Robert A. Hahn, a medical anthropologist at the Centers for Disease Control and Prevention in Atlanta, Georgia. Thirty-seven percent of the babies described as Native American on their birth certificates, Hahn discovered, were described as some other race on their death certificates.

WHEN I STARTED OUT IN ANTHROPOLOGY in the 1970s, I thought anthropologists would stop using race by the 1990s. Why does it persist? At the very least, on a scientific level, it violates the first law of medicine: Do no harm. For every instance in which knowing race helps an investigator, there is probably another instance in which it leads to a missed diagnosis or the premature closing of a police file. At best, it is a proxy for something else. Why not study that something else?

There are good, simple alternatives to classifying by race. In biological studies, from forensics to epidemiology, investigators could focus on traits specific to the problem at hand. If the problem is describing human remains, simply describe those remains as well as possible. In Oklahoma City, for example, the police would have been better off looking for anyone with a dark complexion rather than searching for a "darkly complected Caucasoid." Police officers are used to searching for people with specific traits ("suspect has a smiley-face tattoo on his left bicep"). Why not be equally specific about skin color and other "racial" traits? Epidemiologists, for their part, could focus on likely causal traits. If

skin color is a risk factor, classify people by skin color alone. If the risk factor is a genetic trait, such as type A blood, compare individuals with and without type A blood.

I do not for a moment think that knowing race is a myth eliminates racism. But as long as well-meaning investigators continue to use the concept of race without clearly defining it, they reify race as biology. In so doing, they mislead the public and encourage racist notions. According to the American sociologist Donal E. Muir, those who continue to see race in biology but mean no harm by it are nothing more than "kind racists." By continuing to legitimize race, they inadvertently aid the "mean racists" who wish to do harm. Far too many scientists, unfortunately, still belong to both categories.

ALAN H. GOODMAN is a professor of anthropology at Hampshire College in Amherst, Massachusetts. With Thomas L. Leatherman, he is editing Building a New Biocultural Synthesis, *to be published by the University of Michigan next year. He delivered an invited talk on the topic of this article to the Anthropology Section of the New York Academy of Sciences on October 28, 1996.*

Color Blind

Getting beyond race takes more than a program in the workplace. An excerpt from a new book by ELLIS COSE

IN "THE ETHICS OF LIVING JIM CROW," AN AUTOBIOgraphical essay published in *Uncle Tom's Children* in 1940, Richard Wright told of his first job at an eyeglass lens-grinding company in Jackson, Mississippi. He landed the job, in part, because the boss was impressed with his education, and Wright was promised an opportunity to advance. "I had visions of working my way up. Even Negroes have those visions," wrote Wright. But even though he did his best to please, he discovered, over time, that nobody was teaching him a skill. His attempts to change that only provoked outrage. Finally, a co-worker shook his fist in Wright's face and advised him to stop making trouble: "This is a white man's work around here, and you better watch yourself."

Such sentiments obviously would not be openly voiced in most companies today. The civil rights revolution has seen to that. Still, it seems that every so often we get ugly reminders—of which the Texaco imbroglio is the latest—that Jim Crow's spirit is not yet dead. In 1994, Denny's restaurant chain agreed—in a settlement with the Justice Department—to put a civil rights monitor on its payroll and to cough up $45 million in damages, after a slew of complaints alleging discrimination against customers and employees. The previous year Shoney's, another restaurant chain, settled a suit for over $100 million that alleged, among other things, that managers were told to keep the number of black employees down in certain neighborhoods.

People of color with training and experience are "treated like s—t in too many places on the job," said assistant labor secretary Bernard Anderson, whose responsibilities include the Office of Federal Contract Compliance Programs. Even within the labor department, said Anderson, he had seen racial prejudice. When a black colleague, a Rhodes scholar, appointed two other blacks with impeccable credentials to positions, "the black lawyers were very empowered and encouraged by all of this," recalled Anderson, but a number of the white lawyers . . . were just shaking in their boots." By and by, he said, a "poison pen memorandum" found its way around the department. The missive made insulting, scatological comments, questioned the credentials of the people who had been appointed, and declared that affirmative action had gone too far.

Resentment against minorities often surfaces in places where "diversity" or affirmative action programs are in place. And that resentment often breeds resistance that results not merely in nasty comments but in outright sabotage.

Some time ago, the black employees of a large, international corporation invited me to talk about a previous book, *The Rage of a Privileged Class,* at a corporate-wide event. In talking with my hosts, I quickly discovered that they were not merely interested in my insights. They wanted me to send a message to the management. They were frustrated because a corporate affirmative-action program, of which the management was extremely proud, was not doing them any good. Mid-level managers, it turned out, got diversity points for hiring or promoting minorities, but the corporation had defined minorities in such a way that everyone who was not a U.S.-born white man qualified. In other words, the managers got as much credit for transferring white men from Europe, Australia, and Canada as they did for promoting African Americans. And that is exactly what they were doing, according to the black employees, who wanted me to let the management know, in a nice and subtle way, that such behavior was unacceptable.

I'm not sure what message the management ended up extracting from my speech, but I am sure that the frustrations those black employees felt are widespread—and that the cause lies less in so-called diversity programs than in the widespread tendency to judge minority group members more by color than by ability.

Some two decades ago, I received a brutal lesson in how galling such attitudes can be. At the time, I was a young (maybe twenty-one or twenty-two years old) columnist-reporter for the *Chicago Sun-Times*. Though I had only been in the business a few years, I was acquiring something of a regional reputation. I hoped to break into magazine writing by garnering a few freelance assignments from *Esquire* magazine, so I had made an appointment with one of its editors.

The editor with whom I met was a pleasant and rather gracious man, but what he had to say was sobering. He wasn't sure, he confided, how many black readers *Esquire* had, but was reasonably certain the number was not high. Since I had not inquired about his readership, the statement took me a bit by surprise. I had been a longtime reader of *Esquire*, and it had never previously occurred to me that I was not supposed to be, that it was not me whom *Esquire* had in mind as an audience—never mind as a contributor. I don't know whether the editor bothered to read my clippings, but then, the clips were somehow superfluous; the very fact that I had written them made them so. All the editor saw was a young black guy, and since *Esquire* was not in need of a young black guy, they were not in need of me. I left that office in a state of controlled fury—not just because the editor had rejected me as a writer, but because he had been so busy focusing on my race that he was incapable of seeing *me* or my work.

A nominal commitment to diversity does not necessarily guarantee an appreciably better outcome, as I came to see

> # Do we have the vaguest idea how to create a society that is truly race neutral?

several years ago when I was approached by a newspaper publisher who was in the process of putting together his management team. He was interested, he said, in hiring some minority senior managers, so I gave him some names of people who might be likely candidates. Over the next several months, I watched as he put his team in place—a team, as it turned out, that was totally white. Only after he had largely assembled that group did he begin serious talks with some of the nonwhites I had recommended.

I don't doubt the man's sincerity. He did want to hire some minority managers, and eventually did so. But what was clear to me was that to him, minority recruitment meant the recruitment of people who couldn't be trusted with the organization's most important jobs. His first priority was

hiring people who could do the work—meaning whites—and only after that task was complete would he concern himself with the window dressing of diversity.

Over the years, I have learned that affirmative action in theory and affirmative action in practice are two different things. In the real world it is much more than simply opening up an organization to people who traditionally have been excluded; it is attempting, usually through some contrived measures, to make organizations do what they don't do naturally—and it goes down about as easily as castor oil. Shortly after I announced my resignation as editor of the editorial pages of the New York *Daily News*, I took one of my white staff members out to lunch. He told me he had enjoyed working with me and was sorry to see me go. He had cringed when he heard that I was coming, he confided, for he had feared that I would be just another affirmative action executive, presumably incapable of doing the job competently. He admitted that he had been pleasantly surprised.

I was pleased but also saddened by his confession—pleased that he felt comfortable enough to tell me how he truly felt and saddened that the very fact that a person of color got a high-ranking job would lead him (as it had led so many before him) to question that person's credentials. Yet, having occasionally been the target of affirmative-action recruiters, I am fully aware that (whatever they may say in public) they don't always pay as much attention to credentials as to color. Therefore, I understand clearly why even the ostensible beneficiaries of such recruitment tactics may find affirmative action, as practiced by major corporations, distasteful and even offensive. A decade and a half ago, for instance, I received a call from an associate of an executive search firm who, after verbally tap dancing for several minutes, essentially asked whether I wished to be considered for a job as a corporate director of equal opportunity. I was stunned, for the question made no sense. I was an expert neither on personnel nor on equal-employment law; I was, however, black, which seemed to be the most important qualification. I laughed and told him that I saw my career going in another direction. Still, I wondered just how serious the inquiry could be, since I seemed (to me, at least) so unsuited for the position. Since then, I have received other calls pushing jobs that have seemed every bit as outlandish.

At one point, a man called to discuss the presidency of a major foundation. I confessed I didn't understand why he was calling me, and he assured me that the client was extremely interested in having me apply. The man's earnestness intrigued me enough that I sent him a resume. I never heard from him again, which confirmed, in my mind at any rate, that his interest was anything but genuine. I imagined him sitting in his office with a long list of minority candidates, from whom he would collect resumes and promptly bury them in a file, merely so that his clients would be able to say they had considered minorities. Indeed, when the foundation head was finally named (he was a white man with a long professional association with the foundation trustees), it was clear to me that the supposed search had been a sham. After one takes a few such calls, one realizes that the purpose is often defensibility ("Yes, we took a hard look at fifteen minority candidates, but none quite fit the bill") and that the supposed high-level position is merely bait to attract the interest of people who don't really have a shot—but in whom everyone must pretend they are interested because an affirmative-action program is in place.

It's logical to argue for the replacement of such shameful practices with something better—for some form of meritocracy. Yet affirmative-action critics who extol the virtues of a meritocracy generally ignore the reality of how a real-world so-called meritocracy works. If qualified, capable, and talent-

Twelve Steps Toward Racial Harmony

AMERICANS HAVE LITTLE ALTERNATIVE BUT TO ACCEPT THE POSSIBILITY THAT race will continue to divide us. Yet it is clear that society is more hospitable to minorities and more—racially—egalitarian than it was a few generations ago. There is every likelihood that it can become more so. Hence, we have to ask the question—if only as an experiment in thought: Do we have the vaguest idea how to create a society that is truly race neutral? The short answer, I suspect, is no. Otherwise we would be much further along the way than we are. Still, I believe we can get beyond such platitudes as "Let's just love one another," which is the verbal equivalent of throwing up our hands in noble resignation. Enumerating steps our society could take toward racial sanity is obviously not the same as putting America's racial goblins to rest. It is, however, a necessary prelude to moving the dialogue beyond the realm of reassuring yet empty platitudes. So what would some of those steps be?

1 WE MUST STOP EXPECTING TIME TO SOLVE THE PROBLEM FOR US: In "Guess Who's Coming to Dinner," there is a scene in which Sidney Poitier (who plays a physician in his thirties in love with a young white woman) turns, in a fit of rage, to the actor playing his father. Only when the older generation is dead, Poitier declares, will prejudice wither away. The sobering realization is that Poitier is now older than his "father" was then, and the problem, obviously, remains.

Time doesn't heal all wounds; it certainly doesn't solve all problems. It is often merely an excuse for allowing them to fester. Our problems, including our racial problems, belong to us—not to our descendants.

2 WE MUST RECOGNIZE THAT RACE RELATIONS IS NOT A ZERO–SUM GAME: The presumption that America is a zero-sum society, that if one race advances another must regress, accounts, in large measure, for the often illogical reaction to programs that aim to help minorities. Such thinking even explains some of the hostility between members of so-called minority groups. *Can only one person of color rise within a given organization?* One hopes not. *Does an increase in Latino clout portend a decline in blacks' well-being?* It shouldn't.

Unfortunately, we have too often reveled in political rhetoric that puts across the opposite message; and have too often rewarded those who exploit our anxiety and insecurities—as opposed to those who demonstrate the willingness and ability to harness our faith in each other and in ourselves.

3 WE MUST REALIZE THAT ENDING HATE IS THE BEGINNING, NOT THE END, OF OUR MISSION: Occasionally, I turn on my television and am greeted by some celebrity exhorting me to stop the hate. I always wonder about the target audience for that particular broadside. I suspect that it is aimed mostly at people who don't hate anyone—perhaps as a reminder of our virtue. I certainly can't imagine a card-carrying member of the local Nazi group getting so fired up by the message that he turns to the television and exclaims, "Yes, you're right. I must immediately stop the hate."

Stopping the hate does little to bring people of different races or ethnic groups together. Certainly, it's better than stoking hate, but discrimination and stereotyping are not primarily the result of hatred. If we tell ourselves that the only problem is hate, we avoid facing the reality that it is mostly nice, nonhating people who perpetuate racial inequality.

4 WE MUST ACCEPT THE FACT THAT EQUALITY IS NOT A HALFWAY PROPOSITION: This century has seen huge changes in the status of black Americans. It has also seen the growth of largely segregated school systems, the development and maintenance of segregated neighborhoods, and the congealing of the assumption that blacks and whites belong to fundamentally different communities. The mistake was in the notion that social, economic, and political equality are not interrelated, that it was possible to go on living in largely segregated neighborhoods, socialize in largely segregated circles, and even attend segregated places of worship and yet have a workplace and a polity where race ceased to be a factor. As long as we cling to the notion that equality is fine in some spheres and not in others, we will be clinging to a lie.

5 WE MUST END AMERICAN APARTHEID: Americans have paid much homage to Martin Luther King's dream of a society where people would be judged only by the content of their character—even as they have yanked children out of schools when a delicate racial balance tipped, or planted themselves in neighborhoods determinedly monochromatic, or fought programs that would provide housing for poor blacks outside of the slums. There is something fundamentally incongruous in the idea of judging people by the content of their character and yet consigning so many Americans at birth to communities in which they are written off even before their character has been shaped.

6 WE MUST REPLACE A PRESUMPTION THAT MINORITIES WILL FAIL WITH AN EXPECTATION OF THEIR SUCCESS: When doing research with young drug dealers in California, anthropologist John Ogbu found himself both impressed and immensely saddened. "Those guys have a sense of the economy. They have talents that could be used on Wall Street," he remarked. "They have intelligence—but not the belief that they can succeed in the mainstream." Somewhere along the line, probably long before they became drug dealers, that belief had been wrenched out of them.

Creating an atmosphere in which people learn they cannot achieve is tantamount to creating failure. The various academic programs that do wonders with "at-risk" youths share a rock-hard belief in the ability of the young people in their care. These programs manage to create an atmosphere in which the "success syndrome" can thrive. Instead of focusing so much attention on whether people with less merit are getting various slots, we should be focusing on how to widen—and reward—the pool of meritorious people.

7 WE MUST STOP PLAYING THE BLAME GAME: Too often America's racial debate is sidetracked by a search for racial scapegoats. And more often than not, those scapegoats end up being the people on the other side of the debate. "It's your fault because you're a racist." "No, it's your fault because you expect something for nothing." "It's white skin privilege." "It's reverse racism." And on and on it goes. American culture, with its bellicose talk-show hosts and pugnacious politicians, rewards those who cast aspersions at the top of their lungs. And American law, with its concept of damages and reparations, encourages the practice of allocating blame. Although denying the past is dishonest and even sometimes maddening, obsessing about past wrongs is ultimately futile.

Certainly, loudmouths will always be among us and will continue to say obnoxious and foolish things, but it would be wonderful if more of those engaged in what passes for public discourse would recognize an obvious reality: It hardly matters who is responsible for things being screwed up; the only relevant question is, "How do we make them better?"

8 WE MUST DO A BETTER JOB AT LEVELING THE PLAYING FIELD: As long as roughly a third of black Americans sit on the bottom of the nation's economic pyramid and have little chance of moving up, the United States will have a serious racial problem on its hands. There is simply no way around that cold reality. It is pointless to say that the problem is class, not race, if race and class are tightly linked.

During the past several decades, Americans have witnessed an esoteric debate over whether society must provide equality of opportunity or somehow ensure equality of result. It is, however, something of a phony debate, for the two concepts are not altogether separate things. If America was, in fact, providing equality of opportunity, then we would have something closer to equality of racial result than we do at present. The problem is that equality of opportunity has generally been defined quite narrowly—such as simply letting blacks and whites take the same test, or apply for the same job.

Equality of opportunity is meaningless when inherited wealth is a large determinant of what schools one attends (and even whether one goes to school), what neighborhoods one can live in, and what influences and contacts one is exposed to. *In Black Wealth, White Wealth,* sociologists Melvin Oliver and Tom Shapiro pointed out that most blacks have virtually no wealth—even if they do earn a decent income. Whites with equal educational levels to blacks typically have five to ten times as much wealth, largely because whites are much more likely to inherit or receive gifts of substantial unearned assets. This disparity is a direct result of Jim Crow practices and discriminatory laws and policies.

America is not about to adopt any scheme to redistribute resources materially. What Americans must do, however, if we are at all serious about equality of opportunity, is to make it easier for those without substantial resources to have secure housing outside urban ghettos, to receive a high-quality education, and to have access to decent jobs.

9 WE MUST BECOME SERIOUS ABOUT FIGHTING DISCRIMINATION: In their rush to declare this society colorblind, some Americans have leaped to the conclusion that discrimination has largely disappeared. They explain away what little discrimination they believe exists as the fault of a few isolated individuals or the result of the oversensitivity of minorities.

Making discrimination a felony is probably not a solution, but more aggressive monitoring and prosecution—especially in housing and employment situations—would not be a bad start. Just as one cannot get beyond race by treating different races differently, one cannot get beyond discrimination by refusing to acknowledge it. One can get beyond discrimination only by fighting it vigorously wherever it is found.

10 WE MUST KEEP THE CONVERSATION GOING: Dialogue clearly is no cure-all for racial estrangement. Conversations, as opposed to confrontations, about race are inevitably aimed at a select few—those who make up the empathic elite. Yet, limited as the audience may be, the ongoing discourse is crucial. It gives those who are sincerely interested in examining their attitudes and behavior an opportunity to do so, and, in some instances, can even lead to change.

11 WE MUST SEIZE OPPORTUNITIES FOR INTERRACIAL COLLABORATION: Even those who have no interest in talking about the so-called *racial situation* can, through the process of working with (and having to depend on) people of other races, begin to see beyond skin color. Conversation, in short, has its limits. Only through doing things together—things that have nothing specifically to do with race— will people break down racial barriers. Facing common problems as community groups, as work colleagues, or as classmates can provide a focus and reduce awkwardness in a way that simple conversation cannot.

12 WE MUST STOP LOOKING FOR ONE SOLUTION TO ALL OUR RACIAL PROBLEMS: Meetings on racial justice often resemble nothing so much as a bazaar filled with peddlers offering the all-purpose answer. The reality is that the problem has no single or simple solution. If there is one answer, it lies in recognizing how complex the issue has become and in not using that complexity as an excuse for inaction. In short, if we are to achieve our country, we must attack the enemy on many fronts.

ELLIS COSE

ed minorities and women exist, they say, corporations will reward them because they will recognize that it is within their economic interest to do so. That may well be true. But it is also true that effective executives are trained, not born. They come about because companies make an investment in them, in their so-called human capital, and nurture their careers along—and if corporations only see the potential in white men, those are the people in whom the investments are likely to be made.

> **Our problems, including our racial problems, belong to us— not to our descendants**

John Kotter, a Harvard Business School professor and author of *The General Managers*, discovered that effective executives generally benefited from what he called the "success syndrome." They were constantly provided with opportunities for growth: "They never stagnated for significant periods of time in jobs where there were few growth possibilities." The executives also, to be blunt about it, are often people of relatively modest intellectual endowment. They succeed largely because they are chosen for success.

A true meritocracy would do a much better job of evaluating and choosing a broader variety of people. It would challenge the very way merit is generally imputed and, in giving people ample opportunity to develop and to prove themselves, it would create a truly level playing field.

Simply eliminating affirmative action would not bring such a true meritocracy about. Indeed, a large part of the reason affirmative action is so appealing to so many people is that a meritocracy that fully embraces people of color seems out of reach; and affirmative action is at least one method to get people to accept the fact that talent comes in more than one color.

Yet, by its very nature, affirmative action is polarizing. Wouldn't it be better, argue a growing number of Americans, to let it die in peace? A chorus of conservative critics even invoke the dream of Martin Luther King Jr. to make the case.

King would probably be more astonished than anyone to hear that conservatives now claim him as one of their own, that they have embraced his dream of a color-blind world and invoke it as proof of the immorality and undesirability of gender and racial preferences. But even if he had a bit of trouble accepting his status as a general in the war against affirmative action, he would appreciate the joke. And he would realize that it is the fate of the dead to be reborn as angels to the living. King no doubt would be pleased to have new friends in his fight for justice, but he would approach them with caution. After sharing his disappointment over past alliances with people whose commitment to change did not match his own, King would address his new associates bluntly. "All right," he might say, "I understand why you oppose affirmative action. But tell me: What is *your* plan? What is *your* plan to cast the slums of our cities on the junk heaps of history? What is *your* program to transform the dark yesterdays of segregated education into the bright tomorrows of high-quality, integrated education? What is *your* strategy to smash separatism, to destroy discrimination, to make justice roll down like water and righteousness flow like a mighty stream from every city hall and statehouse in this great and blessed nation?" He might then pause for a reply, his countenance making it unmistakably clear that he would accept neither silence nor sweet nothings as an answer.

How to mend affirmative action

GLENN C. LOURY

My scholarly work on the problem of race relations began with a general inquiry into the theory of economic inequality. Specifically, my 1981 paper, "Intergenerational Transfers and the Distribution of Earnings," which appeared in the journal *Econometrica*, introduced a model of economic achievement in which a person's earnings depended on a random endowment of innate ability and on skills acquired from formal training. The key feature of this theory was that individuals had to rely on their families to pay for their training. In this way, a person's economic opportunities were influenced by his inherited social position. I showed how, under these circumstances, the distribution of income in each generation could be determined by an examination of what had been obtained by the previous generation. My objective with the model was to illustrate how, in the long run, when people depend on resources available within families to finance their acquisition of skills, economic inequality comes to reflect the inherited advantages of birth. A disparity among persons in economic attainment would bear no necessary connection to differences in their innate abilities.

In other research, I applied this mode of reasoning to the problem of group, as distinct from individual, inequality. That analysis began with two observations. First, all societies exhibit significant *social segmentation*. People make choices about whom to befriend, whom to marry, where to live, to which schools to send their children, and so on. Factors like race, ethnicity, social class, and religious affiliation influence these choices of association. Second, the processes through which individuals develop their productive capacities are shaped by custom, convention, and social norms, and are not fully responsive to market forces, or reflective of the innate abilities of persons. Networks of social affiliation are not usually the result of calculated economic decisions. They nevertheless help to determine how resources important to the development of the productive capacities of human beings are made available to individuals.

More concretely, one can say that an adult worker with a given degree of personal efficacy has been "produced" from the "inputs" of education, parenting skills, acculturation, nutrition, and socialization to which he was exposed in his formative years. While some of these "inputs" can be bought and sold, some of the most crucial "factors of production" are only available as by-products from activities of social affiliation. Parenting services are not to be had for purchase on the market, but accrue as the consequence of the social relations between the custodial parents and the child. The allocation of parenting services among a prospective generation of adults is thus the indirect consequence of social activities undertaken by members of the preceding generation. An adolescent's peer group is similarly a derivative consequence of processes of social networking.

I concede that this is an artificial way of thinking about human development, but the artifice is quite useful. For it calls attention to the critical role played by social and cultural resources in the production and reproduction of economic inequality. The relevance of such factors, as an empirical matter, is beyond doubt. The importance of networks, contacts, social background, family connections, and informal associations of all kinds has been amply documented by students of social stratification. In addition, values, attitudes, and beliefs of central import for the attainment of success in life are shaped by the cultural milieu in which a person develops. *Whom* one knows affects *what* one comes to know and, ultimately, what one can *do* with one's God-given talents.

Social capital and inequality

While all of this may seem obvious, the fact is that, prior to my work, formal theories of economic inequality had said little about the role of social background. I was the first economist to use the term "social capital" in reference to these processes by which the social relationships that occur among persons promote or retard their acquisition of traits valued in the market place. A large and growing literature has since emerged in which allowance is taken of the myriad ways that a person's opportunities to develop his natural gifts depend upon the economic achievements of those with whom he is

This essay is excerpted from a paper delivered at Boston University on October 6, 1997 under the title "The Divided Society and the Democratic Idea."

socially affiliated. This literature suggests that unqualified confidence in the equity and efficiency of the income distribution produced by the market is not justified.

In particular, this analysis has an important ethical implication: Because the creation of a skilled work force is a social process, the meritocratic ideal should take into account that no one travels the road to economic and social success alone. The facts that generations overlap, that much of social life lies outside the reach of public regulation, and that prevailing social affiliations influence the development of the intellectual and personal skills of the young, imply that present patterns of inequality—among individuals and between groups—must embody, to some degree, social and economic disparities that have existed in the past. To the extent that past disparities are illegitimate, the propriety of the contemporary order is called into question.

I have employed this framework to explore the legitimacy question with respect to inequality between blacks and whites in America.[1] In a theoretical example, I showed that, notwithstanding the establishment of a legal regime of equal opportunity, historically engendered economic differences between racial groups could well persist into the indefinite future. I concluded that the pronounced racial disparities to be observed in American cities are particularly problematic, since they are, at least in part, the product of an unjust history, propagated across the generations by the segmented social structures of our race-conscious society.

Thus I would argue, as a matter of social ethics, that the government should undertake policies to mitigate the economic marginality of those languishing in the ghettos of America. This is not a reparations argument. When the developmental prospects of an individual depend on the circumstances of those with whom he is socially affiliated, even a minimal commitment to equality of opportunity requires such a policy. In our divided society, and given our tragic past, this implies that public efforts intended to counter the effects of historical disadvantage among blacks are not only consistent with, but indeed are required by, widely embraced democratic ideals.

Color-blind extremists

This argument leads naturally to the question of whether affirmative-action policies are necessary and justified. To emphasize that racial group disparities can be transmitted across generations through subtle and complex social processes is not necessarily to endorse employment or educational preferences based on race. (I will offer in due course a number of reasons to think that these policies should be curtailed.) But recognizing the importance of social segmentation does cause one to doubt the ethical viability, and indeed the logical coherence, of "color-blind absolutism"—the notion that the Constitution requires government agents to ignore the racial identity of citizens. Ironically, recent claims by some conservatives to this effect

bear an eerie resemblance, in form and in substance, to the similarly absolute claims of some card-carrying civil libertarians on behalf of a "wall of separation" between church and state.

Consider that, as a practical matter, the government cannot enforce laws against employment discrimination without taking note of a gross demographic imbalance in an employer's work force. Yet the government's requiring that employment data be reported by race is already a departure from pure color-blind behavior. So too is the practice, nearly universal in the public and private sectors, of targeted outreach efforts designed to increase the representation of blacks in the pool of persons considered for an employment opportunity. Accordingly, the more intellectually consistent of the color-blind absolutists now recommend, as logic would require, that we repeal the civil-rights laws and abandon even those efforts to achieve racial diversity which do not involve preferential treatment. But is that stance consistent with fairness?

More subtly, how can a college educator convey to students the lesson that "not all blacks think alike," with too few blacks on campus for this truth to become evident? Were an American president to assemble a cabinet devoid of racial minority representation, would not the legitimacy of his administration rightly be called into question? What prison warden could afford to ignore the possibility that racial friction among his inmates might threaten the maintenance of order within his institution? Perhaps this is why presidents, prison wardens, and college educators do not behave in a purely color-blind fashion in our divided society.

Coming up with cases that challenge the absolutist claim is not difficult. Can the police consider race when making undercover assignments? Can a black public employee use health insurance benefits to choose a black therapist with whom to discuss race-related anxieties? Can units in a public housing project be let with an eye to sustaining a racially integrated environment? What about a National Science Foundation effort that encourages gifted blacks to pursue careers in fields where few now study? Clearly, there is no general rule that can resolve all of these cases reasonably.

I would venture to say that the study of affirmative action has been too much the preserve of lawyers and philosophers, and has too little engaged the interests of economists and other social scientists. It is as if, for this policy, unlike all others, we could determine a priori the wisdom of its application—as if its practice were always either "right" or "wrong," never simply "prudent" or "unwise." However, although departures from color-blind absolutism are both legitimate and desirable in some circumstances, there are compelling reasons to question the wisdom of relying as heavily as we now do on racial preferences to bring about civic inclusion for black Americans.

Logical stereotyping

One such reason for questioning the wisdom of affirmative action is that the widespread use of preferences can logically be expected to erode the perception of black competence. This

---

[1] See my paper, "A Dynamic Theory of Racial Income Differences," in *Women, Minorities and Employment Discrimination*, ed. P.A. Wallace (Lexington Books, DC Heath, 1977).

point is often misunderstood, so it is worth spelling out in some detail. The argument is not a speculation about the feelings of persons who may or may not be the beneficiaries of affirmative action. Rather, it turns on the rational, statistical inferences that neutral observers are entitled to make about the unknown qualifications of persons who may have been preferred, or rejected, in a selection process.

The main insight is not difficult to grasp. Let some employer use a lower threshold of assessed productivity for the hiring of blacks than whites. The preferential hiring policy defines three categories of individuals within each of the two racial groups which I will call "marginals," "successes," and "failures." Marginals are those whose hiring status is altered by the policy—either whites not hired who otherwise would have been, or blacks hired who otherwise would not have been. Successes are those who would be hired with or without the policy, and failures are those who would be passed over with or without the preferential policy. Let us consider how an outsider who can observe the hiring decision, *but not the employer's productivity assessment,* would estimate the productivity of those subject to this hiring process.

Notice that a lower hiring threshold for blacks causes the outside market to reduce its estimate of the productivity of black successes, since, on average, less is required to achieve that status. In addition, black failures, seen to have been passed over despite a lower hiring threshold, are thereby revealed as especially unproductive. On the other hand, a hiring process favoring blacks must enhance the reputations of white failures, as seen by outsiders, since they may have been artificially held back. And white successes, who are hired despite being disfavored in selection, have thereby been shown to be especially productive.

We have thus reached the result that, among blacks, only marginals gain from the establishment of a preferential hiring program—they do so because the outside observer lumps them together with their superiors, black successes. They thus gain a job and a better reputation than they objectively deserve. Moreover, among whites, only marginals are harmed by the program, for only they lose the chance of securing a job and only they see their reputations harmed by virtue of being placed in the same category as white failures. In practical terms, since marginals are typically a minority of all workers, the outside reputations of most blacks will be lowered, and that of most whites enhanced, by preferential hiring. The inferential logic that leads to this arresting conclusion is particularly insidious, in that it can serve to legitimate otherwise indefensible negative stereotypes about blacks.

A new model of affirmative action

Another reason for being skeptical about the practice of affirmative action is that it can undercut the incentives for blacks to develop their competitive abilities. For instance, preferential treatment can lead to the patronization of black workers and students. By "patronization," I mean the setting of a lower standard of expected accomplishment for blacks than for whites because of the belief that blacks are not as capable of meeting a higher,

common standard. In the 1993 article "Will Affirmative Action Eliminate Negative Stereotypes?" that appeared in the *American Economic Review,* Stephen Coate and I show how behavior of this kind can be based on a self-fulfilling prophesy. That is, observed performance among blacks may be lower precisely because blacks are being patronized, a policy that is undertaken because of the need for an employer or admissions officer to meet affirmative-action guidelines.

Consider a workplace in which a supervisor operating under some affirmative-action guidelines must recommend subordinate workers for promotion. Suppose further that he is keen to promote blacks where possible, and that he monitors his subordinates' performance and bases his recommendations on these observations. Pressure to promote blacks might lead him to de-emphasize deficiencies in the performance of black subordinates, recommending them for promotion when he would not have done so for whites. But his behavior could undermine the ability of black workers to identify and correct their deficiencies. They are denied honest feedback from their supervisor on their performance and are encouraged to think that one can get ahead without attaining the same degree of proficiency as whites.

Alternatively, consider a population of students applying to professional schools for admissions. The schools, due to affirmative-action concerns, are eager to admit a certain percentage of blacks. They believe that to do so they must accept black applicants with test scores and grades below those of some whites whom they reject. If most schools follow this policy, the message sent out to black students is that the level of performance needed to gain admission is lower than that which white students know they must attain. If black and white students are, at least to some extent, responsive to these differing expectations, they might, as a result, achieve grades and test scores reflective of the expectation gap. In this way, the schools' belief that different admissions standards are necessary becomes a self-fulfilling prophecy.

The common theme in these two examples is that the desire to see greater black representation is pursued by using different criteria for the promotion or admission of black and white candidates. But the use of different criteria reduces the incentives that blacks have for developing needed skills. This argument does not presume that blacks are less capable than whites; it is based on the fact that an individual's need to make use of his abilities is undermined when that individual is patronized by the employer or the admissions committee.

This problem could be avoided if, instead of using different criteria of selection, the employers and schools in question sought to meet their desired level of black participation through a concerted effort to enhance performance, while maintaining common standards of evaluation. Call it "developmental," as opposed to "preferential," affirmative action. Such a targeted effort at performance enhancement among black employees or students is definitely not color-blind behavior. It presumes a direct concern about racial inequality and involves allocating benefits to people on the basis of race. What distinguishes it from preferential hiring or admissions, though, is that it takes seriously the fact of differential performance and seeks to reverse it directly, rather than trying to hide from that fact by setting a different threshold of expectation for the performance of blacks.

For example, given that black students are far scarcer than white and Asian students in the fields of math and science, encouraging their entry into these areas without lowering standards—through summer workshops, support for curriculum development at historically black colleges, or the financing of research assistantships for promising graduate students—would be consistent with my distinction between "preferential" and "developmental" affirmative action. Also consistent would be the provision of management assistance to new black-owned businesses, which would then be expected to bid competitively for government contracts, or the provisional admission of black students to the state university, conditional on their raising their academic scores to competitive levels after a year or two of study at a local community college. The key is that the racially targeted assistance be short-lived and preparatory to the entry of its recipients into an arena of competition where they would be assessed in the same way as everyone else.

Racism and responsibility

Unfortunately, economists seem to be the only people persuaded by, or even interested in, this kind of technical argument about affirmative action. Therefore, I turn now, in my capacity as an intellectual and a citizen, to a range of moral and political considerations that may be of broader interest but that still point in the same direction. Begin with an obvious point: The plight of the inner-city underclass—the most intractable aspect of the racial inequality problem today—is not mitigated by affirmative-action policies. Defenders of racial preferences answer by claiming this was never the intent of such policies. But this only leads to my second point: The persistent demand for preferential treatment as necessary to black achievement amounts, over a period of time, to a concession of defeat by middle-class blacks in our struggle for civic equality.

The political discourse over affirmative action harbors a paradoxical subtext: Middle-class blacks seek equality of status with whites by calling attention to their own limited achievements, thereby establishing the need for preferential policies. At the same time, sympathetic white elites, by granting black demands, thereby acknowledge that, without their patronage, black penetration of the upper reaches of American society would be impossible. The paradox is that, although equality is the goal of the enterprise, this manifestly is not an exchange among equals, and it never can be.

Members of the black middle class who stress that, without some special dispensation, they cannot compete with whites are really flattering those whites, while exhibiting their own weakness. And whites who think that, because of societal wrongs, blacks are owed the benefit of the doubt about their qualifications are exercising a noblesse oblige available only to the powerful. This exchange between black weakness and white power has become a basic paradigm for "progressive" race relations in contemporary America. Blacks from privileged backgrounds now routinely engage in a kind of exhibi-

tionism of non-achievement, mournfully citing the higher success rates of whites in one endeavor or another in order to gain leverage for their advocacy on behalf of preferential treatment. That Asians from more modest backgrounds often achieve higher rates of success is not mentioned. But the limited ability of these more fortunate blacks to make inroads on their own can hardly go unnoticed.

It is morally unjustified—and to this African American, humiliating—that preferential treatment based on race should become institutionalized for those of us now enjoying all of the advantages of middle-class life. The thought that my sons would come to see themselves as presumptively disadvantaged because of their race is unbearable to me. They are, in fact, among the richest young people of African descent anywhere on the globe. There is no achievement to which they cannot legitimately aspire. Whatever degree of success they attain in life, the fact that some of their ancestors were slaves and others faced outrageous bigotry will have little to do with it.

Indeed, those ancestors, with only a fraction of the opportunity, and with much of the power structure of the society arrayed against them, managed to educate their children, acquire land, found communal institutions, and mount a successful struggle for equal rights. The generation coming of age during the 1960s, now ensconced in the burgeoning black middle class, enjoy their status primarily because their parents and grandparents faithfully discharged their responsibilities. The benefits of affirmative action, whatever they may have been, pale in comparison to this inheritance.

My grandparents, with their siblings and cousins, left rural Mississippi for Chicago's mean streets in the years after World War I. Facing incredible racial hostility, they nevertheless carved out a place for their children, who went on to acquire property and gain a toe-hold in the professions. For most middle-class blacks this is a familiar story. Our forebears, from slavery onward, performed magnificently under harsh circumstances. It is time now that we and our children begin to do the same. It desecrates the memory of our enslaved ancestors to assert that, with our far greater freedoms, we middle-class blacks should now look to whites, of whatever political persuasion, to ensure that our dreams are realized.

The children of today's black middle class will live their lives in an era of equal opportunity. I recognize that merely by stating this simple fact I will enrage many people; and I do not mean to assert that racial discrimination has disappeared. But I insist that the historic barriers to black participation in the political, social, and economic life of the nation have been lowered dramatically over the past four decades, especially for the wealthiest 20 percent of the black population. Arguably, the time has now come for us to let go of the ready-made excuse that racism provides. And so too, it is time to accept responsibility for what we and our children do, and do not, achieve.

GLENN C. LOURY is University Professor, professor of economics, and Director of the Institution on Race and Social Division at Boston University.

Hip-Hop Nation: The Undeveloped Social Capital of Black Urban America

Lisa Y. Sullivan

Observers of public life and civil society agree that the civic health of a community is largely determined by the availability and abundance of its "social capital." Used in this context, social capital refers to both the informal and formal networks and associations of ordinary citizens who have the capacity to facilitate, coordinate, and cooperate in efforts that benefit the entire community. Although academics like Harvard political scientist Robert Putnam have warned that our current civic crisis has much to do with a decline in formal associational life, my activism and organizing experience in central cities suggests that informal associational life is alive and well—especially among the poor and young.[1] While Putnam may have observed a general decrease in citizen participation in traditional social and civic associations, a significant number of citizens from the inner city are creating and participating in vibrant informal networks of twenty-first century associational life.

For the most part, the social capital of the future remains organized around the immediate needs of individuals seeking new, mutually supportive relationships. Often these new associations center on issues of care and support. In cities ravaged by alcohol, cocaine, heroin addiction, and the nexus of the HIV/AIDS pandemic, networks of care, support, and counseling are some of the strongest, most vibrant, and most visible civic infrastructures existing in poor communities and neighborhoods.

As in the past, others of these informal networks are organized around recreation and social entertainment. For example, between Atlanta and Boston, there is a thriving network of inner city women's basketball enthusiasts who convene regularly for holiday and weekend tournaments. In much the same manner that basketball has served as an informal convener of inner city males and females, tennis, golf, and skiing have become the catalyst of primarily black middle-class networks. These tournaments, ski trips, and racquet clubs are vibrant, thriving, and increasingly common examples of formal black associational life.[2] Likewise, the emergence of book clubs inspired by television talk show host Oprah Winfrey have taken on increased significance in the lives of young middle-class black professional women.

The existence of abundant social capital and vibrant informal networks is most evident among urban youth. In particular, urban youth culture—also known as hip-hop culture and more recently as popular culture—provides a unique and important space for the development and evolution of new styles, leaders, and networks. Within the subcultures of rap artists, musicians, poets, graffiti artists, filmmakers, fashion designers, graphic artists, and party promoters, intricate informal associations exist that are capable of massive mobilization and community cooperation.[3]

A recent public demonstration of this claim was the growth and evolution of the black college event formerly known as "Freaknic." What began in the early 1980s in the Atlanta University Center as a picnic in Piedmont Park sponsored by the DC Metro Club (a campus club for kids from the Washington, D.C., area) grew in a decade to become a major public event that by the spring of 1994 was attracting tens of thousands of college and noncollege young African Americans. Similar examples include the annual black Greek Picnic and Penn Relays in Philadelphia as well as the Myrtle Beach, South Carolina, annual end-of-the-year or commencement celebration. In addition, in urban and suburban retail and commercial space, the visibility of large groupings of young people suggests that the concept of mutual support and informal association is thriving among urban youth.

In an age of youth violence, increased concern about juvenile delinquency, and irrational adult fear, coupled with the predisposition to scapegoat adolescents, it is hard for most to comprehend that the young are highly organized and that their social capital abounds. Although society may not approve, condone, or accept that youth gangs, posses, street organizations, or crews are meaningful and constructive forms of associational life, they exist as the primary networks for inner-city adolescent social development. I am not referring here to organized gangs involved in illicit or illegal business. Instead, I am talking about the neighborhood teenagers who "roll" twenty deep in a pack to the mall on Saturday, and who refer to themselves as crews, posses, or more recently as street organizations.

Evolution of Informal Social Capital Among Urban Youth

Twenty years ago, I was a teenager in the nation's capital. I belonged to several crews. First and foremost, there was my loyalty to the street that nurtured and raised me until I left home at age eighteen for college. Back when neighborhood movie theaters existed in the District of Columbia, all the kids on our street would roll together to see the Saturday matinee. As the oldest child, I was responsible for my younger sister and her friends. At times, my peers teased me about having to babysit the little kids; but I later found out that most of them, too, could not roll unless I did because their parents perceived me as being the most mature child on the block. Back in 1977, I would never have claimed to be a crew leader.

At the movies, our block blended in with the other crews from our community. All of us collectively constituted my second crew: the geographic neighborhood. Now, the older neighborhood teens regularly "beefed" with the leaders of the crews from Riggs Park, Petworth, and Fort Stevens. We had boundaries that distinguished crew affiliation, and we frequently used the battle of go-go bands to determine neighborhood superiority.[4] We challenged neighborhood crews athletically and hosted good old-fashioned block party competitions judged by the best food, the most people, and the best band performance. A successful block party required a high level of community organization and networking of neighborhood associations. Important activities included (1) collecting petition signatures from local residents to close a street to traffic and agree to host the block party; (2) securing the requisite permits from the D.C. police department to hold the block party; (3) renting the stage and sound equipment from the D.C. parks and recreation department; (4) securing in-kind donations of food, paper products, and sodas from local merchants and grocery stores; (5) finding lots of parents willing to "cook out" for hundreds of neighborhood youth from noon until sundown; and (6) arranging for a popular neighborhood leader to serve as master of ceremonies and help coordinate the programmatic activities.

Beyond where I lived, I also belonged to crews that reflected my social independence and interests. There was my tennis court crew, my basketball and softball crew, my crew from high school, and the crew I rolled with to parties and other social activities. All of this associational life was in addition to the "organized" adult-supervised activities that my parents identified. As an average inner-city teenager, my associations and networks were largely organized around my informal crew life.

Crack cocaine, guns, escalating youth violence, increased social despair, misery, and marginalization have transformed the crew over the past twenty years.[5] Now, crossing neighborhood boundaries can be deadly, and guilt by association can lead to being locked up or shot. Nevertheless, the crew remains the locus of youth affiliation. Far too many adults have failed to understand the power and influence of these informal and formal crew associations and their inherent social capital. Sadly, the strength and evidence of the crew is too often visible, active, and effective only in the face of sickness, death, and tragedy. In too many inner-city neighborhoods, wakes and funerals have become massive gatherings for youth in search of refuge and healing from the violence and despair of poverty and neglect.

Whither Black Youth Civic Engagement?

There is no dearth of associational life or social capital among the young, the black, or the poor. The October 1995 Million Man March was an extraordinary example of this fact. Regardless of the controversy surrounding Benjamin Chavis, Louis Farrakhan, and the Nation of Islam, the strategy for mobilizing grassroots support for the march demonstrated the extent to which black nationalist leadership understands the networks and social capital that exist within urban black communities. By utilizing the black press—both radio and print—to get out the message, while organizing at the street corner level, primarily through networks of barbershops, march organizers ensured that the core community would know about (and formulate its own opinion about) the event before mainstream black or white leaders and institutions could challenge its legitimacy. In much the same manner that Harvard professor Henry Louis Gates, Jr., has identified the long-standing existence of a contemporary black theater movement organized around socially relevant themes that appeal to the black poor and working class,[6] the Million Man March effectively evoked the social capital and institutional infrastructure of the black community.

In an important and critical assessment of black civic and political life in the post-civil rights era, political scientist Robert Smith argues with passion and clarity that in the period since passage of the 1964 and 1965 civil rights legislation, black leaders have devoted themselves exclusively to the process of securing mainstream political and economic incorporation, at the expense of an increasingly isolated and marginalized core constituency.[7] Alienated from mainstream American politics and public life, the young and poor have also increasingly found themselves estranged from the black civil rights establishment. Disengaged from traditional black liberal organizations, their social capital has gone underutilized, underdeveloped, and ignored in the late twentieth century.

Smith observes further that in the post-civil rights period, black civil rights organizations have focused narrowly on lobbying congress or litigating in the courts. Neither strategy has required these organizations to broaden their base of political participation to include more or new people in the decisionmaking process. The critical shortcoming, then, is that this top-down, hierarchical, middle-class model of organization and strategy emphasizes elite interaction rather than constituent development and empowerment. Consequently, black civic and political life has been reduced to annual conventions, conferences and meetings, symbolic rallies and marches, and press conferences that habitually omit the participation and inclusion of black urban youth. Predictably, the political strategy of mainstream incorporation has isolated black civil rights leadership from its core constituency: the young and poor.[8]

Beyond this critique, students of black electoral participation have observed that the self-interest of elected officials, regardless of race, has also undermined the civic development of poor black communities.[9] Persistently low voter participation and turnout continue to plague black politics at the local, state, and national levels. Although this phenomenon reflects a larger crisis in American democracy, the nonparticipation of poor black youth in meaningful political discourse, political parties, and nonpartisan political organizations reveals the extent to which civic infrastructure in the black community suffers from atrophy. More than thirty years ago, the preeminent civil rights strategist Bayard Rustin observed that the future of the movement would require a strategic shift from protest to incorporation into mainstream electoral politics.[10] As we approach a new century, it now appears that the civil rights movement is experiencing a crisis of relevancy as the political incorporation strategy has proved unable to solve the major socioeconomic problems facing poor black communities. This profound crisis in black public life includes:

- A decline in organized grassroots community activism
- A decline in philanthropic, union, and nonprofit institutional support for targeted, nonpartisan minority, youth, and low-income voter registration and education initiatives
- Widespread disappointment among black youth with the performance of black

elected and appointed officials, as well as traditional civil rights leaders and clergy
- Deconstruction of the institutions and mechanisms for implementation of civic education and political mobilization in low-income communities

Basically, low voter registration and turnout rates compounded by low civic participation and engagement have reinforced the indifference and unresponsiveness of local, state, and national policymakers toward young black people. The self-fulfilling prophecy of pragmatic electoral politics has come true in most inner-city communities. The least attention is now paid to those neighborhoods and communities that demonstrate a low level of interest and participation in the process that elects its leaders. This is a rule of thumb followed by politicians regardless of their race, ethnicity, or class. It is this reality that explains how and why black inner-city communities have watched the collapse and devastation of their public and civic infrastructure while black mayors, police chiefs, and school superintendents presided.

Toward a More Effective Use of Black Urban Social Capital

Renewing black public life is a necessary prerequisite for restoring both the health of this nation's urban communities and the civic engagement of black youth. It is a task that requires significant resources—intellectual, human, and financial. At the core of what must be done is what public philosopher Harry Boyte has described as popular civic education.[11] Through citizen education, America must renew civic discourse deeply grounded in the culture, traditions, and ways of life of the ordinary people who ultimately must rebuild their communities. The future of black public life is therefore dependent upon community-based citizenship initiatives that emphasize civic literacy, leadership development, community participation, and engagement.

Unfortunately, revival of popular civic education will not rehabilitate black public life on its own merit. Although it is a necessary condition, it is not sufficient for fundamental social change. Instead, a major paradigmatic shift must occur within black public life, coupled with a renewed focus on civic engagement at the neighborhood level. This fundamental shift is necessary for restoring the capacity of the post-civil rights, postindustrial urban black community to affect social change. Without a major transformation of the leadership paradigm that currently guides and dominates black political culture, black public life and its civic infrastructure will not recover from the late twentieth-century socioeconomic crisis.

Historically, public life in the black community has been dominated by loyal, race men. Traditionally, they have led community institutions like the church, schools, businesses, and social and civic organizations. This model of leadership has been predisposed to autocratic, antidemocratic, and egotistical tendencies. As a consequence, generations within the black community have experienced a monolithic leadership paradigm that often validated notions of elite, sexist, hierarchical, antidemocratic, command-and-control relationships with its core black constituency. Entrenched in black political culture and psychology, this model is frequently internalized and replicated by black women and youth.[12]

Few have challenged the presumptions of this model. Even fewer have been willing to acknowledge that the father of twentieth-century black liberalism and elitism, W.E.B. Du Bois, revised his theory of race leadership in 1948. In 1903, when Du Bois published his essay "The Talented Tenth," he defined the commitment to service that the educated few owed the rest of the black community. It was the duty of the enlightened race leaders—the black aristocracy—to lead the unsophisticated black masses. By midcentury, however, Du Bois advanced the idea that a group-centered leadership capable of empowering the masses was a more desired model of race leadership. Thus his reexamined, restated theory of the Talented Tenth evolved into the doctrine of the "Guiding Hundred."

To date, black liberal elites have failed to acknowledge Du Bois's revelation and have therefore failed to transcend his theory of the Talented Tenth. As activist-intellectual Joy James has observed, Du Bois revealed, in the restatement of his thesis on race leadership, a dynamic and evolving analysis that underscored the importance of class and the important social and political agency of ordinary black people.[13] It is therefore quite appropriate that black America's preeminent twentieth-century intellectual must now serve as the point of departure for transcending the promotion of an elite-driven black leadership strategy into the twenty-first century.

It would be a gross mistake to assume that black elitism is the sole source of the contemporary black leadership crisis and its inability to maximize existing social capital. On the contrary, autocratic, nondemocratic, sexist tendencies—particularly among grassroots nationalist organizations—is equally debilitating. The modern civil rights movement makes clear the dependence of black social progress on the leadership of young people and women. Martin Luther King's emerging leadership was inextricably linked to the social capital and civic infrastructure of the resourceful middle-class black women who organized the 1955 Montgomery bus boycott and the mass social action of poor domestic workers and day laborers who walked to work for a solid year in order to desegregate the public transportation system in their segregated city.

Unfortunately, the heroic mythology of Martin (and Malcolm) has in the post-civil rights era paralyzed the development of a new black leadership paradigm. Black America is stuck on the great messianic, charismatic male leadership paradigm, and this nostalgia has significantly warped the community's perception and understanding of its potential social capital.

Again, despite its emphasis on great men, the organizing lessons of the Million Man March demonstrate precisely who possesses the untapped social capital within the black community. In the months preceding the march, it was no accident that organizers chose to actively engage, pursue, and mobilize black women to support the effort. In communities across this nation, black women's social clubs, associations, and informal networks helped raise money and organized buses that delivered a million black men to the nation's capital. Likewise, the coordination and mobilization of young black men, from college campuses to street organizations, was most impressive. More than anything else, the success of the Million Man March mobilization was testimony to the underutilized social capital in black communities across the nation.

The Promise of a New Leadership Paradigm

Restoring black public life, its civic infrastructure, and the promise of urban America requires new vision, new strategies, and a new leadership paradigm. As the nation approaches a new century, finding new ways of doing business around public issues in the black community becomes increasingly important. Doing public business in a new manner requires significant organizational transformation. A twenty-first-century black leadership paradigm will be forced to consider several important points:

• The value of democratic practice within the movement of social change
• The existence of ideological pluralism within the black community
• The need to systematically develop the leadership of black women and youth
• The need to view the leadership contributions of elites as equal and in partnership with ordinary citizens
• The need to replace the charismatic great leader with the collaborative leadership of ordinary citizens

• The need to restore citizenship, democracy, and the belief that ordinary people in local communities can solve their problems and build community capacity with the support of the independent sector, government, and private enterprise

Increasingly, public life and civic engagement require leaders to hear, understand, and consider the views of frustrated, marginalized citizens—especially black youth. It is through collaborative processes that ordinary citizens begin to catalyze, energize, and facilitate their neighbors in community problem solving. In the process, they create new associations, networks, organizations, alliances, partnerships, and forums.

By definition, collaborative leadership brings people to the table and engages them in a process of building trust and shared vision. Consequently, collaborative leaders must be active and involved in building relationships and a credible process that engages citizens in public life. As David Chrislip and Carl Larson have eloquently observed, getting extraordinary things done in the twenty-first century will require a new kind of leadership with a new set of skills.[14] Black public life and civic engagement is no exception to this rule. The traditional hierarchical model of leadership must now give way to more collaborative leadership, willing to include alienated and often marginalized poor black youth in the conversation about the future of their communities.

Sustained by their vision and deeply held belief that ordinary people have the capacity to create their own visions and solve their own problems, collaborative leaders with a commitment to participatory democracy will renew black public life and build a new kind of civic infrastructure that takes full advantage of the abundant social capital of urban America.

Notes

1. See Putnam, R. D. "Bowling Alone: America's Declining Social Capital." *Journal of Democracy,* Jan. 1995, pp. 65–78.
2. For further discussion, see Sullivan, L. "Civil Society at the Margins." *Kettering Review,* Winter 1997, pp. 63–65.
3. For recent mainstream articulations of the importance of hip-hop culture and its impact on the global economy, see Romero, D. J. "Influence of Hip-Hop Resonates Worldwide." *Los Angeles Times,* Mar. 14, 1997, p. 1; and Levine, J. "Badass Sells." *Forbes,* Apr. 21, 1997, pp. 142–148.
4. In much the same manner that rap evolved in New York City, Go Go music is the popular musical expression of inner city youth in Washington, D.C. For further discussion and background, see Wartofsky, A. "Go-Go Goes On." *Washington Post,* Nov. 16, 1996, p. C1.
5. For an excellent discussion of the transformation of social norms among young people in urban communities, see Canada, G. *Fist, Stick, Knife, Gun: A Personal History of Violence in America.* Boston: Beacon Press, 1995; and Taylor, C. *Girls, Gangs, Women, and Drugs.* East Lansing: Michigan State University Press, 1993.
6. For a provocative discussion of social class and black popular culture, see Gates, H. L., Jr. "The Chitlin Circuit." *New Yorker,* Feb. 3, 1997, pp. 44–55.
7. For this important thesis on post-civil rights black politics, see Smith, R. C. *We Have No Leaders: African Americans in the Post-Civil Rights Era.* Albany: State University of New York Press, 1996.
8. For an excellent case study of Detroit's inner-city black community and its relationship to black politics, see Cohen, C., and Dawson, M. "Neighborhood Poverty and African American Politics." *American Political Science Review,* 1993, 87(2), 286.
9. See Steele, J. "Knowledge Is Power: Enhancing Citizen Involvement and Political Participation in Targeted Central Brooklyn Communities." Unpublished paper, Breakthrough Political Consulting, Brooklyn, New York, 1996.
10. See Rustin, B. "From Protest to Politics: The Future of the Civil Rights Movement." In *Down the Line: The Collected Writings of Bayard Rustin.* Chicago: Quadrangle Books, 1971.
11. See Boyte, H. C., and Kari, N. N. *Building America: The Democratic Promise of Public Work.* Philadelphia: Temple University Press, 1996.
12. For a very important essay on black women's leadership development into the twenty-first century, see Noble, J. "Paradigm Shifts Facing Leaders of Black Women's Organizations." In *Voices of Vision: African American Women on the Issues.* National Council of Negro Women, 1996; and for an examination of similar tendencies among black college students, see Sullivan, L. "Beyond Nostalgia: Notes on Black Student Activism." *Socialist Review,* 1990, 4, 21–28.
13. See James, J. *Transcending the Talented Tenth: Black Leaders and American Intellectuals.* New York: Routledge, 1997.
14. See Chrislip, D., and Larson, C. *Collaborative Leadership: How Citizens and Civic Leaders Can Make a Difference.* San Francisco: Jossey-Bass, 1994.

Lisa Y. Sullivan is program consultant for the Rockefeller Foundation, where she facilitates a design team in development of a new and innovative fellowship program for the next generation of American leaders. She was previously director of the field division at the Children's Defense Fund. She has published articles on community service, social problems, and race relations.

Index

Credits/Acknowledgments

Cover design by Charles Vitelli

1. Race and Ethnicity in the American Legal Tradition
Facing overview—Library of Congress photo. 26—AP/Wide World photo by Clark Jones.

2. Immigration and the American Experience
Facing overview—Photo courtesy of James Iannuzzi.

3. Indigenous Ethnic Groups
Facing overview—United Nations photo by Jerry Frank.

4. Hispanic/Latino Americans
Facing overview—© 1998 by PhotoDisc, Inc.

5. African Americans
Facing overview—United Press International photo.

6. Asian Americans
Facing overview—Dushkin/McGraw-Hill photo. 150-154—Pluralism Project photos.

7. The Ethnic Legacy
Facing overview—New York Convention and Visitors Bureau photo.

8. The Ethnic Factor: International Challenges for the 1990s
Facing overview—United Nations photo by Yutaka Nagata.

9. Understanding Cultural Pluralism
Facing overview—United Nations photo by Yutaka Nagata.

ANNUAL EDITIONS ARTICLE REVIEW FORM

■ NAME: _____ DATE: _____

■ TITLE AND NUMBER OF ARTICLE: _____

■ BRIEFLY STATE THE MAIN IDEA OF THIS ARTICLE: _____

_____

■ LIST THREE IMPORTANT FACTS THAT THE AUTHOR USES TO SUPPORT THE MAIN IDEA:

_____

_____

_____

_____

■ WHAT INFORMATION OR IDEAS DISCUSSED IN THIS ARTICLE ARE ALSO DISCUSSED IN YOUR TEXTBOOK OR OTHER READINGS THAT YOU HAVE DONE? LIST THE TEXTBOOK CHAPTERS AND PAGE NUMBERS:

_____

_____

_____

_____

■ LIST ANY EXAMPLES OF BIAS OR FAULTY REASONING THAT YOU FOUND IN THE ARTICLE:

_____

_____

_____

_____

■ LIST ANY NEW TERMS/CONCEPTS THAT WERE DISCUSSED IN THE ARTICLE, AND WRITE A SHORT DEFINITION:

_____

_____

_____

_____

*Your instructor may require you to use this ANNUAL EDITIONS Article Review Form in any number of ways: for articles that are assigned, for extra credit, as a tool to assist in developing assigned papers, or simply for your own reference. Even if it is not required, we encourage you to photocopy and use this page; you will find that reflecting on the articles will greatly enhance the information from your text.

We Want Your Advice

ANNUAL EDITIONS revisions depend on two major opinion sources: one is our Advisory Board, listed in the front of this volume, which works with us in scanning the thousands of articles published in the public press each year; the other is you—the person actually using the book. Please help us and the users of the next edition by completing the prepaid article rating form on this page and returning it to us. Thank you for your help!

ANNUAL EDITIONS: RACE AND ETHNIC RELATIONS 98/99
Article Rating Form

Here is an opportunity for you to have direct input into the next revision of this volume. We would like you to rate each of the 45 articles listed below, using the following scale:

1. **Excellent: should definitely be retained**
2. **Above average: should probably be retained**
3. **Below average: should probably be deleted**
4. **Poor: should definitely be deleted**

Your ratings will play a vital part in the next revision. So please mail this prepaid form to us just as soon as you complete it.
Thanks for your help!

Rating	Article	Rating	Article
	1. *Dred Scott v. Sandford*		25. Understanding Integration: Why Blacks and Whites Must Come Together as Americans
	2. Racial Restrictions in the Law of Citizenship		26. America's Caste System: Will It Change?
	3. *Brown et al. v. Board of Education of Topeka et al.*		27. Misperceived Minorities: 'Good' and 'Bad' Stereotypes Saddle Hispanics and Asian Americans
	4. Retreat into Legalism: The Little Rock School Desegregation Case in Historic Perspective		28. Neighboring Faiths
	5. The Strange Politics of Affirmative Action		29. The Chinese Diaspora
	6. One America in the 21st Century: The President's Initiative on Race		30. The Challenge for U.S. Asians in the Year 2000
	7. Immigration: Bridging Gap between Ideas and Action		31. Migrations to the Thirteen British North American Colonies, 1770–1775: New Estimates
	8. We Asked . . . You Told Us		32. The Settlement of the Old Northwest: Ethnic Pluralism in a Featureless Plain
	9. Ethnicity vs. Assimilation: Seeking a Middle Ground		33. Italian Americans as a Cognizable Racial Group
	10. Newcomers and Established Residents		34. If Names Could Kill: My Name May Be Gambino, But a Notorious Mobster I'm Not
	11. 12th Session of UN Working Group on Indigenous Peoples		35. The End of the Rainbow
	12. American Indians in the 1990s		36. Polish Americans and the Holocaust
	13. Canada Pressed on Indian Rights		37. Belonging in the West
	14. Profile: Rebecca Adamson		38. Ethnicity: An African Predicament
	15. Cape Town's District Six Rises Again		39. Gypsies in Canada: Outcasts Once Again *and* Paradise Found—and Then Lost
	16. A Different Kind of Justice: Truth and Reconciliation in South Africa		40. Eugenics, Anyone?
	17. Specific Hispanics		41. The Geometer of Race
	18. There's More to Racism than Black and White		42. Bred in the Bone?
	19. A Place of Our Own		43. Color Blind
	20. A Balancing Act		44. How to Mend Affirmative Action
	21. Tickled Brown		45. Hip-Hop Nation: The Undeveloped Social Capital of Black Urban America
	22. 10 Most Dramatic Events in African-American History		
	23. Black Politics, the 1996 Elections, and the End of the Second Reconstruction		
	24. Understanding Afrocentrism		

(Continued on next page)

ABOUT YOU

Name _____ Date _____

Are you a teacher? ❏ Or a student? ❏

Your school name _____

Department _____

Address _____

City _____ State _____ Zip _____

School telephone # _____

YOUR COMMENTS ARE IMPORTANT TO US!

Please fill in the following information:

For which course did you use this book? _____

Did you use a text with this *ANNUAL EDITION*? ❏ yes ❏ no

What was the title of the text? _____

What are your general reactions to the *Annual Editions* concept?

Have you read any particular articles recently that you think should be included in the next edition?

Are there any articles you feel should be replaced in the next edition? Why?

Are there any World Wide Web sites you feel should be included in the next edition? Please annotate.

May we contact you for editorial input?

May we quote your comments?

ANNUAL EDITIONS: RACE AND ETHNIC RELATIONS 98/99

BUSINESS REPLY MAIL

| First Class | Permit No. 84 | Guilford, CT |

Postage will be paid by addressee

Dushkin/McGraw·Hill
Sluice Dock
Guilford, CT 06437